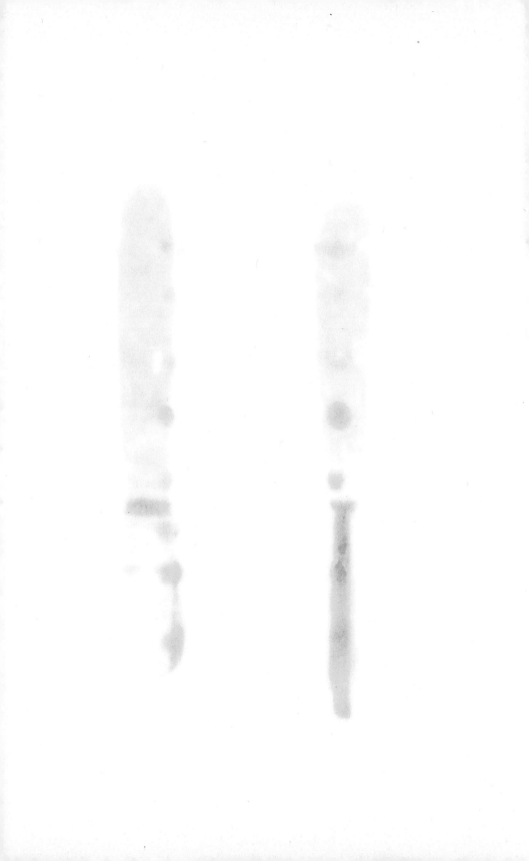

JOHN D. ROCKEFELLER

John D. Rockefeller and William Rainey Harper.

A photograph taken at the Decennial Celebration of the University of Chicago,
June 10, 1901.

John D. Rockefeller

THE HEROIC AGE OF AMERICAN ENTERPRISE

BY

ALLAN NEVINS

Volume Two

NEW YORK

CHARLES SCRIBNER'S SONS

1940

KRAUS REPRINT CO.
New York
1969

Reprinted from the original edition in the
Wesleyan University Library

Contents

Contents

BOOK IV

A MAN AND HIS MONEY

Illustrations

Illustrations

BOOK THREE

YEARS OF POWER

XXVIII

New Horizons in Oil

I T WAS not the Romans that spread upon the world," wrote Lord Bacon, "but the world that spread upon the Romans; and that was the sure way of greatness." It was the world that spread upon petroleum. For twenty years after Drake's discovery man saw little in oil beyond the means of banishing night. Then invention began to make it an instrument of power and speed; the gas engine, the automobile, the Diesel motor, and the airplane rendered it the principal propulsive force of civilization. The search for it spread over all the continents, until new fields had been opened in every clime. Empires came to depend upon it, guarding their pipes and tankers as fiercely as they guarded their food supply. As it thus rose to world-wide puissance, the Standard Oil Company rose with it to a strength and wealth of which its heads had never dreamed, and Rockefeller amassed perhaps the greatest fortune the world had ever seen. We have described the power and efficiency of the organization which he built up; but it was also one of the most dynamic organizations in the world, and its expansion was continuous.

II

"Natural gas? Yes, everybody hereabouts knows that gas lies under part of this country." So citizens of northwestern Ohio would have told any inquirer between the presidencies of Jackson and Hayes. Farmers in digging wells frequently came upon it. It seeped out from rocky hillsides. An ingenious citizen of Findlay about 1838 covered over a well, let the gas through wooden pipes into his house, and burned it in his fireplace through an old gun-barrel. Rockefeller doubtless heard of the gas during his trips as a young grain-buyer. After the Civil War drilling for it was sporadically

3

undertaken, and early in the eighties the search began to be pressed with vigor. By midsummer of 1885 a million cubic feet a day were being used. In May of that year, near the town of Lima, a paper-mill proprietor was driving a gas-well into the Trenton rock at some 1200 feet when the auger suddenly dropped through the stratum, and the amazed driller brought oil to the surface; thick, black, evil-smelling oil. Though the heavy petroleum was at first thought to belong to a lubricating order, men soon found that its sulphur-content had a corrosive effect upon machinery. Within a few weeks more oil was struck at Findlay, and men commenced sinking shafts in every direction.[1]

Thus began production in the Lima-Ohio field. The area was exploited with the same eager rush that had been witnessed in the Bradford field. In 1886 more than a million barrels of oil were obtained; in 1890, more than fifteen million; and in 1896 more than twenty million. As the flood of sulphur-tainted oil poured into the market, prices dropped to the lowest levels in American history, even touching ten cents a barrel.[2] Yet profits were frequently high, for some gushers yielded from 7000 to 10,000 barrels a day. With the same feverish haste, the Lima-Indiana field just across the boundary was opened; during the panic-year 1893 about five hundred wells were drilled here, and some 2,300,000 barrels of crude oil were produced.[3]

It was one of the recurrent strokes of good fortune experienced by the refining industry that these vast new resources became available at the very time that the flow of Pennsylvania oil began to decline; at the very time, moreover, that invention demanded greater supplies of cheap oil, and the United States needed them to maintain its export industry against Russian competition. Timorous men had always feared that the oil basins would be suddenly exhausted. Henry E. Wrigley, a well-known Pennsylvania geologist, predicted in 1879 that six years of the current flow would drain his State.[4] Though time

---

[1] Ralph Arnold and W. J. Kemnitzer, *Petroleum in the United States and Possessions,* 237 ff.

[2] *Idem,* 237.   [3] *Idem,* 250–259.

[4] N. Y. *Shipping and Commercial List,* Aug. 13, 1879. The editor of this paper pointed out that "similar prognostications have often proved delusive." Wrigley, while State geologist of Pennsylvania some years earlier, had made an even rasher prediction.

proved this absurd, had it not been for the huge Lima field the Standard would have faced a period of extreme stringency.

For the great Pennsylvania deposits had unmistakably been drained to the point of diminishing returns. Waste had run riot there; the uncontrollable producers, racing each other to take oil out at any price, had built up a stored surplus which in the later eighties exceeded thirty million barrels, and had thrown away millions more. The first ominous signs of a slackening flow came at the end of the decade. In 1888 production fell to 14,700,000 barrels, and in 1889 remained low. To be sure, in 1890–91 it soared again, reaching the peak figure of 31,425,000 barrels in the latter year; but then it dropped once more, and after 1892 never again touched twenty million barrels.[5] Sunset was descending upon the Regions, so long a fountain of gold. Had the United States been dependent upon the Appalachian pools alone the price of crude oil would have risen to high levels, new industries built on the internal-combustion engine would have been chilled and retarded, and the wells of Russia and the Dutch East Indies would have captured the world market.

While still vaster deposits of oil lay farther west, it would have taken time to discover them and to provide adequate transportation. To most oil men as late as 1885 the presence of petroleum between the Mississippi and the Rockies seemed inconceivable; oil belonged to hilly country—how could it occur in such flat areas? Charles M. Higgins relates that in the middle eighties he heard some one telling John D. Archbold about signs of oil in Oklahoma. "Are you crazy, man?" Archbold demanded. "Why, I'll *drink* every gallon of oil produced west of the Mississippi!"[6] Though oil prospectors were busy in half the States of the Union, west of Indiana they had then accomplished little of note. *The Annual Cyclopædia* in 1886 remarked that "In Kansas, Missouri, Louisiana, and Texas, springs of petroleum appear, but few wells have proved productive. Farther west, in Wyoming, Utah, and Colorado, several localities produce petroleum for local uses."[7] While Kansas was destined in time to become one of the greatest oil areas of the Union, until 1904 its output never in one year exceeded a hundred thousand barrels; and equally negligible in this period was the great Gulf

[5]Arnold and Kemnitzer, *op. cit.,* 103.
[6]Charles M. Higgins to the author, Jan. 17, 1937.   [7]Pp. 681 ff.

Coast field, later so important.[8] In Kentucky also, where wells were drilled even during the Civil War,[9] production never reached ten thousand barrels a year until 1899. California produced half a million barrels in 1892, but most of this was used for fuel.[10]

Rockefeller, as we have said, never exhibited his vision and boldness to greater effect than in insisting upon huge purchases of oil lands in Ohio, Indiana, and West Virginia. His buying and leasing began in 1886, at first quietly. It rapidly increased, so that in six weeks alone (December 1, 1887–January 10, 1888) the Standard paid out $1,500,000 for Ohio lands.[11] At the same time large quantities of Ohio oil from other producers were purchased and tanked. Most of the prairie tracts were bought in small parcels, but in West Virginia some purchases were on a grand scale. Early in 1891 the Standard paid $750,000 for about 20,000 acres in Green County, Pa., and Monongalia and Green Counties, West Va., on which stood a number of oil and gas wells. It was then reported that the trust owned practically all of Gilmer County, West Va., most of Doddridge, and part of Mason, "and every day new tracts are sold to them."[12] As for Ohio, the Standard was credited with about seven tenths of all the State's oil tankage.[13]

Rockefeller confided the development of the Lima-Ohio lands to the Ohio Oil Company, organized September 2, 1887, with a capital of $500,000. He had a great refinery built in Lima in 1886–87, and sent John W. Van Dyke, who had been manager of the old Sone & Fleming plant, to take charge of it.[14] In the spring of 1888 the trust began laying an eight-inch pipe from the Lima fields along the right of way of the Chicago & Atlantic Railroad into Chicago, the railroad making a free grant of the ground in return for the profit from the transportation of pipe and other materials. The National Transit Company had charge of the enterprise. Costs of pumping oil

[8]Arnold and Kemnitzer, op. cit., 470, 471. Oil had been known in coastal Louisiana before the Civil War, and it is said that an unsuccessful well was drilled 415 feet deep in Calcasieu Parish in 1858.

[9]Idem, 575.   [10]Idem, 740–742.

[11]N. Y. World, Jan. 13, 1888.   [12]N. Y. Herald, Feb. 20, 1891.

[13]Bradstreet's, Oct. 25, 1890, p. 682.

[14]Mr. Van Dyke to the author, Nov. 4, 1936. Van Dyke developed a method of increasing the yield of wells in limestone formations by injecting hydrochloric acid under pressure; by dissolving the limestone it created channels through which the oil might flow.

from the Lima district over the flat country to the terminal at 100th Street and the lake front in South Chicago proved only about five cents a barrel, though the pipe was 225 miles in length. Before long work began on a huge new oil refinery at Whiting, Ind.[15] All this enterprise was close to Rockefeller's heart, for he believed that the whole future of the Standard depended upon thrusting westward.

III

The story of the utilization of the sulphur-tainted Lima oil is one of the romances in the Standard annals. Rockefeller ordered tankage built to hold the fast-accumulating stocks, until by the end of 1888 the Standard possessed about forty million barrels of the foul-smelling crude. Even a little sulphur filmed lamp chimneys and rusted machinery, and the Lima fluid had much. But Herman Frasch, patiently working out his process in the No. 5 Plant in Cleveland, converted the oil at one stroke from a dubious asset to a source of tremendous wealth.[16]

In Frasch we meet an erratic, explosive genius. A native of Wurttemberg, he had come to the United States soon after the Civil War with a youthful knowledge of chemistry gained as a druggist's apprentice, and a tremendous enthusiasm for the subject. He found work in a small laboratory of the Philadelphia College of Pharmacy, but as he was particularly interested in industrial chemistry, presently set up his own laboratory. Few industrialists as yet employed chemists in manufacturing. But Frasch made his own way, and began taking out important patents—one of which, in 1876, covered an improved process for refining paraffin wax. It was purchased by the Standard Oil, and Rockefeller was so impressed by it that he induced Frasch to remove to Cleveland in 1877, and devote himself to experiments in petroleum refining. The chemist gave most of his time to this field until in 1885 he went to London, Ontario, and

[15]See article by Alfred Jones in Gary *Post-Tribune*, May 27, 1937, on "John D. Rockefeller First to Industrialize Calumet: Chicago Pipe-Line Factor in Rise from Wilderness." *House Trust Investigation, 1888*, pp. 282 ff., has data on the pipe line.

[16]A biography of Frasch remains to be written. Besides using the printed materials mentioned in the *Dictionary of American Biography*, I have received much information from George A. Burke, A. P. Coombe, John W. Van Dyke, and Doctor William M. Burton, who knew Frasch and his work well.

founded the Empire Oil Company. Though the Ontario oils were also "sour," within a short time he had devised a process for eliminating the sulphur. Then the Standard purchased his plant, his patents, and his services, and Rockefeller brought him to No. 5, where before long his labors were crowned with complete success.

Forty-five years later the Standard had veterans who vividly recalled "the wild Dutchman" or "flying Dutchman," a vibrant, intense little man, full of energy, imperious determination, and hot temper—"a most uncomfortable critter to work with." It has been said that when he began his experiments the Lima field was yielding thirty thousand barrels a day at fourteen cents a barrel, and when he ended them it produced ninety thousand barrels a day at a dollar a barrel. This is an exaggeration, but it has an essence of truth. While most of the credit for the exploit should go to Frasch's genius, some must be reserved for several hardworking Standard men, notably John W. Van Dyke and Doctor William M. Burton, who helped him. The process, based on the use of copper oxides to precipitate the sulphur, could not be applied until certain mechanical as well as chemical problems were solved. The man who became head of the No. 1 works in Cleveland in 1889, a protégé of Frank Rockefeller's named Utley Wedge, also made valuable improvements in the method. It was an inexpensive mode of purification, for the copper oxide could be used again and again.

For seventeen years the Standard had the exclusive use, thanks to its patents, of the Frasch process. Its competitors in the Lima field had to employ the lead-oxide or Canadian method, which was less efficient and more costly, for the lead could not be recovered.[17] The lesson of this stroke was not lost on Rockefeller. The Whiting plant immediately equipped a laboratory to experiment with new refining methods, and placed in charge of it Frasch's assistant, Doctor Burton, a brilliant young Clevelander, holder of a doctorate gained at Johns Hopkins under Ira Remsen. He rose to be assistant superintendent of the refinery and ultimately president of the Standard of Indiana; but other chemists took his place, and the laboratory grew until it counted scores of highly trained men. Rockefeller had all the other large refineries install experimental or testing laboratories, and one

[17]Doctor W. M. Burton to the author, June 3, 1939.

of the latter was placed on the top floor of 26 Broadway.[18] At Whiting, Doctor Burton later introduced the process of "cracking" petroleum which so enormously increased the yield of gasolene. The Standard paid large sums for scientific skill and brains, and it reaped large rewards. The story of its long, patient, and expensive labors to redeem the California asphalt oils is another brilliant romance.

The Whiting refinery was a remarkable creation. The pipe line which Rockefeller built to South Chicago at first supplied fuel oil to steel mills and other industries. It would have been logical to erect the refinery at the pipe-line terminal; but the mephitic smell of early shipments inspired Chicagoans to hold mass meetings of protest, and the Standard began looking for a less populous site. It found one just across the Indiana line, in a flat district of sand and woodland between Lake Michigan and some small glacial lakes not far inland. This was a beautiful semi-wilderness country, better known to duck-hunters and fishermen than farmers.[19] Three trunk railroads and one belt-line crossed the islandlike strip, about three miles long and one wide, which the Standard men selected. Land was quietly purchased. Construction was entrusted to W. P. Cowan, who had succeeded McGregor as superintendent of the Standard works in Cleveland, to James A. Moffett, who had been managing the Pratt works in Brooklyn, and to W. M. Irish of Olean. They took their sketches and plans to William Curtis, the master-mechanic of No. 1 Plant in Cleveland, and he made the blueprints needed—working, for greater secrecy, in his own home. Meanwhile, a purchasing department was established in Chicago. Systematic work began May 5, 1889, when laborers commenced clearing away trees and brush. By the fall of 1890 a mighty plant had been built, with eighty crude-oil stills, and a huge force of executives, technicians, and workmen. Its daily capacity was then 24,000 barrels of crude

[18]See Harold J. Howland, "Standard Oil," *Outlook,* Sept. 28, 1907. A laboratory force of more than a hundred at Whiting was attained before Rockefeller ceased to be president of the Standard Oil in 1911; later it reached two hundred.

[19]See article in the Gary *Post-Tribune* already cited. This emphasizes the pioneering rôle of the Standard. "It was Rockefeller whose genius started the industrial activity that has since made North and Calumet townships among the great manufacturing centers of all time." The Whiting Tract chosen by the Standard lies two miles east of the Indiana-Illinois line.

oil.[20] The town of Whiting sprang up beside the refinery; the roar of engines and machinery filled what was left of the woods, while the smoke of furnaces and machine-shops drifted away over the sand-dunes and the lake.

As the Lima production increased, the Whiting refinery became temporarily the largest in the world. Another six-inch pipe line was laid in 1890 from the Ohio fields to the works.[21] For a time the Whiting men concentrated upon kerosene, gasolene, and naphtha, but their list of products steadily grew. The manufacture of paraffin and candles began in 1893. Grease works commenced operations three years later, an elaborate lubricating establishment was opened about 1900, and other by-products followed. Shipments of light oils were made chiefly in tank cars, and in lake tankers that ran up to Duluth and there unloaded for the Minnesota-Dakota-Manitoba country. But cooperage shops were built to furnish barrels for lubricants, and a can factory to provide oil containers for the Rocky Mountain country, while the Grasselli Chemical Company hastened to throw a factory into East Chicago to provide sulphuric acid. Until 1906 the refinery used Lima oil almost exclusively, and found it quite satisfactory, but it of course turned later to Illinois and mid-continent crudes. Nearly the whole Midwest, Northwest, and Far West came to depend on the Whiting works, which also marketed waxes and other products in the Orient.[22]

The managers of this great Western branch of the Standard were interesting products of the school which Rockefeller and his associates had set up. James A. Moffett had charge of operations as first vice-president of the Standard Oil of Indiana (incorporated early in 1889), while W. P. Cowan was next in command as second vice-president. Moffett had gained his early training under Camden in the Parkersburg area, and his later experience under Pratt and Rogers. He was a tremendously driving, impetuous, and vocal executive. Cowan, a protégé of McGregor's, was slow, calm, somewhat phleg-

---

[20]*Bradstreet's*, Oct. 25, 1890, p. 682. The first stills were charged with crude on Sept. 2, 1890. The first shipment of refined oil was made on Thanksgiving Day, 1890.

[21]N. Y. *Tribune*, June 14, 1890. By this time the productive area in Ohio had vastly expanded, the Standard's purchase and leases keeping up with it.

[22]See series of articles in the *Stanolind Record*, Vol. IV, Nos. 9, 10, 11, 12, July-Oct., 1923; "Some Early Days of Whiting Refinery," by U. G. Swartz.

matic, and lovable. The two able men thus had complementary qualities. Moffett's dynamic, explosive ways and fits of temper were balanced by Cowan's serenity and deliberation.[23]

Both knew their own faults. Doctor Burton relates that Moffett was once talking with him about the head of the paraffin works, who was also slow and phlegmatic. "But he is a good man—like Cowan," said Moffett. "You know, Bill, a man doesn't have to *rant* like I do to get things done. He can just be *positive*."

In his energetic way, Moffett induced Rockefeller to undertake a general overhauling of Western marketing. Control was obtained of a belt railroad running around Chicago, so that the refinery could easily ship its oils in every direction.[24] The Standard had set up a number of new marketing companies in the Middle West; but Rockefeller consented to abandon them, and assigned their marketing activities to the Standard of Indiana. This erected its own efficient sales division. Oil was shipped into cities and towns all over the Middle West and Far West by tank cars, emptied into storage tanks, and distributed by wagons. South of the Ohio River the Standard of Kentucky and Chess, Carley & Co. did much of the marketing; in the Southwest, Waters-Pierce; and in Nebraska and Kansas, the Consolidated Tank Line. Fast as the Whiting works grew, the marketing facilities grew with them. At no point in the manufacturing or distributing was there any friction, any duplication, or the slightest waste—a fact which leaders like Moffett, Cowan, and Burton ascribed fundamentally to Rockefeller's genius for organization.

The profits from the Ohio-Indiana oil, refined at Lima and Whiting, were enormous. As *Bradstreet's* said, "It is one of the greatest bonanzas that was ever struck, and the Comstock and other wonderful mines are not a circumstance to it."[25]

IV

One reason why vast new springs of petroleum were indispensable lay in the constant discovery of new uses, a process which by 1895 had opened dazzling new vistas before the industry.

In the Paris Exposition of 1867 much attention was attracted by a little engine using an explosive mixture of illuminating gas and air,

[23]I have received much on both men from Doctor W. M. Burton and others.
[24]N. Y. *Tribune,* June 14, 1890.   [25]*Bradstreet's,* Oct. 25, 1890.

ignited by an electric spark—perhaps the world's first true internal-combustion engine. Already an American had suggested that the vapor of light hydrocarbons might propel machinery.[26] After 1870 numerous experiments were made with petroleum as an engine fuel. Of course it was fairly easy to burn it under steam boilers, while oil residuum was often utilized in refinery furnaces, and a little later crude oil in steel mills and other plants. In 1875 a steam automobile employing kerosene for fuel was running about the streets of Paris, and three years afterward its inventor, Amedée Boilée, drove it from Paris to Vienna.[27] But for oil refineries the significant experiments were those with internal-combustion engines.

The really practical history of these motors undoubtedly begins with Doctor N. A. Otto of Cologne, who in 1876 invented an engine in which gas (which might be illuminating gas or the vapor of gasolene) was first compressed and then exploded by a spark; an engine which embodied the main four-cycle principle of all gasolene engines of today. From gas he turned to a distillate of oil. But the motors turned out by the Otto Engine Works, which were soon sold all over Europe, were too heavy for road vehicles and were used exclusively for stationary power. It was therefore left for another Wurttemberger, Gottfried Daimler, to take an epochal further step. A well-educated engineer, he had served in the Otto Works from 1872 to 1882. Then, approaching fifty, he established a shop of his own at Cannstadt, where he built light gasolene engines and soon began attaching them to bicycles, tricycles, and finally motor cars. While Otto's engines, and indeed substantially all gas and oil engines built before 1883, were cumbrous machines whose pistons made only 150–250 strokes a minute, Daimler believed that swift motors were quite practicable; motors whose light shafts could attain a speed of 800 or 1000 strokes a minute. Most engineers declared that such velocities were impossible, but in 1883 Daimler built a small engine which proved that he was right. In 1885–86 he made his first successful experiments with a motorcycle, and on March 4, 1887, ran a motorcar propelled by gasolene.[28]

Other men all over Europe hastened to participate in this develop-

[26]Clark, *Manufactures in the United States*, II, 152.

[27]Waldemar Kaempffert, *Popular History of American Invention*, I, 138, 139.

[28]See sketch of Daimler in *American Trade*, July 15, 1900.

ment, and their names in the next generation became famous throughout the world. Germany had Karl Benz, who at Mannheim in 1885 ran a successful gasolene-driven automobile—two-seated, three-wheeled, with solid rubber tires, and a single-cylinder engine. Patenting his machine early in 1886, he manufactured many more of steadily increasing excellence. France had Panhard, Levassor, and Renault. Great Britain had Napier, Lanchester, Royce, and Austin. In the United States, George B. Selden of Rochester had built a gasolene engine in 1877, and made drawings of a "horseless carriage" to be propelled by his motor. Though he failed to obtain funds for improving and marketing his device, in 1895 he did gain a patent which covered the principle of an internal-combustion engine mounted upon a road vehicle.[29]

The first automobile imported into the United States was a Benz displayed at the Chicago World's Fair in 1893. But a year earlier a motorcar had been built and run in America. Charles E. Duryea, with the help of his brother Frank, constructed a "gasolene buggy" which was tested in Springfield, Mass., on April 19, 1892, and which (as rebuilt the next year) stands today in the Smithsonian Museum as the first American car. His two earliest models did not satisfy him, but the third, completed in 1895, embodied many of the principal features of present-day automobiles, and was unmistakably a success. Its four-cylinder engine, with electric ignition, ran smoothly, while it boasted pneumatic tires, an invention of the Englishman Dunlop. The Duryea automobile won a Thanksgiving Day race from Chicago to Waukegan in 1896 for a purse offered by the Chicago *Times-Herald,* making an average speed of about ten miles an hour to finish first among eleven starters. Next year the Duryea brothers built thirteen more automobiles.[30] Meanwhile competitors were appearing. One was a machinist of Kokomo, Ind., named Ellwood Haynes; one a young farmer and mechanic at Detroit named Henry Ford; and one a bicycle manufacturer in Cleveland named Alexander Winton. Ford's first two-cylinder automobile, tested in 1893 soon after Duryea's, made twenty-five to thirty miles an hour.

[29]Kaempffert, *op. cit.,* I, 148, 149.
[30]Charles E. Duryea, "It Doesn't Pay to Pioneer," *Saturday Evening Post,* May 16, 1931; obituaries of Duryea, New York press, Sept. 29, 1938. Duryea says little of Otto, and professes indebtedness to a considerable line of American inventors.

From "Jubilee" published by the Anglo-American Oil Company Ltd.

1. Early tricycle motorcar used in England
2. Early oil tanker propelled by sails
3. Wolfmüller motorcycle

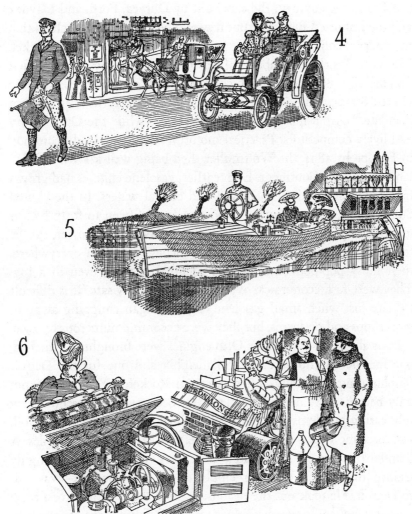

4. Early "Horseless carriage" in England
5. Gasoline launch with engine amidship
6. Early method of filling the automobile in England

It is evident that up to 1896 the automobile was no great consumer of American gasolene. Indeed, that year found only four usable automobiles in the country; the cars built by Duryea, Ford, and Haynes, and the imported Benz car. But it would be an error to conclude that the internal-combustion engine had not as yet affected the oil market. The Otto Works sold about fifteen thousand engines in their first decade, 1876–86, some of which were doubtless imported into the United States, and nearly all of which used some form of petroleum distillate.[31] After 1886 production increased, while the Otto factory had lively competitors. Practical motorcycles became fairly common in Europe by 1894, the Wolfmuller then being well known in England and on the Continent. Even earlier, gasolene engines had grown familiar in small craft on inland and coastal waters. In the United States the "naphtha launch," a boat of from fifteen to forty feet in length equipped with an engine of two or more horsepower, can be traced back to 1884. By 1890 such launches were seen everywhere, their noisy pop-pop unmistakably identifying them even in a fog. They were fast, economical of fuel, and sufficiently safe. It is difficult to state just when small gasolene engines began chugging away in workshops and on farms, but they were becoming numerous by 1900.

In or about 1887 two large Otto engines were brought to America, one for the Cramp yards in Philadelphia and one for the Detroit Shipbuilding Company. They attracted Rockefeller's attention not only because they needed gasolene but because they presented new lubricating problems. The Otto Works had recommended castor oil, but for some reason this would not serve—it clogged the engines. A Standard expert on lubrication, George A. Burke—the first highly trained mechanical engineer employed by the company—was sent to Detroit. He took out the pistons, washed them with kerosene, replaced them, and prescribed No. 23 Red Oil, five gallons of which he had brought from Cleveland. The Standard was proud of this oil, a lubricant having a gravity of 23, a viscosity of more than 200, and a flash-point of about 410 degrees. Pressed out of paraffin, its qualities specially adapted it to engines of great dry inner heat; and when it was applied all trouble with the Otto motor vanished.[32]

During the next ten years numerous engines of the Otto type were

[31]Chicago *Journal of Commerce*, Nov. 24, 1936.
[32]George A. Burke to the author, Nov. 28, 1936.

set up in American plants. They proved especially popular in the electric-light stations then rapidly being built. The Standard supplied them with gasolene, or a distillate halfway between gasolene and kerosene, while it also found in them a widening market for its lubricants. Burke developed the lubricating market by systematic labor. Going to one large plant after another, no matter what its type of power, he hired engineers at the Standard's expense, made careful surveys of the machinery, drew up charts, and offered recommendations for the proper oils. Early in the nineties he established a school for salesmen, giving them a three- to six-months' drill in the correct use of oils, and then sending them out to study plants, make charts, and recommend oil-types. The result soon showed in increased orders and in many expressions of satisfaction with the Standard's service. As time passed the trust encountered sharp competition from other makers of oil—notably Valvoline, Pure Oil, and Kellogg's— who paid their expert salesmen (really lubrication engineers) as much as $15,000 a year. But until after 1900, these firms were interested primarily in heavy oils, leaving the Standard easily foremost in distributing lighter lubricants for internal-combustion engines. When Henry Ford began operating his first car, a Standard salesman named Charles Ross sold him a can of Atlantic Red Oil which he found excellent. The development of lubricants and fuels kept pace with the development of internal-combustion engines, for Rockefeller and his associates saw that it had to do so.[33]

The improvement of the gasolene engine depended upon a whole series of varied advances in technology. The early experiments created a demand for electrical and mechanical appliances—wiring, spark plugs, carburetors, and so on; for new metals and alloys; and for special castings, accessories, and fixtures. These had to be brought to rough perfection and produced in quantity before the gasolene motor was able to compete efficiently with steam.[34] Nevertheless, in the census year 1900 more than 18,500 internal-combustion engines were manufactured in the United States, with a total value of $5,580,-000. Factories were widely scattered over the country, and the size of the motors was increasing. At the Chicago World's Fair in 1893 the largest such engine developed 35 horsepower; at the Paris Expo-

[33]*Idem.*
[34]F. K. Grain, "Age of Gasolene," *Review of Reviews,* XXXII (1905), 320–323.

sition of 1900 a 1000-horsepower engine was shown. These motors rapidly grew familiar to most Americans. They drove boats, they whirled dynamos, they sputtered away in lumber camps, feed-mills, and pump-houses; their staccato in motorcycles and "horseless carriages" would presently rise above the other traffic noises of cities. In the aggregate, by the end of the century they consumed a good deal of naphtha and gasolene.

By that date oil and oil-vapor stoves were also being used in enormous numbers throughout the land, and the business of supplying them with fuel was an important branch of the Standard's activity. Rockefeller had given it much thought and effort, for it offered perplexities. Crude types of oil stoves had been well known as early as 1870, and Professor C. F. Chandler of the Columbia School of Mines in his famous *Report on Petroleum* in 1871 had condemned them all as criminally dangerous. Most of them were so constructed that the naphtha flowed from a small tank into a very hot tube or chamber, where it was vaporized, and from which the vapor then escaped by suitable orifices into burners. Explosions were naturally frequent. "A keg of gunpowder in a building is not as dangerous as one of these stoves," was Chandler's wrathful exclamation as he described how various New Yorkers had been mangled or roasted alive.[35] Yet the stoves were so cheap and convenient that the demand grew.

Naturally, all refiners were interested in encouraging this demand. Throughout the seventies and eighties there was little market for naphtha or gasolene as distinguished from kerosene, and oil companies looked anxiously for outlets. Late in the seventies Rockefeller suggested that the Standard negotiate with a Cleveland manufacturer of vapor stoves named M. L. Hull, and find if by united effort they could not design an apparatus that would be reasonably safe, and could be sold in quantity throughout the vast plains region, from Iowa and Kansas north to the Dakotas, where wood was scarce. C. M. Higgins was sent out to the Middle West to make a survey of the potential market and to talk with Hull. He found local dealers enthusiastic over the idea, and Hull entirely willing to co-operate. A better stove was soon being manufactured. Then, since Hull was old and his work did not prove entirely satisfactory, other manufacturers were approached, and still better designs were put on the market.

[35]*Report on Petroleum*, 32, 33.

Early in the eighties the Standard had a large business in the Middle West and on the Great Plains selling stoves and fuel.[36]

By 1884 both oil-vapor stoves and so-called kerosene stoves or gasolene stoves were widely distributed. Since the former required the vaporization of a light oil, and were dangerous in careless hands, New York and many other cities prohibited the sale either of them or their fuel. They were restricted to the country, and were justly regarded with distrust even there. Yet a competent authority declared: "For those able and willing to exercise a reasonable degree of care, the oil-vapor stove is by far the most agreeable and economical means for light cookery as yet available." With naphtha selling at $3 a barrel or six cents a gallon, the cost of using a vapor stove was very small.[37] Kerosene and gasolene stoves were more popular, and many good designs were on the market. As most of them burned heavier oils than vapor stoves, they were relatively safe; and it was generally agreed that a few simple precautions would have prevented ninety-nine in a hundred of the occasional accidents that were reported. The worst fault of the oil stove in the eighties was that, after perhaps months of efficient service, it would fall into a mysterious fit of sullenness and sootiness. But it was steadily being improved, and the day was at hand when it would be found in nearly every farm and village home. In summer it robbed the kitchen of half its heat; while the average cost of running most models was only about a cent an hour.[38]

In 1891 Rockefeller brought Charles M. Higgins east to New York for the purpose of developing a New England market for stove-fuels in the same way that he had built up the Middle Western market. Higgins set to work, and within two years attained a marked success. But just as he was rubbing his hands over the growing volume of orders, Rockefeller and Ambrose McGregor perceived that the demand for gasolene by makers of the new internal-combustion engines was actually growing at a rate which would not permit the Standard to increase its stove-oil sales. There would not be enough gasolene or naphtha to go around! The campaign in New England was abruptly discontinued—so abruptly that Higgins had to persuade the Chicago stove-manufacturers to take back a large consignment they had ship-

[36]Charles M. Higgins to the author, Oct. 27, 1936.
[37]*American Annual Cyclopædia, 1885,* p. 386.   [38]*Ibid.*

ped to him. They appreciated his predicament, and consented to a reasonable adjustment.[39] One New England inventor of oil stoves, it may be noted, was the well-known manufacturer and social reformer Edward Atkinson. He devised the "Aladdin Oven," in which he asserted that a little more than a quart of kerosene, burned with an ordinary lamp wick, did as much work in roasting or boiling as 120 pounds of coal burned in an ordinary cooking stove.[40]

Even in the illuminating field, the oil industry could rejoice over gains as well as bewail heavy losses. To be sure, during the eighties and nineties the electric light advanced like a conquering army in all urban areas. The world's first central station for incandescent lighting, the Holborn Viaduct station in London, was opened in the early days of 1882 by the English Edison Electric Light Company. The second was Edison's own Pearl Street station in New York, where on December 4, 1882, the current was turned into about four hundred lights. Men eagerly read of the first church lighted by incandescent lamps, the City Temple in London; of the first theatre, the Bijou in Boston; of the first hotel, the Blue Mountain House in the Adirondacks. Yet the inroads of electricity upon sales of kerosene were for many years slow and immaterial. Until the end of the century the incandescent light appeared chiefly in those more thickly populated communities where people had long depended on gas rather than kerosene for illumination.

Meanwhile, ever since the middle seventies there had been a steady increase in the demand for oil as an ingredient of carbureted water-gas, which might better have been called petroleum gas. This new industry grew out of experiments performed by a number of Europeans and Americans, chief among them T. S. C. Lowe, who had been famous during the Civil War as a balloonist and chief of the aeronautic section of the United States Army, and who afterward went into the manufacture of artificial ice and other enterprises; his name is perpetuated by Mount Lowe near Pasadena. In Lowe's process hydrogen was mingled with carbon oxides, and the mixture was then combined with richly carbureted gases, taken usually from petroleum. The first plant to use it was opened at Phoenixville, Pa., in the spring of 1874, and the second was erected at Conshohocken in

[39]Charles M. Higgins to the author, Oct. 27, 1936.
[40]National Cyclopædia of American Biography, IX, 416.

1874–75. They proved so successful that others rapidly sprang up in various parts of the East. For several years the new process was vigorously opposed by makers of coal-gas, but in time many of them adopted it.[41] Not only did water-gas cost less in labor and materials, but its illuminating power was greater. By 1900 more than three fourths of all the gas consumed in America was carbureted water-gas, requiring nearly two hundred million gallons of oil or oil distillate;[42] while much was manufactured abroad. Rockefeller and his partners always evinced a keen interest in this particular market. Here lay the principal reason why William G. Warden became the most prominent figure in Philadelphia utilities, and one of the reasons why William Rockefeller and H. H. Rogers went into gas-manufacture in Boston and New York.

Indeed, no outlet for oil was missed by Rockefeller. It is interesting to find him writing Archbold on August 20, 1888, in the midst of the first Cleveland-Harrison campaign: "Am fearful we shall be cornered this year for bulk cars, for increase and demand will be more than ordinary owing to the torchlight processions." One market alone he disliked; it was his policy to sell as little crude oil as possible. "He thought it much too valuable," a subordinate has said.[43] After the Frasch process was perfected no more crude went to Chicago mills, and he was indifferent to the news of oil-burning locomotives and ships.

It is not impossible that, in the perspective of time, men will speak of a petroleum revolution for the years 1859–1940 as they now speak of the "coal revolution" that took place in England in 1550–1650. What had once been despised in England as a "noxious and disgusting" fuel, dug in surface pits, gradually became indispensable. It gave new impetus to the salt industry, based on the boiling of seawater in huge iron kettles; it gave fresh life to the glass-trade, helping to make window-glass cheap; and as the British forests were exhausted, brewers, tanners, smiths, and other craftsmen took it up. Then the iron industry began employing the fuel on a large scale, and in 1705 the Newcomen engine was patented. Progress in the "petroleum revolution" was much more rapid. First, light and lubri-

[41]Oscar E. Norman, *The Romance of the Gas Industry*, 71, 72.
[42]*Twelfth Census*, X, 711 ff.
[43]Charles M. Higgins to the author, Jan. 13, 1937.

cation; then fuel for various industries; then small gasolene engines; then the automobile; then the aeroplane, the Diesel engine, and other uses—such was the march, until petroleum seemed indispensable to civilization. And in no land was the march so rapid as in America.

v

But until the rise of the automobile the export market was far more important to the Standard than the home market; and Rockefeller had to pay assiduous attention to a competition from other nations which grew fiercer and stronger. In the seventies the United States stood almost alone as a producer of oil for western Europe and Asia, its exports of kerosene rising in that decade from 97,900,000 to 367,325,000 gallons. The eighties witnessed the sudden and powerful entrance of Russia into the world market, while the nineties saw the oil fields of Burma and the Dutch East Indies becoming formidable competitors in certain areas. Nevertheless, American kerosene exports rose to 551,000,000 gallons in 1890, and to 740,000,000 in 1900. Rockefeller for years stood alone, the solitary giant in the world's refining industry. Then lesser but important figures rose beside him— Alfred Nobel, Henri Deterding, Marcus Samuels. Only by keeping prices low and quality high did American manufacturers maintain their unquestioned supremacy. In doing this the Standard played the leading rôle, and to its enterprise, system, and shrewdness must be given credit for the maintenance of American primacy.

The Standard always prided itself on the excellence of its products, and Rockefeller insisted on elaborate precautions. The laboratories he set up in every refinery tested the wares at each stage of manufacture, while the laboratory at 26 Broadway made checking tests on every shipment from the various works. When a tank steamer was loaded at Hunter's Point or Bayonne, a ship-officer took samples from every tank, placed them in a locked case, and sent them to 26 Broadway. When the ship reached London or Bremen, the same officer took another series of samples, put them in another locked case, and sent them back on the next steamer. Tests revealed any deterioration. An unfavorable result was called sharply to the attention of the refinery which had made the product, while warning was sent to the marketing department in Europe to be on the watch for complaints and to permit replacements. Rockefeller and his associates were quick to respond to any criticism. When a protest about the quality of some kerosene was cabled from Norway, three men were instantly dispatched to investigate. They found that fishermen on the lonely Norwegian coast had used the oil in lamps previously employed for burning fish-oil, which had become foul and clogged. Demonstrations convinced the fishermen that they had no real ground for protests. The inquiry had cost the company $5000, but it vindicated the "standard" of the oil.[44]

When the production of the Bradford field became heavy, reports reached the United States that oil of poor character was being shipped overseas. German dealers in 1878–79 made reiterated complaints. The consul at Antwerp, a great oil-importing point, wrote the State Department early in 1879 that unless satisfactory assurances were given for the future, he feared the Belgian government would restrict the shipments of refined oil by heavy duties, or exclude all cargoes that did not meet a fixed standard.[45] Rockefeller had already sent an expert to Europe to investigate the complaints, and he reported that the trouble arose not from imperfect refining, but from the fact that Bradford oil differed sharply in specific gravity and other characteristics from that previously exported, and required different wicks and burners. He believed that it was no more likely to explode than the Allegheny Valley grades, and was as good an illuminant. Efforts were made to convince European dealers of all this, and the Standard marketed new wicks and burners at cost in Europe. It had no use for the oil lamp that Mark Twain described—"the kind that shed a gloom." But the complaints continued.

Germany offered the best market in Europe, and a gathering of dealers at Bremen this spring insisted that the oil, rather than the appliances, was at fault. Especially, they declared, were some of the Standard brands deficient: they demanded better refining to keep the kerosene free from "acids and heavy oils," and better inspection, so that the certificates sent abroad should more accurately represent the merchandise. This was a challenge to the New York Produce

[44]Harold J. Howland, "Standard Oil," *Outlook,* Sept. 28, 1907. See *Consular Report* 84 (1887), 641: "Our petroleum comes in nice, presentable, handy shape, in well-made, fine cases, containing two tin cans of five gallons each, and it is really and truly refined petroleum—a good article."
[45]N. Y. *Tribune,* March 21, 1879.

Exchange, which had established rules upon the quality of oil shipped from the port, and helped supervise the inspection. Moreover, the German dealers asked for careful tests of specific gravity, guarantees of odor as well as color, and more accurate statements of gross weight.[46] When these German complaints were taken up by a committee of the Exchange, they provoked stormy dissent. H. H. Rogers attacked them as nonsense, saying that he did not believe a single gallon of acid-containing oil had ever been exported. An oil-inspector supported him, and other experts declared that the Germans did not know what was meant by "heavy oils." Nevertheless, the complaints made American refiners more careful in treating Bradford crude; while better attention was given to barrels and cargo-stowage, and an improved oil-testing device was adopted.[47]

Somewhat similar complaints came from abroad several years after the Standard began shipping large quantities of kerosene made from Lima oil. In 1893-94 the Standard agents in Germany reported that the government was actually considering the exclusion of such kerosene. Rockefeller and the other members of the Executive Committee decided to send one of the ablest chemists of the country to Berlin with samples, and have him demonstrate the baselessness of the charges. The logical choice was Professor Chandler, who had studied at Göttingen and Berlin, spoke German fluently, had many friends among scientists, and was known all over the world as an expert on petroleum. He asked for a practical refiner to go with him, and Doctor W. M. Burton was chosen. They left for Germany late in 1895, carrying a five-gallon can of ordinary export kerosene made from Lima oil. After an interview with the German Chancellor, Prince Hohenlohe, they talked the matter over with other government officials, fitted up a laboratory, and conclusively showed a German expert assigned to report on the subject that the Lima product was equal to that from the Pennsylvania crude. The government dropped the proposed embargo, and the Standard continued to fill many of its Continental orders with kerosene from Ohio.[48]

American kerosene had spread all over Europe during the seventies, even lighting the lamps of some areas—northern Russia, Galicia,

[46]N. Y. *Times,* April 23, 1879.
[47]N. Y. *Times,* April 28, May 9, 13, 14, 1879.
[48]Doctor W. M. Burton to the author, July 21, 1939.

Rumania—which later became famous for their own oil. By the eighties the Far Eastern market had also become very important. The American consul in Singapore reported in the fall of 1882 that oil was coming from the United States to the Straits Settlements through Penang and Singapore in "immense" quantities. While it was of excellent quality and had caused few accidents, he feared that fires started by the inferior Burma oil used by the lower classes would lead to restrictive legislation—against which he was using his influence.[49] Numerous consular reports in the next few years traced the expansion of American oil-marketing in India, the Malay Peninsula, and China. The Standard Oil sent an energetic and talented agent, W. H. Libby, to the Orient to promote its sales, and he proved brilliantly successful. We find the consul-general in Calcutta early in 1883 praising his work in India, and a little later our minister in China, John R. Young, speaking of him with equal enthusiasm. He had written a circular in the Chinese language setting forth the cheapness and brilliance of kerosene, and Young instructed the American consulates to help distribute this among the natives.[50]

Throughout the eighties and nineties the Standard controlled nearly all the American trade in Asia, Africa, and South America, the independent refiners selling but small quantities. It was a trade with many romantic aspects. Sampans poled by coolies carried case-oil far up the streams of China; oxcarts lumbered with it along the great North Road that Kim travelled in India; it lighted the compounds and palaces of the half-savage native chieftains whom Sir Hugh Clifford has described in his books on Malaysia. Joseph Conrad in his days under the red ensign doubtless watched many a boatful of case-oil unloading in the ports of Oceania. Our consul in Singapore reported in 1887 that the Standard, as yet unworried by foreign competition, transshipped oil there for all the wide regions roundabout. It was sent to the east coast of Sumatra, to the Isthmus of Malacca, to British Burma, to Siam, to French Cochin-China, and to the greater part of Borneo. The consul described the distribution to numerous harbors and far-lying islands of the Dutch and British

---

[49]*Consular Report* 22 (1882), 409.

[50]*Consular Report* 42; pp. 82 ff., 97 ff. It is obviously impossible to give more than a brief sketch of the Standard's export trade under Rockefeller's direction. Full treatment of the subject requires a volume in itself—and some day the volume will be written.

possessions by small steamers, Chinese junks, and Malay prahees.[51]
An equal romance, though of a different kind, attached to the tens
of millions of gallons of oil sent by 1890 to all parts of Latin America
—coastal towns, plantations, ranches, and mining-camps.

But if American "independents" counted for little, foreign competitors soon lifted their heads. In Austria-Hungary early in the
eighties the Standard met the rivalry of the native Galician product,
distinctly inferior to American oil but sustained by the government.
One of the first refiners in Galicia, curiously enough, was James Corrigan of Cleveland, whose works had been bought by the Standard
in 1872. He visited Austria-Hungary in the spring of 1879 to inspect
the fields, concluded that a plant built on American principles would
be successful, and after importing American machinery and opera-
tives, opened a $40,000 refinery in 1880. Though everybody agreed
that the development of the Galician oil-deposits would be a great
boon to the country, Corrigan as a foreigner encountered much
jealousy and opposition. For a time the producers even refused to sell
to him. But by his subborn Irish fighting spirit, obtaining supplies
of American crude oil through Hamburg, he finally broke down
this foolish enmity.[52] Other refineries were set up, and large amounts
of kerosene were soon marketed in the Dual Monarchy; but it never
really affected the world market.

The great antagonist was Russia; and though no history mentions
the Russo-American War of 1885–1910 in oil, that conflict raged constantly and relentlessly. In the Baku field the Russians had a rich
source of supply, and in the three Nobel brothers, Robert Hjalmar,
Ludwig, and Alfred, a gifted and tireless group of industrial captains.
Baku lies on the Caspian Sea, between 500 and 600 miles from the
Black Sea ports of Poti and Batum. The oil-bearing district here
was small, the area worked in 1885 being only about three and a
half miles square, and the wells were not deep. But the field was
distinguished by its enormous yield; many of the four hundred or
more wells threw up jets from one hundred to three hundred feet
high, and one of the Nobel shafts long yielded, whenever opened,
about 1,125,000 gallons a day. In 1884 the production was approximately 1,130,000 tons, as against roughly 3,000,000 tons in the United
States, and the price for crude oil on the spot was but one eighth or

[51]*Consular Report* 84, pp. 641 ff.   [52]*Consular Report* 4, pp. 246 ff.

one tenth of the normal American price.[53] The number of refineries
in the "Black Town" quarter of Baku rose from about 60 in 1884
to 147 in 1889, with the Nobel works much the most important. The
petroleum made an excellent lamp oil, almost free from color or
odor, but giving less illumination than Standard kerosene.[54]

After 1880 Rockefeller and his associates felt a mounting concern
over the threat of the Baku refineries. The American industry depended for the larger part of its returns upon the foreign market,
and expected this market to expand more rapidly than home consumption. Between 1873 and 1880 the Baku field, hampered by poor
transportation, fell short of meeting even Russia's demands. As the
flow of oil increased so did Muscovite consumption, so that American
oil was steadily shipped in from the Baltic. But the Russian importations dropped from 2,700,000 poods in 1873 to 1,700,000 in 1877, and
1,445,000 in 1880. Evidently the vanishing point lay just ahead. Evidently also Russia was fast gaining a position which would enable
her to throw a large surplus upon foreign markets.

This point was attained in the middle eighties. Russian oil then,
with what seemed to unobservant people startling suddenness, began
pouring into the world market. The completion of the Trans-Cau-
casian and Black Sea Railroad made it possible to ship large quantities westward over the mountains to Batum, which became the chief
export center. Moreover, the Russian refiners, and especially the
Nobel brothers, showed an enterprise in water-transportation from
which even Americans had something to learn. They developed
large fleets of tankers on the Caspian, the Black Sea, and the Mediterranean. They shipped great quantities of kerosene up the Volga
into the heart of Russia; and they built many tank cars, which carried oil as far north as the Baltic, where it was transshipped to north
European points. Ludwig Nobel is credited with drafting the original plans, in 1885, for a tank ship divided into watertight compart-
ments in such fashion that the oil could be kept under rigid control,
and yet be rapidly loaded and discharged. The Nobels opened a large
shipyard at Astrakhan on the Caspian, while their Black Sea tankers
were soon passing through the Dardanelles for Smyrna, Naples,

[53]See the historical article on Baku oil in *Bradstreet's,* April 25, 1891.
[54]J. D. Henry, *Baku, An Eventful History;* Charles Marvin, *The Region of
the Eternal Fire.*

Trieste, and other Mediterranean ports.[55] Between 1885 and 1888 they placed themselves in a position to exploit the whole European and Near Eastern market. Simultaneously, Russia began shipping a much larger part of its export-oil abroad in refined form. In 1883 refined petroleum represented only about two fifths of the Russian exports, and in 1890 four fifths.

The appearance of Baku oil was heralded by a chorus of warning reports from American consuls, and alarmist dispatches in American trade journals. From Switzerland, Consul-General Cramer wrote the State Department early in 1885 of the serious threat. He learned that Baku kerosene had substantially supplanted American oil in all Russian markets, and that the Russian government was doing everything possible to provide cheap carriage to western Europe.[56] It was being retailed in St. Petersburg at two cents a pound! From Athens the American consul wrote in the same terms. In Greece the sale of kerosene was a government monopoly, and Standard products had long been exclusively used. But in 1886 the government made a trial importation of 6200 cases of Russian kerosene, and threatened to bring in more.[57] The Beirut consul sent word that although oil was the principal article of American export to Asia Minor, and although it had displaced olive oil as the principal means of illumination, now it was threatened. The Russians had shipped Baku oil into Beirut in the spring of 1885, but its quality was poor. During 1886 it was improved, while its low price enabled it to make heavy inroads on the American market. The Baku tins were a close imitation of those used by the Standard Oil. A gloomy prospect was painted by the consul, who pointed out that transportation from Baku cost only 10 cents a case as against 23 cents from New York.[58]

So the story went for two or three years. In 1885 our consul-general in Vienna reported that sales of American oil were sharply declining. One reason lay in the rising Galician production. Another was that high tariffs were placed on American kerosene, while Russia sent much partially refined petroleum to Trieste and Fiume, where it was admitted almost duty-free, and the refining completed on Austro-

---

[55]J. D. Henry, *op. cit.*, 123 ff.

[56]Feb. 12, 1885; *Consular Report* 53, pp. 204 ff. Robert Nobel settled in Baku in 1875; a few years later his brother Ludwig, known as a great shipbuilder on the Neva, joined him.

[57]*Consular Report* 89, pp. 151 ff.   [58]*Consular Report* 64, pp. 161 ff.

Hungarian soil. He complained also of the systematic use of Standard trade-names by Galician and Russian refiners. In his opinion, American oil interests would do well to erect refineries near Trieste, under Austrian supervision, and ship their crude over in a raw or half-refined state.[59] And the news from Germany, an all-important market, was temporarily dark indeed. The German government appeared to be indulging in outright discrimination against American brands. It lowered the duty on all oil arriving in bulk, whether by land or water, and at the same time raised the tariff on petroleum barrels. This allowed the Russians to ship great quantities of oil across the border in tank cars, but penalized American shippers of barrelled kerosene. Four marks were refunded on every barrel reexported within nine months, but naturally many barrels were lost in the interior of Germany.[60] As for Great Britain, Russian imports suddenly leaped from 7000 barrels in 1888 to 37,000 in 1889, and about 70,000 in 1890.[61]

But as time passed more reassuring news reached Rockefeller at 26 Broadway. The cheap Baku oil lost much of its attraction to Europeans when they discovered that it did not burn as long or brightly as the Standard wares. The Greek government, for example, found its 6200 cases so inferior that the director of the monopoly declared he would buy no more. Indeed, no further attempt was made to dislodge American oil from Greece until the spring of 1892. Similarly, the consul at Beirut exchanged his gloom in 1886 for optimism a year later. The consumers of Russian oil, he reported, had been disappointed by its poor quality and rapid combustion, which made it necessary to burn more lamps to light a room and to refill them oftener; while they suffered from leakage of the badly soldered tins. They were inquiring again for American oil—for the old Standard brands.[62] Hopeful news came also from Great Britain. Our consul at Bristol wrote that while Russian oil in 1885 had seemed about to menace the market for American kerosene, during 1886 the Standard and other exporters had shut the Baku product out by sharp price-reductions. The American companies dominated the ordinary channels of trade, and had built up an unassailable reputation. He commented on the extensive and fast-growing use of tank steamers by

[59]*Consular Report* 64, pp. 151 ff. [61]*Bradstreet's*, May 2, 1891.
[60]*Consular Report* 127, pp. 639 ff. [62]*Consular Report* 89, pp. 364 ff.

American interests, saying that they offered much the cheapest transportation even if they had to return in ballast. The renewed Russian effort to capture the British market in 1887–90 was promptly countered by the Standard with renewed price-cuts.[63]

Reports which Rockefeller read from Standard agents showed that a contest between the southern and northern ports of Europe was involved in the Russo-American war. In 1885–89 the special petroleum harbor at Trieste, and the use of "cistern-cars," enabled that port and Fiume to send oil not only to Switzerland and Italy, but to southern and central Germany. "Quite latterly, however," observed the London *Economist*,[64] "the successful competition of the ports of Hamburg, Bremen, and Antwerp has been acutely felt, because the reduction of the price of American petroleum enables these ports to send it far into the Continent." This was the cheap Lima oil that Rockefeller's foresight and Frasch's skill had made such an asset to the Standard!

The fierce Russian onset was not met by haphazard strokes. It was resisted by hard methodical planning at 26 Broadway, in which Rockefeller took the lead; by a detailed and carefully co-ordinated campaign, whose main features he decided. He had seen to that careful study of the foreign field which we have already noticed. On this foundation was reared a superb marketing structure. The Standard by 1885 had acquired thousands of tons of shipping in the coastwise trade and a great fleet in the foreign trade, and had done its share in perfecting the tank ship.[65] The first tankers were sailing vessels, for it was feared that steam furnaces might start a fire in mid-ocean, but it soon became possible to build safe steamships for the purpose. The real danger lay in explosive gases, particularly in converted ships—usually vessels in whose hold great iron tanks had been set up.[66] But the Standard soon insisted on tankers so well designed and staunchly compartmented that absolute control could be exercised over every pint of oil aboard. Warehouses and storage tanks were obtained at strategic points throughout Europe. Then the

[63]*Consular Report* 82, pp. 186 ff.
[64]*Economist,* Nov. 23, 1889.
[65]Taylor, MS History of the Standard Oil, 93.
[66]Victor Ross, *Evolution of the Oil Industry,* 119 ff.

Standard went on to acquire or incorporate a series of marketing companies in foreign lands, as it had already acquired or incorporated them throughout the United States.

A full list of these companies would be tedious. We have already mentioned the West Indian Oil Refining Company (incorporated 1882), which dealt with the West Indies and part of Latin America. The Anglo-American Oil Company, Ltd. (1887) was purely a Standard Oil enterprise, with no outside partners. So was the Danish Company (1888), which had many subsidiaries scattered throughout Scandinavia. In the German-American Petroleum Company, organized in 1890, the great Standard Oil marketing agency in Germany, the trust had as partners until 1904 the Riedermanns, a firm of energy and ability. It also had Dutch partners in its Netherland agency, the American Petroleum Company. The Societa Italo-Americana del Petrolio was organized under the laws of Italy in 1891, the Standard holding 60 per cent of the stock; it represented a union with the powerful oil-distributing firm of B. Walter Company of Venice. The Standard bought a half interest in a large Canadian marketing company, the Imperial Oil Company, Ltd., in 1898, and incorporated in it other Dominion companies—for example, the Queen City Oil Company, Ltd., of Toronto—in which it had long been dominant. This enumeration of foreign corporations which the Standard controlled might be greatly prolonged. They formed a carefully integrated, highly aggressive phalanx pushing Standard products all over the globe.[67]

Particularly striking was the victory of the Standard Oil in Germany, on the very borders of Russia. The German people had formed a decided preference for the American product if prices could be kept anywhere near equality. To drive back the Baku oil, the Standard slashed rates wherever necessary. It induced, or according to press

[67]Taylor, *op. cit.*, 90 ff., treats this subject in some detail. The consular reports also deal with them. Mr. Taylor states of the Anglo-American Oil Company (p. 93): "It had two sets of books, an American set kept in New York on which was carried as a single item the amount invested in England, and an English set on which was carried, on the other hand, as a single item the amount of the investments in the United States." The Bureau of Corporations reported in 1907 (*Report on the Petroleum Industry, Part II*, 419) that in Great Britain up to 1903 the Standard held the whip hand over Russia and "was able to dictate."

reports quoted by the consul-general in Berlin, *compelled* the principal oil merchants of Bremen, Hamburg, and Stettin to join it in forming the German-American Petroleum Company. The great Bremen firm of Albert Nicholas Schuette & Company was forced into the organization by the Standard's threat to transfer all shipments to two large Hamburg houses if it refused. Tankers flying the flag of the new corporation brought oil in bulk to the north German ports, where vast storage facilities were provided. To avoid the barrel duty, cooperage works were erected at Geestemünde. Storage depots were built in Duisburg, Mannheim, and other interior cities; the whole of Germany was divided into districts assigned to different firms belonging to the combination; and an elaborate marketing organization was perfected.[68] By 1890 the Standard had leased harbor front lands from the municipality of Rotterdam for oil storage, and was making extensive use of Amsterdam and Antwerp as inlets to northern and central Europe.[69] The Russians had strained every nerve. The German-Russian Naphtha Importing Company, a Nobel concern, had purchased an island near Stettin on which to build large storage tanks, and had announced in 1887 that it would sell kerosene for a good deal less than the 18-cent-a-gallon rate then charged by the Standard at retail in north Germany.[70] But the consul at Stettin reported in 1891 that while Russian oil was cheaper, it could not vie in popular esteem with the superior American grade.[71] Only in south Germany and Austria-Hungary was the Russian competition seriously felt. In 1890 the total exports of Russian oil (240,256,000 gallons) were little more than one third the total American exports (692,042,000 gallons); and this lead was maintained.[72]

Invariably the success of the Standard aroused jealousy, and the size of its European operations alarm. The Berlin correspondent of the New York *Sun,* reflecting strong feeling there and in Hamburg, wrote in 1891 that many Germans were apprehensive of the trust. "First it got control of the American . . . refiners, then of the American export business, next of the private shipping interests, then of the European importing business, then of the export from European ports, and now it seems to be trying to seize the entire retail trade."

[68]*Consular Report* 127, pp. 639 ff.; No. 131, 647 ff.
[69]*Consular Report* 116, pp. 41 ff.   [71]*Consular Report* 127, pp. 639 ff.
[70]*Consular Report* 81, pp. 111 ff.   [72]*Bradstreet's,* Dec. 5, 1891.

He had interviewed Max Gaede, director of the Nobel's German-Russian Company:[73]

"According to my information," said Mr. Gaede, "the Standard Oil Company has within the last few months managed to secure a combination of all the large houses in Bremen and Hamburg which are engaged in the coal-oil trade. It paid them big prices for their interests and improvements, and then organized them into a stock company, the German-American Petroleum Company, in which it holds the controlling interest. It bought out Schuette & Company of Bremen and Riedermann & Company of Geestemünde for ten million marks. It paid proportionately large sums to Hamburg houses. All these houses are in the new corporation. It has done the same thing at Rotterdam and Antwerp, where it has formed stock companies, with a capital of about five million guilders each, in order to control the trade of Holland and Belgium. We have just now received the information that the Standard Oil has bought out the firm of Walter & Company, of Venice, who control the oil trade of Italy. This firm had many tank steamers and immense receiving tanks and depots at Venice, Genoa, and Savana, in Italy, and Arth-Goldau, in Switzerland. Now it has been combined with the Standard Oil Company, which of course has a controlling interest, under the name of the Societa Italo-Americana del Petrolio. . . ."

"Cannot the government break the power of the company by special laws?"

"No, it can do nothing. Everything has been done in a strictly legal way. There is apparently no ring, only a regular mercantile corporation. . . ."

Mr. Gaede's talk and manner conveyed the impression that he thought the Standard Oil powerful enough to defeat all opposition, and that, realizing this fact, his company would gracefully surrender if hard pressed, and if a big price were paid for the surrender. Should this take place the Standard would hold uncontrolled sway on the continent. . . .

The first London office of the Anglo-American Company was opened in April, 1888. This corporation helped the Standard's sharp drive against Scottish manufacturers of oil and paraffin from shale. It soon became one of the leading owners of tank steamers in the world, and its ship *Narragansett,* with a capacity of 77,000 barrels of

[73]Quoted in *Bradstreet's,* July 4, 1891. The same issue of *Bradstreet's* quotes the treasurer of the Standard as telling a reporter in New York: "We are pursuing a legitimate business and furnishing oil to Europe and Asia cheaper than any other producer. The only parties who appear to be dissatisfied are the Russian agents. The consumers have not objected. They want to get oil as cheaply as they can, and we can furnish it to them at lower rates than the Russian houses can." But later reports from Europe in *Bradstreet's* (Sept. 12,

refined oil, was for a time the largest tanker afloat. Huge plants for storage and distribution were set up at various points: at Purfleet on the Thames, Birkenhead opposite Liverpool, Avonmouth, Plymouth, Hull, Newcastle, Belfast, and Dublin. Each usually held a three- or four-months' supply, keeping the oil in bulk as long as possible, lest the barrels affect its quality. By the end of the century the company had about three hundred small storage depots in the British Isles, and was making deliveries by some six hundred tank wagons. It had also about five hundred tank cars on British railroads, constantly bringing oil from the seaboard installations to the inland depots.[74] In France the Standard had made in 1888 a friendly arrangement with Duché et Fils, the largest individual importer of crude oil.

Rockefeller and his partners kept the Standard tirelessly busy and ceaselessly vigilant abroad. They had to, for when beaten at one point, Russian oil would appear at another; the Nobel brothers were no mean antagonists. At one time they heard that Russia was gaining a dangerous predominance in India. Consul Ballantine reported in 1891 that during the fiscal year 1889-90 the imports of kerosene through Bombay had been more than three fourths Russian, and less than one fourth American. Again they heard, in 1893, that France and Russia had concluded a bargain by which the French reduced the duties on Baku oil, while the Russians lowered the tariff on about sixty French commodities.[75] Still again they learned, in 1894-95, that the rise in Galician production threatened to leave no room whatever in Austria-Hungary for imports.[76] Pennsylvania producers who had yelled to high heaven over "immediate shipment" prices could have read in the London *Economist* in 1896 that, as a result of overproduction, Galician crude was sold at the producers' cost, for no storage was available.[77] But by hard work Rockefeller and his associates kept

---

Nov. 7, 1891, etc.) make it clear that great numbers of German jobbers, brokers, and retailers were deeply alarmed by the formation of the German-American Petroleum Company, with its enormous power. They fear, said *Bradstreet's*, "lest their trade and occupation may become completely swallowed up by the gigantic maw of the Standard Oil Company." And some of them began a fight which it is impossible to trace here. See the N. Y. *World*, May 24, 1894, for W. H. Libby's operations for the Standard in Germany.

[74]*Petroleum Review*, X, 163 (Feb. 20, 1904).

[75]London *Economist*, Sept. 28, 1895.

[76]*Idem*, Feb. 15, 1896.

[77]*London and China Telegraph*, March 18, 1895.

the Standard exports rising, and the Standard products well entrenched in public esteem. Throughout the world they had the active co-operation of American ministers and consuls. The government was threatening the Standard with prosecution at home; abroad it was helping it sell its wares.

Early in the nineties new sources of supply and new leaders began to appear. By 1894 case-oil from Sumatra was making heavy inroads upon the American market in China. In the Dutch East Indies, American sales continued to grow encouragingly for a time; but the sales of Sumatra oil, and after 1897, from fields opened in Borneo and Java, mounted more rapidly still. The day was plainly at hand when the principal struggle in the Far East would be between American and Dutch East Indian brands. And as the fields in this quarter of the globe were developed, Rockefeller began to hear of men whose names would later become familiar everywhere—of a shrewd English Jew, Marcus Samuels, the first organizer of petroleum transport through the Suez Canal, who became Lord Bearsted; and of a shrewd Dutchman named Henri Deterding.

The Standard always maintained that the foreign market could never have been conquered so promptly, or held so vigorously, without its extraordinary resources in oil, capital, and brains. If it had not been conquered and held, prices of the heavy production of American oil would have dropped into the abyss. This contention was later sharply challenged by the Pure Oil Company and other independents, who declared that *they* would have stepped into the breach. But it is incontestable that they could have done so only slowly and haltingly; and that had it not been for the enormous power and matchless organization of the Standard, the cheaper Russian oil would have wiped out a large part of the American market after 1885.[78] The Standard maintained, again, that in general it did not build up its foreign market at the expense of its domestic customers; that except for special places and periods it did not cut prices abroad while marking them up at home. This contention also was briskly combated by the independents. After Archbold took control of the Standard the price policy unquestionably discriminated against the United States; but the Bureau of Corporations showed

[78]*Federal Industrial Commission Hearings*, I, pp. 124 ff., 273 ff., 562 ff., 617 ff.

that this discrimination did not become marked until 1903–05, long after Rockefeller retired, while evidence given to the Industrial Commission indicates that during the eighties and most of the nineties the Standard's charges abroad were substantially higher than at home. In Europe, according to Standard witnesses, the ordinary price was not merely above that of equivalent grades of kerosene in America, but above the price of even the highest grades.[79] Both the Standard and independents were sometimes accused of shipping poor oil abroad, and indeed it was technically second-grade oil. But ample testimony exists that it was better illuminating oil than the Russian or Dutch products.[80]

The oil market was always primarily a world market, and prices were fixed mainly by world production and world demand. The domain of oil was expanding fast and magnificently. When Rockefeller took up the business of refining it had been a minor and precarious branch of American industry. Twenty years later it was a great world industry, and every year it was becoming greater. To be the principal leader in this domain—and in Europe, Asia, and Latin America as well as the United States nobody questioned Rockefeller's leadership—was to be a figure of world-wide fame and power.

But his power had been won by steps which brought him under incessant fire. From the remarkable story of the organization and growth of the Standard we must turn back to the still more remarkable tale of the efforts of the State and Federal governments to make it amenable to their authority.

[79]*Idem*, I, pp. 568 ff., 791 ff.; *Report of the Commissioner of Corporations on the Petroleum Industry, Part II, Prices and Profits* (1907), pp. 407 ff. The author would not be positive on this subject of price discrimination. A full study would take months of labor in tracing price-fluctuations. But it is clear that *gross* discriminations began under Archbold after Rockefeller had retired.
[80]*Idem*, I, pp. 274 ff.

XXIX

The Rising Storm

WHILE Rockefeller was still living quietly in Cleveland, and the Standard combination was just beginning to crystallize into a trust, the first heavy guns in the bombardment which they were to endure boomed forth in Ohio, Pennsylvania, and New York. To the abortive Ohio investigation of 1879 and the hearings in the Pennsylvania injunction suits we have already referred. Still more important was the resounding Hepburn Investigation in the Empire State.

Rockefeller was undoubtedly steeled to meet these stern interrogatories, this hot cannonade of attack. With his shrewd foresight he was fully aware that his challenge to the great American tenet of free competition—a tenet bound up with American concepts of democracy and enterprise—would soon be answered. But he may well have been astonished by the ultimate scope and fierceness of the assault. He and his associates were arraigned for establishing a monopoly, for using unfair methods to attain it, for acting with swift brutality to repress any new competitive threat, and for interfering in politics to protect their system. The pertinacity with which these charges were pressed, and the general ferocity of the attack, were enough to dismay the stoutest-hearted. For any parallel men had to go back to the Bank war in the thirties, and the more recent Granger assault on the railroads.

In New York City on February 20, 1879, a deputation from the Chamber of Commerce, the Board of Trade and Transportation, and the Produce Exchange called on Mayor Cooper with a memorial to the State Assembly asking for an investigation of "unjust discriminations and other defects existing in the management of the railroads chartered by the State."[1] Merchants from Buffalo to Mon-

[1] N. Y. *Tribune*, Feb. 21, 1879.

tauk had long complained of discriminations against short-haul traffic; of rates higher between Rochester and New York, for example, than between Chicago and New York. They had grumbled that these discriminations were building up great combinations, which suppressed competition in the smaller cities with an iron hand. Mayor Cooper signed the memorial. The Assembly appointed a committee of nine, with Alonzo Barton Hepburn—young, austere, energetic—as chairman; and this body employed as counsel Simon Sterne, who held a place in the front rank of the New York bar.[2]

II

The inquiry, launched June 12 in New York City with the general freight manager of the New York Central as first witness, nominally concerned railroad practices alone, but actually took in much more. It did not enter into some of the more obvious evils chargeable to crooked railroad management, such as stock-watering, speculation in securities, and political activities. Its probings chiefly concerned the abuses that grew out of a partnership between railroads and huge corporations—flour-millers, meat-packers, salt-makers, oil-refiners, and so on. Discriminatory rates required at least two parties, and the shippers were as much on trial as the transportation lines. Many people were becoming convinced that the millers, packers, salt-pool leaders, and others found the railroads only too glad to waltz them down a rose-leaf path to monopoly. In the very week that the memorial was presented *The Nation* published an eloquent article by Colonel Potts which pointed to the Standard Oil as the worst offender in this partnership of railroad and monopolist.[3]

Many small refineries formerly lined the railways along the valleys of the Allegheny River and its tributaries. Under equal rates of rail carriage they enjoyed a moderate prosperity on small profits. They have mainly disappeared; the works have been dismantled; the owners are bankrupt; the laborers and all dependent on them are gone. They have given way to one huge concern, whose annual net revenues are computed by millions, and whose managers can dictate not only what rates the railways may charge, but what proportion thereof they themselves shall receive.

[2]See introduction by George Haven Putnam to Simon Sterne, *Railways in the United States.*
[3]Feb. 20, 1879; article unsigned.

Since the broader findings of the investigation concern us little, they may be briefly dismissed. The inquiry showed that the special rate contracts made between January and August, 1879, on the New York Central alone, were estimated by its officers at 6000.[4] Indeed, for local freight in bulk a uniform tariff did not really exist; every rate was a special rate. Between the same points these rates varied widely from day to day, from shipper to shipper. Chauncey Depew admitted that in recently opened territory discriminations were often "very arbitrary," but this was obviously true everywhere. Favored shippers often got discounts ranging from 50 to 80 per cent. The Central, for example, gave one Utica drygoods merchant a rate of 9 cents while the normal rate was 33 cents; it granted a special low tariff to A. T. Stewart & Co. "to build up and develop their business"; and in 1877 it gave two New York firms a grain-rate from $2\frac{1}{2}$ to 5 cents lower than that allowed other houses, enabling them to control the grain-trade of the metropolis. A Rochester shipper testified that to save 18 cents a hundredweight on consignments to St. Louis, he shipped them into New York and then back through Rochester to Missouri! Other witnesses proved that flour went from Milwaukee to New York, 1030 miles, for 20 cents, but from Rochester to New York, 350 miles, it cost 30![5]

Such disclosures, proving again the universality of rebating, do not interest us here. Neither does the evidence upon the ingenious methods used by some lines to rob certain communities, such as the formation of special elevator associations and coal companies to leech the greatest possible sums out of Buffalo's commerce. What does concern us is the rôle of the Standard in the inquiry. The veil of secrecy that had cloaked many of its acts was rudely torn aside, and in the opinion of the public it was exposed as the outstanding culprit of unfair rate-arrangements with the railroads.

Just one week after the inquiry began, the Standard's name was introduced in connection with charges of discrimination and monopoly. R. G. Vilas, general freight agent of the Erie and brother of

[4]William Larrabee, *The Railroad Question*, 138.
[5]See the five stout volumes of the *Hepburn Committee Testimony* (*Special Committee on Railroads*), *passim*. Vanderbilt and Jewett, in a joint letter on April 18, 1879, denied a single instance of rate discrimination as between individuals. For acid comment upon this statement see the N. Y. *Shipping and Commercial List*, Aug. 27, 1879.

the Standard's auditor, George Vilas, took the stand with testimony on the pooling arrangement of the Erie with the New York Central, Baltimore & Ohio, and Pennsylvania, and on its rates. After dealing with milk traffic and livestock traffic, he turned to the Standard Oil shipments. The following colloquy occurred:[6]

Mr. Sterne: Do you grant the Standard a special rate?

Mr. Vilas: We do. Any one could have the same special rate if his business was as valuable as that of the Standard Oil Company.

Mr. Sterne: Is there any rebate or drawback granted the Standard Oil Company?

Mr. Vilas: There is not. Formerly they had a rebate, but now they have not.

Mr. Sterne: They have ruined twenty or thirty refineries in Pennsylvania, built up a monstrous monopoly—one so strong that the railroads cannot subdue it—and they can afford to dispense with a rebate now.

Josiah Lombard, the independent New York refiner, testified that constant difficulty in obtaining shipments of crude oil had placed his works at a cruel disadvantage compared with the Standard. Several railroads had refused to carry his oil at all:[7]

Mr. Sterne: Mr. Vilas has stated that any shipper who shipped an equal quantity with the Standard Oil Company could obtain the same rate of transportation as the Standard Oil Company obtained; is there any shipper who ships anything like an equal amount of oil with the Standard Oil Company?

Mr. Lombard: I think that if the books of the . . . Erie . . . were examined, it would be found that only ten cars of crude petroleum had been shipped to New York by any shipper outside of the Standard Oil Company or their connections within over a year.

Mr. Sterne: Do you mean to say that the whole shipment, practically, that comes to New York over the New York Central and over the Erie is for the Standard Oil Company and its connections?

Mr. Lombard: I do.

Lombard explained that about a year before neither he nor his agent H. C. Ohlen had been able to get the cars they needed from the Erie because Pratt & Co. had engrossed its facilities; and that the New York Central had also discriminated against him.[8] Other in-

---

[6]N. Y. *Tribune*, June 19, 1879; *Hepburn Committee Testimony*, I, 394, 395. *The Tribune* report differs slightly from the official testimony.

[7]N. Y. *Tribune*, June 24, 1879; *Hepburn Committee Testimony*, I, 709, 710.

[8]N. Y. *Tribune*, June 24, 1879; *Hepburn Committee Testimony*, I, 711.

dependent refiners in the New York area, he declared, when denied proper transportation by the Erie and New York Central, had been compelled to sell to the Standard, merge with it, or go out of business. He specified Denslow & Bush, and Wilson & Anderson. Corroboration was offered by Rufus T. Bush. His firm had been able to obtain crude oil in winter over the Pennsylvania, and in summer over the Erie Canal, but had been refused facilities by the New York Central and Erie. Just one shipment of two cars had come over the last-named line, "loaded by mistake"! He believed that the Standard still received large rebates, and when asked what was the effect of the Standard's railroad arrangements, replied bitterly: "The result has been to crush out and grind out everybody that was not in their interest, and I believe they succeeded with all except five here in New York."

In August the committee, now sitting at Saratoga, heard Jewett of the Erie and William H. Vanderbilt of the Central, both refractory witnesses. Jewett in particular flew into fits of rage. When Sterne asked for a yes or no answer to one query, he angrily replied: "I choose to answer as I please; I am not to be interrupted by you." This arrogant witness proved strangely ignorant of the Erie's shipping arrangements. His refusal to furnish light on several points finally aroused Sterne, who turned fiercely on him. "Do you," the counsel demanded, "as president of a great railway company, do your business so loosely that you do not know whether there is or is not a contract or arrangement in existence with the Standard Oil Company today for the transportation of oil?" Vanderbilt was more amiable, but equally vague and evasive. On rebates, shipping facilities, and special agreements he and other Central men, constantly advised by Chauncey M. Depew, showed a curiously feeble memory. He did not recall the South Improvement Company, was blandly certain that he had never heard of any injustice to Lombard & Ayres, did not know Daniel O'Day "from the side of a house," and could not tell what rate was given to the Standard Oil. Yet the extent of the favors granted under the "evener" agreements of 1875–79 was again brought out.[9]

[9] See George Iles, *Popular Science Monthly*, July, 1883, pp. 289 ff., on the investigation. One New York Central witness, in presenting various documents, grumbled: "I suppose Mr. Sterne will call for our marriage certificates next."

Later some of the competitors whom the Standard had eliminated appeared. Isaac L. Hewitt testified that he had been forced to sell his Cleveland refinery to Rockefeller for fifty cents on the dollar. He quoted Rutter as warning him when he spoke of beginning again: "The fact is, Mr. Hewitt, I am too good a friend of yours to advise you to have anything to do with the oil business."[10] Simon Bernheimer repeated how his Greenpoint, Long Island, refinery, prosperous until 1874, had been pushed to the wall by railroad discriminations, so that in 1876 he sold to the Standard. His works had a capacity of 200,000 barrels a year, but he could get nowhere near that much oil—and he emphasized the fact that profits depended primarily upon quantity. Charles Morehouse told how he had been compelled to sell his lubricating-oil business when the Standard went into the field and took for itself the raw material it had been furnishing him.

The committee brought on the witness stand a number of Standard officials, including Flagler, Rogers, Archbold, and Bostwick. They proved reluctant, obstructive, and at times truculent witnesses. Bostwick, who did not appear until he had been summoned three times, then stood by the witness chair, hat in hand, and denounced the investigation.[11] He took advantage of the pending indictment in Pennsylvania to refuse to answer important questions on the ground that replies might "form a link in the chain of evidence" against him. Admitting that his company worked in harmony with the Standard, he refused to indicate just what harmony meant. All he would say was: "We are in harmony, and if we meet any one in competition with us, we buy him out, or make some arrangement with him, as we think best."[12] Rogers was equally unsatisfactory. As *The Times* reporter put it, "Many of his answers were chiefly characterized by evasiveness."[13] He was certain, he said, that the Standard did not control Charles Pratt & Company. For himself, he had a written agreement "of a personal nature" with various men connected with the Standard. Like Bostwick, he believed that from 90 to 95 per cent of the refiners in the country were by this time working in "harmony." Sterne pressed him on this magic word—what did he mean

[10]*Hepburn Committee Testimony,* II, 2533. The N. Y. *Herald,* Oct. 12, 1879, consistently spells Rockefeller's name Rockafelloe.
[11]N. Y. *Herald,* Oct. 14, 1879.
[12]N. Y. *Times,* Oct. 17, 1879.   [13]*Idem,* Oct. 15, 1879.

by harmony? "I mean just what harmony implies; I live in harmony with my wife." Sterne pointed out that he had a contract with her. "Do you mean that people in harmony with the Standard Oil are married to the Standard Oil Company?" "Not necessarily," flippantly replied Rogers, "so long as they are happy." When further pressed on the definition of harmony, he remarked: "Well, I make an agreement with you to go to Wall Street, and buy at 33, and sell at 40; that is harmony."[14] The courtroom roared at this.

Archbold, representing the Acme, would not confess that his company had any connection with the Standard Oil. He admitted that he was a stockholder, and even a director, of the Standard. But like Rogers, he took refuge in flippancies. When Sterne, vainly laboring to elicit some admission upon the Standard's activities, asked impatiently: "Well, Mr. Archbold, what function do you play in the Standard Oil now as director?" he retorted:

"I am a clamorer for dividends!"

And when Sterne inquired, "What dividends do they pay?" he remarked in his devil-may-care fashion:

"I never have any difficulty in carrying mine off!"[15]

Declaring that the matter was a business secret between himself and the railroads, Archbold persistently refused to reveal the rates at which, as head of the Acme, he shipped oil to New York. Only Hepburn's threat of invoking legislative action lessened his taciturnity. His memory failed him upon the rates he had paid only six months earlier; but he was able to recall that in 1875, as officer of another company, he had received lower rates than as president of the Acme.[16]

The answers of the Standard officials were so unsatisfactory that the irritated committee finally agreed to accept the offer of their counsel to have a questionnaire filled out by Archbold "and others connected with the Standard Oil or with its affiliated companies." But when the questionnaire was returned, the committee found that many of the most important queries had been passed over, and for that reason refused to accept it as final. Members talked of recalling Archbold, Rogers, Bostwick and Pratt for a final examination, but

[14]*Hepburn Committee Testimony,* III, 2617.
[15]*Hepburn Committee Testimony,* III, 2665.
[16]N. Y. *Tribune,* Oct. 1, 1879.

the fact that the committee's time was running short forbade this. Doubtless they would have learned little more if they had.

In one sense the sessions of the committee were disappointing. Inner secrets of railway offices and of various industrial pools and groups, including the Standard combination, were fairly well guarded. Men like Jewett and Archbold came in effect, if not in any technical sense, close to perjury. Jewett's pretended lapses of memory were simply incredible. When Archbold said of the Standard, "Their interests are principally at Cleveland and New York; I know of none outside of those two points in connection with the Standard Oil Company," he was flouting the truth. He knew well enough that the Acme was a Standard "interest." Rogers's denial of any connection between the Standard and Charles Pratt & Company was equally close to perjury. Nevertheless, the committee obtained a mass of important information upon the practices of the railroads, and drew some new facts even from the tight-lipped Standard men. For the first time the general public began to realize how universally rebates and other discriminations had been granted by the railroad.[17]

Of all the combinations, the Standard was left the principal symbol of the monopolistic tendencies fostered by rate-discrimination. For the first time its huge size was fully revealed. H. H. Rogers had admitted that nine tenths of the refiners of the country were "in harmony" with it; and E. G. Patterson, still an enemy of the combination, had given the committee a list of Standard-controlled companies, including the Acme and Charles Pratt & Company. His information was in general fresh and accurate. The fact that the Standard controlled the oil terminals of all four trunk-line railroads was established. New light was thrown upon its services and rewards, 1875–79, as an "evener," and it was made abundantly clear that it and the railroads had worked together to eliminate nearly all the New York independents.

In its final report, submitted to the Legislature on January 22, 1880, the committee bluntly characterized the relations of the Standard with the carriers as a flagrant violation of the first principles of railroad economy and social justice. Calling the Standard "a unique

[17]New York already had a law which authorized the legislature to reduce passenger and freight rates whenever the profits of a line exceeded 10 per cent on the capital actually invested. N. Y. *Shipping and Commercial List,* July 26, 1879.

illustration of the possible outgrowth" of railroad discrimination, it also termed the combination an object-lesson in "the colossal proportions to which monopoly can grow under the laws of this country."[18] It reported that since the Standard had gained control of the refining industry, the railroads obtained much less revenue from oil shipments than they deserved, with the result that they had to increase their rates upon other products to meet this loss. It estimated that of the 12,900,400 barrels shipped from the Regions in the first nine months of 1879, that part which was sent to the seaboard could, and should, have borne a dollar a barrel more in freight charges. In other words, the railroads, and indirectly investors and other shippers, were being deprived of millions of dollars annually for the enrichment of the combination.[19] This part of the report was quickly rendered academic by the completion of the trunk pipe lines. It and other parts were regarded by the Standard men as *ex parte* and unfair. But the testimony before the Hepburn Committee and its report impressed New Yorkers even more than the injunction-suit testimony had impressed Pennsylvanians, and powerfully influenced public opinion throughout the country. The principal commercial organ of New York pronounced the discriminations "illegal, unjust, arbitrary, and tyrannical."[20]

III

Hard on the heels of these three inquiries and the storm over "immediate-shipment" oil came a lawsuit which materially accentuated the public hostility to the trust. It was an action begun by the Standard itself against Scofield, Shurmer & Teagle, refiners in Cleveland. This firm, founded in 1874, represented an amalgamation of Squire & Teagle and Alexander, Scofield & Co. Now the latter company had sold out to the Standard in 1872, its members agreeing not to engage in refining again for ten years. Shurmer had made a similar agreement. Neither pledge has ever been published, so that the exact wording is unknown, but the Standard naturally condemned the re-entry of these men into business as a flagrant breach of contract.

[18]*Hepburn Committee Report*, 40–46. This was published separately from the *Testimony*.

[19]See Sterne's able summary of his report in his *Railways in the United States*, 123 ff.

[20]N. Y. *Shipping and Commercial List*, Oct. 18, 1879.

The new firm had built in 1875 a $65,000 refinery with a capacity of almost 2000 barrels of crude oil a day. As we have seen, after some initial friction the partners entered into an operating arrangement with the Standard. It was agreed that the Standard should supply $10,000 additional capital; that Scofield, Shurmer & Teagle should not refine more than 85,000 barrels of crude a year; that they should have the benefit of the Standard's facilities for buying crude and marketing the product; and that they should be guaranteed $35,000 net return a year. Profits over that figure and up to $70,000 were to go to the Standard, while above $70,000 they were to be divided.[21]

On its face this arrangement seems equitable, and nobody ever pretended that Scofield, Shurmer & Teagle did not enter it willingly. It *guaranteed* them almost 50 per cent a year on their investment, while they actually realized more than 100 per cent while the alliance continued. The Standard had spent huge sums to wipe out weak competitive plants whose price-slashing had dragged the whole industry down to an unprofitable level, and could assert that it was because of these exertions that newcomers now made large profits. It could truthfully say that its arrangements for collecting crude and distributing refined oil cheaply were of high value to all associates. Rockefeller later said of Scofield, Shurmer & Teagle: "The running arrangement was a godsend to them. . . . They got a sure thing and a far better thing than they could have got but for the protection we, at great cost, had secured. . . . We kept a corresponding part of our plant lying idle. This was not a one-sided agreement. It was a contract, with promises made by each side and advantages to each side."[22]

Scofield, Shurmer & Teagle made such large profits that during their first four years under the agreement they took out $315,000 as net proceeds. But they constantly overran the stipulated limit of 85,000 barrels, refining 88,000 the first year, 87,000 the second, 100,000 the third, and 90,000 the fourth. The Standard men naturally protested. Only a reasonable limitation of output, they declared, made profits possible; and they pointed out that their own plants

[21]See the published report of the *Standard Oil vs. William C. Scofield et al.*, Court of Common Pleas, Cuyahoga County, 1880. Rockefeller's affidavit is reproduced in Tarbell, *Standard Oil Company*, II, 324 ff.

[22]Inglis, Conversations with Rockefeller.

could easily have manufactured and sold the additional product. Rockefeller contended, as a logical deduction from this fact, that all the profits on the excess output should go to the Standard. But Scofield, Shurmer & Teagle refused to pay more than half; and when Rockefeller pressed the matter, they declared they would recognize no 85,000-barrel limit at all, and threatened him with a lawsuit if he persisted in restricting their supply of crude oil. They wrote him that they held a large number of orders, and that as he declined to furnish crude at the regular Standard prices, "we shall get it somewhere as best we can, and hold you responsible for the difference in cost."

This cool demand aroused Rockefeller's indignation. He regarded Scofield and Shurmer (but not Teagle) as contract-breakers. "They had no more right to re-engage in business," he declared later, "than a man would have to sell his horse and receive pay for it from a neighbor, and afterward go to his neighbor's stable and call the horse by the old familiar voice and take his halter and lead him back to the old home." They had sold out in 1872, he remarked, when they thought the oil industry foundering. "And then, when we had saved it, they came aboard the ship again and looted it. They were a lot of pirates. You can call them that with justice."[23] In this mood, he had the Standard bring suit to compel them to abide by their quota contract.

The result proved disastrous for the Standard. Scofield, Shurmer & Teagle entered the natural plea that the agreement which they had signed was in restraint of trade, and therefore void—the usual plea made when any recalcitrant member of a pool sought to resist its decrees. To be sure, the definition of an agreement in restraint of trade was then (and still is) far from clear, while the equities of the situation were somewhat debatable. The Standard had compensated the firm for promising not to produce beyond a certain amount; within fifty years the government, for the same object of price-maintenance, was to compensate millions of farmers through the AAA for not producing beyond a set limit, and was to use the NRA to prevent industrial overproduction. Limitation of industrial output by formal or informal agreement is by no means unknown in America today, and is not always frowned upon by the courts. But Scofield, Shurmer insisted that the agreement was against public policy,

[23]*Idem.*

while they also denied that the industry needed any limitation of output. Refinery profits are extremely large, they declared; "it is impossible to supply the demand of the public for oil if the business and refineries of both plaintiff and defendant are . . . run to their full capacities," and restriction would result simply in higher prices "and the establishment of a more perfect monopoly."

Rockefeller was naturally denied the injunction he asked. No court with any regard whatever for public opinion could assist a great monopoly in enforcing a contract to limit output and sustain high prices. Scofield, Shurmer & Teagle were now free to go forward as independent refiners, turning out as much kerosene as they could. But they found that many businessmen, even enemies of the Standard, looked upon their violation of a written contract with disgust; while they naturally met every possible impediment from the Standard and its railroad allies. They had trouble in obtaining crude oil at fair railroad rates, and in selling their refined oil. In 1880, they complained, the Standard was allowed to ship kerosene to Chicago at 65 cents a barrel, while they paid 80; in 1881 the margin became still greater. In an effort to stop this, Scofield, Shurmer & Teagle carried an injunction suit against the Lake Shore through all the Ohio courts. They won the first round in the Court of Common Pleas. They lost the second in the District Court, which held that the Lake Shore had been justified in making a special arrangement with the Standard because of the latter's special rolling stock, terminal equipment, and protection against fire, and the large quantities of oil which it shipped.[24] But the State Supreme Court took a radically different view. It held that the methods of shipment employed by the small firm and the trust were essentially identical, and that the only real distinction lay in the aggregate yearly amounts of freight shipped. This being so, the low rate was a discrimination in favor of capital, and as such violative of the equal rights of citizens; and in trenchant terms, the court pointed to the danger that other powerful combinations, leaguing themselves with the railroads, would drive all small enterprises into bankruptcy.[25]

This hard-fought case and the emphatic final decision attracted

[24]This twenty-three point finding, handed down in the March term, 1884, is most easily available in *House Trust Investigation, 1888*, pp. 553 ff.
[25]Ohio Supreme Court, XLIII, 1886, 571–623.

wide attention. The Lake Shore reluctantly submitted to the Ohio decree. Scofield, Shurmer & Teagle gained little, for they were still unable to compete with their powerful adversary, and within a few years the firm died. But the whole episode, bringing the rebate question again into full view, gravely injured the reputation of the Standard. A number of former Cleveland refiners seized the opportunity to offer testimony or submit sworn affidavits.

One witness in particular, Mrs. Fred M. Backus, told a malignant story which long reverberated and did Rockefeller an outrageous injustice. She was the widow of a Cleveland manufacturer of lubricants. Her husband for years had a special market, was not in competition with the Standard, and remained unaffected by its Cleveland acquisitions. When he died in 1874, Mrs. Backus carried on the business, supporting three children. However, after a time the Standard turned to making lubricants, for which it controlled nearly all the raw materials; and it bought, among others, her establishment.

Mrs. Backus's story was that Rockefeller's competition, together with the general business depression, convinced her that she could not continue; so that when an agent of the Standard came in 1878 to ask if she would sell, she was ready to discuss the matter. But she insisted on talking with Rockefeller personally, and appealed to him on behalf of her children for generous treatment. "He promised me with tears in his eyes that he would stand by me," she asserted later. She declared that she had asked for $200,000, "much below what the stock was worth," but in the end was offered only $79,000, and in sheer desperation accepted this figure. When she begged permission to retain $15,000 in stock, it was abruptly refused. According to her tale, Rockefeller had ruthlessly taken advantage of a defenseless widow, and appropriated her business for little more than a third of its value![26]

But Mrs. Backus misrepresented the whole transaction. This was indicated at the time by evidence which Rockefeller presented in court. Later it was completely established by the testimony of Mrs.

[26]Her story is discussed in John T. Flynn, *God's Gold,* which is hostile to it; in Tarbell, *Standard Oil Company,* I, 203 ff.; and in Rockefeller's *Random Reminiscences,* 96 ff. I have founded my account on the testimony in the Scofield, Shurmer case and letters and affidavits in the Rockefeller Papers. I have also talked with various aged Clevelanders, who unanimously rejected her story. Charles J. Woodbury, *Saturday Evening Post,* Oct. 21, 1911, is scornful of it.

Backus's attorney, her works superintendent, her husband's brother, H. M. Backus, who was an employee and stockholder in the refinery, and Charles J. Woodbury, another responsible employee.[27]

This evidence shows that Mrs. Backus's own valuation of her works was $150,000, not $200,000. Two years earlier, when the business was fairly prosperous, she had been ready to sell for less, but could obtain no assurance of the would-be purchaser's financial capacity. The $150,000 she asked contained as its principal item $71,000 for "works, good will, and successorship." There were additional items for oil on hand, cash, bills receivable, and accrued dividends. The Standard paid $60,000 for the works and good will, and $19,000 for the oil on hand, leaving the other items, valued by her at $60,000, to Mrs. Backus. Her brother-in-law writes: "She got as much more out of these accounts as the Standard Oil Company had given her for the business."[28] She thus received or retained $139,000 for assets which she asserted to be worth $150,000—a difference of only $11,000. Rockefeller's appraisers declared that this was a generous payment. "She had a business dwindling; we bought it from her on liberal terms," said Rockefeller later. And again: "In this case particularly I was moved by kindly consideration to an old employee, Fred Backus, who had been a bookkeeper in my office, who had been for years a consumptive, and who had been a mission Sunday school teacher with me in our boyhood days."[29] For good measure he had added $10,000 to the appraisers' figure. Woodbury, who had been trained by Backus, asserts that the payment for the plant "far exceeded its value."[30]

Mrs. Backus, according to her attorney, was well pleased at the time. She had not been denied permission to retain stock in her company. On the contrary, Rockefeller suggested that she keep part ownership, but she replied that she wished to get out of the business entirely. Later she changed her mind and asked for stock; but since the papers had been prepared for a complete transfer, the request was courteously refused. A few days afterward she wrote a letter of

[27]See Appendix VI for quotations from these documents.
[28]H. M. Backus to John D. Rockefeller, Sept. 18, 1903; Rockefeller Papers.
[29]Inglis, Conversations with Rockefeller.
[30]H. M. Backus to Rockefeller, Sept. 18, 1903; Rockefeller, *Random Reminiscences*, 99; Woodbury, *Saturday Evening Post*, Oct. 21, 1911.

remonstrance to Rockefeller. He then informed her that he would return the plant for what he had paid for it, or would let her have as much as 300 shares for the price the Standard had given—presumably about $30,000. To this letter Mrs. Backus never replied. The reason was stated later by her brother-in-law: "Every one knew she got a high price."

Nevertheless, when the subject was aired in the Scofield, Shurmer case, the widow's hysterical allegations weighed more than calm denials supported by fact. The Backus story was accepted at face value by the public for the next quarter century. Miss Tarbell thus gave it currency. She defends the $200,000 valuation—in reality only $150,000—as based on good will and earnings; and she states that according to a bookkeeper, at the time of the sale the business was earning between $30,000 and $40,000 a year. This is contradicted by other evidence. Woodbury indicates that the plant was unprofitable. H. M. Backus declares that the business had been "left behind," and that the plant was outmoded. Rockefeller, like M. G. Vilas, argued that the entire works could have been reproduced for $20,000, and Miss Tarbell agrees. It is incredible that a $20,000 plant, its machinery "left behind," could be making $30,000 net a year, and if earnings had been even half that high it is unlikely that Mrs. Backus would have discussed the sale. Her entire attitude indicates that the business was bad and getting worse. To get $139,000 out of it was to do well. All things considered, her conduct seems, as her brother-in-law states, to have been unreasonable. She did not suffer from the sale. If she had kept $30,000 worth of stock she would have made a fortune. As it was, this "poor widow" conserved her money shrewdly, and according to Clevelanders died worth about $300,000.

Equally baseless was the story of a Baltimore widow, Mrs. Sylvia C. Hunt, who in 1877 leased her refinery to the Camden Consolidated Oil Company. The lease provided that for a generous rental, and the assumption of all risks and taxes, this Standard subsidiary should control the refinery for a number of years. Rockefeller especially enjoined on Camden that he was to treat Mrs. Hunt kindly.[31] No sooner was the lease signed than she requested that he employ the agent who had been selling her product in the Baltimore market.

[31]Festus P. Summers, *Johnson Newlon Camden,* 200.

This was done. Then she asked that her son be hired. This was also done. Immediately she was back on Camden's doorstep with new requests. The tormented man wrote Rockefeller:[32]

> I really believe that Mrs. Hunt is not in her right mind. I have spent day after day with her, trying to satisfy her, ever since we met in New York, and every time I parted with her she seemed to be well satisfied with the arrangement as it then stood; but never failed to come back with new propositions, all of which I considered kindly, and, in the main, agreed to, in order to avoid having any difficulty with her. Finally before leaving Baltimore the last time, we agreed upon and executed a new lease, modifying the old one, but retaining both. In the new lease we agreed to pay her $7500 a year instead of $5000. She demanded that it extend back to include the first quarter, the rent for which had already been paid. I consented to that and gave her a check for the difference. She then required that for her protection we should agree to buy the refinery at the end of the first five years, in case she desired to sell it. I agreed to do that. She then required, instead of fixing its value at that time, that we should fix now the price to be paid, which I also consented to, and the price was fixed in the lease at $20,000. She then desired that we should release her from personal service as stipulated in the lease. I did not do this in the lease, but addressed her a letter stating that until further notice she was relieved from giving personal attention to the business. The modified lease was drawn up and signed, and a check given for a quarter's rent in advance, including the difference in the first quarter's rent. . . .

Patience could hardly be greater. Mrs. Hunt was taking advantage of the Standard's desire to be liberal. Yet in the end she spread abroad a story of abuse. When Colonel Potts published his *Brief History of the Standard Oil,* he declared (without evidence) that Rockefeller had crushed "her business and her spirit as remorselessly as they would have killed a dog," and Miss Tarbell later quoted the statement.

IV

Then, as time passed, the inevitable happened: A hostile publicist seized upon the facts and suspicions which had darkened the Standard's name, and wove them into a coherent indictment. Antagonism to big business, dormant in the depression period 1873–78, suddenly awoke with the return of prosperity; and a remarkable figure entered the lists against Rockefeller.

[32]Quoted in Summers, *Camden,* 199.

About 1880 a Chicago journalist and lawyer, Henry Demarest Lloyd, who was only thirty-three that year, began displaying a critical interest in the larger American corporations. The son of a New York minister and a graduate of Columbia, he had been admitted to the bar eleven years earlier, had lectured on political economy, and had gone west to join the Chicago *Tribune* early in the seventies. A natural crusader, he had been fired by various reform movements in the seventies—the anti-Tammany revolt, the Liberal Republican onset, the free-trade uprising, the demand for remonetizing silver. In *The Tribune* office he was inspired by its liberal editor Horace White, and its part-owner William Bross, who hated railroad greed. By marrying Bross's daughter Lloyd became a man of wealth. This young idealist was horrified by the myriad iniquities of business during the Great Barbecue. His editorials for *The Tribune* vehemently assailed them: the anthracite monopoly, the railroad juggling, the stockyards combine, even profiteering in Alaska furs and an alleged corner on coffins. Visiting the Pacific Coast in 1881, he learned something of the predatory methods of the men who built the Union Pacific and the Central Pacific. As yet his knowledge of finance was elementary, while he was inclined to be rhetorical, credulous, and cocksure. In 1880, he read to the Chicago Literary Club a plea for railroad regulation called "A Cure for Vanderbiltism." Then he turned to the railroad strike of 1877 and the Hepburn Investigation for more light on the subject. The result was "The Story of a Great Monopoly," an essay which William Dean Howells gave the leading place in *The Atlantic Monthly* for March, 1881.

Until this time criticism of the Standard had been largely confined to the Oil Regions; but Lloyd's vivid article drew national attention to the subject. Moreover, he furnished the first brief, comprehensive, and readable statement of the main allegations against the great oil combination. While the five thick volumes of the Hepburn Committee's hearings had not been widely read, *The Atlantic* article reached a thoughtful public from Maine to Oregon. That issue went through seven printings. Curiously enough, it was little noticed in the press,[33] but it gave multitudes an eager interest in the alleged

[33]The only editorial comment I find in New York newspapers is in *The Daily Graphic*, Feb. 18, 1881.

crimes of the Standard. The London *Railway News* reprinted it and distributed thousands of copies free to English investors. In far corners of the globe—including Australia—it impressed readers. Even Herbert Spencer, speaking in New York in 1882, referred to it: "I hear that a great trader among you deliberately endeavored to crush out every one whose business competed with his own."[34]

Seldom has an article been better timed than Lloyd's. The years of depression, destroying a multitude of weak businesses, had accelerated the process of industrial concentration. Emerging with greater strength than ever, the large corporations were beginning to gain power by rapid strides. Within the next decade big business was to fill the land with monopolies and near-monopolies. Meanwhile the position of the farmer, who had no relief from the relentless competition of Canada, Argentina, and Russia, and who as a debtor was hard hit by poor credit facilities and gold-appreciation, was grim. That of the workingman, without adequate unions or strong leadership, was equally painful. While the lords of industry amassed enormous wealth, took control of numerous legislatures, and by the time of McKinley and Hanna grew intolerably arrogant, the social strains and stresses within the nation became ever more acute. One of the few weapons of the discontented lay in the printing press. Lloyd's article was the first loud stroke in what soon became a mighty tocsin of protest; not the first, for *Chapters of Erie* deserves that title, but the first heard throughout the land.

"That article," wrote Charles Edward Russell, "was a turning-point in our social history; with it dawned upon Americans the first conviction . . . that the republic could no more endure an oligarchy of capitalists than an oligarchy of slave-holders."[35] It would be more accurate to say that it resumed the protests of the Jacksonian era, of William Leggett and Peter Cooper, against the injustices of large-scale capitalism. Lloyd immediately went on to flaming exposures of Jay Gould and the grain-market manipulators; Henry George was soon publishing *Progress and Poverty;* Richard T. Ely was shortly defending labor unions and municipal socialism. The demand for railroad regulation was caught up by a thousand pens. By 1890 the Populist movement was laying the foundation for Roose-

[34]Caro Lloyd, *Life of Henry Demarest Lloyd,* I, 185; Herbert Spencer, *Essays,* III, 484.
[35]Introduction, Lloyd, *Lloyd,* I, vii.

velt's progressivism and Wilson's new freedom. Lloyd could claim a place in the vanguard of what became an irresistible uprising.

It would be beside the point to analyze Lloyd's article in detail. It had errors and weaknesses, but they did not greatly detract from its main significance. It was full of inaccuracies. "Rockefeller," it explained, "had been a bookkeeper in some interior town in Ohio, and afterward made a few thousand dollars by keeping a flour store in Cleveland." More unfortunate were the numerous *non sequiturs*. He began with a vivid description of the railroad strike of 1877, exaggerating the "paralysis" and "anarchy." ("Ironclads were ordered up for the protection of the national capital. Cabinet meetings were continuous." "The large centers of population began to calculate the chances of famine.") Indicting the Standard's monopolistic practices, he charged that an evil combination between the Standard and the Pennsylvania had been largely responsible for the fierce Pittsburgh riots of 1877—though that year saw Tom Scott and Rockefeller locked in battle! Throughout the article *ex parte* statements were accepted without scrutiny.

Facts were also used without regard for their historical background. "Of the fifty-eight refineries in Pittsburgh in 1867 twenty-eight have been crushed out and dismantled, and of the remaining thirty twenty-nine have been bought up or leased by the great monopoly." When the Standard began its absorptions in Pittsburgh during 1874 that city had between twenty-two and thirty refineries (the computation varies),[36] and the Standard of course had nothing whatever to do with "crushing out" weak plants between 1867 and 1874. Lloyd blamed the Standard for the low prices of crude oil caused by the great Bradford field glut. "In 1878," he wrote, "oil went down to 78.75 cents a barrel at the very time the shipments from the wells were 56,000 barrels a day, the largest ever made till that time." Evidently he thought the price of oil should have gone *up* at the very time that production broke all records! He also calmly twisted statistics to suit his purposes:

The average cost, last December, of the one and one-third barrels of petroleum needed to make a barrel of kerosene, was $2.05 at Cleveland. The cost of refining, barrelling, and all expenses, including a refiners' profit of half a dollar a barrel, is, according to the testimony of experts,

[36]Tarbell, *Standard Oil Company*, I, 160.

$2.75 a barrel. To bring it by rail to Chicago costs 70 cents, making the total cost $5.50 for a barrel of fifty gallons, or eleven cents a gallon. The price the Standard charges in Chicago is nineteen and three-fourths cents a gallon, in which . . . there is a tax on the public of eight and three-fourths cents. . . . A family that uses a gallon of kerosene a day pays a yearly tribute to the Standard of $32, the income from $800 in the four per cents.

While the Standard's profit was excessive, it was not so exorbitant as all this! Lloyd includes nothing for the heavy cost of distribution and marketing, nothing for capital investment, plant-depreciation, cost of barrels, risks, and incidentals. His figures also vary amazingly from those of better authorities. The New York Chamber of Commerce states that in 1878 the average market-price of crude in that city was 6.38 cents a gallon; of refined 10.78 cents a gallon. The margin between the two, without allowing for refining-costs, waste, transport, and marketing, was but 4.40 cents a gallon![37]

But however inaccurate and biased, the article in one respect nevertheless hit the mark squarely. The essential indictment was clear to all, and this indictment was what counted. The great railroads had granted secret rates to industrial allies without fear of punishment; these special privileges had enabled some corporations to strike down competitors and erect gigantic monopolies or partial monopolies; and the monopolies were using the money they took from the public to influence newspapers, legislators, and even courts. Lloyd concluded that it was hopeless to push reformative measures in the State legislatures, which were controlled by the corporations. "The Standard has done everything with the Pennsylvania legislature except refine it." The tiger must be caged by the one power stronger than itself, the Federal government. He called for the creation of a Federal agency to make all railroad charges equal, reasonable, stable, and public, to hear complaints against the railroads, and to prosecute infractions of a new Federal law on transportation. Efficient railroad regulation—there lay the remedy!

This was an astute and just demand. Lloyd had struck two keynotes that were to vibrate with rising diapason for the next two decades: dangerous monopolies were springing up everywhere, and the quickest way to halt the process was to destroy the railroad privileges

[37] *Annual Report,* 1878–79, Part II, 98.

which nourished them. When Theodore Roosevelt became President he perceived that rebates furnished monopoly with most of its life-blood, and in the Elkins and Hepburn Acts took steps to destroy them. The East, made resentful by the salt pool, the anthracite combination, and the Standard's control of kerosene, was increasingly troubled by the problem of monopoly. The West and South, objecting more to high rates than to discriminations, had begun to demand railroad regulation in exigent terms. Lloyd's article was one of the first clear demonstrations of the vital connection between the monopoly problem and the railroad problem; and other writers were soon dealing with these Siamese twins in more expert vein.

But if the article hit the truth in this respect, in another it flew beyond it; it created the legend of an utterly ruthless, wicked, and extortionate Standard Oil, pausing at nothing to destroy competitors, rob consumers, and debase the government—a legend that was to grow steadily in the next thirty years. The picture had just sufficient truth to be effective. Some acts of the Standard were quite indefensible; but Lloyd projected on his screen the image of a frightful monster, all horns, hoofs, and scales, romping in crime; an image whose exaggerations made all the more vivid a stereotype upon the national mind. It was a picture which demagogues, sensational journalists, cartoonists, and muckrakers were to keep constantly before the public eye.

Many of Lloyd's statements might have been answered immediately and completely. He implied that all the bankruptcies of all the oil refineries since 1870 were traceable to the Standard's machinations. Readers would never have guessed from his pages that unfettered competition had caused far more bankruptcies than the Standard. "The Standard produces only one fiftieth or one sixtieth of our petroleum, but dictates the price of all, and refines nine-tenths." The oil producers themselves shortly made public admission that prices of crude were fixed by supply and demand, with European buyers in a dominant rôle. Lloyd, again, accused the Standard of bribing railroad heads. "He (Rockefeller) effected secret arrangements with the Pennsylvania, the New York Central, the Erie, and the Atlantic and Great Western. What influences he used to make the railroad managers pliable may probably be guessed from the fact that one quarter of the stock of the Acme Oil Company, a partner in the Standard combination, on which heavy monthly dividends are paid, is owned by persons whose names Rockefeller would never reveal. . . ." This insinuation that railroads held an interest in the Acme had no truth whatever. The facts have been stated by Miss Tarbell in one sentence.[38] "The Acme was capitalized and controlled entirely by Standard men, its stockholders being, in addition to Mr. Archbold, William Rockefeller, William G. Warden, Frank Q. Barstow, and Charles Pratt." Lloyd also accused the Standard of corrupt manipulation of Congress, the Pennsylvania legislature, Governor Hoyt, and the courts, without an iota of evidence.

By prompt action the Standard might have done much to shatter this horned-devil portrait before it became a national stereotype. But Rockefeller preferred secrecy. He committed the error of believing that if he contemptuously ignored attacks they would soon fall into oblivion; that is, he grossly underrated the enormous power of the press, and was blind to the natural inclination of men to believe that an unrefuted charge is a true charge. The popular verdict on Lloyd's article was pronounced by *The Nation,* which said that the tale "is told sensationally, but apparently not more so than the extraordinary and suggestive facts warrant."[39] More than a decade later Lloyd boasted to a friend: "My article of 1881 remains unanswered to this day. . . ."[40] Because it met no reply, he and others thought it unanswerable. Indeed, nothing about the Standard irritated the public so much as its secrecy, which men thought must conceal malpractices of the most wicked character. As J. C. Welch wrote in 1883: "If there was ever anything in this country that was bolted and barred, hedged round, covered over, shielded before and behind, in itself and all its approaches, with secrecy, that thing is the Standard Oil Company."

The only statement the Standard sanctioned was a paper which the loyal hand of J. N. Camden contributed in 1883 to *The North American Review.* Many Standard men felt the storm of attack acutely, and Warden's sons later believed that it shortened their father's life.[41] Yet at this very time some railroads were replying with effect to their critics, and Godkin in *The Nation* was disproving the exaggerated assertions of the Anti-Monopoly League.

[38]*Standard Oil Company,* I, 159.   [39]Feb. 24, 1881.
[40]Lloyd, *Lloyd,* I, 185.
[41]Clarence Warden to the author, Feb. 11, 1937.

To a great extent Rockefeller's silence was part of the general taciturnity of American business in this period. Our industrial leaders have usually been inarticulate; those who possessed gifts of expression, like Carnegie, John Wanamaker, or Abram S. Hewitt, have been rare. Lacking the capacity to defend itself in words, industry was long scornful of such defense. Let journalists, politicians, and political economists chatter; business, self-engrossed, imperturbable, confident that its virtues outweighed its sins, would go on employing millions of men, producing wealth and comfort, raising the standard of life! Morgan, Hill, Frick, Harriman, Huntington, and Rockefeller simply shrugged criticism aside as the work of shallow praters who understood nothing of hard industrial realities. It was not until the criticism began to operate like a great fulcrum on the votes of the American masses, and the State and Federal governments responded, that the chief industrialists awoke to self-defense.

v

The volume of attack now rolled up like a snowball. In the very month of Lloyd's article a new legal assault was begun in Pennsylvania. Auditor-General W. P. Schell on March 23, 1881, requested the Standard Oil of Ohio to report its capital stock and dividends. The company replied that it was not engaged in business in Pennsylvania, and not taxable therein. After a more peremptory demand, the Auditor-General made a rough estimate and sent the Standard a bill for about $3,200,000 in taxes and penalties.[42] Some heated exchanges followed, the upshot of which was that the company filed a list of twenty-five objections. "The Auditor-General," remarked William Rockefeller,[43] "claims that according to the laws of Pennsylvania any corporation doing business within the State is liable to taxation to the full amount of its capital stock and dividends. We say that this is preposterous. If this principle were adopted by all States it would put a stop to all interstate commerce." Actually the claim that the entire capital of an Ohio corporation was taxable by Pennsylvania was a piece of political vaudeville. Of course the physical properties of the Standard in that State, all plainly visible, were taxed by both State and local authorities. But because it bought nearly all

[42]N. Y. *Times,* July 1, Sept. 10, 16, 1881.
[43]N. Y. *Tribune,* Sept. 16, 1881.

its oil in Pennsylvania, the Auditor-General, on the basis of a statute of 1868 to which he gave an entirely novel construction, now proposed to levy upon its whole capital stock as measured by dividends.[44]

Early in 1882 the case was argued before the Court of Common Pleas in Harrisburg.[45] The Standard presented statements by ex-Governor Hartranft, Insurance Commissioner Foster, and Corporation Clerk Frazer, showing that a "foreign" corporation had never before been so taxed. As its attorney said, if it were mulcted in this fashion it might be driven from the State. "That may be little, but it may not be all. The decision that drives this company from the State will drive hundreds more that hitherto have contributed to our prosperity and have also borne their full share of the burdens of taxation. It will not stop there. Our own corporations are in every State. Retaliation will ensue. New York with an untried statute on her books is standing waiting this decision."[46] On April 4 Judge Simonton filed his decision—a complete victory for the Standard. Instead of $3,200,000 he ordered it to pay only $33,277.57 as taxes and penalties for the whole period of 1873–78. And, he declared, when a "foreign" corporation "comes into this State, and engages in business here, and brings just so much of its capital stock as represents the tangible property and assets invested or used here, this proportion and no more is subject to the taxing power of the State."[47] An elementary principle of interstate comity had been upheld and clarified.

Meanwhile, several Standard officers had been brought before a committee of the United States Senate which was inquiring into certain alleged "corners." In December, 1882, Flagler, Benjamin Brewster, and Rockefeller appeared before this body at the Metropolitan

[44]See the long article in the N. Y. *Herald,* Feb. 23, 1882. This states: "The Act (of 1868) was construed for eleven years by the State authorities to mean that a tax was only to be imposed on property within the jurisdiction of the State, and that only so much of the capital stock of a company could be taxed as was used or invested in the State." But Schell's new interpretation "laid the basis of suits against foreign corporations doing business in the State for a tax on the entire sum of their capital stock from 1868 to 1881 inclusive, with interest and penalties." *The Herald* correspondent in Harrisburg called this a test case.

[45]That is, in Dauphin County, Pennsylvania.

[46]N. Y. *Tribune,* Feb. 24, 25, 26, 1882. Attorney-General Palmer argued for the State; Judge Rufus Ranney, M. E. Olmstead, and S. C. T. Dodd, for the Standard.

[47]N. Y. *Herald,* N. Y. *Tribune,* April 5, 1882.

Hotel in New York. All efforts to elicit information as to the exact nature of the trust, the reasons for its formation, the size of the dividends paid, and the interrelation between its parts, failed. They denied any speculation in oil. But they clearly resented the wide range of the questions, which they and S. C. T. Dodd believed had nothing to do with "corners," and which certainly smacked of a general fishing expedition. Three of the queries put to Rockefeller even concerned a silly rumor that the Standard Oil had gone into the cattle-raising business in Indian Territory. He dryly replied to each: "I decline to say." The Standard men also resented the browbeating tactics of the committee's attorney, who frankly expressed the rising public prejudice against the combination. At one point he advised Flagler to answer a question:

"It suits me to go elsewhere for advice," retorted Flagler, "particularly as I am not paying you for it."

"I am not paying you to rob the community; I am trying to expose your robbery," rasped the attorney.[48]

In 1883 a young Democratic reformer, Robert E. Pattison, became governor of Pennsylvania; and on March 1 he sent the legislature a special message asking it to investigate the recent tax-suit against the Standard Oil, which some believed had been fraudulently defeated. He called in especial for an inquiry into certain charges against E. G. Patterson, who after being employed to collect evidence supporting the tax-demand now stood accused of going over to the Standard. Papers relating to Patterson were enclosed. The loss of the $3,200,000 still rankled in Pennsylvania breasts! "Governor Pattison suggests the right way," said the Harrisburg *Independent,* "to get at a monopoly like the Standard Oil Company, grown powerful by its speculative robberies and the criminal recklessness with which it inflates or deflates the price of oil. The Standard has defied the State, and treats its authority with contempt. . . . There is covered up in this business a mass of fraud and speculation which will astonish the people."[49] On the other hand, Patterson's friends—including Lewis Emery, Jr.,—resented the imputations cast upon his integrity, and

[48]See N. Y. *Herald,* Dec. 16, 28, 29, 1882, for Flagler's appearance; Dec. 30, 1882, for Rockefeller. Dodd sat near Rockefeller and "indicated by a series of nods which questions should and which should not be answered."

[49]March 3, 1883.

denounced the proposed investigation.[50] It was "political buncombe," said Emery.

The two houses finally appointed a joint committee of inquiry; the Standard Oil having meanwhile invited a searching investigation.[51] Nothing was developed which supported the stale charge of tax-evasion. But some very significant testimony was given by John D. Archbold in describing how he had brought Patterson over to the Standard's side. He said that about the time the tax case went to trial he had complained to Patterson's counsel, Roger Sherman, of the man's incessant hostility:[52]

In the course of the conversation I referred to Patterson's course in following us up for so long a time, and asked Sherman if it wouldn't be better for him to desist and take a position where he could make a living legitimately; I offered to get Patterson such a position, and Sherman said he would suggest it to Patterson; he did, and it only seemed to make Patterson more bitter against us; at Harrisburg, during the trial, I learned generally that Patterson was casting about for something to do, and I once more offered to get him employment; later on, just after the tax case had been decided against the State, I met Doctor Roberts, of Titusville, in Philadelphia.

He said that Patterson was in Philadelphia, and was feeling greatly cast down because of the defeat of the State; I told him I knew of no reason why he should be, that the case had been fought on its merits; Roberts said he wondered I didn't take steps to have Patterson silenced, his attacks on the company having been annoying and expensive; it was a good thing to silence a barking dog, he said, rather than be kept awake by him; I thought so, too, and said I would be glad to talk with Patterson.

He came to my room at the Continental; I told him that so bright and smart a man as he ought to be in better business than attacking corporations merely because they were successful. Patterson finally said that if we would reimburse him for money he had expended in the litigations and for his trouble he would feel it right to cease his attacks; I finally agreed to pay him a sum of money, and to get him employment. There was not a single word said about his suppressing any evidence or a single

---

[50]Philadelphia *Press*, March 3, 1883. Emery had given Patterson $6000 to find evidence against the Standard Oil; N. Y. *Herald*, Oct. 27, 1883.

[51]Philadelphia *Press*, March 7, 1883.

[52]N. Y. *Herald*, Nov. 17, 1883. The significant headline is, "silencing a barking dog." Emery in his speech of March 2 in the legislature defended Patterson's honesty, saying that he had not sold himself to the Standard, and was at liberty to regather the evidence and demand a reopening of the case. Emery believed that Patterson had been treated shabbily by the State, and called the investigation a reflection upon himself.

word of testimony; I was to pay him $15,000–$7500 down and the balance later—and to employ him for a year in the Enterprise Transit Company at $5000 salary. The only condition was that Patterson was to cease from his vexatious suits.

Patterson gave identical testimony.[53] He made it clear that it was not until after the State had lost its case, and the Attorney-General had rejected his proposal for reopening it, that he had talked with Archbold.[54] But between the lines of both statements could be read a good deal that was not creditable to either Patterson or Archbold.

VI

It was a mixed budget, this list of charges against the Standard Oil. That part of the attack based upon the Standard's use of excessive railroad discriminations and its ambition to achieve monopoly was important and valid; other parts were neither. Mrs. Backus's story was apparently inspired by hysteria, the tax-evasion charge by politics, and the Scofield, Shurmer attack by business jealousy. A good deal of sheer envy and political demagogy unquestionably went into the criticism of the Standard. But, sound and unsound, the charges made a damaging impression upon public opinion. Suspicion of the Standard mounted until many became ready to believe anything of it. It was charged with coercing employees in Long Island City in 1883 to vote the Republican city ticket.[55] It was charged in 1882 with trying to steal part of the East River waterfront.[56] The Harrisburg *Independent* remarked early in 1883: "The Standard Oil Company deems it necessary to obtain the control of some newspapers to enable it to continue its outrageous course toward legitimate competition in its line of trade. It is believed to be the power behind the lately reorganized New York *World*." *The World* had just been sold to Joseph Pulitzer, who made it the principal anti-monopoly and anti-Rockefeller organ in the United States!

Men began to believe anything and everything of the Standard; and particularly did they believe that it was exerting a sinister in-

[53]Substantially identical; cf. N. Y. *Times*, Feb. 27, 1883.

[54]N. Y. *Herald*, Oct. 6, 1883. Patterson testified that he was in Philadelphia on April 11, 12, and 13, 1882, and then he negotiated with Archbold. See N. Y. *Herald*, Oct. 12, 1883, for Patterson's severe cross-examination by Gowen.

[55]N. Y. *Herald*, Nov. 2, 1883. The Standard's plant-managers vehemently denied the charge.

[56]N. Y. *Herald*, Nov. 23, 1882.

fluence in politics. The New York *Times* early in 1883 published a
long article called "A Great Monopoly's Work: An Inner View of
the Standard Oil Company." It was based upon an interview of its
Oil City correspondent with a Cleveland oil man who was said to
have had intimate dealings with the Standard. This nameless informant declared that when the Ohio legislative investigation began,
Rockefeller had hastily prepared packing-cases for the most important
Standard Oil records. The Standard's agent in Columbus was ordered
to telegraph instantly if the committee issued a demand for these
books, and the cases were then to be carted to the station and hurried
by the first express train to New York. Fortunately for the Standard,
the committee "were lobbied into quietness or bulldozed out of an
investigation that might investigate." The oil man went on:[57]

Inside of seven years, the Standard spent $325,000 in Harrisburg. In
five years it spent over $60,000 in Columbus. In the same length of time
but covering different years, it spent $35,000 in Albany. Here was nearly
$500,000 gone—to whom? Who knows? Does Mr. Rockefeller himself?
Does Mr. Flagler or Mr. O. H. Payne? I suppose they know in general
results just what legislation, direct and indirect, was had for their
benefit, and can form some ideas as to what further legislation and investigation that they did not desire was prevented. But no one supposes
for a moment that any of these gentlemen could name the persons to
whose pockets the money might be traced. Their dealing has all been
with agents. The Standard plan has always been to select its agents and
deal with them in general terms. "Produce," says Mr. Rockefeller, "certain
desired results that I shall name to you, and a certain named sum of
money shall be yours. I do not want to know anything about your expense
account. I do not want to know the name of a man with whom you have
dealings. Don't do anything that will involve you in trouble, or that
will be in violation of law. If you do, the entire responsibility lies with
you. This action that we fear is to the injury of our business, and we
desire to prevent it. Now go and use your moral influence to prevent
action, and when you have succeeded I will pay you the sum named for
expenses and for your time." The agent understands what all this means
and goes to work.

This article presented by innuendo a most serious charge. The
readiness of the informant to tell precisely how much the Standard
spent in various State capitals is suspicious, while it is clear that he
made no distinction between legitimate lobbying and bribery. We

[57]May 22, 1883.

shall later examine the Standard's participation in politics. But the point here is not the inaccuracy or accuracy of the charges. It is the fact that so sober a newspaper as the New York *Times* should have given this story of political corruption general currency. It was not known as an anti-Standard organ, as the New York *Herald,* Philadelphia *Press,* and Harrisburg *Independent* were. When it spoke so bluntly of bribery, we may be sure that such stories were generally circulated and generally believed. In the field of public relations the Standard was becoming a city under heavy siege, and Rockefeller was more and more the commander of a beleaguered garrison.

But the great central count of the American people against Rockefeller and his associates in the Standard Oil was that they had set up a monopoly. All else was unimportant compared with it; the miscellaneous attacks merely heightened the antagonism which grew out of this central accusation. And plainly the time was approaching when the State and Federal governments would grapple in deadly earnest with Rockefeller's powerful combination.

XXX

He Should Keep Who Can

E HAVE seen how the tempest against Rockefeller and
the Standard began, and it now remains to show how
it grew. In essence, of course, the story is simple
enough, but it has certain remarkable features, and
some of its main incidents have been strangely misconstrued.

It was axiomatic with Rockefeller and his associates that, having
established a practical monopoly, they must maintain it. For the first
time in American history they had organized a complex, fast-growing, and powerful industry under one central direction. They had
replaced a fierce competition which meant bankruptcy for the weak
and losses for the strong by a unified control which lifted the business to a richly profitable level. The large profits naturally attracted
outsiders. No writer upon the Standard has given due emphasis to
the fact that a very small capital would set up a substantial refining
business, and most writers have not even mentioned it. The lucrative
establishment of Scofield, Shurmer & Teagle in Cleveland cost only
$65,000, while B. B. Campbell testified in 1879 that a manufactory
turning out 3,000 barrels a week could be erected for from $30,000
to $50,000.[1] Now there were innumerable Americans who could com-
mand a capital of $50,000. If the Standard consented, new refineries
would spring up by scores, they would establish new distributing
agencies, and all the old implacable competition would be restored.
It seemed to officers of the Standard that they must do their utmost
to keep newcomers out of the field, for to open the gate to a few
would mean opening it to all.

This implied that the Standard, which in establishing a quasi-
monopoly had taken an attitude deeply repugnant to most Americans, must affront public opinion still further in maintaining it. The

[1]*House Trust Investigation, 1888,* p. 149.

trust of course never possessed a complete monopoly—only a practical monopoly. Its spokesmen declared in 1879 that it did about 90 per cent of the refining business of the country; in 1888, about 80 per cent; and between 1893 and 1899, 82.3 per cent.[2] To maintain order in the industry, Rockefeller could not let the independents expand their segment of the business. The premises which he accepted, or rather the basic conditions of the huge experiment in industrial organization which he had inaugurated, required him to warn off or drive out every possible entrant. Yet Americans believed in a "wholesome" rivalry in industry. They were soon doing their utmost to establish by emphatic affirmations of Congress, legislatures, and courts the rule that a "free and untrammelled traffic of the marketplace" must be preserved.

At bottom, a question of premises was involved. Rockefeller believed in concentration; most Americans believed in unlimited competition. That conflict was basic, and until the climate of opinion in America changed, it defied any compromise.[3] But a subsidiary issue of methods also played its part in the general battle. Rockefeller declared, most earnestly and sincerely, that very unfair weapons were being used in the name of free competition, while his opponents held with equal fervor that his gigantic combination was employing highly improper methods in debarring newcomers from the field. From these opposing convictions sprang a great deal of the heat and rancor of the fight over monopoly in the years 1880–1900.

Rockefeller believed that many of the men who tried to break down the practical monopoly of the Standard Oil were essentially blackmailers, and that many of the politicians who supported them were merely cheap demagogues whipping up a prejudice against great corporations in order to gain votes. His associates believed this just as firmly as he. They used the word "blackmail," of course, in a special sense. Between 1872 and 1890 members of the combination strengthened it by purchasing many refineries, usually at generous valuations; for their policy was to treat established firms generously, and pay well for good will. This held out a bait to other men to set up refineries, press their competition with the Standard, call upon

[2]*Industrial Commission Hearings*, II, 541, 542, 560; Ida M. Tarbell, *History of the Standard Oil Company*, II, 221.
[3]*Cf.* Thorstein Veblen on the rôle of "interstitial" enterprise in economics.

public opinion for assistance, and wait for the heads of the trust to offer them high prices. That a number tried this game is incontestable. Doubtless other outwardly implacable opponents of the Standard had the idea of a sale in the back of their heads; they posed as St. George against the dragon, but if the price went high enough they could couch their lances. All the leaders of the trust became very resentful on this subject, and Rockefeller wrote numerous letters denouncing "blackmailers," of which two will suffice to illustrate his attitude. One was sent on March 7, 1878, to Daniel O'Day at Bradford:[4]

There is a certain man by the name of Doe, of Rouseville, who has been systematically blackmailing us for the last year or two. He is proud of the reputation of having built seven refineries, seems an ugly bad fellow, has made Archbold a great deal of trouble. From what I learn I think Mr. Archbold has rather encouraged him that he would loan him $500 or $1000, some small amount of money, to engage in the producing business. We do not want him to build and it comes like pulling teeth to give him any money or to give him any help. He is the ugliest customer we have seen. We are not settled as to the best way of securing ourselves or managing him in the event of doing anything with him. I suppose we must try and do something. . . .

Mr. Pratt will see you next week, meanwhile please set your wits to work and see if you cannot help us out of this without our tying up any considerable sum of money with this "gentleman." Mr. Pratt is expecting to be with Col. Chester in Buffalo on Tuesday. . . .

Another, sent to Camden just four days later, dealt with some refiners who had been making trouble in the Parkersburg area:[5]

Yours of the 9th at hand and contents noted. Just what I thought of those blackmailers failing to sell out on good high prices for refined during the busy season. They will be sick unto death now having failed in their wicked scheme. A good sweating will be healthy for them and they ought to have it, and it is not money lost to us to have other people see them get it. Our chances for fair play in the future will be better.

I am happy to inform you that we are making some good progress, and while we must look forward to doing the business always *close*, hereafter, I think it possible we may contemplate it with reference to a legitimate manufacturing profit, taking into account all the savings. If you have the producers well in hand and wells, and these people could wait and sell out their works at a loss, thereby making a poor speculation of black-

[4]From New York; Rockefeller Papers.
[5]March 11, 1878; Camden Papers.

mailing, it would probably cure this batch and save you endless trouble in future. Try and exercise patience with these gentlemen as we are doing with some in different quarters, and I believe it will pay to patiently wait.

In brief, Rockefeller discriminated sharply between competition in good faith, and competition as a crass hold-up operation. He similarly discriminated between political leaders who denounced industrial concentration out of a sincere aversion and fear, and those who denounced it as a cheap and easy way to pose as champions of the masses.

But opponents of the Standard and other virtual monopolies also drew a distinction between fair and unfair operations. Iniquitous as they believed monopoly to be, they would not have waxed vehement against great business units for merely using their economies of size to stifle competition. Their chief count against the numerous trusts and consolidations which arose in the eighties and nineties was that they bulwarked their monopolies by a wide variety of cruel and improper acts. Indeed, so widespread did "unfair competition" become that textbooks of economics soon offered examples of a dozen different forms. These included the use of railroad rebates, open or concealed; the lowering of market prices at competitive points only until all competition was destroyed; the operation of bogus "independent" companies; the sale of "fighting brands" or goods of a cheap grade to ruin competitors; the employment of blacklists and boycotts; espionage; the sabotage of competitive plants; and preferential contracts.[6] In the industrial history of this period some allegations of unfair practices became famous. Among them were the charges of espionage and intimidation brought in the "bathtub case" against the Standard Sanitary Manufacturing Company; the charge of using spurious "independents," brought against the International Harvester Company; and that of flagrant coercion brought against the National Cash Register Company. Though the Clayton Act and Federal Trade Commission Act of 1914 attempted to extinguish such abuses, some nevertheless crop out constantly today.

Naturally, a fiercer light beat upon the first great trust than upon its successors. In the history of the use of unfair weapons to wipe out nascent competition the Standard Oil has its chapter, and a chapter with black pages. It should be remembered that it was but one of

[6]W. S. Steevens, *Political Science Quarterly*, XXIV, 282 ff., 460 ff.

many chapters, and that the sugar trust, the whiskey trust, the tobacco trust, the farm implement trust, the match trust, and others
contributed to the general record. Maintenance of monopoly or any
approach thereto meant constant war, and business warfare in the
eighties and nineties was savage and brutal.

II

The case of George Rice unquestionably shows the Standard in
a bad light. Rice was one of the most prominent of the men whom
Rockefeller regarded as a "blackmailer" and the general public as a
champion against monopoly. A Vermonter by birth, he had gone
into oil production at Pithole in 1865, had remained in the Regions
for a decade, sharing in its rising antagonism to Rockefeller, and
then in 1876 had removed to Marietta, Ohio, to set up a small refinery.[7] In this little plant he enlisted his whole family, one daughter
serving as bookkeeper, another as treasurer, and a son-in-law as
general manager. He was a big, hearty man physically, noisy and
blustering in manner, and fond of a shindy. His friends thought him
a brave and earnest fighter for the principles of business freedom;
certainly he showed grit, and the pamphlets he published proved his
ability. Others were not so sure of his devotion to an ideal. In Marietta, opinion still remains divided.[8] The New York *Herald,* an anti-
Standard newspaper, stated in 1891 that members of the petroleum
trade generally regarded him with suspicion, and that some characterized his acts in rather harsh words. "Mr. Rice . . . is the owner
of a refinery in Marietta, O., which he has for years been trying to
induce the Standard to buy. His price is $500,000, a figure which is
said in the trade to be preposterously high."[9] Various Standard officers said that he liked fighting and wanted money.[10] Rockefeller
described him in sharp terms. "He liked to harass, embarrass, annoy
the Standard Oil interests with a view of enabling him to sell his

[7]See George Rice's pamphlet of 1899, *Proposed Testimony . . . Before the
Industrial Commission.*

[8]I have been assisted in obtaining information from old-time citizens of
Marietta by Mr. Charles White of Cleveland. Some regarded Rice as sincere
and honest, others as a man acting for purely selfish ends.

[9]March 20, 1891, "Mr. Rice was willing to profit by the iniquitous Standard
monopoly for half a million dollars," wrote *The Herald* reporter, "but he can't
get his price, and now he wants to annihilate the aforesaid combination."

[10]Charles White to the author, Feb. 4, 1938.

quite unimportant refining interest . . . in a location not desirable, and with a refinery not up to date." He told of an interview:[11]

> He pursued us with litigation, he pursued us with legislative investigation and in all ways possible, and caused us great annoyance on this very question of freight rates. I remember being called myself on one occasion for an examination along these lines, and after a session of some hours, in the presence of his lawyers and greatly to their amusement, I gave old George a good, kindly, plain lecture in which I told him he ought to know better and ought to do better; and he seemed repentant at the time, and said, "Mr. Rockefeller, I'll come and see you."
>
> He was an india-rubber man. He seemed repentant. He'd turn up another day with another lawyer and another case. I said, "Come and see me," and he came to my office. He talked a long time. Only one thing was clear: he wanted $250,000, or he'd raise a ruction. I remember how my associates laughed when I told them. And that was his idea—to raise a row, lose some money and make the Standard Oil lose a good deal, and make a bargain. This is the whole story of George Rice.

Rice himself admitted on the witness stand that in 1882 he had told a representative of the Standard that he would sell out to it for $250,000.[12] Archbold testified under oath that in 1886 Rice demanded, under threat of prosecuting various suits, $250,000 in cash, and $250,000 more in five annual instalments, for a Marietta refinery worth $25,000 or $30,000.[13] Altogether, the man seems to have been quite willing to compound with monopoly. But that does not alter the fact that he was treated badly.

For some years after erecting his Marietta refinery, Rice brought crude oil by barge from Pennsylvania down the Allegheny and Ohio, and sold his refined oil in the East and Middle West. But in 1879 he found that freight charges on his shipments of kerosene from Marietta to the West had been suddenly raised, although the Cleveland tariffs remained unchanged. He therefore turned to the South for a market. East of the Mississippi, from Kentucky to the Gulf, he began selling in competition with Chess, Carley, and west of the river with Waters-Pierce. But at once he met a new difficulty—in 1880 he found himself hampered in getting crude oil from Pennsylvania. The National Transit Company, by Daniel O'Day's orders, suddenly tore up the pipe line which had carried his oil to the river.

---

[11]Inglis, Conversations with Rockefeller.
[12]*Industrial Commission Hearings, 1899,* I, 750. [13]*Idem,* I, 559.

He then had to ship his crude by rail into Pittsburgh, and to build special barge terminals in that city. Thus hampered, he took increasing quantities of oil from the Macksburg area in southeastern Ohio, a small but very productive field less than twenty miles from Marietta; and beginning in 1884 relied upon that district alone.[14]

Rice continued to refine in small quantities (his capacity was two thousand barrels of crude a week), and to distribute his kerosene throughout the South. He indulged in hard price-slashing, marketing at or near cost and boasting that he could undersell the Standard. Undoubtedly his kerosene was inferior to the products made from Pennsylvania oil.[15] Neither Chess, Carley nor Waters-Pierce would brook such opposition, and neither was scrupulous in its choice of weapons. Since most retailers of kerosene were grocers, Chess, Carley prepared to support their dealers in competing on a wide front. They supplied meat, sugar, coffee, and rust-proof oats to stores handling Standard products, and did it at prices which brought customers flocking from rival shops. Rice later testified that they told his retailers that they would keep up this competition to the bitter end, which is probable, and that they had been authorized by the Standard to spend $10,000 to break any store which bought independent kerosene, which is very improbable. Rockefeller later denied any such action. According to Rice, the firm of Chess, Carley actually set up in Columbus, Miss., a new grocery store to undercut him, while the Standard paid his agent in New Orleans $48,000 to cease handling the oil.

At the same time, fresh efforts were made to increase Rice's freight costs. While in New Orleans trying to establish a new agency, he was informed that his rates on kerosene to that city and Memphis had suddenly been doubled. In Louisville, Rice was supplying Wilkerson & Company, and in the spring of 1881 sent them seventy barrels of kerosene. The date of delivery was June 13. So perfectly were Chess, Carley informed of such shipments that three days later they wrote J. M. Culp, general freight agent of the Louisville & Nashville Railroad, describing the transaction, and arrogantly adding:

[14]See Rice's full testimony in *House Trust Investigation, 1888*, pp. 573 ff.
[15]The rule of the best refiners, as Camden's correspondence shows, was to mix equal quantities of Macksburg or West Virginia oil and Pennsylvania oil.

"We suspect [the car] slipped through at the usual fifth-class rate —in fact we might say we know it did—paying only $41.50 freight from here. Charges $57.40. Please turn another screw."

Meanwhile Rice's troubles in obtaining crude oil continued, although he owned some Macksburg wells. He had long carried on a feud with Daniel O'Day, caused by his interference with one of O'Day's pipe-line ventures in 1874.[16] The principal carrier of Macksburg crude was the Cincinnati & Marietta, a small railroad in the hands of a receiver. Both the Standard Oil and Rice were dependent upon it for their Macksburg supplies. In 1884 Daniel O'Day, as manager of the National Transit Company, went to the receiver, Phineas Pease, and informed him that unless the railroad met his terms, the Standard would begin storing all its oil in tanks and build a pipe line to Marietta, thus depriving the bankrupt road of its best oil traffic. His terms were outrageous. He demanded that Pease haul the Standard's crude oil for ten cents a barrel, that it charge all independents thirty-five, and that it turn the extra twenty-five cents collected from rival shippers over to the National Transit Company. The receiver finally agreed, for as he wrote his counsel, compliance was necessary "to save the oil trade along our line, and especially to save the Standard's oil trade, which would amount to seven times as much as Mr. Rice's."[17]

This iniquitous arrangement went into force in March, 1885. A joint agent of the railroad and the National Transit Company was appointed. Collecting thirty-five cents a barrel from all independent shippers, he paid twenty-five to O'Day's organization. George Rice was mulcted along with the others, and vast was his wrath when he discovered the situation. He rapidly laid a pipe to the Muskingum River, by which he fetched his crude oil in barges to Marietta, while he began collecting evidence for a suit against the railroad. On October 13, 1885, he asked the circuit court to order Receiver Pease to report forthwith upon his freight charges and other arrangements connected with the shipment of oil. Judge Baxter immediately granted

[16] See Patrick Boyle's testimony, *Industrial Commission Hearings, 1899,* I, 404. Boyle states that in 1874 Rice, by leasing land, maliciously attempted to prevent O'Day and the National Transit Company from laying a pipe line to connect Macksburg with the Standard refineries in Parkersburg. The attempt failed, but evidently left much ill-feeling.

[17] *Handy et al. vs. Cincinnati & Marietta Railroad, Federal Reporter,* XXXI, 689 ff.

the order. On learning this, the general freight agent hurried to Cleveland to confer with O'Day. The result was that on October 29, twelve days after the court had ordered the report, the treasurer of the National Transit Company sent the joint agent for the railroad and pipe line a check for $340, the amount the pipe line had received upon Rice's shipments, with instructions that he turn the money back to the receiver.[18]

But meanwhile the machinery of the court could not be stopped. When the receiver's report was laid before Judge Baxter, he called for additional information and papers. This brought out the whole sordid story of O'Day's threats and his exaction of a drawback on shipments made by independents. When Judge Baxter pronounced judgment, it was in crushing terms. He scathingly condemned the grant of a rebate, and still more scathingly the seizure of a drawback on competitive business. On the first he wrote: "All unjust discriminations are in violation of the sound public policy, and are forbidden by law. We have had frequent occasions to enunciate and enforce this doctrine in the past few years. If it were not so the managers of railways, in collusion with others in command of large capital, could control the business of the country. The idea is justly abhorrent to all fair minds. No such dangerous power can be tolerated."[19]

Of the second abuse, the drawback, he remarked that it was "a gross, illegal, inexcusable breach of a public trust that calls for the severest reprehension. The discrimination complained of in this case is so wanton and oppressive it could hardly have been accepted by an honest man having due regard for the rights of others, or conceded by a just and competent receiver who comprehended the nature and responsibility of his office; and a judge who would tolerate such a wrong or retain a receiver capable of perpetrating it ought to be impeached and degraded from his position. A good deal more might be said of the unparalleled wrong complained of, but we forbear. The receiver will be removed."[20]

Rockefeller always contended that this collection of a drawback on the shipments of competitors was the only instance of the kind in the Standard's history; and that as soon as the highest officers of the

---

[18]See George Rice's pamphlet, *The Standard Oil Company, First Decade.* Some testimony of his against the Standard is given in *Federal Anti-Trust Decision*, II, *Rice vs. Standard Oil Company*, 635 ff.

[19]*Federal Reporter* XXXI, 689–693.   [20]*Ibid.*

trust heard of it they stopped it. His first point obviously involves terming the payment which the Standard received on competitive pipe-line oil in 1877–79 a commission instead of a drawback. The second deserves careful examination. On March 29, 1890, he told the New York *World:* "We repudiated the contract before it was passed upon by the courts and made full recompense. In a business so large as ours, conducted by so many agents, some things are likely to be done which we cannot approve." To the Industrial Commission he explicitly denied that the Standard had ever collected drawbacks on competitive business. "I know of no such instance. It seems that some arrangement of that nature was entered into by one of our agents in Ohio, being the same case which has been testified to by George Rice. When notice of this agreement was brought to the officers of the company for which it was made it was promptly repudiated, and the money received . . . was refunded. And this was done . . . before we had any knowledge of judicial proceedings." S. C. T. Dodd has left a corroborative statement: "It was the fault of an overzealous agent in Ohio. . . . I know that it was stopped before we had any knowledge, in New York at least, of any action in the courts in relation to it."[21]

Even if we accept this statement, we must condemn the Standard for inexcusable negligence. O'Day was not a local agent, but one of its principal officers, managing its great pipe-line system. The question of rates from the Macksburg field was important, for it bore on the survival or extinction of the independent refineries of southern Ohio. The Standard leaders should have known precisely what contract O'Day had made within a few weeks after it was signed. Instead, on their own showing they did not scrutinize the March contract until October, and did not pronounce it illegal until some days after the court had ordered a full report. Probably O'Day took good care not to send the contract to New York until Judge Baxter's order had made him uneasy. He, too, testified that "our counsel, Mr. Dodd, advised me that we could not do that business and we refunded the money"; but he never stated when he had told Dodd of the contract.[22] The fact that repudiation and reparation coincided with court action was naturally given a sinister interpretation by enemies

[21]*Memoirs of S. C. T. Dodd,* 30.
[22]*House Trust Investigation, 1888,* pp. 275 ff.

of the Standard. At best, the episode was decidedly discreditable.

George Rice continued in business—and continued to take heavy blows. In 1886 the Cincinnati, Washington & Baltimore Railroad unexpectedly raised his freight rates well above those granted the Standard refineries. In 1887 he found that he could not get credit for purchasing tank cars because the bankers were nervous over his endless controversies with the Standard Oil. In the autumn of 1890 the general freight agent of the Little Rock & Memphis Railroad wrote him: "We are hauling your oil. This, of course, we expect as common carriers to be compelled to do. It is a fact nevertheless that on account of handling your oil the Standard Oil Company will not route any of their freight over our lines. As a consequence, we have none of their tanks."[23]

III

Most famous of all the accusations of unfair trade practice levelled against the Standard, and most vigorously exploited by its enemies, were those brought by Charles B. Matthews of Buffalo. His charges of sabotage and other acts gave rise to criminal indictments against five officers of Standard companies, received immense publicity in the newspapers, and were later recounted in detail by Henry Demarest Lloyd and others. Yet these oft-repeated allegations have never been treated with historical objectivity, or subjected to a rigorous analysis.[24]

In the rhetorical pages of Lloyd the story is damaging in the extreme to the Standard organization, if not to Rockefeller. Its essence in this version may be presented in a few paragraphs. In 1866 two Rochester men, Hiram B. Everest and his son Charles, organized the Vacuum Oil Company, which manufactured lubricants by a special process which they believed was protected by patents. In 1879 the Standard, through John D. Archbold, H. H. Rogers, and Ambrose McGregor, bought three fourths of the shares for $200,000. The Everests were paid $10,000 a year for continuing to manage the works for at least five, and if they liked, ten years, the profits of the company

[23]George Rice, *Proposed Testimony. . . . Before the Industrial Commission.*
[24]The full testimony in this case in *House Trust Investigation, 1888,* pp. 801–951, is a document on which some one could found an interesting historical novel. The best newspaper reports are in the N. Y. *World* (friendly to the prosecution) and the N. Y. *Tribune* (friendly to the defense). I have also used files of the Buffalo *Express,* which took the side of the Buffalo Company.

going to the Acme as a subsidiary of the trust. Archbold later testified that the Standard "had no direct relation whatever with the management," though he, Rogers, and McGregor were all directors of the Vacuum Company.

The Vacuum Company had three employees of experience and ability. They were Charles B. Matthews, an ambitious, forceful man who had recently been a farmer in Wyoming Valley; Albert A. Miller, a highly skilled workman; and J. Scott Wilson, an experienced salesman.[25] Discontented with their salaries, they left the company in March, 1881, to set up in Buffalo a rival establishment—the Buffalo Lubricating Oil Company, Ltd. Matthews was to be general manager, Miller superintendent of plant operations, and Wilson head of the sales division. They chose a site, purchased machinery, and looked forward to a prosperous career. But at once they encountered the implacable hostility of the Everests—backed, as they believed, by the united force of the Acme Company and the Standard Oil; a hostility that stopped at almost nothing.

The Everests promptly threatened Matthews and his colleagues with war to the knife and eventual ruin. They warned the three adventurers that the Vacuum Company would bring suit against the Buffalo concern for infringement of patent, and drive it out of the field. Indeed, during 1881–82 the Vacuum Company did bring two suits, which it lost; and after an interval, it perfected an appeal to the Federal Supreme Court, which was still pending as late as the spring of 1887. But this was not all. When Matthews told Charles Everest that he expected to obtain his raw materials from an independent Buffalo refinery, the Atlas Company, the latter replied, "You will wake up some morning and find that there won't be any Atlas Company." Sure enough, the Atlas was shortly absorbed by the Standard combination. The Everests also approached Miller, the technical expert for the new company, and seduced him to come back into their employ; paying him $1500 a year for doing little or

[25]The N. Y. *World,* May 8, 1887, gives a graphic description of Matthews: "Hard knocks have whitened his hair and set firm, hard lines about his face. . . . His eyes are deepset under a protruding forehead and black bushy lashes, and are dark, firm, and searching. His jet-black beard is luxuriant but coarse; his whole head and face bespeak the dogged persistence in following a foe that are characteristic of the man. . . . All strangers are objects of suspicion to him, and his hatred of the Standard monopoly and its men extends to the farthest limit of their network of enterprises and agents."

nothing. And worst of all—according to the version of Lloyd and other haters of the Standard—they tried to wreck the new plant.

The works were completed so rapidly that on June 15, 1881, the first run of oil was made. Miller, secretly bought up by the Everests, was in charge. He ordered an excessively fierce fire built under the still, so hot that the furnace became cherry red; he packed the safety valve with plaster of Paris; and he would have wrecked the plant by an explosion and fire if the valve had not blown open. When it did, a cloud of highly explosive gases floated harmlessly away. This was pure sabotage, endangering life as well as property. When the affair was aired in the criminal court, a lawyer to whom Hiram Everest and the treacherous Miller had talked before the attempted explosion testified that he had warned Miller that he might get a penitentiary sentence if he tried to harm the plant, and that Everest had intimated that protection would be assured. The Buffalo Company went on with its work. But it was handicapped by the loss of Miller's technical skill. Moreover, the Everests systematically maligned it, spreading libelous reports in detraction of its products; while their patent suits trenched heavily upon Matthews's time and energy. The Standard was plainly determined to crush this sturdy competitor.

In desperation, Matthews in the spring of 1883 brought a civil suit against the two Everests for various harmful acts—for falsely representing that the wares of the Buffalo Company were inferior; for attempting to cut off its supply of crude oil; for enticing skilled workmen from its employ; for threatening its customers with law-suits, and so on. A jury awarded him $20,000, which the courts set aside because damages were not proved. A second civil suit was then commenced, in which Archbold, Rogers, the Vacuum Company, the Acme Company, and the Standard Oil were all made co-defendants with the Everests. This time Matthews asked for $250,000 in damages! Meanwhile he had brought charges against Miller, the Everests, Archbold, Rogers, and McGregor before a grand jury. The result was the indictment of these five Standard men for conspiring to burn the works and destroy the business of the Buffalo Lubricating Oil Company. News that they were to stand trial in a criminal court sent a wave of sensational headlines across the continent; and when the case opened on May 3, 1887, in the Court of Oyer and Terminer in Buffalo, reporters from all over the East were present.

The trial, according to Lloyd, furnished a series of startling disclosures. A Rochester attorney named Truesdale testified to a conference with Hiram Everest and Miller, in which they had indicated their wish to damage the new manufactory. Frank R. Beardsley, an employee who assisted Miller on the day of the first run, told how the safety valve was packed and the fires stoked up, and said that catastrophe was escaped only by a lucky chance. The fireman asserted that at Miller's command he had built the hottest fire of his life. Evidence was given by Miller himself that he had been paid $1500 a year to leave the Buffalo Company; while a salesman for the Vacuum Company testified that he had been ordered to assail the quality of the Buffalo products. Espionage on the part of the Standard was also indicated. John Byrne, head of a detective agency, testified that he had hired a laborer in the Buffalo plant to spy upon Matthews and the establishment, had sent reports to S. C. T. Dodd and a Rochester attorney representing the Vacuum Company, and had been paid by checks from Dodd. Matthews testified that in 1882 he had protested to H. H. Rogers against the patent suits, declaring that they were groundless, and that Rogers had growled: "If one court does not sustain the patents, we will carry the case up until you get enough of it!"

In the end, according to Lloyd, the charge of sabotage was fully sustained. The jury found the two Everests guilty of criminal conspiracy. However, after various efforts by counsel to delay sentence, six jurors signed a petition recommending clemency, and the judge let the Everests off with a fine of $250 apiece. Many believed that the judge and jury had been tampered with! As for Archbold, Rogers, and McGregor, the judge ordered the indictments against them dismissed because no connection between them and the alleged criminal acts had been proved; but Matthews asked the public to decide for itself whether these Standard men could really have been guiltless.

This, as we have said, was the story presented with rhetorical flourishes by Henry Demarest Lloyd,[26] and later repeated with strong moral indignation by Ida M. Tarbell. But justice to truth compels

[26]Mrs. F. S. Hayden, daughter of Charles B. Matthews, wrote me on March 5, 1938: "All the information my father had was made available to Mr. Henry D. Lloyd when he wrote *Wealth Against Commonwealth*. In a copy of that book on the fly-leaf father wrote and signed: 'My Dear Son—I give you this book Christmas, 1895. It is not only the best and truest exponent of the

the statement that against it stands an array of facts which Lloyd studiously ignored, though court records and newspaper files plainly and forcibly present them.

To begin with, the defense offered evidence that in leaving the Vacuum Company to set up a rival concern, Matthews, Miller, and Wilson acted unethically. They planned to take the Vacuum process, copy the Vacuum machinery, carry off the Vacuum's list of customers, and sell a product as nearly identical with the Vacuum's as possible.[27] Matthews was apparently obsessed with the idea of making a quick fortune. Miller, as both sides admitted, though valuable for his knowledge of the Vacuum process, was drunken, idle, treacherous, and thoroughly venal.[28] A Corry saloonkeeper testified that Miller said to him: "Here is a palm, black, rough, and itching, and the party that fills it the fullest can get it and me." The third member of the trio, the salesman J. Scott Wilson, shortly became disgusted with his associates and left them. He testified in the Buffalo trial: "I had got in with people who did not keep their agreements or carry out their contracts, and so I left the Buffalo Company as soon as I could."

It was proved that Miller, just before leaving the Vacuum works, went to the iron foundry of Emory Jones in Rochester, where the Vacuum Company kept patterns for its machinery-parts, and there had duplicate castings made for the Buffalo Company. He held au-

---

industrial conditions and dangers of the Republic today but it doubtless gives more of my personal trials and experiences than you will ever find elsewhere in print. The manuscript was entirely rewritten three times to ensure its complete truthfulness and accuracy by my friend Henry Demarest Lloyd of Chicago.' "

[27]On this point see the testimony of Matthews's associate, J. Scott Wilson, *House Trust Investigation, 1888,* p. 917, and press of the day:

Q.—Did he say, "We can go to the Vacuum's customers and say that we have the same processes, same apparatus, and make the same oils as the Vacuum"?

A.—Yes, sir.

Q.—Did he say to you, or in your presence, that he expected to get $100,000 or $150,000 by being bought out by the Standard Company? A.—Yes, sir.

[28]On this point the evidence is conclusive. It was admitted by Miller himself that he first betrayed the Vacuum Company, and then the Buffalo Company. Yet Lloyd portrays him as a deeply wronged man. He was a frequenter of saloons and utterly undependable; his word was worthless. When questioned about his story by a Standard Oil attorney, he remarked: "I've told it a good many times, but I can't always remember it precisely alike"! Even the friendly *World* reporter was disgusted by him.

thority from the Vacuum Company to get such pieces, but did not tell the foundry that they were for a rival plant. It was proved that Wilson took away lists of Vacuum customers. Mrs. Wilson testified that in March, 1881, she heard Matthews tell her husband in a conference at their home: "We must make a good showing, and then the Standard will buy us out."[29] Matthews himself made a significant admission when asked by the Standard attorney about this talk with Wilson:[30]

Q.—Did you not at or about that time, and at that place, say this in substance: "We can go to the customers of the Vacuum Oil Company and say to them, 'We have the same processes and the same apparatus and the same oils as the Vacuum Company, and we have still their old superintendent, Mr. Miller, to manufacture the oils' "?

A.—I might have said something like that in subtance; I do not recollect it, though.

Numerous witnesses denied that there was any "explosion" whatever in the Buffalo plant or any mishandling of the furnaces. The principal witness as to sabotage, Frank R. Beardsley, was a brother-in-law of Matthews. But a laborer in the plant declared that he had observed nothing unusual that day. J. Scott Wilson stated that, returning from a sales trip within one or two days, he had looked about the plant carefully, and "I observed about the still or the works no indication of any harm having come to the stills or to the works in any particular." He heard about the blowing-off of the safety valve, but nobody spoke of any accident or explosion. Thompson McGowan, a graduate of Princeton employed in plant-management by the Standard, testified as a practical expert with twenty years' experience in refining. He said it was the uniform usage to attach safety valves to fire stills, and that there were other outlets for the gases leading to the condensers. Gases began to rise when the oil was heated to 125°, and vapors of varying density were thrown off as the temperature increased. The fire ought to be extremely hot. "When a still is first charged with, say, 175 barrels of petroleum, it is economical to use a big fire so as to get the petroleum heated to a utilizing point as quickly as possible. There is no such thing as making too hot a fire for the first two hours." Asked about the cloud of gas when the safety valve blew open, he said that such escapes were not unusual;

[29]*House Trust Investigation, 1888*, p. 939.　　　[30]*Idem*, 889.

that the cloud must have been a mixture of steam and gas, for the latter alone would not be visible; and that there was no danger whatever of an explosion by such a cloud.

McGowan and other experts testified that the use of plaster of Paris as packing in safety valves was common usage. It was done simply to keep the gases in the still from leaking at points where the valve did not fit tightly. The plaster did not adhere to the iron in a way to prevent proper operation of the valve, but instantly broke when the valve blew open. An independent refiner of Philadelphia, W. E. Cotter, who possessed nineteen years' experience and had specialized in making lubricants, corroborated McGowan's principal points. A blowing off of vapors was common and harmless, he said. Very often the escaping gases caught fire. The result was simply a flash, which led up to the safety valve and burned there until the supply of gas was exhausted. He spoke also of the need for an intensely hot fire.

Q.—Have you seen the firebox under a still during distillation when it was a cherry red?
A.—It is a common occurrence. In fact, it occurs at almost every distillation in my experience.

In fine, this story of "sabotage" by an attempted explosion which might have destroyed property, and possibly have cost several lives, was regarded by these witnesses as a perfect mare's nest. The hot fire kindled by Miller was entirely proper; the packing of the safety-valve with plaster was ordinary practice; the blowing open of such valves was an everyday occurrence. Cotter, who insisted that far from having any ties with the Standard he was its active competitor, and was testifying only out of a sense of fair play, also told of a friendly conversation with Matthews in Philadelphia in 1885:[31]

Q.—In 1885 did Matthews say to you, "This thing of building refineries and expecting the Standard to buy them out seems to be a poor investment," and did you answer, "The Standard's day for buying out refineries is past"? A.—Yes, sir.
Q.—What did he say in reply? A.—He said, "I intend that they shall buy me out, or I shall make it hot for them."

[31]*House Trust Investigation, 1888,* p. 936, gives this statement in expanded form. I use a concise newspaper report. The substance of the two is precisely the same. Matthews (p. 895) confessed talking with Cotter but denied these statements.

Indeed, there can be no question whatever of Matthews's readiness, if not anxiety, to sell out to the Standard. Alfred P. Wright of Buffalo, who hoped to make a commission on the sale, had two conversations with Matthews in the fall of 1885. In the first, Matthews placed a valuation of $300,000 upon his works; in the second, he set his price at $250,000—this to include the abandonment of all legal proceedings, both civil and criminal! Wright, who knew that the Standard regarded the works as worth not more than $70,000, dropped the matter. About the same time, Matthews talked with William O. Allison, former publisher of *The Oil, Paint, and Drug Reporter,* who was known to be close to the Standard. Of this exchange Matthews himself reluctantly testified:

Q.—Did you not say that $250,000 would be accepted? A.—We talked about selling the property. . . .
Q.—Did he not say it was a rather high price for the property? A.—Perhaps so.
Q.—Did you not remark that it might be bought for $250,000? A.—Something of that sort.

As for the charge of espionage, the Standard officers readily admitted the employment of a detective agency which had made reports to S. C. T. Dodd. But the attorneys showed that the contract with the agency carried a statement that Dodd suspected the Buffalo Company of infringing upon the patents owned by the Vacuum Company, and wished data on that subject.

At no point in the trial was any real ground shown for the indictment of Archbold, Rogers, and McGregor, whose inclusion in the proceedings amounted to sheer persecution. Judge Haight made this plain when he ordered the indictments against them quashed. He told the jury that it was obvious that they had no connection with the alleged sabotage, and knew nothing about the Everests' enticement of Miller from the new company. Rogers had acquiesced in bringing the patent suits, but there was nothing illegal in that.

The Everests were found guilty—but guilty of what? The charge was conspiracy to injure the Buffalo Company by various acts, the chief being sabotage, enticement of employees, and the bringing of unfounded suits. The twelve jurors wrangled until a late hour at night, four of them long standing out against conviction. Next morning they returned the verdict "Guilty." But the fact that six jurors asked for clemency, and that Judge Haight fined the Everests only $250 apiece, indicates that the court did not believe them highly culpable. One juror later swore to an affidavit, stating that "it was not the intention of the said jury, in rendering said general verdict, to pronounce the defendants guilty of an attempt or conspiracy to blow up or burn the works of the Buffalo Lubricating Oil Company, Ltd., but the conviction was, in the mind of the deponent, based upon the enticement of the witness Miller from the employ of said company and he believes that the other members of the jury convicted the prisoners on the same ground."[32] Since most of the jurors were farmers, naturally sympathetic to Matthews, while feeling in Buffalo was decidedly hostile to the Standard, the leniency shown the Everests is striking.

Rockefeller at once made a vigorous statement to the press bringing out the strength of the defense.[33] This defense is completely ignored by Lloyd and almost completely by Miss Tarbell. Yet it is clear that it carries great weight. Matthews apparently entered the industry with unclean hands, trying to build a success upon the appropriation of the Vacuum processes, machine-designs, and trade-lists. He brought civil and criminal suits which he was ready to drop if the Standard would pay $250,000 for a business not worth one third that sum. He induced the public prosecutor to indict three prominent businessmen without a shred of evidence that would bear examination in court. If his story of the safety-valve and the near-explosion was not trumped up, it was at least grossly exaggerated. As against this, one of the Everests certainly meditated a retaliation against the Buffalo Company which came near the line of criminality, and the two may really have planned sabotage. On this point the evidence is not clear. We may add that it is not edifying to find H. H. Rogers encouraging a dubious patent-suit against the Vacuum, or S. C. T. Dodd helping make a spy out of one of the

---

[32]This affidavit may be found in *Industrial Commission Hearings, 1899*, I, pp. 234, 235. Five other jurors signed it, four in its entirety, and one as to the recommendation that the Everests be let off with a mere fine.

[33]"The evidence of yesterday," he said to the N. Y. *Tribune* on May 13, "renders it very obvious that a conspiracy was formed and still exists, but not on the part of any of the defendants. The conspiracy was formed to blackmail the Standard Oil Company." He added: "The whole proceeding, at least as far as the Standard was involved, has been a monstrous injustice, the perpetration of which was rendered possible only by prejudice."

Buffalo Company employees. But the Standard group were quite as much sinned against as sinning.[34]

Rockefeller naturally regarded the case as an attempt to harass and blackmail the Standard. Years later his indignation was still hot as he pronounced Matthews "a scheming, trouble-making black-mailer" whose "wicked, defiant purpose" had been to defame honest leaders of the Standard until they paid him to desist.[35] Once during the trial he showed the strongest resentment. This was just after Judge Haight had ordered the indictments against Archbold, Rogers, and McGregor dropped. Attorneys and friends of the Standard set up a delighted murmur, while somebody rushed forward with a bouquet for handsome Harry Rogers. But Rockefeller rose angrily. "I have no congratulations to offer you, Rogers," he grated between set teeth.[36] "What should be done with people who bring an action against men in this way? What should be done?"—and he shook his clenched fist toward the seat which Matthews had occupied. "What an unheard-of thing!" He spoke bluntly to *The Tribune*.[37]

"It was a surprise not only to me, but to all our people, who thought the evidence warranted an acquittal," he said, "as far as the Standard Oil is concerned, it is completely vindicated by the exonera-tion of Messrs. Rogers, Archbold, and McGregor." He went on to predict an appeal. "I feel sorry, however, for the Everests as this blow will be all the more severe on the old gentleman because of bad

[34]The N. Y. *Tribune* published an indignant editorial May 12, 1887, entitled "A Question of Justice." It asked: "How many editors will recognize the fact that the Standard Oil men of New York have been acquitted, will retract charges against them, and do them justice?" After castigating the sensational newspapers, it continued: "Now we shall see how much dishonest pandering to popular prejudice there has been in comments on this matter. For if there were only honest zeal for justice and the public welfare, the journals in ques-tion would reflect that these men have been greatly wronged."

[35]Inglis, Conversations with Rockefeller.

[36]N. Y. *World,* May 11, 1887. Rockefeller, one of the busiest men in America, had then been kept waiting in the courtroom for eight days.

[37]N. Y. *Tribune,* May 16, 1887. John T. Flynn in *God's Gold* quotes the reporter as asking what would be the effect of the verdict upon the Vacuum Company, and cites Rockefeller's answer, "Oh, it will go along just the same as ever," as evidence that he was close to the management of the Vacuum. But reference to the *Tribune* shows that its reporter really asked, "What will be the effect of the verdict upon the Standard Oil Company?" Of the two Everests, the younger had been in active charge, while the father had spent nearly all his time in the West. Rockefeller's statement shows that he barely knew the younger—the active manager.

health and recent family affliction. I have known Mr. Everest for a long time, having met him in Cleveland more than twenty years ago. They are both honorable and upright men, and incapable of doing what is charged against them. . . . So far from the Vacuum Company wishing to crush out rivals, when it began business it had fifty-seven competitors, and now it has ninety-seven. This does not look like a desire to crush out rivals, does it?"

Rockefeller's testimony, given with his usual perfect aplomb, had been interesting.[38] To one query he replied: "I am engaged in the oil-refining business at Cleveland." "Where besides Cleveland?" demanded the district attorney. "I am engaged in it nowhere else." All his utterances were marked by this dry literalness. "Does the Standard own any pipe lines?" asked the attorney. "No, sir." "Are there pipe lines under the control or management of the Standard?" "No, sir." Legally speaking, this was accurate; the Standard Oil of Ohio had no control over the National Transit Company. What the district attorney meant, but did not have the wit to define, was the Standard Oil Trust—which did exercise control over huge pipe-line properties. But the question had no relation to the case anyhow. Rockefeller suavely testified that he knew Archbold, Rogers, and McGregor; that they were engaged in the oil business; and that he had known in 1879 that they contemplated buying control of the Vacuum Oil Company, but that the Standard of Ohio had no interest in the purchase. He left the stand without revealing anything new upon the organization or aims of the trust.

We may record here that Matthews shortly failed. Costs of new litigation may have had something to do with this,[39] while a corrupt partner certainly had a good deal. Matthews blamed the machinations of the Standard for a variety of troubles which he encountered —difficulty in getting crude oil, obstacles in hiring skilled assistants, increases in freight rates, and even higher charges by the Great Lakes steamships. When years later his statement on this last point was read to Rockefeller, the magnate scoffed. "Utterly absurd!" he exclaimed. "I had no influence whatever upon Great Lakes charges."[40]

[38]Graphic accounts are given in the N. Y. *World*, N. Y. *Tribune,* and Buffalo *Express* of May 11, 1887.

[39]A suit by the Vacuum Company for infringement of trade-mark was lost by that company in 1886; Buffalo *Express*, May 18, 1886. The costs were paid by the Vacuum.

[40]Inglis, Conversations with Rockefeller.

Before Everest's damage suit for $250,000 went to trial, a receiver took over his company. Agents representing the Standard then offered to pay a total of $81,000 for the works and their assets, the damage suit to be discontinued. The court, with the approval of most of the stockholders and creditors, ordered this accepted.[41]

IV

Both the charges of Rice against O'Day, and of Matthews against the Everests, conspicuous in all early indictments of the Standard's methods, are obviously unimportant in any broad view of the refining industry. They were admittedly unique and untypical. Nobody seriously asserted after 1881 that the Standard made a *practice* of demanding drawbacks upon competitive shipments. Nobody ever gave substantial evidence of another instance of alleged sabotage. But a different character attaches to the complaints made against the Standard's usages in marketing oil. These outcries came from all parts of the country, they were incessant and long-continued, and they build up the picture of a consistent policy involving unfair methods and very harsh practices. Nothing else did so much, in the years 1883–1900, to make the Standard Oil Trust unpopular. Its marketing organization touched nearly every town and hamlet in the land. When this organization undertook to dictate to all grocery stores and hardware shops which sold kerosene and lubricants, and to force all recalcitrant dealers into line, its practices came under the critical scrutiny of millions of Americans.

One set of complaints is typified by the case of a Brooklyn wholesaler, James H. Tompkins, in 1890. This local Hampden had long dwelt in the Williamsburg area, conducting an establishment at 328 Grand Street. After the Standard became powerful Tompkins bought his oil from it, reselling to customers scattered all over Brooklyn. His trade, partly with grocers and other retailers, partly with private families, kept two wagons busy. Late in the eighties he found that the marketing department of the Standard had bought control of important wholesale stores in his area. These were continued under the names of the old owners, but actually for the Standard's interest. Alarmed and irritated, Tompkins looked about for cheaper supplies; and though he still took most of his oil from the Standard, he began

[41]Lloyd, *Wealth Against Commonwealth*, 292, 293.

buying some at cut rates from independent refiners. Learning of this, the Standard took steps to discipline him.[42]

According to Tompkins, this was done by sending agents to call on all the retailers who dealt with him, and telling them that while oil would be advanced on January 1, 1890, any orders placed immediately would be filled at the existing low prices; the delivery to be made in such amounts and at such times as the retailers desired. Naturally the Standard's agents booked many orders. Prices duly went up two cents a gallon at New Year's. Tompkins had not been warned, and when he called upon his old customers found they were getting all the oil they wanted at lower rates than he could offer. Anxious to hold his trade, he then turned for his entire supply to independent refineries in Pennsylvania. They shipped him oil at low prices, and as his former customers preferred to deal with him, he got most of them back. When the Standard inquired where he was buying his oil, he refused to tell. A price-war immediately opened. The Standard cut prices, and Tompkins met the reduction. The Standard slashed prices again; Tompkins did the same. Other cuts followed until oil was selling three or four cents a gallon cheaper in Williamsburg than elsewhere in the metropolitan district. Tompkins's profits were disappearing, but he held on.

Then the Standard's marketing department resorted to a new step. They had a list of all Tompkins's retail dealers, but not of the families he served. One of his wagons was devoted to these private homes, reaching four hundred to five hundred addresses daily. On March 7 the driver had been absent only a short time when, hurriedly returning, he rushed into the store to say that he had been followed by two suspicious-looking men. Tompkins took steps to ascertain what was afoot. When the wagon began another trip, he stole out after it. One of the spies took the right and the other the left side of the street, Tompkins bringing up the rear; when the horse trotted the shadows trotted too, and the agile Tompkins broke into a spurt. He soon learned what the spies were doing. Whenever the wagon made a delivery, one of them ascertained the name of the house-owner, and jotted his information down in a notebook.[43]

[42]Tompkins's story is given at great length in the N. Y. *World*, March 20, 1890.
[43]*Ibid.*

It was not difficult for Tompkins to deal with this situation. When the wagon made its next morning start, it headed toward Calvary Cemetery, the faithful spies following. Soon the driver touched the horses to a trot. The spies exchanged anxious glances, and when the horses broke into a run, tried to keep pace. Finally the wagon turned a sharp corner, and when the spies puffed up, it had disappeared. They wearily returned to the store to see the horses dozing at the curb, and Tompkins in front with a peculiar smile on his face. Before they had time to rest, he started the wagon off toward East New York on another trip that quickly developed into a race—the spies losing it under the elevated railroad. Once more they trudged back to find the horses dozing, and Tompkins surveying them with an ironic smile. Immediately a third trip began, which turned into another wild-goose chase. So the game went on for several days, Tompkins meanwhile making his usual deliveries in an unmarked wagon. Finally the spies appeared in a buggy drawn by a fast horse, and began taking down names again.

At this point Tompkins carried the matter to the police. A city magistrate assigned two detectives to investigate the matter, and the spies were soon arrested. In court they admitted being in the Standard's employ, and the magistrate told them that on a repetition of the offense, he would send them to jail. Tompkins, relating his story to the New York *World,* appealed to the public for support. "The Standard drivers told some of my customers that they would undersell me, no matter how low I put my prices. Some of my customers have told me about very low prices the Standard made. . . . I have heard of similar warfare on other independent dealers."[44]

This, obviously, is an *ex parte* statement. The Standard would perhaps have alleged that Tompkins had begun the price-cutting, or that he was mixing inferior oils with the Standard's brands. But accusations like those of Tompkins were so numerous that they constitute a formidable indictment of the Standard's methods in marketing. To destroy the outlets for competitive oil it used price-cutting, espionage, and intimidation. Many small dealers testified, like George Rice's customers, that if they handled independent brands rival stores were supplied with cheap groceries to attract buyers.

[44]*Ibid.* Aggressive local price wars and the use of "fighting brands" were common in the history of the Sugar Trust, Tobacco Trust, and other combinations.

Often a mere threat was sufficient. Take the story told to the Industrial Commission of the treatment given in 1888 to a Texas wholesaler, W. W. White, who fitted out wagon trains going over the plains.[45] "He had been buying his oil from the Standard Oil Company, but one day a man came along with some specimens of oil that were very much finer than any he had been able to get, and the price being very satisfactory, he purchased a carload of oil from him. After two or three weeks the car of oil arrived, and the next morning the Standard Oil Company's representative from Fort Worth appeared on the scene and challenged Mr. White's right to buy anybody's oil except theirs and declared that they would not stand it. He finally threatened to establish a store and run White out of business if he insisted on selling any other oil than theirs." White surrendered.

In 1896 the manager of the New England Oil Company complained that the Standard was using every possible means to drive his organization out of western Massachusetts, and was employing underhanded methods.[46] In Holyoke it had reduced the price of oil from 9¼ cents a gallon to 5¼ cents, and offered further concessions to dealers who would agree to take nothing but Standard wares. Going beyond this, declared the manager, it had persuaded the fire department of the city to issue an order stopping the sale of New England Company kerosene. The fire-chief termed it dangerous. When the mayor had an investigation made, it appeared that the New England oil was perfectly safe. At other points competitors complained that the Standard tried to arouse a prejudice against their oils. Frank S. Monnett of Ohio told the Industrial Commission of the systematic price-slashing used in Ohio:[47]

They have a plan of sending agents around—I think competitors call them buzzards—where there is competition, to follow up the competitor's wagon, take the name of the customer and the amount of oil sold, and mail it to the central office of the division. A special agent of the Standard Oil is then sent out who follows up the competitor, making tests. He will clean up the lamp of the customer of the competitor, make a test, and then leave their own oil of as high a grade as the competitor's. If they cannot succeed in that way they then commence cutting rates, and

[45]Testimony of M. L. Lockwood, *Industrial Commission Hearings, 1899*, p. 402.
[46]Manager Warren told his story *in extenso* in the N. Y. *Tribune*, Dec. 14, 1896.
[47]*Industrial Commission Hearings, 1899*, I, 313 ff.

the rates are cut until they are below a living price, or until they have driven out the competitor. Then the man who is inspecting and following the competitor goes to another town where they have competition. When they have driven out competition in a given town the oil goes back again to the old price. They sold oil for four cents at Dayton, where they had competition, while at Urbana it was eight. These towns are but a short distance apart.

This too is an *ex parte* statement; but no reader of the huge array of testimony upon the Standard's operations which became available between 1888 and 1900 can doubt that a great deal of real unfairness entered into its marketing activities.[48] Some practices of Waters, Pierce and Chess, Carley were grossly improper.

v

So important is this subject in any history of Rockefeller's career that certain general observations ought to be set down. Any careful student must conclude that the wild hubbub raised over the Rice and Matthews suits was exaggerated. O'Day's treatment of Rice and the Marietta railroad was certainly outrageous. But there is every reason to accept the statement of Rockefeller and Dodd that they countermanded his action as soon as they learned of it, and that no repetition of this type of offense ever occurred. We have shown how heavy was the discount which must be applied to Matthews's charge.

But the marketing methods of the Standard are a different matter. They constituted a widespread and long-continued abuse of the power of the great combination. To be sure, just what *was* unfair was by no means so clear in 1885 or 1895 as it became a generation later. Throughout this period the use of underselling to drive out a competitor presented a thorny ethical and legal problem. Many States placed no restraint upon it. Other States, by statutes and court decisions, tried to prevent local and temporary price-slashing. But these latter found their laws and decrees hard to enforce; for it was generally accepted as an axiom of the competitive system that the owner of any goods might sell or decline to sell, as he pleased, and if sold might do so without restraint as to prices. It was (and is) also a generally accepted principle that a manufacturer might sell a large

---

[48]See, for example, the testimony of W. H. Clarke of Newark, O., in *Industrial Commission Hearings, 1899,* I, 331 ff.

quantity of goods for a lower price than a small quantity; that is, he might vary his prices. Nevertheless, public sentiment in most localities emphatically condemned the Standard's marketing department for cutting local prices until an independent was eliminated, and then restoring them. It condemned its use of spying, intimidation, and detraction in order to drive marketing rivals out of the field.

In old age Rockefeller uttered a few words regarding some improper acts of the trust. In general, he said, it was a beneficial combination.[49] "But it is nevertheless to be remembered that there might have been representatives of some of the many organizations controlled by the Standard Oil Company who, in their ambition for place and position, might have done and said things, and undoubtedly did and said things, which were never approved of but always condemned by the people who controlled the affairs of the company." This statement applies to O'Day, the Everests, and Henry Clay Pierce. It would have a great deal more force if any evidence existed that Rockefeller and his associates had ever strongly rebuked these men; but it is true that in an oligarchy like the Standard, the trustees could not easily control all their associates. Men on the periphery were often hard to handle, and Carley of Chess, Carley boasted before a House Committee in 1888 that he got his own objects by his own very rough ways. "I was very fortunate in competing; but I want to say that it was not the direction of the Standard Oil Company or at their request; it was simply my way of doing business."[50]

But Rockefeller s statement is to be taken as a comment, not an apology. He believed too fervently in the great organization which he headed ever to apologize for it. To most Americans of that period business meant war, and stern, unsparing war at that, with no blows softened. The Standard Oil Trust, representing a bold experiment in business concentration, occupied a position in which it could not treat competitors gently. No half-way house then seemed feasible between free competition and practical monopoly. The trust had

[49]Inglis, Conversations with Rockefeller.
[50]*House Trust Investigation, 1888*, pp. 534, 535. There is a significant sentence in a letter by Rockefeller to Henry M. Flagler, March 17, 1885: "Colonel Payne is here; and we are negotiating with Carley in reference to some changes in his affairs." Rockefeller Papers.

gained a strength which enabled it to prevent the major price-wars, the sudden sickening drops of the whole national market, the chaotic uncertainty, which from 1865 to 1875 had made refining so dizzy a gamble. It felt that it must maintain its iron grip, for any relaxation would have lost the whole battle. To be tolerant and kindly, to let numerous men like Rice invade the Southern front, men like Matthews lay waste the Northern, and men like Tompkins make wide forays on the Eastern, would have been fatal. It is not strange that in the hard fighting blows were struck below the belt, and that a public which disapproved the mere existence of the trust came to condemn still more strongly its steel-fisted tactics.

XXXI

The Standard in Politics

ROCKEFELLER was keenly aware of the rising public antagonism to the Standard Oil. Riding downtown on the elevated, he doubtless read the New York *Times* editorial of December 11, 1885, upon the George Rice case, entitled "A Great Monopoly's Meanness." It was a blistering excoriation of the trust. "No further disclosures were needed for a complete exhibition of the greed, injustice, and oppression that are a part of the Standard Oil Company's stock in trade," exclaimed *The Times,* "but as an example of the extent to which its bargains with common carriers have been pushed, this story is interesting." Scarcely a week went by without some thrust in Pulitzer's *World* or Bennett's *Herald* at the "anaconda" or "octopus." The anti-Standard feeling long virulent in the Oil Regions and a few refining centers was fast being diffused over most of the country. Expressions of it came in thickening numbers from the Chicago *Tribune*, Springfield *Republican,* Philadelphia *Press,* and other important newspapers. .

Part of this chorus of attack was sincere, part demagogy, and a great part mere habit or convention. The Standard Oil had already become a symbol. During the next decade millions of Western farmers and Eastern workmen were taught to regard Wall Street and Lombard Street, Morgan and Rothschild, as emblems of a brutal money-power. During the same years hosts were taught to see in the dollar-marked Hanna a symbol of corporate control of the government. In the same way multitudes were persuaded that Rockefeller and the Standard typified the most remorseless form of monopoly. What Tom Watson and "Coin" Harvey did for Wall Street, what Hearst and Opper did for Hanna, equally efficient hands were doing for No. 26 Broadway. By 1895 the Standard illustrated the adage about giving a dog a bad name and hanging him. The mixture of fact and fiction heaped upon its head cannot be better studied than in the allegations upon its rôle in politics—some true, some half-true, and some false.

II

The nature of the Standard's relation to government was fixed by its circumstances. Innumerable great American businesses of the period asked for special favors. Manufacturers demanded tariff privileges; mining and manufacturing companies wanted part of the public domain; steamship lines fought for subsidies; till early in the seventies the railroads had gotten land-grants. Many corporations wanted tax-favors from the States, and most railroads were notoriously under-assessed. But other American businesses asked not for favors but exemptions. They wanted to be let alone—no investigations, no regulatory legislation, no penalties for past misdeeds. Obviously, the Standard Oil fell into the second group. It did not want any land-grants, subsidies, or important tariff-favors, and took no part in the active lobbying for these objects. But it did wish to be left untouched and unexamined, and it conducted vigorous defensive operations in the field of government relations.

These activities went back as far as 1876. That year Representative James H. Hopkins of the much-aggrieved city of Pittsburgh offered a bill for regulating interstate commerce, and a resolution for an inquiry by a select committee into railroad rates and practices. The Pennsylvania House and a host of petitioners supported him. His resolution was called up on May 16; it required unanimous consent for consideration, and met an objection from Henry B. Payne, father of the Standard's treasurer. He asked that the investigation be conducted by the regular Commerce Committee instead of a special body, and Hopkins agreeing, a new resolution to that effect passed. When the Commerce Committee met, with Frank Hereford of West Virginia as chairman, J. N. Camden was close at his side as adviser.[1] Camden had recently joined the Standard Oil, and was receiving rebates from the Baltimore & Ohio.

Naturally, the committee did not get very far. Among the wit-

[1] See Hopkins's interview, N. Y. *Herald*, Jan. 19, 1884.

nesses it summoned were A. J. Cassatt of the Pennsylvania; Colonel Payne; E. G. Patterson of the Producers' Union; and Frank Rockefeller.[2] Frank, as an officer of the Pioneer Oil Company, not only charged the Standard with helping the railroads to "even" traffic and collecting a heavy rebate,[3] but also very indiscreetly accused Tom Scott and General Devereux of pocketing part of the rebates which their lines were supposedly paying to the Standard. Of course Scott and Devereux instantly published letters which sizzled with wrath.[4] "Unqualifiedly false" was the mildest term they used—and Frank had to admit that he possessed no proof. Payne, the treasurer of the Standard, told almost nothing. Cassatt admitted making special rates, but refused to say what they were. The committee then heard arguments upon the question whether he should be compelled to tell, but never came to any result. "The entire investigation," Hopkins resentfully said later, "hinged upon the committee's decision, so nothing further was done." He added that Camden had always been present, and that some time after the committee rose, the testimony which it had taken disappeared. Its clerk said that it had been misplaced or taken away, but Representative Reagan of Texas bluntly declared that it had been stolen. "I do not mean," concluded Hopkins in telling of all this some years later, "to reflect upon Mr. Payne, who is a very estimable and innocent-looking old gentleman."

The Hopkins bill died, for the time was not yet ripe for interstate commerce legislation.[5] But Hopkins's story indicates that the Standard had been alert to this investigation, and had effectively employed its most trusted agent in Washington.

This agent was of course Camden, the astute lieutenant of Rockefeller's who had so rapidly consolidated the refining industry in West Virginia and Maryland. As the principal Democratic leader in West Virginia, he possessed invaluable political connections. In 1868 and 1872 he had made two unsuccessful runs for the governorship; and when early in the eighties the party showed strength in the State, he laid plans to be elected to the Federal Senate. By this time his shrewd activities in banking, land-speculation, and petroleum had rendered him wealthy. He was a conspicuous member of the increasing group

---

[2]See *The Critic*, July 19, 1876.   [3]N. Y. *Tribune*, July 8, 1876.
[4]*Railroad Gazette*, July 28, 1876.
[5]The Hopkins Bill gave way to the Reagan Bill.

of men who combined business and politics, and his influence in Wheeling, Annapolis, and Washington was as valuable to the Standard as his executive talents.[6]

In 1878 we find Camden acting as lobbyist in Washington against a House bill placing petroleum on the free list. It was not an important measure, for little oil was yet produced outside the United States and Russia, but on principle Rockefeller desired its defeat. Through H. H. Rogers, he instructed Camden to take steps to maintain the existing tariff protection against Canadian petroleum. Camden immediately appealed to Senator Henry Gassaway Davis and Representative Benjamin Wilson, requesting them to speak to the whole West Virginia delegation. Wilson, a member of the House Ways and Means Committee, then exerted himself to bury the bill, and received Camden's warm thanks.[7]

"My impression is that by managing it prudently we can always have very strong influence with Congress," Camden wrote Flagler in December, 1878.[8] Rockefeller and his associates feared that the bitter attacks which had provoked the injunction suits and conspiracy indictment in Pennsylvania, and the Hepburn Investigation in New York, would result in a Congressional inquiry. Frequent threats were made in the House. Late in May, 1879, Camden went to Washington to observe the situation. On June 2 he wrote George H. Vilas in Cleveland reassuringly: "I do not think it probable that any effort will be made at this session to raise a special committee."[9] He believed that the Reagan bill for railroad regulation might be pushed, but the Standard was much less concerned about this than about an inquiry. Officers of the combination remained uneasy. They were afraid that some committee would look into their secret "evening" agreement with the trunk lines. Early in June they read that the House had instructed the Commerce Committee to report upon possible measures for increasing foreign trade, and it occurred to them that this might be a blind for a dragnet inquiry into oil and railroads! When Rockefeller learned that the committee proposed to conduct its inquiry during the recess, he directed Camden to fight the movement tooth and nail.

[6]F. P. Summers, *Johnson Newlon Camden*, Chs. I–VI.
[7]*Idem*, 212, 213.
[8]Camden Papers, West Virginia University. [9]*Ibid*.

Camden at once began to lobby against the appropriation for the inquiry. He had the assistance of Representative Amos Townsend of Cleveland and John E. Kenna of West Virginia, both members of the Commerce Committee. To Standard officials Camden wrote that Kenna favored the Reagan bill, "but is opposed to the committee investigating the oil question or any other specific branch of trade," for he believed that all investigations should be general in character. After hard work in Washington, Camden returned to Parkersburg and began bombarding congressmen with letters. A note to B. F. Martin of West Virginia on June 21, for example, expressed the hope that if the appropriation came up, "your economic feelings will induce you to vote against it." He significantly added that the committee ought not to sit during the summer. "If a fellow has to go to Washington it ought to be in winter, when the clever men among his acquaintances can be found there."[10]

Late that month he wrote Rockefeller that all danger seemed past. "I do not think we will be troubled with an investigation this summer. . . . I have our friends watching it in Washington, and everything will be done that we are able to do to prevent it." He was right; Congress adjourned without passing the appropriation.[11]

Camden asked for election as Senator in 1881, with most of the Democratic organization solidly behind him. To the party he had given long years of hard labor, his great organizing talents, and large sums of money. He was also supported by most business interests in the State. His opponents naturally made much of his connection with the Standard and his alleged subservience to the Baltimore & Ohio. Many believed, quite mistakenly, that if he went to the Senate he would oppose railroad regulation. Nevertheless, the legislature elected him by a large majority. He was chosen in spite of rather than through corporation influences, and West Virginia took pride in him as an honest and able spokesman. Holding his place 1881-87, he never concealed the fact that he was connected with the Standard Oil and willing to serve it in proper ways; and no one ever adduced any evidence that he acted improperly.

The fact was that after taking his senatorial seat, Camden gradually relinquished his interests in petroleum. While for some years he remained president of two Standard companies, he never again

<hr />

[10]*Ibid.*   [11]Summers, *Camden,* 215, 216.

played a leading rôle in the oil industry, but busied himself with coal-mining and railroads. His loyalty to the trust was explicitly stated in 1883, when he debated its policies with J. C. Welch in *The North American Review*.[12] He maintained that the combination had been of enormous service to the general public. By stabilizing the business it had checked a dry-rot of bankruptcy; it had made oils cheaper, better, and more uniform; it had contributed to the prosperity of hundreds of communities, and given work at high wages to a force equal to the standing army of the United States. While it was not a philanthropic organization, Camden argued that it had done far more for the national welfare than could have been effected by an equivalent capital divided among a hundred quarrelling, losing, perishing organizations. He even made the untenable assertion that the Standard "has never had a contract with a railroad company which a fair-minded man could pronounce to be against public policy, good morals, or good business principles." But as the eighties wore on, he was less and less a Standard man.

His correspondence with Rockefeller and others steadily diminished. No evidence exists that he was ever asked, after becoming senator, to oppose any investigation. The requests made of him seem to have been entirely proper. In 1883 the Standard notified him that the Sultan of Turkey, by a decree in apparent violation of trade stipulations, had practically closed the Constantinople market to American oil. Camden promptly stirred up the State Department and Lew Wallace, minister to Turkey. Not long afterward the Standard asked him to help obtain more favorable trade privileges in Japan, and again he enlisted the aid of the State Department.[13]

Throughout these years Camden made it clear that he believed in Federal regulation of interstate commerce. The problem offered great difficulties, and progress was slow and painful. Congress was divided into three camps, one favoring John H. Reagan's plan for regulation by statute, supported by the courts; one favoring regulation by a permanent commission; and one opposed to any Federal regulation whatever. Sincere men stood in each group. It is usually said that the Standard opposed all Federal control of railroads. The fact seems to be that after 1880 it took no great interest in the matter, for it was then too strong to be dependent on rate-discriminations. In 1887

[12]*North American Review*, CXXXVI, 181–190.   [13]Camden Papers.

Camden supported the Cullom bill for commission regulation, which became law.[14] Indeed, he obtained the passage of an amendment which signally strengthened the provisions aimed against long-and-short-haul discrimination. His papers contain not a word from the Standard on this subject; nor is there a word in the still more voluminous papers of John Sherman to indicate that the Standard Oil ever approached the Ohio senator.[15]

III

Indeed, the charges of Standard activity in Federal politics during the eighties have apparently been overdrawn. After the Hopkins episode, it seems to have indulged in nothing but the lobbying usual on the part of great corporations. Particularly do the allegations connected with the elevation of Henry B. Payne to the Senate fail to withstand analysis; allegations upon which an enormous amount of innuendo was built to prejudice public opinion.

In the year that Rockefeller moved into his Fifty-fourth Street house, 1884, the Ohio legislature had to choose a Democratic successor to Senator George H. Pendleton. Most people supposed that the seat would go again to him or to General Durbin Ward. But when the legislature met in January, Payne's candidacy was pushed with astonishing vigor. Headquarters were opened in Columbus, members lavishly entertained, and aggressive lobbyists employed. His claims for the place were strong. He had been an able, hard-working Representative from the Cleveland district; he was one of the best-known business and civic leaders in northern Ohio, a man of cultivation and integrity. In 1880 Tilden, a shrewd judge of character, had wished the Democratic party to nominate him for President.[16] Among the men active in the canvass was his son, who was reported to have said that it was costing him $100,000. Payne was the choice of the party caucus, with 46 votes against 30 for all others, and his election followed by a wide margin.[17] But his opponents in the Allen G. Thurman wing of the Democracy were bitterly dis-

[14]*Congressional Record.*

[15]So I have been assured by Roy and Jeannette P. Nichols, biographers of John Sherman.

[16]Alexander C. Flick, *Samuel J. Tilden,* 455.

[17]The N. Y. *World,* April 5, 1889, gives the figure 46 to 30 in a long review of the election. Newspapers of 1884 (Cleveland *Leader,* etc., Jan. 9, 10) indicate this is correct.

The most famous business address in the world.

No. 26 Broadway as it appeared when the Standard Oil Company began to occupy it
in the middle eighties; later it was enlarged.

Early uses of gasolene.

A tricycle propelled by a small rear motor; and, *below,* the rear gasolene tanks of a "horseless carriage," the Duryea automobile.

appointed, and they joined Republican newspapers and politicians in spreading rumors that money had effected the result.

Not for two years were these charges taken up.[18] Then, early in 1886, S. K. Donavin, a lieutenant of the Thurman faction, accused Payne in a savage "open letter" of having won his seat by corrupt means. Large sums of money had been ladled out at the Neil House in Columbus, wrote Donavin, by Oliver H. Payne, Colonel William P. Thompson, and John Huntington, men "connected with a corporation known as the Standard Oil Company." The senator expressed contempt for these charges, and called Donavin a low, worthless, foul-mouthed wretch, who had been rolling drunkenly around Washington for weeks. "Anything from him would be a disgrace to the waste-basket."[19] But a Republican House had taken power in Ohio, it ordered an investigation, and a committee was soon examining scores of witnesses. Their testimony was for the most part vague. One poker-playing legislator stated that $500 and $1000 bills had been very common just after the senatorial contest. Various men told of seeing large quantities of money lying about the Payne headquarters. Other witnesses had observed two legislators divide a roll of bills the night after the Democratic caucus. It was alleged that still another legislator, though usually poor, had bought some property that spring. The editor of the Columbus *Sunday Capital* testified that Colonel Payne had offered him money to support Henry B. Payne, but that he had refused when told that he would have to sign a receipt! This editor was not connected with the legislature in any capacity. Donavin himself, when called upon to testify, confessed that his information had been derived from others.[20]

In short, nearly all the evidence was hearsay or circumstantial.[21] The Republican majority of the committee stated in its report that Payne's candidacy had not been announced until a late hour; that "suspicion and charges" were "very prevalent" at the time of the election; and that during the balloting, "numerous remarkable

[18]The Columbus *Times* declared: "The monopoly of the Standard Oil must be destroyed. Its intrusion into political circles must be prevented." Albert H. Walker, *The Payne Bribery Case and the United States Senate.*

[19]N. Y. *Herald*, Jan. 3, 1887. Donavin accused Caspar Lowenstein of taking $1500 to vote for Payne. Lowenstein proved that he had voted for General Ward, and promptly brought suit against Donavin.

[20]See *49th Congress, 1st Session (1886), Senate Misc. Doc. 106.*

[21]See *49th Congress, 1st Session (1886), Senate Report, No. 1490.*

changes" of vote had occurred.[22] The minority report dismissed the evidence as flimsy, largely irrelevant, and prejudiced. Senator Payne pointed out that although he had asked for a public investigation, the sessions had been held behind closed doors; that his offer to testify and to bring in his private books had been ignored; and that the legislature had refused to print the testimony. He branded the whole affair as a partisan attempt to besmear his good name.

The evidence was turned over to the Republican Senate in Washington, with a statement that it justified some further inquiry by a Federal agency. It was difficult to see just how, after a committee sitting in Ohio had been unable to find definite proofs, a body laboring in Washington could do better.[23] Senator Payne himself asked for an investigation. The Senate referred the question and the testimony to its Committee on Privileges and Elections, the members of which were Hoar (chairman), Frye, Teller, Evarts, Logan, Saulsbury, Vance, Pugh, and Eustis—five Republicans and four Democrats. They looked into the matter with care. Strong pressure was brought to bear upon them by Ohio Republicans, who hoped that the seat might be declared vacant. Hoar and Frye were for an inquiry, but Evarts, Logan, and Teller lined up with the Democrats against it, Logan calling the charges "rubbish"; and by a Senate vote of 44 to 17 the issue was dropped.[24] The Washington correspondent of the

[22]Henry Demarest Lloyd says: "None of the matter was presented on mere hearsay or rumor." *Wealth Against Commonwealth*, 377. His own statement then proves that practically all of it was so presented. Some one had *heard* the cashier of a Cleveland bank say that Colonel Payne had indirectly (not directly) withdrawn $65,000; but the cashier did not testify to this. Some had *heard* a State senator say that he had received $5000 to vote for Payne; but the legislator himself did not testify to this. Men were ready to declare that they had *heard* other legislators confess to taking bribes; but none of the accused legislators testified to anything of the sort.

[23]Lloyd asserts: "The State legislature could not compel the witnesses to testify. Only the United States Senate could do this." *Wealth Against Commonwealth*, 383. Actually the powers of the State legislature over Ohio witnesses were greater than those of the Federal Senate.

[24]Lloyd names the four Democratic senators who voted against an investigation, but completely suppresses the fact that three Republican senators stood with them! *Wealth Against Commonwealth*, 383. Both minority and majority reports are to be found in *49th Cong., 1st. Sess., Senate Report No. 1490*. Evarts, Logan, and Teller declared: "We are of opinion that there is no evidence which purports to prove that fraud, corruption, or bribery was employed in the election of Mr. Payne." They were the Republican Senators from New York, Illinois, and Colorado; Evarts had been Secretary of State, Teller had been Secretary of the Interior.

New York *Herald* commented that the three Republican committee-men had withstood "the most desperate attacks by their party journals," and said that their courage deserved the applause of "all honest men." He added: "There has been no more disgraceful attempt to hound men to do dirty work in many years than this in which the Republican politicians of Ohio have been engaged."[25]

At no point did anybody present the slightest evidence that the Standard Oil was interested in Payne's election. He had never possessed any connection with the Standard. His general public record was highly creditable. He was a Democrat, while Rockefeller and most other Standard leaders were Republicans who had openly opposed him in a previous election for the House.[26] While unquestionably Colonel Payne labored hard to put his father in the Senate, his motives need not have been other than filial. In 1887 Payne voted against the Cullom Act, but so did many other senators whose honesty has never been impugned. He explicitly denied that he ever invested a dollar in the Standard, or that it ever did anything to aid him. "The majority of the stockholders are very liberal in their philanthropic contributions," he remarked,[27] "but it contributed not one cent directly or indirectly to my election to this body." Rockefeller later commented:[28]

This was true. I repeat it unqualifiedly. I was opposed to the election of Senator Payne, as a Republican and never anything else but a Republican. And not one farthing of the money of the Standard Oil Company went to his election; nor were the Standard Oil Company favorable to his election, as a company. . . .

This was conclusive. It seems clear that money was spent with inexcusable lavishness by the Payne managers; that probably some of

[25]N. Y. *Herald,* July 22, 1866. Logan said with reference to the attacks on Payne: "There is not an office in the country that would make me do wrong to any man in the Senate for political purposes." The 44 men voting against an investigation included 15 Republicans.

[26]The Cleveland *Leader* of Oct. 8, 1874, had stamped the report that the Standard Oil was supporting Payne for the House as false. "Messrs. Rockefeller, Andrews, and Flagler are not the men to turn their backs upon their party and their political faith." Payne himself complained that in 1871 the Standard Oil men attempted to defeat him for the House.

[27]Lloyd, *Wealth Against Commonwealth,* 386.

[28]Inglis, Conversations with Rockefeller.

it was used corruptly, though proof is lacking; but that it was Oliver Payne's money, and not one cent of it the Standard's.[29]

Equally bizarre was the idea entertained by some writers that William C. Whitney, Cleveland's Secretary of the Navy, was somehow a tool of the Standard. His offense lay in marrying the senator's daughter, Flora Payne, a beautiful girl whom he met long before the Standard came into existence. Senator Hoar asked in 1888: "Is there a Standard Oil Trust in this country or not? . . . If there be such a trust, is it represented in the Cabinet at this moment?"[30]

The suggestion that rugged Grover Cleveland would keep an agent of the Standard Oil in his Cabinet is delightfully amusing. So is the suggestion that the brilliantly headstrong Secretary Whitney would have cared to perform Oliver Payne's bidding. Whitney never had anything to do with petroleum, and a careful searcher of his papers has found not a single drop of Standard Oil on one of them. It is true, however, that the Republican candidate for the Presidency in 1880, Garfield, wrote a Cleveland friend that "the situation in Indiana is such that Mr. Rockafeller (sic) can do us immense service if he will. . . . Do not think that this relates to the raising of means. Mr. Rockafeller can do what is even more important than that." The friend made inquiries and reported that Mr. Rockefeller was "all right."[31] Just what Garfield meant is a mystery, for at that date Rockefeller had no Indiana interests whatever.

IV

It was in State politics that the Standard was really active, and particularly in Pennsylvania politics. Here, as elsewhere, its rôle was primarily defensive. In view of the intense hostility of most people in the Oil Regions, and of the heavy attacks by the producers, Gowen, Colonel Potts, the Tidewater Pipe-Line, and independent refiners, it was imperative that the Standard take steps to defend itself. The trust would have suffered heavily had it not, and since Harrisburg was probably the most corrupt capital in the Union, it was soon fighting fire with fire.

[29] *49th Cong., 1st Sess., Senate Report 1490.*

[30] *Congressional Record.* Hoar, who had no difficulty in voting for Blaine for President, believed no Democrat could be really honest.

[31] Mr. Mark Hirsch, biographer of Whitney, derides the idea of Standard influence over him. For Garfield, see R. G. Caldwell, *James A. Garfield,* 304.

The reputation of Harrisburg as a political Gomorrah went back to the thirties, when Nicholas Biddle had bribed many legislators to recharter his United States Bank. During the fifties the Pennsylvania Railroad gained an ascendancy over the government, which Tom Scott strengthened after the Civil War by his alliance with the Cameron machine; young Don Cameron becoming president of a principal branch of the Pennsylvania, the Northern Central. In 1879 the railroad's efforts to push through a bill appropriating $4,000,000 to cover the damages it had suffered in the great riots of 1877 raised a tremendous scandal. An investigation by a legislative committee revealed quite shameless bribery, $600 having been paid for a vote and $1,000 for a speech. Members had been bought, snarled the Harrisburg *Independent,* "as if they were so many hogs fattened for the market." Log-rolling favors had also been promised. Lewis Emery, Jr., stated that a railroad attorney had assured him that if he voted properly, the free pipe-line bill, the bill against railroad discriminations, and another measure much desired by the Oil Regions would be passed. The riot-compensation measure failed, but it left a long-remembered stench.

If this episode typified one kind of corruption met in Harrisburg, the recurrent "strike" bills represented a more frequent variety. In Albany and Harrisburg every session saw measures introduced in a palpable effort to blackmail some rich company into quick payments to stop further action; bills to slash trolley fares or gas charges, for example. All volumes on State politics from 1860 to 1910 mention these "strike" bills. Theodore Roosevelt says in his autobiography that at Albany he found them incessant. The Standard, like other corporations, was necessarily always on its guard against them. It had to employ lawyers and lobbyists to protect its legitimate interests. In districts where it owned large properties and hired thousands of men—in Pittsburgh, Philadelphia, Titusville, Bradford—it expected the locally elected legislators to pay just as much attention to its rights as Emery and other Regions members paid to the rights of well-owners and independent pipe-line companies. During the eighties two State senators, Cooper and Laird, with one still more prominent Republican leader, George W. Delamater, were known in Pennsylvania as Standard Oil spokesmen. They fought the free pipe-line bill till it passed in 1883, and opposed a bill passed at the same session to prevent the further consolidation of pipe lines. They worked year in and year out with the Standard's expert lobbyists.[32]

It is impossible to say how many "strike" bills were aimed at the Standard, or how far it went in the use of money. The anonymous Clevelander who declared that in seven years it had spent $325,000 in Harrisburg was obviously making a guess, and frankly admitted his inability to estimate how much had been used improperly. However, one punitive measure, the Billingsley Bill of 1887, was met by the Standard with a counterattack which apparently involved bribery.

If the Billingsley Bill was not a "strike" measure it came very near it. The measure purported to lay down rules for the regulation of pipe lines and storage tanks. In part it was prompted by a desire to harass and punish the Standard; in part it arose from an honest feeling among well-owners that the charges of the Standard tanks and pipe lines were exorbitant. The trust asked twenty cents a barrel for collecting oil and carrying it to the railroads or trunk pipe lines. This sum by the later eighties amounted to a fifth, fourth, or sometimes even a third of the whole value of the crude oil. Producers pointed out that in the old days of competitive pipe lines, the real if not nominal charge had often been ten or fifteen cents; and that since then the cost of pipe had been greatly reduced, and its quality much improved. "We think five cents would be sufficient compensation," one producer told the House Committee investigating trusts in 1888.[33]

To these complaints the Standard men replied that the rate was entirely fair. They laid free pipes to any well, which meant a heavy investment. Whenever a field was rapidly exhausted, the pipes had to be dug up or abandoned before they had paid for themselves. Interest charges on the $30,000,000 which the Standard had invested in pipe lines were high, maintenance and patrol cost large sums, and depreciation was rapid. Since the trust was responsible for oil in its custody, whenever a tank was set on fire by lightning or carelessness it had to foot the bill.

Obviously, a searching State investigation was needed to determine the proper charge. Apparently the Standard rate was really exces-

[32]I have obtained much information on Pennsylvania political affairs from the scrapbooks of Congressman John Dalzell of Pittsburgh, which the University of Pittsburgh had kindly loaned me.
[33]*House Trust Investigation, 1888,* p. 71.

sive, and a careful inquiry would probably have reduced it by a few cents. Instead, the bill fixed a maximum pipeage rate of ten cents a barrel; forbade a charge of more than one-sixtieth of a cent a day per barrel for tanking oil; and cut the allowance for waste in tanks from three per cent to one.[34] When the petroleum was tanked on credit balance, no charge whatever was to be levied for the first month's storage. The penalties provided for violation were excessively severe. A company, officers, or agent charging more than the prescribed sums was to be fined $1000 to $2000 for the first offense, and $2000 and $5000 for all subsequent infractions; guilty individuals could be sentenced to jail terms of from sixty days to a year; and the company and officers were made liable for double any damages sustained by reason of their violation of the law.

Miss Tarbell remarks that "the Billingsley Bill was as bad as it could be," and that the rates' fixed "were in nearly every case less than the cost."[35] Even Lewis Emery and other supporters of the measure had to apologize for it, and to admit that a thorough recasting was needed before it became law. The right of appeal to the courts against unfair or confiscatory rate-making laws had now been firmly established; and the badly drawn Billingsley Bill could not have withstood the briefest judicial scrutiny—though in the meantime it might accomplish great damage. Since the major pipe lines were engaged in interstate commerce, the State could obviously not regulate them. It could regulate the local lines, but they were all linked with the larger systems, so that State regulation would have created two classes of oil in the pipes, an intolerable situation.

Yet for a time the bill seemed likely to pass. It was supported by the Knights of Labor, which had demanded such legislation in its State convention the previous year. The well-owners were naturally almost a unit behind it. Many other citizens stood with them because they believed that it would hamper the Standard in carrying oil outside the State, and do much to restore an independent refining industry in the Regions, Pittsburgh, and Philadelphia. Such anti-monopoly organs as the Harrisburg *Independent,* Philadelphia *Press,* and New York *World* applauded it. "The bill is undoubtedly a fair one," declared the *Press.*[36] "It applies a remedy to exorbitant storage

---

[34]Full text of the bill in Tarbell, *Standard Oil Company,* II, 357–360.
[35]*Idem,* II, 122. [36]Philadelphia *Press,* April 20, 1887.

and pipeage charges, which appears to be possible of accomplishment only by law. . . ." Only the Standard, the brokers and speculators in crude oil, a few producers, and a general group of conservative businessmen opposed it. Greatly disturbed, the Standard attempted to arrange a compromise meeting with Regions leaders in New York; while it sharply reduced its charges for tankage and its deductions for waste.[37]

On April 12, 1887, the bill reached its final vote in the House. Great delegations of oil men had poured into Harrisburg to witness the defeat of the Standard, and the galleries and lobbies were packed by excited spectators. Only a few Standard adherents were present, a dejected and silent group. Various telegrams asking for the passage of the bill were read, as were remonstrances from the Philadelphia Petroleum and Stock Exchanges, and President Satterfield of the Union Oil Company; but there was no debate. When ex-speaker Graham told the House that the subject ought to be thoroughly discussed, he was interrupted by impatient cries of "Question! Question!" Amid deep silence the roll call began. The instant it was announced that the result stood 133 yeas and 39 nays, pandemonium was loosed; amid yells of exultation the spectators rushed for the corridors, and the members hurriedly took a ten-minute recess. Men danced wildly through the rotunda, shaking hands, slapping backs, and even hugging one another. Within a few minutes the telegraph was announcing a sharp drop in the price of crude oil. But this hardly damped the general joy, for the producers believed that it had been engineered by the Standard in an effort to affect the Senate. The Philadelphia *Press* proclaimed that at last an effective protest had been registered "against the aggressive greed of the Standard Oil Company."[38]

But alas for the producers! The Senate took an attitude very different from that of the House. For two weeks lobbyists on both sides labored frenziedly. One of the Philadelphia bosses, Senator McManes, who had been supporting the bill, suddenly turned against it. Of the Pittsburgh (Allegheny County) senators, two were against the measure, one for it, and one uncertain. Day by day the feeling mounted. The last week in April found the Senate corridors filled with pro-

[37]See Philadelphia *Press,* Harrisburg *Independent,* N. Y. *Tribune* and *World,* March, April, 1887.
[38]See Harrisburg, Regions, and Philadelphia papers, April 13, 1887.

ducers arguing for the measure. It was the people's bill, they declared, and if it were not passed the voters in the fifteen northwestern counties of Pennsylvania would swing over to the Democratic party. Men were talking of running Billingsley for governor on a Democratic and Anti-Standard platform. Moreover, the oil men threatened to attack the Republican organization in the Middle West and Northwest. Monopoly was fast becoming a national issue, and if the Regions joined the Knights of Labor in supporting the Democratic party in 1888, the Republicans might lose Pennsylvania. Meanwhile the Standard lobbyists were predicting that oil would drop from eighty-five to fifty cents if the bill passed, while large business groups which detested the Knights were attacking the measure. No issue in a long generation had aroused such angry class feeling.

The debate on the 28th revealed this bitter antagonism. Two opponents, Senators Delamater and Rutan, riddled the uneconomic and unconstitutional features of the bill, and taunted its supporters with demagogy. Senators from the Regions angrily retorted. At one point Lewis Emery, Jr., rose to a personal explanation. He had the clerk read extracts from the Oil City *Derrick* and Titusville *Herald* charging that he had offered to sell his Philadelphia refinery and his support to the Standard for $750,000, with affidavits from various men that these charges contained no truth whatever. He arraigned the two newspapers as organs of the Standard. Then, turning to the east side of the chamber, he called upon the spectators standing back of the seats to move aside. They did so, revealing W. T. Scheide of the Standard's National Transit Company placidly sitting against the wall. Pointing his finger, Emery cried: "There sits a man, Scheide by name, who has vilified me on the floor of the Senate. . . . He has said that he believed these infamous charges to be true. He knows they are false. . . . If I could get at him I would sue that man and the rest of the Standard people who utter these falsehoods."[39]

The final vote was an unexpected defeat for the oil producers. Confident that they would muster an easy majority, they had filled the lobby and corridors with crowds ready to stage another celebration. But the ballot showed 18 yeas, 25 nays. A groan of despair went up from the spectators. Next day many conservative newspapers declared that the oil business had narrowly escaped a dangerous experi-

[39]The Philadelphia *Press*, April 29, 1887, describes this scene.

ment. The New York *Tribune* remarked that the passage of the measure "would have plunged the petroleum industry into disastrous confusion, contest, and litigation." Now that it was beaten, "an enormous load will be lifted from commercial and speculative interests, and the future value of crude oil will be measured with closer reference to commercial considerations."[40] Writing long afterward, and from full knowledge of the facts, Miss Tarbell stated that the defeat of the bill "really was merited."[41]

But the anti-Standard journals were cynical. "The Oil Region is a great region, but it isn't as big as the Standard Oil Company," commented the Philadelphia *Press*. "We mention this in both sorrow and anger." And the New York *World* caustically declared: "There is many a slip between the House and the Senate, especially when the lobbyist is on hand with material for 'explaining things.'"

These hints of corruption were but faint echoes of the angry accusations hurled at the trust by the producers, who were certain that it had bribed at least five senators. When Miss Tarbell wrote her history of the Standard, she intimated her belief that its agents had used the "sinews of war" in an improper way. Recording that Emery had publicly charged Delamater with receiving $65,000 for his services to the Standard, she added that it was "a charge which, so far as the writer knows, has never been either proved or disproved."

The author of this volume has seen evidence which Senator Emery and Miss Tarbell did not possess, and in place of their empty accusations can offer a definite statement. The Standard lobbyists, fighting what seemed to them a "strike" measure, apparently did employ bribery. One of Delamater's principal aides in assisting the Standard at Harrisburg was a shrewd politician from the Oil Regions named W. H. Andrews, who was employed by the trust from 1887 to 1895, and served it faithfully while he held in succession the offices of representative from Crawford County, state senator from that and a neighboring county, and Republican State Chairman. In the summer of 1938 the author was shown his papers by his son, Mr. W. S. Andrews. They were for the most part kept in a battered suitcase in the Merchants' Bank of Meadville, and consisted of original letters and memoranda, a large number of photographs of letters and documents, and several typed manuscripts. The letters included a

[40]April 29, 1887.   [41]Tarbell, *Standard Oil Company*, II, 125.

number from S. C. T. Dodd and M. F. Elliott, attorneys for the Standard, some from Quay and other Republican leaders, and a few from John D. Archbold. They indicated that Andrews had been in highly confidential relations with Archbold and the two Standard attorneys; and a letter from Andrews's secretary stated that the trust had paid him $6,000 a year in quarterly instalments. His own memoranda indicated that he had been given a large expense account. All the letters from Archbold, Dodd, and Elliott seemed on their faces innocent enough; they merely instructed Andrews to watch certain legislation, oppose certain hostile steps, and make certain counter-moves.[42]

The typed manuscripts, however, possessed a different character. Andrews late in life went to New Mexico, invested heavily and unfortunately in land, and quarrelled with Archbold because the latter failed to give him some expected political and financial assistance. As a result of the quarrel he wrote a story of Standard Oil lobbying, as carried on by an unidentified person called X. According to the story, this man had on two occasions used large sums to corrupt Pennsylvania legislators; and the before-mentioned memoranda on small slips of paper, carrying hastily pencilled names and amounts, indicated just what had been paid. The first occasion was in 1887, in defeating the Billingsley Bill; the second was in 1895, in securing passage of the Marshall Bill to permit a great unification of pipe lines. The memoranda, which the author has inspected with care, indicate that bribes ranging from $400 to $1000 or more a person had been paid in 1887 for votes. Admittedly, the narrative was written by a disgruntled employee, whose motives were vengeful; and the pencilled slips, though yellow with age, did not in themselves amount to proof. But taken altogether, the circumstances of the defeat of the Billingsley Bill, the detailed typewritten narrative, the supporting memoranda, and the story told by Andrews's son, a man of education and character, convinced the author that bribery had been employed. The materials may yet be published.[43]

[42]I inspected these materials August 8, 9, 1938, and Doctor Paul H. Giddens saw some of them at the same time. I also have letters from Mr. W. S. Andrews upon their contents.

[43]Mr. W. S. Andrews told me that after W. H. Andrews became an enemy of the Standard, Lewis Emery, Jr., encouraged him to reveal the secrets of Standard activities in Harrisburg, while Joseph Seep tried to dissuade him.

At Columbus the Standard's influence was beyond doubt constantly felt from the middle seventies onward. The principal charge levelled against the combination was that it acted to suppress the legislative investigation begun in 1879. That winter, according to the New York *Times* informant already quoted, "the company had in its direct employ a member of the House, a member of the Senate, an ex-member of the House, and three outsiders, one of the last being a newspaperman. And of all this collection only two, they that were the outsiders exclusive of the newspaperman, knew that they were not the only paid lobbyists on the ground." He added that when the investigating committee was finally appointed, "it was composed of men of such moral and financial capacity as suited the Standard to a dot. Of course the whole thing ended in a farce." The Ohio legislature of 1885 was also accused of defeating a free pipe-line bill under Standard pressure.[44]

v

While the Standard had no publicity agent until long after the end of the century, certain newspapers in Cleveland and the Regions habitually spoke for it. Indeed, for obvious reasons, after 1880 no Cleveland journal except Scripps's anti-corporation *Penny Press* was hostile to it. The Standard paid heavy taxes with never a protest, it had covered much of one ward with its manufactories, it employed many thousands of men, and it poured out huge sums in wages every day. *The Herald* and *Plain-Dealer* were distinctly friendly, and often spoke of the trust with pride; while *The Leader,* which had sometimes attacked it sharply in the seventies, thereafter seldom offered a word of criticism. Rockefeller was not without honor in his own city.

The Oil Regions press, at first a unit in assailing the Standard, was soon divided. Rockefeller early became aware that the newspapers of the Allegheny Valley, led by the Titusville *Courier,* were

---

[44]This legislature was called the "coal-oil legislature." J. F. Hudson, *The Railways and the Republic,* 467. The anti-monopoly press of the period contained many vague charges. See the Philadelphia *Press,* July 20, 1887: "The Standard Oil is engaged in its annual effort to run and ruin the Ohio Democracy, and there is little doubt of its success. When the Standard manipulators once place a mortgage on a political organization, they either boss the property or foreclose on it." It would be interesting to know just what the editor had in mind.

doing him and the Standard enormous harm. It is said that he called
in a discreet agent and gave him careful instruction. This man
opened negotiations for the purchase of the Oil City *Derrick,* and
since it was not doing well, easily obtained control. Gradual changes
were made in the staff, while the tone of the paper changed first to
tolerance, then partial friendliness, and finally open support. The
publisher was Patrick C. Boyle, an effervescent, talented Irishman,
who by 1890 was also controlling the Bradford *Era* and the Toledo
Commercial in the interests of the Standard. Financially he seems
to have been largely independent of the trust, and boasted that he
had obtained *The Commercial* for $35,000 of his own hard cash;
but there was no doubt as to his allegiance. Naturally he was much
hated, and one editor even denounced him as "too lazy to make the
fire for his wife." Another fulminated: "Machiavelli was not more
crafty; Borgia was not more perfidious; Judas was not more base."
Other Regions journals by 1890 had become respectful to the Standard—the Titusville *Herald,* the Oil City *Blizzard,* and the Bradford
Evening Sun. In New York the leading trade publication of the petroleum industry, *The Oil, Paint, and Drug Reporter,* became known as
a Standard organ, though its financial relations with the trust were
never made clear.[45]

Throughout the East the conservative newspapers, led by the New
York *Tribune* and Philadelphia *Public Ledger,* consistently treated
the Standard with respect; but radical journals caught the tone of
the New York *World* and *Herald* and the Philadelphia *Press,* bringing the wildest accusations against it. Any rumor was caught up and
accepted as true. If there was a State in the Union where the Standard had no influence, it was Tennessee. Yet in the spring of 1887 *The
Press* published a report that small dealers in Tennessee blamed the
Standard for a new law placing a State tax on all sellers of refined
petroleum, and the editor added: "The Standard will never be satisfied, we fear, until it gets legislation making it a felony for anybody
to compete with it." The New York *Sun* credited the Standard
with a desire to buy the unused Ohio Canal, running from Cleveland
to the Ohio River. Its purpose, said the news story, might be either
to build steam packets for carrying oil on the canal, or to drain it

[45]See the attack in the Bradford *Era,* Aug. 14, 1878, on *The Derrick* (otherwise called *The Organ*), which indicates that it took the side of the Standard
as early as 1876. *The Era* also liked to call it *The Emetic.*

and use the bed for a pipe line! At any rate, it was a corrupt scheme: "It is no secret at Columbus that the gang of State legislators could be induced to sell the State House and grounds if they were sufficiently bribed."[46] The New York *Herald* printed reams of material upon the alleged plot of the Standard to get Albany to pass a so-called Bulkhead Bill which, ostensibly fixing a new dock line on the East River, would (it said) really give the trust full and exclusive control of two miles of waterfront. Year after year the Bulkhead Bill came up, and year after year it was defeated. It was clearly controversial, and may have been an undesirable measure. But *The Herald* habitually called it "a gigantic robbery," "a scheme of land-grabbing," and "the Standard Oil's job."[47]

The New York *World* rang every possible change upon its accusation that the Standard Oil was a corrupt force politically as well as industrially, yet it almost never presented a shred of evidence. When in 1887 the Buffalo conspiracy case resulted in the complete acquittal of Rogers, Archbold, and McGregor, and *The Tribune* called upon Pulitzer to acknowledge that his charges against these men had been groundless,[48] *The World* simply replied with more innuendos. It commented upon a report that one of the Standard attorneys had irritated the jury by shouting. "This was indeed directly against all the Standard Oil Company's traditions and methods. It never shouts nor employs a brass band when it sets out to seize a legislature, control a court of justice, or crush a rival."[49]

The World was certain this spring that a bill to bridge the Hudson at Poughkeepsie was a wicked Standard Oil scheme, though it failed to show why. The paper declared that the measure had been "crookedly reported: that a scandal was likely to grow out of the committee action favoring it: that it had a coal-oil odor: and that if thoroughly investigated the affair would prove as nauseous as the Billingsley episode." It added: "The disposition to rush the bill through displays

[46]Philadelphia *Press*, May 3, 1887; N. Y. *Sun*, Nov. 28, 1884.

[47]See the N. Y. *Herald* for the spring months of 1887, 1888, and 1889. Such headlines as "The Oily Toils" and "Fighting the Standard Grab" adorned the news-stories. Apparently there was a good excuse for allowing piers to be pushed farther out into the East River, but it was alleged that through "joker" provisions the Standard would monopolize access to the piers. See *The Herald*, Dec. 20, 1888—Jan. 25, 1889, for a stirring fight over the Standard's lease of Pier 26. *The Herald* liked to talk of "Bostwick's East River."

[48]See the N. Y. *Tribune* editorial, "A Question of Justice," May 12, 1887.

[49]N. Y. *World*, May 18, 1887.

the thoroughness of organization of the Standard Oil lobby at all the State capitals."[50] On May 18, 1887, Pulitzer brought his attacks to a climax in a four-column article of the fiercest denunciation. When the nineteenth century had passed into history, it predicted, men would be astonished to find that the United States had "tolerated the presence of the most gigantic, the most cruel, impudent, pitiless, and grasping monopoly that ever fastened upon a country." It was like the simoon, blasting everything with its breath; like the upas tree, killing every creature beneath its branches; like the maelstrom, engulfing everything; like a cancer, corrupting all around it. Exhausting his similes, *The World* writer turned to sarcasm:

"Certain ribald and envious persons have asserted that the Standard Oil Company is aiming at the control of the solar system. . . . It is but an act of justice to state that this is not the case. The Standard Oil Company is entirely satisfied at present with controlling the earth."

Through such methods, by 1888 the Standard's opponents had fixed upon the public mind their stereotype of a hideous, merciless, and insatiable organism, which menaced the life of the nation. Jay Cooke's son-in-law William Barney, travelling west on a Great Lakes steamboat with a typical businessman of Milwaukee, heard him burst forth: "There is not a law in the decalogue they haven't broken!"[51] A multitude shared this belief. Early in 1887 Congress debated the long-pending Cullom Bill for the Federal regulation of interstate commerce. Repeated references were made to the history of the trust as proving the need for thorough control. Senator Coke remarked:[52] "The Standard Oil enormity, through which one company is by discrimination and by undue preference permitted to monopolize the entire oil trade of the country, bankrupting and destroying all who dare to attempt competition, is familiar to all." Representative Nelson quoted Arthur T. Hadley as saying that the Standard was "fostered by a system of special rates until it became strong enough to dictate its own terms," and cited the "turn another screw" letter as an example of its "extortion."[53] Representative Brown of Ohio, who believed the bill too mild, thought he saw "the cunning hand of the Standard Oil Company in it."[54] So the comments went.

[50]N. Y. *World,* May 6, 1887.
[51]Mr. William Barney told me this, Feb. 11, 1938.
[52]*Congressional Record,* Jan. 11, 1887, p. 526.
[53]*Idem,* Jan. 19, 1887, p. 815.   [54]*Idem,* Jan. 20, 1887, p. 868.

In 1890 a long-celebrated battle was waged in Pennsylvania between George W. Delamater as Republican candidate for governor and Robert E. Pattison as Democratic nominee. Delamater was notoriously friendly to all corporations, and hostile to reform; he had been rammed down the throat of the party by Boss Quay, who was anxious to pay off certain political and financial debts. Independent-minded Republicans, led by Emery, Rudolph Blankenburg, Henry C. Lea, Wharton Barker, and A. K. McClure, revolted. From end to end of the State the Pennsylvania Railroad and the Standard were denounced as eager to make of Delamater a cat's-paw governor. On Election Day he was overwhelmed, and the victory of Pattison brought into office a man of proved hostility to the Standard and other large corporations.

Yet the fact was that in politics the Standard's rôle had been almost entirely defensive. However much might be charged against the trust, it could never be accused of battening upon the American people by virtue of special legislative favors. Decade after decade "infant industries" (and some quite adult) made millions out of a tariff which enabled them to raise home prices to levels outrageously in excess of costs. Year after year lumber magnates, mining magnates, and cattle magnates stole parcels of the public domain. Year after year steamship companies asked for subsidies, and the G. A. R. demanded more pensions. The Federal government under Harrison held open a vast grab-bag to special interests. But the Standard throughout this period wanted little except to be left alone. It used the lobbying methods of the day, it was not queasy about its tools, it fought a corrupt "strike" bill by a corrupt counterstroke; but its political activities, good, bad, and indifferent, were in the main devoted to warding off attack. Rockefeller had devised a great experiment in monopoly, he had put it into practical operation in the face of general denunciation, and he did not wish it smashed.

But how much did Rockefeller himself know of the political operations of the Standard? The answer is clear: he knew nothing, for he took pains not to learn. He new no more than Benjamin Harrison or William McKinley knew of the campaign funds and the inside history of the campaign methods of Quay and Hanna which elected them to the Presidency in 1888 and 1896.

S. C. T. Dodd, in the interesting memoirs he wrote for his children, disclaimed any special knowledge of Standard Oil lobbying. "I kept clear of all mingling with politics and legislative business, except when I went to make a public argument before some committee of the legislature, which I did on several occasions. I know of no instance of the Standard Oil Company desiring legislation in its favor. It was often opposed to proposed legislation, but so far as I know, used legitimate means in its opposition."[55] Mr. Dodd obviously did not try to learn too much during the Billingsley affair.

Rockefeller also said repeatedly that he had no knowledge whatever of the use of improper means to influence legislative bodies, and was firmly opposed to their employment. This is certainly true. But Archbold never made any such statement, and Archbold, O'Day, and others were probably careful not to tell the head of the trust about some of their operations; nor was he more inquisitive than other corporate leaders of the day. It is said that Rockefeller was once at a watering place near Cleveland when a former member of the Ohio legislature approached. Introducing himself, he remarked: "I did what I could in that little matter at Columbus, Mr. Rockefeller, and I am glad that the Standard came to no harm." "I am glad to know you personally, sir," replied Rockefeller, "but I have no idea to what you have reference in the matter of legislation"; and entering his carriage, he took up the reins and drove away.[56] The story may be fiction—and it may well be true.

[55] S. C. T. Dodd, *Memoirs*, 31. [56] N. Y. *Times*, Feb. 27, 1883.

XXXII

The Trust Against the Wall

O N A cold February day in 1888, Chairman Frank B. Arnold
of the New York Senate committee for investigating
trusts rapped for order in the large room of the Superior
Court in New York City, jammed with spectators, and
announced, "Mr. John D. Rockefeller will now take the stand."
There was an instant craning of necks. Rockefeller rose from a row
of seats occupied by Standard officials and their three attorneys—
Joseph H. Choate, with his classical features and serious, intellectual
air; S. C. T. Dodd, bulky, ruddy, and cheerful; and former Representative J. B. Camp, thin, dark, and nervous looking. Already the
Senate committee had inquired into alleged monopolies in milk,
sugar, rubber, and cottonseed oil. Such well-known business executives as Henry O. Havemeyer, attended by such distinguished lawyers as Elihu Root and William Nelson Cromwell, had appeared
before it. But the public took a special interest in Rockefeller—"the
father of trusts, the king of monopolists, the czar of the oil business,
the $15-a-week clerk of fifteen years ago, the autocrat of today, who
handles a business worth $20,000,000 per annum, and relentlessly
crushes all competitors into the slough of failure and bankruptcy,"
to quote the hostile *World;*[1] the leader "who stands head and shoulders above all businessmen in the country," as *The Herald* put it.[2]

Next day the newspapers agreed that Rockefeller had handled the
Standard's case in masterly fashion. *The Tribune* reporter, describ-

[1] N. Y. *World,* Feb. 28, 1888.

[2] N. Y. *Herald,* Feb. 28, 1888. *The Herald* states that "when a hard question
was put to him he always turned to see if his lawyers looked worried, and if
they did he never could (er-ah-a-a-er-you-know-er-that-is) understand the precise point his questioner was trying to get at, and when he saw that the lawyer
had for the moment forgotten the point he hastened on to some more agreeable subject."

ing him as the embodiment of sweetness and light, remarked that the trust had done well to make him its principal spokesman. Questions were put by the committee's counsel—the keen-witted, sarcastic George Bliss, and that stagy former Confederate, General Roger A. Pryor, long-haired, long-nosed, and fond of shaking a long index finger. But their probings never disturbed Rockefeller's serenity. Immaculate in a frock coat, his brown hair and light-brown mustache both close-cropped, his eyes "sad and dreamy," he assumed a manner which now seemed mildly reproachful and now tenderly persuasive, but which never betrayed the slightest vexation.[3]

"It was a glorious picture," remarked the ironic *World,* "which this prince of philanthropists presented. Ah, how he glowed as he told of the glorious missionary work which the trust had accomplished! Beginning with $70,000,000 capital, which by thrift and care it has increased to $90,000,000, this charity has paid from 7 to 10 per cent a year of profits, while it has improved the plant, has steadily reduced the price of kerosene (it may be said parenthetically that the price of crude has dropped correspondingly), has improved upon the quality of its products, has never cut under antagonists in the way of freight discriminations or price, has never done anything to injure the business of competitors, and is on the best of terms with refining companies outside the trust. In tones so gentle that the wild birds of the wood would not be frightened this gilded monopolist told all this and more." *The Herald* spoke in the same vein:

We had our own opinion of the Standard Oil monopoly, and it was not entirely favorable. We rather regarded it, in fact, as a $90,000,000 ogre. . . . Mr. Rockefeller, however, on taking the stand, proved conclusively that it is the greatest philanthropy of the age, a sort of missionary society engaged in spreading the evangelical light of kerosene oil over the dark places in a naughty world.

Colonel Bliss did his utmost to draw a confession of weakness from Mr. Rockefeller, but that gentleman, with a bland smile which resembled the beautiful spring, maintained that the Standard Oil is without spot

[3]N. Y. *Herald, World, Sun,* Feb. 28, 1888. *The Herald* on Feb. 29 published a bit of doggerel:

> Since attorneys have fussed
> O'er the Standard Oil Trust,
> Rockefeller, who serves nought but Mammon,
> Has convinced each law fox
> By his guile in the box
> He's the o-r-ig-in-al-l "oily" Gammon.

or blemish. It has none of the wicked traits of a monopoly, and maintains the sweetest and most fraternal relations with its competitors. It has never crushed anybody or crowded him out of business. It has never fixed prices, never endeavored to control the market, and never made any little arrangement with the railroads which was to the disadvantage of other dealers. . . .

The only thing this company lacks is a chaplain. . . . Robin Hood had his Friar Tuck, and why not they? A twenty-five thousand dollar chaplain, who would open their meetings with religious services, and expound to them the law of charity, which has already netted them from ten to twenty millions apiece, is the only thing needed to put the Standard Oil at the head of the evangelical associations of the age.

Rockefeller told the committee little that it had not known before. He named the trustees, now only eight, for Payne's retirement had left a vacancy. He disclosed the fact that the trust now had about 700 shareholders. He testified that the trustees, who met quarterly in New York, kept a record book; and this was produced, but proved quite barren of interest. Rockefeller spoke feelingly of Russian competition, remarking that the Rothschilds, Nobels, and other large capitalists were exploiting the almost limitless supply of Russian oil, were copying all the advanced American ideas, and threatened to flood the world market. When asked if the trust formed in 1882 had not been preceded by "a trust company called the Southern Improvement Company," he said no; he admitted that he had heard of a company by that name, but denied that he had been in it. Some writers have treated this statement as a quibble; but of course Rockefeller always frankly confessed his connection with the South Improvement Company, and in this answer to Pryor it appears that he was simply denying that there had been an earlier *trust*. At the close, he placed in the record a list of 111 competing refineries as evidence that the Standard Oil did not enjoy an absolute monopoly.

In the course of his testimony one important document was revealed for the first time—the trust agreement of 1882. When asked to show it, Rockefeller hesitated but a moment before replying, "I will"; and Dodd thereupon took from his pocket a severely legal-looking paper and passed it to the magnate. Choate instantly dropped his air of lassitude, rose, and requested that the details of the agreement should not be published. "There are very important private interests that ought not, under the guise of public investigation, to be interfered with." But after a conference, he withdrew this objection, and Bliss read the tiresome paper in full.[4]

Archbold, who immediately followed, made a less favorable impression. Small, bright-eyed, and boyish-looking, he showed not only a nimble mind but a quick temper. When Chairman Arnold read extracts from printed testimony tending to prove that the Standard had obtained rebates, Archbold hotly characterized these statements as "dogmatic, intemperate, and without a basis of fact throughout," and intimated that the press was addicted to publishing irresponsible attacks upon the Standard simply because it was the popular thing to do. The by-laws of the trust were revealed while he was on the stand. He explained the workings of the executive committee, and with marked evasiveness admitted that the proxy committee controlled the selection of the officers and boards of directors of the various component companies. But the records of this proxy committee were in Flagler's hands, and Flagler was in Florida. Before retiring, Archbold defended the trust agreement as entirely harmless, saying:

It was made as a simple and effective form of holding the interests which had been theretofore acquired. We were advised by counsel that neither the Standard Oil Company of Ohio nor indeed any other single corporation could successfully or safely, perhaps, hold them. They were varied in nature; the property was widespread, located in many different states, the laws of which were in many cases restrictive of the rights of corporations, and the trusteeship was suggested as a simple method of bringing together these properties so as to provide for an evidence of ownership, a token of ownership that would be marketable, that would give the interests a market value, a basis for trading, and that would enable an administrative oversight in the simplest possible way.

This New York investigation was a loose, hasty, and inconsequential affair which proved a disappointment to the public. The legislature, spurred on by popular demands for the suppression of monopolistic combinations, had ordered an inquiry into their formation and effects. This covered sugar, petroleum, cottonseed oil, milk, meat, furniture, glass, rubber, and other commodities of general use, emphasis being given the first five. The committee found that the American Cotton Oil Trust had been in existence since 1884, and embraced about seventy corporations, but had not been

[4] N. Y. *World, Tribune,* March 1, 1888.

profitable, having paid only a single dividend of 1 per cent. It found that the Sugar Trust dated from October 24, 1887, and had united about 85 per cent of the sugar refiners of the Atlantic Coast. It extracted a good deal of information about combinations in copper, oilcloth, bagging, milk and the grain trade. It learned just how the Standard Oil Trust was controlled by the trustees, the executive committee, and the proxy committee, and it obtained a list of the forty-one companies and partnerships bound up in it.[5]

The committee admitted that its work had been far from thorough, and reached no striking conclusions. There was nothing new in its denunciation of various trusts, or its warning that if they kept on growing both producer and consumer would be at their mercy. In its final report, dated May 10, the members divided sharply. Chairman Arnold and three others took a rather optimistic view of the situation. They declared that a rigid line should be drawn between good and bad combinations; that the former should not be unnecessarily restrained; and that new legislation should not be passed until it became clear that the common law was inadequate. "The more that is known of trusts the less they are feared," said this majority group. A minority report, however, differed.[6]

The chief accomplishment of the inquiry lay in bringing out certain facts which the public had theretofore known vaguely rather than definitely. One was the rapid growth in the number of monopolistic combinations. On adjournment the chairman remarked that new Alps upon Alps arose, and that if all the trusts were to be investigated the committee would have to be made a permanent body.[7] Another interesting result was the disclosure of the high profits made by some combinations. It was shown that in half a dozen years the Standard's holdings had more than doubled in value, and its dividends had exceeded $50,000,000. Equally important was the proof that trusts had a tendency to raise prices. Thus it was demonstrated that the Copper Trust had advanced the

[5]This list is in John Moody, *The Truth About the Trusts*, 121, 122.

[6]The full investigation is given in *Report of the Committee on General Laws on the Investigation Relative to Trusts, Transmitted to the Legislature, March 6, 1888.* The testimony and appendices fill 689 pages, which include a 15-page report by the committee, and a 2-page minority report. Later, beginning Dec. 12, 1888, new evidence was taken filling 207 pages. It will hereafter be cited as *State Senate Investigation.*

[7]N. Y. *World, Sun,* March 7, 1888.

price of copper from twelve to seventeen cents a pound; the Sugar Trust had exorbitantly increased the price of sugar; and the Jute Trust had doubled the price of bags.

Finally, the exhibition of the size and wealth of the largest combinations was decidedly alarming to thoughtful observers. Even the New York *Tribune* expressed apprehension.[8] It quoted with approval the committee's statement that the $150,000,000 property of the Standard Oil, controlled by eight energetic, aggressive, and highly able men, was "the most active and possibly the most formidable moneyed power on the continent." This property might again double in value by 1894; and the fact that its managers were able to wield their huge power in secret, publishing no reports or minutes, seemed highly disturbing. As the Senate committee declared, the thirty-nine corporations of the Standard had "turned their affairs over to an organization having no legal existence, independent of all authority, able to do anything it wanted anywhere, and to this point working in absolute darkness."[9] While the snowbanks left by the great blizzard of 1888 still lay in the Capitol grounds, the legislature began debating anti-trust legislation. No action was taken this year or the next; but popular hatred of the great new aggregations by no means diminished.

II

By this time, indeed, the demand for both State and Federal action against monopolistic combinations was becoming irresistible. From every part of the nation arose calls for action. The principal complaints against the trust were two. To begin with, it was what E. L. Godkin called the sphinx of industrial organizations, working in almost total darkness and mystery.[10] Neither public nor shareholders could call it to account. Though the Standard agreement provided that "the trustees shall render at each annual meeting a statement of the affairs of the trust," essential operations were kept secret, no real discussion took place, and no statement was printed.

[8]See N. Y. *Tribune,* May 8, 1888.
[9]The Standard Oil Trust agreement did provide for annual meetings, and declared that "The board of trustees shall have its principal office in the city of New York, unless changed by a vote of the board of trustees." *State Senate Investigation, 1888,* p. 463.
[10]N. Y. *Nation,* May 5, 1887.

No limit existed upon capital or debt. The trust could engage in any kind of business anywhere; it stood outside the law, and was irresponsible to the last degree. In the second place, the public believed that all trusts were set up in order to establish a tyrannous control of production and raise prices. Their object, taken as a fast-growing group, was to circumvent what Americans regarded as the grand law of free competition, and to do so over the whole of a vast continent.

The generally prosperous years since 1880 had witnessed a marked expansion of American business. Before the Civil War the United States had stood fifth among the manufacturing nations of the globe; now it was racing almost neck and neck with Great Britain for first place, and was destined before the end of the century to surpass her. In the decade of the eighties the United States set up a world's record, which still remains unbroken, for the laying of railroad trackage. Industrial payrolls increased during the ten years by approximately a billion dollars. As the country thus attained gigantic stature in manufacturing, its production in numerous fields outstripped consumption, and business leaders were from time to time driven half desperate by gluts, price-slashing, and losses. They could continue their price wars until the weaker companies went bankrupt and a few large corporations arose on their ruins; or they could combine, limit production, and regulate prices. Industry after industry elected the second course. The road to monopoly was smoothed by various factors. Combinations were assisted by the high tariff wall that shut out foreign goods, the fast-growing railroad system that brought nationwide markets within reach and so favored the growth of great national businesses, the railroad-rate discrimination which boosted the big concern and crippled the little one, and the inadequate laws for policing business. Moreover, business leaders had before their envious eyes the example of Rockefeller's great combination, which amassed tens of millions.

By 1888 combinations of monopolistic tendency were appearing everywhere, and in protean forms. Some were built upon patents, like the Bessemer Steel Association, the match combination, and the barbed-wire combination. Some were pools: the whiskey pool of the early eighties, the wall-paper pool, the iron-pipe pool, and others. Some were called syndicates. By 1887 a single syndicate in the coke industry of southwestern Pennsylvania controlled 8300 ovens, and the competitive factor was reduced to three small firms which sold only the product of 850 ovens. The history of the meat-packing industry exhibited a succession of stockyards syndicates and rings of livestock eveners.

Anthracite coal was still in the hands of a small group of corporations working with a remarkable unity of purpose. The manufacture of cottonseed oil had been brought under the control of a combination which by 1886 marketed 98 per cent of the output. Henry M. Flagler was a stockholder, and one J. H. Flagler (of no traceable relationship) was president.[11] *The Nation* stated, of the Standard Oil Trust: "It has blazed the way for all the others, and has excited the investing public with a vision of equally large profits to be derived from the magical name of trusts. It has kindled a new form of madness in the speculating public, such as the South Sea Company bred after its kind in London a century and a half ago."[12] Everywhere small business units were being bought out, bankrupted, or forced to merge; and in one department of trade after another aggressive leaders were striving to weld the largest units into an unbreakable monopoly. Pulpit, press, and politicians inveighed against the tendency. It was erecting a Modern Feudalism, exclaimed James F. Hudson in *The North American Review;* a domination of great and irresponsible rulers of industry, whose power, like that of the feudal barons, burdened the people and even overshadowed the national government.[13]

Of all the forms of combination, trusts most alarmed the American people. After all, monopolies based upon patent rights were essentially transitory, and would break up as soon as the patents expired or were superseded. Pools had never proved really stable or formidable. As they had no legal standing, it was always difficult to hold members to their agreements; and in any event, they were but temporary expedients, seldom attempting to establish prices or policies over a protracted period. Price-fixing associations

[11]The story went around Wall Street that the cottonseed oil organizers had paid the Standard trustees $250,000 for a copy of the trust agreement—the first copy ever seen outside the Standard Oil Trust rooms. This was probably a fiction, but it shows how much the idea was thought to be worth. Flynn, *God's Gold,* 278.
[12]N. Y. *Nation,* May 5, 1887.
[13]*North American Review,* CXLIV (1887), 277–290.

were even less dependable. It was no uncommon event for a manufacturer to station a salesman outside his building, and as soon as a
price agreement had been reached, to stroll casually to a window,
adjust the shade in a prearranged way, and thus indicate to the
watcher the level agreed upon—after which the salesman would
rush forth to undercut the price his employer was even then pledging himself to maintain![14] Syndicates were precarious. But the trust
as Rockefeller and S. C. T. Dodd had perfected it held all the units
of a great industry in an unbreakable grip.

Emulation of the Standard thus became an important factor in
the movement toward concentration and control, and its organization was directly imitated by the Whiskey Trust, Sugar Trust, and
Lead Trust.[15] All three industries were familiar with excessive production, price-slashing, and heavy losses. As early as 1881 the whiskey distillers had set up a pool, the Western Export Association,
which took its name from the fact that it intended to export the
surplus product to maintain domestic prices. The pool had worked
poorly, and in desperation the principal distillers in 1887 formed
the Distillers' and Cattle Feeders' Trust, copying the Standard Oil
agreement. About eighty establishments were brought together,
most of which were shortly closed down, leaving the manufacturer
of spirits centralized in a dozen great plants. Nine trustees received
the stock of all the component companies, issuing trust certificates
in exchange. In sugar manufacturing, many refineries had been
forced out of business by the relentless competition. By 1887 only
twenty-six were left, operated by twenty-three companies. Under
Henry O. Havemeyer, a trust was created which controlled more
than four fifths of the nation's sugar production. This time there
were eleven trustees. Dismantling many weak plants, they carried
on most of their manufacturing in four huge refineries able to utilize
every economy of large-scale operation. The National Lead Company united white lead smelters and refineries in precisely the same
fashion.[16]

The attacks of press and politicians upon the trusts were both
natural and healthful; for it was not merely important, but essen-

[14]Arundel Cotter, *United States Steel, A Corporation with a Soul.*
[15]*State Senate Investigation, 1888,* p. 463.
[16]*House Trust Investigation, 1888, passim;* Moody, *The Truth About the
Trusts,* 56, 61 ff.

tial, that the reign of free competition be protected in the United States. But from the vantage point of a later day we can see that many crusaders were blind to the larger tendencies of the time. They did not realize that industrial concentration was now a world-wide movement, and that Europe was creating cartels and other combinations as energetically as America. They grossly underestimated the evils of unrestrained competition, and ignored the fact that such combinations as Rockefeller's originated in an attempt to mitigate or abolish the unendurable rigors of *laissez faire*. They refused to comprehend the power of the current, and took decades to realize that a policy of mere obstruction would fail—that some program must be adopted which would save the good combinations and punish or reform the bad. Had the attackers been wiser, they would have been less ferocious.

We can see, too, that a good deal of hypocrisy entered into the uproar. Monopoly and size have no correlation. Some of the greediest and most pernicious monopolists in the country operated petty businesses. In countless villages and towns, certain shopkeepers, implement dealers, produce buyers, and undertakers held monopolies, and wrung merciless exactions from the consuming public. All over the Middle West, farmers and villagers paid tribute to men who operated the only dry goods store, hardware store, or shoe store within reach. It was a fortunate town in the wheat States which had more than one grain elevator. When the Standard bought oil it graded that oil fairly, and paid a fair world-price for it. But a host of elevator men from Ohio to California graded No. 1 wheat as No. 2, and No. 2 wheat as No. 3, while a host of commission men paid cruelly unfair prices to the farmer—facts abundantly proved when the Western States established regulatory boards. Yet a large part of the denunciation of big business came from small merchants and buyers who practised monopoly whenever they had a chance. A great part of it came from Republicans who turned around and voted blindly for high tariffs which did much to nurture monopoly.

When the campaign of 1888 drew on, all the national platforms included stern pronouncements against monopolistic combinations. The Republicans called for State and Federal laws to halt their oppression of the people. The Democrats denounced them, and pointed to the high tariff as their parent. The Prohibitionists asserted that they must be stamped out. "The paramount issues," declared the Union Labor party, "are the abolition of usury, monopoly, and Trusts." Public opinion had crystallized rapidly. As early as 1884 Ben Butler had run for President as candidate of an Anti-Monopoly party, but his organization had taken a vague position, calling merely for effective government regulation of "transportation, money, and the transmission of intelligence" as controlled by "giant monopolies"—that is, railroads, banks, and the Western Union Company. No party had then mentioned industrial combinations.

III

The inquiry conducted by the House Committee on Manufactures early in 1888—one for which Samuel J. Randall and the New York *World* were chiefly responsible—was the most important scrutiny of industrial tendencies in America since the Hepburn Investigation. The Sugar Trust and Standard Oil Trust were exhaustively studied. Some two hundred pages of testimony were taken on the former, leaving no doubt that it enjoyed a monopoly. The committee, with Henry Bacon of New York as chairman, then on April 6 turned its guns upon the Standard Oil.

Franklin B. Gowen, eager to break the Standard as he had broken the Molly Maguires, was counsel and chief questioner. Handsome of face and figure, richly dressed, ready of tongue, he was making his last great public appearance. He was as ambitious, energetic, and quick-witted as ever. A long list of interesting witnesses were catechized: Emery, George Rice, Matthews of Buffalo, and B. B. Campbell among the Standard's enemies; Cassatt among railroad men; and Rockefeller, Archbold, Flagler, and Carley of the Standard executives. Various episodes in the Standard's history were thoroughly explored. Detailed information was spread upon the record respecting the war with the Empire Transportation Company, O'Day's iniquitous arrangement for a drawback on George Rice's shipments over the Marietta railroad, the Buffalo conspiracy case, and the defeat of the Billingsley Bill. A valuable collection of documentary evidence was introduced.

Of course Gowen laid stress upon the railroad rebating. Archbold retorted with his usual breezy, facetious bluntness:[17]

---

[17]*House Trust Investigation, 1888*, p. 316.

Q. You got the very best terms you could out of the railroads?
A. Yes, sir.
Q. No matter what other people got?
A. I was not attending to business for other people.
Q. But you were at all times willing to do the best you could for yourself?
A. To make the best arrangement I could for the concern for which I was dealing.
Q. Irrespective of any considerations as to whether the obligations of the railroads as common carriers authorized them to do so or not?
A. That was a matter for them to consider and not me.
Q. You did not intend to keep their consciences?
A. I would have had a hard job, I am afraid.

He insisted upon the universality of rebating before the Interstate Commerce Act:[18]

Q. Did you familiarize yourself with the rates open to the public at the same time?
A. I had knowledge always of the nominal rates; everybody had; but there was a long period during which everybody who shipped oil knew that the rates on the public schedules were only nominal, and that it was a question of special contract always.

Archbold insisted that the Standard had preferred what he called net rates, "without any question of rebating."[19] He remarked that the company at times played one railroad against another, and had also used the Great Lakes and Erie Canal. "Our object has always been to reduce rates and cheapen the produce and increase its consumption by making the lowest price possible to the consumer." He admitted that the Standard Oil had for some time past possessed an agreement with the Pennsylvania Railroad assuring the latter a fixed proportion of the crude-oil traffic—26 per cent; and that this agreement practically cut off any possibility of rate competition between the Standard pipe lines and the Pennsylvania. But, he added, the rate was already so low that the Pennsylvania occasionally grumbled that it yielded them no profit. When questioned as to the Standard's practical control of the refining business, he denied that it rested upon any other basis than superior efficiency. Neither railroad rebates nor any other special privilege was a real factor, he maintained:[20]

[18]*Idem*, 317.   [19]*Idem*, 316, 317.   [20]*Idem*, 333, 334.

Q. . . . I desire to know whether there exists anything . . . that would prevent capital entering into the same field competing with you, and if there be anything whatever of that sort I desire to know it.

A. There is nothing of the kind. Our hold on this trade and our position in it is, we believe—and we believe we can show to any fair tribunal of inquiry—the result of the application of better methods and of better business principles than have been brought against us, and on that basis only can we hold it or survive, and the people who come to tell you differently tell you what is false, and which we can prove false to the utmost particular. They are people who have failed through their lack of ability to succeed, and who would not succeed under any circumstances. They are soreheads and strikers. . . .

These defiant generalities did not satisfy Gowen. Pacing the floor, he pressed Archbold hard. Let us come down to the solid regions of actual fact, he demanded; you were paid rebates, "and you were paid that not only upon the oil which you shipped, but also upon the oil which others shipped." Archbold, flushing with anger, flatly denied this. But under continued questioning, he said merely that he had "no knowledge of any such case," and "did not believe" that it ever occurred.[21] He admitted that the Standard dismantled many refineries, perhaps fifty in all. But when Gowen asserted that this must have involved a great deal of waste for which the Standard's customers had to pay, he sharply demurred. "I think the consolidation of the business into large and thoroughly modern establishments has more than counterbalanced, in the aggregate business, any such expense."[22]

In his questions as to rebates paid the Standard upon its competitors' oil, Gowen of course had in mind the testimony given by Cassatt in 1879. The vice-president of the Pennsylvania had then revealed that his railroad was paying the American Transfer Company, a Standard subsidiary, 22½ cents a barrel on all crude oil received. This, he said, was "a commission to them to aid in securing us our share of the trade." Archbold took Cassatt's view that this was a commission; Gowen and other independent observers held that it was an iniquitous drawback exacted to cripple the Standard's rivals. Lewis Emery, Jr., testified, on the basis of an elaborate computation of his own, that the four great trunk-line railroads which paid this 22½-cent drawback or "commission" to the Standard Oil

[21]*Idem*, 334.   [22]*Idem*, 347.

had thus given the trust, in the seventeen months, October 17, 1877, to March 31, 1879, a total of $10,155,218 in rebates.[23] It was these railroad favors and nothing else, he asserted, which had enabled the Standard to build up its great monopoly:

Q. Had you any doubt in your own mind that if you had had at your refinery in Philadelphia the same rates as the Standard and the same good oil, your refinery would have been successful?

A. It would certainly have been successful; I could have made $75,000 a year.

Flagler's testimony, offered with readiness and grace of manner, gave the public a full view of the financial arrangements of the trust and of its high profits. He recited the fact that its original capital of $70,000,000 had been increased to about $90,000,000, and gave the actual market value of the shares in April 1888, as about $154,000,000. Since its formation the trust had averaged earnings of about 13 per cent a year; about 7 per cent annually had been paid to the stockholders in cash, 3 per cent in stock dividends, and the remaining 3 per cent held in the treasury. Any corporation which steadily made 13 per cent a year was doing very well indeed.

Rockefeller, called to the stand on April 30, was treated with great respect. Gowen, who seemed afraid of him, courteously announced that he would be asked very few questions. Already the precise and gently pontifical aspect which he presented to the public in his later years had begun to descend upon him. He emphasized the good intentions of the trust. "We think our American petroleum is a very cheap light. It is our pleasure to try to make it so." But on one specific point after another he was vague and uninforming. He could not tell the committee what percentage of its export oil the Standard sold at the seaboard, and what share it carried overseas. He could not hazard a statement as to the price of Scottish shale oil. He could not say whether the trust held any natural gas properties in Indiana. Representative Smith burst out impatiently at one point: "Well, Mr. Rockefeller, in getting testimony here we find among you officials that there is a very great shortness of memory in not knowing this or that or the other, and yet the testimony goes to show that you are doing an immense business, and there seems to be nobody that knows anything positively about it."

[23]*Idem,* 242.

Rockefeller gazed pityingly at him, and responded that the business was too vast and complex for him to master all its details. Immediately afterward he remarked that the trust had no books—"No, sir; we have no system of bookkeeping"—each separate company keeping its own accounts. But this statement he shortly modified:

Q. Who actually handles that money [the profits of subordinate corporations]?
A. The treasurer of the trust.
Q. Who is he? A. Mr. Brewster.
Q. Does he keep books of these transactions? A. He has a record, to know what money comes in.
Q. Call it record, or books, or whatever is most appropriate. Does he keep a record of receipts from those different corporations and payments made to holders of certificates?
A. He must have some record. I do not know just what his system of bookkeeping is. There must be some record; yes, sir.
Q. You are the president of the nine trustees? A. Yes, sir.
Q. You have never seen those books? A. I do not think I have ever seen those books.
Q. Has any member of that nine, to your knowledge, ever seen those books?
A. I do not know that they have. If such accounts are kept, Mr. Brewster must have seen them.

Nothing could be more gently evasive. When Rockefeller was asked even a simple question as to the number of shares which the Standard Oil Trust had issued in exchange for one share of Standard Oil of Ohio, he replied: "I could not tell that from memory. I cannot remember about these different companies."[24] When he left the stand he had contributed far less information than Archbold, Flagler, or O'Day. But at least he had not contributed actual misinformation, as O'Day did.

Of the witnesses hostile to the Standard, it was not Emery, Rice, or Matthews who made the deepest impression, for their charges had long been public. The most novel evidence came from such figures as Harlow Dow of Memphis. Dow was a kerosene distributor, who, buying from independent refineries, had come into sharp collision with the Standard. He and the trust had waged a bitter warfare throughout the area from Charleston, W. Va., to Cairo

[24]*Idem,* 393.

and Memphis, and he offered data to show that the Chesapeake, Ohio & Southwestern Railroad had strongly favored the Standard. Because of the large bulk shipments by the trust the officials had given it fourth-class rates while charging Dow first-class; and this discrimination held good even when both the Standard and Dow were shipping in small barrel lots. The Illinois Central had used him no better.

In some towns the railroad rate practices had driven Dow completely out of business; in others he had maintained a foothold by delivering his kerosene in steamboats or wagons. But even near Memphis the struggle had been grim and deadly. The Standard, thanks to its railroad privileges, could place kerosene in Ripley, Dyersburgh, Newburn, Obion, and other towns, all within 100 miles of Memphis, for 56 to 68 cents a barrel less than he could. He testified, for example, that he had once sold to thirteen out of the sixteen or seventeen dealers in Newburn, but could now sell to none. The situation was the same in Covington. He could haul his oil by wagon as far as forty miles from Memphis for less than the Illinois Central charged him. Dow also testified that after he had bought a tank wagon to distribute kerosene to certain communities and had operated it profitably for a year, the Standard went into those towns and began selling oil through grocery stores for 7½ cents a gallon. "I stopped the wagon and it has been idle in the stable ever since."[25]

Such testimony was interestingly corroborated by J. M. Culp, general freight agent of the Louisville & Nashville, and F. D. Carley, former president of Chess, Carley. At first Culp was reticent about rates. He refused to say whether he kept any books showing rebates. But finally he admitted that up to April 5, 1888, his railroad had allowed specially low rates to the Standard and to Chess, Carley. This was because they furnished a large amount of business, shipped to many points not reached by other companies, and abstained from sending oil to Memphis, New Orleans, Vicksburg, and Mobile by river. Carley had now retired and was living at Tuxedo Park, N. Y. He frankly and indeed proudly declared that his policy had been to crack every competitive head that bobbed up, and crack it hard. His arm of the Standard had owned nearly all the tank cars

[25]*Idem*, 416, 417.

running on the L. & N.; and .whenever a competitor introduced others, he was promptly disciplined. "For instance, a man named Pettit got on some tanks at New Orleans. . . . I dropped the price on him pretty lively. (Laughter.)"[26]

Carley was asked whether he had not frequently entered into direct competition with grocers and hardware dealers in still other commodities than oil in order to compel them to buy the Standard brands of kerosene. "Almost invariably; I did that always," he replied. He also made it clear that in thus savagely assailing all opponents he followed the policy which he had marked out while an independent:[27]

Q. You were active and made a great many efforts to enlarge your business and drive other people out of competition. Was it not a point of your business character that you would drive out competition?

A. I was very fortunate in competing; but I want to say that it was not by the direction of the Standard Oil Company or at their request. It was simply my way of doing business. I thought it was cheaper in the long run to make the price cheap and be done with it, than to fritter away the time with a competitor in a little competition. I put the price down to the bone. (Laughter.)

Q. You put it down so as to kill him outright?

A. I did not look to him.

The most amusing episode of the hearing was offered by the gyrations of Culp and Carley when confronted with the famous turn-another-screw letter which A. B. Hathaway of Chess, Carley had sent to Culp after Rice's competitive shipment of oil had gone through at a low rate. Both were eager to explain it away. But though they testified on the same day, they offered entirely different explanations! Culp remarked that he simply couldn't understand the letter.[28] "The man who wrote this must evidently have been crazy. He afterwards died in the insane asylum." Carley, however, regarded Hathaway as eminently sane! He was a stenographer in the Louisville office of Chess, Carley. One of his duties was to make sure that competitive shipments over the L. & N. were not, through office carelessness, accepted at "a rate lower than the regular rate." Such carelessness, he testified, was fairly frequent. "He would say to me, Mr. Carley, there is another carload gone through to Wilker-

[26]*Idem*, 520–525, for Culp's testimony; 526–537, for Carley's.
[27]*Idem*, 534, 536.   [28]*Idem*, 524.

son, or whoever it might be. I said, I do not think it is right on the part of the road. Can you not get them to stop it? I mentioned it to them before. They said it was the fault of the clerk; that it was clerical. I used to complain to Hathaway, and as he had been in the office and was very familiar with them he writes this letter to ask them to tighten the machinery of their office up there, using this unfortunate expression which has been thrust in my face for several years. (Laughter.)"[29]

Altogether, the House Committee presented the Standard in just as unfavorable a light as the Sugar Trust. The complaints of producers, independent refiners, and small distributors were thoroughly reviewed. Their testimony as to rebating offered little that was really novel. But evidence was given which strongly indicated that the pipe-line charges had been excessive. It was again proved that two important men connected with the trust, O'Day and Carley, had committed acts against competitors which could not be defended. The large profits of the Standard were once more exhibited; the coercive power which it had exercised over trunk-line railroads was brought out in detail; and the secrecy which had surrounded many of its operations was emphasized.

In reporting to Congress on July 30, 1888, the committee offered some brief and noncommittal conclusions upon the Standard Oil Trust. "This form of combination," it declared, "was obviously devised for the purpose of relieving the trust and trustees from the charge of any breach of the conspiracy laws of the various States, or of being a combination to regulate or control the price of any commodity." It did not condemn the trust or its operations in so many words, nor did it offer recommendations for any new law. But to most readers the testimony spoke for itself.

IV

As the House Committee and the New York Senate Committee adjourned, legislators began to prepare bills aimed against these new aggregations of capital. The spring of 1889 found the subject heatedly discussed in half the State Capitols of the land. Numerous States already had constitutional or statutory provisions prohibiting any combination in restraint of trade. Between 1888 and 1896 either

[29]*Idem*, 530.

these were greatly strengthened, or new and more definite statutes were enacted. Michigan, Kansas, Tennessee, and Idaho acted as early as 1889, and a still larger group of States in 1890, while New York finally passed a drastic law in 1892.[30]

The promise of both major parties in 1888 to deal severely with trusts and other monopolies made action by the next session of Congress inevitable. Fourteen bills were placed before the House in 1888, while John Sherman introduced one in the Senate. On December 4, 1889, Sherman resubmitted his measure as Senate Bill No. 1, entitled "A bill to declare unlawful, trusts and combinations in restraint of trade and production." A spirited discussion began. As the result of much floor debate and committee work, a measure—to which Sherman of Ohio, Hoar of Massachusetts, George of Mississippi, and Edmunds of Vermont all contributed—was gradually hammered into shape.[31] Passed by a bipartisan and indeed almost unanimous vote, it was signed by President Harrison on July 2, 1890. The so-called Sherman Anti-Trust Act was brief. Its two essential articles declared that "every contract, combination in the form of trust or otherwise, or conspiracy, in restraint of trade or commerce among the several States or with foreign nations, is hereby declared to be illegal"; and that every person who should monopolize or attempt to monopolize any part of trade among the States or with foreign nations was punishable by fine, imprisonment, or both.[32]

In the discussions of the bill both inside and outside Congress the Standard Oil Trust was naturally treated as the principal culprit. Sherman himself remarked: "I do not wish to single out the Standard Oil Company, which is a great and powerful corporation, composed in part of citizens of my own State, and some of the very best men I know of. Still, they are controlling and can control the market as absolutely as they choose. . . ." He referred to it as able to buy not only cars but railroads. Teller of Colorado accused it of having advanced the price of oil to the injury of 65,000,000 Ameri-

[30]Charles H. Van Hise, *Concentration and Control*, 192 ff.; H. R. Seager, "The Recent Trust Decisions," *Political Science Quarterly*, XXVI, 582.

[31]G. F. Hoar describes his own contribution in *Autobiography of Seventy Years*, II, 363; Shelby M. Cullom states in *Fifty Years of Public Service*, 274, that Edmunds was the principal author. See Ida M. Tarbell, *The Nationalization of Business*, 214 ff.

[32]*U. S. Statutes at Large*, XXVI, 209, 210.

cans. Edmunds remarked, on the other hand, that while "the oil trust certainly has reduced the price of oil immensely, that does not alter the wrong of the principle of any trust." Culbertson of Texas, a State where the Waters, Pierce group had treated competitors roughly, denounced the methods of the Standard angrily. Like the dressed-beef combination, he said, the trust had reached into every local market and taken every independent dealer by the throat.[33]

By this time Camden had left the Senate, and the Standard was without any avowed spokesman there. No evidence exists that it attempted to impede the proposed anti-trust legislation. Indeed, it was helpless to do so, for public hostility was so intense that any discoverable move on its part would simply have led to more extreme action. The only course open to great monopolies was to bow to the storm while searching for some means of circumventing the new laws. But it is significant that in the midst of the debate Rockefeller took the highly unusual step of giving an interview to his leading assailant, the New York *World*.

Great courtesy was exhibited on both sides. *The World* reporter, plainly awed by his opportunity, opened his story respectfully.[34] "Rockefeller! There is something rich in the word. It suggests solid wealth. It has the ring of a solid gold coin. Even if the name had not been for years associated by the public with one of the most stupendous business enterprises of the century, it would still convey to the mind the idea of . . . ventures energetically pushed and successfully prosecuted." He thought the offices of the trust pleasantly modest. "Two or three moderately sized rooms, carpeted and supplied with the ordinary chairs and desks, form the headquarters in the city of this great trust with nearly one hundred million dollars of capital. A subdued tone is the noticeable feature of the offices. People who come and go in numbers speak in a low tone of voice. There is an absence of bustle and noise. While transactions involving millions may be involved, the negotiations are conducted in a quiet, methodical manner, apparently free from excitement. There is no exclusiveness, however, every person who has business to transact with the president . . . receiving his due share of attention." Rockefeller proved urbane and cordial. He was "a man well but

[33]See *Congressional Record*, February–April, 1890, for the debates.
[34]N. Y. *World*, March 29, 1890.

plainly dressed, a little above the average height, well proportioned, weighing probably 180 pounds, with an intelligent and pleasant countenance, fair complexion, sandy hair and mustache intermixed with grey, a somewhat prominent nose, mild grey eyes, and an agreeably expressive mouth. Mr. Rockefeller at first scarcely looks his age, but on a closer scrutiny it can be seen that the care and thought required in his vast business undertakings have left their impress. . . . "

This reporter obtained from Rockefeller an elaborate defense of the trust against the charges of oppression and monopoly levelled against it. In his story the interviewer said a good word of his own for the Standard. It had been a pioneer in its methods, he wrote. No one had ever seriously charged that it was open to the grave objections brought against combinations that sought to control the supply and increase the cost of food and other necessaries of life. And *The World* carried a surprisingly moderate editorial.[35]

The claim that the problem of the transportation of oil at the time of the development of the great oil fields required a vast accumulation of capital as the first step towards its solution is doubtless well founded, and the ample resources and energetic efforts of the combination have unquestionably brought the oil trade of the United States to the magnitude it has attained at home and abroad. But Mr. Rockefeller will find it difficult to persuade the general public that the Standard Oil Trust has no monopolistic tendencies or that its hand is never felt in politics.

President Rockefeller's story shows to what astounding dimensions the operations of the Standard Oil Trust have grown, and what an important position the company fills in the commercial world. It will serve to remind Congress that legislation on such vast interests should be intelligent in character, while firmly and effectively restrictive of the evil tendencies of such powerful and dangerous moneyed combinations.

Some observers expected that the first energetic effort to break up the Standard Oil Trust would come from the Department of Justice under the Sherman Act. They wondered, to be sure, just how energetic it would be. President Harrison had little interest in the trust question. In none of his messages to Congress after the passage of the Act did he mention it.[36] Nor did Attorney-General Miller do

---

[35]*Idem.*

[36]Oswald W. Knauth, *Policy of the United States Towards Industrial Monopoly*, 66.

so until his last report in December, 1892. But Republican senators in the course of debate had repeatedly indicated their belief that the Administration would deal sharply with these "tyrannies, grinding tyrannies," as Edmunds had termed the Sugar Trust and Standard Oil.

However, the first attack upon Rockefeller's great organization was launched from an unexpected quarter. On May 9, 1890, the press announced that the attorney-general of Ohio had filed a petition in the Supreme Court of the State for the dissolution of the Standard Oil Company. The St. George who thus rode forth against the dragon was David K. Watson, and the battle which he was beginning had the eager interest of the whole nation.

XXXIII

The Trust "Dissolved"

As the campaign against the trusts, fierce with its drums and banners, gathered headway, Rockefeller saw at least as far into the future as such anti-trust leaders as J. H. Reagan of Texas and John Sherman of Ohio.[1] He realized by 1890 that the Federal and State governments were attempting to put an end to all monopolies and quasi-monopolies, to exterminate them as the little people of H. G. Wells's *Food of the Gods* tried to exterminate the giants. They were writing more and more drastic legislation, initiating more and more energetic prosecutions. But in this they came into conflict with a powerful and, as Rockefeller believed, an irresistible tendency of the times. A great part of American business had determined to achieve security by a degree of centralization which carried it far along the road to monopoly. The business leaders in this movement would not submit to fettering legislation without a Samson struggle. They were as able and determined a group as the senators, governors, and Presidents; they had powerful weapons at hand. Industrial organizations could take as many forms as Proteus, while the wide variance in State incorporation laws gave them numerous cities of refuge. Ingenuity would be pitted against ingenuity, resolution against resolution.

News reached Rockefeller in the spring of 1889 that three States had just passed drastic laws against trusts. At 26 Broadway he read with keen interest the dispatches in *Bradstreet's* and other journals. Missouri, Kansas, and Texas in varying terms, but with almost equal severity, had outlawed all trusts, pools, or other combinations which tended to control prices and prevent a full and free competition in trade or transportation. And they had put teeth into their laws.

[1]H. R. Seager, "The Recent Trust Decisions," *Political Science Quarterly,* XXVI, 581–614.

Missouri had provided that purchasers of articles from monopolistic combinations were not liable for the price, and could plead the law to estop collection. Kansas had declared that any purchaser injured by a trust or similar combination might recover the full sums he had paid. The Texas law voided all contracts in violation of the act, and made persons outside the State liable to indictment for any violation, the commission of which did not necessarily require personal presence in Texas. While much doubt was expressed as to the enforceability of these statutes, *Bradstreet's* reported that "the State officials will make an earnest effort."[2]

Journals and magazines continued to dilate upon what William Barry, in *The Forum* for June, 1889, called "The Moloch of Monopoly." Late that summer the annual assembly of the Chautauqua Association witnessed a remarkable incident. Doctor Washington Gladden had been invited to speak and had chosen a topic which seemed innocuous. But he cut loose from all restraint in a ferocious assault upon the Standard Oil and its methods. The Chautauqua meeting included many visitors from northwestern Pennsylvania, where not a few people gratefully remembered how during the Bradford boom the Standard had provided facilities for storing and transporting oil that was running to waste. Bishop John H. Vincent, head of the Chautauqua, in accordance with his rule of never presenting one side alone of a controversial issue, immediately telegraphed Rockefeller an explanation and invited the Standard to send a representative to explain its point of view. Rockefeller at once despatched the English-born economist, George Gunton, who took the platform for a lively debate with Gladden.[3]

Gunton proved one of those maddeningly calm persons who never lose their tempers or their heads. He would place rows of figures on a blackboard and expound them with dispassionate calm. Gladden, more excitable, would rush to the board, shake his fist at the figures, and denounce them as utterly misleading. The audience, divided half and half, vociferously cheered both disputants. Both debaters

[2]*Bradstreet's,* June 15, 1889. The same journal, Jan. 19, 1889, describes the "peculiar" anti-trust bill introduced into the New York legislature, which "will satisfy neither the advocates nor the opponents of trusts." It predicted that the bill would fail, as it did.

[3]The debate is described in *Bradstreet's,* Aug. 31, 1889. A full account was given me by Doctor George E. Vincent, son of Bishop Vincent, in May, 1939.

agreed that the tendency in industry toward combination and the concentration of capital was healthful. But Gladden maintained that the trusts were trying to destroy competition utterly, while he contended that men like Gunton exaggerated the service which such combinations had performed in reducing costs.[4]

Yet despite minatory laws and hostile clamor, trusts continued to multiply. An English writer in *The Contemporary Review* during the summer of 1890 declared that American citizens already had to deal with them from the cradle to the grave.[5] With humorous exaggeration, he remarked that there were trusts "in kerosene oil, sugar, cottonseed oil, steel, rubber, steel beams, cartridges, lead, iron, nails, straw, paper, linseed oil, coal." Where would the consolidating tendency end? Could it really be checked? All over the country now the attorney-generals of States were dusting off their old conspiracy laws or leafing through the new anti-trust statutes, and discussing methods of action.[6] Charles F. Tabor of New York was pressing a double attack upon the Sugar Trust.[7]

In Ohio, Attorney-General David E. Watson undoubtedly read of the New York suits, and doubtless heard of the Western State officials who were riding like knight-errants into the lists. In 1889 he was suddenly spurred to action. Coming out of the State Capitol in Columbus one day, he crossed the street, and according to his custom halted at a bookstore. He picked up a small 110-page volume called *Trusts: The Recent Combinations in Trade,* by William W. Cook of the New York bar. This was primarily a legal treatise, although it contained some pages on the anti-trust movement. It included the trust deeds of the Standard Oil and the Sugar Trust, with a summary of the New York investigation.[8] Cook did not believe that the new trusts could long survive. In all probability, he boldly predicted, the States through their attorney-generals or legislatures would soon "forfeit or repeal the charters which have

[4] See N. Y. *Tribune,* Aug., 1889.
[5] R. Donald, "Trusts in the United States," *Contemporary,* 57: 829. See also "Progress of Trusts in the United States," *Spectator,* 64: 788.
[6] See A. J. Eddy, *The Law of Combinations* (1901), I, *passim.*
[7] *N. Y. vs. North River Sugar Refining Co., 121 N. Y.;* 582 ff.
[8] Cook wrote in his preface: "This fragment of the great law of corporations is written to throw light upon a dark subject. During the past twelve months certain mysterious combinations of manufacturers, called "Trusts," have sprung into prominence." He discussed their causes, legality, influence, and future; and the book went at once into a second edition.

been misused and perverted from the purposes of their creation."[9]

This volume, like much else written in those days, was a challenge to public prosecutors to do their duty. An evening over the book fired Watson, young and energetic, to accept the challenge. Miss Tarbell tells us that this was the first time that he had ever seen the Standard's trust agreement; yet it had been public property for a year and a half, and tom-toms had been beaten over it from the Hudson to the Sacramento. Miss Tarbell further remarks that he "saw at once that, if it was a bona fide agreement, the Standard Oil Company of Ohio was and had for seven years been violating the laws of the State of Ohio by taking the affairs of the company from the directors and placing them in the hands of trustees, nearly all of whom were non-residents of the State."[10] He at least saw that there was a good *chance* to prove this.

Within a few weeks the Republicans re-elected Watson attorney-general, and he set to work in earnest. Miss Tarbell states that because he doubted the correctness of the trust agreement as printed, he inquired into its authenticity, and sent for the reports of the investigations by the New York Senate and Federal House.[11] But it is not likely that he had many misgivings as to the accuracy of the agreement. Its text had been given to the New York Committee by Rockefeller himself, of course in carefully verified form. What Watson undoubtedly searched for in the New York and Federal reports was something much more important and elusive—for evidence that the practical affairs, the active management, of the Standard Oil of Ohio, had really been transferred to the officers of the trust. If he could find this, he could prove that the Ohio company had acted illegally. Both in New York and Washington the Standard Oil officers had refused to admit such a transfer, and had labored arduously to conceal the facts. But the evidence nevertheless pointed to an unescapable conclusion: this Ohio company *had,* in practice if not in law, handed over its properties, its business activities, and all its responsibilities to the nine trustees.

Watson not only studied the report of the House Committee, but went to Washington to consult Representative James Buchanan of New Jersey, a Republican and an experienced attorney, who had

---

[9]Wood, *op. cit.,* 31, 62, 63.
[10]Tarbell, *Standard Oil Company,* II, 142.   [11]*Ibid.*

been one of the most persistent questioners of the Standard Oil men. Watson told him that he was meditating a *quo warranto* action against the Standard Oil of Ohio for breaking the laws of the State. "You would not *dare* do that, would you?" demanded Buchanan. When Watson explained that his conception of duty required him to enforce the law no matter how formidable the violator might be, Buchanan raised his eyebrows.

"I admire your courage," he remarked, "but I would not do it."[12]

Evidently Buchanan had an exaggerated notion of the power exercised by the Standard Oil in Ohio. As a matter of fact, the agitation against trusts was as vociferous in that State as elsewhere, and more political capital was to be made out of attacking them than ignoring them. The Democratic platform in the State campaign of 1888 had denounced them roundly. Since action against the Standard was certain to be popular, Watson showed no great courage in following where Attorney-General Tabor of New York had already led. The latter was already scoring a success, for early in 1889 Judge George C. Barrett, in a special term of the Supreme Court, had handed down a decision adverse to the Sugar Trust.[13] On May 8, 1890, Watson filed his *quo warranto* petition in the Supreme Court of Ohio. This document recited that the Standard had transferred substantially all its shares to the officers of the Standard Oil Trust, most of them non-residents of Ohio, and that these trustees selected the directors of the Standard Oil of Ohio, and managed its affairs. As such management by outsiders violated the State law, he asked that the company be held to have forfeited its corporate rights and powers, and be dissolved.

It is an exaggeration to say, as some writers have done, that this petition fell upon Rockefeller "like a thunderbolt."[14] He had unquestionably been expecting some such attack ever since the trust agreement had been published. He and his attorneys knew perfectly well that when the Sugar Trust was being haled before the courts of New York, when the so-called Chicago Gas Trust was being arraigned before the tribunals of Illinois, and when the Cotton Oil Trust was forestalling court action by abandoning the trust plan, the Standard could not long escape. The whole tenor

[12]*Idem,* 143.   [13]*American Annual Cyclopædia, 1889,* p. 796.
[14]Tarbell, *Standard Oil Company,* II, 144.

of the testimony by Rockefeller, Flagler, and Archbold in the recent investigations had indicated that they anticipated an assault on the component companies of the trust upon the ground that they had illegally surrendered their management to another organization. S. C. T. Dodd and his associates at once cleared their decks for action. After some delay, they filed a carefully drawn answer, the essence of which was that the Standard Oil of Ohio had never given up its powers and privileges to the trust, and still managed its own business.

Meanwhile, extraordinary pressure was brought to bear upon Watson to discontinue his suit. Conservative Ohio newspapers criticized him, and Ohio businessmen protested. It was rumored that efforts were being made to buy him off. Republicans of prominence joined in the campaign of suasion, among them Mark Hanna, already the most influential political leader in Ohio, and the close ally of John Sherman and William McKinley. Hanna was desperately busy during the autumn of 1890 in an attempt to help McKinley gain re-election to Congress. But McKinley had just given his name to one of the worst tariff bills in American history; he was defeated, and fellow Republicans were routed all over the nation, losing control of the House. Hanna then looked about for means of strengthening the party. On November 21 he sent Watson an impassioned letter of protest. This epistle was subsequently, at Hanna's request, destroyed. But soon after its destruction Watson let it be known that, as a safeguard against misrepresentation, he had kept a copy. The transcript which he made public read as follows:[15]

Dear Sir:
Some months ago when I saw the announcement through the papers that you had begun a suit against the Standard Oil Co. in the Supreme Court, I intended, if opportunity presented, to talk with you, and failing in the personal interview, to write you a letter, but the subject passed out of my mind. Recently while in New York, I learned from my friend, Mr. John D. Rockefeller, that such suit was still pending, and without any solicitation on his part or suggestion from him, I determined to write you, believing that both political and business interests justified me in doing so. While I am not personally interested in the Standard Oil Co., many of my closest friends are, and I have no doubt that many of the business associations with which I am connected are equally open to attack. The

[15]Herbert Croly, *Life of Mark Hanna*, 267, 268.

simple fact is, as you will discover, if you have not already done so, that in these modern days most commercial interests are properly and necessarily taking on the form of organization for the safety of investors, and the improvement of all conditions upon which business is done. There is no greater mistake for a man in or out of public place to make than to assume that he owes any duty to the public or can in any manner advance his own position or interests by attacking the organizations under which experience has taught business can best be done. From a party standpoint, interested in the success of the Republican party, and regarding you as in the line of political promotion, I must say that the identification of your office with litigation of this character is a great mistake. There is no public demand for a raid upon organized capital. For years the business of manufacturing oil has been done with great success at Cleveland, competition has been open and free, and the public has been greatly benefited by the manner in which the oil business has been carried on. The Standard Oil Company is officered and managed by some of the best and strongest men in the country. They are pretty much all Republicans and have been most liberal in their contributions to the party, as I personally know, Mr. Rockefeller always quietly doing his share. . . .

Very truly yours,

M. A. Hanna.

Hanna's biographer, Herbert Croly, admits that most of this letter is doubtless authentic. He rejects, however, the statement attributed to Hanna that many businesses with which he was connected were equally open to attack, and the clause about a public officer not owing any duty to the public. These he thinks fabrications. However this may be, there is no question as to the authenticity of a second letter which Hanna sent Watson on December 27, 1890.[16] In this he said that he had known the men who organized the Standard Oil for thirty years, and most of them were intimate friends; that no industry had been of greater benefit to Cleveland; that the businessmen of the city were indignant over this attack, and would make their resentment felt; and that politically Watson had made a sad mistake.

This spectacle of Mark Hanna reproaching the attorney-general for attempting to enforce the law is decidedly sad; but Hanna never made any bones about his attachment to big business, and we can well believe his statement that he was writing without any solicitation from Rockefeller. It is pleasant to record that the attorney-general did not flinch.

[16]*Idem*, 269.

II

Watson had retained John W. Warrington of Cincinnati to assist him. Their amended petition alleged that after the trust agreements of January, 1882, the stock of the Standard Oil of Ohio had been transferred to trustees; that the trustees, who issued certificates in return, had thereafter chosen the directors of the Standard Oil of Ohio, and controlled its management; that the company had never made any complaint because its stockholders and officers had thus surrendered their stock, but instead had acquiesced; and that because its stockholders and officers had entered into the trust agreement, and permitted the corporate business and property to be conducted and controlled by the trustees, the company had forfeited its rights, powers, privileges, and franchises. In their brief Watson and Warrington went beyond this. The company had not only submitted to the domination of an agency unknown to the statute, they said. It had united in carrying out an agreement inimical to the public interest.[17]

For the defense Rockefeller added Joseph H. Choate to the regular Standard Oil attorneys, Dodd and Kline. These men denied that the Standard Oil of Ohio was ever a party to the trust agreement. On the contrary, they declared, the transfer of its stock had been merely the act of its *stockholders*. They denied that its business was conducted by the trust. On the contrary, it was conducted solely by the board of directors, who were chosen not by the trustees but by the holders of a majority of the stock. They contended that no relationship existed between the trustees and the Ohio company; merely a relationship between the trustees and the individual stockholders who had given up their stock for trust certificates. The attorneys further asserted that if the signing of the trust agreements should be held a cause for forfeiture of charter, then the statute of limitations would intervene, for the agreements had been executed more than five years before Watson acted.[18]

[17]The dissolution suit is covered in John Lewis, ed., *American Railroad and Corporation Reports*, V, 679–711 (Chicago, 1892); *Standard Oil Trust Cases, Ohio.*

[18]The argument of the defense is thus summarized in *Ballantine on Corporations*, by Henry Winthrop Ballantine (1927; pp. 28, 29): "The defense was based upon the argument that the corporation was a legal entity, separate

No testimony was taken in the case. The court decided it upon the pleadings, assuming for the purposes of the hearing that all the allegations of the answer were true.

Rockefeller doubtless expected—like everybody else—that the decision would go against the Standard. In New York the general term of the Supreme Court the previous fall had dealt harshly with the Sugar Trust and the North River Sugar Refining Company, declaring the former illegal, and deciding that the latter must forfeit its property, which would pass under a receiver. To these decrees the Sugar Trust was ready to bow. Nobody at 26 Broadway was therefore astonished when on March 2, 1890, the Supreme Court of Ohio decided against the defendants. An able opinion by Judge T. A. Minshall held that the Standard Oil of Ohio was actually controlled and managed by the trust—"indirectly, it is true, but none the less effectually." It held also that the trust had violated the common law. Its object was to establish a virtual monopoly of producing, refining, and dealing in petroleum and its products throughout the country, so that it might control prices; and all such associations were contrary to sound public policy. Judge Minshall added:

Much has been said in favor of the objects of the Standard Oil Trust and what it has accomplished. It may be true that it has improved the quality and cheapened the cost of petroleum and its products to the consumer. But such is not one of the usual or general results of a monopoly; and it is the policy of the law to regard, not what may, but what usually happens. Experience has shown that it is not wise to trust human cupidity where it has the opportunity to aggrandize itself at the expense of others.

The judgment against the Standard, on its face, was merely a decision upon a technical question of corporate law. This had been true also of the New York decision against the North River Sugar Refining Company. But in both cases the real reason for the decision went beyond law—it lay in the belief of the courts that sound

---

from its stockholders; that in it were vested all the property and powers of the company, and that it could only be affected by such acts and arguments as might be done or executed on its behalf by its corporate agencies, acting within the legitimate scope of their powers; that its stockholders were not the corporation; that their shares were their individual property, and that they might each and all dispose of and make such agreements affecting their shares as might best suit their private interests; and that no such acts and agreements of the stockholders could be ascribed to the company as a separate entity, though done and concurred in by each and all of its stockholders."

public policy required the disruption of such monopolistic organizations. Because of the statute of limitations the charter of the Standard Oil of Ohio was not annulled. But the company was forbidden to maintain the trust agreement, to recognize further the transfer of stock, or to permit the trustees to control its affairs. It also had to pay the costs of the suit.[19]

While the New York *World* and Philadelphia *Press* were exultant in their comments, Kline hurried to New York to join Choate and Dodd in consulting with Rockefeller and the other trustees. According to *The Tribune,* no uneasiness was exhibited at 26 Broadway. The officers told a reporter that the decision would not affect the business of the Standard group or interfere with its plans. Nevertheless, anxious daily meetings were held during the next week. The great question, of course, was whether Rockefeller would merely accept the severance of the old relationship between the Standard Oil of Ohio and the Standard Oil Trust, or break up the trust altogether. That question was answered when on March 10 he announced, through S. C. T. Dodd, that because of the general public hostility toward such combinations, the entire trust would be terminated.

This determination was formally communicated to the Ohio Supreme Court by Kline. He wrote that no appeal would be made, that the trust as a whole would be dissolved, and that the trustees asked only for leisure to do this in an orderly manner. Kline also explained to the judges, sitting in chamber with the attorney-general, just why a good deal of time would be required. The trustees held all but seven shares of the stock of the Standard of Ohio, and nearly ten years had elapsed since they had issued trust certificates in exchange for this stock. Of course these certificates had since passed through many hands. It would take time to find all the new owners, and to induce them to exchange their certificates for stock in the Standard of Ohio. Chief Justice Spear informally promised Kline that adequate time would be allowed.

Rockefeller and his partners had seen that they really possessed no alternative. An appeal would quickly have been lost; the trust itself was open to attack in the Federal courts under the new Sher-

[19] *Annual Report of the Attorney General of Ohio, 1892,* p. 18; *Standard Oil Trust Cases, Ohio.*

man Act; and the attorney-general at Albany had prepared papers and was ready to file them against the New York companies if they remained in the trust.[20] The nine trustees acted at once. On March 11, 1892, all holders of trust certificates were notified by mail and by advertisements that a meeting would be held at 26 Broadway ten days later to vote upon the proposed termination of the agreement, and also to take such further action as might be necessary.

Precisely what Rockefeller thought of the Ohio decision we do not know, for he gave out no interview. But there can be little doubt that he held, like Dodd, that the trust had been harmless and that the attack upon it was unfair. "I believed then, and still believe," Dodd states in his *Memoirs,* "that the trust was perfectly legal, but as public opinion was against it, it was not surprising that the court invented a principle of law in order to condemn it." Both men sincerely defended the trust on moral and business grounds. Dodd used to extol it as ardently as a delighted artist talks of a great picture, until even skeptics half doubted whether his enthusiasm was not justified! But both were ready to accept the decree. Nor can there be much doubt that both Rockefeller and Dodd at first looked forward to the genuine termination of the trust. They did not realize all the difficulties ahead, or foresee the bitter reluctance of many holders of trust certificates to give them up. Kline convinced Chief Justice Spear that they honestly intended a dissolution. Dodd writes in his *Memoirs:* "I then took steps towards the disintegration of the combination, intending that each company should afterwards act independently."[21] Of course, "independent" action would not preclude a general understanding, a community of purpose. The Sugar Trust, as a *trust,* was dissolved at this time, and reborn under New Jersey laws as a consolidation. Other trusts were broken up and moulded into new forms—retaining all their old efficiency. Rockefeller and his associates expected to reshape their combination in some fashion; for they would never willingly surrender the order and prosperity which they had given the industry—they would never break up their magnificent alliance of property and brains.

The press of the nation frankly assumed this. As practical men, the editors knew that the great movement for industrial concentra-

[20]N. Y. *Herald,* March 2, 1892.   [21]S. C. T. Dodd, *Memoirs,* 30.

tion could not be stopped by a few State attorney-generals and a few courts. The Philadelphia *Times* remarked:[22] "It is not probable that the dissolution of the trust will for some time, at least, affect the monopoly of the oil business which it now holds." The Philadelphia *Inquirer* commented that it is not human nature to throw up 12 per cent dividends.[23] "And the fuss that is being made over the proposed dissolution is just a little premature. The ten years for which the trust was organized have expired, and its call for another meeting is more likely issued for the purpose of renewing in some shape the present profitable agreement than to dissolve the trust." The Philadelphia *Press* declared that the law would be obeyed in letter, but the spirit of the old trust would still survive: that "in a business way it is more alive than ever."[24] Its editorial was headed, "A Change of Form, Not Substance"; and it shrewdly predicted that the heads of the trust would soon make use of the loose New Jersey corporation act in reorganizing their holdings. Already a score of monopolistic or semi-monopolistic aggregations had been reorganized under the New Jersey law, their total capital exceeding $250,000,000.[25] The New York *Tribune* declared: "While the trust dies, there will be no sacrifice of interests of the certificate holders, and the great aggregation of capital known as the Standard will still be managed by the same men and will retain its control of the transporting and refining of petroleum." *The World* was certain that the dissolution would be but a pretense. And *The Herald* warned its readers: "The trust in form will be abolished, but by some other name it may prove to be just as obnoxious."[26]

On March 21 a fateful air hung about the corridors of 26 Broadway. At the appointed hour the meeting began, with Rockefeller in the chair and Archbold serving as secretary. Three of the eight trustees—William Rockefeller, Henry M. Flagler, and Benjamin Brewster—were absent. Some three hundred certificate-holders and onlookers squeezed into a room built for two hundred. But there

[22]*Ibid.*   [23]March 12, 1893.   [24]March 12, 1892.
[25]March 22, 1892. The *Press* sharply attacked the New Jersey law. "It looks easy now to use a loose general corporation act which requires no reports, little paid-up capital, and ignores the experience of centuries in the management of corporations; but this short cut to secret and irresponsible control is sure in the end to breed lawsuits like mushrooms."
[26]N. Y. *Tribune, World, Herald,* March 11-13, 1892.

was no drama. The proceedings were brief and harmonious.[27]

S. C. T. Dodd made a long speech of explanation and defense. He argued once more that the Standard Oil Trust had always been precisely what it purported to be, a fiduciary obligation placed upon a few for the benefit of the many. It was not set up to concentrate a new control over component corporations in a few hands, he said, because the men chosen as trustees had always held the voting power by virtue of their absolute ownership of a majority of the stocks. It was not created to reduce competition, because the companies whose stocks were placed in trust were not competing companies, and could not be as long as their stocks were owned by a few persons. It was not established to limit production or increase prices, but on the contrary to increase production, cheapen costs of manufacture, and lower prices. After these rather specious remarks, which did not touch the essential issue—for the trust had really been set up to bulwark and govern a pre-existing approach to monopoly— Dodd went on to say that the Standard had become the victim of imitators who had adapted the trust plan to very different purposes. They had made such perverted use of it that the public had come to define a trust as a combination to suppress competition, reduce production, and increase prices. "Public opinion has now unwisely been roused against combinations for such purposes" to such an extent, he said, that nearly twenty States had passed legislation of more or less severity against them. All such arrangements were now miscalled trusts, and all trusts were popularly condemned. For this reason, if for no other, dissolution was expedient.[28]

The original trust agreement had provided that if at any time after ten years two thirds of the certificate-holders should vote to terminate it, it should thereupon be dissolved. The trustees should take charge of the distribution of property, and continue to hold their offices for that purpose. A unanimous vote of the stockholders present, representing 808,504 shares out of a total of 972,500, was registered for a dissolution, and Rockefeller and his seven associates began the work of division. "It will take about four months," *The Tribune* reporter optimistically predicted.[29]

[27]A record of proceedings was published as a pamphlet, *Dissolution of the Standard Oil Trust*. See also the *Standard Oil Case in the Supreme Court of Ohio*, 80, 81.

[28]*Idem*.

[29]N. Y. *Tribune*, March 22, 1892.

III

Was this distribution, undertaken in good faith, pushed forward in that spirit? Was a complete distribution really possible, so that, in Dodd's phrase, "each company should afterwards act independently?"[30] There were now about 1600 holders of Standard Oil Trust certificates; could each somehow be given his due share in the Standard Oil companies?

The dissolution arrangement provided that after four months the trustees could no longer vote the stocks held by them in trust. To that extent the old centralization of management would be swiftly broken down. But in view of the large individual holdings of stocks by the eight liquidating trustees—the two Rockefellers, Archbold, Flagler, Benjamin Brewster, W. H. Tilford, O. B. Jennings, and H. H. Rogers—and in view of the close community of interest long since established among the various companies, would this action have any practical effect? The holders of trust certificates were expected to give up their paper, and accept stock in the constituent companies of the defunct trust. But would they consent to do so?

Obviously, if each certificate-holder were given the value of his certificates in stock of *one* company, so that John Doe received shares in one corporation and Richard Roe shares in another, the return to competition would be facilitated. But could this be equitably arranged? For ten years certificates had been widely bought and sold. The buyers believed they were getting part-ownership in *all* constituent companies. If John Doe were now assigned a share in the Standard Oil of Ohio, while Richard Roe got shares in the Standard of New Jersey, they would undoubtedly protest that they did not want holdings in these particular companies; that the appraisal was incorrect; and that they were being cheated. In fact, not only protests but legal resistance would be certain. Dodd hastened to announce that each certificate-holder would get a carefully proportioned share in each of the twenty component companies. (Forty companies had originally been parties to the trust agreement, but only twenty were now controlled by the trustees.)[31] Any

[30]S. C. T. Dodd, *Memoirs*, 30.

[31]*Industrial Commission Hearings, 1899,* Vol. I, 301. The maximum number of companies in the combination at one time was 84. Prior to the dissolution the stocks of 64 had been transferred to the remaining 20; for example, 23 to

other mode of distribution would in fact be impracticable and un-just. Each man would get a part of the omelette, not a bit of some original egg![32]

The eight trustees therefore issued to each certificate-holder a so-called assignment of legal title in the stock of all the twenty companies. The document given to Rockefeller (No. A 365) was typical. It recited that "Whereas John D. Rockefeller is the owner of 256,854/972,500 of the amount of corporate stocks held by the trustees of the Standard Oil Trust in each of the several corporations whose stocks were held by such trust on the 1st day of July, 1892," and whereas he had surrendered his trust certificates for this amount, the trustees "do hereby assign and transfer to John D. Rockefeller and his assigns the legal title to the aforesaid amount of the said stocks and authorize the proper officers of the said corporations to transfer upon their books and to issue corporate certificates for the required amount of their respective capital stocks. . . ."[33] The several companies were to issue stock certificates for whole shares, and scrip for fractions of shares. Dodd was able to assure the stock-holders: "Your interests will be the same as now. The various corporations will continue to do the same business as heretofore, and your proportion of the earnings will not be changed."

What thereupon happened was both simple and natural. Within a short time after the dissolution, the holders of a majority of the trust certificates surrendered these papers to the trustees, and received assignments of legal title to stock and scrip in the twenty companies. They presented these assignments and obtained a *pro rata* share of the stocks. Rockefeller and the other seven trustees all did this. But *the total number of certificate-holders* who did so was very small. The large owners took action, but the little fellows did not. Sixteen or seventeen men, including the eight trustees, held more than half of the 972,500 shares in the trust. Nearly 1600 men and women held comparatively small amounts, and the great ma-

the Standard of New Jersey, 11 to the Standard of New York, 11 to the Anglo-American Oil Company, and so on. See Frank B. Kellogg's argument before the Supreme Court, 1910, *Standard Oil of N. J., Appellant, vs. United States, Appellee, U. S.* 92.

[32]All this is covered in Walter F. Taylor, MS History of the Standard Oil; and there is a good short history in the *Report of the Commissioner of Corporations on the Petroleum Industry, Part I*, 76–84.

[33]*Standard Oil Trust Cases, Ohio*, 450.

jority of these refused to act. As Joseph H. Choate pregnantly said
in 1894: "There is no power that this company can exercise to
compel me and other indifferent certificate-holders, if you please,
to come forward and convert our trust certificates."

These hundreds of lesser investors continued to hold their trust
certificates; or they held liquidation certificates, as the papers issued
by the liquidating trustees in exchange for trust certificates were
called; or they held assignments of legal interest issued in exchange
for trust certificates or liquidation certificates. They did not, and
would not, take stock. At the end of the first year after the dissolution of the trust, 477,881 shares remained uncancelled. At the close
of the second, third, and fourth years the figure was precisely the
same—477,881.[34]

As Dodd says in his *Memoirs,* the stockholders bitterly disliked the
idea of dissolution, and were determined to prevent it from becoming a reality. The investors who held these trust certificates, liquidation certificates, or assignments of legal interest—all of which were
briskly traded in and passed from hand to hand—received their
dividends from the liquidating trustees just as prior to the dissolution they had received them from the trustees. In fact, the small
investor had the best of reasons for declining to give up his trust
certificate and accept stock in exchange; for refusing to surrender
his one piece of paper and take twenty pieces instead. His one piece
of paper was readily salable. But there was no ready market for the
stock of the twenty separate companies, and if he held such stock
his investment was frozen. Nor was there any way in which the
courts could compel the market to refuse to recognize the trust
certificate or liquidation certificate as the basic unit of trading, and
to begin trading in shares of the twenty separate companies. The
latter simply did not pass current. Between 1892 and 1899, writes
Taylor, "there was not a share of stock (leaving out of account
directors' qualifying shares) in any of the twenty companies transferred from one holder to another except as part of the equivalent
in stocks of the twenty companies in one or more Standard Oil
Trust certificates."

In effect, the trust still stood intact!

In a technical legal sense, the plan adopted for the dissolution

[34]*Ohio vs. Standard Oil Company,* 109.

of the trust literally carried out the decree of the Ohio Supreme Court. The complaint which Attorney-General Watson had made was that the Standard of Ohio had permitted its stock to be transferred to the trustees under the trust agreement and managed by them; the judgment of the Supreme Court had forbidden the company to enter into or perform the trust agreement. The dissolution plan literally complied with the judgment. It abolished the trust agreement entirely. It restored precisely the condition of affairs which had existed before the trust agreement of 1882 was drawn up. That is, it threw the Standard of Ohio back to the position it had occupied in 1879–92 under the old Keith, Vilas, and Chester trust agreement, when the ownership of the company's stock was entirely separate and independent from the ownership of the stock of the other companies.

The fact was, of course, that a technical compliance totally failed to meet the real wishes of court or public. Although the court decree had concerned only the *form* of the organization into which the Standard of Ohio had entered, the real reason which prompted the attorney-general and Supreme Court of Ohio to act lay in the *fact* of the combination. The form was a trifle; what Ohio and the country at large wished to attack was the substance of the great alliance of companies, and the substance remained.

For the management of the trust was not affected in the least. The great combination was still directed as completely as before by Rockefeller and his associates; "The ablest group of businessmen in the country," said the Philadelphia *Press*.[35] The same men who, as trustees under the old trust agreement, had elected themselves or their nominees directors of the various constituent companies, now as holders of the majority of the stock in each of these companies still chose themselves or their nominees as directors. Now as before—in fact, almost daily—they met and deliberated on the affairs of the vast aggregations of interests. They did so not as trustees, but as legal owners of a majority of the stock in the constituent companies. As they and the holders of the outstanding trust certificates continued each to have the same proportional interest in every one of the twenty companies as in the remaining nineteen, the whole Standard Oil business could still be governed as a single enterprise.

[35]March 22, 1892.

The monopolistic power of the organization was unbroken. If the government was to shatter it, that must be done by some far heavier blow than that struck by the Supreme Court of Ohio.

But could it be done at all? That was the burning question which the foes of monopoly faced as they looked to the future. As the first impetus of prosecutions in the States was lost, and as Richard Olney became attorney-general under Cleveland, the outlook was far from bright.

XXXIV

Citizen of New York

W E HAVE seen that in the late seventies the Rockefeller family began coming to New York just after Christmas, staying until early spring. Their first residence was the quiet, dignified Windsor Hotel at Fifth Avenue and Forty-sixth Street, the one great hostelry that the upper Avenue boasted; the home for a time of Andrew Carnegie and Edwin Booth. But, beginning in 1880 or 1881, the family arrived soon after Thanksgiving, and spent the entire winter at the Buckingham, a residential hotel on the site later taken by Saks' department store.[1] At first they ate in the hotel dining-room, but soon had their meals served in their own quarters. In early spring the family would return to Cleveland, where the two houses were kept in readiness for their use. The Euclid Avenue home was occupied for perhaps a fortnight each spring and fall, and used every Sunday, but Forest Hill was the principal Cleveland residence.

During the early eighties the better part of upper New York—that is, above Forty-second Street—was still a brownstone-and-brick residential area. Fifth and Madison Avenues were lined with substantial and handsome houses, above which peered the spires of St. Patrick's Cathedral and the Reformed Church. An atmosphere of quiet pervaded the district, for business had hardly begun to assail it. Columbia College still occupied its old-fashioned building at Madison and Forty-ninth; Rutgers Female Institute still stood not far distant on Fifth Avenue, a stark battlemented building with weeping willows in front. Below Forty-second Street the central area of the island, all the way down to Madison Square, was rapidly

[1] For a picture and description of the Buckingham see advertising columns, N. Y. *Times,* Oct. 28, 1894.

filling with hotels, theatres, and shops. Citizens had realized with a start the extent of the northward trend when in 1879 Augustin Daly built his new theatre near Thirtieth, and four years later the Metropolitan Opera House was opened with a gala performance. But the reaches above Bryant Park remained well outside the commercial maelstrom. Upper Fifth Avenue was becoming distinguished by a group of palatial residences, the most beautiful being the William K. Vanderbilt and the Cornelius Vanderbilt houses.[2]

By the beginning of 1884 Rockefeller had become a legal resident of New York. Comfortable as the Buckingham was, he regarded the hotel as ill-suited for family life, and looked about for a permanent home. He and his wife thought of buying the Fifth Avenue house later occupied by E. H. Harriman;[3] but that fall they determined upon the four-story-and-basement house at 4 West Fifty-fourth Street, just off the Avenue, paying a reputed price of $600,000. Solidly built of brownstone, it was sufficiently imposing to be called a mansion, though too tall, narrow, and gaunt-looking to be really handsome. At this time it was twenty years old, having been erected by William P. Williams in 1864-5. Unlike most city houses, it possessed ample yard space.[4] A photograph of 1866 shows that it then rose in isolated and ugly dignity; fronting north, it had on the west a lawn fifty feet wide, and on the east another of seventy-five feet, containing some young trees, a fountain, and a summer-house.[5] The house had been recently occupied by Mrs. Arabella Worsham, who that summer married the railroad magnate Collis P. Huntington, and the Rockefellers took it with her furniture, rugs, and hangings intact. Just to the south was the celebrated tract of land which elderly citizens still called the Elgin Gardens, the property which Columbia College had received in 1814 from Doctor Hosack, and which included the twelve acres of the present-day Rockefeller Center. Just opposite on the north was St. Luke's Hospital, with

---

[2]I. N. Phelps Stokes, *New York Past and Present: Its History and Landmarks,* 1524-1939. 48-50.

[3]Mr. John D. Rockefeller, Jr., to the author.

[4]Mr. John D. Rockefeller, Jr., has a letter written by Thomas E. Wallace, at the age of eighty-two, stating that his uncle, Adam H. Embeer, a masterbuilder, was in charge of the construction, and that the building went up about the same time as St. Luke's Hospital.

[5]This photograph is reproduced in the *Rockefeller Center Weekly,* Nov. 7, 1935.

wide and well-shaded grounds. As no high buildings stood near, the upper windows commanded spacious views on all sides.

The interior was as attractive as its exterior was plain.[6] On the first floor the visitor entered a handsome reception hall, with dark mahogany panelling and a large fireplace surmounted by a carved mantel. Nearly all the rest of the floor was occupied by three large rooms, which if necessary could be thrown together by sliding back the wide connecting doors. That on the front was the main living-room, perhaps twenty-five feet in width by forty in length, lighted by two tall windows on Fifty-fourth Street, and a third on the garden. The woodwork was rosewood, polished to resemble mahogany; the walls were covered with garnet-colored velvet brocade, and the furniture was massive. Another large fireplace gave opportunity for a blazing fire in winter. This room opened at the rear into a somewhat smaller apartment, decorated in the Moorish style and lighted by eastern windows. Still farther back lay the dining-room. The three apartments were often used together for church meetings and charitable gatherings, and a speaker standing in the doorway between the main room and Moorish room could be heard by several hundred guests. Behind the dining-room, with a southern exposure, lay the conservatory.

On the second floor was the large library, its windows facing north on Fifty-fourth Street and east toward Fifth Avenue. Well-filled bookcases, some good paintings (Rockefeller soon owned a Troyon, two Meissoniers, a Daubigny, a Rosa Bonheur, and other pictures of value),[7] and another huge fireplace gave it an air of comfort, and the family spent more time here than downstairs. Back of the library was Mrs. Rockefeller's dressing-room, cheerful with its light-colored inlaid wood and silk-covered walls. Still farther back was the bedroom which, with its heavy ebony furniture, is now preserved in the Museum of the City of New York as an interesting illustration of the period. Adjoining it was Rockefeller's dressing-room, where he was shaved every morning in an adjustable wicker-backed chair. A massive staircase of carved mahogany connected the two floors, and the landings were lighted by good stained-glass

[6]The house was demolished in 1936, and the site loaned to the Museum of Modern Art for an outdoor exhibition area.

[7]N. Y. *World*, Dec. 3, 1893, "Rockefeller at Home." William Rockefeller was credited with a larger art collection.

windows; the first of which, with three panels of Renaissance design, was called the "three sisters." There was also an elevator, which the occupants started and stopped by pulling ropes.

The third floor contained bedrooms and sitting-rooms, while on the fourth were the servants' quarters, and a suite which at a later date was used by John D. Rockefeller, Jr., as bedroom and sitting-room. From his northeast window the young man could look across Fifth Avenue to Madison, and when guests were expected sometimes watched them alight from the Madison Avenue street-car.[8] A few servants were quartered downstairs on the ground-floor level. The house as a whole was dignified, solid-looking, roomy, and comfortable. Its bright rosewood and mahogany woodwork, its fireplaces, and its many windows made it cheery. It had none of the pretentiousness of A. T. Stewart's gleaming white-marble mansion at the corner of Fifth Avenue and Thirty-fourth, or of the turreted Renaissance houses of the Vanderbilts; it boasted of no such private art gallery as August Belmont's or William H. Aspinwall's. It was not fitted for entertaining on a sumptuous scale. But it suited the Rockefellers precisely.

For the side yards Rockefeller found a unique use. He was always extremely fond of skating. His son recalls that in Cleveland he once got up a few minutes after midnight on a bitter Monday morning to direct his employees in flooding a pond; he would not let such work be done on Sunday, but he wished a smooth surface for the next day's sport. In New York he had the area beside and behind the house cemented over and surrounded by a curved coping. In freezing weather water was turned on, and the horseshoe-shaped space became an excellent rink. He, his children, and scores of friends delighted in it. The basement hallway was fitted up with boxes where guests kept their skates, and sometimes a hundred pairs lay there.[9] At night, under gleaming electric lights, the yard offered a gay scene; while early in the morning passers-by might see Rockefeller, in overcoat and silk hat, taking some sedate turns on the ice before he went down to work.

Still devoted to horses, he purchased from Flagler a stable on Fifty-fifth Street near Sixth Avenue, with a Scot named Alexander McLean in charge. The carriage room contained several light vehicles—road-wagon, brougham, cart, and victoria—and large plate-glass cases holding the coach and cart harness.[10] In the stable proper were five box-stalls and eight or ten open stalls. Rockefeller kept some of his horses in Cleveland, for they were too valuable to be driven over hard pavements; the others were taken back and forth each year. His favorite pair in New York were first "Magic" and "Enchantress," and later "Flash" and "Midnight," the two latter being able to cover a mile in 2:19½ and 2:18¼ respectively. A well-matched team of black geldings, they had sometimes trotted a quarter of a mile at Fleetwood in 33 seconds.[11] Two other horses were named "Hilton" and "Trifle," while a chestnut team was kept for Mrs. Rockefeller's landau. A great stable pet was the Yorkshire terrier "Rags," who could sometimes be seen taking a nap on the broad back of one of the carriage horses.

Rockefeller was one of the best of the many drivers of fast trotting horses in Central Park and on the roadways north of town. He liked to pick up a race on Seventh Avenue or the "Vanderbilt mile" north of Macomb's Dam Bridge with his brother William, or one of the Standard men—Flagler, E. T. Bedford, or Horace Hutchins. Whenever possible, he left his office early to drive before dark, and the children frequently waited at the stable. "Other drivers," states his son, "would often lose their tempers when horses broke or pulled hard; Father never. If a horse was excitable or difficult, he always kept his temper, and patiently, quietly worked with the animal until he steadied it. Frequently I have seen him driving at a very rapid pace through Central Park, in the middle of the roadway through two streams of traffic, pushing always a little to the left, as he explained to me, so as to open his way through, but keeping margin enough on his right so that if the approaching traffic did not swing over in time to let him through he would still have room enough to pass." His method of driving had a kinship with his procedure in business.

He was particularly fond of winter sleighing. A letter to his son early in 1888 exuberantly records: "Aunty and I went to the Harlem River with Flash and Midnight in a new cutter which

[10]See N. Y. *Herald*, "Horses that Live in Grand Style," Feb. 23, 1890. Before buying from Flagler, Rockefeller had a stable at 21 West 55th.
[11]See the N. Y. *Tribune* article, "An Old Roadhouse Gone," April 19, 1896. The writer needlessly remarks that Rockefeller paid no attention to roadhouses.

Rockefeller's four children: Bessie, Edith, Alta, and John.

Above: Rockefeller's father, William Avery Rockefeller, and his uncle, Egbert Rockefeller.
Below: John D. Rockefeller, Jr. (*right*), with a playmate at Forest Hill.

cost $300. Very extravagant I know but the sleighing is so good [I] could not resist the temptation to buy it and hope to get the worth of our money. I drove four times day before yesterday and three times yesterday making an aggregate in the two days of about eighty miles. Don't you think I am rather an enthusiastic youth?"[12] His relaxations were always those of a man of action.

From the beginning No. 4 West Fifty-fourth Street became a center of hospitality for church people, charitable workers, and groups of Standard Oil executives. Entertaining was restricted to these groups, for the house was never used for "society" affairs. Some of Rockefeller's associates have recalled the animated meetings there, and the gaiety with which he unbent. Mr. M. G. Vilas once came for breakfast with some other Standard men. They gathered at table while Rockefeller was detained elsewhere. When he entered he took the seat at the head of the board, looked about, and said: "Well, gentlemen, what do we have for breakfast this morning?" Archbold at once spoke up: "We have Baptist fish, Mr. Rockefeller." "Baptist fish?" echoed Rockefeller. "And what kind of fish is that?" "That," Archbold slyly replied, "is the kind of fish that doesn't stay good very long after it is taken out of the water."[13]

William Rockefeller, Henry M. Flagler, and Benjamin Brewster all lived literally within a stone's throw of Rockefeller on Fifth Avenue, and he could see them by taking a two-minute walk. Other Standard associates and many church friends were near. Adjoining Rockefeller's house on the Avenue, residences were presently erected for Seward Webb and Hamilton McKay Twombly, two highly cultivated men. Until near the end of the century the district was a true neighborhood.

II

Home, church, and office—these were the three poles about which Rockefeller's life in the eighties revolved. He had three homes, the two in Cleveland and one in New York; he had two churches, the Fifth Avenue and the Euclid Avenue Baptist Churches; and he had two offices, the Standard Block in Cleveland, and 26 Broadway in New York. While his life was crowded with labor and responsibility, he tried to keep its routine simple. He cared nothing for receptions

[12]Jan. 20, 1888; Rockefeller Papers. [13]Mr. Vilas gave me this story in 1936.

and dinners, never went to the theatre, and heard most of his music at home. Outdoor pastimes furnished his principal recreation; to driving, skating, and swimming he added systematic horseback riding before 1890, and bicycling soon afterward.

The removal to Forest Hill for the summer was the pleasantest event of the year for the family. It opened to the children a vista of glorious play, and to Mrs. Rockefeller long hours out of doors. To Rockefeller himself Forest Hill meant exercise, relaxation, and increased vitality, and his attachment to the place underwent no diminution for a quarter of a century. "Oh, I like Forest Hill much better than any other home!" he used to exclaim.[14] Here he spent some of the most active days of his life. He remodelled the house, improved his half-mile race track, built an artificial lake, enlarged the stables, and constructed many miles of drives and walks. Moreover, in the decade from 1884 to 1894 he was more his children's companion than ever before or after.

They were all old enough to share a busy outdoor life with him. From John, who was ten at the beginning of the period, to Bessie, who was eighteen, they all spent much time with "Father," for he encouraged their companionship. He drove downtown every morning, and usually returned at lunch to spend the remainder of the day. "I have a definite and vivid recollection," writes John D. Rockefeller, Jr., "of his spending much time with us children in the summers, driving. He used to drive a pair of trotting-horses in a light, two-seated surrey that would take three beside himself, and in this carriage we all of us had long drives with him about the country; he used also to take a buggy for two which he drove a great deal. I recall vividly Father walking with us children in the woods, frequently and year after year. I recall his teaching us to row on the little lake, his teaching us to swim, and his going often with us to the lake for these purposes. . . . I recall no time during my early days, from let us say 1880 to 1888, when Father was not our frequent and daily companion in these outdoor occupations."[15]

[14]So Mr. H. D. Sims, one of Rockefeller's secretaries, told me Nov. 24, 1936.
[15]John D. Rockefeller, Jr., to the author. In the family circle he had many gay and boyish ways. He would frequently sing at table. He liked to balance a cracker on his nose, and snapping it into the air, catch it in his mouth. He would also balance plates on his nose; and his nieces record how often they feared for Mrs. Rockefeller's best porcelain!

Rockefeller emphatically expressed his regret that he did not have more leisure for his son and three daughters. And he was not only a companion in their sports, but an earnest guide in more sober occupations. Alta and John were encouraged to do their part in developing the grounds. They were given several men to help them construct paths through the woods, and John soon learned a good deal about landscape design. By 1890 he had taken much of the burden of supervising Forest Hill from his father's shoulders, and was looking after the tree-planting, road-building, and upkeep of the grounds. All of the children when small worked in the vegetable garden, where each had a small crop. John one day ran into a hornet's nest; "I was so badly stung," he writes, "that I was not interested to resume gardening as a career." They all pulled weeds from the lawn at a penny for ten weeds, while as John grew older he broke stones for the road, and chopped wood at fifteen cents an hour.

On the circular half-mile course at Forest Hill, a fast track, Rockefeller drove whenever he did not have time for the country roads. Here also he taught the children to ride, first on Welsh and Shetland ponies, and later on horses.[16] For a time in middle life his doctor prescribed horseback riding. His son recalls watching him trot from the Euclid Avenue home to Forest Hill behind the family carriage, his spirited horse rearing and curveting without disturbing him in the slightest. Another sport which he enjoyed with the children as they grew older was bicycling. On moonlight nights they often went out in a body on the Forest Hill footpaths and roads. The leader, tying a handkerchief to his seat, would seek the most difficult paths, testing the skill of the others in following the winding course. Sometimes the glimmering moonlight would lead them off the road, and the entire party would be spilled in a delighted heap. For a time Rockefeller made a standing offer that to all Forest Hill guests who learned to ride on the place he would give a bicycle. In all his amusements he showed an unconventional spirit. He constructed ingenious and unorthodox devices to keep the youngsters afloat while learning to swim. On hot summer days he would swim around the lake, nearly a mile, with his straw hat on his head to

[16]A letter of the spring of 1882 shows that Rockefeller was then negotiating for a pony "for a little boy of seven years of age. Something lazy and surely safe." To A. S. Odell, April 21, 1882; Rockefeller Papers.

keep it cool.[17] His son also remembers how they would go out together to test the thickness of the ice for skating. As the water was deep, they took long narrow boards under their arms to hold them up if they broke through. "That was characteristic of Father," writes the son. "He always took the utmost care to examine any project thoroughly; then when convinced it was safe, put it through without any further question."[18]

Altogether it was a gay and happy family. Indoors they often played household games at night, and Rockefeller entered into blind-man's buff with all the zest of Bob Cratchit, giving the sport excitement by his quick and daring lunges. Once in the Euclid Avenue house he ran full tilt into a doorway, cutting his forehead. Doctor H. F. Biggar, a homeopathic physician, was summoned to take some stitches, and became not only the family physician, but one of Rockefeller's favorite companions.[19] The children were kept assiduously at their practice on musical instruments, played in the Sunday school orchestra in Cleveland, and gave frequent home concerts.[20] Family prayers were held at 7:30 sharp every day. Then they all trooped in to breakfast, where each member of the circle was expected to read from any letter of general interest. As the children grew older they were encouraged to bring in their friends for meals, which were merry and talkative occasions.

All home activities were carried on with a careful eye to character-building. Once Rockefeller proposed to buy tricycles for all the youngsters. "No," demurred his wife, "we will just buy one for all of them. If they have just one they will learn to give up to each other." The parents set an example of courtesy and patience in their own behavior. "I cannot remember ever having heard the voices of either Father or Mother raised in anger or complaint in speaking to any of us children," says John D. Rockefeller, Jr. No coddling was permitted. The son, to improve his health, spent parts of two winters in his teens (apparently 1887–88 and 1888–89) at

[17]Inglis, Conversations with Rockefeller.
[18]Memorandum by John D. Rockefeller, Jr.
[19]John D. Rockefeller, Jr., to the author. Doctor Biggar published in 1908 a pamphlet called "Loiterings in Europe with Mr. J. H. Wade, Colonel William Edwards, Senator H. B. Payne, Summer 1885." It throws light on his character; a slow, humorous, likeable man.
[20]See N. Y. Herald, June 9, 1895, on the place of music in the Rockefeller home.

Forest Hill in outdoor work. He rose early, and labored as hard as the men on the estate chopping wood, burning brush, and doing odd jobs. Rockefeller also set an example of courage. "I have never known Father to show the slightest fear, either physical or moral," writes his son. "I remember one fall evening in Cleveland we were at supper when we heard the burglar alarm ring upstairs and a maid called down that there was a burglar in one of the bedrooms. Father started at once for the back door to intercept the burglar in his flight. As he went out he called, 'Where is my revolver?' The burglar slid down a pillar and escaped. I also recall a time when I was about fifteen years of age when there was much anarchistic agitation in New York, accompanied by many threats of violence to Father. I was going to Cleveland at the time, and as Father drove me to the station I begged him to get adequate protection for himself. 'Have no anxiety, John,' he said. 'I can take care of myself. If any man were foolish enough to attack me, it would go hard with him.'"

Rockefeller's personal tastes remained for the most part extremely simple. He took no interest in clothes, and though he dressed neatly, his family found difficulty in getting him to renew his suits before they became shiny. He did at one time buy great numbers of shoes in an effort to find comfortable footwear, finally hitting upon a shoe with a cork inner sole. When his son gave him a handsome fur coat, he wore it once or twice, sent it to storage, and finally gave it back to the son. He much preferred a plain cloth coat, with perhaps a sweater underneath for driving on very cold days. At table he always ate sparingly; he disliked hot dishes, and would usually wait for the food to cool, telling his family and guests to go right along with the meal while he talked. One of the dishes of which he was fondest was bread and milk, a fact which gave rise to queer stories about his supposed dyspepsia—though except for a few years in the early nineties his digestion was excellent. He was also fond of eating an apple just before he went to bed, and his children remember that for years he used to keep a paper sack of them on the sill outside his bedroom window. The cuisine of the household was always plain; they had no French chef or rich foods.

The Rockefellers inculcated in each child the obligation to give to church and charities, and these gifts were made from the youngsters' own earnings. In time the children cast their eyes about and observed that many of their youthful friends did less work and had more money than they. This was true, for example, of William Rockefeller's children. "We felt we were in a terrible plight compared with them!" said John D. Rockefeller, Jr., afterward. But their upbringing gave them a simple, wholesome attitude toward life, and a clear idea of the value of money.

Their training left them for years naïvely unaware of the importance of their father in the outside world—for Rockefeller himself said nothing to indicate it. Soon after the family removed to New York, Bessie went with some Vassar classmates to select furniture for a college clubroom. They made a choice, but did not have money enough to pay for it. The girls suggested that the dealer send the furniture, and they would mail him the money. He declined, but remarked that if they knew a New York businessman who would vouch for them, the shipment could be arranged. "My father is in business," spoke up Bessie. "He will vouch for us." "And who is your father?" inquired the dealer. "His name is Mr. Rockefeller," said the girl innocently. "John D. Rockefeller; he is in the oil business." The merchant gasped and looked at her queerly. "John D. Rockefeller your father!" he exclaimed. He ordered the furniture packed and shipped immediately. Bessie was unaware that the name had some magic quality, and thinking that he had changed his mind out of kindness, thanked him prettily![21]

When John D. Rockefeller, Jr., grew up and had children of his own, he instituted the same discipline. One of his sons was becoming fairly well-grown when he one day admired a handsome boat that a young friend of wealthy family had bought. He was frankly envious. "Get one for yourself," suggested the friend. "Why don't you have your father buy it?" The son rebuked the proposed extravagance with asperity. "Who do you think we are?" he demanded. "Vanderbilts?"

The established schedule of the family, which varied little from year to year, kept them in New York from middle or late October for about seven months. Late May usually saw them in the Euclid Avenue house, where they remained for several weeks. Then they went to Forest Hill for the summer, coming back to the Euclid Avenue house in the fall for another fortnight. These movings were

[21]See McLaurin, *Sketches in Crude Oil*, 368, 369, for one version.

formidable affairs for Mrs. Rockefeller, but her husband seems to have given them little attention. The son later recalled the pleasant excitement that attended the shift from the Euclid Avenue place to the hilltop estate. "It was quite an undertaking. I can see the old spring wagon, first loaded with trunks, and then making another trip with boxes, packages, violins, and nondescript personal effects which the various members of the family wanted to have moved and could not conveniently carry. There was always a big box called a 'book box' which from the time I was about twelve I usually packed. This carried books, small boxes, music, and other odds and ends that could be easily lost or mislaid, and that needed protection in transit." This fragmentary picture indicates the careful organization which governed household affairs, and the useful part each child was given to play in the family activity.

Only one of Rockefeller's discoverable letters contains any account of his life at Forest Hill, but that is written with evident zest. It was sent to his mother, who had remained with William in New York, under date of June 8, 1895:[22]

I hope you will not judge us harshly for not writing before. It was quite an undertaking to close up the house in New York, and do all the other things connected with the change and opening of our home here, which by the bye, we find as neat as wax. The girls did themselves credit, and we were very much gratified. The house seems very inviting and pleasant, and the lawn is in good condition. We are all now well established and settled. Uncle Rudd [husband of Rockefeller's sister Mary] took tea with us last night, and spent the evening. . . . Frank has not yet returned. Had some delay on account of changes in his help just before the time he decided to leave Kansas. Forest Hill is looking very beautiful; trees are growing; the lake was full of water; we let out some to repair the banks. William reports Mary leaves tomorrow with the children for Vermont. . . .

I shall leave for New York next Monday and see you during the week. I return Friday night with Bessie and the other girls. Many friends here [are] inquiring after you and would be very happy to see you. Your rooms at Forest Hill seem very lonesome, and we hope you will not permit them to remain vacant all the summer. The robins already begin to inquire for you, and we can have the whole lawn full if you will only come back to greet them.

We have great quantities of wild strawberries. Many more than ever before. I know you would enjoy picking them. . . .

[22]Rockefeller Papers.

III

As the years passed they brought changes in the family circle. We have seen that Rockefeller's sister Lucy died in 1878. She had been closer to her brother than any of the other children; she had a singularly serene, sweet, well-balanced personality, and to his last years Rockefeller still spoke of her with evident emotion. Her husband, Pierson D. Briggs, who had charge of the Standard's purchasing division in Cleveland, remained a great favorite with the family. He came frequently to the Euclid Avenue house and Forest Hill, always bringing John and his sisters some small gift.[23] Mrs. Rockefeller's father, Harvey B. Spelman, died in the fall of 1881 in Cleveland, and thereafter Mrs. Spelman spent much time with her daughter. She was a vigorous, well-read, and interesting woman, still strongly concerned with temperance and a devoted worker for the W. C. T. U. Because of her feeling, and that of Mr. and Mrs. Rockefeller themselves, all the Rockefeller children joined the Loyal Legion temperance society in their youth, and all signed a total abstinence pledge.

Rockefeller's mother during the later 1880's divided her time among the children. Most of the year she was with Mrs. William C. Rudd at 33 Cheshire Street in Cleveland; but she visited Frank, Will, and John impartially—keenly interested in their life, always serene, and as deeply religious as ever. We have a letter which she wrote her grandson from the Cheshire Street house on March 20, 1886. Enclosed with it was a note from William Avery Rockefeller dated March 10, but bearing no place-name, and containing no clue as to his whereabouts. It is worth quoting in full, for it reveals the old gentleman as vigorous and high-spirited as ever:[24]

Mr. J. R. Jun   10th March, 1886.

Sir. I have bought a small rifle for M. Wm. R. Jun & it shoots nicely at 40 rods. I will visit you all at Forest Hill in July if all is well &c & if Wm. R. Junior comes up there you & I will show him What shooting is I never shall forget the pleasant hours we spent at Forest Hill—& your beautiful shooting. Please write me a long letter giving me all the news and hand it to Grand Ma Mrs. E. R & she will mail it with hers dont fail to write me at once   Very truly yours
                                                    Grand Pa.

[23]John D. Rockefeller, Jr., to the author.   [24]Rockefeller Papers.

On the back of the note the grandmother added her own injunction: "Johnnie if you wish to write a letter to Grandpa send it by Aunt Helen to me and I will send it to him." Already William Avery Rockefeller had given John a .22-caliber rifle and had taught him to fix a rest, sight carefully, and shoot straight.

Grandmother Rockefeller died at William's house on Fifth Avenue, March 28, 1889, in her seventy-sixth year. The two sons, John and William, that same day sent identic notes, signed by both, to all close relatives. "She had not felt as well as usual for the last four or five months," they recorded, "although she had kept about. She took to her bed some two weeks since, and gradually failed, until Tuesday morning, when she had a slight stroke of paralysis, which left her right side completely paralyzed. She could not speak to us since the stroke, but was conscious until the last, and very peaceful and resigned. She knew us all and did all her strength would permit to show her affection, appreciation, and Christian resignation. This peaceful death will leave a lasting impression upon us all. It will be treasured as one of the beautiful memories of a lifetime. We go with her remains to her home in Cleveland tomorrow, and she will be buried there on Sunday in the Lake View Cemetery, where the other members of our family have been laid. . . ."[25] Funeral services were held in the Euclid Avenue house, and the sons acted as pallbearers; but her husband was not present.

Though William Avery Rockefeller occasionally came to New York, his movements were unpredictable. His long absences in the West must have troubled his oldest son. He was gone for months and even years at a time, one explanation being that his asthma required a dry Western climate; one Standard official later thought that he spent much time in New Mexico, and it is not impossible. Nothing was impossible to this adventurous and roving spirit. He was also very fond of Frank's large and finely equipped ranch in Kansas. Early in 1885 he visited the city, for an autograph-book which John D. Rockefeller, Jr., had acquired bears evidence of the sturdy old man's presence. Under date of February 28 it carries a bold entry from his septuagenarian hand. Characteristically, he did not write a moral precept—as his son had done in 1883, penning the injunction: "Dare to be true. Papa."—but set down a forthright

[25]Copy supplied by the Van Duyne family of Moravia, N. Y.

assertion of his identity. "I was born in Ancrum Duches County New York on the 13th day of Nov. 1810—William A. Rockefeller." One can still see the flourish with which he wrote the line. Incidentally, this declaration contradicts the oft-repeated statement that he was born at Granger, N. Y., not far from Ancram.

One of the last recorded visits of William Avery Rockefeller to the metropolis was in the fall of 1890. He was as vigorous as ever, talking enthusiastically of hunting and outdoor adventure in the West. One of the Standard attorneys was much impressed by his physical strength, hearty sociability, and absolute independence of demeanor.[26] His brother Egbert came down from Richford to see him; and John D. Rockefeller, Jr., writing his sister Bessie, told how much they all liked the two upstanding old men:[27]

We so enjoyed seeing Grandfather; he is just eighty years old, but as jolly and entertaining as can be, and as he lives in the West we only see him once in every two or three years. Thursday afternoon Mother came home from Worcester, where she had been for ten days. . . . That same afternoon Grandfather and Uncle Bert came to stay with us for a few days.

Uncle is a farmer from Owego, New York, and has only been to the city once, and then on business, so that he knew nothing about the life that is led here, and he has been much interested to ride in the park and see all the fine carriages and horses besides the many other sights of interest to one accustomed only to country life. He is such a dear, simpleminded old man, and so appreciative of anything done for him that it is a great pleasure to make his visit as enjoyable as possible. Grandfather said to me the other day when we were driving together, "Uncle Bert is so happily disappointed in your family and Uncle Will's." I said why how do you mean. "Well," he said, "he told me that he supposed you would all be stiff and high-minded and hardly pay any attention to an old country man like him, and he is so delighted to find you all so social and entertaining. And," he said, "he does enjoy everything he sees here so much. Why, he talks to me until nearly eleven o'clock every night, telling me all about it." This morning Uncle went to church with us and on the way we stopped in at the cathedral that he might see what a fine building it is. When we came out he said, "Well, that do beat all I ever see," and so with everything he sees.

The three daughters were given their early education at home. Bessie, the oldest, then went directly to a seminary founded and administered at Rye, N. Y., by the brilliant Mrs. Life, formerly

[26]Mr. George Welwood Murray to the author.
[27]Oct. 18, 1890; Rockefeller Papers.

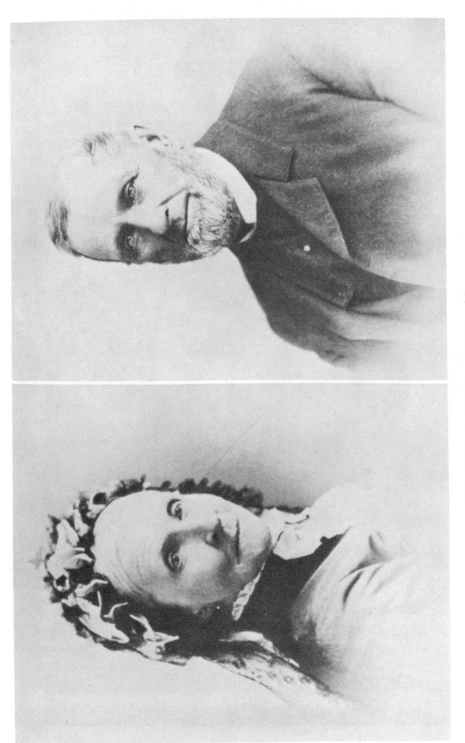

John D. Rockefeller's parents in old age.

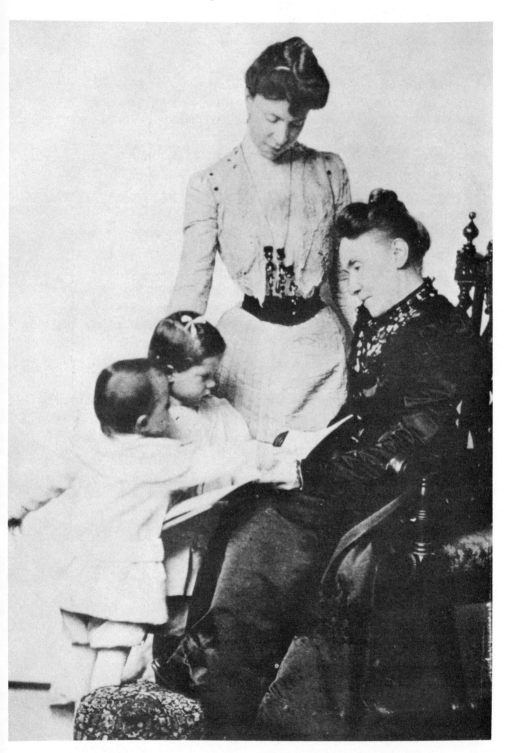

Mrs. John D. Rockefeller with Edith Rockefeller McCormick
and her two children.

Susan LaMonte of Owego—the Rye Female Seminary, long one of the best-known and most successful schools of its kind in America. It drew pupils from far and near. Among Bessie's schoolmates were her cousins, the daughters of William Rockefeller and Mr. Briggs. After graduation she took her degree at Vassar. Alta and Edith were first trained by governesses, then attended Miss Nott's private classes in New York, and finally went to the Rye Seminary. At week ends the three girls often brought schoolmates down to the West Fifty-fourth Street house, which was given a new liveliness by the gay young people.

Bessie was the first to marry. An old friendship subsisted between the Rockefeller family and that of Doctor Augustus H. Strong, a former Cleveland minister who had become head of the Rochester Theological Seminary. As a young man Charles A. Strong visited Forest Hill. John D. Rockefeller, Jr., recalls him sitting in the crotch of a beech tree, reading the "Bab Ballads" to the Rockefeller children beneath, while all burst into frequent fits of laughter. A warm attachment grew up between him and Bessie, and on March 22, 1889, they were married at the West Fifty-fourth Street house before about three hundred guests. Alta and Edith acted as brides-maids, and a reception and dinner at Delmonico's followed.[28] Young Strong, who had been teaching philosophy at Bryn Mawr, wished to complete his studies abroad; and next day the couple sailed for Europe—the bride, Lucy Spelman wrote, carrying "a face as bright as the sun above her."[29]

Alta, who had inherited her father's gift for organization, became deeply interested in various charities. It has sometimes been said that she was born deaf;[30] actually, the hearing of one ear was slightly affected by an attack of scarlet fever, which at the age of eight or nine she caught from her brother. The disability was slight, and she mastered the knack of turning her head so quickly toward any one who spoke that few were conscious of it. She played the piano well and sang with faultless tone. Later, in Carlsbad, she was partially cured. In Cleveland she founded a settlement house in the Italian quarter of the east side, not far from Forest Hill. Her father supplied

[28]The wedding is described in the N. Y. *Herald, Tribune,* March 23, 1889.
[29]Lucy Spelman to the Reverend Mr. Dixon, March 31, 1889.
[30]So John T. Flynn states in *God's Gold,* 270.

funds, while she gave the hard work which made "Alta House" a genuine success.[31] She did a good deal of reading and other work at St. Luke's Hospital, while she also managed a remarkably efficient sewing-school for girls, first on Forty-seventh and later Fiftieth Street, using volunteer teachers. In both the Cleveland and New York churches, too, she was indefatigable, teaching Sunday school classes with marked success. Edith's interests, by contrast, were linguistic, artistic, and musical.

Rockefeller decided that his son should be taught not by tutors but in schools where the boy would rub shoulders with others of his own age. The lad attended four different schools, the last of which was founded by Rockefeller and his brother William—the Browning School.[32] Browning was a gifted teacher who had been training a group of boys which included V. Everit Macy, Albert Herter, and Tracy Dows. Quarters were taken first at Fifth Avenue and Forty-fifth, and later at 29 West Fifty-fifth, and a number of John's associates were brought in. Among the pupils were Everett Colby, his older brother Howard Colby, William's youngest son, Percy, and the sons of B. M. Hawks, superintendent of William's estate at Greenwich, Conn. Characteristically, William tactfully but firmly arranged that the two last young men should later repay him the cost of their schooling. "They ought to have a sense of the value of what they were getting," he told Hawks. "I will make a formal compact with them. Probably I shall never ask them for the money, but I want them to realize that schooling is expensive." Rockefeller likewise gave his son a sense of the importance of school. No study was allowed on Sunday, and sometimes the boy rose long before dawn on Monday to finish his lessons. "School work did not come easy to me," he said later, "and I was determined to do the best I could. Father never expected more than that, but he did expect *that*. Whatever my marks, even if I was far from the head of the class, I was never censured if I had done my best." At nineteen, John finished his preparatory work and entered Brown.

[31]Described in the N. Y. *Herald*, Feb. 25, 1894.
[32]A memorandum by Mr. John D. Rockefeller, Jr., Feb. 15, 1937, fully describes his schooling. He pays a warm tribute to Mr. Browning's personality. After the first year the school had twenty-five more boys, and it is still in existence.

IV

Outside his home, Rockefeller continued to find in the church his principal source of intellectual stimulus and spiritual refreshment. In the Fifth Avenue congregation he immediately became a principal figure. Indeed, he was now one of the leading Baptists of the country, and acquainted with all the principal educators and ministers in a denomination then surprisingly rich in talent. The Fifty-fourth Street house was seldom without some clerical guest. In Cleveland, the Reverend Mr. George T. Dowling served as pastor of Rockefeller's church from 1877 to 1888, when he was succeeded by the Reverend L. A. Crandall; both earnest and hardworking rather than brilliant. The minister of the Fifth Avenue Church when Rockefeller settled in New York was Thomas Armitage, an Englishman by birth, who served the congregation more than forty years. The sermons of these men were an important part of Rockefeller's mental nutriment. He still had no taste for books, though Mrs. Rockefeller, her sister, and the children read a great deal, and he sometimes listened. Only once in his letters does he touch a literary note, writing his son from Forest Hill in the fall of 1892: "Mother and I are plodding on peacefully, sleeping and eating quite well; reading books and trying to store our minds with useful knowledge."[33] But, as he wrote a friend, he did get ideas and ideals from sermons: "I greatly enjoy the many noble and talented men we have in the ministry, and need their good preaching to wind me up, like an old clock, once or twice a week."[34]

His Christianity remained that of the primitive church in that the congregation was always a fellowship to him. In the fall of 1888 he lingered in Cleveland later than usual. An important negotiation affecting the Tidewater Pipe-Line and Josiah Lombard's refinery was before the Executive Committee in New York; S. C. T. Dodd was worried by anti-trust bills; William Rockefeller was ill—but still he stayed on. A letter to Archbold gave his reasons.[35] "I have a large company of Sunday school workers at my house tomorrow night, and Thursday afternoon was going to attend a meeting in reference

[33]Nov. 7, 1892; Rockefeller Papers.
[34]To Doctor J. E. Clough, June 13, 1885; Rockefeller Papers.
[35]Sept. 25, 1888; Rockefeller Papers.

to establishing a home for aged people; and Sunday is the last of eleven years' pastorate of Rev. Dowling—hence my desire to remain over, if it will not be to the inconvenience of our affairs." In Cleveland, Rockefeller continued to act as Sunday school superintendent, and excerpts from his discourses sometimes got into the papers. Mrs. Rockefeller continued to supervise the infant department. Both parents and children were regular attendants at the Friday night prayer-meetings, and the whole family made a point of going to the Sunday school picnic.[36] Once each summer all the Sunday school teachers came out to Forest Hill; some drove about the estate, some walked, some rowed, they had dinner together, and afterward they listened to good music.

More and more time had to be devoted by Rockefeller to his philanthropies, which were becoming extensive. In 1885 he gave away more than $155,000; in 1887 he gave $284,116; and in 1891 his benefactions exceeded a half million dollars, while in 1892 they aggregated $1,353,520. The range covered by his gifts was large, with education receiving more and more emphasis. Hardly a Baptist college in the land failed to get assistance, while he was giving to numerous other colleges, including Barnard and Vassar. He insisted with increasing rigidity upon the two principles which we have already defined: that he would not give alone, but would expect others to do something toward matching his gifts, and that he would never give until he had been convinced that the money would be used economically and efficiently. His benefactions should stimulate the spirit of philanthropy in others, not repress it, and they should go to assist organizations that had vitality, not to bolster dying causes. In the spring of 1886 a number of Baptist leaders undertook to raise money for foreign missions by a drive among Sunday school students. Rockefeller expressed warm approval of the movement because it would stimulate the interest of Sunday school members, and would add to the resources of a missionary effort already sturdily organized. The great difficulty in such work, he wrote, "is that many individuals and churches content themselves with giving comparatively little or nothing, and this is owing, in

---

[36]Professor O. J. Campbell of Columbia University used as a small boy to attend these picnics.

part, I assume, to a lack of information in reference to the great needs."[37] At the same time he was interested in a *concerted* effort to raise $150,000 for home missions. If all assisted, he declared, success would be easy. "Poor as the Baptist denomination is, I think our people will not consent to the society going to protest yet. Put me down for $30,000."

Pledging $1000 a year for a missionary chapel, he asserted that he would not help unless success was assured, and would therefore expect "all who pledge to pay as they are called on." When his mother sent him a plea from a cousin whom he did not know, his refusal was emphatic. "I decided [I] would not comply with the request contained in it. I want to know surely, in giving, that I am putting money where it will do the most good." By 1877 his giving was already carefully budgeted. Replying to a request from Chauncey M. Depew for a gift to the Hahnemann Hospital in New York, he asked that the committee "pass me by in this instance, as I have just made pledges to other hospitals of some $25,000 or $30,000."[38] In all his personal charities, he insisted that the only true rule was to help people to help themselves. Sending a poor young man $50, he asked for a note, adding: "It will be injurious for him to receive from others what he can in any way secure for himself by his own efforts."[39] And a visit to a famous New York institution elicited a dubious verdict:

"We all went to the Five Points House of Industry on Thanksgiving Day, and were much interested. One feature, however, we decidedly objected to, but I have not had sufficient time to confer with the managers and get their idea of the policy of feeding all the tramps that come. My impression is that they only do it once a year. I would give them work and make them earn their food."

It is interesting to note that Rockefeller objected strongly to church fairs and other undignified methods of raising funds. But he believed that public dinners for gaining pledges might be effective. "The English people succeed well in getting subscriptions at such dinners," he wrote, "and I don't know why we should not."

[37]To A. T. Osborne, March 3, 1886; Rockefeller Papers.
[38]May 16, 1887; Rockefeller Papers.
[39]To Amy L. Lyon, March 31, 1887; Rockefeller Papers.

v

During the eighties Rockefeller began to take time to travel
widely. One of his earliest journeys was to Florida, with Henry M.
Flagler, in or about the winter of 1883. Rumors flew in the wake
of the two men, who were said to have millions for good Florida
investments. Doctor Andrew Anderson of St. Augustine arranged
that they should spend some time at his home, and met them in
Jacksonville, then the railhead. They went aboard the steamboat
Sylvan Glen on St. John's River, took another boat, the *John Syl-
vester,* up to Piccolata Landing, and thence travelled by a hissing
little peanut-roaster train to St. Augustine. That evening, sitting
before a warm coal fire in Anderson's house, they discussed the
prospects of Florida with him and his friend George P. Lorillard.
It was a momentous visit, for the golden cloud that floated about
Flagler's head was in due time to condense in a shower of millions
upon Florida soil. In 1884 the Rockefeller family, accompanied by
Doctor Biggar of Cleveland and Doctor Judson of New York (son
of the great missionary Adoniram Judson), visited California. Two
years later, in the summer of 1886, Rockefeller took his whole family
west to the Yellowstone, visiting Chicago, Milwaukee, Minneapolis,
and St. Paul on the way. And in 1888 a family party of twelve,
including Doctor Biggar and President Strong of the Rochester
Theological Seminary, went to Europe for three months. Visiting
Italy, Switzerland, France, and England, they met no celebrities,
but devoted long hours every day to sightseeing.

Early in this tour Rockefeller became convinced that the courier
whom he had engaged before going abroad was cheating him outrageously. After he had accumulated sufficient evidence, he said
to the man, very mildly and pleasantly: "Hereafter I will pay all the
bills." The courier was taken aback. "In that case, Mr. Rockefeller,
you will have no further need for my services," he curtly remarked—
thinking to bluff Rockefeller. But the millionaire, without abating
his friendliness of manner, accepted the resignation on the spot,
paying the man in full, and obtaining a release for the unexpired
period for which he had been engaged.

"After that," writes John D. Rockefeller, Jr., "how hard Father
worked in managing the party! I can see him now going over the

long French bills, studying each item, many of them being unintelligible to him. 'Poulets!' he would exclaim, 'what are poulets, John?' Or again, 'Bougies, bougies—what in the world is a bougie?' And so on down the bill. Father was never willing to pay a bill which he did not know to be correct in all of its items. Such care in small things might seem penurious to some people, yet to him it was the working out of a life principle." It might be added that it was an object-lesson to the children whom Rockefeller was training so patiently and carefully.

Some additional reminiscences of Rockefeller on this trip are furnished by the Reverend Doctor John H. Eager, who was in charge of a Baptist mission in Rome.[40] He had met Rockefeller in New York, and obtained a gift from him. When the magnate arrived in Rome, Mr. Eager expected him to attend one of the large English churches. Instead, the family took their places the first Sunday with the Italian congregation, and listened with edification to the spirited rendering which the Italians gave to various Moody and Sankey hymns. Taking tea with Doctor Eager, Rockefeller talked·at length with him and the Waldensian pastor of one of the Baptist churches in Rome; and learning that the latter was bringing up a large family on three hundred lira a month, gave him a sum which, says Doctor Eager, the pastor remembered gratefully all his life. But however generous with his gifts, Rockefeller was careful in managing the party. Doctor Eager goes on:

The last day the Rockefellers were in Rome I called at the hotel to say good-by. They had their meals in their own private dining-room, and settled their bill at the close of the week. When I arrived they were just beginning to examine the last week's account. Some one remarked, "They have two chickens down here for Thursday dinner, but we had only one." After a brief pause some one else replied, "No, you are mistaken; I am sure that we had two chickens." Mr. Rockefeller listened for a while to the discussion, and then said quietly: "I can settle that very easily. John, did you have a chicken leg?" "Yes." "Alta, did you have a chicken leg?" "Yes." "Well, Mother, I think I remember that you had one. Is that right?" "Yes," said the mother, "I know that I had one, and no chicken has three legs. The bill is correct." This manner of settling the dispute made a lasting impression on me, and though this happened more than forty years ago I still see the faces of that family group and hear the

[40]A long memorandum was prepared by Doctor Eager, then eighty-seven, in 1937, and made available to me through his son, Mr. George T. Eager.

tone of Mr. Rockefeller's voice as he so quietly and so uniquely settled that dispute.

"When we travelled as a family," writes the son, "Mother and Father always made it a point to find some little church on Sunday, wherever we might be, and not only to attend the services, but to get acquainted with the minister; and often they made some little special contribution to him and his work."[41]

Once Rockefeller and his son broke away from the rest of the party for a few days of strenuous exercise in Switzerland. They travelled rapidly by rail and coach, and did much hard climbing. The son recalls that they arrived at Zermatt one evening, had supper, and went to bed immediately to rest for a long tramp the next day. Called at four A.M., they set out in a cold drizzle on horseback, and rode up to the snow line. Then they pushed forward on foot, roped to their guides, over a glacier and down on the other side of the mountain. "Father was so tired by the time we got to the first little inn that he went to bed, and I thought he would not be able to continue the journey that day. After a couple of hours' rest, however, and some food, he started out again, and walked several hours more down the mountain-side until one of the guides, who had gone ahead, brought back a horse." At fifty he was still capable of strenuous exercise.

VI

It remains to say something of Rockefeller's habits as a businessman. By 1885 he had thoroughly systematized his work, and although its burden was so heavy that before 1890 his health seemed giving way, he handled it without fuss or confusion. Ever since 1877 he had employed a faithful private secretary, George D. Rogers, who relieved him of minor details, signing ninety-nine in a hundred of his checks. He had efficient personal aides at 26 Broadway, in the Standard Block in Cleveland, and at the Forest Hill house, where he kept a telegrapher in summer. Daily in winter he went downtown on the elevated, reaching his office about nine; every evening he left about five.

In that pre-skyscraper age 26 Broadway was considered a rather grand structure. With Trinity Church, the gilded pile of the Stock

[41]John D. Rockefeller, Jr., to the author.

Exchange at Wall and Broad, the United States Treasury Building at Nassau and Wall, and the new and handsome Custom House, it was one of the downtown landmarks. "The building is of enormous extent on Broadway," wrote a local reporter.[42] "And in the rear it runs back a great distance, affording accommodations for an army of people." It had four elevators, and was pronounced by another writer "the very essence of convenience in all physical facilities."[43] Work was commenced in the spring of 1896 upon a six-story addition, making fifteen stories in all.[44] The upper floors were always busy with employees rushing from office to office. But the heads of the trust seldom appeared, and moved with dignity. "When the secretary of the Standard Oil Company goes from the third to the fourth floor he puts on his hat and makes the journey as though performing a ceremonious call," writes a newspaperman. This reporter succeeded in talking with Rockefeller. "He is modest, retiring, gentle-mannered, and without the human vanities which we associate with great millionaires," he declared.

Though Rockefeller was no longer "all business," he worked at a pace which would soon have brought ordinary men to a breakdown. Much of his important labor was done in the conference room, but it was nevertheless gruelling. The busy committees which furnished executive direction to the Standard aggregation revolved about him as center and head. His was the brain which was expected to master the ocean of information which constantly welled up from these committees, to reduce it to order, to draw deductions from it, and to lay down far-sighted policies. Each body—the Committee on Manufactures, the Export Committee, the Lubricating Committee, the Production Committee, and so on—was ceaselessly collecting data, and applying this information to the conduct of its work. The Export Committee, for example, knew day by day what supplies of crude and refined oil were being produced in different areas of the globe; what was the cost of production; what quantities were being shipped to Britain, to Germany, to South America, to China,

[42]*Truth*, X, p. 6; July, 1891. John T. Flynn, *God's Gold*, 270, treats as remarkable the fact that the trust boldly listed itself under that name in the city directory. But however much the trust concealed some of its *functions* it never concealed its existence, to which Flagler had publicly testified in 1882.

[43]N. Y. *World*, Oct. 10, 1886.

[44]*Oil, Paint, and Drug Reporter*, May 4, 1896.

to far-off islands; what was the cost of shipment; what was the
quality of the oil; what prices were asked; what laws and customs-
organizations were interfering with American trade; what were the
weak and strong links in the Standard's foreign organization. It
knew where each tank ship was, and followed every shift in marine
insurance. The Committee on Manufactures collected information
from a thousand sources on the latest chemical and technological
advances; on the expense of refining oil; on costs of fifty by-products; on plant design, fuel charges, labor problems, and deprecia-
tion; on changes in customer-demand; on complaints as to quality.
Not a new well of size was opened in the country but 26 Broadway
was informed of it. Not a foot of competitive pipe line was laid
but 26 Broadway instantly knew it. And the brain which was expected to know most about all this, to master the intricacies of the
field of battle, and to lay down a fresh strategic plan for every
new shift of circumstances, was Rockefeller's.

Such business correspondence as survives throws not a little light
on his ideas and temper. He had a way of encouraging his associates
to renewed effort with brief notes:[45]

(To F. Q. Barstow, July 12, 1884)

Yours 9th at hand, and it is gratifying. Col. Payne has also read it
with much interest. I hope there is no mistake about it. We are also feeling much gratified with the progress made in meeting competition at
Cleveland. We have the capacity to do all this home trade as well as the
export, and I hope we can devise ways and means to accomplish it later
on; at all events we must continue to strive for it in every department.

(To John D. Archbold, August 23, 1884)

For your esteemed favors of the 16th, 18th, 19th, and encouraging and
interesting telegram please accept many thanks.

The Acme showed well. Long may she wave. We must have close competition with our Buffalo competitors in the local trade. It is inevitable
and among other reasons because almost all other branches of business
are paying little or no profit and the merchant or manufacturer who barely
exists takes encouragement in times like these.

Am gratified with the report from Chambers, and hope we can continue
to hold out with the best illuminator in the world at the *lowest* price.
I trust progress will be made with Lombard.

[45]All these quotations are from the Rockefeller Papers. But most business
correspondence of the Standard Oil has long since been destroyed.

Rockefeller in relaxation.

Above: At Leamington, England, with Mrs. Rockefeller, Miss Spelman, Mr. Prentice, Alta Rockefeller Prentice, and Miss Caroline Platt. *Below:* Playing shuffleboard on shipboard, and with grandchildren in the snow.

Rockefeller with a grandchild (*top*), and great-grandchild (*below*).

When he did not have any needed fact, he requested it. We find him writing from Cleveland on October 6, 1884, to J. Crowell of 44 Broadway thanking him for assistance. "My desire to have information from you was to keep close up with each department of the business." A fortnight later, the day before he left for New York, he was urging Archbold to have the Executive Committee evince a little more boldness:

I hope if crude oil goes down again in the neighborhood of 60 [cents a barrel] our Executive Committee will not allow any amount of statistics or information from Vandergrift, Scheide, and others to prevent their buying oil. The day I sent you the request to buy on a scale at 61¾ 25M and increase 1000 each ¼ down, when you responded we had only $54,000 on hand that morning after paying drafts. I noticed at evening the bank balances were nearly $300,000, but were we obliged to borrow money to buy oil at 62¢ or 63¢ and under, up to one million barrels or so, I think we would be fully justified in doing it, and please kindly represent in Committee these as my sentiments. We must try and not lose our nerve when the market gets to the bottom as some people almost always do.

A letter a few months later shows that this recommended policy of buying crude oil at low levels even if money had to be borrowed for the purchase had been followed; while a significant passage in it indicates how much independence Carley retained, and another reveals that Warden was turning more and more from the Standard Oil to his public utility investments:

(To Henry M. Flagler, March 17, 1885)

Our business matters are moving along smoothly. At the time we bought crude, of which we advised you, some days since, we borrowed $300,000 for 45 days at 4%, also something over $600,000 on our governments, but the accumulations since will leave us, say tonight, about even, paying off the debts, or possibly $150,000 short of that.

The thermometer is this morning 14 degrees above zero, and today is a regular March day, cold, with the wind from the West and a chilling air.

Colonel Payne is here; and we are negotiating with Carley in reference to some changes in his affairs.

Mr. Pratt and Mr. Archbold have gone to Parkersburg to bid on the property, and we have agreed upon the outline of an arrangement with the Garrett party in respect to the lubricating business, dividing to us each 47½% and to an outsider—a mutual friend—5%.

Our local trade has kept up nicely, but we have very little export trade, though confidently expected soon.

Mr. Warden sold 3000 shares Trust at 95, which we will absorb for the Donald party, Squire, and others. This is rather above the current market now; purchases could be made for one or two points less, of small amounts, and [I] think those inclined to buy are not doing much but talk buy.

Another letter, relating to some issue which troubled the Pennsylvania group, shows how carefully changes in policy were debated beforehand:

(To William G. Warden, May 2, 1885)

We want to have our Executive Committee hear the representatives of Cleveland, Pittsburgh, Titusville, and New York local trade departments, and then I trust we shall be able to arrive at some equitable, reasonable, fair solution of this question. We certainly must not reach a decision without giving everybody the opportunity to be heard. I trust that the conclusions, when reached, will meet with your approval and that of our good friends in Pittsburgh.

I confess, I am not fully up to the question; however [I] am seeking after information and think we shall have no trouble, when we get the testimony all in, to reach the right decision.

The year 1885 brought that sudden portentous invasion of the world market by Russian oil which we have already described. It deeply alarmed Rockefeller. When the Standard's agent in Hamburg, Charles F. L. Meissner, sent on May 19 a detailed account of the invasion, Rockefeller urged his associates to take instant and aggressive action. They must face the necessity for increasing their bulk shipments of oil, and for reorganizing their distribution.

(To the Executive Committee, June 6, 1885)

I am at a loss to understand how the bulk transportation could have been carried on to the extent referred to [by Meissner] in Switzerland and elsewhere, without our having received more information about it.

I have shared the feeling, entertained by a part, at least, of our Committee, that it would not be necessary for us to enter this department of business in Europe, but the statements in this letter demand our careful consideration, and I think we should immediately proceed with further investigations and not blindly set ourselves against what may possibly prove an important safeguard to our business.

As one of the practical things to meet any competition, I would be quite willing to reduce the price of refined oil for export ⅛ cent now, and [would be] as favorable to continuing the margin between crude and refined close, and not allow ourselves to change from this policy on a flush of orders which we are likely to have now at any time.

Should we decide to make investment in the bulk transportation there are good arguments in favor of having representatives in the different countries who are at present established there in the petroleum business, although the tendency in our own country is to own the departments and direct them entirely ourselves, as we find it quite difficult to control the individual interests in the way we deem most desirable for the protection of our manufacturing department.

We are neither old nor sleepy, and must "be up and doing, with a heart for any fate; still achieving, still pursuing; learn to labor and to wait."

Charles Pratt had always been especially interested in the export trade, and Rockefeller urged him to assist in swift dispositions to meet the Russian threat:

(To Pratt, June 26, 1885)

Yours 24th at hand, and carefully noted. Please not forget, we are not always to have such a condition of things in the oil market as has existed for the last year or so. We have been educated to believe that if we only wait prices will adjust themselves to our views. This state of things cannot continue much longer, unless we get a large increase of production, and the part of wisdom for us is to be ready to adapt ourselves promptly to the changing conditions.

One of the reasons I have been so desirous to buy on the dull markets, has been the fear that when the change came, in view of what I have said above, we would not be quick enough for our own good. Please make this a matter of special study and go into training in connection with Mr. Flagler, so we may not be (excuse the expression) left.

But while Rockefeller was always urging rapid and progressive action, while he was always ready to take risks in borrowing money to buy crude oil or absorb a corporation, he was extremely conservative when it came to paying dividends. In this he differed from most business leaders, who demanded large and immediate gains.

(To Henry M. Flagler, June 29, 1885)

As I cannot be at the quarterly meeting, I desire to say, I agree with you that it is not best for us to increase our regular dividends above 6%, at all events, not now; but from present indications, judge we can pay, in addition to the regular one and a half dollars per share July 10th, another dollar per share, in about forty-five days after, that is, dividing the time equally between the regular July and October dividends, and I am in favor of doing this.

As you say, it does not commit us to increase of dividends in the future, nor will it prevent us from making another extra one when we are warranted in doing so. I am certain we are more likely to make mistakes by increasing our dividends than to go carefully and conservatively along as we have been doing.

Have had a conversation with Mr. Harkness and he approves of the dividends as above. I failed to see Colonel Payne, and he will not return to the city in time for you to receive a letter from me before the quarterly meeting, though I am entirely safe in saying, we have no one who takes a more conservative view about paying dividends than he. His expression to me has been uniformly to go very carefully indeed in this matter.

If today's prices are maintained it would of course have been better for our shareholders had we invested our surplus money in crude oil at around 80, as a number of our Committee desired to do, but that is past now, and I have no complaint to make, and am thankful we have as much crude on hand as we have. I hope the extra dividend as above suggested will be entirely satisfactory to all of our Committee, and surely we have all occasion to be very thankful for all the success that has attended us in our business, especially during a time when almost every other interest has greatly suffered in the general depression.

As we have said, he was anxious to keep the price of kerosene low:

(To H. C. Folger, Jr., September 21, 1885)

I am in receipt of yours of the 19th inst., with the interesting statement of the reduction of cost of manufacturing, being a copy of our communication to Mr. Barstow, Secretary of the Manufacturing Committee, of the 16th inst.

I am much gratified. Let the good work go on. We must ever remember we are refining oil for the poor man and he must have it cheap and good. Please present my congratulations to the Manufacturing Committee, and say that I am confident we shall continue to make progress in different ways in our manufacturing department.

(To John D. Archbold, June 30, 1886)

I return herewith letters from Mr. Chambers to Mr. Libby of the 4th and 5th of June, forwarded me from the Committee to Mr. Curtiss, June 28th, which I have carefully read.

I think the lesson we should draw is to continue making the best goods, so far as possible reduce the cost of manufacture, be content with a small profit, and continue wisely seeking for orders.

Of course one reason for keeping market prices low was to discourage competition, and Rockefeller stated as much to a partner travelling in Europe:

(To Benjamin Brewster, August 3, 1886)

Our returns for the first six months are coming very satisfactorily indeed. Indeed, I think we have made more money than we ought, and that the margin of profit is unduly stimulating to our competitors, notably in the oil regions. We are not free from the annoyance and trouble incident to this smooth-running business, but it seems to me we have every reason to be grateful when we compare it with any other.

While few of his letters in these years contain any comment upon competition, one does throw light upon Rockefeller's attitude toward independent refineries. He was quite willing to tolerate them as long as he could be sure they would not demoralize the markets. Just after Christmas in 1885 he wrote the vice-president of the Standard Oil of Ohio on the subject. After congratulating him on the reduction in expenditures for coal at the Ohio refineries, and informing him with evident satisfaction that shares in the Trust had sold at 130 before the recent dividends, and were now being tightly held, Rockefeller went on:[46]

I presented in the [Executive] Committee yours of 22d and 24th in regard to the anxiety of the outside refiners at Cleveland to have us market their oils, and the question of purchase of the Goodwillie property. It was thought, if we marketed their oil for them, questions might afterwards arise which would make it necessary for us to show them our books. For example, if they were dissatisfied with our returns, and should get more, etc.

How would it be for us to consider the question of buying from them for cash, instead of marketing? This is a suggestion of Mr. Pratt's. Our people are rather inclined not to buy any more refineries at present, and think the arrangements we have with the Cleveland refiners are a greater protection to us than if we owned all the refineries in Cleveland.

After a pretty earnest discussion on the question, we are rather inclined to delay any action for further thoughtful consideration.

Since the meeting, it has occurred to me that an arrangement might

[46]To W. T. Thompson, Dec. 28, 1885; Rockefeller Papers.

be made, advantageous to Goodwillie and us, to rent his refinery and take him on a salary, if we had a place for him. I assume we can surely manufacture cheaper than they, and market more advantageously; and if they would be reasonable, we ought to be able to rent so as to get some profit for ourselves, and be as good, or better, for them than continuing the business as at present. Goodwillie might desire to rent his refinery on the basis of what he can make, and be free from the risk of fire and bad debts, etc., and give us the benefit of our decreased cost of manufacturing and merchandizing. What would you think of this? And it might result in our arranging with others later, on the same plan.

A letter about three years later shows that fresh negotiations with some of these Cleveland independents were under way, and that Rockefeller was anxious that no unfair pressure should be used. His brother Frank was again with the Standard, and Rockefeller wrote to him on January 20, 1888, as an intermediary:

We want to be exceedingly careful in reference to the gentlemen referred to or any others who at any time may be considering with us the question of adjusting their relations as proposed in these cases.

Let nothing be said or done to unjustly or unfairly influence their minds. I believe you fully appreciate the importance of this and will see to it, that this spirit is carefully observed by any and all men representing Standard Oil Co. of Ohio in any negotiations, but I send this message from extra precaution feeling it very important.

Once more we must emphasize the fact that the decisions of the Standard Oil represented an agreement by a group of men, not the fiat of one. Control was by a directorate, not a dictator; the press was fond of calling Rockefeller "the oil king," but his rule was far from absolute. While his word usually prevailed, this was because it was supported by keener insight, more expert knowledge, and riper wisdom, not merely by a larger block of stock. The sentence above referring to "a pretty earnest" discussion, ending in a determination to give the matter "further thoughtful consideration," is significant.

The debates upon policy sometimes indicated a major line of cleavage. We have already spoken of the "Pratt group" as a self-conscious element in the organization. We must add that a shadowy but none the less real line can be traced between the Westerners and Easterners in the trust. Rockefeller, his brother William, Flagler, Ambrose McGregor, and Colonel Payne felt a special comradeship arising from their pioneering work with the Standard Oil of Ohio. Archbold, Camden, and W. P. Thompson were drawn to them; and during the later eighties, Archbold became Rockefeller's most resourceful lieutenant. The two Pratts and H. H. Rogers stood apart. Their opposition to expansion on a grand scale in the Lima area was allied to their chilliness toward Western men. Subordinates who came from Cleveland to 26 Broadway felt that these three did not quite "belong." Yet there was seldom any open friction, and Rockefeller never took cognizance of such ill-feeling as smouldered beneath the surface.

Indeed, his letters show that he did more than anybody else to propagate that "Standard Oil spirit" of which his officers always spoke proudly, and rival business organizations with jealous hostility. This was a spirit of aggressive loyalty. To work for the Standard was to belong to a special fraternity, and the constant attacks upon it simply cemented a feeling of group loyalty. Part of this devotion was the natural result of his policy of high wages and salaries, good working conditions, and short hours. Part of it arose from a feeling that Rockefeller and the Standard would take good care of all those who helped take care of the organization. But part of it was rooted in personal regard for Rockefeller, whose kindly consideration for his employees was clearly manifested. Mention has been made of his numerous letters inquiring after the health of the officers and urging special vacations. We find him announcing in a typical note that he has at last persuaded Joseph Seep and Daniel O'Day to hire much-needed assistance. We find him constantly urging mutual help: "Kindly keep D. O'Day posted on anything new on gas properties in Ohio, and he will follow them up." We find him even writing two letters about an aged pump-station engineer near Owego named Hiram Odell, whose privilege of using a tricycle on the Lackawanna Railroad to ride three miles to and from work daily had been suddenly cut off. The man found the long walk a hardship, and Rockefeller tactfully mentioned the matter to the attorney for the road.[47] "It occurred to me that possibly sometime when you saw Mr. Sloane, and he was in a good humor, it might do to mention this man's name. I should esteem it a favor if he would permit him to ride the tricycle . . . It will be

[47] To J. B. Trevor, July 18, 1885; Rockefeller Papers.

a cup of cold water which I am sure will be much appreciated."

No one who had business relations with Rockefeller ever doubted his intellectual power—the shrewdness of his mind, the penetration of his vision, the precision of his logic. Those who knew him only in business, or who, like the general public, saw only the results of his talent for organization, thought of him as a cold, hard, inexorable force. There can be no question that intellectual power was his most distinguishing quality, and that in practical affairs he seemed the most emotionless of men. But his intimates knew another side of the man; they knew that he was thoroughly and warmly human, that he brought geniality and even gaiety to his daily contacts, and that he always manifested a conscientious regard for the welfare of his friends and associates.

XXXV

Towers in the West

Long before 1890 Rockefeller found the task of dealing with the applications for gifts exhausting. Every mail brought its crowding appeals; every day brought its pertinacious callers. As a friend put it, he was "constantly hunted, stalked, and hounded almost like a wild animal."[1]

"The good people who wanted me to help them with their good work seemed to come in crowds," he later recalled with a touch of his dry humor. "They brought their trunks and lived with me. I was glad to see them, too, for they were good people and earnest—they were all earnest. So they talked with me at the breakfast table and they rode downtown with me so as to miss no opportunity. When I left my office in the evening they were waiting to ride home with me. At dinner they talked to me, and after dinner . . . these good people would pull up their chairs and tell their stories . . ."[2]

As his wealth grew Rockefeller attempted constantly to obey the principle which he repeatedly enunciated: "A man should make all he can and give all he can." But as his fortune rolled up portentously, the task of giving money discreetly became unexpectedly burdensome. It was all too easy to find good, unselfish people willing to take it! Late in life he was playing golf with Doctor Cornelius Woelfkin. The frank pastor was impressed by a specially skilful shot. "Mr. Rockefeller," he remarked, "I would give one million dollars of your money if I could make a shot like that." "Yes," responded Rockefeller dryly, "there are lots of people who would give a million dollars of my money for less worthy causes than that!"[3] Rockefeller wished to give to well-established or estab-

[1]Frederick T. Gates, MS Autobiography, 302.
[2]Philadelphia *Public Ledger,* Oct. 8, 1908.
[3]Mr. Harold V. Milligan had this story from Doctor Woelfkin.

lishable causes and institutions; to give in a way that would stimulate other gifts and enlist numerous supporters; to give to undertakings that would persist after his support was removed; and to give for objects not merely sound, but the soundest within the range of his investigations. To meet these conditions required onerous labor and anxious thought.

For evident reasons, the organization which was in the best position to help him was the Baptist Church. He had become its most powerful layman. It contained a number of highly cultivated, disinterested, and sagacious men who were well acquainted with social and economic issues; men like President James M. Taylor of Vassar, Jacob Gould Schurman of Cornell, W. H. P. Faunce, soon to be president of Brown, Augustus H. Strong of the Rochester Theological Seminary, and Thomas W. Goodspeed and William Rainey Harper of the Morgan Park Theological Seminary near Chicago. They represented the liberal element so prominent in the Baptist tradition ever since the days of John Bunyan and Roger Williams. Probably no sect in the country contained more alert, energetic, and broadly trained leaders. The church was aiding home and foreign missions, and supporting colleges, theological schools, and Negro training schools. Already Rockefeller was giving generously to these labors, and it was inevitable that under church guidance his benefactions should extend more and more heavily into the college field. Carnegie was to enter certain pursuits, notably the building of libraries and promotion of international peace, which appealed to his personal tastes; Rockefeller, advised by the best brains of his denomination and ignoring his personal inclinations, was to make his principal gifts in education.

II

Between the Civil War and 1900 our colleges and universities felt two great impulses toward renovation and expansion. The first followed hard upon the conflict. Under the leadership of such men as Charles W. Eliot, Andrew D. White, and Daniel Coit Gilman, and with the aid lent by the Morrill Act, the revolution in scientific thought, and technological advances, higher education was virtually remade.[4] The second impulse appeared as the century entered its last

[4] C. F. Thwing, *History of Higher Education in America*, 418–445.

decade. In 1890 the United States could still boast of but two really distinguished faculties, those of Harvard and Johns Hopkins. But by 1905 the scene had changed with startling rapidity. Leland Stanford opened its doors in 1891, the University of Chicago in 1892, and Clark University in 1894. David Starr Jordan, G. Stanley Hall, and William Rainey Harper appeared, and with them such other new statesmen of education as Nicholas Murray Butler at Columbia, Edmund J. James at Illinois, and Simon Patten at Princeton. James Bryce, writing in 1905, hailed the far-reaching changes wrought in fifteen years as without a parallel in the world.[5] "Roughly speaking," he declared, "America has now not less than fifteen or twenty seats of learning fit to be ranked beside the universities of Germany, France, and England as regards the completeness of the instruction they provide and the thoroughness at which they aim." Faculties had been expanded; new departments had been incorporated; and differentiation and specialization had been accompanied by a spectacular growth of libraries and laboratories. Graduate schools, which had been merely infant undertakings in 1880, were sturdily enrolling hundreds of students each at a dozen centers. The universities had shot up suddenly to maturity.

This spectacular development in the years after 1890 was called forth by the increasing complexity and power of American civilization. The simple Grant era could do without large faculties, without scholarly and scientific research, without exacting professional schools, without means of teaching pharmacology, pedagogy, chemical engineering, landscaping, sociology, astronomy, or ceramics; the specialized America of 1900 could not. It was made possible, again, by the increasing wealth of the nation, much of it concentrated in the hands of men able to dispose of huge surplus estates. Had riches been more equally diffused, had no multimillionaires existed in the republic, the State universities might have grown with deliberate sturdiness; but the old endowed universities could never have taken those impressive strides which set the pace and example for publicly supported institutions. Such swift and far-reaching innovations as distinguished new universities like Chicago and Leland Stanford, and old universities like Columbia and Harvard, were made possible by munificent gifts.

[5]"America Revisited," *Outlook*, March 25, April 1, 1905.

It has never been pointed out that this educational renascence of the nineties coincided with a striking fact: the arrival at old age of the whole generation of business leaders who had begun their careers in the boom years of the eighteen-sixties. A host of young men had entered manufacturing, transportation, and finance when the industrial revolution was just being completed. They represented the greatest aggregate of business genius that the world has ever seen. Some, like Rockefeller, Carnegie, Morgan, and Armour, had been hard at work in the war years of rich contracts and rising prices; some, like Washington B. Duke, fought in the ranks and entered business when peace came. As the industrial revolution conquered the nation, they began to build up such huge fortunes as the United States will assuredly never again permit. This aggressive generation of money-makers, very properly termed captains of industry, was reaching middle age by 1880, while by 1890 its members were growing old and satiated. The impulse to give was unescapable in a land so full of idealism, and higher education was the principal beneficiary. Leland Stanford founded his university in 1885; Jonas Clark announced the prospective establishment of his in 1887. In the history of Columbia University the happy decade beginning in 1890 is studded with the names of openhanded givers who had helped skim the cream from the natural resources of the continent, and who under a growing weight of years thought now of distribution; such names as Havemeyer, Schermerhorn, Milbank, Pulitzer, and Morgan.[6] All the men named had been young in 1865, all had profited from the tremendous release of exploitive energy after the war, and all were vying in generosity.

It was certain that Rockefeller would take a prominent and early place in this galaxy of philanthropists. He was one of the older figures in the generation we have described—born in 1839, and in business for himself since 1859; he was far on the road to the greatest fortune of them all; and he possessed an ingrained habit of giving, and of giving in sums large compared with his resources. He was still in the thick of complicated affairs, dominating a vast industry which had expanded to cover the habitable globe. To the crowding problems and incessant battles of this industry he had to give most of his attention. But he was more and more aware of the

[6]Frederick P. Keppel gives a list in Appendix F of his *Columbia University*.

duties imposed by the unexpected weight of his fortune. It presented two responsibilities to which he was keenly alive—the lesser of investment, and the greater of philanthropy.

For many years he had insisted that a great part of the Standard Oil profits be put back into equipment and expansion, while from those dividends which were declared he had reinvested heavily in Standard stock. As late as the middle nineties he purchased large blocks from Flagler, then immersed in his Florida ventures.[7] But long before 1890 he was diversifying his investments, for the Standard no longer sufficed. When the trust was formed in 1882, Rockefeller had more than one fourth of its shares, while fifteen years later he owned approximately three tenths.[8] This trust gushed forth such a stream of wealth as no other closely held corporation in the world's history had ever paid, and its annual dividends indicate accurately the rate at which income was flowing into Rockefeller's coffers. In 1887 they reached almost eight and one-half millions, and in 1888 they amounted to $13,705,000. Then, dropping back again in 1889 to $10,620,000, they moved forward again in 1890 to more than eleven millions. For the six years 1885–90 inclusive, the total dividends paid by the Standard Oil Trust fell very little short of sixty millions, of which Rockefeller's share was between fifteen and twenty millions. In the next half-dozen years they totalled more than eighty millions, of which he received a similar proportion.[9]

To invest this money he still possessed no proper mechanism. He depended on the advice of partners, bankers, and friends, with results that he admits in his *Recollections* were unfortunate.[10] The lack of efficient system in his benefactions was equally distressing. He had begun giving when he earned but a few dollars a week, and had progressed to giving in hundreds of thousands—always with the liberalism he had shown when, as an ill-paid clerk in the Puritan atmosphere of the Western Reserve, he had made gifts to

[7]See his statement in *Corrigan vs. Rockefeller, Testimony Before Arbitrators*.
[8]On Jan. 1, 1882, Rockefeller held 191,700 shares of trust certificates out of a total of 700,000; Taylor, MS History of Standard Oil, Appendix 3. In 1895 he bought 2500 shares in one lot from James Corrigan, 3700 shares from Flagler.
[9]A table of profits 1883–1906 inclusive, with three years missing, is in *Defendants' Brief, U. S. vs. Standard Oil Company*, 145 ff. See Appendix III.
[10]*Random Reminiscences*, 115 ff.

"Catholic orphans" and a Negro church. With characteristic method, he had adopted careful rules for his philanthropies. But he
needed an investigative and administrative office for the work.

Rockefeller undoubtedly read Carnegie's article "Wealth" in *The
North American Review* for June, 1889. This was the essay which
so excited Allen Thorndike Rice, the editor, that on reading the
manuscript he at once hurried to Carnegie's house, telling him:
"It is the finest article I have ever published in the review. I promised Lord Wolseley first place in the June number, but this will
lead the magazine." He asked Carnegie to read it aloud. But Rice
stopped Carnegie when the ironmaster reached the sentence: "Of
every thousand dollars spent in so-called charity today, it is probable that $900 is unwisely spent, indeed, so spent as to produce
the very evils which it is meant to mitigate or cure." "Make it $950,"
suggested Rice. Carnegie did so.[11] Rockefeller knew well how much
money went to foolish benefactions. Of all his intimates, Charles
Pratt had perhaps given most shrewdly. A devout Baptist, Pratt
had been urged by many friends to found a theological seminary,
while others asked him to establish a medical school; but he was
interested chiefly in industrial development and in helping young
people to fit themselves for the practical arts. He travelled widely
to visit engineering schools in America and Europe, and often talked
with Rockefeller about his observations. Then, late in 1885, he
began building the Pratt Institute in Brooklyn; and when he died
in 1894, his gifts of not far from four millions had made it a
flourishing institution.[12]

It was inevitable, as we have said, that Rockefeller should give to
education. But it was not at all inevitable that his first great gift
should go to found a university. And it was far from inevitable—
indeed, for a time it seemed most unlikely—that this institution
should be established in the West. The steps by which he was led
to create the University of Chicago as one of the principal seats of
learning in America constitute a story of absorbing interest, for it
involves a clash of powerful wills, a conflict of weighty sectional
interests, and a division affecting Rockefeller's own family.

[11]Burton J. Hendrick, *Andrew Carnegie*, I, 330.
[12]Sarah K. Bolton, *Famous Givers and Their Gifts*, 108–128.

III

East against West; a specialized as against a comprehensive ideal of higher education; a sectarian as against a quasi-secular view—these were the lines along which the conflict between Rockefeller's advisers ultimately developed. The leaders of the church wished him to give to higher education. But one set of opinions found a champion in the strong brain and imperious will of Augustus H. Strong; an opposite set in the still more powerful minds and equally tenacious wills of William Rainey Harper, Thomas W. Goodspeed, and Frederick T. Gates. The contest developed slowly, but in the end it became an implacable battle. While Doctor Strong and his Eastern supporters urged Rockefeller to create a great Baptist university in New York, Doctors Harper, Goodspeed, and Gates pressed him to establish it in Chicago. A third group spoke for Washington, but it hardly counted. Every one knows that Rockefeller ultimately cast the die for Chicago in 1889, but the story of how he reached this decision has never been fully told. His final determination was founded partly upon reasons of educational policy and partly upon sectional considerations, but most of all upon personal factors—upon his faith in the genius of William Rainey Harper, and in the talents and enthusiasm of Goodspeed and Gates.

A priori, all the advantages of position lay with Doctor Strong. He had known Rockefeller longer than had any other Baptist leader; his family became closely connected with Rockefeller's by marriage; he held a position of immense theological prestige; and at an early date he had evolved a plan for a great university—a super-university—which was truly inspiring. The friendship between Rockefeller and Doctor Strong dated back to the years just after the Civil War, when Strong, a vigorous young graduate of Yale, was pastor of the First Baptist Church of Cleveland.[18] He was three years Rockefeller's senior. In 1872 he went east to become president of the Rochester Theological Seminary, then and during the forty years of his administration the principal citadel of Baptist orthodoxy. But the friendship remained close. Rockefeller could not but be impressed by the force and positiveness of Doctor Strong's

[18]*Dictionary of American Biography; Rochester Hist. Soc. Pubs.,* I (1922).

stalwart though narrow personality.[14] In learning, in dignity, in elevation of character, in strength of will, and, alas! in rigidity of doctrine, no Baptist leader surpassed him. His character had a touch of Torquemada in it. Yet despite his lack of liberalism, he was a man of broad cultivation, and he wielded a trenchant and powerful pen. He frequently visited Rockefeller in Cleveland and later in New York City.[15] As we have noted, in 1888 young Strong married Rockefeller's daughter. Doctor Strong enjoyed opportunities of access to Rockefeller that were denied to most men.

Moreover, Doctor Strong's plan for a great super-university in New York had a nobility that appealed to any imagination. By 1880 he realized as clearly as Rockefeller himself that the latter was destined to amass one of the greatest of American fortunes. He wished to help Rockefeller use this huge fortune aright. What was the principal need of the Baptist denomination?—what, indeed, of the United States? An institution of learning, church-controlled, possessing the richest endowment in the world; employing the most distinguished faculty in America; devoting itself entirely to post-graduate work upon a grand scale; drawing the most brilliant young men of the nation to its doors by hundreds of fellowships and scholarships, and turning out a constant stream of teachers, writers, ministers, and other professional men who would lift all American civilization to a higher level. This was Doctor Strong's vision.[16] Johns Hopkins, with meager resources, had accomplished much until it began devoting an excessive attention—or so he thought—to undergraduate teaching. But his super-university would do ten times more. It would revitalize the Baptist Church, strengthen Protestant Christianity throughout the land, and become the principal cultural asset of the nation. Before 1885 Strong had unfolded his plan, with eloquence and enthusiasm, to his friend. Rockefeller, he proposed, should give $20,000,000 to set up this great post-graduate university, rising full-panoplied on precisely that part of Morningside Heights in New York which Columbia University now occupies.

[14]See Doctor Goodspeed's memorandum on his character in the Harper Papers, University of Chicago.

[15]John D. Rockefeller, Jr., to the author, May 3, 1939.

[16]Conrad H. Moehlman, "How the Baptist Super-University Planned for New York City was Built in Chicago," *Colgate-Rochester Divinity School Bulletin*, XI, 119–134. Doctor Moehlman has sent me valuable information.

But Strong addressed himself to the wrong capitalist: he should have chosen Carnegie rather than Rockefeller. The warmly imaginative Scot, with his love for the grandiose and with a mind which, as his biographer has said, moved in rushes of pure intuition,[17] might have responded to this vision of raising overnight on Morningside Heights the greatest university in the world. But Rockefeller had a very different mind and personality. It cannot too often be said that all his life he intensely distrusted an emotional approach to problems, acting by the cold, clear light of his intellect alone; that his mind did not move by swift intuitive rushes, but by slow, careful, and incredibly acute ratiocination, making sure stage by stage of a course of action projected far into the future. It was the mind of a great tactician brooding over his brigades and corps, and foreseeing not only the immediate moves but every other move to the end of the campaign. While benevolent in the best sense of the word, his benevolence was always cool, shrewd, and realistic; it was never for a moment guided by sentiment or much affected by imagination. He came to regard Doctor Strong, for all his learning, intellectual power, and fervor, as impractical, and to distrust Doctor Strong's vision precisely because too much grandiosity and imagination entered into it. It is true that Doctor Strong finally worked out his plan in some detail, laying down specifications for the highly paid faculty and the hundreds of graduate fellowships; but he did not correlate, in a way that Rockefeller could regard as practical, his super-university with the actual demands of the country and the church. He left that essential link unforged.[18]

IV

Meanwhile, by 1886 the first educational demands had reached Rockefeller from the West. They made little impression upon him at the outset for precisely the same reason that Doctor Strong's proposals made little impression; that is, for reasons connected with the minds and personalities of the petitioners. These first petitioners were the president and secretary of the Morgan Park Theological Seminary near Chicago, Doctors G. W. Northrup and Thomas W.

[17]Burton J. Hendrick to the author.
[18]Strong published a pamphlet, "The Church and the University: With a Detailed Argument and Plan," which exists in only two known copies.

Goodspeed; men of great ability, energy, and learning—but once more, in Rockefeller's opinion, a little impractical.

As early as 1880 Rockefeller's pastor in Cleveland had called his attention to the needs of the Morgan Park school, established thirteen years earlier. As a result, Rockefeller in 1882 became vice-president of the Theological Union of Chicago, a body which supported the Seminary; and this post he held until early in the nineties. He gave generously to the Seminary—$40,000 the first year, and contributions of varying size thereafter. He maintained a large correspondence with President Northrup and Secretary Goodspeed.[19] From them he heard much about the school's problems and about the teachers at Morgan Park, including the gifted young professor of Hebrew, William Rainey Harper, a native of Ohio and a graduate of Yale. He heard much also of the old University of Chicago, founded by Stephen A. Douglas and others in 1856, with which Morgan Park Seminary was connected, and which was gradually collapsing under a mountain of debt.[20] But his interest was in the Seminary, not in this so-called University—really a very weak and precarious freshwater college.

Rockefeller was therefore a highly sympathetic spectator when in 1886 a double calamity fell upon the Morgan Park Seminary. The struggling little University of Chicago received its death-blow when an insurance company foreclosed a debt of $100,000 upon its site and buildings. At the same time Doctor Harper, the most precociously brilliant figure that Western education had yet known, was invited to become the first Woolsey Professor of Biblical Literature at Yale. The Seminary, bulwarked by its endowment of a quarter of a million dollars, was in no immediate danger. But with its supply of students reduced, for the old University had been an invaluable feeder, and with its most powerful teacher gone to Yale, it would face a troubled future. No one realized this better than Rockefeller, who during four years had kept closely in touch with its work. When he first heard, by way of New Haven, that Harper might be called to Yale, he had hastened to write a warning letter to Goodspeed.[21]

Under the shock of this double blow, Doctor Northrup, Doctor

---

[19]Rockefeller Papers.
[20]See George Fort Milton, *The Eve of Conflict*, 4, for Douglas's sponsorship.
[21]Rockefeller to Goodspeed, April 5, 1886; Harper Papers.

Goodspeed, and their colleagues devised a hasty plan which they laid before Rockefeller as rapidly as the mails could carry their letters east. They proposed that the fragments of the ruined University of Chicago should be picked up and re-established at Morgan Park, with Harper as president and also as head of the Department of Hebrew in the Morgan Park Seminary. Doctor Goodspeed, temperamentally sanguine, believed that Harper could thus still be restrained from going to Yale. He believed also that the businessmen of Chicago would assist them. "There is profound interest felt by very many Western men in the re-establishment of the University," he wrote, with something more of wishful thinking than sober regard for facts. No real concern was discernible among any but impecunious churchmen. Rockefeller knew this, for the University would never have collapsed had many people taken a profound interest in its work. He knew that it had never been aught but a weak and ill-equipped institution; he knew that its hasty re-establishment would serve no useful purpose. He therefore replied to the impulsive and optimistic Doctor Goodspeed in April, 1886, in terms of indifference about the University but of lively concern about William Rainey Harper. "I really do not know what to say about the University," he wrote.[22] But he declared emphatically that every effort should be made to keep Doctor Harper, and expressed his readiness to make a special contribution to that end. For the Seminary and its ablest teacher Rockefeller plainly cared a great deal; for a hurried, ill-planned, and shortsighted attempt to galvanize a rickety little college, which had never possessed a proper faculty, library, or course of study, into a semblance of renewed life, he cared nothing at all.

Within the next few weeks Harper accepted the Yale offer. During June the last lecture was given and the last examination held at the first University of Chicago. In dejection, Goodspeed considered accepting the presidency of Kalamazoo College, one of the best Baptist schools in the West. When he informed Rockefeller of his inclination to take the post, he received an immediate and characteristic reply:[23]

Yours 10th at hand, and I regret much to see that it is your purpose to leave the Seminary. What will they do? It had never occurred to me but that you and the other standbys were permanent there and that in

[22]April 7, 1886; Harper Papers.   [23]June 14, 1886; Harper Papers.

contributing to the Theological Seminary I was placing money where
it would remain doing good for ages; but what is to be the outcome of a
change of administration? I cannot advise you, I do not know what is
best, but I am anxious in respect to the future of the Seminary and by
no means unmindful of yours. I have felt great confidence in you and
it will take some time to adjust myself to any change. I trust that what
is done will prove to be for the Seminary and yourself the very best thing.
I shall be very happy to receive your advice that you decide to stay.

This was an adroit letter. Rockefeller made it very clear that he
felt grieved by Goodspeed's apparent decision to leave the Seminary,
and hoped he would reconsider. Yet he was far too skilful a diplo-
matist to be betrayed into language which might later justify Goodspeed in basing any appeal for contributions to the Seminary upon
Rockefeller's wish that he should identify his own future with it.
He wished Goodspeed to do his duty without any inducements, explicit or implicit! And Goodspeed did so; he immediately wrote[24]
that he would remain. Many years later, in a memorandum upon
Rockefeller's letter, he spoke of "the extraordinary alertness of his
[Rockefeller's] mind and his skill in balanced phrasing."[25]

In remaining at Morgan Park, Goodspeed was of course actuated
by a desire to help keep alive his project for a revived University of
Chicago, to be placed in close association with the Seminary. He
missed no opportunity to impress this upon Rockefeller's mind.
"Chicago," he wrote, "is the place of all others in the world to build
a great Baptist University." If the movement he was still nursing
during the summer of 1886 failed, he declared that another would be
commenced in 1887. The school would grow till in the course of time
it equalled Yale and Harvard. No great sum would be required;
for outside Chicago land could be got for nothing, a building erected
without cost, "and a start made with little expense." The Western
Baptists could maintain the institution once it was well launched.
"We need here a college. The seminary needs it. Our cause needs it
and I cannot but believe it is certain to come. . . ." The time was
at hand when this would be a living question, and "I hope you will
feel that you can take it into your heart and in your plans."[26] Toward the end of the year he wrote again. Offers were being made

[24]Goodspeed to Rockefeller, June 15, 1886; Harper Papers.
[25]Harper Papers.
[26]Goodspeed to Rockefeller, June 16, 1886; Harper Papers.

by men interested in founding a new university at Morgan Park. He would like permission from Rockefeller to lay before him the question of aiding in its establishment. But once more the industrialist, realizing that no plans had been fully canvassed, and that no certainty of a general support yet existed, refused. He wrote:[27]

> Yours 28th at hand. There is hardly a chance I could give the least encouragement for assistance in respect to the University, but I will carefully read the communication you suggest. I am pleased to note the progress of the work at the Seminary.

V

Meanwhile, Doctor Strong was more intent than ever upon his plan for a super-university in New York. He had prepared a careful memorandum on the subject, which bears no date. In this he pointed out that no true university yet existed in America; that is, no such university as Berlin, Oxford, or Cambridge. The colleges of the United States were struggling to "emerge from the Academical to the University condition." Even at Harvard all but 500 of the registrants were undergraduates and not properly university students at all; of the $10,000,000 of property owned by Harvard, not more than $1,000,000 was applicable to university purposes. Johns Hopkins came nearer being a true university, he wrote, than any other institution in America. But even there marked shortcomings existed.

"Now where are we Baptists?" continued Doctor Strong's memorandum to Rockefeller. "We have no university at all. No Law Schools, no Medical Schools, no Advanced Scientific Schools, no means of preparing our own teachers in Greek, or Mathematics, or Science. For all these we have to send our sons to other universities, either in this country or abroad. Against Harvard's 1500, or Yale's 1200 students, our largest number is 300 at Brown. The only approach to professional instruction is our theological seminaries, and the largest of these numbers no more than 50 well-prepared students, by which I mean college graduates—while Union and Princeton have their 150 each. Our theological seminaries are the greatest advance we have made yet. One of them, or better still two or three united, might make the nucleus and beginning of a Baptist university." He pointed out that no real approach to a university could be

[27]Rockefeller to Goodspeed, December 31, 1886; Harper Papers.

found in New York, although the metropolis was the very place where the greatest of American seats of learning must inevitably rise. If Rockefeller moved promptly, he and the church could seize possession of the ground before any other denomination, and begin their work there "unhampered by child's clothes, untrammelled by an academical or college department." The opportunity would not long be open, for already Seth Low was urging that Columbia College should turn herself into a true university.

The best sources for advice, Doctor Strong declared, were Presidents Eliot of Harvard and Gilman of Johns Hopkins. He was anxious to have Rockefeller confer with them, and to avoid "the narrow men, educated at very small colleges, who have no true conception of higher education." It was his hope that Eliot, Gilman, and Rockefeller might meet with him in the same room, where they could all discuss the subject carefully. "I have great faith in your wisdom when you have the facts before you," he concluded. But Rockefeller still showed no responsiveness, for he was not yet convinced.

It is evident from a study of the papers of Rockefeller, Goodspeed, and Strong that in his sternly unresponsive attitude to both Eastern and Western pleas the industrialist was actuated by a broad general apprehension that he was being asked to do something impractical. The two schemes were poles apart. Doctor Strong had a grandiose vision of a $20,000,000 super-university dedicated to advanced teaching and research; Doctor Goodspeed had a plan for reviving, with a few hundred thousands at most, the weakest of all the weak Baptist colleges. Yet to a believer in hard-based business realities both undertakings were open to the same objections. The shrewdest, least emotional, and most farsighted of American industrialists perceived three fatal weaknesses in each. First, neither scheme possessed a really firm foundation in popular demand; Doctor Strong had never proved that American culture was eager for a colossal new graduate institution, or could properly employ its hundreds of graduates each year, and Doctor Goodspeed had not demonstrated that a small Baptist college at Morgan Park was keenly desired by the Western constituency which had just let the so-called University die. In the second place, neither scheme was assured of co-operative financial support by a large group of interested men. Since becoming very rich, Rockefeller had tried to insist that his larger gifts should be matched dollar for dollar, or at least half-dollar for dollar, by other givers. But Doctor Strong had thus far envisaged him as the sole creator and supporter of the super-university in New York; while Doctor Goodspeed had offered no evidence that the hitherto lukewarm Chicagoans would give their "university" any important aid if revived. It was a church college; the Baptists of Chicago included no really rich men; and other denominations were indifferent.[28] Third, and most important of all, Rockefeller did not regard the sponsors of either scheme as possessing quite the business enterprise and administrative capacity needed to carry it to success. He felt a high admiration for Doctor Strong's learning, piety, and zeal, but he comprehended the dogmatic narrowness and essential unworldliness of the man. In expounding Baptist orthodoxy at Rochester, Strong was tremendously effective; but he was not the man to launch or govern a complex, broadly planned, and liberal institution of higher education. Rockefeller also felt a warm admiration for the varied gifts of President Northrup and Secretary Goodspeed at Morgan Park Seminary.[29] But he believed that Doctor Northrup was too exclusively the scholar, and Doctor Goodspeed was rather too impetuous and optimistic, to be safely entrusted with great practical undertakings. Until these three fundamental objections were overcome, Rockefeller would yield to neither the West nor the East.

Throughout 1887 and 1888 he stood firm. Both Rochester and Morgan Park plied him with eloquent arguments and plaintive entreaties. In Rockefeller's papers are two letters written him by Doctor Strong and Doctor Goodspeed on the same day—January 4, 1887. Both struck the same note; a note of just that emotional character which was most repugnant to Rockefeller's temperament. "I feel profoundly about the re-establishment of our University," Doctor Goodspeed wrote. "I would be willing to risk a good deal personally in the effort to found a new and first-rate Baptist University in this great center. It is likely to take a long and hard struggle. I shrink from it. If some one else could be found to undertake it, I would earnestly entreat you to help the enterprise. But when I think that

[28]Thomas W. Goodspeed, *History of the University of Chicago*, 12 ff., describes the difficulties.

[29]Goodspeed, *History*, 21, calls Northrup "a great executive and a great teacher." Goodspeed's MS Autobiography, kindly lent me by the University, reveals his own energy, vision, learning, and administrative capacity.

it may be necessary for me to take up the burden, I am deterred by the thought and I shall make no earnest appeal, I fear." This was hardly an attitude that would encourage Mr. Rockefeller to give the sums that Doctor Goodspeed desired. Doctor Strong wrote in an equally emotional vein. "With the largest constituency, or certainly next to the largest," he pleaded, "we are allowing other denominations to capture our best young men, to take possession of the strategic points, and to organize their own triumph and our downfall in the near future. But I must not trench upon a subject which I laid before you several years ago, promising that I would not open it again except at your suggestion. It has haunted me day and night for years, but I have had to keep my mouth shut. Meanwhile, years are passing, and we are hurrying on to meet God. How can we leave the world in peace, when our chance to meet the one great need of our time in the body of Christians to which we belong is allowed to slip by unimproved?"[30]

At one time Rockefeller did seem to waver under Doctor Strong's incessant pleas. In 1887 he made that first trip abroad which we have already described. Doctor Strong accompanied him, and had every opportunity to expound his plans for a great metropolitan university. On their return, Rockefeller seemed half-converted. Early in November he invited William Rainey Harper to spend Saturday with him in New York. "I enjoyed myself exceedingly," Harper writes,[31] "lunching with him at noon, driving for two or three hours in the afternoon, and visiting with him in the evening." In this talk of several hours Rockefeller put Harper through a close examination, asking him all about his family, his studies, and his ambitions; while he also told Harper that he was thinking of putting $8,000,000 or $10,000,000 into the founding of a great university in New York of which he wished Harper to be head. But perhaps he was merely talking in tentative fashion to elicit Harper's ideas. It is certain that as November went on his interest waned. On the 30th he wrote Strong that he had decided to postpone the question of a New York university indefinitely, and at once informed Harper of this decision. His reasons were not stated.[32] But Doctor Goodspeed later made a shrewd guess that he had been offended by a series of

[30]Copies in the Harper Papers.
[31]Harper to Goodspeed, November 7, 1887; Harper Papers.
[32]Strong Papers; Harper Papers.

letters from Strong, each more urgent than the last, culminating in one which laid upon him the duty of founding the university as something demanded by the voice of God. This was too much, and Rockefeller revolted.[33]

Doctor Goodspeed's appeals during 1887 and the first months of 1888 continued to be couched in very general terms. His vision of a revived college at Morgan Park as yet lacked specific details and distinguishing features. He suggested that Rockefeller should give $100,000 on the express stipulation that $100,000 more be raised at the earliest moment possible, but he did not state just how the $200,-000 should be expended. He was terribly in earnest; but much as Rockefeller liked and admired Doctor Goodspeed, he could not but feel that his plans were altogether too vague. Doctor Strong, equally persistent and more impassioned, did offer some concrete if not wholly practical data. He drew up for Rockefeller a detailed plan for the proposed university which he headed, "A Postscript to My Letter of Three or Four Weeks Ago—Demanding No Answer." He emphasized again his desire to establish a true university after the best European models. But it was plain that the narrowness and rigidity so characteristic of the man stamped all his ideas. "My plan," he wrote, "is that all the work of the University should be Christian; based upon the Bible; that it should begin with education for the ministry and center around the studies relating to God and his revelations. . . . Gradually I would branch out into a complete university system, including both law and medicine."[34] Mr. Rockefeller might be pardoned for doubting if the learned theologian were the best man to entrust with $20,000,000 in founding a university.

Moreover, Doctor Strong in his abounding zeal was not wholly tactful. In one letter of 1887 he tried to appeal to selfish motives. After sketching again the "incalculable" effect which a great university in New York would have in vitalizing the denomination, he wrote that he wished "in all affection for your family and yourself" to urge a personal consideration. "Would it not make the noblest work as well as the noblest recreation of your life if, not neglecting other and distant interests, you should devote yourself mainly to the travel and investigation connected with the establishment of [this]

[33]Goodspeed, MS Autobiography.   [34]No date; Harper Papers.

institution in New York . . .? Could you give your son a nobler education during the next ten years than to have him grow up amid the discussions and interviews connected with such a plan? Could you leave him with a nobler work in life than to be the Solomon for whom you like another David made the preparations?"[35] Rockefeller had always insisted upon completely divorcing himself from any active control over his money-gifts when once made; and this suggestion that he and his son should exploit the proposed university for their own "recreation," education, and dignity did not appeal to him in the least. A little later Doctor Strong made a still more untactful plea. Pressing Rockefeller hard in his pertinacious way, he wrote him late in 1887 that the founding of the super-university would create a much-needed fund of popular good will:[36]

Very many people do not understand you and they very unjustly accuse you. Your friends love and admire you, but very many are not your friends. Your present gifts, to education and to the churches, do not stem the tide of aspersion as would the establishment of an institution for the public good, so great that it has manifestly cost a large self-sacrifice to build it. Your means are pretty well known, and "take a boy of your size" is what people say. Here is something of your size. George Peabody even in his manhood was only a money-maker—a man who secluded himself, as I understand. He never gave much money away, and he was a man disliked and avoided. How completely the fame of George Peabody's moneymaking, and of his early unpopularity, has been lost! He changed in his later days; began to make benevolence and not moneymaking his principal aim in life; immediately got a name for charity and public spirit; now he is remembered for nothing else. You have the opportunity of turning the unfavorable judgments of the world at large into favorable judgments—and not only that—of going down to history as one of the world's greatest benefactors.

It need not be said that Rockefeller had too much self-respect not to resent this intimation. In his opinion it was neither necessary nor right for him to use great money gifts to purchase the good opinion of the world. Yet he showed no irritation. Doctor Strong had expressed the deepest agitation. "I feel as if I could hardly go through the strain of meditating and praying about this for another year," he wrote. "I had almost rather leave my testimony and die. But I do not believe you will decline." It was a quietly firm negative that

[35]Strong to Rockefeller, February 22, 1887; Harper Papers.
[36]Strong to Rockefeller, November 26, 1887; Harper Papers.

he received. "Yours of the 26th at hand," Rockefeller wrote.[37] "For
all the reasons, I have decided to indefinitely postpone the consideration of the question of the university or the theological seminary
in New York."

Thus the impasse continued. Rockefeller's fortune was steadily
increasing; yet he did not feel justified in giving until some clearly
practical plan, fixed in a clearly practical situation, and to be controlled by highly practical men, was offered to him. As late as February 4, 1888, Doctor George C. Lorimer wrote Rockefeller that,
after patient effort, he had not been able to find a Western Baptist
willing to give even $25,000 to revive the old University in Chi-
cago.[38] "The difficulty," he wrote, "is to make a start in such a way
as to inspire confidence and hope all along the line." It was plain
that some new elements must be introduced into the situation.

But fortunately, between May, 1888, and May, 1889, all those elements appeared. In those twelve months nothing less than a decisive revolution in the situation was wrought—a revolution which
made possible the University of Chicago.

VI

This revolution was initiated by the establishment in May, 1888,
of the American Baptist Education Society. Many groups in the
church had become deeply concerned over the feeble and chaotic
condition of the Baptist colleges and seminaries, especially west of
the Alleghenies. A convention was therefore called to meet in
Washington to found a special society for raising funds and making
plans to better the situation. The principal leader of the movement
was Doctor Henry Morehouse, a graduate of Rochester Theological
Seminary who after service as a minister had become head of the
Home Missionary Society. He was supported by most Western and
Southern Baptists and by some prominent New Englanders like
Doctor Henry L. Wayland, but opposed by Doctor Strong and by
most Easterners. The convention brought together 427 delegates
from 36 States and Territories, a remarkable outpouring. Its de-

[37]Rockefeller to Strong, November 30, 1887; Harper Papers.
[38]Harper Papers. Doctor Strong, while generously commending the idea of
a college in Chicago, sneered at the smallness of Doctor Goodspeed's ideas.
"A $100,000 college will be nothing but a great high school." Strong to Rocke-
feller, February 15, 1887; Harper Papers. Yet he called Goodspeed "the only
really level-headed man I know out there."

liberations showed that while the Eastern churches controlled the more wealth, the Western churches had the more members and votes; and the Society was forthwith organized on a broadly representative basis. This was a victory, as one of its officers later wrote, "of the moneyless and educationally destitute West and South over the moneyed and educationally well-provided Eastern and New England States."[39]

The establishment of this society was important in itself, but still more important in bringing into the situation an entirely new figure, destined to exert a profound influence over Rockefeller's whole later career; a man whose importance in various spheres of American effort is yet to be properly recognized by historians— Frederick T. Gates of Minneapolis. It is not strange that Doctor Goodspeed in his history of the University of Chicago should unconsciously underrate Gates's rôle. To Doctor Goodspeed and Doctor Strong, Gates was at first simply another Baptist minister with a strong interest in education. When he was appointed executive secretary of the new society it seemed to these men that nothing had occurred save the addition of another energetic cleric to the group which was studying educational problems. But from Rockefeller's point of view, it soon became clear that the addition of Gates had radically changed the whole equation. When he was first named, Rockefeller had probably never heard of him. But the two men had not long corresponded, and had held only one or two conferences, before Rockefeller realized that he could at last begin to discuss a great educational gift upon a practical and dependable basis; that in Gates he had found a man who, when assisted by those earlier workers in the field, Goodspeed and Harper, could build a firm bridge between visions and realities.

It has been customary to treat Frederick T. Gates as a minister who developed an interest in education and philanthropy.[40] Actually this is misleading. Gates was essentially a businessman with a talent for large affairs, a keen interest in the power of money, and a passion for seeing it expended with the greatest possible efficiency. He was, in short, a man after Rockefeller's own heart. It is true that, graduating from Rochester University and Rochester

[39]Frederick T. Gates, MS Autobiography, 172–174.
[40]*Dictionary of American Biography*, VII, 182, 183.

Seminary, he had now spent eight years in the ministry. But in working his way through high school and college he had been in turn teacher, farmer, bank-clerk, and salesman. During his Minneapolis ministry he had raised the church debt, written for newspapers, helped the wealthy miller George A. Pillsbury draw up his will, and conducted a successful campaign for $60,000 to found a Baptist Academy. Devoutly religious he unquestionably was; but at heart he was a businessman, shrewd, alert, aggressive, and capable of driving hard bargains. The time was not far distant when this former minister, coming to New York, would essay to teach Wall Street itself some lessons, and would do it! It should be added that he had a dynamic alertness, a compelling personality, and a gift of eloquence which he liked to exercise upon one hearer as much as upon ten thousand.

He at once demonstrated his remarkable qualities by the way in which he set to work. He has left a manuscript autobiography, and it needs only a little study of this and of his letters to disclose three facts. First, when this self-made leader of the church became head of the Education Society, he was already convinced that the denomination needed its principal educational institution in Chicago, not New York. Doctor Goodspeed in his history asserts that he was not—that he was still open-minded as between East and West. But Doctor Goodspeed had either not seen or had forgotten the letters which Gates sent to Doctor Morehouse within a month after his appointment. He wrote on June 21, 1888, that he was "figuring underground with the Chicago University matter through Doctor Smith to see if there is anything in it, if so whether the Education Society can be of service. Confidentially, my present opinion is that there is a greater case, better prospect, more need, and for the Society better outcome here than anywhere else. If we can take hold of that matter, raise half a million . . . and set an institution on its feet, we shall have done more for education than in any other way. . . ."[41] In the second place, Gates believed that he could immediately convince Rockefeller and others both of the crying need for a strong university in the West, and the possibility of enlisting a broad popular support for it. Finally, it is evident that he looked forward to the task of money-raising with positive elation.

[41]Harper Papers.

Indeed, a few years later Gates drew up a number of rules for raising money which throw a penetrating ray of light upon his personality and methods.[42] Written for the financial agent of a Western college, they were founded upon his own experience. He urged would-be collectors of money to dress well, with "costly" clothes, immaculate linen, and well-brushed shoes. "See also that your hands are kept clean." They should hunt in pairs, for a call by two men would have greater dignity than a call by one; but only one should talk. They were to have "an elegant personal card" each to present at the office door. At the outset they were to ask for only a *few minutes* of the prospective giver's time, and by plunging into the heart of the subject create the impression that the call would be short. "Enter the room in genial and radiant good nature," urged Gates; allow no provocation to disturb this good-humor, and "keep your victim also good-natured, and this throughout." Rule No. 6 ran: "If you find him big with gift, do not rush too eagerly to the birth. Let him feel that *he* is *giving* it, not that it is being taken from him with violence." Rule No. 8 advised: "Appeal only to the nobler motives. His own mind will suggest to him the lower and selfish ones. But he will not wish you to suppose that he has thought of them. . . ." Rule No. 10 also had a cynical ring: "Let the victim talk freely, especially in the earlier part of the interview, while you use the opportunity to study his peculiarities. Never argue with him. Never contradict him. . . . If he is talkative, let him talk, talk, talk. Give your fish the reel, and listen with deep interest."

When this highly realistic man took hold of the situation, he was certain to bring some new result out of it. Gates steered the shrewdest possible course. As soon as elected, he informed Doctor Strong and others that he intended to do what they had previously advocated—to make a survey of the Baptist educational field; and they promised him their support. He at once circulated an elaborate questionnaire on educational needs throughout the denomination. Then, taking the results and all the other matter on education he could find, he settled down at Racine to digest his data. Looking out over Lake Michigan, he pondered long on the best available remedy for the anemic state of Baptist education. Various proposals had been made: special funds, new endowments for old colleges,

---

[42]Dated April 20, 1891; General Education Board files.

and fresh institutions in Washington, New York, and other cities. But he quickly became confirmed in the view that the primary need was the establishment of "a powerful college to become later a University, on the ruins of the old University of Chicago."[43] He then wrote out his whole argument in an eloquent report which he laid before a Baptist Conference in Chicago on October 15, 1888 —a report entitled "The Need for a Baptist University in Chicago, as illustrated by a Study of Baptist Collegiate Education in the West."

Gates himself has well described its effect on the Chicago gathering. "To say that the . . . facts produced a sensation would be mild language. The brothers were 'all torn up' over it. They were astonished, astounded, confounded, dumbfounded, amazed, bewildered, overwhelmed. . . . It was these terrible truths about Western education, every one pointing to the necessity for a great University at Chicago and that at once, that slew the brethren. The truth has never before been told, but I told it for once." His paper produced the same effect when delivered in Washington and Boston; and a copy of it soon lay on Rockefeller's desk.[44]

Gates showed that the States lying between Pennsylvania and the Rockies and north of the Ohio River contained almost one half the Baptists of the nation; but that the educational facilities of the church in this area were wretched beyond belief. The Baptists had eleven so-called colleges there, but their property and endowments were worth only $881,000. In the previous year they had enrolled 1257 students, but of these three fourths were in preparatory departments. All but one of the colleges, Des Moines, were in little obscure towns of impecunious population. Their combined libraries aggregated only 25,000 volumes; the average salary paid their teachers was $1015. Gates of course did not deny that the eleven colleges all represented a fine aspiration and heroic self-sacrifice; or that the four oldest, best-known, and most largely attended, Kalamazoo, Shurtleff, William Jewell, and Franklin, had large possibilities of usefulness. But the showing as a whole was discreditable to the denomination. In these same States the Methodists possessed twenty-one colleges, which possessed more than $5,300,000 worth of prop-

[43]MS Autobiography, 181.
[44]Goodspeed wrote Gates October 15, 1888: "The paper stirred my heart. I want it to stir another's [Rockefeller's] heart." Harper Papers.

erty, and which enrolled almost 5700 students. Gates came out vigorously for a great Baptist institution in the largest city of the Middle West:

Of many things which must be done to remedy our need the first and most important, as it seems to me, is to found a great college, ultimately to be a university, in Chicago. We need in Chicago an institution with an endowment of several millions, with buildings, library, and other appliances equal to any on the continent; an institution commanding the services of the ablest specialists in every department, giving the highest classical as well as scientific culture, and aiming to counteract the western tendency to a merely superficial and utilitarian education—an institution wholly under Baptist control as a chartered right, loyal to Christ and His church, employing none but Christians in any department of instruction, a school not only evangelical but evangelistic. . . .

It is not too much to say that this report, with the expressions of instant approval which it evoked throughout the denomination, made Rockefeller's choice of the West for his first gift unescapable. There lay the most exigent need. There his money *must* go if it went to higher education at all. Within a few months, on December 3, 1888, the executive board of the Education Society met in Washington, and when Gates laid his proposals before it, they were unanimously approved. Every one present understood that this action would have a powerful effect upon Rockefeller. As Gates put it, Rockefeller had been "waiting to hear the voice of the denomination." That practical basis for giving which he had missed in the proposals of Doctor Strong and Doctor Goodspeed was now fast being supplied.

And another factor of unquestionable importance in Rockefeller's changing views was the position taken by William Rainey Harper, whose genius, learning, and energy he fully appreciated. While Harper had told both Rockefeller and Strong that he would be ready to devote his life to a university in New York, his heart really lay with the Western enterprise—and Rockefeller saw it. With Harper, any university would soon become great; without him, its future might be dubious. Two letters which the young educator wrote to Goodspeed in the fall of 1888, just as Gates's report was brought out, show both his own feelings and the way in which Rockefeller was at last veering to the Western choice. The first, dated October 13, described how he had met Rockefeller at Vassar

College, where both spent a week end. They enjoyed a long talk after Harper's Sunday morning lecture, and that evening rode to New York on the same train. Harper wrote:[45]

> ... The chief question was the one of the educational problem. ... Again and again he referred to his dealings with you and Doctor Northrup in the kindest terms, and on one occasion when President Taylor was present he broke out in the exclamation: "I never read a letter from Doctor Goodspeed without feeling better for having read it." There are no two men in the country of whom he thinks so much as of you two. He stands ready after the holidays to do something for Chicago. It will have to be managed, however, very carefully; but the chief point of my letter is this: in our discussion of the general question he showed great interest in the Educational Society (I mean the new one) and above all talked for hours in reference to the scheme for establishing the great university at Chicago instead of in New York. This surprised me very much. As soon as I began to see how the matter struck him I pushed it and I lost no opportunity of emphasizing this point. The long and the short of it is I feel confident that his mind has turned, and that it is a possible thing to have the money which he proposed to spend in New York diverted to Chicago.
>
> He himself made out a list of reasons why it would be better to go to Chicago than to remain in New York. Among other things the fact that there would be an entire uniformity of the thing, which could hardly be expected if the university were established in New York.
>
> Mr. Rockefeller left me with the understanding that he would at once communicate with Mr. Colby in reference to the matter and led me to infer that the question would receive his careful attention at once.

Rockefeller had indeed taken a keen interest in the new Education Society. He had corresponded with Doctor Morehouse upon its work, and sent it money—$3000, for example, at the beginning of October.[46] Harper's second letter was written November 5, after another meeting with Rockefeller at Vassar. It shows that the millionaire's imagination was becoming fired by a plan at once large and practicable:[47]

> I spent ten hours yesterday with Mr. Rockefeller; he came to Poughkeepsie. The result of our interview was the telegram which I sent you last night. He is practically committed to the thing. The great plan which now lies open to us is: (1) a college and university at Chicago; (2) a theological seminary of high grade in New York City; (3) the organization of colleges in the West. This is the way the thing presents itself to

[45]Harper Papers.
[46]Morehouse to Gates, October 6, 1888; Harper Papers.
[47]Harper to Goodspeed, November 5, 1888; Harper Papers.

him, and the order in which the things are to be done. He is very much in earnest, or surely, he would not have come up to Poughkeepsie. He had not read Gates's paper, but I gave him the substance and it fired him up. President Taylor was with me in the greatest part of the interview and backed up everything I said. He is a strong ally.

As Harper wrote, Rockefeller intended to inspect Cornell University and consult three Baptist professors there, E. Benjamin Andrews, Jacob Gould Schurman, and one other whom Harper did not name. He wished to learn how the proposed university struck them, and whether their services would be available. Meanwhile, he was anxious that the subject should not be discussed in such a way that rumors would get into print. Harper at once telegraphed Goodspeed to come east and join the group that was going to Ithaca. They were to meet at Rockefeller's house at seven-thirty the following Friday evening. "I believe," wrote Harper, "that this is the most important step which has been taken in the matter of the Chicago University. It is absolutely certain that the thing is to be done; it is now only a question as to what scale. I have every time claimed that nothing less than four millions would be satisfactory to begin with, and have expressed my desire for five. Just what he wants to do and what his definite ideas are I cannot yet tell. I have never known him to be so interested in anything, and this promises much."

It will be seen that Rockefeller, very characteristically, was getting as much expert advice as possible. He had talked with President Taylor of Vassar at length.

"Wouldn't it be best, Doctor Taylor," he had inquired, with shrewd anxiety to make sure that he was getting a sincere and considered answer, "to place the university, if it is to be established, in Washington?"

Taylor at once took strong ground in favor of Chicago. He remarked that more and more of the young men to be educated in Baptist institutions would come from the West.

"Well, Doctor Taylor," Rockefeller persisted, "is it certain that a large university is the principal need after all? Might it not be best to give the money to establish or strengthen colleges instead?"

On this point Taylor was hesitant; he thought the small colleges were doing more for the denomination than a great institution could do, and pointed to some examples. "But, Mr. Rockefeller," he added, "I would be glad to see the great university established. Why not do both?" Taylor talked with Rockefeller in New York as well as at Vassar, and at 4 West Fifty-fourth Street found the printed deliberations of the May meeting upon the educational question lying on Rockefeller's table.[48]

VII

But while Rockefeller was thus turning toward the Chicago idea, Strong was as determined as ever. Late in October the good doctor appeared in Cleveland to address the Ohio Baptist Education Society on "The Church and the University." He did not reveal many details of his plan (though he argued for the New York site), or allude to Rockefeller. The speech was delivered with his characteristic force and fervor. As he wrote later, "the audience seemed impressed, if not stunned." Rockefeller, who attended the lecture, shook Strong's hand with the enigmatic remark, "You have given me some new ideas, Doctor Strong—some new ideas!"[49] Just what these ideas were he did not say. Doctor Strong was now becoming profoundly excited, and his feelings were more and more intensely enlisted. He shortly published his Cleveland address, together with *A Detailed Argument and Plan,* and circulated them widely among Baptist leaders. The plan contained some excellent features. He wished to spend $2,000,000 out of the first $5,000,000 upon the library; to pay professors the then enormous sum of $5000 a year; and to erect strong departments of theology, law, and medicine. There were also some bad features. The tone of the university must be aggressively Christian, no "infidel" teachers were to be allowed, and the president must be a regularly ordained minister.

Meanwhile Goodspeed, after coming east for the Ithaca trip, set down on paper the first financial plan that had any resemblance to the plan ultimately adopted. Rockefeller had indicated his strong belief in conditional and co-operative giving. Goodspeed wrote him suggesting that "your proposition take this form": an initial gift of $1,500,000; a promise to match every other gift of $100,000 with $200,000 more, until a total of $4,000,000 was reached; his proportion of these gifts to be paid in ten annual instalments, and his offer to

[48]Morehouse to Gates, October 15, 1888; Harper Papers.
[49]Strong to Harper, November 6, 1888; Harper Papers.

continue in force throughout the decade.[50] This plan would have required Rockefeller to give $3,160,000, while others furnished only $840,000—hardly a fair apportionment; but it marked a long step in the right direction. While Goodspeed was thus active, Harper informed Doctor Strong that he was in favor of a Western university. And he received in reply a letter that spoke of an anguished heart. "Much as I respect your judgment," wrote Strong, "I think you are wrong in advising Mr. Rockefeller to separate Theology from the other departments of the University, and put the University at Chicago."[51] Chicago, he went on, was the place for a first-class college; New York was the place for a great university, to hold the primacy in American education. Waxing heated, he declared that "the establishment of a mongrel institution in Chicago, which is neither fish, flesh, nor fowl, neither University, College, nor Academy, but all three combined, would create no more of a ripple on the surface of our educational ocean than the work of Madison University now does."

The meeting between Goodspeed and Rockefeller in New York early in November was undoubtedly an immense stimulant to both. Goodspeed wrote jubilantly of it to his sons. They talked for two hours, and the millionaire was evidently nearing a decision. "Mr. Rockefeller has been self-moved in this new interest in the question," wrote Goodspeed. "He is profoundly in earnest. His heart is in this matter. He is full of it, and I feel a great hope kindling in my mind. His mind works fast, and I do not think we shall have to wait long for something decisive."[52] Harper, who was now frequently dining with Rockefeller, felt similarly encouraged. Before mid-November he reported that their frequent talks were resulting in progress. Rockefeller fully understood the necessity of the undertaking, and would be ready within a short time to make a definite proposal to the denomination. If Harper's advice were followed, this would come through the Education Society.[53] Then Rockefeller unexpectedly went up to Yale to talk with Harper, who sent an exultant letter upon their deliberations to Goodspeed:[54]

[50]Goodspeed to Rockefeller, November 13, 1888.
[51]Strong to Harper, November 18, 1888; Harper Papers.
[52]Goodspeed, *History*, 47.
[53]Harper to Gates, November 13, 1888; Harper Papers.
[54]Harper to Goodspeed, November 19, 1888; Harper Papers.

He was with me from 7:30 to 10 Saturday night and all day yesterday. Almost the only thing we discussed was the University of Chicago. He has made a good deal of progress since you and I visited him. He told me of the letter which he had written you and sent to the Grand Union Hotel. He did not tell me exactly what was in it, but I think that he felt your last proposition was a little out of proportion. He is clear on the point of the four million dollars, and he proposes to give one million and a half of the first two, and one million and a half of the second two. I am sure that this is the way it will come out. He is anxious now to have the thing agitated from an impersonal standpoint, and to have the denomination express themselves and commit themselves to a University. Whether he will be ready to make a bona fide proposition to the National Education Society, which will probably meet December 13, is a question.

He is settled in reference to two or three things: First, that you must have a leading hand in the new university, in the charge of its financial matters. I think he is pretty well settled also in reference to the repurchase of the old site. . . . His chief anxiety now seems to be, first, to have those who oppose the scheme present their objections, in order that he may consider them, and secondly, to get the thing started without alienating Doctor Strong. An arrangement has been made by which he will join me at Vassar College next Sunday, with Mrs. Rockefeller, and we shall there discuss the matter with Doctor Robinson of Brown, who is to preach there. I thought that perhaps Doctor Robinson would be able to present the objections, if anybody could. . . .

But President Robinson was also in favor of placing the university in Chicago! When Rockefeller talked with him, he expressed stern opposition to Doctor Strong's plan. Goodspeed was glad to hear this. Indeed, sentiment in the Baptist Church was now fast becoming a unit. The principal denominational organ, *The Examiner,* was speaking eloquently in favor of an institution in Chicago.

At this point, with the decision practically made, Doctor Strong struck hard—and struck, alas! below the belt. His rigid, dogmatic temper, his intense emotionalism, and his agony in seeing the great dream of his lifetime flash, like a pricked bubble, into nothingness, forced him into an unfair step. Doubtless, to do him justice, he did not realize just what an Iago-stroke it was.

Harper was at this time making weekly trips from New Haven to deliver a brilliant series of lectures at Vassar. Their subject-matter was the prophetic element in the Old Testament, upon which he later published a book. Doctor Strong, a trustee of Vassar, had sent his daughter to the college, and she sat in Doctor Harper's course. Taking her notes, Strong scrutinized them, and easily persuaded himself that they convicted Harper of heretical views. Forthwith, he sat down and wrote Rockefeller, who was also a trustee, declaring that Harper's lectures proved him an unbeliever in the supernatural element in the New Testament, and a dangerous man! As a matter of fact, the position of the young theologian had been no more radical than that taken at the time in leading Baptist seminaries, and he at no point rejected the supernatural element in the Old Testament. It is difficult not to agree with Harper's immediate conclusion: "His [Strong's] purpose was of course to injure me, feeling sure that in injuring me he would injure the chances of the University of Chicago—else why should he write to Mr. Rockefeller concerning this matter?"[55]

Harper first heard of the complaints when, after a period of silence on Rockefeller's part, he went down to New York to see what was the matter. He found Rockefeller very busy at his office.

"What progress has been made, Mr. Rockefeller, in reference to the Chicago matter?" was Harper's first question.

"I have made little progress, Doctor Harper," answered the industrialist. "My wife has been sick and I have been very anxious about her. My time has been taken up with the consideration of petitions from many sources—I have never known them so numerous. Montreal has come down upon me. Richmond, with a great reinforcement, has come down upon me. From every quarter the demands are growing more numerous, and more insistent. Besides, you cannot imagine how many people have been volunteering their opinions in reference to the Chicago matter. You would be amazed to know the peculiar statements of many who have called to see me. I have been keeping my ears open and hearing everything. Young Strong, who is stopping with me now, thinks that nothing but a college is needed at Chicago. I find a good many who think thus; but I am so tired that I haven't really strength to consider the matter. I did not ask you to come and see me Sunday because I spent the day in bed; Christmas, too, I spent in bed—I was so tired. I have had some unusually worrying business matters in the

[55]Harper to Gates, December 28, 1888; Harper Papers.

last three weeks; still, the thing is on my mind and I want to hear more about it."[56]

Harper could see that Rockefeller felt some special worry to which he did not like to give utterance. And finally it came out— Doctor Strong had charged Harper with being a Kuenenite, almost a rationalist! (Abraham Kuenen, a Dutch theologian, had published in 1875 a study of Hebrew prophecy attacking those who rested theological dogmas upon the fulfillment of prophecy; and his book filled the narrower American theologians with horror.) Of course Harper at once protested. He returned to New Haven seriously disturbed. There he soon received a letter from Strong himself, taking him sternly to task, and asking him to assert his belief in the literal interpretation of all Old Testament transactions, and all New Testament references to the Old. This was on the basis of Miss Strong's fragmentary reports, or as Harper put it, "a schoolgirl's notes."[57]

Intensely agitated, Harper wrote two long letters to Gates in one day. He was half angry, half sorrowful. "I feel this morning as if I were ready to pull out of the whole concern," he exploded. He believed that Rockefeller had not been influenced by the charges, and this was true. While Rockefeller, like Strong, was a fundamentalist, their outlook was very different; for Strong insisted that all Baptists must think like him if they were to be orthodox, while Rockefeller was quite willing to let others hold their own views. What now worried Rockefeller was the fear of a church schism. After years of uncertainty, the denomination had at last apparently reached an agreement on the educational question; and was it to be riven apart again? Harper looked with foreboding on the future. Rockefeller would expect him to explain the charges away—and Harper could readily do this. "But I am not going to be drawn into a fight over these matters even if I am to be deposed from the Vassar teaching by Doctor Strong's attitude because he is a member of the Board of Trustees—a deposition ostensibly for heresy, but really to bring me into discredit, so that I shall have no influence

[56]Harper to Gates, December 28, 1888 (two letters of this date); Harper Papers.
[57]Ibid.; cf. T. W. Goodspeed, *William Rainey Harper*, passim; History, 107 ff.

in the Chicago matter. . . . The question is whether the brethren in the West will stand by me or not."

Fortunately, churchmen both East and West did stand by him, and with vigor. Doctor Northrup and President Taylor wrote letters to Strong which fully endorsed and supported Harper. President Taylor, who had heard all the lectures, insisted with great emphasis on Harper's fairness, reverence, belief in the supernatural, and essential conservatism. At the height of the controversy, Harper urged Gates to come east early in January, 1889, and talk with Rockefeller. At the same time Northrup wrote the millionaire a six-page typewritten letter covering, as he remarked, four points:[58]

1.—Harper and Strong (explanatory, confirmatory, irenical, etc.).
2.—Strong (appreciation—good and strong).
3.—Harper (appreciation—better and stronger).
4.—Rockefeller and the Chicago University (best and strongest).

VIII

It is evident from Rockefeller's letters that Doctor Strong had made but little impression upon him. The magnate wrote Doctor Harper in a rather worried tone. "It would break my heart if I did not believe you would stay in the fold all right. For all the reasons I believe you will. Be sure you do. I know you will understand and not take offense at my suggestion about writing." But he was not really shaken for an instant in his resolve to help found an institution of learning in Chicago. To an unnamed minister lunching with him early in January he said that he had substantially decided to give several hundred thousands toward a million-dollar fund for the purpose. Doctor Strong was soon compelled to recede from his charges. And later in January Harper, spending three hours with Rockefeller, found the industrialist quite explicit as to his interest in Chicago. Delighted beyond measure by this burst of dawn after long darkness, Harper set down his impressions in nine points:[59]

1.—He is certainly planning to do something for Chicago.
2.—He is kept from it by the large amount of money he is giving to other objects—an amount greater by many thousands than in any preceding year; partly by the pressing calls which are coming from every direction (e.g., Broadus is pushing him unmercifully for $50,000 for Louis-

[58]Northrup to Harper, January 3, 1888; Harper Papers.
[59]Harper to Goodspeed, January 27, 1889; Harper Papers.

ville, as a thank-offering for Mrs. R's recovery; he will not get it); Gilman of Johns Hopkins has been at him; Pres. Willing of Columbia(n) has tried to get at him, etc., etc., etc., etc.; it makes one tired merely to see the list.

3.—Gates made a good impression; he likes him.

4.—Strong has accomplished something but not much.

5.—He will give the money (which is to be given) to the Education Society, allowing it to appropriate it at its pleasure; but in every case he must be allowed to endorse the appropriation.

6.—He will give it at the rate of so much a year for a certain number of years—how much, and for how many years I could not get him to indicate, though I tried very hard.

7.—He will decide soon. . . .

8.—He is more tired than ever of Strong, and the New York plan is N. G.

9.—He agreed that, everything considered, I would better stay at New Haven for a period not exceeding five years. . . . He would like the arrangement to be for only three years at most.

And, concluded Harper, he had never been so kind, never so interested, and never so anxious to do just the right thing.

This statement that Rockefeller was more tired of Strong than ever carried implications tragic to the aggressive theologian. He was tired of Strong's pertinacity, of his narrow dogmatism, of his emotionalism. He could not avoid contrasting the breadth and serene energy of Harper with Doctor Strong's harsh fanaticism; and he realized that it would be as dangerous to entrust the guidance of a great university to the latter as it would be safe to entrust it to Harper. All this time he said and wrote nothing to Doctor Strong. But as the latter became increasingly conscious of Rockefeller's tacit disfavor, he fell into deep despondency. "The man is mad, daft," wrote Goodspeed,[60] while Gates, who heard from persons close to him, declared:[61] "Strong is melancholy, a profoundly unhappy and disappointed man, I fear almost desperate." Yet the doctor had labored better than he knew. Some distinct and admirable features of his grandiose plan were to be embodied in the future University of Chicago.

Meanwhile, the executive board of the Education Society had met in Washington in the last days of 1888, and Gates had sub-

[60]To Harper, January 22, 1889; Harper Papers.
[61]To Morehouse, January 3, 1889; Harper Papers.

mitted a report urging united support for the founding of a new university in Chicago. The board unanimously approved the Chicago plan. Then Gates sent Rockefeller a letter—since the industrialist was too busy to see him—intended to resolve some of the last difficulties lying before the great project.

Rockefeller, as Gates learned, still felt two grounds for perplexity. Harper and others were urging him to give a large sum of money and erect a university of great immediate strength. Others were advising him that only a college was needed. He inclined to some compromise action, partly because (as Gates surmised) he did not have three or four millions immediately available, and partly because he believed in letting institutions grow from modest beginnings and prove their worth.[62] He was also troubled over the question whether Doctor Harper would take charge of the institution. Of course the brilliant Yale professor would gladly accept the presidency of a great university; but if Rockefeller established merely a college, would Harper consent to be its head? Gates suggested a way past these perplexities. In a long letter, he proposed that Rockefeller at once set up a college, but with plans for its early expansion into a university; and that Harper remain at Yale, giving his advice while the institution was in its formative stage, and then become head as it grew larger.

Characteristically, Rockefeller gave no indication of his feeling about Gates's ideas. But he did write Harper that he had come to feel that it might be wisest to give Chicago a college, and leave the university to a later date.[63]

A little later he had Gates and Morehouse lunch with him. The talk at table was on general subjects. But after they had risen, Rockefeller quietly suggested that since he was about to leave for Cleveland, and Gates was going back to Chicago, they take the same train. They did so.

"Of course I was on the crest of anticipation," the secretary wrote later,[64] "expecting a long, interesting, and possibly decisive conversation." He thought it would be best to let the head of the Standard Oil open the Chicago subject. While waiting for him to do so, he studied his companion. "I observed the neatness of Mr. Rockefeller's

[62]Gates, MS Autobiography.
[63]Rockefeller to Harper, January 15, 1889; Harper Papers.
[64] MS Autobiography, 200.

clothing," Gates writes. "It was spotless but very quiet and inconspicuous, though of the costliest materials and workmanship. There was a conspicuous absence of jewelry and ornament. No watch guard or chain was visible, no rings, and not even a pin in his necktie." He was struck by the rich man's solution of the problem of tipping; he held out a handful of change, and let waiters and porters take what they thought their due. To his parents he reported: "Mr. Rockefeller is on the whole the greatest man I ever saw. He is the broadest, clearest-headed, most universal in his sympathies, most calmly self-poised, most devoted to what he regards as duty, least influenced by considerations of position, or the authority of advocates of special causes. A child with a clear case would have just as much weight with him as the most eminent of men." By way of supplement Gates added years later: "He impressed me with his extreme reserve, without the least sign of austerity. In his talk I was impressed with his quiet ease, the simplicity and directness of his speech, the penetration, experience, and yet reserve of it. He had then been in business for thirty-five years and during most of his time had been a national storm center in business. His look, manner, conversation, and general carriage were those of a man who had cultivated and acquired an easy and habitual self-command."

Of Rockefeller's reserve the secretary indeed had an unpleasant dose. All evening he waited vainly for his companion to open up the great subject. When they retired, Gates felt a miserable, disappointed man. But Rockefeller appreciated the educator's forbearance. Next morning he began to question Gates closely about the Education Society. After talking freely of its personnel and of Gates's part in its work, he remarked that the Society might "become a relief to him"; that is, he thought of making important gifts through it. In parting he remarked that his mind moved slowly, and requested that the interview be held confidential. Gates was encouraged.[65]

He had good reason, for the situation was now approaching its climax. On this trip Rockefeller was really "sizing up" Gates, and assuring himself of the secretary's capacity and dependability.[66] He was more than satisfied, and from the date of that train-journey the

[65]*Ibid.* [66]Goodspeed, *History,* 56.

dynamic Gates began to take the leading part in the negotiations. Harper was meanwhile writing Goodspeed that he thought the University might be given a triple headship: one man to have charge of financial affairs, buildings, and other material matters, one to direct the faculty and courses of instruction, and a third to help make policies. He, watching affairs from New Haven and making frequent trips to Chicago, would be the third man! This plan was the temporary aberration of a great mind, and Harper immediately dropped it; but it showed that he fully appreciated Rockefeller's desire that he direct the course of the new institution.[67] Once Rockefeller was certain that Gates could be trusted as he already trusted Goodspeed, and once he felt a fair assurance that Harper's incomparable services would be at his disposal, he would be ready to move decisively. When Gates suggested that the executive committee of the Society should appoint a group of men to go to Chicago, talk with leading churchmen, inspect available sites, and discuss details, Rockefeller warmly approved the step. He wished this body to prepare a *definite* plan, including proposals for raising funds from other sources, and an outline of the departments of the university. He himself suggested several members of the committee, which, minutely advised by Gates, began its work in March. Its nine members included Harper, E. Benjamin Andrews, President Taylor, Doctor Duncan, Doctor Morehouse, and Charles L. Colby.

IX

All the factors essential to a final decision by Rockefeller had now been, or were rapidly being, supplied. First, the existence of a genuine need and of a real popular demand had been established by Gates's telling report. Second, the denomination had been fairly united behind a course of action; Morehouse, Gates, and others had done that. Third, the scheme for a Western university was now being placed upon that foundation of provisional and co-operative giving upon which Rockefeller based all his philanthropies. He would give but moderate sums until it had taken root, and others would be asked to give with him. Gates and Goodspeed, both adept in money-raising, would help find the funds. Finally, the personal elements that were all-important to action by Rockefeller had now

[67]Goodspeed, *History,* 56, 57.

been supplied. Three men stood ready to offer the new Western university precisely the leadership it would require. With the shrewd Gates as principal money-raiser and guardian of funds; with Doctor Goodspeed to furnish his wide influence in the West, his learning, and his business capacity; and with Doctor Harper to supply his genius for creative planning, the university was assured of success. These three men, so different yet so complementary, were figures whom any institution might be proud to have in the forefront of its history; and their united enthusiasm for the project made Rockefeller feel that it was at last safe to act. Having reached that conclusion, he moved with characteristic decision.

The final scene has been memorably described by Gates. In May, Rockefeller called him to New York just before the annual Baptist gathering, which was to be held in Boston. The report of the committee which had visited Chicago was now ready, and contemplated an expenditure of not less than $1,400,000 within four years. Rockefeller and Gates spent the evening together, and next morning Gates came back to breakfast. After the meal they stepped out upon the street and paced to and fro in front of the house. It was a delicious spring day. They agreed that at least $1,000,000 would be required to found the institution—that no smaller fund would command confidence. Rockefeller spoke of giving $400,000; but Gates told him that he must do more—that nothing less than $600,-000 from him as against $400,000 from the denomination would give any promise of success. They must go before the people of Chicago and the West with the task more than half done.

"At last," writes Gates, "at a certain point near Fifth Avenue, Mr. Rockefeller stopped, faced me, and yielded the point. Never shall I forget the thrill of that moment. I have since been intimately associated with him. I have seen him give $10,000,000, $30,000,000, $100,000,000, but no gift of his has ever thrilled me as did the first great gift of $600,000, on that May morning after those months of anxious suspense."

XXXVI

The Rise of a University

THE date set for the meeting of the Baptist Education Society in Boston this year—1889—was May 18, and the place was Tremont Temple. Gates journeyed northward with an elated heart. As the general church convention was being held at the same time, he found several hundred delegates present. The executive board of the Society had reported in favor of the establishment of a well-equipped college, later to become a university, in Chicago; and a motion was immediately made by Doctor Alvah Hovey that this action be endorsed. Several speakers were heard. Among them was Doctor Strong, who declared that although he still believed that education properly began at the top, and that it would have been wisest to found a university first, he would give his cordial blessing to the college. The way was thus opened for unanimous approval of the report. Then Gates, as secretary, stepped forward.

"I hold in my hand," he said, "a letter from our great patron of education, Mr. John D. Rockefeller—" Here he was halted by wild applause and enthusiasm.

"A letter," he went on, "in which, on the basis of the resolutions adopted by our board, he promises that he will give six hundred thousand dollars——"

Again he was interrupted by tremendous cheering and hand-clapping, long sustained. When order was restored, the assemblage rose and united in singing, "Praise God from Whom All Blessings Flow." Thereupon it sent Rockefeller a telegram announcing that the denomination had received "with unparalleled enthusiasm and gratitude" the announcement of his "princely gift."[1]

Rockefeller had exacted from Gates a promise that the pledge of

[1]*American Baptist Yearbook, 1889;* New York newspapers.

$600,000 should be kept entirely secret until the Education Society had committed itself to the establishment of the college in Chicago. If the Society had failed to do this, then the pledge was to be returned to him undelivered. He wished the denomination to make up its mind upon the new institution in perfect independence. Indeed, he and Gates had spent a long time at 26 Broadway mulling over the pledge, and revising its form again and again.[2]

II

The two tasks of primary importance which now had to be faced were the raising of the $400,000 needed to meet the stipulations of Rockefeller's gift, and the selection of a president for the new institution. Both presented some unexpected difficulties.

Doctors Gates and Goodspeed assumed charge of the campaign for obtaining the additional funds. The latter did so with a heavy heart, for he had hoped and labored to obtain an unconditional grant from Rockefeller, and the failure to do so filled him with depression. He feared that so large a sum could never be raised. "If I know all that is to be known," he wrote Harper, "then God help us."[3] It was with the greatest reluctance that he committed himself to the effort, but when Gates agreed to move to Morgan Park and devote himself wholly to the campaign, he was fairly forced into it. Rockefeller's pledge had given them a year for the work. Goodspeed thought this inadequate, but Gates felt long afterward that they would have done better if given only three months. The very length of the period granted for solicitation caused money and pledges to come in haltingly.[4] Appeals were directed to four bodies: to Baptists in and near Chicago, to Baptists outside that area, to businessmen and other prominent citizens, and to the general public everywhere. One of the first steps was to distribute pleas to all the Chicago congregations and to about twelve hundred ministers elsewhere in the West. But in and near the city much of the work was done by personal solicitation. The rule was not to press for contributions, and never to suggest the amount to be given, but as far as possible to let no man say "No."

Within two months the fund amounted to $200,000, given chiefly

[2]Gates to Goodspeed, Jan. 9, 1915; Harper Papers.
[3]Goodspeed, MS Autobiography.   [4]Gates, MS Autobiography.

by Baptists. Then came the rub, and every new cent was won by hard effort and argument. For both Gates and Goodspeed the canvass became an exhausting and harrowing experience. The former pronounced it the most disagreeable, depressing, and anxious work of his life. "It placed a heavy shadow on the year, removed only at the very end by success." That first fund, he added, "cost more brain work, anguish, tears, prayers, and shoe leather than all the millions that have since gone into the University."[5] Goodspeed called it "a desperate struggle against what often seemed insurmountable obstacles."[6] But victory was won at last. The Baptists of the city and its vicinity gave $233,000; businessmen of Chicago $70,000; and people outside the city area $116,000—making a total of about $419,000. Prominent among the donors were the alumni of the old University and a Jewish group. Finally, the merchant Marshall Field offered as a site a ten-acre tract valued at $125,000.[7] Rockefeller's principle of conditional giving had after all been vindicated.

III

With an endowment assured, it remained to plan the institution's work and assemble its staff. This offered problems of a crucial character. Marshall Field's gift had determined the site of the school. The land fronted on the Midway Plaisance, between Jackson and Washington Parks, an ideal site; and an additional area of a block and a half was shortly purchased from Field. When the May meetings of the Baptist denomination were held in Chicago in 1890, Gates told the story of a year's progress with an eloquence which aroused the strongest enthusiasm. Once more the concourse rose spontaneously to sing the Doxology. The Education Society immediately appointed the Board of Trustees, two thirds of whom were to be Baptists. Then important events followed in rapid succession. On July 9, the Trustees held their first meeting; on September 8, the

[5]Gates to Goodspeed, Jan. 9, 1915; Harper Papers.
[6]Goodspeed, MS Autobiography. Gates wrote Harper on Feb. 3, 1890: "We are unusually well received and even welcomed in business offices of millionaires, and though they hesitate or postpone they feel *flattered* by the visit." Harper Papers.
[7]Goodspeed, *History,* 87 ff. Alumni of the old university gave $30,000; the Jewish group $27,000. Rockefeller sent Marshall Field on Jan. 24, 1890, a cordial personal letter of congratulation and fellowship.

original University was renamed "The Old University"; and on September 10, the University of Chicago was incorporated. Finally, the most important step of all was taken when on September 18 William Rainey Harper was unanimously elected to the presidency —though it was not yet certain he would accept.[8]

Rockefeller watched all this with keen sympathy. A rapid succession of letters from Gates and Goodspeed chronicled every step in their work. To a proposal that the institution be given his name he returned a decided negative. In this he showed better taste than some other American capitalists who, for gifts totalling far less than his, have not only permitted but often insisted that their names be borne in perpetuity by the institutions they helped to found. He also showed good sense, for "The University of Chicago" was the only appropriate name. He was consulted as to the choice of Trustees; but the selection of men for this body was made chiefly by Gates and Goodspeed, who in collecting funds had become acquainted with a number of able citizens certain to manifest a continuing interest. The roster included such well-known Chicagoans as Herman H. Kohlsaat, E. Nelson Blake, Charles L. Hutchinson, and Martin A. Ryerson. Both Rockefeller and Marshall Field approved the list before it was finally voted upon. Rockefeller was undoubtedly pleased by the report which the executive board of the Education Society submitted in May, 1890, defining three characteristics which should stamp the new institution. It should be Christian, and should be forever under Baptist auspices, but it should "be conducted in a spirit of the widest liberality," inviting to its halls the largest possible number of students from "every class."

When Doctor Harper hesitated to accept the presidency, Rockefeller was seriously disturbed. Yale naturally made great efforts to keep the brilliant young professor, still only thirty-four. President Dwight strenuously opposed his leaving, and unfairly asserted that since the university had done so much for him, he was in duty bound to remain indefinitely! Letters poured in from alumni and friends of Yale. Several of the ablest men of the faculty earnestly assured him he would make the mistake of his life if he went out to Chicago, where he would have to spend years in building a weak institution up to a level where it could command a little prestige.

[8]Goodspeed, *History*, 96 ff.; *William Rainey Harper*, 93.

Meanwhile, a flood of letters came from Western Baptists, old Morgan Park associates, and educators like Bishop John H. Vincent and Doctor Richard T. Ely, pleading that he go to Chicago. One reason why he hesitated was that, although a born executive, his heart was really in Biblical scholarship—or so he thought. Believing that he could not conduct a university and continue research and writing, he doubted whether he should give up his life's work.[9]

But another and larger reason lay in the fact that he did not believe a true university could be founded by gifts of a million dollars and ten acres of land. Though Harper held that the West was the proper seat of the new institution, he had really been captivated by Strong's vision of a great university, the equal of Oxford or Berlin, devoted mainly to graduate work. He had thought that Goodspeed made a vital mistake when he asked merely for a college; he had bitterly reproached the Western group when they reduced their initial request to a million dollars. Until almost the end he had persisted in misunderstanding Rockefeller's intentions, crediting him with the wish to found a rich and powerful university in the European sense in Chicago. Even near the close of 1888 he had believed that the institution of Doctor Strong's dreams was to rise there.[10] Goodspeed assured him that as Rockefeller's wealth increased, his vision would expand and he would endow the University; while Gates reminded him that even if a university were planned, a college would necessarily be the first work. But when the final decision was taken, Harper was grieved and hesitant. He by no means closed his mind to the presidency. On June 4, 1890, he wrote Goodspeed that he was "inclined to consider the Chicago question."[11] But he clung to all his old ambitions for the institution.

As soon as it was evident that he would be the unanimous choice of the Trustees, and that Rockefeller earnestly wished him to take the place, he made this fact perfectly clear. He insisted that more money must be obtained to accomplish what the intellectual world anticipated. "There must in some way be an assurance of an additional million," Harper wrote Gates on July 31. "How this is to be obtained, or where, is the question. If Mr. R. is in dead earnest, possibly the case will not be so difficult as we may think." This

[9] See Goodspeed, *History,* 106 ff.
[10] Goodspeed, MS Autobiography.   [11] Harper Papers.

letter of course found its way to Rockefeller's desk. Within a week, on August 5, the industrialist was inviting Harper to visit him:[12]

I agree with the Board of Trustees of Chicago University that you are the man for President, and if you take it I shall expect great results. I cannot conceive of a position where you can do the world more good; and I confidently expect we will add funds from time to time to those already pledged, to place it upon the most favored basis financially. I do not forget that the effort to establish the University grew out of your suggestion to me at Vassar, and I regard you as the father of the institution, starting out under God with such great promise of future usefulness.

In reply, Doctor Harper spoke frankly of his belief that greater resources were needed. The church and indeed the whole country, he wrote, were expecting the University to be from the very beginning an institution of the highest rank and character. Already it was being talked of in the same breath with Yale, Harvard, and Princeton, with Johns Hopkins, Cornell, and Michigan. No one expected its standards to be lower than those of the best American institutions; and yet, with the money available, he did not perceive how it could equal them. "Naturally we ought to be willing to begin small and grow, but in these days when things are done so rapidly, and with the example of Johns Hopkins before our eyes, it seems a great pity to wait for growth when we might be born full-fledged."[13]

He discussed the situation with Rockefeller in Cleveland. Then, on August 17, he held a conference with Gates, and the two agreed upon an eight-point arrangement under which all of Doctor Harper's principal requests were to be met. The first part of it embodied a plan whereby he could become president of the University, and at the same time maintain his chosen life-work of Old Testament research, criticism, and instruction. Under this plan, the Morgan Park Theological Seminary was to become an integral part of the University; the instruction in Hebrew and Old Testament criticism was to be transferred to university chairs; and Doctor Harper was to be made principal professor, with full authority over the department offering this instruction. The seventh and most significant article of the agreement went tersely to the heart of the financial problem. "Mr. Rockefeller," it ran, "to give one million dollars as

[12]*Ibid.*   [13]*Ibid.*

a new, unconditional gift, a part of which would go for aid to the Seminary in carrying out the plan." The eighth article stipulated that Doctor Harper was to visit Rockefeller, and accept the presidency on the basis of this program.[14]

Seldom, if ever, has a wealthy man been held up in this fashion! Rockefeller had committed himself to the establishment of a great university. He wished one particular man for president, and knew that the University could not attain its highest success without him. Now this man was coolly informing him that he would not come unless another million dollars was paid into the endowment.

But Rockefeller was quite willing to be held up! Gates laid the eight-point agreement before him at once, and found it acceptable. Harper spent September 4 and 5 in Cleveland, where he and Rockefeller devoted nearly the entire day to the discussion of details. The industrialist then wrote a letter promising an additional million, and gave it to Harper for delivery to the Trustees; while Harper began to act upon the theory that he was committed to the presidency. The very day after the interview he wrote Goodspeed that he wished half a dozen acts performed, intimating that he hoped for immediate progress and would accept all necessary responsibility. On the basis of this indicated willingness, the Trustees on September 18 elected him president. Though he was given six months in which to make his final decision, everybody understood that his acceptance was certain.[15] Indeed, he at once took in hand the plan of organization for the University. Always a terrific worker, he began to concentrate upon the institution the tremendous energy and zeal which, with his powerful brain, enthusiasm for scholarship, and wide knowledge of the teaching world, made him such an admirable choice for the presidency.

IV

From this point all should have gone smoothly; but a new and unanticipated difficulty soon gave Rockefeller fresh anxiety. Doctor Harper was keenly sensitive to public opinion, especially on matters of conscience. He suddenly began to worry lest his doctrinal position should subject the University to embarrassment. Already Doctor Strong had attacked him for his supposed radicalism. What if the

[14]Goodspeed, *History*, 121, 122.   [15]*Ibid.*, 122.

attack were renewed? What if the friends of the Morgan Park Seminary did not consider him sufficiently orthodox to warrant uniting the two institutions under his leadership? After sleepless nights, he called Gates, Goodspeed, and others together, and laid the matter before them. They of course assured him that his fears were groundless.[16]

For a time Harper's mind seemed tranquil, and he began considering candidates for faculty positions. Nevertheless, it soon became evident that his secret anxieties were still preying upon him. His correspondents in Chicago did their utmost to hearten him. They believed he had been overworking, and begged him to drop all university business for a few weeks. Not until later did they learn that some unnamed person had been writing him "strictly private" letters, advising him that he was in honor bound to make a full statement of his doctrinal position to Rockefeller—perhaps also to the public. Finally, Harper in November, 1891, burst forth with all his troubles in a letter to Goodspeed. This epistle irritated Goodspeed, who immediately destroyed it. "We have settled that matter and I will not reopen it," he informed Harper.[17] Gates, learning of the matter, added his assurances that the president-elect need feel no uneasiness.

But the conscience-ridden Harper decided that he must make a full statement to Rockefeller, and in a long letter of January 8, 1891, did so. He began by reviewing his difficulties with Doctor Strong in 1888, adding: "There is no doubt that the way in which I present Bible truth differs largely from that of leading men of the Baptist denomination." He believed it the will of God that he continue teaching in this way. He could not accept a position in which that privilege would be denied him, yet he did not wish to bring down on the new institution the distrust of the denomination. He could teach what he believed the truth at Yale, with hearty and constant encouragement from the president and the theological faculty; but could he teach it at Chicago? He felt that he ought to lay the exact situation before Rockefeller.[18]

"If my positions are so far away from those of the rank and file of the denomination as to make me unfit to hold the office of

[16]This whole matter is covered in Goodspeed, *History*, 122–130.
[17]*Ibid.*, 123.   [18]*Ibid.*, 124, 125.

president," he added, "it ought to be known before I accept it. . . . If this is true you ought to know it. I therefore propose to you that you select three or four gentlemen, *e.g.,* Doctor Morehouse, Doctor Rhoades, Mr. Faunce, and that you give me the opportunity of laying before you and before them the exact facts, in order that (1) I may know whether I shall have the privilege of teaching my views in the University of Chicago, and (2) I may decide in case this privilege is not granted me, whether, under all the circumstances, it is wise for the University and for myself to accept the position."

Rockefeller was highly displeased by this strange proposal; and making no immediate reply, he kept the anxious Doctor Harper waiting for several weeks. It did not seem to him that Harper, having received an additional million for the University as a condition of his acceptance, should now be raising new difficulties. Nor did Rockefeller believe that he ought to be asked to pass upon nice points of theological doctrine, or to assume the responsibility of deciding what Harper should teach and should not teach. He had neither the qualifications, the time, nor the inclination for that task!

He did call Doctor Morehouse, the founder of the Education Society, into conference. The two lunched together twice, and apparently agreed in taking a rather impatient view of Harper's proposals. At any rate, Rockefeller had Doctor Morehouse draft a long letter to the president-elect, which he approved before it was mailed on February 2, 1891.

In this letter, Rockefeller and Morehouse were sternly frank. They pointed out that in view of the antecedent understanding between Harper and Rockefeller, when Harper delivered to the Trustees the letter promising a million dollars he thereby ratified his acceptance of the presidency. As the letter bound Rockefeller, so it bound Harper. After matters had gone so far the introduction of new conditions as prerequisite to the formal acceptance of the presidency was unpleasant. If pressed, this would result in a serious impairment of the cordial relations between Rockefeller and the University. Rockefeller also made it clear that he could not pass upon questions of Old Testament interpretation. As for the proposed conference with various theologians on the subject, he preferred to abide by the decision of the men whom Harper had already consulted in Chicago. "The brethren named by you," ran the letter, "would be reluctant practically to sit in judgment upon the candor or the competency of those with whom you have already conferred." Finally, Rockefeller and Morehouse turned to Harper's question whether it would be right, if he could not teach his views, to accept the presidency. This, they asserted, was a purely hypothetical question, and it was not wise to introduce a new and quite unnecessary complication at this critical stage in the university enterprise.

"The private committal has been made," Morehouse concluded, "and the chief patron of the enterprise is not prepared to give his consent to a reopening of the question or a reversal of the decision."

This ended the curious episode. The letter lifted Doctor Harper out of his morbidity, and thereafter he took the view that, having put his hand to the plow, he must not look back. On February 5 he resigned at Yale, and eleven days later sent the Trustees in Chicago his acceptance of the presidency. The news was received with unalloyed pleasure throughout the educational world. Doctor Wallace Buttrick, pastor at New Haven, wrote Harper with true Baptist fervor: "I thank you and congratulate the Universe."[19] Rockefeller urged the president to take a good rest before he entered on his duties, adding: "And now, my dear Doctor Harper, I will not undertake to express what I feel toward you and your work, and could not if I would. My hopes are high."[20]

v

The founder had realized when he made his original gift of $600,000 that the sum would be only a small beginning. This fact accounted for the readiness with which he had added a million more as soon as Harper asked for it—a million which rendered possible the immediate expansion of the college into a university. His letter to the Trustees, dated September 16, 1890, declared that of the new fund, $800,000 was to be used as endowment for non-professional graduate instruction and fellowships, while the remaining $200,000 was to go to the Divinity School.

When Rockefeller thus made it possible to convert the college into a university, numerous Westerners assured him that Chicago would respond quickly and generously, and make large contributions for buildings and equipment. But although for some time the

[19]*Ibid.*, 129.   [20]Inglis, MS Biography, 422.

country remained prosperous, although Chicago was growing rapidly and looking forward to a great World's Fair, little was accomplished. Purse-strings remained tied. Some of Rockefeller's Western correspondents wrote him in despondent terms. They had expected that immediately after his gifts a campus would be laid out, handsome buildings would begin to rise, and appointments to the faculty would be announced. When nothing of the kind happened, they leaped at the conclusion that the city was unwilling to do its share, and was waiting for him to carry the entire burden.[21] These letters depressed Rockefeller. When Gates called in the spring of 1891, he found the president of the Standard much discouraged. They talked the matter over frankly. Gates expatiated upon various hopeful facts—a recent gift by Martin A. Ryerson, the action the Trustees had just taken to raise $500,000 for buildings, the prospect that several hundred thousand might be obtained elsewhere, the support of the newspapers, and the profound sense of responsibility manifested by the Trustees. All this helped to lift from Rockefeller's mind the fear that he would have to support the University unaided by the rich metropolis of Western business.

In their talk, Rockefeller impressed upon Gates that he did not wish the officers of the University to come running to him to make up every annual deficit, or to demand small gifts for every emergency. These injunctions Gates took much to heart.[22] He at once asked Harper to estimate the absolutely minimum expenses for the year beginning July 1, 1891, and also for the subsequent year. When Harper did so, his figures rendered it plain that for at least three years the University would have to rely upon special contributions in addition to all its income from endowment. This offered precisely the situation which Rockefeller wished to see guarded against. The University would begin operations, it would soon run into debt, and then its Trustees would beseech him to lift it out of its difficulties. Gates had fully entered into the founder's ideas on this point, and approved them. He had written Rockefeller: "While Doctor Harper undoubtedly expects that you will give more to the University, I feel confident that he will be equally active and eager with every one else from whom there is the least hope of funds. He will by no means confine his importunities to yourself,

[21]Goodspeed, *History*, 177.   [22]Gates, MS Autobiography.

and I feel confident that you can dismiss, with a light heart, the anxieties of last Sunday."

To this Rockefeller replied, three days later: "It is an added indication to me that we can work together *to help the world.*"[23] Already he had asked Gates to come to New York and assist him in his benevolent work, and Gates had promised to do so.

It was therefore in a dual capacity, as one of the men engaged in organizing the University of Chicago, and as a confidential agent for Rockefeller, that Gates studied the two tentative budget-sheets which Harper laid before him. He did not in the least like their implication that special contributions would be needed for current expenses. As educator, he knew that this meant trouble for the infant University. As unofficial agent for Rockefeller, he knew that it meant trouble for the millionaire founder. He strongly objected to any budget that did not keep within current income. For several months the question of budgetary expenditure remained in a confused state. Then Harper began to find that his efforts to detach able teachers from other faculties and bring them to Chicago were impeded by the prevalent belief that the University was not on a stable financial basis. "Am completely discouraged," he wrote Gates on December 26, 1891. "We have not a head professor after nine months of constant work. Not one of the men that we want can be moved from a good position at a salary of six thousand dollars. I am in despair."[24]

By this time Gates had resigned his secretaryship, entered the employ of Rockefeller, and taken up his headquarters in New York. He held a conference with Harper a few days later. This convinced him that the situation was indeed serious. The University was to open its doors and begin instruction within nine months, on October 1, 1892; and where was the instructing force? Following his talk with the president, he discussed the matter with Rockefeller, who sent him to Chicago to make a study of the situation. Arriving late in January, Gates discovered that the foundation of two build-

[23]April 30, 1891; Harper Papers.
[24]Goodspeed, *History*, 178. Gates feared in 1891–92 that Harper was undertaking too many outside activities to do the university full justice. Rockefeller on July 21, 1891, sent Harper a gentle rebuke upon "the danger of spreading out too thin." Subsequently Harper asked Faunce if he thought he were doing too much. Faunce said *yes,* and Harper cancelled thirty-six lectures—to Gates's jubilation. Harper Papers.

ings, a lecture hall and a dormitory, had been completed, and that a number of "head professors" had at last been obtained. They included William Gardner Hale and J. Laurence Laughlin of Cornell as professors of Latin and political economy respectively; Harry Pratt Judson of the University of Minnesota as professor of history; and William I. Knapp of Yale as professor of Romance languages and literature. But the financial outlook was less promising. It had been agreed that the salary list for the first year must not exceed $100,000. The interest on investments was expected to reach $40,000, and the net income from tuition $35,000. This left an estimated deficit for the first year of $25,000, which the Trustees had already made up from their own pockets.

"Some of it was from poor men," wrote Gates. "I may as well say here that I am utterly appalled at the inadequacy of the provision now in sight to take care of the work thrust upon the institution the *first year*."[25]

VI

At the beginning of February, Rockefeller received from Gates a long and eloquent report on the position of the University. It was an exhaustive review of the whole situation, covering probable attendance, the faculty, the spirit of the Trustees, the site and buildings, and equipment. But above all, it was a fervent plea for an increased endowment. Gates, naturally of sanguine temperament, waxed enthusiastic as he described the immense possibilities of the University. It was to be truly national in all its attractions. Already seven hundred students, graduate and undergraduate, seemed assured. Harper wished to make final arrangements with "men of immense value," and did not dare because he was so handicapped financially. The Trustees were showing a capacity, generosity, vision, and zeal that wholly surpassed Gates's expectations. The site was precisely right. "You see the thing is growing and spreading out in every direction, beyond my dreams." Yet no fund was in prospect for even a little apparatus; no money, beyond students' fees, for even a few books; no provision for heating, lighting, and janitors' service; nothing for clerks, secretaries, and administrative costs. Gates continued:[26]

In round numbers the institution ought now to have the promise of

[25]Goodspeed, *History*, 179.　　　　[26]*Idem*, 180, 181.

two million dollars or income from same beginning October 1 next. . . . It is my profound and unalterable conviction that, if your funds will admit, you will not be able, at any later time, to reap the manifold and various profits now likely to be secured by now offering, at once, the sum of two million dollars or the income thereof (principal to be pledged), to be operative October 1 next.

He added various arguments, and reinforced them by six complete exhibits. One exhibit dealt with the professors needed, and showed that the minimum income required to provide a decent faculty was $164,000. Harper had insisted that much more should be spent, but Gates had kept him down to that figure. Other increases in the budget were equally exigent. Gates, carried away by his cause, grew almost eloquent. "Finally, in justification of Harper, Northrup, Goodspeed, and all of us," he wrote, "let me say that none of us dreamed at the first of the magnitude of the opportunities, the promise, the occasion. It has grown on our wondering eyes month by month. . . . I stand in awe of this thing. God is in it in a most wonderful way. It is a miracle."[27]

It was Rockefeller's habit, once he had thoroughly tested a partner or aide, to repose the utmost confidence in him. He completely trusted Gates's judgment, while he had been impressed by the evidence of public faith in the new University, and public admiration for the effort which had established it. He was now fast recovering from an illness which had kept him half-prostrated all winter. As soon as he read Gates's report, he telegraphed:

"It is of course a surprise. Can say nothing encouraging, but deem it desirable to have an interview with you."

This conference was held at Forest Hill on February 10. Rockefeller raised some questions which Gates was unable to answer, and next day the latter returned to Chicago for a talk with the Trustees. On the 20th he was back again at Forest Hill; and this time he did not leave until Rockefeller had promised the University an additional million, and until they had virtually agreed upon the form of letter making the gift and specifying the uses to which it was to be put. This letter, dated February 23, was addressed to the Trustees:[28]

[27]*Idem*, 180–182.

[28]*Idem*, 182. "Now that it is all over," Gates wrote Goodspeed on Feb. 23, 1892, "I find myself singularly lacking in any feeling of exultation. The responsibility we have all assumed, the necessity of great care, forethought, and prudence, weigh upon me, and cloud any spirit of joy." Harper Papers.

Gentlemen:

I will give to the University of Chicago one thousand five per cent bonds of the par value of one million dollars, principal and interest payable in gold. The principal of the fund is to remain forever a further endowment for the University, the income to be used only for the current expenses and not for lands, buildings, or repairs. I reserve the right to designate, at my option, the expenses to which the income shall be applied.

I will deliver these bonds March 1, 1892, bearing accrued interest from December 1, 1891.

I make this gift as a special thank-offering to Almighty God for returning health.

Sincerely yours,

John D. Rockefeller.

Since interest on the million began December 1, 1891, more than $41,600 from this source would be available by the time the University opened; and this, together with the regular annual income, would provide in the first year more than $90,000 for current expenses. Rockefeller stipulated in an accompanying letter of designation that $70,500 of the income should be employed for salaries, $10,000 for fellowships, $5,000 for books and apparatus, and the remainder for incidentals. He added that if gifts from others should provide the funds needed for any of these purposes, the designation would then be waived, and the money might be used in any way.

Though Rockefeller had been pressed hard by Gates, he made this offering with good will. "When the decision was finally arrived at," Gates wrote to Goodspeed, "it was hearty, cheerful, not to say glad." The response in Chicago was all that he could have wished. Goodspeed wrote Gates that the feeling was one of universal gratification. "Mr. Field said the other morning, after expressing his satisfaction with the gift and his admiration for Mr. Rockefeller, 'Now Chicago must put a million dollars into the buildings of the University.'" The Chicago *Evening Post* carried an editorial entitled, "Chicago's Turn Next," and the press teemed with delighted reference to the University and its future.[29]

And well might the city be enthusiastic. Doctor Harper was now meeting the most brilliant success in obtaining his faculty. He was besieged by applicants for positions; more than a thousand men and

---

[29]*Idem,* 182, 183. Harper's papers show that he twice applied to William Rockefeller for a gift to the university, and twice (April 13, Oct. 21, 1891) was refused.

women either wrote letters or came to see him in person. On July 10, 1892, writing that "life at Chicago has become a great burden, so many people after me," he fled to Chautauqua for a little peace. In seeking professors, he attempted to find the ablest men in the country, already distinguished and in some instances famous. He would simply refuse to take "No" for an answer; it was not until a man had declined half a dozen times, each negative more emphatic than the last, that he gave up. But he did not have to confess many defeats. As the faculty was constituted the first year, it included seven men and one woman who had been presidents of other institutions of higher learning. Among them, Thomas C. Chamberlin had been head of the University of Wisconsin, and Albion W. Small of Colby. Harper wished to make Alice Freeman Palmer, then head of Wellesley College, the dean of women at Chicago; and "What an acquisition she would be!" Gates wrote approvingly. She immediately gave the position of women in the University a standing that would otherwise have been impossible.

Among the other teachers were Hermann E. von Holst, whom Harper brought from Germany to fill the chair of history; Frederick Starr, who became assistant professor of anthropology; Richard Green Moulton, who came from England to be extension professor of English literature; and Emil G. Hirsch, professor of rabbinical literature and philosophy.[30] To gain his early faculty, Harper robbed his neighbors' hen-roosts shamelessly. His raids upon Yale, Harvard, Cornell, Clark, and other institutions aroused a chorus of rage and denunciation—at which Chicagoans merely smiled. It need not be said that Rockefeller had nothing to do with the appointments. The historian of the University tells us that, among the hundreds of written applications that he had examined, one alone referred to the founder. "I have friends," wrote this man, "who will gladly ask John D. Rockefeller to give me his recommendation." No doubt this was true. But the writer did not know, states Goodspeed, "that Mr. Rockefeller never, under any circumstances, could be induced to recommend the employment or dismissal of a member of the faculty or give any advice whatever regarding the teaching

[30]It is pleasant to note that Harper thought of calling Doctor Strong into the faculty. He had met the doctor in Rochester in the fall of 1891 and found him kindness itself. "I love the man better as I know him better," he wrote Gates, Nov. 6, 1891. Harper Papers.

force." Nevertheless, Rockefeller did follow with great interest the accessions to the teaching staff.

He watched with equal interest the work now being done in Chicago to match his own donations. On April 7, 1892, Field offered to give $100,000 upon condition that a total of $1,000,000 were raised within sixty days; a period that he shortly extended to ninety days. For a time it seemed doubtful whether the condition could be met. At the end of the second month only a little over half of the amount had been subscribed. But within a few days a gift of $150,000 from Silas B. Cobb, an early settler of Chicago, lent a strong impulse to the campaign, and before the allotted time was up $1,000,000 had been subscribed. Of this, Sidney A. Kent gave $235,000. The million-dollar fund assured the erection of eight buildings in addition to those already under way, and provided the University with a group of structures whose dignity and spaciousness befitted its high standards. With total resources of more than four million dollars, the institution now seemed certain of taking a place, at the outset, in the very front rank of American universities.

Thus the heads of the University, with rising confidence, approached October 1, 1892, the great day on which it was to throw open its doors and begin its work of investigation and enlightenment. Harry Pratt Judson, in some reminiscences published long afterward, writes that he spent the previous night working with Doctor Harper on some details of the opening. They labored until nearly midnight. When they had finished, Harper threw himself back on the sofa and exclaimed: "I wonder if there will be a single student there tomorrow!" The next morning the bells sounded, the 120 members of the faculty waited in their classrooms, and nearly six hundred students began the work of the year. The University of Chicago had commenced its great career.

VII

From the outset Rockefeller had tried to make it clear that he intended to exercise not the slightest control over the operations of the University.[31] A very different course had been followed by

---

[31]The Harper Papers show that both Rockefeller and Gates repeatedly emphasized this to Harper.

Ezra Cornell with the institution he founded on Lake Cayuga, by Senator Leland Stanford with the university he had founded in memory of his son, and by Jonas Clark with Clark University. But having assured himself that the new institution was in the very best hands possible, Rockefeller was content to leave its direction to Doctor Harper and his aides. Gates did give advice upon the University's management of its funds, but in *propria persona,* not as Rockefeller's agent. At the very outset the founder seized an opportunity of making his position perfectly plain.

The Trustees of the University had wished to mark the opening day by formal exercises. President Harper had also looked forward to something of the sort, and had exacted from Rockefeller a promise that he would come to Chicago for the occasion.[32] But as the day approached he decided that it would be better to have no ceremony. He wished the labors of the University to begin that day just "as if it were the continuation of a work which had been conducted for a thousand years." When a majority of the Board demurred, he laid the matter before Rockefeller for a decision, writing of the Trustees' perplexity:[33]

They realize the great debt of gratitude due to you for your many and magnificent donations. They recognize your deep and personal interest in the University. They feel that the question ought not to be decided one way or the other without consulting you. I venture, therefore, to trouble you to give the matter at least a passing thought, and, if it is in accordance with your judgment, to indicate to me what, under all the circumstances, seems to you to be the proper thing.

Now this was precisely what Rockefeller did not wish to do. If the Trustees and president of the University of Chicago asked him to decide whether formal opening exercises should be held, how many other problems might they not lay before him? Harper's letter gave him a much-desired excuse for defining his relations with the University. Compared with this definition, which he meant to make explicit, the question of the opening exercises seemed to him a triviality. He did say that his judgment was against any formal ceremonies, and that even if they were held it would "be hardly possible for him to attend."[34] But he dictated a careful mes-

[32]Goodspeed, *History*, 242.   [33]Harper Papers.
[34]Harper Papers; Goodspeed, *History*, 243.

sage to the Trustees on the subject uppermost in his mind. Gates, at his direction, wrote Harper:

A prefatory word regarding his [Mr. Rockefeller's] counsel in general. While he is, of course, closely interested in the conduct of the institution, he has refrained from making suggestions, and would prefer in general not to take an active part in the counsels of the management. He prefers to rest the whole weight of the management on the shoulders of the proper officers. Donors can be certain that their gifts will be preserved and made continuously and largely useful, after their own voices can no longer be heard, only in so far as they see wisdom and skill in the management, quite independently of themselves, now. No management can gain skill except as it exercises its functions independently, with the privilege of making errors and the authority to correct them. The only way to assure a wise management during the whole future of the institution is to continue the method employed hitherto in the selection of the members of the Board, which is to make the most careful, the nicest possible choice of new men to fill the necessary vacancies, as they shall from time to time occur, and so keep the Board at all times up to the highest point of skill and efficiency. . . .

You will understand that I have tried to give accurately Mr. Rockefeller's views, as he expressed them a day or two ago, without any admixture of my own.

In later years Rockefeller's advice was seldom asked; rarely, if ever, given.[35] He never interfered with any question of instruction; he never knew anything whatever about the dismissal or retention of any instructor; and he never concerned himself with the opinions expressed in any University publication.

Upon one point, and only one, his views were always known, and Gates lost few opportunities of underlining them. Rockefeller always believed that the University should cut its financial suit according to its cloth—that it should keep strictly within its budget. It ought never to incur heavy new expenses until it had obtained a definite pledge that he or somebody else would provide the money required. Harper, a man of powerful imagination, his dreams always reaching beyond the practical demands of the moment, his energy inexhaustible, who believed in launching new enterprises with a firm faith that God would provide, could not conform to this cold businesslike view. He thought that the University was not in

[35]Goodspeed, *History*, 35.

From the Chicago "Daily News," February, 1900

Popular conception of Dr. Harper and Rockefeller

(This cartoon, from the Chicago *Daily News* of February, 1900, actually did violence to the facts. Doctor Harper never applied directly to Rockefeller for a gift to the University)

a healthy condition unless it was constantly exceeding its budget. He was insatiable in his desires for money, while Gates was the guardian of the treasury; and the result was frequent tension between him and Gates—though their differences never really ruptured their friendship.[36]

VIII

Before the University had completed its first year (for it had adopted the quarter system, and the year did not end in the spring) the great panic of 1893 had descended upon the United States. The financial crisis caused appalling hardships to institutions of every character. Factories closed their doors; railroads by scores went into receiverships; banks failed; the credit of the government itself was imperilled, and President Cleveland soon found that he could maintain gold payments only by making costly bond issues. The University of Chicago had undertaken a gigantic work, which would have taxed its resources to the utmost even in ordinary times. It could not possibly have met the heavy strain so suddenly thrown upon it but for Rockefeller's protecting generosity.

Fortunately for the University, Rockefeller had made it a Christmas gift in 1892 of another million dollars. Doctor Harper had begun asking for this money just before the opening. He was anxious, he wrote Gates, to publish his first annual report on October 1, and to accompany it with the announcement of another gift from the founder. The institution stood in dire need of more funds for buildings. Would Rockefeller not give an additional million, without condition, on the simple understanding that the University would find still another million elsewhere at once? He believed he could raise a large sum among Chicagoans. "But I cannot secure this additional money for buildings without another act of

[36]Murray, counsel to Rockefeller and a close friend of Gates, assured me on May 23, 1938, that while there was often an *appearance* of friction between Gates and Harper, there was very seldom—and not for long—the reality. The Harper papers contain many evidences of an affectionate intimacy. "Cheer up, old friend," writes Gates to Harper, Nov. 19, 1892. "Trust in God, eat well, sleep well, and do not overwork." This was when Gates knew but poor Harper didn't, that Rockefeller was about to give another million!

grace on the part of Mr. Rockefeller."[37] To this appeal Gates had at first replied in rather discouraging terms, intimating that the founder would not give anything more until the machinery was in successful working operation. Harper had thereupon fallen into a state of extreme depression, writing notes full of gloom and despair, and even threatening to resign forthwith. "I am compelled to think that the work here is too much for me," he mournfully declared on December 13. "Some other man will have to take hold in one form or another." Indeed, the financial difficulties which loomed up might have struck terror to the stoutest heart. Rockefeller's fourth donation therefore came in the nick of time. Dated December 25, 1892, his letter of gift provided $1,000,000 "to remain forever a further endowment."[38]

This new gift was not immediately deliverable, and no income from the bonds would be available until 1894. To meet the immediate financial exigencies, therefore, Rockefeller gave $150,000 outright, making it applicable to any University need; while Martin Ryerson, head of the Board of Trustees, advanced $100,000. Then in the fall of 1893, when the panic seemed at its height, Rockefeller unexpectedly made another large gift. The officers of the University had just launched a campaign to raise $350,000 more, and thus obtain a conditional gift of $100,000 from Martin Ryerson. Rockefeller wrote the Trustees on October 31, 1893, that he would contribute $500,000 with the proviso that the terms of the Ryerson grant should be fulfilled.[39]

Despite the terrible economic storm, the stipulations attached to this gift were met. Banks were still failing, railroads still going into receivership; the farmers of the West were rising in a maddened revolt; the final dollars were collected as the fierce Pullman riots were about to break out. When the work was done, the University possessed another round million, of which half had come in a lump sum from Rockefeller. Doctor Harper had already given thanks in a public address. "The gift of so large a sum as half a million to be used outright for the purpose of equipment was a gift under all the circumstances not to have been expected of Mr. Rockefeller. He

[37]Goodspeed, *History*, 267, 268.   [38]Harper Papers.
[39]Goodspeed, *History*, 276.

had plainly indicated that he would care for instruction, and he had also expressed the hope that Chicago would care for buildings and equipment. He realized, however, the peculiar situation in which we found ourselves—the financial stringency which defied every effort to secure money. Seeing our necessities and appreciating all that we had tried to do, he has come forward in a new and unexpected way, and the University has stronger evidence than ever before of his deep interest in its work."[40]

Even in these years of depression, the activities, the student-body, and the expenditures of the University all increased. The annual expenses went soaring up—above $500,000, above $600,000, then in 1896–97 to nearly $700,000. The deficits went up too; all efforts to hold them somewhere near the $50,000-a-year mark collapsed in 1896–97, when they amounted to nearly double that sum. Rockefeller was troubled by this inability of the University to make two ends meet. Through Gates, he served warning after warning upon the authorities.[41] At one point he made an effort to halt the march toward financial trouble. Near the close of 1894 he subscribed $175,000 toward the current expenses of the coming academic year, with a proviso that if he found that the expenditures were exceeding the income, he should be at liberty to make no further payments on the pledge. But he soon concluded that a better way to meet the situation would be to add so handsomely to the endowment that the income would amply cover all the yearly costs.

The result was his great $3,000,000 subscription of October 30, 1895. It had not come unheralded. Early that month he had sent Gates to Chicago to talk with the Trustees and officers, and Gates had spent three days in a close examination of the whole situation. He found that both the needs and the opportunities were manifestly great; and though the representatives of the University never thought of so munificent a donation as was actually impending, they doubtless cherished strong hopes as they put him aboard his train. The answer did not come for three weeks, when Gates returned, bearing a letter from Rockefeller. We can well imagine the air of quiet exultation with which the ambassador took this missive from his pocket, and the histrionic emphasis with which he read

---

[40]*Idem*, 277.   [41]Harper Papers.

it to the Trustees. That Board meeting, as the historian of the University remarks, "was one of enthusiasm and rejoicing long to be remembered." The joy of the University prompted an immediate celebration. The students kindled an immense bonfire in the middle of the campus; President Harper, Secretary Goodspeed, and various Trustees and professors addressed a happy gathering in Kent Theatre. The Chicago papers, with editorials of congratulation, spread Rockefeller's letter to the Trustees (dated October 30, 1895) before the public. It gave one million outright, and two millions in amounts equal to the contributions of others, if paid in before January 1, 1900.[42]

In explaining the unexpected size of this gift, Gates long afterward wrote Goodspeed a letter embodying an idea which it was unfortunate that Harper never grasped; for its essence was that Rockefeller always gave much more generously under terms of freedom than under terms of constraint. "The reason I discouraged Doctor Harper and yourself in asking for so large a gift was not because I did not believe the University needed it and not because I did not propose to urge it with all my might. The University needed every cent of it, and I proposed to secure it if it was in any way possible. What I wanted to do was, by whittling down the requests of the University, to give Mr. Rockefeller an opportunity of seeming at least to do voluntarily *more* than was asked, to seem to act freely and not under compulsion; to give him a chance to seem to express his benevolence other than by paying an inevitable tax, and I thought he would be far more likely to give the $3,000,000 if *less were asked for* than if the more were asked. He was restless and irritable because he was not even allowed the privilege of seeming to give to the University freely. . . ." This was based on a shrewd view of Rockefeller's psychology.[43]

Under the terms of this new gift, the University confronted the task of raising $2,000,000 from other persons before the end of the decade; that is, within a little more than four years. It seemed a formidable undertaking. In fact, it remained an extremely difficult task even after Helen Culver, in the closing days of 1895, turned over to the University properties which she valued at $1,000,000.[44]

[42]Goodspeed, *History,* 278–280.   [43]May 22, 1915; Harper Papers.
[44]Gates sent "Most hearty congratulations" to Harper on Dec. 18, 1895; Harper Papers.

Month by month, year by year, the fund grew—but not fast enough. Rockefeller, perceiving that more time was needed, extended the period until April 1, 1900. Additional gifts were made, but still not enough. The last day but one arrived, with the Trustees and officers of the University in a state of intense anxiety. With it came a telegram from Gates, which President Harper must have torn open with an apprehensive heart. It read: "Wire me Saturday noon (March 31) how much you lack in fulfilling conditions." The information was at once despatched. Then came another telegram from Gates which banished every apprehension:[45]

"I have secured valid pledges from friends of University sufficient to cover whatever may be found on examination to be the actual shortage in the amount necessary to entitle the University to the full amount of Mr. Rockefeller's pledge of October 30, 1895, and you can therefore announce the success of the movement."

The University never made any inquiry as to the identity of the "friends" thus mentioned. Its heads suspected that they were found in Rockefeller's own family. But Rockefeller accepted the subscriptions as valid, and when duly paid in, they were duplicated by him. Thus as a result of his pledge of October 30, 1895, more than $5,000,000 was added to the resources of the University; an amount which, coming at a critical period in its adolescent growth, was simply invaluable.

But great as this accretion was, it represented not an end, but a beginning. In December, 1900, as a new Christmas gift, Rockefeller gave $1,500,000 more, of which two thirds was for endowment and one third for general purposes. The following year came another Christmas gift of $1,000,000, and in December, 1902, $1,000,000 more; making in all, by that date, a total of almost $10,000,000 furnished to the University. And even this proved but a beginning.

IX

While making this succession of gifts he had continued, primarily through Doctor Gates, to press upon the University the importance of whittling its expenditures to fit its means. Year after year he had contributed large sums to meet its deficit. He did this cheerfully,

[45]Harper Papers.

not grudgingly. Yet he was not pleased by these deficits, and still less did he like the reflection that they had been incurred with a full comprehension of the fact that he alone could meet them. The University committed itself to great expenditures upon which he was not consulted; it thus placed itself, year after year, in straitened circumstances from which, if not extricated, it would suffer irreparable damage; and it then came to its founder with what amounted to a peremptory demand for salvation. If he had been appealed to at the outset, and presented with a plan for the enterprises which later caused the deficit, he would have given with far greater satisfaction. As it was, he could not but feel that an element of improvidence, and even of recklessness, entered into the management of the University. He knew that any business managed in this way would soon come to grief.[46]

As deficit followed deficit, the situation grew more and more strained, and his irritation over the compulsion which Harper seemed to be placing upon him was increasingly clear. Finally there came a crisis when he insisted upon a clearer understanding between himself and the University. This was early in 1897. The University officers had just submitted a budget for the year 1897-98 which showed that the margin between estimated receipts and estimated expenditures would reach about $200,000—all of which Mr. Rockefeller would be expected to supply. Indeed, it appears that the University debt was approaching $500,000, and that it was in a position of real peril.[47] The secretary and comptroller of the University, Doctor Goodspeed and Mr. H. A. Rust, were summoned to New York to discuss the situation with Gates. Two long and somewhat painful interviews ensued.[48] The University officers pointed out once more that Doctor Harper and his aides had been laying the foundations of a great enterprise, and that the commendable largeness of the plan upon which it had been conceived was itself the principal cause of the recurrent deficits. In reply, Gates declared that Rockefeller was perfectly familiar with this plea for university expansion, and realized its force; that he was indeed thoroughly in favor

[46]I have talked with Professor Samuel Harper, son of Doctor Harper, and with sons of Doctor Goodspeed and Doctor Gates. There can be no question whatever of the good faith and high intentions of all the men concerned.
[47]Doctor Goodspeed so states in his autobiography.
[48]Described in Goodspeed, *History,* 284-289.

of expansion, but he by no means fully approved the way in which it had been accomplished.

This policy, wrote Gates, "involved, of necessity, in order to save the large funds already contributed by him, and to save the institution from ruin, three or four millions from himself, and not only was he not consulted on the policy which rendered these immense gifts from him compulsory, but every injunction he gave, in advance, was on distinctly the opposite lines of procedure."[49]

In the end an agreement was reached upon some healthful reforms. The University arranged to set up a committee on expenditures, comprising the president, secretary, and comptroller, which was to supervise expenditures within the budgetary limits, and so far as possible keep them below the budget estimates. It was to sit as often as required, even daily if necessary, and to pass upon the requisitions of the departments. Beginning with this year, moreover, the widest publicity was given the University's financial condition by the publication of annual budgets and annual reports of receipts, expenditures, and assets. Up to this time it had never issued a treasurer's report, because, as the treasurer admitted, it had never dared disclose the facts to the public!

When these conferences in New York closed, Gates sent a full report of all that had been said to the members—for a stenographer had taken down every word. He appended to this report a careful statement, dictated in its essentials by Rockefeller himself, defining anew the attitude of the principal benefactor toward the University. Rockefeller ordered this placed in his safety-deposit vault as an expression to posterity (to quote Gates's later phrase) "of his total dissent from Doctor Harper's policy of building the University on air, rather than on a sound financial basis."[50] But the statement was also intended, in part, to guard against any impression that Rockefeller was reluctant in his giving, or took a shortsighted and narrow view of the potentialities and duties of the University.

"It does not follow from this," wrote Gates in reviewing Rocke-

[49]Gates later wrote Goodspeed: "I thought at the time that the policy of Doctor Harper looked like compulsion, but was not intended to be compulsion. . . . From what I *now* know, from what I have heard *since,* I could not say with the same assurance that on Doctor Harper's part compulsion was not *intended.*" May 22, 1915; Harry Pratt Judson Papers. Goodspeed indicates in his MS Autobiography that he agreed.

[50]Gates to Goodspeed, May 22, 1915; Harry Pratt Judson Papers.

feller's wish that debts and deficits be avoided, "that Mr. Rockefeller's conceptions of a university are, or ever have been, less broad than those, for instance, of Doctor Harper, or that his ideals of what the University of Chicago may become, are now, or ever have been, less expansive or magnificent. Before he had ever been approached in behalf of an institution at Chicago, he had visited great universities in our own and in foreign lands, and he had intimately contemplated for years the plan of an institution involving far greater expense than any now involved at Chicago. His conservatism is not now, nor has it ever been, due to any narrowness of conception. Nor have his prudence and caution arisen from any reluctance to contribute. The story of his gifts, so numerous, so ready, so vast, always leading and inspiring others, testifies to his willingness to give."

The real causes of Rockefeller's repeated admonitions upon the avoidance of heavy liabilities, he went on, lay elsewhere. For one reason, Rockefeller felt it important to gain and maintain public confidence. If the University were believed to be shaky financially, if men feared that bankruptcy stared it in the face, then nobody would feel like giving to it. Only through secrecy as to its annual deficits, and through Rockefeller's repeated interposition to meet them, had the University kept a brave and imposing front before the world. Only this fair front, in turn, had made possible the great gifts of Miss Culver and others. Then again, Rockefeller, while cherishing views no less broad than those of Doctor Harper and ideals no less high, had realized the importance of time in an undertaking so vast. He knew that he was inexperienced—that Doctor Harper and other University officers were also inexperienced in this great work. He wished to avoid nervous haste in building the University. And he was moved by still other considerations:[51]

Again, Mr. Rockefeller has his eye not on the transitory present, but on the long future. He is unspeakably more interested in the tendencies, policies, and character of the management than in any present success, however brilliant.

Lastly, he has known from the first, what he has only lately disclosed to others, this namely, how largely he might, under favorable conditions, become interested in the University of Chicago, and he has known that he would, himself, give, not only far more cheerfully, but also far more

[51]Goodspeed, *History*, 286, 287.

largely under a conservative and prudent management that avoids debts and deficits.

Finally, let me add that Mr. Rockefeller, rejoicing in all that has been achieved, recognizes and extols the great qualities of leadership, enthusiasm, and organizing ability in Doctor Harper, without which the present development of the University would have been impossible. He looks to the Trustees, whose invaluable services he also heartily recognizes, not to chill this ardor, or discourage it, but to guide it into channels of solid and permanent prosperity.

It is important to note that one of the University officers who knew the situation best, Doctor Goodspeed, always agreed with Rockefeller and Gates and sided against Harper in this difference. At the New York conference in 1897 he warmly defended Harper's course. But he confesses in his unpublished autobiography that this was not because he was fully convinced of its wisdom, but out of a sense of loyalty to him and the Trustees. Indeed, he remarks that the issue made "something of a breach" between Harper and himself. "It sometimes seemed as though Doctor Harper was deliberately forcing the Founder's hand, and had adopted this as a thoroughly considered and permanent policy." Without being dogmatic on the subject, Goodspeed strongly leaned toward Gates's view that Rockefeller would have given more freely, rapidly, and largely had he not felt that Harper was deliberately forcing his hand. He thought that the strained relations which developed between Harper and Rockefeller were altogether unnecessary and most unfortunate:

The difficulties all arose from the different ideals of these two great men in entering on the undertaking. The one began with the conception of a high-grade college developing as the funds increased into a great university. The other began with the ideal of a great university to start with, the college being only an incident and an important part of the larger conception. My own views coincided with those of the founder, as did those of Mr. Gates. We did not accept them from him, we had them from the beginning. They seemed to us the logical and necessary method of developing a great university. Had Doctor Harper held them we should have been saved many unhappy years. I do not undertake to say who was right. . . . All that can be said with certainty is this, that no sooner did President Judson begin to administer the University on this other policy, regulating the expenditure by the income, than the founder began to make new endowment contributions on an unprecedented scale, and a new era of development set in. . . .

x

Twice during the first ten years of the University, and only twice, Rockefeller visited the campus. He came first for the quinquennial celebration of July, 1896. It was a gala occasion for the University and the city. He watched the laying of several cornerstones; heard Professor Bernard Moses of the University of California speak on "The Condition and Prospects of Democracy"; sat under sermons by Doctor George A. Smith of Glasgow, and Doctor W. H. P. Faunce; and heard the students sing:

> John D. Rockefeller, wonderful man is he
> Gives all his spare change to the U. of C.

At a convocation held in a large tent in the central quadrangle he listened to four addresses of greeting by as many representatives of the Trustees, the Divinity School, the faculties, and the students.[52] It was impossible for him not to respond, although he had previously exacted from President Harper a promise that he should not be asked to speak. He praised the extraordinary growth of the University. "It is due to you of Chicago, to your enterprising businessmen, to your public-spirited men, to say that in no other city on this continent, in no other city in the round world, could there have been accomplished what you have accomplished." He thanked the Trustees, the president, and all the others who had given their aid to an enterprise in which he had been, as he said, a silent partner. "It is but a beginning," he remarked—and the huge audience broke into spontaneous applause. Fearing that some had drawn a mistaken inference from the statement, he instantly added, as soon as the applause died away, "and you are going on; you have the privilege to complete it." For a moment, says one who was present, his hearers felt that the entire financial burden of the future of the University had been rolled from the founder's shoulders to their own![53] But he quickly reassured them.

"I believe in the work," he went on. "It is the best investment I ever made in my life. Why shouldn't people give to the University of Chicago money, time, their best efforts? Why not? It is the

[52]The University of Chicago Library has volumes of newspaper clippings which I have consulted.

[53]Goodspeed, *History*, 397, 398.

grandest opportunity ever presented. Where were gathered, ever, a better Board of Trustees, a better faculty? I am profoundly, profoundly thankful that I ever had anything to do with this affair. The good Lord gave me the money, and how could I withhold it from Chicago?"

This episode illuminated certain of Rockefeller's characteristics. The officers, the students, and the city had hoped and half expected that he would utilize the ceremonies to announce some great new gift, or at least to make some new promise of a specific character. Andrew Carnegie in his place would probably have responded to the mass-emotion of the occasion by some new grant of funds. But Rockefeller, as we have repeatedly said, disliked and distrusted any display of emotion. He was not to be carried off his feet by a sea of faces, a crash of applause. Hence his instant effort to correct the impression that *he* intended to complete single-handed the work so well begun. But when he saw how crestfallen his audience became, he was quick to speak an encouraging word, and to indicate—albeit in general terms—that he was still inclined to give generously.

Rockefeller was present again at the decennial celebration in June, 1901; a still more imposing occasion, for the University had grown steadily, and the cornerstones of three new buildings were laid. Once more he was the central figure at a convocation held on June 18 in a great tent set up in the central quadrangle. Once more he praised the work done by the University officers and its friends in the city; a work "greater by far than our most sanguine expectations" of 1895 had envisaged. He gave the students some fatherly advice on the importance of service. Success did not necessarily mean reaching a conspicuous place, he told them; it was enough to fit into some useful niche, and to do the day's work in the best possible way. The chances of success had steadily increased in America. "Success is attained by industry, perseverance, and pluck coupled with any amount of hard work, and you need not expect to achieve it in any other way." And again he spoke of the unparalleled contribution made by the city of Chicago to the rapid growth of the institution, and of the magnificent promise which the University offered to the city, the country, and indeed the whole world. "The success of the University of Chicago is assured, and we are here today rejoicing in that success. All praise to Chicago! Long may

she live, to foster and develop this sturdy representative of her enterprise and public spirit!"[54]

XI

It was inevitable that Rockefeller's motives in founding and supporting the University of Chicago should be impugned. *The International Socialist Review* shortly published a pack of playing cards
with Rockefeller as king of spades, and across his breast ran the
spirited verse:

> I love to oil the college wheels
> And grease the pulpit stairs
> Where workmen learn to scorn the strike
> And trust to Heaven and prayers.[55]

He oiled the college wheels—so the theory ran—that his ill-gotten
wealth might take on an odor of sanctity; and that eminent University men, from Doctor Harper down, might preach economic
doctrines which tended to support Rockefeller's business practices.
It is certain that this malevolent theory for years received a wide
popular acceptance. Doctor Richard T. Ely, invited to accept a chair
in the University of Chicago, refused because of his fear that some
limitation might be placed upon his work of investigation, teaching,
and publishing. Later he confessed that this was sheer folly, that
the utmost freedom prevailed at Chicago, and that his refusal had
been a serious error; but his apprehensions and beliefs were the
apprehensions and beliefs of many others. When almost immediately a *Journal of Political Economy* was established at the University under Doctor J. Laurence Laughlin, it was thought by some
observers that it paid inadequate attention to the problems of industrial combinations and trusts when they were a subject of burning
interest to Americans. The charge that Laughlin ignored these
problems is still sometimes repeated.[56]

It would have been unfortunate had Laughlin failed to deal with
the trust question, for it needed discussion; but as a matter of fact,
he by no means ignored it.[57] *The Journal* for 1899 contained two

[54]*Idem*, 401, 402.   [55]New York *Evening Post*, May 20, 1909.
[56]The files do show early reviews of books upon monopoly and the regulation of great corporations.
[57]These are the views of veteran teachers at the University of Chicago with
whom I have talked.

long articles on "The Chicago Trust Conference" and "Trusts from an Economic Standpoint," as well as a note on "Trusts and the Tariff." In 1901 it offered some pages on "Trusts in Europe." The volume for 1904 presents Veblen's amusing essay on "An Early Experiment in Trusts," with a judicious article on "The Trust Problem." Three years later Laughlin turned a large part of his magazine over to the topic. Anna Youngman published two highly significant articles on "The Tendency of Modern Combination," offering the first frank and thorough treatment of the Standard Oil investments yet printed. The same volume published Gilbert H. Montague's "Transportation Phase of the Oil Industry," an objective appraisal of the Bureau of Corporations' report on that subject. It is true that in the early nineties no articles on trusts appeared. But this was probably because Laughlin's economic opinions were paleolithic. To call him conservative would be a euphemism, for he was abysmally reactionary. For another reason, he may really have felt somewhat constrained in the treatment of business by the fact that the Trustees numbered important industrial leaders, and that the contributions of Chicago businessmen were indispensable. Robert Herrick in his novel, *Chimes,* has some pungent sentences upon the local leaders from whom Doctor Harper was gathering tribute to erect the "plant" for "higher things."[58] They included the McCormicks, the Swifts, Mrs. George Pullman, Philip D. Armour, Samuel Insull, and various railroad heads. Thought of the Trustees and these donors as well as of Rockefeller may to some extent have deterred Laughlin in the first years from raising embarrassing issues in *The Journal.*

Years later Laughlin wrote Mr. John T. Flynn that his articles "were chosen solely for their economic quality." He went on: "We could discuss trusts or any economic subject. No one ever tried to use our columns for their private purposes."[59] Unquestionably this was true; nobody ever dreamed of dictating what Laughlin should or should not discuss. If he felt any inhibitions they must be blamed upon his own conservatism, his social connections, and perhaps his timidity.

The papers of Harper and Rockefeller contain evidence that Rockefeller and Gates leaned backwards in their anxiety to have nothing

[58]P. 43.   [59]Flynn, *God's Gold,* 307.

to do with any part of the University's secular work. Just after Cleveland's Venezuelan message, for example, von Holst made a public statement criticizing it severely. Harper differed with him, and came out in another public utterance saying so.[60] This worried Gates as seeming to be an effort to reprimand a professor for his opinions, and he telegraphed Harper: "Von Holst's views correspond with best thought here does your virtual correction of same as published here lend color to recent criticism of University sensitiveness to utterances of professors?"[61] A few days later von Holst sent Gates a private expression of his views. The latter, instead of replying to him directly, enclosed his response to Harper. "I feel strongly," he wrote Harper, "on this colossal recklessness and folly of President Cleveland's, and I feel *with* von Holst. I want to join hands with him, or perhaps better shake hands. If there is any impropriety or if it will not be a pleasure to you be free to return me the letter. Answer."[62] Assuredly in all this Gates displayed a sensitive regard both for academic freedom and for the feelings of Harper. And assuredly in all this he spoke equally for Rockefeller. In May, 1893, Mr. and Mrs. Rockefeller declined an invitation to attend a University convocation. One of their chief reasons was stated by Gates to Harper: "There are, as you know, advantages to the University . . . in the disinterested way in which Mr. Rockefeller has given his money. These advantages will be in *some* degree impaired, if he allows himself to be the recipient of the honors which the city is of course willing to bestow."[63]

In the theological field Rockefeller did press certain purely negative views upon the University. In 1896 it was proposed to begin publication of an *American Journal of Theology*. Rockefeller had no objection to the issuance of such a journal by the Divinity School. Indeed, he pointed out that he had no right to object, for that school had its own Trustees and represented the denomination as a whole. But he did protest against issuance of *The Journal* by the University. This was because the University, Gates wrote Harper in Rockefeller's behalf,[64] "is in a peculiar sense the creation of Mr. Rockefeller

[60]New York *Sun,* Dec. 22, 23, 1895.   [61]Dec. 23, 1895; Harper Papers.

[62]Dec. 27, 1895; Harper Papers.

[63]May 29, 1893; Harper Papers. The whole letter shows that both Mr. and Mrs. Rockefeller modestly shrank from the public appearances they would be required to make.

[64]May 17, 1896; Harper Papers.

himself. He has given nearly all its permanent funds, and he has received many letters from every part of the country complaining of the attitude which the University has seemed to take regarding the Bible, holding him responsible for what is a real or fancied injury to religion. He prefers that the denomination shall settle its own theological affairs. He founded in Chicago a secular institution of learning. He had no thought of the University entering the theological arena. He would prefer that the great power and prestige, financial and moral, of the University should not be thrown into the theological scale on either side. The sphere of theology should be relegated to the Divinity School, and the denomination may hold the Divinity School responsible."

This request was not improper, and Harper acceded to it. *The Journal* appeared under the rubric, "Edited by the Divinity Faculty of the University of Chicago."[65] Much less reasonable was Rockefeller's protest when, in the first months of university work, Joseph Jefferson made a characteristically delightful address to the students after one of the daily chapel services. Many conservative Baptists retained the old Puritan animosity to the theatre as inimical to morals, and they filled Rockefeller's mail with angry warnings that his University was entering upon a godless path. In view of the uneasy attitude of many churchmen toward the new institution, the invitation to Jefferson had perhaps been indiscreet. Ex-President E. G. Robinson of Brown so regarded it. He wrote Rockefeller that the "mistake" was regretted and would not occur again.[66] But it appears that Rockefeller took it altogether too seriously. Gates went west and made earnest representations to Harper, who sent the founder an unnecessarily contrite letter:[67]

We were surprised to learn that Mr. Jefferson's speaking in the chapel had led to conclusions which, so far as our feelings were concerned, were without foundation. The responsibility for his address rested wholly upon myself. From the beginning it was proposed to bring to the university, in connection with the chapel exercises, the best known men in the various lines of human activity. It was in accordance with the best purpose in the world, and . . . it was not supposed by any of us that in the doing of it we would be understood to be endorsing the theatre in general. . . . The whole event must be regarded as a mistake.

[65]After the first issue appeared, Gates protested to Harper that the "masthead" did not make it sufficiently clear that the Divinity School was responsible.
[66]Dec. 19, 1892; Harper Papers.   [67]Dec. 18, 1892; Harper Papers.

We were all glad to learn anew of your deep personal interest in the religious condition of the university, and I am sure that the visit of Mr. Gates, which was prompted by this interest on your part, will prove to be an occasion of great assistance to us.

But within a few years actors and actresses spoke unabashed before university audiences, the drama was always studied freely, and students gave their own dramatic representations.

This practically exhausts the list of Rockefeller's suggestions to—they cannot be called interferences with—the University officers. In 1894 he intimated to Harper, through Gates, that if a medical school were established he wished it to embrace homeopathic as well as allopathic instruction.[68] This reflected the influence of Doctor Biggar; but a medical school was far in the future, and when Rockefeller gave money for it he did not repeat this unhappy suggestion. A careful search has revealed no other requests but has instead disclosed a consistent determination to leave the University to its own heads.

When Doctor Edward W. Bemis was dropped from the faculty, unfriendly critics talked of an interference with teaching rights. Bemis had come from Vanderbilt University in 1891 to the University Extension faculty as associate professor of political economy. His views were radical compared with those of Doctor Laughlin. Personally he was bumptious, tactless, and offensive. Laughlin objected to his work, and he was transferred to the Department of Sociology under Doctor Albion W. Small. He had published an excellent article on the Homestead strike in *The Journal of Political Economy* for June, 1894. Just after the Pullman strike that year he made a speech in the First Presbyterian Church in which he mildly criticized the railroads—which deserved very severe criticism indeed. At that time feeling ran high on the subject in Chicago. The great majority of propertied citizens abhorred Debs and believed that the city had been saved from a reign of terror by Cleveland's timely use of Federal troops. Bemis's speech caused President Harper great annoyance. The head of the University could not put his head inside a Chicago club without being pounced upon by truculent citizens, demanding: "What kind of fools and agitators do you have teach-

[68]Gates to Harper, Dec. 18, 1894; Harper Papers. Rockefeller had the bizarre view that homeopathy represented a progressive and "aggressive" step in medicine.

ing sociology, anyhow?" Harper therefore sent Bemis a tart letter, with the admonition: "I propose that during the remainder of your connection with the University you exercise great care in public utterances about questions that are agitating the minds of the people."[69] This incident was soon closed. But Bemis continued to receive newspaper publicity, some of it undesirable in character. Eventually he was denied a reappointment—Doctor Harper having much earlier asked him to look about for another position.

Many leaped at the conclusion that he was dropped from the faculty because his views were obnoxious to Rockefeller. This was absurd, for Rockefeller had probably never heard of him, and certainly neither knew nor cared anything about his teaching. But even had Rockefeller been irritated by Bemis's ideas, he would never have spoken of the matter, for he made no suggestions whatever regarding University management. The fact was that Bemis, while able, honest, and useful, was highly addicted to controversy and lacking in discretion. Laughlin later wrote that he had been dropped "because he was not of University caliber. He was an agitator, not a scholar."[70] If Laughlin meant that Bemis was not of the cast of mind which best suits a university, he was probably correct in this statement. Bemis soon became noted as an expert on public utility problems, and was employed by Brand Whitlock and others in contests between municipalities and utility corporations. In that field he did valuable work for public regulation or ownership of rapid-transit facilities and electric-light plants. But he was known in the academic world as a trouble-maker. Doctor Richard T. Ely, who investigated the matter, has pooh-poohed the idea that any issue of academic freedom was involved, and said that the University acted entirely within its rights.[71]

In any event, Rockefeller cared nothing about the University publications or the utterances of the University faculty. He asked less and expected less from the University of Chicago than any other great benefactor of a similar institution had ever asked or expected. He refused to let it take his name. He refused to assume

[69]University Scrapbooks.   [70]Flynn, *God's Gold*, 308.
[71]Doctor Ely to the author, Jan. 12, 1939. See Bemis's article on "Academic Freedom" in *The Independent*, Aug. 17, 1899. Professor Samuel Harper emphasizes his father's insistence upon absolute freedom of thought and expression in theological matters from the beginning.

the slightest voice in its management. He declined to visit it except on two great occasions when a refusal would have been construed as ungracious; and then his visits were brief and his rôle in the proceedings was as inconspicuous as he could make it. Not until after his death was even a building on the campus named for him —the chapel then becoming Rockefeller Memorial Chapel. He asked, in fact, for nothing, though he was deeply appreciative of what gratitude was shown him, and said so. He was one of the best friends of academic freedom in the country, for by giving the institution tens of millions without the slightest interjection of his own personality, he set a valuable example to all other wealthy men. When Edwin E. Slosson published his series of articles on "Twelve Great American Universities" in 1912, he categorically declared that—as the whole intellectual world then knew—the university which Rockefeller founded was one of the freest centers of research, publishing, and teaching on the globe.

XXXVII

New Lieutenants

B UT in this story of the University we have pushed ahead of a
more fundamental theme, the general management of
Rockefeller's investment on the one hand, and of his philanthropies on the other. It is a subject full of interesting incident and even drama, and we can best take it up on a March day
in 1891—a day when Frederick T. Gates was conferring with
Rockefeller at 26 Broadway upon University affairs. As he rose to
leave Rockefeller halted him. "Sit down, Mr. Gates," he remarked.
"I wish to talk with you on another matter."[1]

Gates knew that twenty years of overwork had recently brought
Rockefeller to the verge of a breakdown. His doctors had peremptorily ordered him to stay away from the office as far as he could,
and throw off as many cares as possible; for though not attacked
by any organic ailment, he required quiet and rest. Gates also knew
that Rockefeller had been keenly studying him, his methods and
characteristics. This scrutiny had become steadily closer since the
fall of 1888, when he had read Gates's report on Baptist education.
Early in 1889 he had written Harper that "I like Mr. Gates," and
that "I have made up my mind to act in my educational benefactions through the American Baptist Education Society"—that is,
Gates's organization. The head of the Standard had often asked
Gates searching questions in order to appraise his judgment. The
former clergyman, who prided himself on his vein of hard business
realism, was therefore not astonished when Rockefeller went on:

"I am in trouble, Mr. Gates. The pressure of these appeals for
gifts has become too great for endurance. I haven't the time or
strength, with all my heavy business responsibilities, to deal with
these demands properly. I am so constituted as to be unable to give

[1]Gates, MS Autobiography, 298, 299, details the interview.

away money with any satisfaction until I have made the most careful inquiry as to the worthiness of the cause. These investigations are now taking more of my time and energy than the Standard Oil itself. Either I must shift part of the burden, or stop giving entirely. And I cannot do the latter."

"Indeed you cannot, Mr. Rockefeller," said Gates, with strong conviction.

"Well, I must have a helper," continued Rockefeller. "I have been watching you. I think you are the man. I want you to come to New York and open an office here. You can aid me in my benefactions by taking interviews and inquiries, and reporting the results for action. What do you say?"

Though Gates was far from realizing the full extent of the responsibilities to which this invitation would lead him, he accepted without hesitation. He still thought of Rockefeller's philanthropies in terms of millions, not hundreds of millions, and as applied to American objects, not to work throughout the world. Even so, he foresaw great opportunities for power and for usefulness. He felt no misgiving about his capacity to execute the work; and it fortunately grew by slow degrees, so that he could adapt himself to its demands. At first his principal anxiety concerned the social isolation to which he was condemning himself. "I guessed," he wrote later,[2] "that any man known to be making disinterested inquiries into appeals for charities made to Mr. Rockefeller would be surveyed with no friendly eye . . . I saw myself largely cut off from disinterested friendships, and almost of necessity a center of intrigue and dislike." He had seen something of the quarrels which burst forth among suppliants for Rockefeller's money, and of the chagrin felt by those who were refused.

In September, 1891, Gates took up his duties in an office in the Temple Court Building on Nassau Street, meanwhile continuing for a time his work as secretary of the Education Society. Written appeals were referred to his desk, while the doorman at 26 Broadway sent all personal applicants to him. He was soon appalled by the volume of the demands. By this time the newspapers had widely publicized Rockefeller's position as one of the richest men in the world; an article on great American fortunes in the New York

[2]*Idem*, 299.

Herald in 1892, for example, estimated the Rockefeller holdings at about $125,000,000. It was·no sinecure that Gates had accepted. His employer had been driven almost desperate.

"Neither in the privacy of his home, nor at table, nor in the aisles of his church, nor on his trips to and from his office, nor during his business hours, nor anywhere else, was Mr. Rockefeller secure from insistent appeals," writes Gates. "Nor, if asked to write, were solicitors willing to do so. If in New York, they demanded personal interviews. Mr. Rockefeller was . . . hounded almost like a wild animal. . . . But he had determined to escape. He meant what he said. And so, nearly all comers, near or remote, friend or guest, high or low, were blandly sent to my office at Temple Court. I did my best to soothe ruffled feelings, to listen fully to every plea, and to weigh fairly the merits of every cause. I found not a few of Mr. Rockefeller's habitual charities to be worthless and practically fraudulent. But on the other hand I gradually developed and introduced into all his charities the principle of scientific giving, and he found himself in no long time laying aside retail giving almost wholly, and entering safely and pleasurably into the field of wholesale philanthropy."[3]

Rockefeller, who had long before ceased to be a "detail man" in business, was still immersed in the minutiæ of his philanthropies. He cautioned Doctor Harper in 1892 against overworking: "You cannot carry all the details. I have spoken particularly to Mr. Gates on this subject. A multitude of people will stand ready to take your time, but many of them must be attended to by others."[4] Yet he had been breaking his own rule. He had been giving to a long list of Baptist churches—a lawsuit in 1896, for example, revealed how strongly he had been supporting the Tabernacle Baptist Church in lower New York[5]—and to missions, hospitals, and asylums. Gates took steps to strengthen the central Baptist agency for aiding poor churches, and then insisted that all applications must be sent to this agency. This rule precipitated some resentful battles, for naturally all the churches on Rockefeller's list wished to stay there; but Gates stood firm. He laid down the same principle in dealing with ministers, missionaries, and social workers. A multitude of them had

[3]*Idem,* 302, 303.
[4]April 2, 1892; Harper Papers.   [5]N. Y. *Herald,* May 19, 1896.

been getting money directly from Rockefeller. After strengthening the various church boards which had appropriate jurisdiction, Gates referred all letters to their secretaries. Rockefeller of course retained a very extensive private list of charities, but even in this the secretary weeded out numerous items. Of the huge stream of current appeals, Gates found that the great majority were personal, selfish, and often unreasonable. They came from all parts of America and the world, and from all types of humanity. A large proportion were illiterate. Year by year they increased. Once, just after Rockefeller announced a large gift, Gates had the pleas counted, and found that they totalled more than 15,000 the first week, and more than 50,000 the first month![6] A single steamer on one occasion brought some 5000 begging letters from Europe. No wonder Rockefeller had approached nervous prostration![7]

II

The man whom Rockefeller thus selected as his principal aide in philanthropy was as remarkable as any of his partners in business. In sheer ability he matched Flagler, Rogers, and perhaps even Archbold. Despite certain shortcomings, he possessed an unusual combination of gifts: insight, genuine imagination, analytical power, and vision, backed by unquenchable energy, courage, and an evangelistic fervor. He was largely a self-educated man, and though he labored hard to enlarge his knowledge, and possessed a highly disciplined mind, some observers thought his culture never really ran deep.[8] He was often impulsive and sometimes inconsistent. His enthusiasm and his pulpit training combined to give him a histrionic tendency. He liked to make orations, whether to an audience of one or ten thousand, and he could sometimes talk with the fierce emotionalism of a revivalist. Yet behind all his rhetoric, his impulsive acts, his zest and *brio,* lay a shrewd, wary, and highly practical mind. "I never saw him excited," testifies one close associate.[9] At bottom, as we have said, he was a businessman rather than a min-

[6]MS Autobiography, 307.

[7]"I hope I am improving, but I have not been to the office for weeks," Rockefeller wrote Harper May 15, 1891; Harper Papers.

[8]Mr. Jerome D. Greene has given me a balanced estimate of Gates. Files of the Rockefeller Institute for Medical Research contain memorial addresses by John D. Rockefeller, Jr., Doctor W. H. Welch, and Doctor Simon Flexner.

[9]Mr. George Welwood Murray to the author, May 23, 1938.

ister or social worker, and he soon gained a reputation for cautious, adroit, and hardheaded (some also believed rather hardfisted) conduct in business affairs. He liked to think that, with a different training and opportunities, he might have had a career much like Rockefeller's, and it is certainly true that he would have made a very successful business captain. To all his enterprises he brought an immense gusto; and though of medium height and average build, his personality was so dynamic that he stood out in any crowd.

Gates, who was not quite thirty-eight when he entered Rockefeller's employ, had been born on a farm in Broome County, N. Y., about ten miles north of the Susquehanna.[10] His father, who had previously studied medicine, became a Baptist minister, and when Frederick was one year old, took charge of the home church at Lamb's Corners, N. Y., at a pitiful salary. It will be seen that Gates and Rockefeller sprang from the same environment—from Baptist homes of meager income in rural New York. The elder Gates soon removed to the neighboring village of Center Lisle, where the boy was brought up in a strictly puritanical atmosphere which he afterward condemned. He always recalled with resentment that when he was three a thoughtless neighbor showed him a corpse. He equally resented the dreary monotony of the Sundays, when no play was permitted. "The best that religion had to offer me as a boy," he writes, "was death and heaven, the very things I most dreaded—being a normal, healthy boy." Because his grade school was worthless, his mind never really awoke until he entered high school.

The father, serving for a time at Mott's Corners and then at Ovid, N. Y., was always under the heel of bitter poverty. "There was no church treasurer," writes Gates of the former place. "People handed their church subscriptions to my father from time to time in cash, as it became convenient. Father's usual salary amounted to about $250 per annum, and his 'donation' added $50 more. His wood was usually furnished, and we had trifling presents. So we were always poor, and during the Civil War we became progressively poorer, because while the salary did not rise, the cost of living did. Father's was probably a typical case of the country pastor. He had to keep a horse, because his church membership was scattered, and expected

10MS Autobiography; *Dictionary of American Biography.*

Frederick T. Gates: Rockefeller's first great associate
in planning the benefactions.

Raymond B. Fosdick and George E. Vincent: Two later leaders
in planning the benefactions.

the usual amount of pastoral visits and preaching at out-stations. He had to dress in ministerial broadcloth and wear a silk hat; he must take papers and magazines, buy and read books, and his wife and family must dress respectably. Father always had to pay a rental of not less, I think, than $50 a year for his house. He received a few wedding fees of from $2 to $5, but never, I believe, a funeral fee. Never while he lived in the State of New York did Father receive as much as $400 in money in any one year."[11] It is clear that Gates remembered this poverty with a sense of injustice. There was impatience, too, in his recollection of some of the crudities of rural religion—the public baptisms in the creek, with hymns, and prayer, and the revivals.

Entering the home mission service, Gates's father was sent to Forest City, Kan., and in 1868 the boy entered Highland University at Highland in that State. The "university," which was on the high-school level, was conducted by a Dartmouth graduate, and gave really excellent instruction. But young Gates's career there was short. At fifteen he had to quit his classes and teach school to earn money, and he kept this up for three winters, helping to lift the debt on his father's farm. While teaching he became converted, this being an intellectual rather than emotional experience, for it was the ideas of Christ which appealed to the lad. "His teachings, particularly his social and moral teachings, became attractive, and I was drawn to his person and character, and felt that throughout my life I wanted to side with him and his friends against the world and his enemies. Such, frankly, was the only 'conversion' I ever had."

Then the youthful Gates began to gather business experience. First, he worked in a bank, where his shrewdness and inflexible honesty—for he refused to pre-date a letter—pleased his employer. He canvassed for a patent harrow so successfully that he earned $1500. When not otherwise occupied, he continued his studies at Highland. In 1875, with his own money in his pocket, he entered the University of Rochester, then even more than Brown the leading Baptist institution of the country. President Martin B. Anderson, an eloquent speaker and true scholar, was the heart and soul of the institution, and exercised a profound influence upon Gates. He not only taught the young man a good deal of economics, but radiated

[11]MS Autobiography, 70.

inspiration. He would exhort the students: "Hold on! You will succeed! The world wants men of will, of brains, of energy! It may
be ten or fifteen or twenty-five years before the world finds you out.
But no matter, fight on! The world wants you."[12] Such exhortations
caused Gates to give serious thought to his vocation. Doctor Anderson urged him to teach, but that did not appeal to his dynamic
nature—"I wanted to be an actor in life." He thought of the law,
but it seemed too selfish. "Starting with the fundamental proposition that I was to give my life to doing good, the sole question to
be determined was in what vocation I could be of most service.
With such knowledge of myself and of life as was then at my
command, I concluded that I could be of more service in the
ministry than elsewhere."[13] He entered Rochester Theological Seminary in 1877. Its staff was able, though too bookish and too limited
in vision; and it gave Gates everything requisite to success as a
preacher except the most essential thing of all—"namely, something
interesting and useful to say."[14]

This remark by Gates contains a great deal of wisdom. A preacher
is worthless until he has some message, and no amount of theological study will furnish it. He can gain it only from careful
reading, from experience of life, from long reflection, and from
study of economic, sociological, and political problems. After two
years as minister, Gates realized this. Forthwith he threw overboard
his cargo of theological and philosophical learning, and began to
study the English Bible, the daily problems of his congregation,
and the pressing issues of the day. He had become pastor of a small
and poor congregation in Minneapolis. But he labored hard to lift
the church debt. He attracted attention by two essays in the Minneapolis *Tribune* advocating a happier observance of Sunday, this
being his first important step on the road of modernism and independent thinking. His sermons began to receive notice, and his
congregation became larger and more important.

Then occurred the significant event we have already mentioned—
George A. Pillsbury, the wealthiest Baptist of the Northwest, called
on him, revealed that he had an incurable disease, and asked for
advice upon his will. Should he give $200,000 to a Baptist school,

---

[12]The autobiography gives a chapter to Doctor Anderson, pp. 111–132.
[13]MS Autobiography, 135.   [14]*Idem,* 139, 140.

the Owatonna Academy? He feared that the denomination would take no real interest in it. Gates proposed a shrewd plan for making sure of this interest: that Pillsbury give $50,000 at once on condition that the Baptists raise an equal sum, and leave the other $150,000 in his will. Pillsbury accepted the advice. Faced with the task of raising $50,000, Baptist leaders commissioned Gates to travel about Minnesota and solicit funds. Resigning his pastorate, he employed such businesslike methods that he soon had $60,000. He was asked to become principal of the school, now called Pillsbury Academy, and was also tentatively offered the presidency of the University of Rochester. Then, while his plans were still uncertain, he attended the stormy meeting in Washington from which the Education Society sprang.

It is evident that by 1892 Gates possessed a varied experience. He had been student, teacher, farmer, bank clerk, salesman, minister, and money-raiser; he had become a leader in the Baptist denomination, and was one of the best-trusted advisers of the heads of the University of Chicago. This training had matured his native gifts. Despite his enthusiasm, he was tough-minded, and never let personal considerations interfere with his business judgment. His decision in 1888 in favor of a new university in Chicago showed his ability to pierce quickly to essentials; his masterly use of his report on Baptist education that year to crystallize sentiment for the University revealed his practical grasp. His imagination and fervor sometimes produced curious results; they would carry him temporarily away, and when he brought himself up with a jerk observers would accuse him of inconsistency, and even of a jesuitical vein. He combined strong altruism in some directions with strong self-interest in others. When he began advising Rockefeller in business as well as philanthropy his dualism of character increased, for he could be as cold, hard, skeptical, and adroit in managing investments as he could be warm, responsive, and enthusiastic in helping pour funds into some educational or social enterprise to which he had been converted. Altogether, he was a versatile and impressive man; and even while his associates saw his inconsistencies and foibles, they admired him.[15]

[15]Doctor Welch in his memorial address calls him "a great man"; he and Doctor Flexner emphasize his vision and passion for labor.

III

Gates, first employed as Rockefeller's counsel in philanthropy, was soon looking after investments as well. Shortly after he came to New York, Rockefeller suggested that whenever on his frequent educational trips he happened to be near one of Rockefeller's properties, he take a day off, visit it, learn all he could, and report. Gates was reluctant. He warned Rockefeller that he was not expert in business. But Rockefeller persisted, and having uttered the warning, writes Gates, "I could not refuse." In his *Random Reminiscences,* Rockefeller explains that he chose Gates for his great common sense.[16] But actually he was better prepared than either he or Rockefeller knew.[17]

"Much of my life," he writes, "had been in fact an unconscious preparation for successful business. My interesting experience in selling harrows, my months as a clerk in a country store, and as cashier of a country bank, my interest in my father's financial affairs and the ways and means of paying our debts, my studies of political economy under Doctor Anderson, my close study of the finances of our church building in Minneapolis, a habit of looking at things in their financial tendencies and relations, my study of denominational finances at home and abroad, all these things had given me a business experience and my mind a financial turn."

By 1890 Rockefeller's fast-growing investments badly needed expert attention. His partial breakdown in 1891–92 increased the need for assistance, while the panic of 1893 revealed numerous errors of judgment. He had been too busy with the multifarious responsibilities of the Standard Oil during the eighties to pay proper attention to his surplus wealth. Remarking in his reminiscences that he had made some especially unfortunate investments in the Pacific Northwest, he indicates that he knew little about them. They "included a good many different industries, mines, steel mills, paper mills, a nail factory, railroads, lumber fields, smelting properties, and other investments about which I have now forgotten. I was a minority stockholder in all these enterprises, and had no part in their management." He goes on to say that "not all of them were profitable." This was an understatement, for most of them

[16]*Random Reminiscences,* 116.   [17]MS Autobiography, 310, 311.

were losing money. The flush years of the late eighties had led to a wild boom in some parts of the Far Northwest. Was not James J. Hill just driving his Great Northern through to Puget Sound? When the panic came the inflated valuations collapsed. "Most of these properties," admits Rockefeller, "I had not even seen, having relied upon the investigations of others respecting their worth."[18]

The fact was that he had been led into very unwise purchases by two enthusiastic participants in the Northwestern boom, Colgate Hoyt and Charles L. Colby. Both were members of the Fifth Avenue Baptist Church. Hoyt, a dapper man with bright staring eyes and flowing mustache, shrewd and plausible, had sprung from an old Cleveland family, and married a daughter of John Sherman. Rockefeller had known him when he was associated with Truman P. Handy. An active banker and broker, with offices at 36 Wall Street, he became president of the American Steel Barge Company and director in numerous transportation and financial corporations.[19] Colby, son of the Boston merchant Gardner Colby who endowed Colby College, had lived for many years in Wisconsin, helping his father construct and extend the Wisconsin Central, and serving in the legislature. He had made a trip to the Northwest and Alaska, and been fired by the idea of developing the rich resources of the Puget Sound area.

As energetic partners, Colby and Hoyt in the years 1890–91 interested themselves in developing from the raw wilderness what is now the city of Everett, Wash.—so named after Colby's able son. The Great Northern was expected to make it a terminal. They founded the Everett Land Company, which bought 5000 acres, cleared off the trees, built a wharf and ramshackle hotel, and platted lots for sale. They induced Eastern industrialists to set up a paper mill and a nail factory. They themselves established a shipbuilding plant to turn out whaleback steamships. Some Seattle citizens had discovered in the mountains behind Everett what they thought were marvellous deposits of minerals. Colby and Hoyt sent thither an expert mining engineer named Dickerman, who reported that he had found a wonderful vein of lead ore, which ran entirely through a mountain. On the strength of this report, the partners organized

---

[18] *Random Reminiscences*, 115, 116.
[19] *King's Notable New Yorkers*, 1896–99, p. 600.

a mining company, arranged to build a railroad from Everett up into the range, erected a concentrator for the ore at the mountain hamlet of Monte Cristo, and put up a smelter at Everett. They employed one of the most brilliant engineers of the country, a brother of Nicholas Murray Butler, to take charge.[20] An exciting wave of real-estate speculation swept over the town. Land boosters from all over the country swarmed into Everett and opened offices. Five banks opened their doors. Numerous hotels (one owned by the Everett Land Company) and shops served the 2500 people who quickly arrived. A street-railway company was organized. Colby and Hoyt sold lots on the two main avenues for $1000 to $2500 apiece, and the speculators kited them to $6000 and $10,000! A number of Baptists back east, hearing that Rockefeller was investing heavily in Everett enterprises, hastened to take land there.

For Hoyt, coming to 4 West Fifty-fourth Street and riding downtown to work on the elevated with Rockefeller, had given the magnate some of his and Colby's roseate faith in the future of the Northwest.[21] There seemed good reason for this faith. The Northern Pacific had reached Puget Sound in 1886, following a curved oxbow route through the State of Washington. Later Hill's Great Northern had started building to Puget Sound. It was obvious that Hill meant to strike almost due west from Spokane, thus shortening the route to the Sound and tapping the wealthy interior country of Washington. The Northern Pacific had therefore decided to build its own line from Spokane to salt water, cutting off the oxbow and competing with the Great Northern for the new country. Colby and Hoyt, who were on the executive committee of the Northern Pacific, had planned their town of Everett just where this railroad was expected to strike the Sound. They also hoped for a great Oriental trade. Hoyt in particular was an enthusiast who believed of each new venture, like Colonel Mulberry Sellers, that "There's millions in it!" Rockefeller held the mistaken theory that he could not do better than trust men who, giving all their time to specific investments, placed in them large sums of their own; that he thus had the benefit of their brains and labor. Unfortunately, he found that their judg-

---

[20]I am indebted to President Butler for information; President Butler and Gates used to meet at the station when the engineer came in from the West.

[21]John D. Rockefeller, Jr., to the author, April 14, 1938.

ment might be poor, and that they might invest far less than he did. Though at first a minority owner in these unsound ventures, later, in order to salvage his investments, he had to acquire majority holdings and take over the management.

"Little by little," states his son,[22] "Father found himself carrying the load for all of them; the others getting out. Eventually he owned as much as 80 per cent of most of them. They were boom affairs, and like most boom affairs, they never panned out."

For the panic of 1893 crushed the Everett boom as a pile-driver would crush an egg. Three of the five banks immediately shut their doors. Half the population fled, and hotels and shops folded up. The Everett Land Company was obviously bankrupt; it hastily made an issue of mortgage bonds, of which Rockefeller took a large proportion, and in 1894 it defaulted on the interest. The paper mill, the nail mill, and the shipbuilding company (which actually built one whaleback) were left floundering. It would obviously require much time and expert attention to salvage any considerable part of Rockefeller's large investment.

But these delusive enterprises at Everett by no means stood alone. The South had also enjoyed a land-boom in the late eighties; and the first mission confided to Gates was to report on an iron furnace in Alabama. The son of an old Southern friend had induced Rockefeller to invest some $30,000 there. In company with this promoter, Gates visited the town. The furnace, manufacturing pig-iron, was already under a receivership, its operations completely suspended. A brief inquiry showed that it could never make a profit. It showed also that the plant had been set up and a so-called college established in the town merely in order to help sell lots. Many people, particularly Baptist ministers scattered over the country, had bought the lots, but the town was utterly dead. Gates made an incisive report, which Rockefeller in his *Reminiscences* calls a model document—though at the time, he characteristically gave Gates no word of appreciation. When they next met, he told the secretary that he had sent the shares to be sold at auction.

As another investment in iron, Rockefeller held nearly $600,000

[22]Mr. Everett Colby has also given me valuable information. Not the slightest question of the good intentions or complete integrity of Messrs. Hoyt and Colby ever arose. For mistakes of judgment, many of them natural in a boom period, they themselves paid heavily.

par value of bonds of the West Superior Iron & Steel Company of West Superior, Wis. Colby and Hoyt had sold them in entire good faith, receiving a fee, says Gates, of $50,000. Rockefeller believed that the company was prosperous, making profits of $1000 a day; but he asked Gates to visit the plant when he was next in that area. Several months later Gates registered at the elegant hotel of the West Superior Land Company. He carried a letter from the president of the steel company in New York asking the manager of the works to furnish him with full information. But he encountered difficulty in obtaining an entry. The manager was out of town; the plant-superintendent refused to give him any data; and he suspected the worst even before he ran across the president of the land company at his hotel. This man frankly told him that the steel company was subordinate to the land company, and had been organized to help boom the town and sell lots at high prices. In short, the Alabama situation had been duplicated on a larger scale.[23]

And when Gates investigated the mortgage securing the bonds, he found evidence of the grossest dishonesty. He obtained a printed copy of the mortgage, and took it to the county seat to see if it was identical with the recorded document. It was. He then took authoritative maps, and tried to ascertain if the mill actually stood within the boundaries described in the mortgage. At once he found that it did not; it covered merely some vacant lots near by! He found also that of 570 city lots which were supposed to be mortgaged, only 449 were actually covered. He learned that forty acres of the town site of West Superior included in the mortgage had not been acquired by the steel company until sixteen months after the instrument was recorded. The mortgage stipulated that all the money raised by bond sales should be used in erecting improvements on the land; but actually the plant had cost $100,000 less than the bondholders had put in. For every $750 invested by the bondholders, the stockholders were supposedly to put in $250; but they had really put in nothing. Instead of making $1000 a day, as was represented, the plant was losing about that much. Apparently no attempt whatever had been made by Rockefeller's broker-friends to verify any of the assurances they had transmitted to him.

When the manager returned, Gates found that he was willing to

[23]MS Autobiography, 405–414.

talk frankly. They discussed costs of ore, labor, fuel, freights, and selling, and talked of prices. The manager admitted that they possessed a very narrow market, and were unable to compete with the great Chicago and Pittsburgh mills. The company could exist only by sufferance of its competitors.

Hurrying back to Cleveland, Gates went out to Forest Hill and told Rockefeller the almost incredible story of his deception. Hardly able to believe what he had heard, Rockefeller asked him to remain at Forest Hill until one of the Wall Street friends who had sold the bonds could be summoned. This gentleman soon arrived. He frantically denied every one of the allegations, but had nothing to meet Gates's proofs except protestations and lamentations. He even shed tears of rage and fear. But several days later, when he had completed his own investigation, he had to come to Rockefeller and admit that Gates had been correct in every detail. The mortgage was rewritten, and in the end guaranteed by the land company; but Rockefeller had learned with amazement of the recklessness of his brokers.

Colby & Hoyt, indeed, had led Rockefeller into about a score of very large investments east and west—some even outside the United States. The aggregate sum involved was several millions. Gates was staggered by the blind trust he had reposed in these men. Absorbed in the direction of the enormous Standard Oil empire, Rockefeller by 1890 had found his fortune surpassing his wildest dreams, and his annual income approaching $10,000,000. He had no time for a searching personal examination of investment opportunities. When Colby & Hoyt, men experienced in business, told him that they had become satisfied that a new enterprise was safe and profitable, and offered him a share of it with other ground-floor participants, he had been ready to go in without much inquiry. He reasoned that since they were much less able to stand a loss than he, their investigation would be thorough and their supervision careful. But the shock of the West Superior disclosures taught him a lesson.

Within a few weeks Rockefeller, learning that Gates had business for the Education Society in Colorado, asked him to investigate the San Miguel Consolidated Mines, in which he held some 25,000 shares. The promoter of this company was a Cleveland man who had gone to Telluride, Colo., and on a shoulder of the Rockies, some 11,000 feet high, had acquired a number of claims. He declared them extremely rich in gold. All that he needed to bring forth glittering profits was some capital to harness his splendid waterpower, build stamp-mills, and sink shafts. He consented to let a few favored Cleveland friends become his partners in developing the Consolidated shafts, selling them stock at a dollar a share. Several visited his mountain home, enjoying the scenery, eating at his bountiful table, and listening to his eloquent predictions; and some stayed for weeks. Having sunk all their available cash in the Consolidated, which still needed more, they favored Rockefeller with a share in the property that was now about to bloom into another Comstock Lode.

Gates accepted the commission with reluctance, for he feared he could add nothing to the reports of so many intelligent men. As he neared Denver, he resolved that he would not rely upon any examination of his own—he would seek expert advice. He made inquiries of the president of the Denver & Rio Grande, who referred to the promoter in a way that aroused his suspicion. Then he called on the head of the First National Bank for the name of a good mining engineer, and was directed to a man who had made a great reputation at Telluride.

"To his office we went," writes Gates. "I presented to this engineer Mr. Rockefeller's card, on which he had written 'Introducing Mr. Gates'—I still have that card of more than a quarter of a century ago. 'What!' he shouted. 'Do you mean to say that John D. Rockefeller has invested money in that damned swindle?' And when I humbly confessed the truth, his eyes flashed, his face flushed, and he strode to and fro, making the air blue with oaths and imprecations."

The Consolidated consisted of nothing but some twenty-odd claims which had all been abandoned as worthless. The promoter had come to Telluride as a cook, knew nothing about mines, and was using the invested money to pay himself a salary of $15,000 a year. He had always met his Eastern friends at the State line, had kept them, with the aid of a cunning secretary, so closely engaged during their sojourn that they could not speak a word to disinterested men, and had always accompanied them home beyond Denver. Gates was the only man who had escaped his clutches. The stamp-

mill was simply a blind to keep up the deception. Gates dealt with
the officers of the company summarily. He called them to his hotel
in Telluride. There he told them that he had already obtained all
the facts; that they had made a great mistake when they invited
Mr. Rockefeller in as partner; and that Rockefeller would sell out
to them at cost. He quickly had a note for Rockefeller's stock in
his pocket—but the note was never paid.

This third shock awakened Rockefeller to the necessity of organizing his investments. His faith in the sagacity of a number of
friends and agents had been painfully misplaced. It was plain that
he must have an office with a competent staff to maintain a continuous investigation of his investments. Obviously Gates was the
man needed to head this office. When the secretary returned to
New York, Rockefeller asked him to drop his Temple Court quarters and take an office at 26 Broadway. "That," writes Gates, "is
how I came to be a businessman."

The post was willingly accepted, for Gates was growing attached
to Rockefeller. In a letter to his parents early in 1893 he wrote:[24]

Mr. Rockefeller is as pleasant as ever or more so than ever. He is a
man of marvelous insight, tact, and skill. He does not diminish as one
gets better acquainted with him. He has the art of managing men. And
he is not, as the enemies of the Standard Oil Company imagine, a dis-
honorable or dishonest man. He is shrewd and keen and knows which
end of a bargain to take hold of. He does not mean to be cheated, though
he sometimes is, in the multiplicity of his business interests. Nor on the
other hand have I ever seen him disposed to do an unfair thing or take
an unfair advantage. He is tenderhearted too if there arises an occasion,
but Mother herself is not quicker to detect hypocrisy, fraud, or sharp
practice. In fact, he often reminds me of Mother in his keen scent for
the motives and purposes of others, and I suppose a certain share of the
same thing which I have inherited from her is one of the qualities which
he relies upon in me. He is chary of praise. Me he never praises to my
face. But I hear of good words about me to others. He is confiding great
interests to me, and I am exercising great caution, taking no step until I
know where my foot is going down, and whither it leads. He never
hurries me into any decisions or allows others to hurry me, but always,
on the contrary, while giving me plenty of rope, encourages me to take
my time.

[24]MS Autobiography, 429 ff.

IV

All of Rockefeller's files were thrown open to Gates. He at once gave up every possible moment to studying the investments. Some twenty corporations in which Rockefeller was part owner he found sick and dying—the balance-sheet of every one ending in red ink. And as the panic of 1893 precipitated a long, gruelling depression, salvage operations became almost impossible, for no stockholder but Rockefeller was in a position to furnish funds for further development. Forced sales or receiverships were unavoidable. Rockefeller had determined to dissociate himself immediately from all further business relations with the friends who had led him into bad investments. This severance, accomplished amicably but more slowly than both men would have liked, was handled by Gates. In some instances he bought out other shareholders to obtain complete control; in others, he sold Rockefeller's stock. When he finished, Rockefeller was the dominant figure in thirteen or fourteen corporations, and Gates was made president of all or nearly all of them.[25]

The heaviest labors in this reorganization were imposed by the various corporations in the Puget Sound area. Rockefeller and Gates found affairs there in a dismaying mess. The town of Everett and all its enterprises were prostrate. Gates, who made repeated visits to the district, set up a practical directorate of three men: Francis H. Brownell, the very able attorney for the Everett Land Company and other corporations; William C. Butler, the mining engineer; and J. B. Crooker, who had been a Minneapolis parishioner. They sent him suggestions and recommendations. Rockefeller quickly cut his losses in the land company. He also got out of the hotel and street-railway company as rapidly as possible. His large holdings in the nail-mill Gates was able to dispose of later to the American Steel & Wire Company. Rockefeller owned most of the lead-smelting works (the Puget Sound Reduction Company), and after Butler had operated these for a time with ores from the Cœur d'Alene, Gates sold them to the Guggenheim interests. He likewise disposed of Rockefeller's controlling share in the Puget Sound Pulp & Paper

[25]Messrs. Francis H. Brownell, Henry E. Cooper, and Jerome D. Greene have given me information on this salvaging.

Company to a capable young Englishman, William Howarth, who
had been its manager, and to A. H. B. Jordan, its superintendent.
Under their progressive management and with reviving business, the
paper company ultimately became a prosperous enterprise. On all
these companies Rockefeller took losses—sometimes heavy.

A heavy loss had to be accepted also on the Everett & Monte
Cristo Railroad, running sixty miles into the mountains, and terminating in a vast amphitheatre of crags. Costing nearly $2,000,000,
it had been built to carry down to the smelter the inexhaustible
masses of gold, silver, lead, and arsenic ores supposed to lie in these
ranges. Claims had been staked out with fancy names—the Monte
Cristo, the Pride of the Mountains, and so on. Butler, however,
quickly found that they were practically worthless; the lead veins
were rich only within a shallow area, while in the other mines the
ore was too poor to be worth extracting. The railroad had been built
—in large part with Rockefeller's money—before the mines were
properly explored! The original expert had known about iron, but
nothing else. Soon after Gates took charge a heavy spring freshet
washed out part of the railroad, and he sold the remainder to the
Northern Pacific. But he did get some enjoyment from the line
while he remained in charge. "The scenery of these snow-capped
mountains," he writes, "was hardly less imposing and awe-inspiring
than the Alps around the Jungfrau and Matterhorn. In my annual
trips I used to ride up on the cow-catcher and be regaled at dinner
with the delicious trout caught in the stream."

Yet, taken as a whole, these Northwestern ventures did not turn
out badly. One corporation offered large possibilities for profit, and
Gates's quick eye fastened upon it—the Everett Timber & Investment Company. He bought out the other stockholders for a hundred
cents on the dollar. Mr. Brownell took charge, and began the wholesale purchase of standing timber, acquiring about 50,000 acres in
Washington and 40,000 on Vancouver Island within a few years.
Having been an attorney for lumber companies, Brownell showed
admirable judgment. Before long, prices rose, and as buyers appeared Gates sold tracts of timber, often at five or six times what
they had cost. "I was able to report to Mr. Rockefeller before I
left him," he boasts, "that I had already made enough out of the
Timber and Investment Company to repay him all his Puget Sound

losses, and there remained an unsold surplus of one billion feet, at least, on which there had already accrued two or three millions more of profit. So . . . Mr. Rockefeller came out in the end with millions of profit."[26]

In all this Gates showed remarkable business sagacity. "Of all the minds with which I have come into contact," testifies Mr. Brownell, "his was the finest; a photographic memory, a wonderful power of analysis, and an independence which never let him be carried away by others." Gates also began giving advice on general subjects to Rockefeller. Intensely loyal, he, like William Rainey Harper and other Baptist leaders, was deeply grieved by the abusive attacks rained upon the head of the Standard. Near the close of 1895 Harper sent him a copy of *The Outlook* containing some vitriolic comments on Rockefeller by the Reverend Doctor Washington Gladden. Ever since his debate at Chautauqua with Gunton, Doctor Gladden had been the foremost figure in the American pulpit in public hostility to the Standard. He had a national reputation. Gates was already familiar with the article. "It is, on the whole, the worst I have ever seen," he wrote Harper. "I do not know what can be done about it, if anything. Gladden has evidently been reading the Lloyd book."[27] But he shortly made up his mind that Rockefeller's policy of silence under assault was a mistake, and he exerted his influence in favor of a more spirited attitude. There were other men among Rockefeller's associates who felt as strongly as he did.

Already one step had been taken to give the public a more favorable view of the Standard. It had installed at the Chicago World's Fair in 1893 an attractive exhibit showing the methods of drilling, piping, refining, and distributing oil. It had even driven two new wells for the special purpose of obtaining good "cores" showing the various rock-strata which overlie oil-bearing sands. Daniel O'Day had expended an enormous amount of time and ingenuity upon models of the pumping, piping, and storage facilities, while all the innumerable oil products were interestingly displayed.[28]

It is not strange that Rockefeller quickly came to trust Gates implicitly. As he writes in his *Reminiscences,* he found in his new

[26]MS Autobiography, 429–433; information by Mr. Francis H. Brownell.
[27]Harper to Gates, Dec. 3, 1895; Gates to Harper, Dec. 9, 1895. Harper Papers.
[28]N. Y. *Herald,* April 30, 1893.

assistant "rare business ability, very highly developed and very honorably exercised, overshadowed by a passion to accomplish some great and far-reaching benefits to mankind." Gates was wont to lay his plans, always carefully thought out, in lucid written form before his employer. Once they were accepted, Rockefeller financed them without another word, and to whatever extent Gates asked. He provided Gates with every facility for conducting his work— with confidence, credit, information, and the best of office assistance. In this he simply followed a lifelong rule: to provide conveniences for any energetic, sagacious, and conscientious assistant, whatever his rank or place, which would make his work as easy, and his success as nearly certain, as possible. "I had every needed tool," asserts Gates, "and the machinery was well oiled and without the least friction. No man of serious business responsibilities ever had a happier business life than I. No man was ever furnished with more of the external elements of success, or given better opportunities."[29] Any officer of the Standard could have said as much.

For his part, Gates soon became convinced that Rockefeller was not only a business genius, but one of the most honest and public-spirited industrialists that America had produced. If he had ever questioned Rockefeller's probity or given any credence to the attacks upon him, his doubts completely disappeared. "In all my acquaintance with him," wrote Gates at the end of his career, "acquaintance covering periods of trial and temptation, never have I ever known him to depart one hair's breath from the best standards of business rectitude. Every newspaper story I ever have seen, of his supposed complicity in shady transactions, in doubtful mining promotions, in artificial booms, in conspiracies to create panic, in operations of the so-called 'Standard Oil crowd' in the formation of monopolies, or in the manipulation of freeze-outs, have been falsehoods one and all, without even a shred or semblance of basic truth. He has of necessity been annually a large investor. He has bought and he has sold stocks and bonds. It has been necessary for him to keep in touch with the market, to know its feel, and to interpret it as best he could. He has never been a 'bull' or a 'bear.' He has always followed the market, never sought to direct it. In every one of our great panics he did everything possible to sustain

[29]MS Autobiography, 687–694.

prices, and has always been a heavy loser. And when the panic was on and the credit of banks and individuals exhausted he has placed his securities at the . . . call of . . . distressed debtors."[30] Of course Gates knew nothing of the early history of the Standard Oil

v

In 1897 a new and still more important lieutenant took his stand at Rockefeller's side—his twenty-three-year-old son, John D. Rockefeller, Jr., was graduated from Brown this year. The young man was well trained. After leaving the Browning School, he had at first intended to go to Yale, and had taken preliminary examinations and secured a room there. But several of his friends were going to Brown; he decided that the smaller college would give .him better opportunities for forming friendships and entering undergraduate activities; and he spent four happy years in Providence. He was a member of Alpha Delta Phi, was junior class president, and in his senior year managed the football team so efficiently that he turned a deficit into a surplus. He made the players carry their own suitcases on train trips! He had studied hard, covering a fairly wide range of liberal arts courses, and making a consistently good though not brilliant scholastic record. President E. Benjamin Andrews, who in these years courageously maintained his free-silver convictions, and who showed independence and rectitude in many other ways, profoundly impressed young Rockefeller.

But what particularly distinguished the son was his remarkable earnestness and conscientiousness, and his sense of devotion to great objects. He had no thought of making a career for himself; he was anxious above all to be of service to his father—and to the public. All his home tuition had made him singularly unselfish and purposeful. At a later date some one told John D. Rockefeller, Sr., that his two greatest successes were the founding of the Institute for Medical Research, and the training of his son. "The boy's mother should get all the credit for the last," said Rockefeller. However this may be, his training had been ideal not for a businessman—though he had qualifications for that rôle—but for the trustee of a great fortune. It had been suggested that he enter a law school; several friends invited him to go around the world with them. But

[30]*Idem.*

he put these proposals aside. "I felt that I had no time for either," he writes; "that if I was going to learn to help Father in the care of his affairs, the sooner my apprenticeship under his guidance began, the better." Early in October he reported at 26 Broadway.

His father did nothing either to push or to guide the novice. "He never said one word to me about what I was to do, nor did he say a word to any one else in the office," writes the son.[31] "He intended that I should make my own way." By this time Rockefeller was withdrawing from the direction of the Standard, and seldom came downtown. The son had no difficulty in deciding that his career was to lie in dealing with the now colossal and constantly growing fortune—that is, in the work of investment and giving. If he had wished to be a money-maker, he would have joined the management of the Standard as William Rockefeller's oldest son did. But he was anxious instead to help protect the accumulations that already promised to become an ever-mounting burden, and distribute them for the public good. He did represent his father's interests in the Standard's affairs, when necessary, as in other corporations, and for a year or two was vice-president and director of the Standard of New Jersey. But he took no active part in its control. Instead of going into Archbold's office, he entered that of Gates.

The younger Rockefeller gained experience in various ways, and went through much the same course of sprouts that most beginners have to hoe. He had his ups and downs, and one mishap was a bruising affair. It seemed important that he should obtain some acquaintance with security values by buying and selling; and his sister Alta and he became partners in stock investments, dividing their profits and losses. Somehow David Lamar, later termed the Wolf of Wall Street, became acquainted with several of young Rockefeller's associates, and told them of certain attractive deals in leather stocks in which he said that the very astute James R. Keene was interested. Little by little John D. Rockefeller, Jr., was drawn into a speculation in which he believed that he was acting with Keene. His commitments became greater and greater. Actually Keene had nothing to do with the matter; and when Lamar was supposed to be buying in Keene's name for the joint enterprise, he was really selling for his own account. At last, when called upon

[31]Memorandum by John D. Rockefeller, Jr.

to produce certain amounts of stock, he was unable to do so. Young Mr. Rockefeller peremptorily asked him to call at his office. He appeared very tardily, and one look at his flushed face convinced the young man that he was a swindler. The total loss approached a million; but as the son writes, the elder Rockefeller showed an astonishing comprehension, generosity, and patience:[32]

Never shall I forget my shame and humiliation as I went up to report the affair to Father. I had not the money to meet the loss; there was nothing else to do.

Father listened to the story. He did not utter one word of complaint or rebuke. He asked a good many questions—you know how hard he can bear down in asking questions—and probed into every detail of the transaction. It was hard to answer: "Why did you do so-and-so?" "Did you think to ask so-and-so?"

When he had heard the whole story, Father simply said: "All right. I'll take care of it, John." That was all. There was no reproach, not even a warning as to the future. But could any man have given his son a greater incentive to do right and try his hardest to learn the right than Father gave by what he did not say? He wanted me to learn in the hard school of experience how to protect myself, and he was so generous and big that he uttered no word of reproof for my costly mistake.

The younger Rockefeller applied himself assiduously to studying account books and other office records. He spent much time with Gates in talking with applicants for gifts, and made numerous investigations of institutions which asked for funds. He participated in important conferences. He joined Gates in analyzing investments and examining properties, and on several occasions went out to examine the Puget Sound and other Western holdings. Inevitably, he learned a great deal from the older man, who was endlessly patient in explaining details. Since he attended meetings at which important decisions were reached and contracts entered into, it was natural that before long he should begin to sign contracts and business agreements for his father. He never had a power of attorney or any other specific authority, but that was not necessary. Rockefeller quickly learned that the son's sense of responsibility and caution was remarkable, and that his judgment was entirely trustworthy.

It happened that "Junior," as most people called him, appeared on

[32]*Ibid.*

the scene just when his services were most needed. The fortune had begun to grow with a tremendous new rush. By 1897 petroleum had become a spectacular source of power as well as light. Gasolene took its place beside kerosene as an indispensable commodity all over the world. The growth of the business was phenomenal. In 1900 and again in 1901 the net earnings of the Standard exceeded fifty millions. In 1902 they were almost sixty-five millions, and in 1903 more than eighty millions. Rockefeller, less and less interested in business, more and more interested in giving, was indeed in danger of being crushed by his accumulations. And he found in Gates and his son just the combination of qualities he needed: Gates endowed primarily with imagination, fire, and vision, the son endowed primarily with hard sense, caution, public spirit, and conscientiousness.

The office force during the later nineties included the before-mentioned George D. Rogers, who had served since the seventies, had been Rockefeller's first personal secretary, and knew all his wishes in small business matters perfectly. Methodical, conscientious, and accurate, he could be trusted with any amount of detail, but he had insufficient grasp or imagination to grow into a larger position. Mr. Lovett, who had come to 26 Broadway as telegrapher (taking the New York end of Rockefeller's private wire from Cleveland during the summers), studied routine investment securities, and gave buying and selling orders. An able college friend of the junior Rockefeller, Henry E. Cooper, presently came in to advise upon investments. One of the most valuable employees was Mrs. Tuttle, a veteran telegrapher, stenographer, and filing-clerk, who had long held charge of the Cleveland end of the telegraph, often living for months at Forest Hill. Another elderly employee named Carey had charge of insurance, deeds, and legal records generally. There were a bookkeeper, and a young man who looked after all the accounts of Rockefeller's houses, stables, and grounds.

The younger Rockefeller shortly took charge of the office, managing it very efficiently. He and Gates shared the burden of investigating philanthropic needs and investment opportunities, dividing their time almost equally between the two tasks. They soon had the same wide range of acquaintances in both fields. Never was there even a momentary misunderstanding or instance of friction between them, though in temperament they were utterly unlike. The elder Rockefeller of course retained the final decision in all large matters, and upon some worked closely with his two assistants. The two men had different ways of presenting their material to him; the son usually did so verbally, while Gates wrote careful reports. Indeed, Gates had been quick to grasp the fact that the overburdened Rockefeller wished information brought before him in the most thoroughly digested form possible. He was willing to read long memoranda, but only when they had been stripped to essentials. In 1895 Harper sent Gates an article by one of his faculty on the University of Chicago as a Christian institution, asking him to call it to Rockefeller's attention. "I despair of getting Mr. Rockefeller to listen to it," replied Gates,[33] "as he generally requests the gist of the thing instead of the reading. I can give that to him thoroughly." Gates rapidly mastered the art of penning reports on various topics —philanthropic, industrial, financial, educational, and what not— that were masterpieces of condensed and lucid analysis. The younger Rockefeller learned to make brief and convincing oral statements.

But none of the major projects of the two men was accepted without careful scrutiny, and Rockefeller often acted only after long hesitation and inquiry. Studying a report, he would say: "I'll let the idea simmer." Then, after reflection and perhaps investigation, he would act. But often he did not wait to be prompted in his philanthropies. Talking with his son or Gates about some line of work, he would say:

"I'm ready to make a further gift if you think it wise."[34]

VI

With these two lieutenants, Rockefeller had blunter, franker, and more expert advice than for years past. It was one of the penalties of his increasing wealth and power that he had met with more subserviency than was good for his affairs. One of the traits of William Rainey Harper which pleased him most was the man's absolute spiritual independence. Doctor Harper used to enjoin upon his University associates, "No feudal attitude toward Mr. Rockefeller!"[35] He himself delighted in contradicting and opposing Rockefeller in

[33]Gates to Harper, May 11, 1895; Harper Papers.
[34]Mr. John D. Rockefeller, Jr., to the author, Feb. 18, 1939.
[35]Doctor William R. Harper, Jr., to the author.

discussions. He would say no simply to demonstrate his independence. Of course John had no difficulty in asserting himself against his father, who he knew liked opposition. And fortunately Gates, who sometimes showed even too much self-confidence and self-assertion, took the same stand. He could be as plain-spoken as if he had the millions and Rockefeller were his employee.[36]

Gates used to admonish Rockefeller, to preach to him: "Your fortune is rolling up, rolling up like an avalanche! You must keep up with it! You must distribute it faster than it grows! If you do not, it will crush you, and your children, and your children's children!" He prided himself on showing no reserve. As he writes of Rockefeller:[37]

Within the limits of the respect and deference due him, I felt that he was entitled to my ultimate thought frankly expressed. Of course I came to know him well, and could at any time predict with considerable accuracy his attitude on any question I might submit. But as I have already said, I did not consciously allow his anticipated views to control or to modify my own views in the least degree. On the contrary, where I knew there would be a conflict of view I took special pains to fortify my position instead of yielding it or concealing it.

I used to reason that any one could buy for a few dollars a machine into which he could talk, and by turning the crank get back his own words and thoughts accurately registered. If Mr. Rockefeller wanted a human machine of that kind he could get plenty of such shrewd and cautious men who after a little while could read him and anticipate his thought. But their real value would be no more than that of a talking machine. . . .

I was there to present my own views with courtesy indeed but with absolute and undeviating frankness and truth. This therefore I always did. I usually came to clear and fortified judgments which I sometimes expressed strongly. I have no doubt that at times I irritated him. If so, he had great skill in concealing it. He was indeed very patient and very considerate. On the other hand, his deliberation was sometime extreme; his reluctance to argue and speak out his thoughts fully, his skill in not exposing the slightest surface for attack, his long silences so that we could not locate even his objections, were baffling. He knew how to keep the reins in his own hands.

It was indeed one of Rockefeller's errors, both in business and philanthropy, that he placed somewhat too great a value upon harmony. He liked unruffled board meetings, and though he en-

---

[36]Mr. Jerome D. Greene to the author, Feb. 26, March 2, 1939.
[37]MS Autobiography.

couraged hearty debate, was averse to contention. He never adequately realized the value of a clash of convinced minds and strong wills; he never fully comprehended that a dispute which generates heat usually kindles light.[38] It was another heavy error that he was much too taciturn about his purposes, beliefs, and skepticisms. This ingrained reticence crippled discussion and argument. After Gates became his aide, and still more after the son emerged as mediator between Rockefeller and the world, these faults were less injurious.

It is true that Gates sometimes irritated Rockefeller; but rather by his evangelistic passion, his bursts of emotion, his way of addressing the magnate as Gladstone addressed Queen Victoria, than by his contradictions and arguments. Two men so totally unlike would sometimes fray each other's nerves. Gates sometimes complained of Rockefeller's repressed nature and enigmatic mind. It was not Rockefeller's way to complain, but he had moments of impatience. Yet his confidence never really wavered, for he realized how shrewd, honest, and alert an aide he had acquired. In 1917 he gave B. C. Forbes a public tribute to Gates. "We all owe much to Mr. Gates. . . . He combines business skill and philanthropic aptitude to a higher degree than any other man I have ever known."[39]

By rapid steps in the nineties, Rockefeller and his two lieutenants systematized the investments. The Northwestern millions were slowly salvaged. An accidental investment in Minnesota ore-lands bloomed into a huge property and a reverberating controversy, the story of which demands a special chapter; while it also led Rockefeller into building up the greatest fleet of carriers the Great Lakes had yet seen. The head of the Standard owned shares in the Brooklyn Union Gas, the Consolidated Gas, various natural gas companies in Ohio, coal mines in the same State, the New York Central, Lackawanna, and other Eastern railroads, and the American Linseed Oil Company; he had a small interest in the National City Bank; and his real-estate holdings were considerable.

He was also led during the nineties into close association with George Gould, a choice almost as unfortunate as that of Colby and

---

[38]Various associates have insisted on this. But John D. Rockefeller, Jr., disagrees: "I have often heard Father speak of the earnest and heated debates among the Standard Oil officers and directors, and often of sharp differences of opinion and hard fights."

[39]*Forbes's Magazine*, Sept. 29, 1917.

Hoyt. On Jay Gould's death in 1892, George received almost complete control of the estate. He was then twenty-eight, shy, unaggressive, and unprepossessing. A great sportsman, addicted to boxing, fencing, hunting, yachting, and tennis, he did much to popularize polo in the United States. He liked luxury, and late in the nineties built the magnificent residence called Georgian Court, one of the show places of the country. As the world later learned, he maintained two establishments and two sets of children at the same time. Outwardly, such a man would seem one of the last in the world to appeal to Rockefeller; but the Standard Oil leader, who met him through the philanthropic Helen Gould, found him attractive.

Gould's business career was so dramatic and in the end so tragic that it is strange that no novelist or playwright has made use of the theme. Inheriting the control of the Western Union, Missouri Pacific, Manhattan Street Railway, Texas & Pacific, International & Great Northern, and Wabash, he was one of the great railroad kings of the country. The four Western roads were the basis of the "Gould system," which he and his trustees agreed should be conserved and developed. For some years Rockefeller lent large sums in this work of development. As Gould pressed his policy of expansion, there opened before him the vision of a railroad empire extending from ocean to ocean. In the East it seemed desirable that the Wabash should have an outlet on the Atlantic in place of the Buffalo terminus. Gould was encouraged in this ambition by Carnegie and other steel men who were dissatisfied by the Pennsylvania's treatment of Pittsburgh. He therefore threw a line from Toledo to Baltimore by way of Pittsburgh. The entrance into Pittsburgh, studded with tunnels and trestles, was one of the most expensive railroad stretches ever built, costing $380,000 a mile for sixty miles. From beginning to end the Pennsylvania Railroad did its utmost to hamper and defeat the project, even tearing down the Western Union poles and wires on its right of way because Gould controlled the Western Union.[40]

In the West the young railroad magnate became engaged in equally heavy battles. A struggle developed between him and Harri-

[40]E. M. Gilmer, "The Goulds," *Cosmopolitan*, XLVI, 603–615; J. L. Cowan, "Freeing a City from a Railroad's Control," *World's Work*, IX, 5712–5722; Burton J. Hendrick, "The Passing of a Great Railroad Dynasty," *McClure's*, XXXVIII, 483–501; Frank H. Spearman, *The Strategy of Great Railroads*.

man, for the two had fallen out over the ownership of the Colorado
Fuel & Iron Company—a property into which Rockefeller put
money. In consequence, about the turn of the century Harriman's
Union Pacific began discriminating against Gould's Missouri Pacific.
The young man launched an effective counter-attack in the winter
of 1901–02, when he obtained control of the Denver & Rio Grande,
and thus paralleled the Union Pacific all the way to Salt Lake City.
Harriman then, after the death of Collis P. Huntington in 1901,
bought control of the Southern Pacific. Owning great trunk lines
both north and south of the Gould roads, he began squeezing the
latter unmercifully. Gould thereupon chartered the Western Pacific
Company, and began building his own line from Salt Lake to San
Francisco, completing it in 1911. But meanwhile the panic of 1907
had thrown his ill-ballasted craft, carrying far too much sail, on its
beam ends. In the sequel, he lost road after road.

Rockefeller invested much money in the Missouri Pacific and
Missouri, Kansas & Texas, his son becoming a director in both lines.
On Gould's advice, he also invested in the Santa Fé, New York
Central, and Manhattan Street Railway Company. The minority
interest which he obtained in the Colorado Fuel & Iron, a company
operating twenty-four mines in Colorado, proved sufficient to maintain control, and the younger Rockefeller, Gates, and another able
assistant, Jerome D. Greene, all served on the board. As Gould
became deeply involved in battles east and west and his star declined,
it required astute management to make sure that some of the investments into which he had led Rockefeller did not show cruel
losses; but the management was supplied.[41]

Meanwhile, the flow of gifts was also being systematized and
accelerated. Besides the grants to the University of Chicago, and
other large benefactions which we shall describe elsewhere, Rockefeller was making a steady succession of lesser donations. They included gifts to a long array of colleges and universities—Barnard,
Wellesley, Vassar, Cornell, Brown, Denison, Lincoln Memorial,
Nebraska, Syracuse; gifts to Newton Seminary, Rochester Seminary,
and other divinity schools; gifts to the Y. M. C. A., to missions and
settlement-houses, and to other social agencies; gifts to churches,

[41]Information from Messrs. John D. Rockefeller, Jr., and Henry E. Cooper;
Gates's MS Autobiography; Julian Ralph, "John Davison Rockefeller," *Cosmopolitan*, XXXIII (1902), 162 ff.

hospitals, and asylums. No grant was made without careful inquiry, or without guarantees of continuing usefulness.

In making these generous gifts, Rockefeller, his son, and Gates all acted on the same principle and were animated by the same spirit. It is now clear that in one sense the colossal fortune was largely an accident. Economic conditions would not have permitted such an accumulation before the Civil War, while our economic and social legislation would not have permitted it after the World War; it was a phenomenon possible only in a limited period of our history. Moreover, its ultimate magnitude far surpassed anything of which Rockefeller had initially dreamed. It constituted a tremendous responsibility, a vast opportunity for doing good; and he felt himself not so much its owner as its trustee or manager. He soon learned that the American public (perhaps because they felt that the fortune was largely an historical accident) did not express any special gratitude for the mere fact of its distribution. But discerning people did feel grateful for the care which Rockefeller put into his trusteeship. He, his son, and Gates were determined to employ it as scientifically and thoughtfully as possible. For the devoted labor, forethought, and imagination which they gave to this task, they deserved very warm thanks indeed. We may add that there grew up in Rockefeller's mind, as the years passed, a semi-mystic conviction that God had given him the money to be used for the welfare of mankind. He reflected that he had always been a giver, and had always given by the light of fixed rules, conscientiously and wisely; and it seemed to him that Providence had perhaps rewarded him by making him the greatest trustee, the largest distributor of its bounty, in all history.

XXXVIII

The Standard's First Rival

FROM the day that Hezekiah of Judah revolted against Sennacherib, no empire, however powerful, has been safe from attack. Rockefeller, who had built up an unprecedented combination and accomplished wonders in consolidating its position, was well aware that a host of enemies could gather overnight. So long as the numerous competing refineries remained small, scattered, and disorganized, the Standard was safe; but what if a large group of them united? Early in the eighties the Tidewater Company had tried to break down his monopoly, but he had quickly forced it to an agreement which recognized his supremacy. Now in the nineties a new effort—the effort of Lewis Emery, Jr., and his partners in the Pure Oil Company—was made to conquer part of the Standard's domain. From the story of Rockefeller's fortune we must turn back to the oil industry, and to the first really successful co-operative enterprises launched by the indomitable men of the Regions.

While the Standard had been holding its own abroad and enlarging its sales at home, the producers in the Oil Regions had fared much less happily. Just as in these years the farmers of the Great Plains began to smother themselves in their own grain, so the well-owners seemed likely to drown themselves in their own oil. In 1886 the flow from the Appalachian field exceeded 26,600,000 barrels. Once before, in 1881, it had slightly surpassed this level; but the situation in 1886 differed in two striking particulars from that at any earlier date. The flood of Russian oil was now being fully loosed upon the European and Near Eastern markets, threatening a sharp restriction of American export shipments. And still more ominously, Lima petroleum was pouring forth like a spring freshet. So rapidly were new wells being drilled that the Lima production leaped from 650,000 barrels in 1886 to more than five millions in 1887.

Year after year the anxious well-owners had looked forward to a golden day when the flow of oil would slacken and prices would rise. Back in the middle seventies they had spoken of four-dollar oil as their just due. But the centennial year saw oil reach the $4 mark for the last time, and during fifteen years after 1877 it never even for a single month averaged $2. Early in the eighties a dollar a barrel was regarded as a high return, of which men talked longingly while the quotations drooped around 70 or 80 cents; and by 1887 even 75 cents a barrel was hailed as a good price, for the midsummer bids fell as low as 54 cents.[1] Times had changed indeed. Only those producers whose wells flowed copiously, or whose expenses could be kept extremely low, were making any profit.

Ragged, down at the heels, and discouraged, the Regions men knew that their difficulty lay not only in high production but in the huge surplus which they were carrying from previous years. This weighed upon the industry like some old man of the sea. Year after year more crude oil had been pumped from the Pennsylvania valleys than the world could use. In the spring of 1887 the stocks on hand were estimated at about 31,000,000 barrels, or more than had yet been produced in any single year, and twice as much as the whole production of 1878.[2] It was held at considerable expense, it was steadily deteriorating, and it kept the market depressed. Probably no other industry in the world at the time, not even grain-growing, had such a colossal carry-over of raw materials. The main cause of the overproduction was simple: too many men "went on in a wild way hunting new oil, and when they found it they would develop it rapidly," as one irate producer testified.

The hard-beset well-owners in 1888 estimated the cost of producing a barrel of Pennsylvania oil at about $1.15, and inasmuch as the average price that year was 66 cents, they believed that they had lost about ten million dollars. No doubt this was an exaggeration, while many marginal producers deserved to be squeezed out. But it was plain to everybody that the flush years were past and that men once rich were growing poor. The well-known producer called

[1]Boyle, *Derrick's Handbook,* 711, 794 ff.
[2]Figures given in *House Trust Investigation, 1888,* p. 34; *Derrick's Handbook,* 807 ff.

"Farmer" Dean told Federal investigators that whereas in 1872 he could have listed seventy friends in the Regions able to draw their checks for $50,000 to $100,000, now he could think of only one who could sign his name for $25,000. For most people the hard times meant "economy and struggle to get a living out of the industry." Drillers who in prosperous years had been paid $6 a day and expenses were now glad to take $3 flat; ordinary laborers got a dollar a day and were idle much of the year. This growing poverty in the Regions had helped to generate the widespread feeling of bitterness and vindictiveness against the Standard Oil. The trust was getting rich while most oil men were desperately poor.[3]

Worst of all to farsighted Pennsylvania producers was the grim certainty that as the rich Lima field was developed, their plight would become still more distressing. In 1888 Ohio crude sold at 15 cents a barrel, while Pennsylvania's brought 70 to 80 cents. The difference in quality, after Frasch perfected his process, by no means justified this discrepancy. It cost only one third more to refine the Ohio oil, or about an additional 13 cents a barrel, while the finished product was salable for nearly as much as Pennsylvania kerosene. The Standard was now mixing Lima and Pennsylvania oils in some refineries, and obtained the same price for the resulting kerosene as for its purest brands. Obviously, when Ohio oil became available in large quantities, its competition would cost the Regions dear; and it became available with astonishing speed, for the output in 1888 leaped to almost ten million barrels, and in 1890 exceeded fifteen million!

II

The decline in prices naturally produced a new uprising in the Regions, and this revolt rapidly developed toward two very different objectives. The more immediate aim was to cut down crude-oil production, get rid of the huge surplus, and thus raise prices at the well-head. The secondary object was to strike once more at the Standard's monopoly by a co-operative enterprise in piping, refining, and exporting oil. Rockefeller dealt with this movement after his own incisive and logical fashion. In the great effort of producers to reduce the flow of oil and raise prices he co-operated wholeheartedly —and that effort scored a magnificent success. But when the Regions

[3]*House Trust Investigation, 1888*, pp. 34, 38, 90.

men attempted competition in piping and refining, he struck hard
to defeat them.

It was natural for producers to blame the Standard for the ruin-
ously low levels at which crude oil sold. They believed that its
buyers fixed the price of petroleum to suit themselves, and did it in
such a way that the Standard took an exorbitant share of whatever
profits the oil industry could make. Beyond doubt the Standard held
a monopolistic position in the American market and for at least
short periods could manipulate prices without difficulty. As Henry
Havemeyer said in the sugar-trust investigations, any combination
which manufactured 80 per cent of a commodity could raise or
depress the value of raw materials. It could refuse to buy for long
intervals, or could buy heavily and rapidly. But the oil market—
since about seven tenths of American oil went abroad—was fundamentally a world market. The producers themselves soon admitted
that, whatever the Standard's sins, the two main causes of poor
prices were simply overproduction, and the huge annual carry-over.
As one Regions leader told a House Committee in 1888: "The Standard attributed all our troubles to existing stocks over supply . . .
and they convinced our committee, and finally the committee convinced our assembly, that that *was* the trouble. . . ." The surplus or
carry-over for the five years beginning 1882 was never lower than
33,395,000 barrels, and at the beginning of 1885 actually approached
37,000,000. It was incubus enough to ruin any industry.[4]

German buyers of both crude and refined petroleum kept agents
in the Regions and in New York who were familiar with stocks and
current production. English dealers had equally well-informed representatives. Their reports to London and Berlin did much to fix
the price-level in the world market, and in 1884–88 the surplus and
the increase in Russian shipments led most buyers to take a bearish
attitude. Another factor in determining prices was speculation.
The tanked oil was represented by certificates, which the oil-ex-
changes dealt in just as the wheat-pit in Chicago traded in ware-
house receipts. The greater the tanked surplus the larger the volume
of certificates, and the easier it was to depress prices. In the spring
of 1888 an executive committee of the associated producers issued an
intelligent analysis of the price situation, in which the much-hated

[4]Figures in *House Trust Investigation, 1888*, p. 115.

Standard was not even mentioned. The depression, they stated, was "due to two causes: one, the existence of 31,000,000 barrels of crude petroleum stored in tanks in advance of consumption, and the other, the continued selling short by speculators who were not interested in the business of production of petroleum,[5] nor indeed in any legitimate business connected with petroleum in any way, but who persisted in selling short, gambling on the hope of differences in their favor."

In the days of heartsick disillusionment which followed the defeat of the Billingsley Bill on April 28, 1887, the angry producers who lingered in Harrisburg began to think more realistically than for years past. They realized that they were under the harrow. Their leaders eloquently assured them that they must awake, arise, or be forever fallen. And in the next few weeks they launched a movement which resulted in the rapid enrollment of about 2000 members in a new Producers' Protective Association. Thus for the third time an exigent crisis had brought forth an attempt at combination. The challenge of the South Improvement Company in 1872 had resulted in a Petroleum Producers' Union; the Standard's conquest of the last independent pipe lines in 1877 had given birth to a second Union. Now in 1887 another stern effort was undertaken. A fresh group of leaders had arisen—Lewis Emery, Jr., David Kirk, Thomas W. Phillips, Rufus Scott, and others—in place of the old circle headed by William Hasson and B. B. Campbell. As enterprising and aggressive as their predecessors, they had larger business connections, and were destined to meet with greater success.

Head and shoulders above the others rose that Regions Bobadil, the impetuous and irrepressible Emery, a man of multifarious enterprises who loved nothing so much as a shindy. "He was never happy unless he had two or three lawsuits on hand," Ida M. Tarbell has told the author.[6] A graduate of Hillsdale College in Michigan, he had come to the Regions just after the war, made money, lost it in the panic of 1873, and by lucky strikes and sheer ability made it again. Having settled in Bradford, he became the principal business-

[5]This statement, dated Butler, Pa., April 18, 1888, and signed by T. W. Phillips and five other prominent producers, is in *House Trust Investigation, 1888,* pp. 110–112.

[6]Gifted with great constructive powers, he was in some ways (as Miss Grace E. Emery writes the author) "twenty years ahead of his time."

man and political figure of the town. He was interested in wells, pipe lines, and refining. Gaining election to the Assembly in 1878 and the State Senate two years later, he distinguished himself at Harrisburg as an opponent of monopoly. With his snapping blue eyes, bristling mustache, and strong chin, he looked the born fighter that he was.[7] He might have quoted Don Quixote to Sancho Panza: "Tell me, what greater pleasure can there be in the world, or what delight can equal that of winning a battle and triumphing over one's enemy? None, beyond all doubt." The veteran David Kirk, who was drilling six oil wells when Fort Sumter was fired on, who had lost a fortune when the Pithole field was exhausted, and who had amassed another by organizing and managing the McCalmont Oil Company, was also a man to be reckoned with. He had served two terms in Congress. And Thomas W. Phillips, a burly former minister who had become the largest individual producer in Pennsylvania, his output averaging at least 6000 barrels a day, was a pillar of strength to the new movement.[8]

By June, 1887, the Producers' Protective Association was well launched, and by October its framework was complete. The 2000 members formed thirty-six local assemblies scattered through ten counties of Pennsylvania and two of New York. Their constitution provided for a general assembly, an executive board of nine, and a president, vice-president, secretary, and treasurer. Phillips was the first head. The order was secret, and no person connected in any capacity with the Standard Oil was allowed to join. According to the platform adopted in June, they intended "to protect and defend their industry against the aggressions of monopolistic transporters, refiners, buyers, and sellers of their product." To this end they were "to encourage and assist as far as possible the refining and marketing of their product, and the sale direct to the consumer by the producer."

To suggest the co-operative shipping, refining, and marketing of oil, however, was a great deal easier than to take practical steps in that direction. Many schemes were offered and many proposals

[7]See account of Emery in Philadelphia *Public Ledger,* Nov. 20, 1924; I have talked with many residents of the Regions about him.

[8]A good sketch of Kirk may be found in Boyle, *Derrick's Handbook,* 668; of Phillips in D. R. Crum, ed., *Romance of American Petroleum and Gas,* 329, 330.

debated. But as David Kirk later confessed, "We found we would have trouble to get capital and means."[9] They could not reach the few independent refineries on the seaboard without a pipe line, and pipes could not be laid without money and labor. As late as August, the Association still assumed a menacing attitude toward the Standard. Its general assembly, meeting in Bradford, proposed to duplicate both the main pipe lines of the Standard to New York, Buffalo, Pittsburgh, and Philadelphia, and the minor lines ramifying throughout the Regions. It threatened also to employ attorneys and detectives for a new prosecution of the Standard leaders upon charges of criminal conspiracy.[10] But sensible men comprehended that a third proposal made at this August meeting, and sent to the local units for ratification, a proposal for stopping all drills and shutting down all wells, was far more urgent. They realized also that such an embargo could not succeed without the Standard's help!

Phillips flatly refused to join in any shutdown movement unless the Standard joined too. Other practical men agreed with him, and as Kirk later testified, "it was deemed best to appoint a committee to wait on the Standard and see what they would do before going into a fight."[11] A second good reason existed for seeking an agreement. It was evident that a shutdown, if effective, would advance prices not only on the new production of oil, but on the 31,000,000-barrel surplus which was already above ground. Much of this was owned by the Standard, and no producer believed that it ought to reap huge profits without making any sacrifices or taking any risks.

For his part, Rockefeller was quite willing to come to an amicable arrangement with the Association. He had always complained of the anarchy of the Regions and the frequent glut of oil. He had often asserted, as in the New York investigation of 1888, that the producers needed only to organize themselves and regulate the flow of crude oil in order to obtain fair prices. He had two good reasons for supporting the shutdown movement. In the first place, it would contribute to a greater harmony between the producers and the

[9]*House Trust Investigation, 1888*, p. 33.

[10]Philadelphia *Press*, Aug. 4, 1887. At the very beginning, just after the Billingsley defeat, Emery and his associates wished to unite the producers behind legislative action against the trust in Pennsylvania, New York, Ohio, and other States, and in Congress; to introduce anti-monopoly bills, and fight for them along a wide front.

[11]*New York Senate Committee on Trusts, 1888*, p. 445.

Standard, and, by reducing the distress throughout the Regions, lessen the bitterness which had produced the Billingsley Bill. In the second place, a rise in crude oil would make it easier for the Standard to maintain profitable prices for refined oil in Europe. He therefore welcomed the overtures of the Union,[12] and, after conferences at Saratoga and Niagara Falls, a satisfactory agreement was reached.

The arrangement made was simple. The Standard, which owned nearly one third of the 31,000,000 barrels of crude on hand, admitted that it ought not to take all of the prospective profits upon this amount. It consented to sell the Producers' Association one half of its holdings, or 5,000,000 barrels, at 62 cents a barrel, the market price on the day of the contract. The Association for its part agreed to reduce production by 17,500 barrels a day. If at the end of the year the Association could show that the reduction had reached this figure, then it was to pocket the profits on the 5,000,000 barrels, deducting storage, fire losses, and insurance. A shutdown would of course throw many drillers, mechanics, and laborers out of work. President Phillips therefore suggested that all the profits on 1,000,000 barrels out of the Association's 5,000,000 be set aside for the workmen, and that the Standard appropriate the profits of an additional 1,000,000 for the same purpose. The workingmen would thus receive the difference, on 2,000,000 barrels, between the original 62-cent price and the enhanced price following the shutdown. Rockefeller immediately assented.[13]

The great embargo became effective November 1, 1887. Three contracts had been prepared by the Producers' Association: one for the shutting in, partial or complete, of wells; one to stop men from shooting, cleaning-out, or otherwise increasing the flow from wells which were not shut in; and one for abstention from drilling new wells. The first was of course the most important. Nearly a thousand signatures were obtained, some of which represented many wells.

[12]*Idem*, p. 449. Rockefeller said that his great object was "accomplishing a harmonious feeling as between the interests of the Standard Oil Trust and the producers of petroleum"; and that he wished to co-operate to alleviate "the great distress throughout the oil-producing region." He added that the higher prices did work a hardship in the contest against Russian oil, "which we recognize and which we are feeling somewhat." In the Turkish market the Standard had given up all profits to hold customers.

[13]*House Trust Investigation, 1888*, pp. 34, 35. The agreement between the Standard and the producers is given on pp. 69, 70.

According to careful estimates, the reduction in flow amounted to about 18,500 barrels a day. This was impressive, and it had an instant effect on the market. Stocks began to fall off at the rate of a million barrels a month, and the price late in December touched 90 cents. Production for the year was nearly four million barrels less than in 1886. During the first three months of 1888 prices repeatedly rose above 95 cents. The movement was clearly proving a success. By agreement with the Standard, in March the Producers' Association sold 250,000 barrels of stored oil at a profit of some $77,000, and advanced $85,000 to the well-drillers' union as a partial recompense for loss of wages.[14]

But it became evident, as the first flush of enthusiasm cooled, that any protracted regimentation of the loose industry would be impossible. Some well-owners refused to sign the agreements, waiting for a "free ride" to better prices. Others signed and then broke their word. Violence broke out, and the derricks of various new wells were dynamited, with resultant injury to the prestige of the associators. Moreover, speculation on the oil exchanges remained uncurbed, and various bear-movements, suddenly reducing prices, alarmed many well-owners. Honest producers complained that whenever their strenuous efforts brought oil up to a decent level, gamblers rushed in to depress the market. By the early summer of 1888 crude was quoted at 70 to 80 cents a barrel.

Obviously, since the profit which the Producers' Association hoped to make on its 5,000,000 barrels depended upon the price-rise above 62 cents, these quotations did not look very tempting. Adherents tended to fall away. The Producers' Association continued a vigorous existence during the remainder of 1888, and managed to hold production for Pennsylvania and New York to 16,500,000 barrels. But 1889 found the shutdown movement waning. Production in these States spurted back that year to 21,500,000 and in 1890 to 28,500,000 barrels, the latter a record figure.

Yet if the Association failed to give any long-continued stability to the market, it did score two very real successes. It got rid of that old man of the sea, the burdensome surplus, and it sold its stored holdings at a small profit. The first achievement was of course the

---

[14]*House Trust Investigation, 1888,* pp. 36–62; Boyle, *Derrick's Handbook,* 752, 805.

more important. The stocks of Pennsylvania oil on hand at the end of 1888 amounted to 18,600,000 barrels; at the close of 1889 they were down to 10,900,000 barrels; and at the end of 1890 they were below 9,300,000 barrels. This last figure was about one fourth of the carry-over existing a half-dozen years earlier. The crushing incubus had been dislodged, and Pennsylvania well-owners could stand upright again.[15]

As for the stored oil, the last of it was sold in June, 1889, at a small but gratifying profit. The Association had parted with 1,500,000 barrels at various times to meet expenses, still retaining 3,500,000. On this the Standard Oil held an option which would expire July 1. Early in June it was rumored that a Wall Street group was being formed to bid against the Standard, and one report even declared that it was offering a dollar a barrel. Representatives of the Association came to New York on the 27th to discuss a sale with any bidders, President Phillips heading the delegation. Rockefeller and other Standard men spent most of the 28th in negotiations with them at the Fifth Avenue Hotel, where late that evening an agreement was reached by which Rockefeller paid the market-rate, 91½ cents. As the oil had cost 62 cents, and interest and storage added 22 more, this gave the producers a profit of 7 cents a barrel. The transaction was announced under such headlines as "Largest Oil Deal Ever Made," and next day the Standard's check for slightly more than $3,200,000 was handed to Phillips. On this one sale the Association had gained approximately $245,000, a very satisfactory reward.[16]

Thus ended the great shutdown movement of 1887–89, doubtless the largest restrictive undertaking known up to that time in any American industry. It had benefited every one concerned—the producers by raising Pennsylvania prices, Rockefeller by lifting Ohio prices and helping stabilize the western European market, the Association by yielding a neat profit. It had shown that Rockefeller was willing to assist the Regions, and had improved the feeling between him and the oil men. A reporter for the New York *World*

[15]After the property of one opponent of the Association had been dynamited, the N. Y. *World* (May 7, 1888) remarked: "The event shows that there are wild spirits yet in the Oil Regions who will take the law in their own hands if it ever comes to a pinch."

[16]N. Y. *Herald, Tribune, World*, June 27–30, 1889.

found President Phillips ready to give him generous credit for his co-operation, and wrote:[17]

President Phillips was asked last night if he regarded this settlement as a satisfactory outcome of the enterprise. He said the prices on the oil set aside for the laboring men had yielded a good profit, some of it as much as thirty cents a barrel, but the producers' 3,500,000 barrels had not been so profitable. He thought the Standard Company was as much disappointed in this as the producers, as he thought their object was to help the producers a little more. It was his opinion that the Association had acted wisely in not selling this oil when the market was higher, say at 93, when a former large lot was sold, as such a sale at that time would have broken the market seriously.

III

The organizers of the Producers' Protective Association could now turn back to their original object, the co-operative piping, refining, and marketing of oil; an object which meant a declaration of war upon the Standard. Leaders like Emery impatiently awaited the opening of hostilities. During 1888–89 one group of Regions men had been busy promoting the Co-operative Oil Company, Ltd., while another had been engrossed with plans for the United Oil Company, Ltd. The executive board of the Association thought the latter the more promising, and created a special committee under Hascal L. Taylor of the Union Oil Company to study the scheme and report on its development. Taylor possessed great experience, ability, and shrewdness, and since his Union Oil Company was one of the largest and oldest producing firms in the Regions, he seemed a logical choice.[18]

The special committee energetically worked out plans for building pipe lines and making alliances with independent refineries. It thoroughly investigated the marketing question both at home and overseas. Large German distributors, owning tankers and oil depots, were approached. The undertaking began to loom up as a genuine threat to the Standard. Then suddenly the producers were left aghast by a report from New York that the Standard had knocked some of the principal supports from under the scheme by

[17]June 29, 1889.
[18]He "was with the producers in every move they made during the shutdown"; Venango *Spectator,* June 12, 1890.

buying up Taylor's Union Oil Company and three other large oil-producing corporations—the Forest, the Washington, and the Anchor companies.

It must be realized that throughout the later eighties the Standard had steadily continued its expansion. In 1887–88, for example, it had purchased the Philadelphia refineries of Malcolm Lloyd and Logan, Emery & Weaver. In 1889–90 it had suddenly acquired three important properties in the Pittsburgh area—the huge Globe refinery, the Freedom refinery, and the Western Atlantic Pipe-Line running from Pittsburgh down to the Washington County field; while another Globe refinery had been bought in Philadelphia. The purchase of these Globe plants removed a dangerous threat.[19] They were owned by four very rich men, J. M. Craig and D. P. Reighard of Pittsburgh and P. A. B. Widener and W. L. Elkins of Philadelphia, who could have put enormous sums of money into them. Reighard was a stubborn independent, while Craig, whose daring speculations on the Pittsburgh oil exchange had earned him the title of "the young oil prince," held valuable wells. According to the Pittsburgh *Leader,* this acquisition was "the most important gobble by the Standard Oil Company since the day of the dismantling of Pittsburgh refineries aggregating millions in value."[20] Preservation of the monopoly made the step indispensable.

Nor was the Standard's expansion into the Pennsylvania oil-producing area an unexpected move. It had long owned some small properties there, for various refining companies which it had acquired in the Regions had possessed wells, and it had continued operating them. Moreover, Rockefeller had bought largely and aggressively in Ohio and West Virginia. Good evidence exists that long before the purchases of 1890 he had determined to enter Pennsylvania production upon a large scale. John W. Van Dyke has said so. The New York *World,* announcing the acquisition of the four corporations, remarked that "according to current reports, they [the Standard] have been quietly buying up the stock of these companies

[19] Taylor, MS History of the Standard Oil, 105, 106, states that 45 per cent of the stock of the Western Atlantic Pipe-Line was acquired. The Globe Refining Company of Pittsburgh had been incorporated in 1888, the Globe Refining Company of Philadelphia in 1889. See *Bradstreet's,* March 17, 1888, for the purchase of the Lloyd and the Logan, Emery & Weaver refineries.
[20] Pittsburgh *Leader,* Nov. 8, 1889.

during at least three years, and got a large holding before these operating companies knew what was being done." This would carry the purchasing policy back to 1887, and indicate that Rockefeller had decided to buy Pennsylvania lands at about the same time that he moved to take over large Ohio tracts. Oil Regions newspapers, writing of the purchases, stated that the Forest and Anchor companies "have been practically under the control of the Standard for years."[21] Nevertheless, many observers were staggered when the Standard overnight became the most important producer in the Regions.

Eastern newspapers announced the fact on June 6, 1890. "Bought Up By the Trust," ran *The World's* headline. The Union Oil Company had been capitalized at $4,000,000, the Forest at $2,000,000, the Anchor at $1,200,000, and the Washington at $5,000,000. Altogether they owned about 300,000 acres, partly in Pennsylvania and partly in West Virginia. Their total production was estimated at 7600 barrels daily.[22] Since the Standard already possessed wells in these areas yielding about 1000 barrels a day, its aggregate flow in the Appalachian field now reached 2,750,000 barrels a year. According to its usual practice, it made no statement about the prices paid. But owners of the companies were allowed to take cash or Standard Oil Trust certificates at $170 a share, as they pleased, and during 1890 about 35,600 trust certificates were issued to former stockholders in the Union and Forest companies.[23]

Beyond doubt, Rockefeller was glad to execute these purchases at a moment when they dealt a heavy blow to the plan for the cooperative refining and marketing of oil. The producers had declared war upon the Standard, which had no choice but to strike back. It was Rockefeller's business to cripple the attack, if he could, before it got started.

And cripple it—temporarily—he did. Vast was the wrath of the producers when they learned that Taylor, head of the very committee planning independent action, had sold his company to the trust; vast was their wrath against his partners, J. L. and J. C.

[21]Van Dyke to the author, Nov. 10, 1936; N. Y. *World,* June 6, 1890; Venango *Spectator,* June 12, 1890.

[22]See New York, Philadelphia, and Pittsburgh newspapers, June 5-15, 1890, on this sale.

[23]*James Corrigan vs. John D. Rockefeller, 1897, Plaintiff's Exhibit,* 52.

McKinney. At a meeting of the executive board, Taylor and J. L. McKinney were angrily taxed with treason and invited to resign. Yet immediately afterward the Standard struck another staggering blow. It offered President Phillips of the Protective Association $750,000 for about 7500 acres in Butler County, on which stood approximately 125 producing wells; and Phillips accepted! He stated that he saw no reason to hold out after other men had given up their acreage, and plumed himself upon not joining the Standard's personnel. Repeatedly he was asked to do so. "Each time I absolutely refused to consent to this proposition, and finally stated that if they would insist upon that as a condition, I would not sell."[24] Phillips's associates accepted payment chiefly in cash, but partly in trust certificates. At the same time another company, the North Pennsylvania, was bought up, its owners taking more than 2500 certificates. Altogether, during 1890 more than 40,000 certificates were issued for oil-producing properties, so that western Pennsylvania was now full of Standard shareholders.[25] Many observers feared that the Standard would push forward until it owned nine tenths of the wells of the nation. "The trust officials," declared one such Jeremiah,[26] "are going to gobble up all the oil fields in the country, and then they will be able to do just as they please." This was absurd, for the oil-producing areas were now expanding rapidly.

Nevertheless, from this time onward it was the fixed policy of the Standard to increase its holdings of oil-bearing land. It continued to buy heavily in Ohio and Indiana, and conservatively in Pennsylvania. In West Virginia it leased large blocks of land, holding most of them for future development. It showed great ability in production, for it had sufficient capital to drill deep wells in fields where the oil lay far underground. Along with the land the Standard acquired valuable men. "I regard this transaction as one of the best strokes the Standard ever accomplished," commented a shrewd observer in June, 1890. "It not only secures to it a large proportion of the output of crude oil and some large tracts of rich territory but it enlists in its service many of the most efficient and able explorers and managers of producing property in the United States."[27] Though Phillips would not join the trust, the McKinney brothers

[24]Testimony in *Pure Oil Company vs. Standard Oil Trust*, 279.
[25]Taylor, MS History of the Standard Oil.
[26]N. Y. *World*, June 6, 1890.   [27]N. Y. *Tribune*, June 5, 1890.

did; and so did many young men who proved invaluable as new Middle Western tracts were opened up.

IV

For a time the defection of Taylor, Phillips, and the McKinneys seemed likely to destroy the dream of a great co-operative effort in refining. Consternation spread through the producers' ranks. Only the courage of a few devoted men, chief among them Lewis Emery, Jr., David Kirk, Michael Murphy, and two Regions attorneys, Roger Sherman and J. W. Lee, kept the undertaking alive. They called a meeting of the General Assembly for January 28, 1891, at Warren, Pa., where a committee of nine was appointed. It whipped into shape the plan long vaguely in the minds of Emery, Lee, and others. The united well-owners would create transportation facilities, refineries, and marketing agencies for all the oil they produced, and endeavor to cut off that oil from the Standard. They would do this through a limited-liability partnership, which should store crude oil, build pipe lines, and refine it in independent plants already existing or to be built.[28]

The Regions press began booming the new scheme. Officers of the Producers' Association energetically toured the Regions, asking for subscriptions. Within a few weeks more than a thousand well-owners had promised financial support; and this made it possible to set up the Producers' Oil Company, Ltd., with J. W. Lee as president and a capital of $600,000. To guarantee a supply of crude oil the company hastily erected four iron tanks at Corapolis, Pa., near the rich new McDonald oil field.[29] To obtain facilities for shipping crude oil abroad, it simultaneously made an agreement with the Columbia Oil Company at Bayonne, owners of a large independent refinery and of a waterfront terminal. The producers immediately had fifty tank cars built and prepared to ship crude oil abroad. Unfortunately, the market at the moment was unfavorable, while the railroads fixed their charges for hauling the cars at a prohibitive level.

Emery and his associates therefore determined to join hands with

[28]Philadelphia *Press;* Bradford, Warren, and Titusville papers, Jan. 28–31, 1891.
[29]Boyle, *Derrick's Handbook,* 520.

a number of independent refineries which had sprung up in the Regions during the previous decade. These plants, all small, had of recent years been hard pressed to maintain their existence. The only method by which most of them could ship their refined oil to the coast was in barrels, for neither they nor the Pennsylvania Railroad owned tank cars, and the Standard naturally refused to rent any to the independents. In 1888 the Pennsylvania, doubtless under Standard pressure, had raised its charge from 52 to 66 cents a barrel, while making no change in the rate on tank cars. This new tariff was almost prohibitive. The despairing independents at once appealed to the Interstate Commerce Commission, but no decision had as yet been rendered, and they were meanwhile on the verge of bankruptcy. Naturally they flamed with anger against both the Pennsylvania and the Standard, and were only too glad to form an alliance with the embattled producers.

The upshot was the emergence in 1892 of a new corporation, the Producers' and Refiners' Oil Company, Ltd., in which about fifteen refineries combined with a thousand or more well-owners. Of its capital of $250,000 the Producers' Oil Company furnished $160,000. Its first step was to lay local pipe lines from the wells to the Titusville and Oil City refineries. Oil began flowing on January 8, 1893, and the charge was only 15 cents a barrel as against the 20-cent charge of the Standard lines. A good beginning had been made.

But it was a bare beginning, for the independent refineries in the Regions could never take any large proportion of the oil produced there. Before the well-owners could achieve success, they must gain an independent outlet on the seaboard. Here several large independent refineries existed, and if cheap supplies of raw material were assured, more could be built. A great trunk pipe line was indispensable. With the determination which made him so formidable, Emery began to explore the possibilities. At first he thought of imitating the Tidewater and constructing a line to Williamsport on the Reading Railroad. But Gowen lay in his grave, and the new heads of the Reading proved chilly to Emery's advances. "If we sign an oil-carrying contract with you," they said, "we shall disturb our relations with the Standard Oil Trust; and we cannot afford to do it."[30] With startling audacity, Emery then drew up a plan for laying

[30]See testimony in *Pure Oil Co. vs. Standard Oil Co.,* 369 ff.

not one but two trunk pipe lines eastward, the first to carry crude oil and the second to carry refined. It had been generally assumed that refined oil could not be pumped over long distances without injury, but Emery believed the idea a fallacy. He proposed to carry his lines along the northern boundary of Pennsylvania eastward to a point near Hancock, N. Y., where they would connect with the New York, Ontario & Western Railroad. This would transport the oil to Cornwall-on-the-Hudson, whence it could be carried to storage tanks or refineries on New York harbor.

In September, 1892, Emery set up the United States Pipe Line Company with a capital of $600,000, and that same year began buying a right of way through northern Pennsylvania. The great enterprise which men hoped would bring forth a strong competitor of the Standard Oil had been fully launched.

v

Co-operative enterprise in the United States—the enterprise of a great producing group—had never before achieved so impressive a result. The Regions men had formed the Producers' Oil Company, Ltd., and this corporation had built pipe lines in western Pennsylvania and erected tank facilities at Bayonne. They had founded the Producers' and Refiners' Company, which had laid a pipe line between the independent refineries of the Oil City-Titusville district and the new McDonald and McCurdy fields southwest of Pittsburgh. They had assisted Emery to create his United States Pipe Line to lay conduits from Bradford to New York Bay. Three vigorous companies thus stood arrayed against the Standard, their supporters animated by a profound hatred. "The feeling against the Standard Oil Trust was never so strong in western New York and Pennsylvania as it is today," wrote a good observer in the spring of 1894.

It was certain that the Standard would bring all its cohorts into action, and leave no weapon untouched. This was the most formidable threat it had yet faced. For a short time, said Emery later, he made steady progress in buying a right of way for his pipe line, for "the Standard Oil did not get on to our operations." But not for long.

For when the Standard awoke it moved with characteristic swiftness and determination. "They came along there," Emery testified, "and bought strips of land right across our right of way in Pennsylvania; buying strips of land a mile and a half long, throwing us into court at every instance they could."[31] The principal agent of the trust was J. M. Brewer, who spent two weeks travelling from Shinglehouse to Tioga, tendering leases to all the farmers. Simultaneously, the Erie Railroad did all that it could to block the line. When construction gangs attempted to lay pipes under the tracks near Hancock, N. Y., hostilities broke out. Emery had gone to Hancock to watch his men, and subsequently gave a vivid description of the fracas. "We were met first with two derricks and two locomotives, a flatcar containing lumber, and a little brass cannon that had been used for shooting holes through the tank that was run off the track; and a car holding about seventy-five men. The moment we got there with our men they supposed, of course, we were going to connect up those two pipes. They threw off the old slabs and stuff, and they built a sort of cob fire over each end of the pipe. They threw off the lumber and they built a house on each side of the track, and put two men in them with Winchesters; and we stayed there three months, looking one another in the eyes. We never got under the track. We spent $70,000."[32]

But while thus stopped at Hancock, Emery was not idle elsewhere. Secretly executing a swift flank movement, he obtained a right of way from northern Pennsylvania to Wilkes-Barre on the Central Railroad of New Jersey, which promised to carry the oil to New York Bay until the pipe lines could be completed across New Jersey. By midsummer of 1893 the pipes had been laid to Wilkes-Barre. Emery's company then had a four-inch pipe for crude oil 180 miles long connecting the Bradford field with the Central of New Jersey, and a five-inch pipe for refined oil joining the independent refineries of Titusville, Bradford, and other Regions points with the same railroad. The producers were at last free from the tyranny of the Pennsylvania and the Erie.[33]

Beyond question, the opposition of the Erie officials to the new

[31]*Pure Oil Co. vs. Standard Oil Co.*, 369 ff; N. Y. *World*, May 24, 25, 1894.
[32]*Industrial Commission Hearings*, 1899, I, 653. See also N. Y. *World*, Nov. 29, 1892. The *World* reported that the Erie garrison "is furnished with canthooks, grappling irons, skiffs, bars, dynamite, powder, and ropes."
[33]N. Y. *World*, May 24, 1894.

lines was inspired partly by its own interests, and partly by pressure from the Standard. It was obvious that the piping of refined oil would deprive the railroads of a considerable part of their carrying-trade. They had reconciled themselves to the loss of crude-oil shipments; but to lose the kerosene as well would be a heavy blow. As for the Standard, its strength had always depended largely upon its control of transportation. It was the Erie's best customer, and naturally called upon the railroad to defend it against new competitors. One Standard official about this time dropped an illuminating remark upon the pressure which the trust exerted upon its allies: "We ask our friends on the railroad and in the New Jersey legislature to look after our interests."[34] Rockefeller felt that he simply could not afford to let an independent group of refiners obtain an independent low-cost outlet to the coast; it would vitally menace the control he had given the industry. The trust had stopped new lines in the past, and it urged the Erie and Pennsylvania to help it stop this one. As the Standard's attorney, John G. Milburn, later stated, this pressure was "an ugly feature" of the trust's history, but "it's all in the record."[35]

As soon as Emery's refined-oil line was completed to Wilkes-Barre, the entire industry breathlessly awaited its trial. Standard officials freely predicted its doom. An anxious group gathered on the appointed day at Wilkes-Barre terminal. Pipes were now made so well that no one seriously feared leakage. But would the oil lose color? Would it become muddy? Would its inflammability be increased? As soon as it began pouring from the pipes, the watchers realized that its color and odor were not impaired in the slightest. When it was tested in lamps, they found that the flash-point had actually been raised by its agitation in the pipes, so that it was safer than barrelled oil. Moreover, a stream of 110° fire-test oil (export kerosene) could be sent through the pipes and followed immediately by 150° fire-test oil (domestic kerosene) with complete separation—not more than a few barrels of the two grades mixing.

The experiment was an unqualified success. To some this seemed the greatest advance in oil transportation since Byron D. Benson had turned the valve of the first pipe laid across the Alleghenies.

[34]Tarbell, *Standard Oil*, II, 187.
[35]Comment on Taylor's MS History of the Standard; Rockefeller Papers.

Actually the feat proved of little importance. The Standard, with its corps of expert technicians, had long been aware that it could carry refined oil by pipe line, but had not cared to do so. It adopted the policy instead of planting refineries where they best served various sections of the trade—the Whiting refinery in the Middle West, the Richmond, Cal., refinery a little later in the Far West, the Corsicana and Chanson refineries in Texas, and so on. The New York and Philadelphia refineries of course served the export trade. To this day comparatively little refined oil is transported by pipe lines in the United States.

Enthusiasm among the producers and independent refiners now amounted to a high pitch. At last victory seemed alighting on the green hills of the Regions. Public sentiment was with them, and laws against monopoly were being enforced by both State and Federal agencies. They had a strong organization, adequate capital, abundant raw material, nearly a score of refineries, and free access to the seaboard. Plans were laid for a closer union. A merger between the United States Pipe Line and the local lines of the Producers' and Refiners' Company was discussed, while men talked of a strong new company to unite wells, refineries, pipes, and marketing agencies in one huge unit. The outlook, by the fall of 1893, seemed roseate.

But two lions stood in the path. One was the general business depression, which was now spreading with fearful rapidity, bringing millions to poverty, and making it more difficult to sell even such a necessity as kerosene. The other was the Standard Oil. Rockefeller had determined upon drastic action against this group which was intent upon humbling the trust. Left to itself, the depression would have tended to reduce crude oil to 60 cents a barrel or less, just as it was reducing wheat to 30 cents a bushel and corn to 10. The tremendous production in the Ohio and Indiana fields—rising from 16,000,000 barrels in 1893 to well over 20,200,000 in 1895—would have aided in this reduction in prices. But there can be little doubt that the Standard also lent a hand in manipulating the rates for both crude and refined oil in a way calculated to discourage the new co-operative enterprise.

Prices went down, down, down—and those of refined oil were held down. Crude petroleum during July and August, 1893, ruled

below 60 cents and even touched 56. Meanwhile, quotations of
refined oil were dropping even more severely. Up to 1891 the
average export price in New York had never been below 7 cents
a gallon. But in that year it went down to 6.85 cents, and in 1892
to 6.07 cents.[36] Thus, as one chronicler wrote, "began two years of
depression and gloom that proved desolating throughout the producing districts of Pennsylvania. The property of many men went
under the hammer. There were a number of suicides, and men
became insane from their losses. Many of the members of the Producers' Company could not pay their assessments. But the heroic
quality was not wanting, and many small producers went without
the comforts of life to pay their instalments as they matured."[37] All
over the nation, these were years of suffering and despair; the years
of Coxey's army, the Homestead massacre, the Pullman strike, and
the desperate Populist uprising.

Yet, as the panic of 1893 brought relentless deflation and a general drop in the price-level, a curious phenomenon occurred in the
oil industry. The price of crude oil sharply recovered, while that
of refined continued falling. The average quotation for crude, which
had been 66 cents a barrel in 1891 and 55 cents in 1892, rose again
to 64 cents in 1893, and to 83¾ cents in 1894. Meanwhile, the
average price of refined oil dropped from 6.07 cents a gallon in
1892 to 5.24 in 1893, and 5.19 in 1894. In midwinter of 1893–94
it stood at 5.15 cents.[38] It seemed to many observers remarkable that
kerosene should go so low while raw petroleum was rising, and
should do so at just the moment when a strong movement for independent refining was getting under way.

VI

As between the jaws of a gigantic, inexorable vise, all refiners,
but especially the weak independents, were caught during 1893–94
between these rising prices for crude and falling prices for kerosene.
The pincer-movement of the market substantially wiped out any
margin of profit, particularly for export oil. It threatened to crush
the independents to death. What caused it? All opponents of monopoly pointed to the Standard, and indeed, this episode offers one

[36]Boyle, *Derrick's Handbook*, 767 ff.   [37]N. Y. *World*, May 24, 1894.
[38]*Industrial Commission Hearings*, 1899, I, 547.

of the classic counts in the indictment of the trust. The Standard in rebuttal asserted that the movement was simply the consequence of unescapable natural forces. It argued that the reduced volume of Pennsylvania oil sent crude prices higher, while the world-wide depression and the bitter Russian competition in Europe forced refined oil downward. Any manipulation of the kind alleged, declares Taylor, would have cost the Standard Oil immeasurably more than it could have gained.[39]

This explanation is not convincing. It is true that the pincer-movement reduced the Standard's profits, but by no means as disastrously as it affected the independent refiners. The total net earnings of the trust for 1892 were $19,175,000, or almost 15 per cent of its net assets. In 1893 these earnings slipped downward to $15,457,000, and in 1894 to $15,544,000, being respectively 11.7 and 11.4 per cent of the net assets.[40] Now, a corporate organization whose net profits, after ample write-offs for depreciation, exceed $15,000,000 a year during a period of the gravest national depression—whose profits run between 11 and 12 per cent of the invested capital—is not suffering. Yet in these years some independent refiners made no profits whatever, and several of the largest were forced in desperation to sell out to the Standard Oil. No doubt the great depression and the heavy sales of Baku oil in Europe were really factors in keeping refined oil low. But it is impossible to believe that the Standard did not exert its immense influence in the same direction, expecting to cripple the independent movement. Experienced oil men declared that it could have equalized prices, and refused. Said *The World* in an expert account:[41]

The eleven hundred men who formed the Producers' Oil Company, Ltd., were given to understand directly from the main offices of the oil magnates, 26 Broadway, that if they persevered in their efforts to defy the trust the price of crude oil would be placed where the producers would not pay the assessments necessary to complete their stock subscriptions, it being well known that the members of the Producers' Company were given three years to complete their payments. . . .

The Standard Trust arbitrarily fixes the price of oil. There is a pretence kept up by purchases and sales at the Oil City Exchange, but the Oil Ex-

---

[39]Taylor, MS History of the Standard, 109.
[40]*Defendants' Brief, United States vs. Standard Oil Company*, 145 ff.
[41]N. Y. *World*, May 24, 1894.

change quotations are controlled by the agents of the trust. The Oil Exchange in Oil City used to be the scene of extensive operations in the product. Of late years there has practically been but little or nothing done. The forms in exchange business are, however, maintained, even to the minutiae of ringing a bell at the hour of three in the afternoon, when the Exchange is to close. Representatives of the Oil Trust occasionally go in and offer to sell or buy 1000 barrels at a price fixed in advance by Joseph Seep, the trust agent. Then, on this entirely arbitrary proceeding, the sales of oil throughout the United States as well as Europe are based.

Some exaggeration is evident in this, for the Standard did not fix prices of crude or refined oil single-handed. In the years 1894–95 it did a little more than 82 per cent of the manufacturing of petroleum products in the United States; and obviously the refiners of the other 18 per cent helped to fix prices. So did the many speculators who dealt in oil and oil-certificates. So did the Russian and Dutch producers and refiners. The market was largely a world market, and numerous elements of supply and demand, cost and profit, affected the level. But 82 per cent control did permit price-fixing for considerable periods, and the charge of manipulation seems justified. The Standard could have widened the spread between crude-oil prices and refined-oil prices in 1893–94—could have held the pincers apart—and for selfish reasons it declined to do so.

Just how painful the pinch became in 1893–94 is evident from a table later printed by the Bureau of Corporations, showing the average yearly price of Pennsylvania crude at the wells, and of export oil at New York, with the resulting margin:[42]

Year	Pa. Crude (cents per gallon)	Export oil (cents per gallon)	Margin
1888	2.07	7.49	5.42
1889	2.19	7.12	4.93
1890	2.06	7.31	5.25
1891	1.59	6.93	5.34
1892	1.32	6.07	4.75
1893	1.52	5.23	3.71
1894	1.99	5.19	3.20
1895	3.18	7.36	4.18
1896	2.84	6.97	4.13

Nota Bene { 1893, 1894 }

For independents caught between the pincers, the situation was

[42]Bureau of Corporations, *Report on the Petroleum Industry: Part II, Prices and Profits*, 622, 623.

made more painful by certain basic facts of the refining industry. All refiners of Pennsylvania oil were under the necessity of exporting about 40 per cent of their product. Most American States now had laws requiring a 150° test for marketable kerosene, while most European nations were satisfied with a 110° test. High-test or water-white kerosene therefore was sold at home, and low-test kerosene abroad. It was roughly estimated at this period that Pennsylvania crude oil produced on the average 10 per cent of benzine, 35 per cent of high-test domestic oil, 40 per cent of low-test export oil, and 15 per cent of tar, paraffin, and residuum, Refiners therefore found it absolutely necessary to obtain a market for their export oil; they could not throw away two fifths of their production. If they lost heavily on exports, they would soon go bankrupt. And in 1893–94 they were losing heavily!

The World, which accused the Standard Oil of deliberately tightening the pincers, called its plan "one of the most daring and unprincipled in the history of American commerce." A *World* writer showed that at one time in the spring of 1894 a barrel of refined oil for export was actually cheaper than a barrel of crude. "These figures tell the whole story of the crushing blight cast upon the oil trade by the Standard monopoly." Naturally, independent refiners who took cruel losses abroad had to recoup themselves in the domestic market. But here, too, the Standard Oil forced the fighting. It brought its own prices down so low that the independents were glad to sell their high-test oil at the refineries, during the winter of 1893–94, for 2¾ cents a gallon. When spring came they were almost exhausted. "Their condition is now pitiable," declared *The World*. "No one of the refiners under this cruel persecution but is making losses in the refining of oil. They cannot, without jeopardizing their entire investments, stop operations. . . ."[43]

Yet, during this Valley Forge winter, most of the independents grimly tightened their belts and polished their accoutrements. Losing far more money than they could afford, denied credit at the banks (through Standard pressure, they alleged), fearing a still darker future, they defiantly held fast. Their stake in the movement was now too heavy to give up until they were utterly routed. It was estimated that they had invested almost $2,500,000 in various

[43] N. Y. *World*, May 24, 1894.

facilities. Of this the United States Pipe Line Company and the Producers' and Refiners' pipes represented $1,200,000 and $450,000 respectively; refineries in Oil City, Titusville, Bradford, and Warren $400,000; refineries on New York Bay $200,000; and Atlantic terminal facilities $200,000 more.[44] Generally speaking, the same men held stock in all the different companies and enterprises, so that it was impossible for one group to desert the others.[45]

When spring came in 1894, three Regions refiners did give way. One was no less a person than John Fertig of Titusville. A Regions pioneer who had sunk his first well the year Lincoln was elected, he had become wealthy by energetic drilling; he had served as mayor of Titusville and State senator, and been Democratic candidate for lieutenant-governor. He was the principal organizer of the National Oil Company, which owned important wells and pipe lines, a Titusville refinery, a tank-car system, and distributing stations scattered all the way from Providence to St. Paul. His companions in surrender were H. P. Burwald of Titusville and S. Y. Ramage of Reno, Pa. Their plants were among the largest independent outfits. Going to New York, they consulted the leaders at 26 Broadway. Rockefeller gave them no hope that prices would improve, but offered to buy their works at fair figures. The three accepted, and returning home, announced their withdrawal to their stunned colleagues. The Standard shortly dismantled their refineries. By these purchases, the Standard also acquired the stock which the three men owned in the United States Pipe Line and the Producers' and Refiners' Oil Company—this seeming to many its principal reason for buying.[46]

Even earlier, the new venture had lost the support of one important figure outside the Regions—John E. Borne, the senior partner of Borne, Scrymser & Company. Their Elizabethport Refining Works in New Jersey were rated the largest independent establishment in the country, and had a daily capacity of 1000 barrels of oil. Borne, eager to have crude oil delivered by the new line

[44]*Ibid.*

[45]J. W. Lee testified: "All four are owned by substantially the same persons and operated together"; *Industrial Commission Hearings,* 1899, I, 261.

[46]"They wished to assume of get control of these pipe lines; they did not care a snap for the refineries. They made that statement." T. B. Westgate, *Industrial Commission Hearings,* 1899, I, 370.

at his works, had taken a considerable block of stock and become a director. His firm had also induced Cord Meyer, the Brooklyn sugar manufacturer, to take $50,000 in shares. But in 1893 Borne unexpectedly resigned his directorship, and began to work in close harmony with the Standard interests, while Cord Meyer announced that he had turned his stock over to Borne. The Standard thus obtained a larger block of stock, while the new pipe line was deprived of the Elizabethport refinery as an outlet. Within a short time this establishment was closed, and Borne, Scrymser as a unit of the Standard devoted themselves to compounding lubricants.[47]

These defections were a serious blow, and they added to the dense gloom now pervading the Regions; but Emery and Lee were indomitable. They took immediate steps to put heart into the other independents. In a speech delivered with his usual impetuous fervor, Emery assured a gathering of oil men that while crude was rising, no monopoly could long maintain so abnormal an economic situation. Before many months elapsed a just relation between the cost of raw materials and the price of the finished product must reestablish itself. In this faith, he and others were ready to raise funds to support the more precarious independents. A campaign for this purpose was set on foot in the Regions; and as its leaders matured their plans in the summer and fall of 1894, they determined to form a new corporation to act as financial bulwark for the independent movement.

Two mass meetings of the independent interests early in 1895 put this plan into effect. The first was held January 24 at Butler, with special trains, badges, music, and prodigious enthusiasm. When David Kirk presented the resolution for a new financing company—the Pure Oil Company—it was passed by a tremendous chorus of ayes. Nearly fifty different producing or refining organizations promised their support. Then and there men subscribed $75,000, while Kirk announced next day that $1,000,000 in assets were within sight. Various companies had offered to supply 1000 tank cars. Not less than $600,000 in cash would be paid into the treasury, and the remainder of the $1,000,000 would be represented by refineries, pipe lines, and other equipment. With these resources, he defiantly predicted that the Pure Oil Company would carry the

[47]N. Y. *World,* May 24, 1894.

war into the enemy's country. "We will erect a plant in every city
in the United States where the Standard has one now. . . . We
mean to force the Standard into a fair price for our products, and
take the monopoly of the oil market out of its hands." As he said,
many Standard refineries had been built when material and machinery were high, and since the panic the united independents
could duplicate them for far less money.[48]

At the second meeting, held in Bradford on February 13, Emery
and Kirk presented a more detailed plan. The $1,000,000 capital
of the Pure Oil Company, they proposed, should be divided into
100,000 shares. Thirty independent refiners had promised to turn
over their entire holdings, including 500 tank cars, and accept stock
in exchange. Special safeguards were to be provided against the
boring-from-within policies attributed to the Standard. To prevent
interference by the monopoly, declared the prospectus written by
Emery, Kirk, and Lee, "the voting power of one-half of the stock
of the Pure Oil Company is placed by the owners in the hands of
five champions of this right of independence, who are bound by the
terms of a permanent trust bond to vote only for such men and
measures as shall forever make this company INDEPENDENT, so
that no sales of interest will carry with them any power to jeopardize
the policy or existence of the company, or the investments of its
remaining members." Already the concept of the corporation as
solely or even primarily a financing body had faded, and it was
understood that it was to go into all branches of the oil business.
Its backers expected to control much of the Pennsylvania output,
and they were planning to use natural gas as fuel in their refineries.[49]

Thus, early in 1895 plans were completed for the strongest organization of independents yet seen in the oil business. Before the year
ended the Pure Oil Company had been incorporated in New Jersey
with Kirk as president and James W. Lee as vice-president. Its
200,000 shares at $50 par value each found ready takers.[50]

VII

It was founded at an auspicious moment, for the early months of
1895 witnessed one of the greatest booms in petroleum history. In

---

[48]Philadelphia *Press*, Jan. 26, 1895.   [49]*Idem*, Feb. 14, 1895.
[50]*Oil, Paint, and Drug Reporter*, Dec. 21, 1895.

March prices of crude oil suddenly began soaring, and refined oil soon followed. Not in twenty years had such a sudden and general revival of the oil business taken place. The boom occupied most of April, at the end of which month oil had begun to fall again; but it remained at fairly high levels—levels which gave every producer and efficient refiner handsome profits. The bitter winter of hard times turned within a few weeks to a bright and golden spring.

The fundamental reason for this boom was patent to every one; a simple shortage of oil. Between 1891 and 1893 the total production of the eastern fields (New York, Pennsylvania and southeastern Ohio) had dropped from nearly 36,000,000 barrels to less than 31,400,000. In 1894 the output went down to 30,800,000 barrels. Meanwhile, the production of Lima oil was inadequate to make up the deficit.[51] Stocks fell off with alarming rapidity. Yet at the same time world demand was mounting steadily. Up to 1892, the grand total of American exports of oil had never in any single year reached 695,000,000 gallons, but in 1894 it reached very nearly 900,000,000 gallons. And after the first shock of the depression wore off, it became evident that domestic demand was also increasing. Oil stoves were now being manufactured and sold in large quantities, while an improved type of parlor lamp rapidly made its way into a multitude of homes. In some American cities consumption nearly or quite doubled within two years. The well-informed Philadelphia *Press* stated early in 1895 that oil production was running 5,000,000 to 6,000,000 barrels a month behind consumption, and while this was an overstatement, a distinct shortage did seem at hand. Standard Oil reports in April showed that daily refinery consumption was running 8300 barrels ahead of daily consumption. At that time the stocks of Pennsylvania oil were down from their normal level of about 15,000,000 barrels to about 3,000,000.[52]

During the first half of April prices went up, up, still up. "Golden Grease" ran a headline in the New York *World* early that month, while the sub-head announced: "Supply of the Pennsylvania Stuff Seems to Be Short." In just one week, April 6–13, the price of crude in western Pennsylvania doubled, reaching two dollars a barrel. Parts of Pittsburgh were taking on the appearance of an oil-boom

[51]Boyle, *Derrick's Handbook,* 805, 812, 813.
[52]Philadelphia *Press,* April 15, 1895.

town. In streets near the Oil Exchange animated groups were peering over maps, running imaginary pipe lines to new oil-belts, and discussing leases and sales. A wildcat derrick was rushed up just outside the city line; a girdle of speculative oil leases was quickly thrown about the smoky metropolis. A similar excitement seized other parts of Pennsylvania and West Virginia. Hesitation was vanishing like a fog before the golden sun of high prices. "Give us territory!" was the only cry. Large sums were hurriedly invested in "wildcatting," and still more in redrilling old areas to deeper levels. During 1894 oil lands had sold at $200 a barrel—that is, a ten-barrel-a-day well had been worth $2000. But now the value of lands had suddenly doubled. Properties long regarded as worthless were being reopened, for it paid to pump a five-barrel-a-day well. Stories were being circulated of speculators who had bought old wells for a few hundred dollars, installed a little machinery, and sold the property for thousands.[53]

For years now Rockefeller had compelled the Standard to lease and purchase oil lands vigorously. Operations had been pushed all the way from Pennsylvania to Tennessee, where Thomas Hughes's famous Anglo-American settlement of Rugby was leased to the Standard in 1895 for oil exploitation, while in the Lima fields the Standard had long been much the largest investor. The trust had been credited early in 1889, for example, with spending $1,600,000 within six weeks for oil territory in Ohio. But now the trust redoubled its operations. For one producing company in the Sisterville field of West Virginia it paid $475,000. Rockefeller purchased the Venture Oil Company, with a property near McDonald, Pa., comprising eighty-eight wells, for $550,000, though a few weeks earlier this might have sold for half the price. For the Rose & Byron holdings in the old Bradford field, nearly a mile square, with thirteen small wells, he paid $250,000. In the summer of 1895 he took over all the oil properties of William L. Mellon of Pittsburgh. This, the largest oil deal in years, involving millions of dollars, gave the Standard the great Crescent Pipe Line from western Pennsylvania to Delaware Bay, many gathering lines, and rich oil wells.

Numerous men were buying in competition. A happy feature of the rising price of prospective oil lands was that many little

[53]Pittsburgh *Leader*, Philadelphia *Press*, April 1–20, 1895.

fellows profited. Farmers, pumpers, shopkeepers, and others who had leased land in or near the Sisterville and McDonald fields when the rushes began, now cashed in with alacrity. Some larger investors did very well too. Theodore Barnsdall had held from 15,000 to 20,000 acres in Elk County, W. Va., for which Rockefeller had vainly offered him $1,500,000 in 1893, and which two years later he regarded it as worth more than $4,000,000.[54]

As the boom increased a wild speculation in oil certificates reached New York. "Uncle Russell Sage," wrote a reporter on April 11, "wore a pained expression yesterday. A few days ago he had in his strongbox a lot of oil certificates, fifty of them. They called for 1000 barrels of crude oil each, and he had taken them in when oil was selling for about sixty cents. On Thursday certificates were selling at $1.30, and Uncle Russell let them go and pocketed more than 100 per cent profit. He was joyful and went uptown on his dead-head El pass, humming a merry tune as he thought of the $40,000 he had made. Yesterday the opening price of oil was two and a half cents higher, and at the close $1.50 was bid without bringing out any certificates. Then a wail went up from the bombproof office at 71 Broadway." So far as possible, the Standard fought the speculators. Joseph Seep, head of Rockefeller's buying organization, had announced in January that he would pay merely the rates justified by the foreign and domestic market, and discourage gamblers. As prices soared, loose talk was heard that the Standard was in grave peril because it did not have oil enough to fill its great pipe-line system, for to build smaller pipe lines and plants would cost a fortune. But in mid-April oil reached its highest point, selling at $2.50 to $2.70. Then it began falling till on May 1 it stood at $1.85 to $1.95. The boom was over! Regions men who had been boasting that the Standard would be "seriously if not fatally" damaged now expressed a fervent hope that it would check the drop and stabilize prices again.

Of course well-informed observers had laughed over the fairy stories of the coming downfall of the trust. The fact was that in 1895 not far from a third of all the oil yielded in the United States

[54]These facts are drawn from N. Y., Philadelphia, and Pittsburgh papers of March to June, 1895, which are full of the boom and of details of Standard Oil operations.

was produced by the Standard. Of the 30,892,000 barrels pumped in Pennsylvania it produced 9,120,000; of the 21,720,000 pumped in the Lima field, it produced 8,810,000. The total flow of its wells fell just short of 16,000,000 barrels, or more than the entire American yield as late as 1878! Moreover, it controlled almost the whole stock of Lima oil above ground, not far from 20,000,000 barrels. No danger had existed of a shortage in its refineries.[55] On the contrary, the advance in prices had brought it huge profits. The first rise of 70 cents in Lima-Ohio oil alone was estimated by *The World* to have added $14,000,000 to its assets. Since in the Pennsylvania field the Standard now received about 25,000 barrels of oil a day from its own wells, a net advance of $1 a barrel meant increased receipts of $25,000 daily. The editors of *The World* justly remarked that Rockefeller and his partners "seem to be doing pretty well."

Indeed, the Standard was soon proving its vigor by sustaining the market during some tense days in which an excessively rapid drop would have ruined many producers and refiners. A *World* dispatch just after the downward turn stated that its power "was never more forcibly illustrated than it was in the oil market today. Had it not been for 'the Old House,' as it was called," the industry would have suffered "a crash the like of which was never witnessed in oildom."[56] Crude would have gone to $1.50 or less. But the Standard's purchasing agents saw to it that the decline was not only gradual, but was halted at levels which still gave a profit to marginal producers. Late in June the Pittsburgh price remained about $1.60 a barrel, and it was deduced that Rockefeller and his partners, who needed a large flow of oil for the world market, were anxious to give exploration and production a reasonable stimulus.

This long-remembered boom in oil had varied results. One was a sustained increase in oil prospecting, drilling, and producing. In every field more wells were sunk. By 1896 the flow of petroleum in the Appalachian area had risen again to almost 34,000,000 barrels, while in the Lima field it had broken all records with more than 25,000,000. Another result was that the hard-pressed independents suddenly found the means to place their enterprises on a solid foundation. The sponsors of the Pure Oil Company were able to

[55]*Industrial Commission Hearings,* 1899, I, 561.
[56]N. Y. *World,* April 18, 1895.

raise capital, lay pipe lines, buy machinery, and push energetically into the foreign market. Emery's prophecy that the price of kerosene could not be kept abnormally low had been justified. Finally, the greatest result of all was that while the United States was still sunk in the trough of a great depression, with the balance of trade heavily against the nation, and with gold flowing out to Europe, the petroleum industry suddenly rose to a plane of affluence. It sold large quantities of refined oil in Europe for gold at prices which did much to improve exchange. In 1895 the export sales of oil and oil products amounted to $56,223,000, and in 1896 to $62,764,000. The remittances which paid for these shipments aided Cleveland in his final struggle to maintain the gold standard, and indirectly did something to promote the victory of McKinley over Bryan in the great free-silver battle. Even *The World* admitted that the boom, which it attributed to the Standard Oil, had "stimulated prosperity vastly."[57]

VIII

From the time of this brief but remarkable boom in oil prices, the success of the new independent enterprises was never gravely in doubt. To be sure, they still encountered obstacle after obstacle. Those interested in the full story of the efforts made to defeat the Pure Oil Company and its allies will find it graphically related in the first volume of the Industrial Commission hearings in 1899. There Emery, Lee, Phillips and other officers relate how the Standard Oil assiduously bought up stock in the Producers' Oil Company, Ltd., until it held 29,764 shares out of 60,000.[58] It then "sold" these shares (at a heavy loss) to J. J. Carter of Titusville, who owned 300 more; and with more than half the stock, Carter made a de-

[57]Boyle, *Derrick's Handbook*, 805, 813, 818; N. Y. *World*, April 20, 1895.
[58]See the full account in N. Y. *World*, May 25, 1894. *The World* stated: "In the banks scattered about the oil regions, operators and refiners constantly run up against Standard influence. There are bank directors who object to taking the securities of the company [Producers' Company] as collateral, denounce them openly at board meetings, and say they will be made worthless. The trust keeps posted regarding the financial affairs of nearly all the operators. By means of espionage in the banks by directors, the amount of paper in circulation is noted, and weak producers are picked out and made the subject of the trust's approaches. Despite all that has been done against it, the Producers' Oil Company has kept its head above water, and the assessments due by the members have been paid, excepting about $25,000."

termined effort to gain control of the company and bring it into harmony with the Standard. He was defeated by the fact that the company was a limited partnership, and both the company by-laws and Pennsylvania statutes denied membership to any man unless he were elected by a majority of the partners. "It is a very queer law," said Archbold ruefully; but it sufficed to maintain the company's independence.[59] The Standard also acquired large blocks of stock in the United States Pipe Line, and gained the right to elect a director of that corporation; but the independents easily maintained their majority control.[60]

Meanwhile, the Lehigh Valley, Pennsylvania, and Lackawanna Railroads were doing everything possible to impede the progress of Emery's pipe line. They all denied him passage under their tracks. He labored frantically to circumvent them. Searching old titles, he obtained possession of a forgotten acre of land which enabled him to tunnel under the Pennsylvania.[61] When he reached the Lackawanna line near Washington, N. J., he resorted to lawless tactics, sending out fifty brawny laborers one dark Saturday night to lay his pipes and guard them. The railroad hurried its forces to the spot, and squirted boiling water from locomotives at Emery's men, while fighting raged with picks and spades. Farmers rallied to assist the pipe layers, while the local G. A. R. sent them its army muskets! Emery eventually lost his case in the courts.[62] But he nevertheless carried his pipe line eastward to a junction only fifty miles from New York, from which he obtained railroad transportation to the bay at satisfactory rates. When the independents arranged with the well-known dealer Julius Poth of Mannheim to conduct most of their German marketing,[63] the Standard suddenly brought Poth into its own marketing corporation, the Deutsche-Amerikanische Company. The independents alleged that he had been tricked into deserting them, but the Standard maintained that the shoe was on the other foot—that he had first been tricked into leaving them, and they had then persuaded him to come back.

[59]*Industrial Commission Hearings*, 1899, I, 179 ff., 270 ff., 578.
[60]Taylor, MS History of the Standard Oil, 109.
[61]*Industrial Commission Hearings*, 1899, I, 652–655.
[62]*Oil, Paint, and Drug Reporter*, April–July, 1896; see *Industrial Commission Hearings*, I, 1899, 653, 654, for Emery's story, and p. 529 for the Lackawanna's side.
[63]*Bradstreet's*, May 14, 1892.

Again, when the independents began marketing their kerosene in New York City, the Standard sharply reduced its prices to meet their competition.[64] According to J. W. Lee, within a few weeks it cut its rate from 9½ cents a gallon to 5½, or below cost; but it should be added that Archbold made a sweeping denial of any improper price-slashing.[65]

All along the front the independents encountered a withering fire; yet they gained ground. The four companies, to obtain greater strength and security, shortly united in one. A meeting was held in 1897 at Taylor's Hotel in Jersey City—the historic hotel which had been Jay Gould's stronghold in the Erie War—to lay plans for reorganizing the Pure Oil Company and giving it control of the other three; and after a long period of wrangling the scheme went through. The capital of the Pure Oil Company was increased to $10,000,000, and a majority of the stock of the other companies passed into its hands. It thus became an extremely powerful organization, the independence of which was guaranteed by various safeguards.

When this occurred, the Standard Oil had one really formidable antagonist engaged in the production, refining, and marketing of oil. By 1903 the Pure Oil Company possessed nearly 1000 stockholders, most of them producers. Its wells produced some 8000 barrels of oil daily, which were pumped through 1500 miles of crude-oil pipe line, and 400 miles of refined-oil pipe. It controlled fourteen refineries. Besides having one large tanker, the *Pennoil,* it chartered several others. It owned fully equipped oil depots and marketing systems in England, Holland, and Germany, and sold kerosene, naphtha, and other products at both wholesale and retail in New York and Philadelphia. Its officers were able and progressive. At long last the Oil Regions could boast that, while they had not wiped the Standard from the map of the United States as with a sponge, they had at least furnished it an efficient competitor.[66]

[64]On this highly controversial question of Herr Poth's action, see *Industrial Commission Hearings,* 1899, I, 531 (Archbold); 273 ff. (Lee); 617 (Emery).
[65]*Industrial Commission Hearings,* 1899, I, 265 ff. (Lee); 528 ff. (Archbold). Lee testified that the Pure Oil lost money in New York every month from the opening of 1896 to the spring of 1899.
[66]Patrick Boyle describes the reorganization of the Pure Oil Company, *Industrial Commission Hearings,* 1899, I, 462 ff.

XXXIX

The Trust Changes Armor

W HEN the fierce economic storm of 1893–97 fell upon America, blasting its industries as the simoon withers a green land, most people ceased to think of any problems but those which demanded an immediate answer. Newspaper headlines were occupied by bankruptcies, the Pullman strike, Coxey's army, the Populist movement, Cleveland's bond issues, the tariff, and, after 1895, the bloody rebellion in Cuba. For several years the trust question passed into the background. Every one had been thinking of the menace of monopoly in 1890; five years later only a minority were thinking of it. Those monsters the trusts still dragged their scaly folds across the land. Observers counted nearly a hundred of them. But they did not ramp and breathe blue fire as defiantly as of old, and the demand for a St. George was less strident. When most businesses were struggling hard to keep alive, it seemed inopportune to launch a noisy campaign for punishing wicked corporations.

Even in prosperous days, the Harrison administration had never paid anxious heed to the anti-trust clamor. And when rugged Cleveland returned to power, he did hardly more than his predecessor to enforce the Sherman Act. Overwhelmed with exigent troubles, he was compelled to postpone many problems until the wild economic storm blew over. He had long been committed to the theory that high tariffs were the principal bulwark of monopoly, and he made a valiant effort to break that wall down; but he did little else. Attorney-General Olney so grossly mismanaged the one great suit of the administration, levelled against the Sugar Trust, that for half a dozen years afterward few men felt any confidence in the efficacy of the Federal law.

Yet a powerful undercurrent of popular anxiety regarding the trusts remained. The plain people of the nation bitterly opposed them and demanded their extermination. Extermination was the word, for few and feeble were the voices that proposed regulation. One of the deepest roots of the great movement of protest which Bryan headed in 1896 lay in the popular antagonism to predatory business combinations. One by one, States were still passing acts against monopolies.[1] It was evident that as soon as the economic crisis ended, the battle against the great industrial giants would be stubbornly renewed. Thanks to the teachings of Weaver, Altgeld, Bryan, La Follette, and many more, a new movement in behalf of free competition would arise, bringing with it stronger laws and more determined prosecutions.

II

The principal token of the continuing anxiety felt by Americans over the trust problem was the publication in 1894 of Henry Demarest Lloyd's *Wealth Against Commonwealth,* one of the famous polemics in American history. "As much an epoch-making book as *Uncle Tom's Cabin,*" wrote Edward Everett Hale. Never since his first article on the Standard Oil in *The Atlantic* had Lloyd ceased to take a deep interest in the progress of that corporation. To him it typified all that was dangerous and hateful in American business. He had other irons in the fire—municipal reform, for example; but when he read of the trust investigations in 1888 by the New York Senate and the Federal House, his anger against the monopoly was rekindled. He resolved to expose its misdeeds in their full length and breadth. "I consider . . . the rise and progress of the oil monopoly to be on the whole the most characteristic thing in our business civilization," he wrote. His time was all his own, for, his rich father-in-law having given him an independent income, he had ceased active journalistic labor.[2] He had a winter home in Winnetka, a summer home on Narragansett Bay, and ample funds for travel and secretarial hire.

Setting to work with a huge accumulation of documents, reports, records of lawsuits, and press clippings, Lloyd built up his volume. He was not a writer of high literary gifts, and not a patient scholar

[1]Jeremiah Jenks and W. E. Clark, *The Trust Problem,* 245, 246.
[2]Caro Lloyd, *Lloyd,* I, 79, 182–183.

or careful investigator, but simply an intensely earnest and very rhetorical journalist. He spent three years digesting his evidence against the Standard Oil (with a little additional material upon the Beef Trust), into a volume of 536 pages, recasting it four times. Profiting from the example of other effective controversialists, notably Henry George in *Progress and Poverty* and Helen Hunt Jackson in *A Century of Dishonor,* he made his book crisp and dramatic. At the same time, he was aware that he must render it as nearly impregnable as possible. He dared not put in too much detail, for that would repel readers, or leave out too much, for then he would lack proof for his assertions. He must exhaust his evidence where it was strong, adroitly guard his statements where it was weak. His attack on the Standard must be as well documented as a work of history, and yet sufficiently simple to be understood by the workingman or clerk.[3]

Lloyd was extremely nervous over the reception his book would meet. "The gun needs to be loaded carefully," he wrote Richard T. Ely; "the query uppermost in my mind is, which is going to be the most dangerous place, in front of it or behind?" As the chapters were completed he sent them to specialists and attorneys for verification. C. B. Matthews of Buffalo had furnished him with full materials upon the alleged attempt of the Everests to destroy his lubricating works, and this section of the book was submitted to Adelbert Moot of Buffalo. City officials of Toledo scrutinized the pages relating to their million-dollar suit in 1893 against the opponents of a city pipe line to the natural gas fields of Ohio.[4] The entire manuscript was scanned by Roger Sherman, the brilliant attorney for independent interests in the Oil Regions. Throughout the volume Lloyd avoided the use of proper names, personal or corporate, wherever he could. Rockefeller's name does not appear in the index, nor those of Flagler, Archbold, Rogers, or Colonel Payne. Again and again the author spoke of the "oil combination"

[3]The Wisconsin Historical Society Library has what Lloyd calls his "working copy" of *Wealth Against Commonwealth,* with marginal jottings giving evidence which he felt served further to substantiate his case. Lloyd had access to the papers of Roger Sherman and others, and gathered a great deal of material upon Rockefeller and the Standard after his book appeared.

[4]See the letters of A. E. Macomber of Toledo to Lloyd; Lloyd Papers. Roger Sherman read the MS with care in 1893. "Have no fears for your book!" he reassured Lloyd on June 5, 1893; Lloyd Papers.

where it was perfectly evident that he meant the Standard Oil Trust. It was the "oil combination," for example, which had thwarted the efforts of Toledo to obtain cheap natural gas. He later explained that he avoided names because he wished to fix the reader's attention upon principles, not personalities. But this explanation did not fit the facts, for the whole force of the book depended upon an ascription of guilt to definite persons and a definite corporation. They were clearly indicated but not named. George Rice and others thought this a great pity; but obviously, the principal reason lay in Lloyd's fear of the libel laws.[5]

After four publishers had rejected the manuscript, William Dean Howells helped persuade Harper & Brothers to bring it out in September, 1894; but it was copyrighted in Lloyd's name, perhaps because the publishers feared legal action.[6] The book was happily timed. It appeared just after Cleveland's use of troops in the Pullman strike had planted in millions of breasts a bitter antagonism to great corporations, and an indignant conviction that predatory wealth was finding the government an ally rather than an opponent. The country was full of poverty and discontent. Never before had the contrast between penury and riches seemed so stark and glaring. Within the next ten months the decisions in the Sugar Trust case and income tax case apparently proved the shameless subservience of the Supreme Court majority to plutocratic interests. Lloyd's book was (after the works of Charles Francis and Henry Adams on the Erie scandals and James Parton on the Tweed Ring) the first distinct contribution to that literature of muckraking which within the next dozen years was to become so impressive in scope and volume. Other polemics were being published in these years—Jacob Riis's *How the Other Half Lives, Coin's Financial School,* and in fictional form Hamlin Garland's *Main-Travelled Roads.* They all found an eager public, but none of them produced so arresting an impression as Lloyd's work. His treatise swiftly became famous, and its stories and arguments were rapidly mas-

[5]Harpers were distinctly nervous over libel suits. See their letter to Lloyd, July 13, 1893, and also George Rice to Lloyd, Oct. 12, 1894; Lloyd Papers.
[6]Lloyd sent his check for $500 before typesetting began; Lloyd Papers. He wrote Richard T. Ely, Oct. 26, 1898: "I of course think very highly of the Harpers because they had the courage to print my book. I have never supposed that they did very much in the way of pushing."

tered by hundreds of thousands. Many read it with fascination. Ministers used it as a text, journalists drew from it for their editorials, a few bold professors employed it in their courses, and Robert Louis Stevenson even thought of founding a novel upon some of its incidents.[7] "A very capable, clever fellow," Stevenson wrote of Lloyd from Saranac Lake.[8]

Any later-day judgment upon the book must insist upon a sharp distinction. As a polemic for the times it was magnificent; as a piece of industrial history for study by posterity it was almost utterly worthless. But since it was written as a polemic, it must be pronounced a success. It produced precisely the effect that Lloyd intended. No reader could fail to respond to its vitality and interest. The narrative was swift and vivid; the bits of exposition were touched by piquant epigram. Dialogue, taken authentically from court records or the reports of investigating committees, was frequently employed. The page-headings were unfailingly pungent and sometimes sensational: "Judgment Day Law," "Evolution of Volcanoes," "Secular Tithes," "How Judges Are Made," "The Victim Punished First," "The Presidency at the Bargain-Counter," "Sale of Indulgences." John Burroughs reported that after an hour's reading of the highly colored pages he had to go out and kick stumps. Howells called it "intensely fascinating," a "kinetoscopic impression of the abomination it treats of." In England John A. Hobson read it with approval and W. T. Stead pronounced it a really great book, while in Russia it was praised by Tolstoy. More than any other work, it fixed upon the public mind of America that stereotype of Rockefeller and the Standard Oil as indescribably cruel, greedy, and wicked which was to remain there for decades. It created a stage Rockefeller as unreal as the stage Irishman or stage Jew or stage Mark Hanna.

There can be no question that Lloyd was sincere, with the terrible sincerity of a hot-gospeller ridden by his creed. His letters to friends show just the same fervor as his book. It is true, he writes "Golden Rule" Jones, that the bulk of American businessmen are pursuing unscrupulous methods.[9] "Still, they have been forced into

[7]Caro Lloyd, *Lloyd*, I, 197.   [8]To George Iles, Dec. 14, 1887.
[9]Aug. 7, 1899, Lloyd Papers.

them by the initial unscrupulousness of a few radicals. My study
. . . of the oil business convinces me that in the early development
the majority of the people concerned were willing to live and let
live, and sought success only by the ordinary methods of business
competition. This normal state of affairs was rudely interrupted by
the entrance of a very small knot of very reckless men who were
willing to commit crime itself for the purpose of obtaining the
success they desired. . . . It seems to me that the essentially criminal character of what was done by these radicals ought to be
sharply discriminated from the conduct of the rest of the business
community. To say that all are doing the same thing but that the
monopolists have only done it a little faster and a little more than
the others, seems to me to throw the protection of an undeserved
condonation over the deeds of men who, as the adjudicated records
show, ought to be in the penitentiary." That statement reveals a
profound misunderstanding of the history of the oil industry and
the conditions that led Rockefeller to intervene to restore order (as
he believed) in an anarchic, man-killing chaos; but it flames with
sincerity. So do Lloyd's letters to many others. He had a wide correspondence—with Altgeld, Sidney Webb, Clarence Darrow, John
Swinton, Frances E. Willard, Jane Addams, Florence Kelley, W. D.
Howells, Gompers, Ely, Henry George and many others whose
names do him honor. To all he wrote with the same passionate
earnestness. He fired them all with his own zeal and eloquence. The
charge that he was "a millionaire Socialist" was inaccurate. As he
wrote a friend in 1895,[10] he had never identified himself with the
Socialist organization, detested the class-struggle ideas of the Marx-
ians, and leaned to the Fabian movement.

But any critical scrutiny of the book in the light of present-day
knowledge of business history and economic principles shows that
it was full of prejudice, distortion, and misinterpretation. The
proportions of the work were bad. More than one tenth of it was
given to the Matthews-Everest affair in Buffalo; and this was described as an episode "which has let us see how the employees of
a trust coolly debated with lawyers the policy of blowing up a competitor's works," although the Standard Oil defendants in the trial

[10]To George A. Gates, May 23, 1895, Lloyd Papers.

growing out of that affair had been acquitted.[11] The case of the defense was totally ignored. A good deal more than another tenth was allotted to the Toledo gas war, though it had such tenuous relations with the history of the Standard Oil that later Miss Tarbell did not even mention it in her book.[12]

Lloyd swallowed whole the malicious story told by the Widow Backus of her "ruin,"[13] though he had available or could have procured all the material which we have used in exploding it. He insisted that the South Improvement Company, which actually never did any business whatever, was responsible for the "singular ruin" which afflicted the Oil Regions in 1872. ("Many committed suicide," he wrote. "Hundreds were driven into bankruptcy and insane asylums.")[14] He likewise made the untenable assertion that the Standard Oil Trust was simply the South Improvement Company redivivus. Thirty pages were devoted to accusations and innuendoes treating Henry B. Payne and Secretary William C. Whitney as tools of the Standard.[15] ("The Senate Votes to Be a Market," ran one page-heading; "Public Office for a Private Trust," ran another.) Everything in sight was blamed upon the Standard. For example, even the Standard's co-operation with the Producers' Protective Association in 1887 to effect a shutoff and get rid of the huge surplus of stored oil that was weighing down the market was treated as a crime.[16] The blowing up of the derricks of well-owners who

[11]Pp. 244–298. To call the Everests, who were heads of the Vacuum Oil Company, "employees of the trust," is to misdefine their relation to the Standard Oil Trust. The judge specifically decided that the Standard Oil officers knew nothing whatever of the alleged sabotage plot; and the testimony of a juror shows that even Everest was not convicted on that count. One of the most striking of Lloyd's innuendoes occurs on pages 250–252. On pages 250, 251, he explains that an explosion did *not* occur in the Buffalo plant; on page 252 he coolly begins a paragraph, "Several years after the Buffalo explosion"! This chapter seems to the author one of the most dishonest pieces of so-called history he has ever read.

[12]Pp. 299–368. Rockefeller told W. O. Inglis that various outside men had joined with Standard Oil interests in the companies selling natural gas to Toledo. "I had nothing to do personally with this enterprise."

[13]Pp. 73–83.   [14]Pp. 38–60.   [15]Pp. 369–404.

[16]Pp. 152 ff. One of Lloyd's egregious blunders was his treatment of prices after the panic of 1893. As we have seen, a classic count against the trust lay in its operation of the "pincers movement" of 1893–94 to injure independent refiners; lowering the price of refined oil while the price of crude rose. But Lloyd abused the Standard for not making the price of refined oil still cheaper!

refused to aid in this shutoff was laid at the door of the Standard, when it was actually the work of the angry producers![17]

All these false and misleading materials were mingled with much that was entirely true and convincing. No present-day student of corporation history would trust the book at any point. But immense numbers of people in the nineties were not in a frame of mind to read it critically. They found it the first full and coherent story of the Standard Oil to be put into print; they noted that a great part of it was based directly upon legal documents, and that the Standard made no real effort to reply to it. They naturally accepted it as a truthful indictment.

The reception which the book met from press and public leaders, to be sure, was mixed. Many newspapers hailed it with raptures. "It is an exhaustive and impressive showing that he makes," said the Chicago *Tribune,* on which Lloyd had long worked. "A masterly and successful attempt to illustrate the movement of business feudalization in this country," declared the Chicago *Evening Post.* "Not a book of an hour or a day, but of a life," said the Brooklyn *Standard-Union.* "A stronger indictment of the present dominant forces in industry has not been put in print," remarked the Springfield *Republican. The Review of Reviews* declared that "his massing of facts is irresistible"; *The Outlook* that the volume was "the most powerful book on economics" since *Progress and Poverty.* Lloyd scattered complimentary copies broadcast. He sent them to John Ruskin, Bernard Shaw, Sidney and Beatrice Webb, and other prominent people in England; to senators, labor leaders, professors, writers, and reformers in America. Many who were thus favored returned enthusiastic encomiums. The collection of Lloyd's papers at the University of Wisconsin is full of notes from readers declaring that he had opened their eyes to this great evil; that they had never guessed how far-reaching were its crimes; and that he should distribute a cheap edition in hundreds of thousands of copies. "Astounding, infuriating!" wrote Howells. John Bascom publicly declared that the book "ought to mark an era of resistance to the many and utterly unscrupulous forms of monopoly" which

[17]P. 154. Honest study of Regions newspapers would have shown Lloyd that in the year of the "immediate shipment" quarrel, for example, they were imploring the Regions men to stop disgracing themselves by acts of lawlessness.

had arisen, and delivered a fierce attack upon Rockefeller: "The president of such a company has no right to endow a university; to put a gift on the altar of patriotism. . . . This man has sown the land with offenses from boundary to boundary."[18]

But other men and journals treated the book sharply. The German scholar Ernest von Halle in his careful *Trusts or Industrial Combinations* pronounced it "only a *chronique scandaleuse.*" An Oil Regions critic remarked that it belonged to the school of "hysterical economics."[19] The New York *Times,* though unfriendly to the Standard, condemned Lloyd's tone. "He has neither judicial fairness of mind nor self-control. The volume is defaced by passion and is made unwholesome by intolerance."[20] The New York *Morning Advertiser* thought that nothing more false and prejudiced had been printed in recent years. "The wonder is that a work so manifestly malicious and dishonest could have found a reputable publisher."[21] *The Literary World* objected to the fevered declamation and rank sentimentalism of his style.[22] The New York *Tribune* and *Sun* practically ignored it, though the latter was strongly anti-Standard. Even *The World* damned the book with faint praise: "However much any one may disagree with Mr. Lloyd, he cannot fail to thank him for the admirable manner in which he has gathered and digested his facts."

The foremost critical magazine of the country, *The Nation,* whose literary editor, Wendell Phillips Garrison, son of the great Abolitionist, was a friend of Lloyd's, published a scathing review. The book was a signal illustration of the rhetorical blunder of overstatement, it remarked. A temperate resumé of the evidence against the Standard would have been a most damaging indictment; "instead, we have over five hundred octavo pages of the wildest rant." The reviewer accused Lloyd of seeing Standard Oil devils behind every bush, and of finding their malign handiwork in every possible disaster or crime. If his tirades were to be credited, the Standard leaders had not only controlled legislatures and Congresses, but had swayed the action of the British Parliament, and seduced the Czar

---

[18]*The North and West,* Jan. 31, 1895.
[19]Doctor David H. Wheeler of Meadville, Pa., *Central Christian Advocate,* Jan. 9, 1895.
[20]Dec. 20, 1894.
[21]Aug. 1, 1895.
[22]Nov. 3, 1894.
[23]Oct. 13, 1894.

of Russia. They had almost monopolized the light-producing substances of the globe, "and we doubt if Mr. Lloyd feels that the human race is altogether secure in the possession of sunlight." Nor was *The Nation* attracted by his closing picture of the beauties of Socialism. "He appears to us to exhibit in his writing such indifference to truth, such incoherency of thought, such intemperance of speech and such violence of passion, as to make him an undesirable leader." Apart from the wild exaggeration of the book, *The Nation* found that it had two grave faults. One was its vagueness at critical points and its refusal to name names. The second was even more serious:

> Mr. Lloyd calls witnesses without discrimination. Some of them are crack-brained, by his own admission. Some of them testify that they were bribed to commit arson and other crimes by the mysterious leaders of the Standard Oil Company. A dog would not be hung upon such evidence. Nor can Mr. Lloyd's citations of the testimony of reputable witnesses be allowed much weight, for he is so bitter in his advocacy that it would be grossly unfair to pass judgment upon his *ex parte* statement. . . .
>
> Upon the whole, Mr. Lloyd's book is eminently calculated to arouse incredulity in the mind of any reader who understands the nature of evidence. Were we not satisfied from evidence *aliunde* that the managers of the Standard Oil Company had violated both law and justice in their attempts to suppress competition, we should be inclined to acquit them after reading this screed. It is quite beyond belief that these men should be capable of the height and depth of wickedness attributed to them, even if they possessed the superhuman powers with which they are credited. It is plain upon Mr. Lloyd's showing that their competitors would be no better than they if they had similar opportunities, and it is impossible to arouse sympathy for men whose complaint is that they were not allowed to make enormous profits; for it appears to have been the policy of the Standard Company to buy out its rivals at reasonable rates.

Yet Lloyd was entitled to regard his book as a success. Once more Rockefeller and his associates erred in not meeting the attack with a vigorous and emphatic defense. They had it in their power, if they had supplied the evidence to some careful and effective writer, to traverse and confute many of Lloyd's pages. But to do this would have involved making damaging admissions at various points, and for that they were not prepared. It would have dragged the Standard Oil leaders into direct controversy, which they were anxious to avoid. Rockefeller, as always before, believed a dignified silence the best policy. He did not comprehend until too late that it was construed as an admission of guilt all along the line. One spokesman for the Standard, George Gunton (who much later, in 1906, was stated by his wife to be receiving a yearly retainer of $15,000 from the corporation), did attempt a partial rejoinder.[24] In an article in his own review, *The Social Economist* for July, 1895, he assailed Lloyd's book for unfair quotation and the suppression of rebutting evidence. Lloyd shortly replied,[25] and Gunton published a second article. There the matter rested until the Standard Oil offered to give full opportunity for investigation to a committee of ministers and economists. This was through the Reverend B. Fay Mills of Fort Edward, N. Y., who on April 21, 1896, wrote the Reverend E. E. Hale:

I recently was in New York City, and took pains to arrange an interview with the authorities of the Standard Oil Trust. I told them plainly how I had felt concerning the organization, and that I believed that my convictions were shared by a great number of the more intelligent Christian people of this country, and asked them if they would like the opportunity of presenting any explanations or defense in connection with the serious charges which have been brought against them, from time to time, especially in Mr. Lloyd's book. I was received with the greatest courtesy, and spent several hours with two men—one of them Mr. Rockefeller's personal representative, who manages all his business affairs outside of the Standard Oil—Mr. Gates; and the other Colonel Dodd, who is the Solicitor of the Trust. I went entirely through Mr. Lloyd's book with them, taking up all the charges contained therein seriatim. It would be too much (with the limited time at my disposal, and hearing thus only their statement of the case) to say that I thought these various charges were disproved by them; but of this I felt very clear: that all of these charges were at least susceptible of reasonable explanation, and possibly, of disproof. They stated that it had been the policy of the Standard Oil from the beginning, never to deny or attempt to disprove charges made against them in a public manner, but that all of the actions of the Company had been— from any reasonable standpoint—thoroughly moral, and that they challenged all reasonable investigation of the charges made against them, and of their methods.

The object of my writing you this letter, is not to express any personal opinion at this time, but in response to the very urgent request of Mr.

[24]Caro Lloyd, *Lloyd*, I, 211. When Gunton wrote an article for *The Political Science Quarterly*, the Standard distributed 10,000 copies; Lloyd Papers.
[25]Boston *Herald*, Oct. 23, 1895.

Rockefeller that I write to you, with his authority, stating that all the charges made against the Standard Oil Company, of various forms of immorality, are unfounded and false, and that he is pleased to extend you an invitation—either alone or in company with others—to visit their offices in New York, where he himself and the solicitor of the Standard Oil Trust, will be glad to take their own time and to put all the facilities of their office at your disposal—for your investigation of the serious charges made against them. They would not want to do this, except for one whom they believed to be honestly desiring to know the truth for the best purposes. . . .

But though much correspondence ensued, and Richard T. Ely was invited to join the inquiry, the plan fell through.

Lloyd not only succeeded in fixing an ugly stereotype of Rocke- feller and the Standard Oil Trust upon the public mind. He was able to persuade many readers that their misdeeds were in kind as well as degree far worse than the misdeeds of American business in general. He himself, in his hysterical fashion, seems to have believed this firmly. We find him writing George Rice that people have been deluded by the Standard's claim that it has cheapened oil: "This the public—dear fools—believe, and it entirely reconciles them—knavish fools—to the piracies, treasons, and murders by which the fabled cheapness has been brought to them." This loose talk about murder did not befit a man who pretended to be a careful economist. To another correspondent he writes of "the condottieri of the monopoly." We have already quoted his statement about "the essentially criminal character of what was done," and his assertion that the heads of the Standard "ought to be in the penitentiary." His unpublished letters are replete with such epithets as "robbery" and "depredation." To him, Rockefeller and his partners were the arch-criminals of the century. Jay Gould, Frick, Russell Sage, Carnegie, Morgan, Armour, Collis P. Huntington—these all might be open to certain charges; but the really wicked men were the Standard's leaders.[26] They had committed "crimes" and ought to be in the "penitentiary."

Lloyd, as we have said, persuaded many readers of this. Actually when Rockefeller began to struggle upward, the oil business was disorderly and lawless in the extreme. When he and Flagler ac-

[26]Lloyd to Rice, Nov. 20, 1891; Lloyd to A. Von der Leyen, Jan. 1, 1895; Lloyd Papers.

cepted their first rebates, rebating was the general practice. When other businessmen were crushing competitors ruthlessly, he bought them out at generous figures. Among industrial leaders of his time he stood out as conspicuously constructive and clean-handed. The touch of Jay Gould upon any property was death, and he wrecked railroad after railroad simply to increase his own fortune. The builders of the Union Pacific, led by Oakes Ames, perpetrated a gigantic fraud upon the government, while the architects of the Central Pacific actually outdid them. A great part of Morgan's fortune was built up by sheer manipulation of stocks. An equally great part of Carnegie's was obtained from a high protective tariff upon iron and steel which mulcted every resident of the United States. When Lloyd published his book the bloodshed and agony which had followed Frick's treatment of poor workingmen at Homestead, and Pullman's of strikers just outside Chicago, were fresh in the public mind. Workingmen for the Standard Oil, as every one knew, were always a little better paid and a little more contented than those for similar companies. Yet Lloyd thought the Standard leaders the worst of all! He should have lived to read Mark Sullivan's comparison of Rockefeller with Carnegie: "Of the methods of the two men, Rockefeller's were the more humane toward competitors." Or John T. Flynn's statement:[27]

Rockefeller's great fortune was not only the most honestly acquired, but was amassed in the building of a great constructive producing business and in the development of a new system in industry. . . . It is therefore . . . the least tainted of all the great fortunes of his day.

III

In 1896 the hard-fought battle between Bryan and McKinley filled the nation with shouting, excitement, and suspense. To the battle of the dollars, the life-and-death struggle between gold and silver, every other issue was subordinated. The Republican platform did not even mention trusts and monopolies. The Democratic platform contained a mere passing reference coupled with a recommendation for stricter control of railroads: "The absorption of wealth by the few, the consolidation of our leading railroad systems, and the formation of trusts and pools require a stricter control

[27]Flynn, *God's Gold,* 5; Sullivan, *Our Times,* II, 343.

by the Federal Government of those arteries of commerce." This was less pointed than the Gold Democratic plank, which declared that the party recognized "the obligation of all good citizens to resist every illegal trust, combination, or attempt against the just rights of monopoly." It was well known that McKinley was friendly toward great corporations. During his four years as governor of Ohio he had done nothing whatever to harass them, while his attorney-general, John K. Richards, had been equally disinclined to assail the Standard Oil or any other combination. Mark Hanna, who stood at McKinley's elbow, frankly asserted that the Sherman Act was unwise and that any prosecution of trusts would be injurious. The election of McKinley was received with gratification by all the large business interests of the country, and when he appointed the conservative Joseph McKenna of California head of the Department of Justice, most men agreed that monopolies had little to fear.

Yet actually the future was uncertain. The progressive torrent had been checked but not permanently dammed back. Such leaders as La Follette, Cummins, Altgeld, and Bryan remained vociferously active, and antagonism to the trusts was one of their sincerest tenets. In Ohio a new governor, A. S. Bushnell, took office in 1896. His attitude was cautious, but the attorney-general elected with him, Frank S. Monnett, had very different qualities.

Monnett was young, energetic, and ambitious, and had caught the inspiration of the bold progressive ideas which shortly made famous such other Ohioans as Brand Whitlock, Tom L. Johnson, and "Golden Rule" Jones. The son of a Methodist minister, and a graduate of Ohio Wesleyan University, he was not forty years of age. Like his predecessor Watson, he believed in executing the laws and the court decrees. He would doubtless soon have turned his attention to the Standard Oil of Ohio even had he been left alone. But the irrepressible George Rice of Marietta furnished some evidence which hastened his action; evidence which to both men constituted proof that the Standard of Ohio had never obeyed the decision that it must sever relations with the Standard Oil Trust.

Rice's allegations were interesting. For purposes of his own, he had obtained in October, 1892, a certificate for six shares of the Standard Oil Trust. Though the trust was supposed to be in dissolution, he was never asked to send these shares in for cancellation. He received regular dividends on them. Within a short time he bought a seventh share, represented by an "assignment of legal interest," on which dividends were also paid. Rice presently transferred this seventh share to an agent with instructions that it be sent to the Standard Oil Trust for liquidation—that is, for division into twenty pieces of paper representing twenty interests in the companies composing the trust.

Of course he was demanding a very troublesome operation. S. C. T. Dodd wrote to him, objecting that the transfer would cut up the trust share into a "multitude of almost infinitesimal fractions of corporate shares." He offered to buy the certificate at market value, or to assist Rice to purchase more certificates until he held enough to call for full corporate shares in each of the twenty companies. But Rice refused to follow either course. He intended to cause the Standard organization as much trouble as possible. As a matter of fact, in 1897 he would have had to hold 194½ shares in the Standard Oil Trust in order to be entitled to not less than one full share in each of the twenty companies; and as trust shares were worth $340, this would have cost him about $66,000! The law was on his side, and he was finally sent his scrip. In one company he received 50/9,725ths of a share, and in another 100/9,725ths. On such fractional parts of shares the rule was not to pay dividends.

Rice, who concluded that the Standard officers were making no real effort to dissolve the trust, then consulted various attorneys. One was David K. Watson, who retained all his old animosity toward the Standard Oil. In 1897 Rice and he laid all the available evidence before the attorney-general. By this time prosperity was returning, the thrust toward concentration in business was stronger than ever, and public hostility against trusts was fiercely reawakening. Monnett, who was planning onslaughts upon the Tobacco Trust and other alleged monopolies, at once took up the case. On November 9, 1897, he filed information with the State Supreme Court, alleging that the Standard Oil of Ohio stood in contempt of its decision of 1892. An answer was demanded by January 15, 1898.

The legal issue was simple. The State intended to punish the Standard of Ohio for contempt on the ground that its officers had never honestly intended to sever it from the Standard Oil Trust.

Indeed, asserted Monnett, they had actually adopted a scheme to prevent a severance, for under the name and guise of liquidation, the Trust Agreement was steadily being continued. The only essential difference was that the nine men who had formerly been Trustees of the Standard Oil Trust were now liquidating Trustees. They managed the companies as a unit, and the Standard of Ohio was still an integral part of a great monopoly.

It was obvious, however, that the State would find this contention difficult to prove. The Standard of Ohio could maintain that the Trust Agreement had been formally abolished, and the situation previous to its adoption restored. This was true. The companies in the Standard organization were now held together in merely the same loose way as between 1879 and 1882. To be sure, the stock of all the companies was in much the same hands as before, and the holders had not broken it up into twenty parts. But could anybody prove this the fault of Rockefeller and the other Trustees? These nine men had turned back to the Standard of Ohio all of its stock in their hands. They had not induced other holders to surrender their trust shares; but then they had no coercive power. They might quote Choate's statement to the attorney-general of New York several years earlier. "I happen to own one hundred shares in the Standard Oil Trust, and I have never gone forward and claimed my aliquot shares. Why not? Because I would get ten in one company, and twenty in another company, and two or three fifths in another. There is no power that this company can exercise to compel me and other indifferent certificate-holders, if you please, to come forward and convert our trust certificates."

As a matter of fact, Monnett was quite unable to prove his case against the Standard of Ohio. The contempt suit failed. Miss Tarbell states that his term having expired January 1, 1900, his successor suppressed the anti-trust suits; but this is not true of the contempt case. It was closed by a clear-cut decision of the Ohio Supreme Court on December 11, 1900:[28]

This day this cause came on to be heard upon the information against

[28]Given in *U. S. vs. Standard Oil Co., Record,* Vol. XXII, 525. Newspapers stated that Chief Justice Shanck and Judges Burkett and Davis were for dismissing the case; Judges Minshall, Williams, and Spear wished to declare the Standard in contempt. The tie vote meant a victory for the Standard. N. Y. *World, Herald,* Dec. 12, 1900.

said defendant for contempt heretofore filed herein, and the evidence produced by said parties: On consideration wherof, the Court being fully
advised in the premises does find that said defendant is not guilty. It is
therefore considered and adjudged that said information be and it is dismissed, and that said defendant recover its costs, herein expended.

But before this decision was reached, Rockefeller and his associates had been brought before the public again in dramatic fashion.
The suit, as Miss Tarbell correctly says, "proved one of the most
sensational ever instituted against the Standard Oil combination."
It achieved certain of Rice's and Monnett's aims even though it
failed.

Three arresting features marked this famous case. One was the
reappearance of Rockefeller, with other Standard Oil officials, upon
the witness stand. Another was the controversy which sprang up
over the alleged burning of certain books and records by the Standard Oil of Ohio. And still another was the furious dispute aroused
by Attorney-General Monnett's hasty charges of attempted bribery
on the part of Standard Oil officials.

Rockefeller found on his desk in November, 1897, a long list of
questions from the attorney-general upon the operations and position of the Standard Oil of Ohio. To some, as president of the
company, he made satisfactory answers; to others he objected. His
information showed that the plans for dissolving the trust had been
at a complete standstill from the fall of 1892 until 1897, with
477,881 shares persistently reported uncancelled. In the summer of
1896 the number dropped to 477,880—George Rice had cancelled his
one share! But after contempt proceedings began in 1897, the process
of cancellation had received a mysterious impulse. Within three
months, more than 100,000 shares were exchanged for new stock.[29]
Although Monnett learned a good deal from Rockefeller's answers,
he still needed more information. He therefore asked the court to
appoint a master commissioner to take evidence in New York;
and by agreement between him and the Standard, Allen T. Brinsmade was named—a choice which Monnett and his friends later
thought very regrettable.

Rockefeller appeared before Brinsmade in a suite of the New
Amsterdam Hotel on October 11, 1898. Lawyers and witnesses gath-

[29]*Ohio vs. Standard Oil Company*, 109.

ered cosily about a large table. Although he testified from ten until four-thirty, with an hour for lunch, he probably did not utter a thousand words. "Rockefeller Imitates a Clam," ran *The World* headline. Incessant objections came from his legal advisers, who sat immediately behind him and would not let him respond to any question until they had assented; and half of the objections precipitated wordy arguments. Next day Rockefeller took the stand again. Once more the legal sparring exhausted all observers. Monnett would ask a long involved question; the Standard attorneys would demur; argument would rage for weary minutes; and finally, if the objection were overruled, Rockefeller would answer in slow, measured words—"seldom in response to the meaning of the question put," wrote one reporter.[30] *The World* gave a graphic sketch of "the richest man in the country":[31]

Tall and spare, with a slight stoop of the shoulders, he looked very well dressed, in a black frock coat, trousers of small gray check, a silk hat that was not of this fall's block, a standing collar, and a Teck scarf of dark red with a little black figure in it. . . . When he spoke it was in a low, monotonous, but not unmusical tone of voice, that could scarcely be heard across the room.

Mr. Rockefeller has a long head, which is well shaped. His chin is narrow and sharp. His cheekbones are rather prominent and his cheeks rather hollow, except when he indulges in his common habit of closing his mouth and puffing his cheeks out, as though he were blowing into a bugle. His complexion is good, having a faint but natural flush. His eyes are deep-set, rather small, of a steel-gray color, and quizzical, except when he is aroused from the seeming apathy that his face usually expresses. Then the eyes become very bright and look straight at his questioner.

"The art of forgetting," added *The World* reporter, "which is one of the most valuable virtues that a monopolist can have when under cross-examination, is possessed by Mr. Rockefeller in its highest degree."

When Rockefeller was told late on the second day that he need not appear again, he plainly evinced relief. The serious air he had worn gave way to a cheery smile. For a time he listened to a wrangle between counsel over summoning Flagler to the stand. He nodded pleasantly to several friends, and was still in a happy mood when suddenly confronted by George Rice. Rockefeller cordially extended

[30]N. Y. *Sun,* Oct. 12, 1898.　　　　[31]N. Y. *World,* Oct. 12, 1898.

his hand, remarking: "How are you, Mr. Rice? We are getting to be old men now, eh? Don't you wish you had taken my advice years ago?"[32]

They began talking, with many curious eyes fixed on them. *The World* reporter thought he heard Rice admit that he should have taken Rockefeller's advice. But a moment later Rice burst out: "Well, you ruined me, anyhow!"

"Oh, pshaw, pshaw!" retorted Rockefeller mildly as he moved away.

The most important evidence which Rockefeller offered was the list of fifteen holders of Standard Oil Trust certificates who late in 1897 had suddenly turned over more than 100,000 shares for cancellation. So irritated was Monnett by his bland reticence that he attempted to have him and the secretary of the Standard of Ohio cited for contempt; but the court refused. Monnett was also overruled when he moved to rescind the order appointing Brinsmade as master commissioner.[33]

Then suddenly emerged the controversy over the alleged burning of important books. The attorney-general was deeply dissatisfied with the hearings in New York. He believed that the Standard of Ohio was not really conducting its own business; that, as still a part of the trust, it was controlled from 26 Broadway. He had learned from Rockefeller that about 13,600 shares of the company were yet represented by trust certificates. Of course these trust certificates paid very handsome dividends. Did not part of such payments come from the Standard of Ohio? The officers of the Ohio company denied this. They had paid no dividends whatever since 1892, they declared, but had used the earnings to improve their plant and increase their reserves. The dividends paid on trust certificates came from the other nineteen companies. But Monnett, still unconvinced, demanded that the Standard of Ohio produce the books which would show gross and net earnings since 1892, and the precise disposition made of them.

This demand alarmed Rockefeller and his associates. The Ohio legislature earlier this year had passed a drastic anti-trust law, drafted by Monnett, prescribing stiff criminal penalties for any infractions,

[32]N. Y. *World, Herald, Sun,* Oct. 13, 1898.
[33]Review of case in N. Y. *World,* March 6, 1899.

and granting civil damages to all injured complainants.[34] The crusading attorney-general had hastened to push litigation against railroad companies, insurance companies, banks, the Western Union, and other businesses; and among others, he filed suits against four companies which he believed to be constituent members of the Standard Oil Trust—the Standard of Ohio, the Ohio Oil Company, the Buckeye Pipe Line, and the Solar Refining Company. Officers of the Standard may or may not have been confident that the books would sustain their contention that they had paid no dividends since 1892 to holders of trust certificates. But it is certain that they feared the books would yield evidence damaging to them in the four anti-trust suits—that is, evidence revealing a combination of monopolistic tendency. Virgil P. Kline therefore advised the secretary of the Standard of Ohio, F. B. Squire, who was also the dominant figure in the company, to refuse to produce the books. Squire pleaded that they might be used to incriminate him and the corporation; moreover, he asserted that to enforce their production in the contempt case would be an act of unwarranted search and seizure. When the court supported Monnett, and on December 7, 1898, ordered the Standard of Ohio to produce its books for 1892–97, Squire simply repeated his refusal.[35] He defied the court.

Did he take any other steps? Before Christmas Monnett placed witnesses on the stand to show that Virgil P. Kline had received a warning of the court's order, and that the Standard of Ohio had forthwith burned its journals, ledgers, and other documents. One of his witnesses, a rabbi of a congregation of Bohemian Jews in Cleveland, gave some vague hearsay testimony.[36] But an employee named O'Hearn asserted that sixteen large boxes of packaged material from the Standard offices had been carted to one of the company plants; and another employee, John McNierney, swore that on November 19 and 21, 1898, great quantities of books and papers had been burned. The officers asserted that these were worthless —mere waste paper. "We burn old books in storage every ten years," said Kline, "but none have been destroyed pertinent to this investigation." When the attorney-general demanded proof of this by

[34]Act of April 19, 1898, effective July 1.
[35]N. Y. *World*, March 25, 1899; *Standard Oil Case in Supreme Court of Ohio*, 1897–98, pt. II, 248.
[36]N. Y. *Tribune*, Dec. 22, 1898.

production of the true books, the company refused, arguing that they might incriminate it. Throughout the winter of 1898–99 the quarrel dragged on, growing steadily more acrimonious.

In a last effort to obtain information, Monnett returned to New York and resumed the hearings under Brinsmade on March 17, 1899, at the Hoffmann House. This time Archbold was the principal witness. George Rice, portly, amiable, and eccentric, again watched the proceedings from a front seat. Archbold made a bad impression on the witness stand, showing none of Rockefeller's equanimity, and evincing a bitter antagonism to Rice, whom he plainly regarded as a frustrated "blackmailer" in the oil business. "There is nothing to you but wind and weight!" he snorted in one exchange.[37]

Throughout a long day Monnett did his utmost to extract some damaging testimony from Archbold, but without success. Every incisive question brought the Standard's lawyers to their feet with objections. At one point Monnett, losing his patience, turned on him with the sharp inquiry: "What do you think we are all here for?" "Buncombe, all buncombe," interjected Archbold.[38] When asked if the officers had encountered any difficulties in dissolving the trust, Archbold grew eloquent in explaining their troubles. They were still meeting grave obstacles, he explained. They did not know where many holders of trust shares lived, while others would not turn them in to be exchanged for other paper. To take precipitate steps would injure many worthy people.

"If we had acted in any other manner than we did it would have resulted in the ruin of many widows and orphans and hospitals and——"

"Were you one of those orphans?" demanded Monnett, sarcastically.[39]

The second day witnessed a vitriolic quarrel between Archbold and Monnett's assistant, W. L. Flagg. Archbold from the outset showed a truculent attitude on the stand. When Flagg whispered some advice to Monnett, he shouted, with clenched fists, "You keep still, or I'll expose you right here." Flagg retorted by calling him a cur, and Archbold came back with: "You dog, you miserable

[37]N. Y. *World*, March 18, 1899.
[38]*Ibid.*   [39]*Ibid.*

whelp!" When Flagg termed Archbold a liar, the magnate went him two adjectives better: "You are a dirty, stinking liar!" Brinsmade stopped this disgraceful exhibition, and ordered the speeches stricken from the record. But the affair made good newspaper headlines next day: "like a barroom brawl," commented *The World*. The press disliked Archbold, who lost his temper much too readily, and was rude to reporters. He called the witnesses who had testified to book-burning "semi-anarchists"![40]

On the last day Monnett expected two independent refiners to take the stand with testimony against the Buckeye Pipe Line Company. For some reason they refused to do so. Newspapers hostile to the Standard declared that they had been intimidated. *The World* reporter found one of them, Levi Smith, a veteran oil man of Warren, Pa., at the Astor Hotel. When it was suggested that he would be called upon to testify by Monnett, Smith replied in some agitation:[41]

"Not on your life! If he wants me I will take the midnight train for home. I dare not testify. The railroads would put me back on the old basis of rates in a minute!"

With this second hearing a virtual failure, Monnett had to conclude his case. The press of Ohio had taken sides acrimoniously for and against his suits. Most of the newspapers aligned with Foraker's faction in State politics had applauded Monnett. Most of the newspapers under Hanna's influence had been hostile to him. He had attacked so many companies all the way from Toledo to Marietta, driving some out of the State, that he had aroused deep antagonism. Governor Bushnell caustically remarked in the spring of 1899: "So many suits have been commenced recently by Mr. Monnett that I have not been able to familiarize myself with them." Early in December, 1898, about the time of the alleged destruction of books, a large number of Ohio journals suddenly began publishing complimentary notices of the Standard Oil Company as news and editorial matter, coupling with it uncomplimentary allusions to the attorney-general. As this appeared in precisely the same form in numerous newspapers, it had obviously been paid for. On investigation, Monnett found that it was actually advertising matter, placed

[40]N. Y. *World, Herald, Tribune*, March 19, 1890.
[41]N. Y. *Herald*, March 7; N. Y. *World*, March 21, 1899.

through the agency of Malcolm Jennings of Cleveland. When he subpœnaed Jennings and demanded a sworn list of all the newspapers, Jennings refused on the ground that such an order invaded his private rights. The attorney-general committed him to jail, but Jennings promptly obtained a writ of habeas corpus. Unquestionably the hostile newspaper reports and editorials, whether inspired by Hanna or paid for by the Standard, injured Monnett and crippled his efforts. Many businessmen of the State were convinced that he was trying to persecute and harass legitimate business.[42]

By the spring of 1899 Monnett seemed to be striking out recklessly. Apparently he saw that he was being checkmated by the Standard, and in desperation acted rashly. The evidence as to bookburning did have a nasty look, while the evidence as to the virtual buying of various newspapers was equally sinister. But when the attorney-general brought charges of bribery he had no real evidence to support his statements, and his assertions merely injured himself. Eager as the Standard Oil doubtless was to defeat his suits, it was certainly not guilty of such folly (to say nothing of dishonesty) as to attempt to corrupt the fanatical Monnett.

Monnett asserted that on or about January 10, 1899, a friend in Cleveland called him on the telephone to arrange a meeting, which took place January 25 in Columbus. The friend told Monnett that several men in New York had been commissioned by the Standard Oil to have the suits stopped; that they had been telephoning him by long distance from a place known to be the resort of prominent politicians; that among them was Abner McKinley, brother of the President; and that they had arranged to offer Monnett, if necessary, $400,000. This was to be left in money, stock, or trust certificates in a safe-deposit box in New York, to which Monnett was to be given the key! In return he was simply to consent to dilatory motions, for which the Standard's attorneys would accept the blame, and let the case drag along without coming to final issue.[43] Attorneys for the Standard pronounced this story too ridiculous for comment. When they called upon Monnett for the names of his Cleveland friend and the New York agents, he at first refused to furnish any information, saying that the names were confidential. Thus left unsupported, his allegations failed to impress anybody.

[42]N. Y. *World*, March 6, 1899.   [43]*Ibid.*

A little later, however, he filed a statement declaring that the agents who offered the bribe were F. B. Squire, Frank Rockefeller, and Charles N. Haskell. They indignantly repudiated the charge, which the court ordered dismissed and stricken from the record.[44]

It is possible that Monnett was the subject of a delusion, or was concocting a malicious story to arouse prejudice against the Standard Oil. It is more probable that a group of crooks thought that they would investigate the possibility of bribing him for some payment between $100,000 and $400,000, and, if they met a favorable response, would then attempt to collect $500,000 or more from the Standard Oil, pocketing the difference. Evidence sustaining this conjecture may be found in a statement by George Rice that Monnett had been offered $500,000, "less a fee of $100,000 to be retained by the person attempting the bribe."[45]

IV

Whether because of the Ohio prosecution, or for more fundamental reasons, Rockefeller and his associates by the beginning of 1899 had resolved to alter the form of the great Standard Oil organization completely. Probably Monnett's suit hastened this action, but it would doubtless have been taken within a short time had the suit never been commenced. Holding the convictions and ambitions that they did, Rockefeller and Archbold could never consent to a complete disruption of their powerful organization. Yet their practical position since the Ohio decree of 1892 was insecure, for it depended upon continued ownership of a majority of the stock of the twenty companies by a very small group willing to act as a unit. Moreover, it did not fall within any recognized form of legal organization, and therefore invited attack. A change was really overdue.

The tendency toward what Van Hise calls concentration and control in industry was now altogether too powerful to be checked.

[44]*Annual Report*, Atty. Gen. Ohio, 1899, p. 42. The N. Y. *World* published a dispatch saying that the "Oil Trust agents" had made the $400,000 proposal by long-distance telephone from the Windsor Hotel in N. Y. But it had to retract this statement when the telephone records at the hotel showed no telephone calls to or from Columbus or Cleveland for a week prior or subsequent to Jan. 19, 1890. *World*, March 6, 7, 1899.

[45]*Ann. Report*, Atty. Gen. Ohio, 1899, pp. 30–43; N. Y. *Herald*, March 4–8, 1899, for Rice's statement and Monnett's comment.

When the first anti-trust laws were passed, and when the Ohio decision of 1892 against the Standard Oil was followed in 1894 by an Illinois decision against the whiskey monopoly, the trusts had two principal courses to follow. They could dissolve their trust agreements and go the full length of consolidation, the member companies selling out to a single centralized corporation; or they could resort to the still new and little-known device of the holding company. The Sugar Trust chose the first alternative. The twenty-odd refining entities dissolved their trust agreement in 1891, but the properties were immediately taken over by a huge new corporation, the American Sugar Refining Company. Henry O. Havemeyer was shortly asked to explain the difference between the old trust and the new consolidation. He replied that "the trust was attacked and the courts decided that it was illegal, and a company was organized in New Jersey which bought outright and paid for the different companies, which were the constituent companies of the trust."

The use of holding companies on a broad scale was made possible by a New Jersey law of 1888, clarified and broadened in 1889, 1893, and 1896. Until this time the States had generally refused to let one corporation hold the stock of another, save by special enactment. Shrewd executives were quick to see the possibilities which the New Jersey law offered for business reorganization. Nevertheless, for a number of years the holding company remained a little-tried agency, which few attorneys were bold enough to urge upon their clients; and Rockefeller and S. C. T. Dodd rightly regarded it with caution. Between 1889 and 1898, only one of the ten major monopolistic combinations then formed or reorganized took the holding-company shape—the American Cotton Oil Company. The others (though often reincorporating under New Jersey law) tended to resort to outright fusion. The Standard Oil combination assumed a waiting attitude while its heads pondered all aspects of the question.

Such patient study was characteristic of Rockefeller, and so was the shrewdness of the decision at which he arrived. He saw that the holding company offered definite advantages over any other form of organization. It was both simpler and less expensive for one central corporation to acquire stock control (that is, mere majority ownership) in other companies than to buy the property of these companies by direct fusion. The operation could be accomplished by gradual steps, without publicity, and without arousing antagonism. It required no action by the stockholders of the companies acquired, and it did not affect the position of bondholders in the least. Moreover, the outstanding stock of any controlled company could later be bought in, perhaps gradually, if such action seemed wise. Rockefeller and Archbold probably also believed that a great combination based on holding-company control might be less exposed to anti-trust attacks than a monopolistic consolidation. Time soon proved that the holding company made possible a far more rapid development of gigantic business organizations than by any other method. Only through use of it, or some kindred legal device, would it have been feasible to create such great enterprises, their capital ultimately running into the billions, as the American Telephone and Telegraph Company and the United States Steel Corporation.[46]

In turning to the new form, Rockefeller and his associates were encouraged by the decision of the Supreme Court in the Sugar Trust case of 1895. This held that manufacturing was not interstate commerce, and that the acquisition by a corporation of competing manufactories in other States did not bring it under the interdiction of the Sherman Act.[47] The holding company after this decision, and after the New Jersey amendments of 1896, seemed safe—and safety was tempting. Even if Monnett failed to void the charters of four Ohio companies, further attacks (if the Standard Oil remained in its anomalous position) would certainly be made by other States. "Trust-busting" was becoming highly popular.

The result was that in June, 1899, a great holding company emerged to take charge of the Standard Oil aggregation. The charter of the Standard Oil of New Jersey was amended; its capital was increased from $10,000,000 to $110,000,000; and it was given 1,000,000 shares of common and 100,000 of preferred. On June 19 the directors authorized the company to exchange this stock for the outstanding certificates of the defunct Standard Oil Trust, and for the stock of the twenty constituent companies. This was done

[46]Cf. J. C. Bonbright and G. C. Means, "Holding Companies," *Encyclopedia of the Social Sciences,* VII, 403 ff.
[47]*U. S. vs. E. C. Knight Co.,* 156, U. S., 1 ff.

at the rate of one share of the New Jersey common stock for a designated fractional share of New Jersey preferred stock and designated fractional shares of each of the other twenty companies. The fractional share in every instance was the fractional share to which the holder of a Standard Oil Trust certificate became entitled on the distribution of stocks by the Standard Oil Trustees in 1892. The total amount of common stock of the Standard of New Jersey to be issued under the resolution was 972,500 shares; that is to say, one share for every share of trust certificates outstanding in 1892. The greater part of the stock of the twenty companies was immediately turned in for common stock of the Standard of New Jersey.

This reorganization of course had no effect whatever upon the continuity of the Standard Oil management. The same men remained in the same control, carrying out the same policies in the same way. There had in fact been no break in the continuity of the Standard's management since it became the master of Cleveland in 1872 and reached out to conquer other fields; and there was to be none until 1911. The president of the Standard Oil of New Jersey was John D. Rockefeller, and the vice-president John D. Archbold. The fourteen directors included, besides these two men, Henry M. Flagler, H. H. Rogers, William Rockefeller, Charles M. Pratt, W. H. Tilford, Frank Q. Barstow, E. T. Bedford, Walter Jennings, James A. Moffett, Oliver H. Payne, C. W. Harkness, and John D. Rockefeller, Jr. Of the fourteen, six had been connected with the Standard business since the seventies. The stockholders of the Standard of New Jersey in 1899 numbered about 3500.[49]

This great holding company immediately took its place as one of the richest and most powerful corporations on the globe. Made up at the outset of twenty constitutent companies, it soon began purchasing control of others, adding to its list year by year. In 1900 the total net assets of the Standard organization were $205,480,000, and the net profits more than $55,500,000. By 1906 the total net assets were just short of $360,000,000 and the total net earnings exceeded $83,120,000. The corporation was a colossus of such size and wealth as nobody—save perhaps Rockefeller—would have dreamed possible twenty-five years before.[50]

[48]Taylor, MS History, 161.   [49]*Ind. Comm. Hearings*, 1899, I.
[50]Taylor, 127, 170.

V

But the Standard Oil of New Jersey was far from being the only business giant of these years, or even the largest. During 1897–98 the United States passed rapidly from depression to prosperity. The election of McKinley, the discovery of gold in the Klondike, the rapid increase of gold production in South Africa, the contracts let in the Spanish War, the national self-confidence engendered by victory, the coincidence of bumper crops with a vigorous European demand, and the upward curve of the economic cycle, combined to make American business strong and hopeful. The turn of the century witnessed a remarkable expansion of manufacturing, and a marked accentuation of the movement toward concentration in industry. New Jersey reaped a golden harvest. In the three years 1899–1901 the State chartered an average of 2172 companies annually, and took in an average of more than $550,000 a year in filing fees, while the annual franchise tax by 1901 exceeded $1,625,000. It paid to protect big business![51] The New Jersey Guarantee & Trust Company of Camden had on its doors 770 corporation names.

New "trusts" sprang up on every hand; not trusts in the strict sense of the word, for they were outlawed, but in the loose new sense of any organization of monopolistic tendency. Some represented the complete fusion of various companies; some a union under the ægis of a holding company; some a simple federation or community of interest. By 1904 John Moody was able to begin *The Truth About the Trusts* with the arresting statement: "There are in the United States today an aggregation of over 440 large industrial, franchise, and transportation trusts of an important and active character, with a total floating capital of $20,379,162,511."[52] In this flush period of consolidation appeared the first $1,000,000,000 company, the United States Steel Corporation; its stock and bonds, indeed, representing nearly $1,500,000,000. Organized in 1901, it was a typical holding company, the eleven constituent corporations within a short time owning a controlling interest in about 170 subsidiary companies.[53] The Copper Trust (Amalgamated Copper

---

[51]S. McReynolds, "The Home of the Trust," *World's Work*, IV (1902), 2526–2532.

[52]P. xi.   [53]H. U. Faulkner, *American Economic History*, 524.

Company) was incorporated under the New Jersey law in 1899 with a capital of $75,000,000. The Smelters' Trust (American Smelting and Refining Company), another holding company, appeared that same year. The new Tobacco Trust (Consolidated Tobacco Company) emerged in 1901. Lesser combinations were legion. Cartoonists who depicted them as dinosaurs or megatheria were able to paint the American scene, stretching far and wide, as swarming with these monsters.

Many observers believed with Hanna and Aldrich that they should be let alone. Many believed with Bryan and La Follette that they should be sent to join the saber-toothed tiger. Some were wondering whether these yet untamed monsters ought not to be divided between the good and the bad, the beneficial and pernicious, the latter to be slaughtered and the former to be led around with rings in their noses. Since it was plain that great business combinations had come to stay, why not make the best of them? The debate on these questions began to grow strident. Meanwhile, Rockefeller would have echoed S. C. T. Dodd's confident words: "You might as well endeavor to stay the formation of the clouds, the falling of the rains, or the flowing of the streams, as to attempt by any means or in any manner to prevent organization of industry, association of persons, and the aggregation of capital to any extent that the ever-growing trade of the world may demand."

XL

Iron Men and Glittering Gold

ROMPTED by Messrs. Colby and Hoyt, Rockefeller during the
years 1885–91 had made various investments in iron mines.
They included an important holding in Cuba, where the
Colby-Hoyt interests, acting through the Spanish-American
Iron Company, had bought about 4000 acres near Santiago, sunk
shafts, built a costly railroad and dock, and were just ready to begin
shipping ore when the panic of 1893 began. They included also
several mines on the Gogebic range in Wisconsin, including two
of the richest, the Aurora and Tilden. Finally, he held properties in
Michigan and Minnesota. Like other enterprises of the Colby-Hoyt
group, some of these purchases represented more of sanguine enthusiasm than cool realism. When Rockefeller found in 1892 how
badly he had been misled elsewhere, he began to survey these mines
with a distrustful eye, and requested Gates to give them early
attention. When Gates did so, he was at once attracted by the possibilities of the rich new Missabe field in Minnesota.[1]

Far and away the richest ore deposits in the world have been
found about Superior, the chill deep lake that lies within a veritable
rim of iron.[2] During the fifteen years preceding the panic, a development unequalled in history had taken place there. To be sure,
the Marquette field in northern Michigan had been opened up
before the Civil War; but the great era of exploitation had not begun
until much later. In 1877 the railroad builders forced an entry into
the valuable Menominee range in the Michigan peninsula, providing outlets on upper Lake Michigan. In 1884, amid wild speculative
excitement, they opened up the rich Gogebic range, lying athwart

[1] Gates, MS Autobiography, Chapter 40.
[2] The phrase is used by Chase Osborne.

359

the Wisconsin-Michigan line just beneath the western end of Lake Superior; the first ore being taken from the Colby mine.[3] A vast deal of wildcat stock-peddling accompanied the early mining operations on the Gogebic; yet the field had remarkable deposits of ore, rich in iron that was ideally suited to the Bessemer process.

At about the same time, iron began to be taken from the extensive Vermilion range north of the western tip of Lake Superior, in Minnesota. Here some early gold-hunters had stumbled upon a huge gray-black cliff of hematite ore, rising naked above the trees and bushes. The astute Charlemagne Tower, a Philadelphia capitalist, was credited with obtaining about 17,000 acres of rich mineral land here for only $40,000;[4] a railroad was pushed through nearly seventy miles of swamp and rocky wilderness from the lake, and by 1892 this bleak, remote area was shipping annually more than 1,000,000 tons of excellent ore. The development, practically monopolized by Tower's company, was orderly and prudent. The three enormous fields, the Menominee, Gogebic, and Vermilion, riveted the attention of the world and remade the iron industry of the United States.[5]

Yet they represented merely a beginning; for other rich fields were to be found—one the greatest known to history. The early discoveries set scouts searching the woods west and north of Lake Superior, where it was generally believed there lay great quantities of iron. Among the men firmest in the faith was Leonidas Merritt, a native of Chautauqua County, N. Y., who had come to Minnesota with his father in boyhood, settled at Oneota (now part of Duluth), and served in the Civil War.[6] He was a man of stubborn grit, who had walked 150 miles to get into the army, "and packed my grub."[7] After the war he went into lumbering and seafaring on the lakes. A little group of Merritts, five of Lon's brothers and three nephews, finally became lean, hard-bitten, indefatigable explorers for pine timber. Some of them were convinced that the Missabe hills, full of iron-veined rocks, where the compass needle spun about like a whirligig, held richer ore deposits than the Ver-

[3]H. R. Mussey, *Combination in the Iron Mining Industry,* 84.
[4]Paul De Kruif, *Seven Iron Men,* 49.
[5]Stewart Holbrook, *Iron Brew, passim.*
[6]Paul De Kruif, *Seven Iron Men;* W. W. Folsom, *History of Minnesota,* IV, 18.
[7]*Transcript of Record, Alfred Merritt vs. John D. Rockefeller et al.* This will hereafter be cited as *Merritt vs. Rockefeller.*

milion range. At various spots they came upon ochre-tinged dirt and felt certain that somewhere excavations would show iron. For years they failed of any real proof, for explorers then believed that the iron ore would show itself in outcropping mineral veins, whereas actually it lay in loose flat beds beneath the surface. But the Merritts never gave up. They went into the woods with hundred-pound packs looking for pine and iron, and came out thirty days later "skin poor."[8] Derision was hurled at these "lumberjacks" because they tried to locate nonmagnetic ore with needles, but they kept on.

Paul De Kruif has ably sketched these men of the true pioneer breed, with both its faults and virtues. Leonidas, five feet eight, his 180 pounds all bone, muscle, and sinew, walrus-mustached, grim-jawed, loved the wilderness which he cruised for fifteen years. He had an encyclopædic knowledge of woodcraft. In everything he undertook he was self-confident and even cocksure. In many ways he was very ignorant. He was impulsive, and could be bitterly stubborn. One of his convictions was that the iron outcrop would always be found on the south side of the Missabe range, for his father had said so. He alternated between flush days of prosperity and lean months of poverty; sometimes he would take up timberland cheap, sell it dear for the white pine, and have money to lend to friends or give to less energetic relatives, but more frequently he was poor. Apparently a mystic faith animated the spirit of this courageous pioneer, so uncouth in manner, so roughly dressed in Mackinaw pants, heavy socks, cowhide boots, and flannel shirt; a feeling that God had purposely laid down iron in these cliffs and basins just beside the mighty lakes whose ships could easily carry it to the East and to Europe, and that it was his duty to find it. A photograph of seven Merritt men standing in front of their father's hotel shows the strength of their rugged, thick-set frames, and indicates the intensity of their energy.[9] Leonidas, the most restless and imaginative, inspired his brother Alfred, a superlative lumberjack, and Cassius, the best ranger in the State.

"The Merritt family saw this thing big from the start," said Alfred later.[10] Indeed, they saw it too big. Lon always talked and acted in the epic manner; his experiences were all battles, and he

---

[8]*Merritt vs. Rockefeller,* 1886, 1887.
[9]In De Kruif, *Seven Iron Men,* 102.   [10]De Kruif, 123.

thought in empires. In 1887 they made a careful survey of the Missabe region, running diagonals across the formation and mapping the lines of attraction with a dip needle.[11] Then Lon helped lobby through the legislature a new law which permitted any one who paid $25 to hold not more than 160 acres for a year on a prospecting-lease, and anybody who paid $100 to hold a similar area for not more than fifty years on a mining-lease. The result was that in 1890 he took out 141 leases of mineral land, while other Merritts filed on a good deal more.[12] In the fall of that year an exploring party sent out by the family struck ore in quantity on the Missabe range. The next summer further explorations revealed rich deposits at various points, and it was evident to the blindest that another huge iron field had been discovered.[13] The Merritts had meanwhile organized the Biwabik Mountain Iron Company—with not a cent in the treasury.[14]

One of the Merritts later gave a vivid description of the new area.[15] Imagine, he said, a great tract in which deep basinlike lakes and ponds had suddenly found their water displaced by equal quantities of soft ore; the basins then being covered over with glacial deposits to a depth of from one to forty feet, on which dense pine forests had sprung up. The Missabe range, about 120 miles in length, is a watershed separating the streams which run north to Hudson's Bay or east to the St. Lawrence from those which flow south to the Caribbean. Hence the Indian name, "Grandmother of Them All." It was on the southern slope—precisely as the elder Merritt had said—that the ore-bodies occurred. Lon Merritt has related how in 1891 the family cut a road nearly thirty miles through the woods to the basin later famous as the Mountain Iron Mine. They carried a diamond drill because all miners knew that drills were needed to reach iron ore! Their first explorations were con-

[11]Walter Van Brunt, *Duluth and St. Louis County*, I, 398.

[12]De Kruif describes the lobbying and quotes Lon Merritt as making the remarkable statement that he got the law passed "so the land could be taken up by comparatively poor people, and not be bought up at $5 or $10 an acre by some rich syndicate." *Op. cit.*, 123, 124. By this he means he got it passed so that the widespread Merritt family could take it up for less than $1 an acre!

[13]Folsom, *Minnesota*, IV, 18, 19.

[14]De Kruif, *Seven Iron Men*, 126, 127.

[15]*Merritt vs. Rockefeller, Transcript of Record; cf. Federal Reporter*, LXXVI, 909 ff.

ducted on the rim of the basin, where they found plenty of taconite. But they reasoned that the heart of the basin would contain the richest ore deposits, and, leading a German miner to the center, they ordered, "Sink a shaft here." It did not occur to them that ore could be found without considerable digging. "Yet," said Lon, "if we had gotten mad and kicked the ground right where we stood we would have thrown out 64 per cent ore, if we had kicked it hard enough to kick off the pine needles." The pig-headed German refused to dig in the center, and they compromised by going half-way up the slope, where they struck ore at twelve or fourteen feet. Taking a bushel of this ore into Duluth to be tested, they found that they had tapped a fortune.[16]

But the hundreds of millions of tons of ore in the Missabe range were commercially worthless until a railroad could be built to carry them to market. The Merritts fruitlessly tried to persuade either the St. Paul & Duluth, or the Lake Superior & Missabe (which soon became a branch of the Northern Pacific), to extend its tracks to the district. But the roads "did not seem to realize the value of the range," said Alf later.[17] Then they organized their own company. By the fall of 1892 it had built forty-five miles of rough track to connect with the Duluth, Missabe & Northern, which had a terminal at Superior. Next year the road was extended deeper into the Missabe, and more than 600,000 tons were shipped over it. Already, in 1892, Henry Oliver of Pittsburgh had leased the Missabe Mountain Mine from the Merritt boys for $75,000 in cash and a royalty of 65 cents a ton, guaranteeing to take at least 400,000 tons a year from it. Within ten years more than 40,000,000 long tons of ore were shipped out over that line, and Minnesota had become the largest ore producer in the Union.[18]

But before this result was achieved, the Merritts had undergone some extraordinary vicissitudes, with which Rockefeller and Gates were closely connected.

[16]*Transcript of Record.*

[17]*Stanley Committee Hearings, Investigation of United States Steel,* 1845, 1846. Hereafter cited as *Stanley Committee Hearings.*

[18]H. R. Mussey, *Combination in the Mining Industry,* covers this development.

II

By lease, purchase, and other means the Merritts rapidly obtained equities in a large number of mining properties along the range. In particular, they owned about 40 per cent of the stock in six mining corporations, the beds of which were estimated to contain from 25,000,000 to 50,000,000 tons of ore.[19] They later declared that in the summer of 1893 they held control of all these companies. They also had an equity in a land company and in the Duluth, Missabe & Northern, which by that time comprised sixty-six miles of poorly built, dirt-roadbed track connecting the Missabe with Lake Superior. The line had cost $660,000, but no less than $1,200,000 in first mortgage gold bonds and $1,200,000 par value of stock had been issued against it! Of these securities the Merritts held one fifth and other investors four fifths.

But to acquire their equities in these various properties, the Merritts had run deeply into debt. At the end of 1892 they owed fully $2,000,000, and probably much more.[20] They expected to extend the railroad twenty-nine miles to Duluth, and build ore docks there. Paul De Kruif writes that Lon, "fierce-eyed, supremely confident, bull-necked, and looking like a dressed-up blacksmith," was ordering hundreds of ore cars and planning to lay a network of rails over the whole Missabe district and on northward, even to Winnipeg. He was anxious for all his family and friends to get shares of the properties, and assisted them recklessly. "When I found out what I was worth," he said, "I endorsed paper, loaned money from our bank."[21]

They were headed for trouble. All the omens, as 1893 opened, pointed to hard times ahead. But the brothers had an indomitable faith in the mines and railroad which they partly owned. Even if a panic came, they believed that the depression would be brief.

---

[19]Gates in *The Truth About Mr. Rockefeller and the Merritts* says five mining companies. The Merritts in their legal briefs in *Merritt vs. Rockefeller* enumerate the six: the Mountain Iron Company, Missabe Mountain Iron Company, Biwabik Mountain Iron Company, Great Northern Mining Company, Great Western Mining Company, and Shaw Mining Company. There were also two other corporations, the Missabe & Northern Townsite Company, and the Duluth, Missabe & Northern Railroad Company.

[20]Gates, *The Truth About Mr. Rockefeller*, 3–6; *Iron Age*, 1892–93.

[21]*Seven Iron Men*, 173, 174.

Their partners in the railroad, chiefly Minnesota contractors and bankers, sternly opposed the Duluth extension and the ore docks. After all, was the line not usable as it stood? But the Merritts, showing what De Kruif calls "maniacal eagerness," broke with these partners and went ahead. A very large sum of money was required. While the brothers fondly estimated that $1,600,000 would finance the new construction, the event proved that more than twice that much was needed. To get rid of various obstructive associates, the Merritts bought their stocks for $665,000, paying wholly with time-notes. This price, in view of the fact that the whole road cost only $660,000, and that bonds for $1,200,000 were outstanding, was preposterous. All the stocks owned by the Merritts were then put in the names of trusted friends in order to keep the brothers' creditors from seizing them. These operations aroused in certain Duluth circles a resentment that even yet is not forgotten.[22]

Having thus gained full if precarious control of the railroad, the Merritts went ahead with plans for financing the extension. They had talked over the problem of ore transportation on the lakes with a young New York financier, Charles H. Wetmore, who was associated with the American Steel Barge Company in which Colby and Hoyt were so heavily interested. This barge company built and operated the "whaleback" type of ship then regarded as hopeful, but now long since abandoned. They consulted with Wetmore again. Why should he not try to interest Rockefeller in the Missabe field and the railroad?—for every one knew that Colby and Hoyt were close to Rockefeller. Young Wetmore himself enjoyed no direct connection with the head of the Standard. He never in his life had more than three or four interviews with Rockefeller, for he was simply an independent promoter of uncertain judgment and scanty financial resources. But through Messrs. Colby and Hoyt he could easily gain access to Gates. The Merritts convinced him of the enormous wealth in their holdings, and he formed a close alliance with them. They endorsed each other's notes; when the brothers

[22]Conversation with Mr. George Welwood Murray, who spent much time in Duluth; and with Mr. Herbert L. Satterlee, who represented Wetmore in the purchase of mining properties. Mr. Satterlee was once seated with Lon Merritt in the Duluth, Missabe & Northern railroad offices. A brisk young man with a legal paper entered. "Have you seen Mr. Leonidas Merritt about?" he asked. "Just went down toward the roundhouse there," responded Lon. And as the server went out one door, he disappeared through another!

came to New York they all lunched together at Delmonico's; they united their collateral to obtain loans; and eventually the Merritts used Wetmore's office in Wall Street. Wetmore bought shares for himself and his friends in mines along the Missabe, the Merritts helping him find choice locations. And he undertook to sell $1,600,-000 worth of bonds for the Duluth, Missabe & Northern.

In this undertaking he quickly interested Gates. The former Minneapolis clergyman visited Duluth in the spring of 1893, and went to the Missabe in the private car fitted up by Lon and Alfred. On his recommendation, Rockefeller took $400,000 of the bonds. But Wetmore found the task of selling the other three fourths of the issue extremely difficult, disposing of them slowly and at heavy reductions.[23] Few wanted the securities of a small, distant ore-carrying railroad, running to still undeveloped mines in an unknown district.

And at this difficult moment for the Merritts the panic of 1893 fell upon the country. The iron industry was quickly prostrated. Blast furnaces and rolling mills closed down. Stocks of the five mining companies held by the Merritts, traded only in Duluth, fell to a fraction of their former value. By July, writes Gates,[24] "the Merritts could not have sold their stocks in the open market . . . for more than one half their debts," and other evidence confirms this. Indeed, they never denied that they were really insolvent.

Their position, in fact, was soon desperate. They were head over heels in debt; they had given a wildly exorbitant price to get control of a sixty-six mile railroad; they were concealing their ownership of various properties to baffle their creditors. They had let contracts for railroad extension and docks, and had no funds for payment. Wetmore was compelled to borrow money in driblets from the banks, putting up his unsold bonds, at a heavy discount, for collateral. Rockefeller had flatly refused to join the Colby-Hoyt syndicate and Wetmore in buying Missabe lands. In fact, Gates thrice between January 18 and March 8, 1893, sent Wetmore or the Colbys a formal statement that Rockefeller would neither invest in nor loan money on Missabe mines.[25] What were the brothers to do? Whither could they turn? As the spring came on, they were

[23]Folwell, *Minnesota*, IV, 29; Flynn, *God's Gold*, 315.
[24]Gates, *The Truth About Mr. Rockefeller*, 3.
[25]Gates, *The Truth About Mr. Rockefeller*, 7.

in danger of losing the collateral they had pledged—of losing everything.[26]

Only a rapid alliance with powerful financial interests could save them. In this emergency Wetmore and the Merritts evolved a grandiose plan, which was unfolded to Gates by Joseph L. Colby on March 16, 1893. A great corporation was to be formed. It was to take in the Minnesota Iron Company, founded about ten years earlier by Charlemagne Tower and others to exploit the Vermilion range;[27] the Colby-Hoyt interests on the Gogebic range, in which Rockefeller had a share; and the Wetmore-Merritt interests on the Missabe range, with their undeveloped mines and unfinished railroad. Discussion of the scheme lasted for almost two months. Estimates were drawn up, and conferences held. But irreconcilable differences developed. Then the Merritts evolved still anothr plan, this time for uniting the Wetmore-Merritt interests on the Missabe with all but one of the Colby-Hoyt interests on the Gogebic. To this the Colbys refused their assent.[28] The Merritts stood facing an impasse. Gates has vividly described their predicament:

The failure of the second attempt to consolidate left the Merritt-Wetmore syndicate in despair. It was impossible to get money for the railroad, for the mines or for themselves, anywhere, at any price. May and June went by, with conditions worse every hour. The Merritts in Duluth had let their contracts for the big dock and for the extensions of the railroad; the contractors were at work with hundreds of men; the railroad debt was piling up at the rate of $10,000 per day; the mines were idle; and no money was forthcoming from the East. The financial arrangements planned in the spring had completely broken down. The railroad was trembling on the brink of a receivership. Interest on the bonds was not paid. Suits were actually begun. There were labor riots on the Missabe range. Contractors were knocked down on the Merritt Railroad by their enraged men. Knives were drawn. Men actually entered the railroad offices in Duluth and demanded cash on their pay checks at the end of drawn revolvers. The personal affairs of the Merritts themselves were in no better shape. Some of their creditors were jumping on them and threatening to sell their collateral.

"Must have some money at once to save the Merritt boys' collateral, which means control of best properties," so Leonidas Merritt wires me in

---

[26]Folwell, *Minnesota*, IV, 29.   [27]*Idem*, 11.

[28]The consolidation agreement progressed so far that a contract was actually signed by Lon Merritt and Wetmore; *Transcript of Record*, 577.

July. The complete financial collapse of the Merritt-Wetmore syndicate, of the Merritts personally, and of the Duluth, Missabe & Northern Railroad is now a mere question of days.

But Rockefeller owned $400,000 of the bonds sold to finance the railroad extension. Having invested so much, he and Gates reluctantly concluded that he might well go further in trying to save the line. Wetmore and Leonidas Merritt came to Gates early in July with a series of proposals which meant the transfer to Rockefeller's broad shoulders of the load now crushing them. Their ideas were discussed, amended, and finally agreed to in a series of contracts closed during July and August. For convenience they were shortly bound together in one contract dated August 28.[29]

These contracts resulted in the formation of the Lake Superior Consolidated Iron Mines Company—a holding company chartered July 21, 1893, under New Jersey laws. The Merritts turned over to it the equity they held in the five mining companies and the railroad and ore-docks, while Rockefeller transferred to it all his own iron holdings; that is, his stocks and other securities in the Aurora Iron Mining Company, the Penokee & Gogebic Consolidated Mines, the Spanish-American Iron Company, the West Superior Iron & Steel Company, and two Missabe mines which he had recently bought from the Merritts. He further advanced $500,000 to meet the immediate needs of the railroad—and later added $1,500,000 more. He also lent Merritt and Wetmore, in partnership, considerable sums in cash, while he advanced the Merritts personally $150,000 to enable them to hold on to their collateral. He was bailing them out of a hopeless situation. A Duluth man, A. D. Thomson, who had interests in several Merritt companies, was in New York this summer. He later testified that he met Lon Merritt at the Metropole Hotel; and Lon said "plain, clear, decisive, that he and C. W. Wetmore were trying to get John D. Rockefeller in by degrees into this thing, five thousand dollars today, ten tomorrow, as much as they could every day, and lead him along by degrees until some day he would wake up and find he was in so deep that he would have to go in and save the corporation and every one connected with it."

To assist the Consolidated Iron Company, Rockefeller agreed to

[29]See *Analysis of Contracts* printed in *Alfred Merritt vs. John D. Rockefeller et al.*, U. S. Circuit Court, District of Minnesota.

buy at market rates all the iron it could ship that fall from its principal Missabe property, the Mountain Iron Mine. For his share in the company, he took first-mortgage 6 per cent bonds of $4,299,000 par value.[30] This gave him a paper profit, over the value of the mining securities he had put in, of perhaps $1,250,000; but the bonds were actually not salable at any price whatever.[31] The Merritts took stock, Alf alone receiving 29,676 shares in the Consolidated, worth at par almost $3,000,000; and they thus controlled its operations to suit themselves.[32]

Being inexperienced, ill-advised, and greedy, the Merritts used their control of the Consolidated Company to issue excessive amounts of stock. They first estimated the cash value of all its mines at $7,000,000. Then, after mutual adjustments and the addition of a new mining property believed to be worth $400,000, they decided in secret family conclave that the value was $10,525,000! To be safe, they immediately doubled this, making the whole $21,050,000. Gates suggested that the railroad shares be added, and at $200 a share, "so as to come in on a reasonably just parity."[33] This came to about $5,000,000, making the total of Consolidated stock, at par, $26,-050,000. According to Gates, the Merritt brothers received about $10,000,000 of this. That is, they had exchanged about $2,000,000 worth of mining and railroad stocks—bought largely with other people's money—for five times as much in the highly watered stock of the new company. They and they alone were responsible for watering it. They hoped to sell great quantities of it at par, $10 a share. This was large in comparison with the money thus far invested, though eventually it proved small in comparison with the actual value of the Missabe mines.

When the vital contract was accepted by Rockefeller on July 12, Lon Merritt was overjoyed. Gates, watching Rockefeller sign, telephoned the good news to Wetmore's office. Lon Merritt immediately begged permission to come over and shake Rockefeller's hand. He did so, and the two men, with Gates looking on, chatted pleasantly for several minutes. They talked of the Minnesota climate, and Merritt began to extol the Missabe range. Rockefeller listened

[30]*Transcript of Record*, 177; 441.
[31]Gates, *The Truth About Mr. Rockefeller*, 10; cf. *Iron Age*, Sept. 7, 1893.
[32]*Transcript of Record*, 362.
[33]Gates, *The Truth About Mr. Rockefeller*, 10.

politely for a moment, and then terminated the call. They never met again. Gates comments:[34]

The contract creating the Lake Superior Consolidated Iron Mines in the midst of the panic saved and finished the railroad, opened the mines, and carried the Merritts successfully through the panic without the loss of one dollar or one share of stock. The Merritts were jubilant. "We have passed the danger point." "The days are past when we rate ourselves as paupers." "Perfect confidence is restored." "We are taking care of everything without trouble, and this without any collateral." So ran their letters and telegrams for weeks and months after.

This seems to be a correct statement. Indeed, Merritt on August 10 wrote a St. Paul friend that he had been employed every hour for three months in trying to bring the consolidation to a successful end; that the bad financial situation had steadily blocked his efforts; that his arrangements had failed again and again; but that at last a connection with "able people" was enabling him "to get such advances as will relieve the situation for all time."[35] Rockefeller had shown characteristic caution in taking bonds instead of stock. He acted precisely as Andrew Carnegie did when, selling his steel interests to the United States Steel Corporation, he also chose bonds and not stock. The bonds were a first mortgage upon all properties of the Consolidated. Actually the value hidden in the Missabe mines was so huge that, as time proved, Rockefeller would have been wise to accept even the heavily watered stock that the Merritts issued.

The railroad was at once pushed through to completion.[36] The Merritts gathered up the widely scattered mining stocks which their creditors held as security, and exchanged them for the new Consolidated stock. Minority holders in the mines were admitted to the new Consolidated Company on the same terms as the Merritts themselves. This was not accomplished without a struggle, for the Merritts counted enemies among these holders, and were reluctant to let them in on the ground floor. But Gates, supported by Rockefeller and George Welwood Murray, Rockefeller's counsel, insisted. Everybody was treated alike.[37]

From this point all should have gone as merry as a wedding bell.

[34]*Idem*, 11.   [35]*Idem*, 11, 12.
[36]Folwell, *Minnesota*, IV, 29.
[37]Gates, *The Truth About Mr. Rockefeller*, 12, 13.

Why was it that the Merritts soon fell into fresh difficulties, and began fiercely assailing Rockefeller—whom Lon had just greeted as a saviour?

III

The Merritts had hoped to sell off the Consolidated stock rapidly enough to lighten their load of debt and regain solvency. But on the heels of the panic a heavy depression gripped the nation. With the greatest difficulty Cleveland forced Congress to repeal the Sherman Silver-Purchase Act, but even this brought no relief. The gold reserve in the Treasury sank till as the year ended a bond issue to replenish it was inescapable. Banks continued to shut their doors, railroads to go bankrupt, factories to shut down. Confidence in the industrial future of the country vanished. Hard-pressed for money, men refused to invest in even the most attractive enterprises. Far from selling large quantities of stock at $10 a share, the Merritts found it difficult to dispose of even small amounts at $8 or $8.50.[38]

The fact was that most investors did not regard the Missabe mines as a safe enterprise. Iron-ore prices, high in 1890–92, had dropped to levels which offered little chance for profit. The huge extent of the resources opened during the previous decade in the Menominee, Vermilion, Gogebic, and Missabe fields threatened a glutted market even when the iron industry of the nation recovered. While the Merritts fondly believed they held nearly all the best mines of the Missabe, in reality rich competitive pits were owned there by others. In particular, the Minnesota Iron Company had important holdings, and in 1893 its Duluth & Iron Range Railroad had built a fifteen-mile spur straight through the eastern half of the range. Finally, many iron manufacturers doubted whether it was practicable to use the loose Missabe ores, and it was certain that several years would have to be devoted to experimentation and the redesigning of furnaces before any large-scale employment was possible.

Some of these considerations gave Rockefeller, Gates, and the

---

[38]*Comparative Analysis of Pleadings, Alfred Merritt vs. John D. Rockefeller,* p. 24. Both Lon and Alf Merritt later testified before the Stanley Committee that Rockefeller deliberately depressed the price of the stock. Congressman Gardiner of Massachusetts ridiculed this, pointing out that Rockefeller could not control the market. *Transcript of Record,* p. 1907. Nearly all stocks in 1893–94 descended to preposterously low levels.

Merritts great anxiety. Prices of Bessemer pig-iron dropped from $24.50 a ton in January, 1889, to $11 in December, 1893—and iron-ore prices fell with them.[39] When 1893 opened, 253 furnaces were in blast in the United States; when it closed, only 137. The trade then seemed in the depths of depression, yet within six months it had fallen to a still lower abyss. No one knew when it would recover, and some doubted if it would ever reach predepression levels. A historian of the mining industry characterizes this period as one of "ruinous prices, contracted credit, limited consumption, sharp competition, ineffectual attempts at combination to hold up prices, failure of the weak companies, and growth of the strong ones. . . ."[40] Mining companies without funds faced death. The low price of ore, and the high cost of steam-shovels and other equipment, necessitated large-scale operation and heavy investments. Year by year great ore bodies were discovered in new corners of the Missabe range. The Merritts, controlling the Consolidated, had little capital; some of their competitors had much, and used money as well as brains, enterprise, and science more liberally than they could.

Even had times been good the Missabe ores would have come into use slowly. To be sure, they could be mined cheaply. Early in 1893 it was estimated that they could be laid down in Cleveland at $3 a ton, far less than the price of Gogebic or Vermilion shipments.[41] But they differed completely from the hard ores, which were quarried like rocks and went into the furnaces looking like stones and rubble. The soft and powdery Missabe product varied in consistency from a loose clayey mass when wet to a fine dust when dry. When this loose, powdery ore was charged in furnaces designed for rocklike mixtures, the results were unfortunate. Sometimes the ore packed in heavy masses, and then suddenly exploded, wrecking the furnaces. Sometimes the terrific force of the blast blew it out of the top in a fine hot dust, settling on the surrounding buildings or countryside, and provoking lawsuits. A new type of furnace had to be designed, and existing furnaces were dismantled and remodelled to conform to it.[42] Charles M. Schwab thought the ores

[39]*Report, American Iron and Steel Association,* 1903, pp. 85 ff.
[40]Mussey, *Mining Industry,* 112.   [41]*Idem,* 113.
[42]Mussey, *Mining Industry,* 113; Gates, *The Truth About Mr. Rockefeller,* 4. Charles M. Schwab, in talking with the author, expatiated upon the magnitude of these difficulties, June 15, 1939.

excessively "lean," containing a low percentage of iron. For some years experts made hostile reports, and it was upon such expert advice that the Northern Pacific and the St. Paul & Duluth refused to build to the fields. The Merritts acquired and always evinced a strong hatred of scientific men.

"Speaking with substantial accuracy," writes Gates, "no mining company made $1 out of mining Missabe ores for the first ten years after their discovery."

Having failed to sell stock in adequate quantities, the Merritts naturally turned to Rockefeller. Their obligations were maturing, and creditors pressed them hard. As the clouds lowered blackly, Andrus Merritt on September 30, 1893, asked Rockefeller for a loan of $100,000—this request having no relation whatever to the contracts. On October 2, Gates, the alert watchdog of Rockefeller's funds, sent back a decided refusal. He pointed out that Rockefeller had already invested between $1,500,000 and $2,000,000 in the Merritts' enterprises, and that the strain upon him from other quarters was very great:[43]

Other enterprises with which he has been long associated, and other men who have long been his friends, have been constantly coming to him during these hard times for assistance, and as the Senate continues inactive [*i.e.,* refuses to pass the silver-purchase repeal] they are coming to him in larger numbers and with more urgency than ever before. I have today on my desk urgent imperative appeals to save old friends from ruin amounting to many hundreds of thousands of dollars. I have incurred the enmity of important business enterprises with which Mr. Rockefeller is connected because I have had to decline to assist them within the last few days. Each of them supposes it would not make any great difference to Mr. Rockefeller were he to help him out, forgetful that his request is one of many which make an aggregate absolutely impossible in these times for any man or combination of men to carry.

At that date, as Rockefeller's books later showed, he had advanced almost $6,000,000 in cash to fifty-eight different men and companies, all desperate and all unable to obtain money at the banks. To do this he had himself borrowed between $3,000,000 and $4,000,000, and had overdrawn his bank account more than $30,000.[44]

[43]Gates, *The Truth About Mr. Rockefeller,* 14.

[44]The table of daily rates for money compiled by Rogers Gould of the New York Stock Exchange shows that during a great part of the terrible summer of 1893 the interest rate on loans in New York averaged ⅛ per cent a day, or at the rate of slightly more than 50 per cent a year!

When 1894 opened, the position of the Merritts had become intolerable. They had not raised enough money in the first place. Violent seas had washed away their Duluth docks, and a heavy iron structure had to be built on a foundation of cement-filled iron cylinders, sixty feet deep, sunk in the sand. In January they astonished Gates, who was ignorant of the extent of their liabilities, by proposing to sell 90,000 shares of Consolidated stock to Rockefeller at $10 a share, or $900,000. The stock was paying no dividends and offered no early prospect of any. As the Merritts later admitted, they could not have gotten above $8 a share in the open market. Rockefeller accepted the offer, making the purchase in two blocks, February 1 and February 21, 1894.[45] He paid for the stock, but granted the Merritts an option to recover 55,000 shares within one year at the same price, with 6 per cent interest. According to Gates, his motive in giving this option was purely benevolent—and indeed, he could have had no other. He wished to allow the Merritts a full year, or more if they needed it, to work their way to solid ground. Late in 1893 rumors that Rockefeller had allied himself with the Merritts for selfish ends, set afoot by Minnesotans whom the Merritts had antagonized, caused Wetmore to send Rockefeller an indignant denial, to which Lon Merritt added a postscript:[46]

When in December last I concluded an arrangement with the Merritts and their associates to assist them in the extension of the Duluth, Missabe, & Northern Railway Company, my object was simply to secure the transportation of the Missabe ores for the American Steel Barge Company.

The bitter attacks made by the Minnesota Iron Company last January and February upon the contracts which I had concluded, made it necessary, in order to protect all interests, that an investment should be made in the stock of the Railway Company, and that further advances for this purpose should be made to the Merritts. This contest for the control of the Railway threw me into the most intimate association with the Merritts; and my investigations impressed me with the great value of the interests which they controlled, and the almost unlimited opportunities for profit

[45]*Transcript of Record,* 360–362, 418, 419.
[46]In the papers of George Welwood Murray. Some thought Wetmore a slippery fellow; see Anna Youngman on his operations, *Journal of Political Economy,* XV, 201 (April, 1907). She shows that he converted $90,000 of the Merritts' bonds to his own use, and that as his associates the Merritts "elected to waive the tort committed." But Mr. Satterlee assures the author that he was quite honest.

which lay open to the Barge Company if it maintained close relations with the Missabe Railway and the mines tributary to it.

The idea of a great combination of mining interests in the Missabe and elsewhere also suggested itself to me. Upon my return from the West I sought earnestly to interest you further than as a mere subscriber to the Railway Bonds. I need not rehearse the events of last summer. As they progressed I saw the possibility of carrying out my ideas of a great combination. I had won the confidence of the Merritts for myself and for you. I esteemed you most highly in every relation of business and private life. I had been associated with you in many enterprises, to which I knew of my own knowledge how generous your support had been; and I knew also of your kindly assistance to friends in their business troubles. I felt that the best service I could render to the Merritts was to bring them into close association with you; and this I sought earnestly and successfully to accomplish.

Every step that has been taken, resulting in the great combination of mining and railway interests now concluded, with the single exception, so far as I can remember, of the purchase of the railway stock by the Consolidated Company, which I believe was first suggested by Mr. Gates, was planned and proposed by me and urged upon you.

With the exception stated I do not recall any contract leading to the consolidation, whose essential terms were not first suggested by myself, and in every case you fulfilled, without question, every obligation which was imposed upon you by these contracts.

The financial crisis of last summer made it necessary to make heavier demands upon you than any of us anticipated. Had I foreseen the extent and severity of that crisis, I certainly should not have attempted to effect the consolidation of mining interests which has been accomplished.

All these extraordinary and unforeseen demands upon your time and resources have been met by you in my opinion most generously. This is the simple truth and I am glad to say it to you. . . .

Yours very truly,
C. W. Wetmore.

I have carefully read the above statement of facts signed by Mr. Wetmore and very cheerfully certify to their accuracy.

Leonidas Merritt.

IV

The option which Rockefeller had given the Merritts for repurchasing their stock expired in a year; but they needed only to ask for an extension to receive it. Indeed, Rockefeller carried one brother, Lewis J. Merritt, with his son Hulett, for more than seven years on a freely given renewal of options. They finally sold their stock to the United States Steel and were millionaires. Had Lon and Alf Merritt pursued the same course, Gates avers, they would have received the same treatment; and they could have delivered their 55,000 shares to the United States Steel in 1901 for $9,190,000 cash.[47] But they failed to redeem the stock, or to ask for an extension. Instead, they turned to open warfare with Rockefeller.

Why? Gates's explanation is that they had fallen under the influence of a Duluth lawyer of uncertain antecedents, Anak A. Harris. He was a veritable Sampson Brass; but whereas Sampson Brass had a sister named Sally, Harris had a son called Henry. The elder Harris was now beginning practice for the fourth time in the fourth State. He was looking hard for clients—and money; and the Merritts fell in his path. First he represented them in an unpleasant suit they brought against their old companies for compensation, claiming extravagant sums for services. Then, on July 10, 1894, the elder Harris turned up at 26 Broadway and asked to see Rockefeller. Gates's version of the call is interesting.[48]

"Mr. Rockefeller was not meeting strangers. I declined to see Harris. Two members of the office staff were delegated to meet him. He said that he had once transacted some business for a company with which he believed Mr. Rockefeller to be connected, that he was now counsel for several of Mr. Rockefeller's acquaintances, and that they could vouch for him. He said he did not want trouble with Mr. Rockefeller, that he had great influence with the Merritts, and that he could dissuade the Merritts from bringing suits against Mr. Rockefeller personally. If Mr. Rockefeller would buy this Consolidated stock which he had with him in considerable quantity, at a price considerably above the market, he would have no personal difficulties with the Merritts. Harris came in on three successive days. His words were recorded. We refused to pay the extra price for his stock, and Harris went away in a huff."

Following this rebuff, Harris on behalf of Alfred Merritt sued Rockefeller for $1,226,400. He alleged that the Merritts had purchased the Cuban and Gogebic mining stock from Rockefeller in the consolidation agreement of the previous year under fraudulent misrepresentations, first by Rockefeller personally and then by Gates

[47]Gates, *The Truth About Mr. Rockefeller*, 15.
[48]*Idem*, 16, 17.

as his agent.[49] Alf Merritt arrived at his figure by asserting that his share of the stocks in the Missabe companies turned over to the Consolidated was worth $1,533,000, and that the Consolidated stock he received in exchange was worth only $306,600—leaving a difference of $1,226,400. This was a test suit. Every one understood that if Alf recovered one and a quarter millions, the other Merritts would obtain huge sums. Indeed, according to Harris's calculation, the Merritts had been damaged, by giving about $2,000,000 in mortgage bonds to Rockefeller for the mining properties which he placed in the Consolidated, to the tune of some $10,000,000!

As a matter of fact, the mines which Rockefeller had turned over to the Consolidated Company in 1893 were valuable properties, which seem to have been worth all that he said they were. Engineers and other experts later testified to this effect.[50] The Cuban mines were subsequently sold to the Pennsylvania Steel Company; by 1911 more than 6,000,000 tons of ore had been shipped from them, and they had proved very profitable. The Gogebic mines consistently yielded high-grade ore in large quantities. Both the Aurora Mine and Tilden Mine on that range long remained among the richest in Wisconsin, producing millions of tons at profitable rates. The Tilden, in reality a group of mines, later passed into the possession of the United States Steel and was rated among the best of its Gogebic assets. To be sure, in the fearful depression all mining properties depreciated in value, and good ore holdings, like good railroads and good factories, were forced into temporary receiverships.[51] About January 1, 1894, Rockefeller learned that the Penokee & Gogebic Company (operating the Tilden Mine) was embarrassed. Before this was generally known, or had affected the price of stock in the Consolidated, he offered (January 8) to repurchase from the Consolidated all the Penokee & Gogebic, Aurora, Spanish-American, and West Superior Iron & Steel properties for the same price, payable in the same manner, as upon his sale thereof. This offer the

[49]I have used the voluminous testimony, briefs, and comparative analysis of pleadings in this famous case of *Alfred Merritt vs. John D. Rockefeller et al.*, United States Circuit Court, District of Minnesota, made available to me by Mr. George Welwood Murray. *Cf.* Anna Youngman, *ut supra,* for the Merritts' unsuccessful suit against the American Steel Barge Company.

[50]See *Transcript of Record,* 452 ff.; *Federal Reporter,* LXXVI, 909 ff.

[51]*Cf.* Mussey, *Mining Industry,* 114, 115, for the numerous bankruptcies of Missabe mining companies.

Merritts rejected.[52] But shortly thereafter Rockefeller did repurchase all the bonds of the West Superior Iron & Steel which he had sold. In addition, he gave up in round numbers $2,150,000 of his first-mortgage bonds of the Consolidated for cancellation; taking instead stock of the Consolidated at par, though its open market value was then but one tenth or less of its par rating. The bonded debt of the Consolidated was thus reduced to $1,500,000.[53]

"The effect of this transaction," stated Rockefeller's attorneys later,[54] "was that the defendant presented to the Consolidated Mines something more than $1,700,000—a sum in excess of the face value of all the bonds received by him from it for his Penokee & Gogebic and Spanish-American properties." And Gates writes:[55] "I am not here to praise Mr. Rockefeller. . . . I cannot resist saying, however, that if a more honorable, prompt, and spontaneous act, wholly free from legal obligation, is recorded in the history of American finance, than this of Mr. Rockefeller's, I have yet to learn of the fact."

It is unpleasant to think ill of the hardy, tenacious Merritts. But it is evident that, travelling in a private car, eating at Delmonico's, dreaming of tens of millions, Lon and Alf had changed from their forest-cruising days. Men like Wetmore and Anak Harris had corrupted their moral fiber. They had plunged recklessly; the panic had caught them hopelessly overextended; they had turned to Rockefeller for rescue; borrowing more and more, they had put up their much-valued stock for help; and even yet they needed money. Anak Harris, when some of the properties Rockefeller had put into the Consolidated became embarrassed, showed them a cheap way out. They would sue the unpopular Rockefeller in a Northwestern area, where public feeling against Wall Street was intense. They would charge him with misrepresenting the properties he had put into the Consolidated. They would get their stock back, and more to boot.

This, or something very near it, would seem to be what happened. It is significant that Paul De Kruif, in writing of the seven

[52]*Transcript of Record*, 384, 502–506; *Comparative Analysis of Pleadings*, 11.
[53]*Comparative Analysis of Pleadings*, 12. These bonds were taken back by the company not at par, but at 90; but the company gave Rockefeller the stock at par. No one could accuse him of a lack of generosity.
[54]*Brief for Plaintiff in Error*, 9.
[55]*The Truth About Mr. Rockefeller*, 18, 19.

iron men, entirely skips the events from the summer of 1894 to the Stanley Committee hearings many years later, thus passing over every vital point of their relations with Rockefeller from the moment they turned against him. The story was apparently too damaging to explore. To be sure, not quite all the fault may have been on one side. The author suspects that Gates, precise, clear-headed, and realistic, never understood the speculative Merritts. He suspects that Gates, always a hard dealer in business and at this time anxious to prove his capacity to Rockefeller, may have acted with more vigor than tact. But the Merritts clearly behaved very badly.

Into the litigation which Harris thus provoked it is unnecessary to go at length. Gates always regarded it as essentially a conspiracy to extort money. So did Rockefeller's attorney, Mr. George Welwood Murray. So did Mr. Francis H. Brownell, later chairman of the American Smelting & Refining Company, who was conversant with the details.[56] Beyond doubt outright mendacity entered into the testimony given by Lon and Alf. In the Duluth courtroom they asserted that Rockefeller had talked with them at length in June, 1893, before they signed the July contract, and made loquacious misstatements about the value of his Cuban and Gogebic properties. Actually Rockefeller had not seen them until mid-July; had chatted for five minutes only; and had said not a word about business.[57] To this both Gates and George D. Rogers, Rockefeller's confidential secretary, explicitly swore.[58] Leonidas and Alfred also testified that on August 17 they had talked with Gates, who rivalled Rockefeller

[56]Mr. Murray to the author, May 23, 1937; Mr. Brownell to the author, Dec. 6, 1939.

[57]Lon Merritt quoted Rockefeller's precise words: "These properties I would like to put in with you, they are prosperous, and if the matter could be arranged, I would be very glad to consolidate the matter with you, and I would be proud to be a partner of yours, that is of yourself and brothers, in such a consolidation." *Transcript of Record*, 228. It is obvious that Rockefeller never talked in this way. Lon went on: "He said the Penokee-Gogebic was a large shipper of ore, the Penokee-Gogebic and Aurora mines were large shippers of ore, and their being in the markets with large amounts of ore that are already known in market, it would be a great advantage to the consolidation, and would help us greatly. He said that the Spanish-American was a great mine situated in the Island of Cuba, and was all ready to mine, they had a railroad built to it, and that the ores could be mined very cheaply, and they could be shipped as far as the Allegheny Mountains, and compete with the best Lake Superior ores." *Transcript of Record*, 228, 229.

[58]*Transcript of Record*, 439.

in misrepresentation. Gates was able to prove that the whole afternoon of the 17th he had spent at the Farmers' Loan & Trust Company, in a committee meeting on Northern Pacific affairs; that he had returned to the office and written a detailed account of the meeting for Rockefeller, who was in Cleveland; and that he had then taken the 4:20 train home. The allegations about misrepresentation were absurd on several counts. For one reason, the Merritts were constantly in the Wetmore office, which was cheek by jowl with the Colby office; they were constantly talking with Messrs. Colby, Hoyt, and Wetmore about the Cuban and Wisconsin mines; and the books of these mines were almost under their eyes—Wetmore being counsel for and stockholder in some or all the companies. For another reason, the assertions they attributed to Rockefeller, though never uttered, would have been true statements. Mr. Murray writes:[59]

In the final sifting of the testimony, Harris dropped all the alleged misrepresentations but three. These were that the companies owning the Wisconsin and Cuban mines were "solvent and prosperous"; that they "owed very little money outside their funded indebtedness"; and that the securities Mr. Rockefeller was to put in were "gilt edged." The statements were not made; had they been made they would have been true.

The trial began in Duluth on June 5, 1895, before Judge Riner of the Federal Circuit Court. The jury was obviously prejudiced in favor of a group of Minnesotans who were suing one of the richest and worst-hated men in the world. Moreover, the Merritts owed sums great and small to a host of Duluth citizens, and the prospect of obtaining millions of Rockefeller's money for circulation in Duluth was attractive to many people.[60] Local feeling, whipped up by the Merritts, had become intense. Mr. Murray, who was supported as counsel by Judge Shaw, of Minneapolis, had prepared strong printed briefs on various points in the case. As it dragged on he learned that two detectives were shadowing him. "It would not have been surprising," he wrote later,[61] "had some irresponsible member of the Merritt clan taken a shot at one or more of our group." In the end, he became so convinced that the Merritts had utterly failed to make out a case that he hoped the judge would dis-

---

[59]Quoted in *The Truth About Mr. Rockefeller*, 23.   [60]*Idem*, 24.
[61]In his brochure on *Milbank, Tweed, Hope, and Webb*, 37.

miss the suit. But in that new city, with its wild-West atmosphere, a jurist had been known to abandon the bench in terror of an aroused public sentiment. The judge told Shaw at his hotel the night before: "I shall be glad to hear Mr. Murray tomorrow morning on his motion for non-suit, but I am going to send the case to the jury."[62]

The jury decided in favor of Alfred Merritt, awarding him $940,000 damages. On appeal, the case then reached the Circuit Court of Appeals in St. Louis late in January, 1896. Murray argued it at length. This was the year of the McKinley-Bryan contest, and the court withheld its decision until the Monday following Election Day. The verdict was unanimously reversed, Judge Walter H. Sanborn writing the opinion; and a new trial was ordered. The judgment closed (76 Federal 909): "We are convinced that damages so enormous could not have been reasonably expected from, and could not have been the natural or probable consequences of, so relatively small an increase of the mortgage debt of so gigantic a corporation. This view is confirmed by the fact that the reduction of the mortgage debt of this corporation more than $2,000,000 by an exchange of its first-mortgage bonds and accrued interest for its stock at par in January, 1894, did not appreciate or change the market value of this stock by so much as 1 per cent of its par value." The judgment was reversed with costs, and the case was remanded to the lower court, on the ground of the errors in the court ruling relative to the plaintiffs' damages. There were other allegations of error, but on these the court did not pass at all.

Having lost their case, the Merritts began to consider ways and means of settling out of court with Rockefeller. Their precious lawyer, Harris, deserted them and treacherously attempted to sell to the Standard's attorney in Duluth, Joseph B. Cotton, for $25,000, a telegram that would have gravely injured the Merritt case. This telegram, sent by Leonidas Merritt in New York to his secretary in Duluth, and dated July 12, 1893, stated that he had that day talked with Rockefeller. This was the interview he had tried to place in June! Of course Cotton refused to have anything to do with the offer. Harris at about the same time made overtures to a travelling auditor of Rockefeller's looking toward a settlement. Rockefeller

---

[62]*Idem*, 36.

refused to treat with him on any terms whatever. The Merritts then turned to another attorney, J. L. Washburne of Duluth, and opened negotiations through him. Within a short time the suit was compromised out of court, Rockefeller paying $525,000, and the whole Merritt clan signing a complete retraction of the charges against him.[63]

Why the payment of $525,000 if Rockefeller felt confident of winning the suit? His representatives have given several reasons. It put an immediate end to vexatious litigation which, in view of the prejudice of juries against rich men, and the fact that the retrial would be held in Duluth, might still have offered difficulties.[64] All of the large and influential Merritt clan were nursing claims, to be presented on the basis of any verdict that any one might get; and now, to the number of twenty-three, they signed explicit disclaimers. Again, the Merritts owed large sums to numerous creditors. These creditors had turned over to the Merritts mining property which they, often without payment, had put into the Consolidated Company; and Rockefeller had by now purchased enough stock to gain control of the Consolidated. With his mines and railroads, Rockefeller was under the necessity of carrying on a huge business in Minnesota among these creditors, and needed their good will; indeed, he needed the good will and brains of some of the Merritts

[63]J. L. Washburne, in negotiating this settlement with Gates and Murray as the Merritts' representatives, came to New York; and he constantly showed them telegrams from Minnesota, at every stage of the negotiations, as evidence of his good faith. But according to Mr. Murray, Rockefeller's agents later learned that all the while Washburne had Andrus Merritt, the most vindictive of the brothers, in Brooklyn, and consulted with him every night, the two then concocting the telegram! Eventually the sum of $500,000 was agreed upon. But the Merritts then trotted in another of the clan, who insisted on $25,000 more for himself. "If he hadn't got it he would have kicked over the traces and spoiled everything." George Welwood Murray to the author, May 23, 1938.

[64]Mr. Murray instances the case of McKinley vs. Lake Superior Consolidated Iron Mines as an example of the responsiveness of Duluth courts to local sentiment. "In the McKinley case the presiding judge, after sitting two or three days while we were seeking a jury, quit the bench saying that he had an appointment in Winona, and had arranged with the Senior Circuit Judge that Judge Riner of Wyoming would arrive the next morning. We all thought (I think both sides) that he was scared, the local feeling was so intense. In that case the jury disagreed. The McKinleys were heavily in debt, largely to the banks in Duluth. During every day of the trial, presidents of all the banks took a front seat directly opposite the jury." *Milbank, Tweed, Hope, and Webb,* 35, 36.

themselves—which he ultimately secured. It seemed wise to give the family money with which to pay their obligations. Finally, Rockefeller received a complete retraction, and a practical admission of wrongdoing, with the right to publish it. It read as follows:

Certain matters of difference have existed between the undersigned and Mr. John D. Rockefeller, and a certain litigation has been pending between the undersigned Alfred Merritt and Mr. Rockefeller, in which litigation it was claimed that certain misrepresentations were made by Mr. Rockefeller and those acting for him concerning certain properties sold by him to Lake Superior Consolidated Iron Mines. It is hereby declared that from recent independent investigations made by us or under our direction we have become satisfied that no misrepresentation was made or fraud committed by Mr. Rockefeller or by his agents and attorneys for him, upon the sale by him of any property to us or any of us, or to Lake Superior Consolidated Iron Mines, or upon the purchase by him from one or more of us of any stocks or interests in any mining or railway company or companies, or upon the pledge by us or either of us to him of stocks and securities belonging to one or more of us; and we hereby withdraw all such charges and claims and exonerate Mr. Rockefeller and his attorneys therefrom.

The Merritts also agreed that they "do and will continue to extend their hearty good will" to Rockefeller and his companies.

It will be seen that Rockefeller and Gates insisted not merely upon a withdrawal of the charge of fraud, but upon a reasoned and detailed explanation of why the Merritts withdrew it. The signers declared that they had made independent investigations, and that these had convinced them that no misrepresentation had ever been offered or fraudulent act committed. "Personally," George Welwood Murray stated years afterward,[65] "I was extremely glad that the settlement was made. It permitted us to go ahead with free minds in the development of the property."

Although the case was now absolutely closed, it had reverberations which we shall examine later. It may be noted here that within eight months, Alf Merritt, on behalf of himself and some brothers, brought suit against Anak A. Harris & Son for the recovery of certain mining stocks which they alleged that Harris was fraudulently withholding. The facts brought out in this suit were highly revealing. It was shown that Alf had contracted with Harris about three

[65]Mr. Murray to the author, May 22, 1938.

years earlier to conduct a legal contest against Rockefeller for $10,000 a year. For two reasons—to assure Harris of his money, and to keep the securities out of the hands of the Merritt creditors— Alf Merritt had handed over to the lawyer mining stocks of value. Now the lawyer refused to give them up, and also refused to return certain documents connected with the Rockefeller and other suits unless he were paid $25,000. Why that particular sum? It suggests that he thought this the value of the telegram which proved that Lon Merritt's story of his call on Rockefeller was pure fiction. The testimony in this case exposed various disreputable activities on the part of the two Harrises, and elicited from Mr. Cotton, Rockefeller's Duluth attorney, the full story of Henry E. Harris's effort to sell the telegram to Rockefeller. It was one of the Merritt brothers who called Cotton to the stand to tell this story. The Harrises lost their case, and shortly left Duluth under a cloud of disgrace.

Gates in his history of the case asks a rhetorical question: "Was the whole attack on Mr. Rockefeller a frame-up between the Harrises and the Merritts, and was their conspiracy completely exposed by the conspirators themselves when they fell out?" To this question he evidently thought that the answer was clear—and so did others who knew the full story of the affair.[66]

No one should be misled by the high values which the Missabe property, now in Rockefeller's hands, later attained. Some of the best steel men of the land thought for years that he would lose heavily by his venture.[67] The rise in value did not come until times had entirely changed, and until Rockefeller had put into the property millions of money and eight years of Rockefeller management.

v

Not dissimilar in origin was another suit pushed against Rockefeller—a suit which, arraying his brother Frank against him, awoke

[66]*The Truth About Mr. Rockefeller,* 29, 30; Mr. Murray to the author, May 23, 1938; Francis H. Brownell to the author, Dec. 6, 1939. Mr. Brownell writes: "Lon Merritt was a ruthless, not to say unprincipled, pioneer of a type quite prevalent in the early West. This is shown by (1) his getting a bill through the legislature to enable him to obtain control of the Missabe acreage at the expense of the State of Minnesota and its people; (2) selling stock of his mining company on a basis which today perhaps would land him in the penitentiary; (3) his frequent misrepresentations to his creditors and others."
[67]Charles M. Schwab to the author, June 15, 1939.

sensational echoes. Here too a designing lawyer was concerned in pressing it, and here also Rockefeller won a full legal victory. But it aroused malicious comment and, like the Merritt case, strengthened the wall of distrust and hatred that encircled Rockefeller.

James Corrigan was one of the most picturesque, belligerent, two-fisted citizens that Cleveland ever boasted. He was a powerfully built, big-chested, squint-eyed adventurer, Irish in blood and Episcopalian in religion, who loved action and combat. He cared little for clothes, society, or amusement. "He wanted to do things, and if he had a place to sleep and enough to eat was satisfied." He liked money, but as a symbol of success rather than a means to luxury. For a time he and his brother John were oil refiners, but Rockefeller bought them out, Jim thus acquiring a sizable block of Standard stock. Later he went into steel and lake shipping. His temper was well illustrated by his intolerant attitude toward labor organizers. Once when a strike occurred at the Corrigan, McKinney steel mill in Rochester, Corrigan faced a crowd of angry workmen. He stalked across the yard in front of them, drew a line on the ground with his stick, and shaking his fist, shouted: "I dare you to cross that line!" He later explained: "I had bought all those revolvers and wanted to get some good out of them. I wish I could have winged some of those hunkies!" Cleveland is still full of stories about his bellicosity, humor, and energy.[68]

Early in the eighties Corrigan and Frank Rockefeller had bought the Franklin Iron Mining Company in Wisconsin. Indeed, as businessmen Jim and Frank often "hunted in couples," as one observer put it.[69] They were alike in being breezy, self-assertive, daring men, sometimes reckless in their undertakings. They had gone into debt, and when the panic of 1893 broke they came in succession, first Corrigan and then Frank, to John D. Rockefeller for aid. He loaned them large sums of money in several different instalments, Corrigan putting up 2500 certificates in the Standard Oil Trust as part security. As John T. Flynn says, it was "a perfectly good business transaction."[70] But as the depression lengthened and their iron property became a heavier burden, they found themselves deeply involved. Finally, at their request, Rockefeller in March, 1895, assisted

[68]Conversations with various Clevelanders, April 20–24, 1939.
[69]Mr. Murray to the author, May 23, 1938.
[70]Flynn, God's Gold, 364.

them by paying Corrigan $420,000 for his Standard Oil stock, taking it at $168 a share. This was its highest market value on the day of the sale, and much more than Corrigan could have obtained had he dumped so large a block in Wall Street. Moreover, to get so large a sum on any moderate terms in that severe crisis was a decided favor. But even this accommodation did not save Jim and Frank from disaster. They were shortly compelled to sell outsiders their Franklin Iron Mine Company at a very low valuation.

Having taken these losses—just such losses as multitudes of businessmen had to accept in the depression of 1893–97—Jim and Frank persuaded themselves that the fault did not lie with their own recklessness and carelessness, but with John D. Rockefeller. They asserted that he had paid them too little for the Standard Oil stock; that he had no legal right to buy this stock, for he was a trustee, and a trustee may not legally purchase from a *cestui que trust;* that he concealed the fact that the trust possessed a surplus, and had falsely alleged that it was earning no money; and that by pressing them for payment of their debts, he had compelled them to sacrifice the Franklin company for a fourth its worth. They told a story whose defects and contradictions were later ably analyzed by Rockefeller's attorneys. The brief prepared by Messrs. Murray and Kline shows:[71]

1. That Corrigan owed Rockefeller about $250,000, for which 2500 shares of Standard Oil Trust certificates were pledged as security. This transaction stood by itself.

2. That Corrigan had borrowed $140,000 from Rockefeller, giving a mortgage upon "certain vessel property" on the lakes, and owed interest on this sum.

3. That Corrigan was also liable to Rockefeller as endorser on upwards of $135,000 of Franklin Mine paper, and on upwards of $130,000 more of paper signed by Frank Rockefeller and endorsed by Corrigan. For this total of about $265,000, Corrigan had pledged with Rockefeller about 5000 shares of Franklin Mine stock. This also was a separate transaction.

Rockefeller then made a generous contract with Corrigan, by execution of which several objects important to the latter were accomplished:

1. Corrigan received $420,000 in cash, selling Rockefeller his 2500 shares of Standard Trust certificates for this sum.

2. The amount due from Corrigan under Item 1 above, and the interest due under Item 2, aggregating more than $250,000, were cancelled outright.

[71]Supplemental brief, *Corrigan vs. Rockefeller,* office of Mr. Murray. This is my own summary.

3. Rockefeller loaned Corrigan, on new notes, $80,000 more.

4. Of the $420,000 that Rockefeller paid Corrigan for the trust certificates, the latter at once returned $140,000, which together with the lake vessels mentioned above was retained as collateral security for the old loan of $140,000, the new loan of $80,000, and the $135,000 of Corrigan's own Franklin Mine indebtedness.

5. Rockefeller surrendered to Corrigan the 4500 shares of Franklin Mine stock, and absolutely released him from liability as endorser of Frank Rockefeller's note for $130,000.

If this was not wholly generous, what could be? Rockefeller had released Corrigan from liability on Frank's paper; he had cancelled part of Corrigan's debt; and he had accepted a very small security for the remainder. When Corrigan later demanded that an additional sum be paid for the trust certificates, he did not ask to be reinstated as endorser of Frank Rockefeller's paper. He forgot that!

With the encouragement of a Cleveland attorney, Judge Stevenson Burke,[72] Corrigan—after the lapse of two years and three months— commenced a suit to compel Rockefeller to return the 2500 shares of trust certificates, or to pay $500 a share for them; alleging that when he bought them he knew well that the real value was more than $168, and had lied about it. Of course as the depression ended, Standard Oil shares, like railroad shares, industrial stocks, and most other forms of property, rose in value. Wide fluctuations occurred, first up, then down, but on the whole they advanced. Judge Burke told Corrigan that the more frequently he warned Rockefeller of the rise the better his case would be. Every few weeks a note from Corrigan would reach Rockefeller's desk: "I call your attention to the fact that the price of Standard Oil stock is now so-and-so."[73]

The case was submitted to arbitrators—William A. Lynch of Canton, Ohio, partner of Judge Day, later McKinley's Secretary of State, and William G. Choate and William D. Guthrie of New York. Rockefeller's attorneys easily showed that he was not a trustee for Standard Oil stockholders in the old and strict sense of the term; the nine trustees, of whom he was one, were really directors of the combination. In New York and Ohio the terms "trustee" and "director" were legally interchangeable. They easily

[72]Various Clevelanders have assured me that Judge Burke would cook up a suit for love of battle and money. Others have told me he was above reproach in all professional matters.

[73]Mr. Murray to the author, May 23, 1938.

showed that Rockefeller had possessed no information that the stock would rise in value. He had bought 100 shares in the summer of 1893 for as little as $135, and he had sold 500 shares in September, 1893, for $140. In January, 1895, he had bought 500 shares from Archbold for $168, precisely the sum he paid Corrigan the following month. In the first three months of that year he himself sold a number of shares at $168. Indeed, during the worst stress of the depression Rockefeller had been so far from believing in a great future rise of Standard Oil securities that, pressed for money, he had sold all his own "floating" shares and those of Mrs. Rockefeller and the children. Mr. Murray brought into the courtroom the books of the Standard Oil Trust, which had never before been outside 26 Broadway, to demonstrate that it had no hidden surplus.[74]

The arbitrators on April 20, 1899, unanimously decided in Rockefeller's favor. They agreed in stating that the charges were baseless.[75] "On the contrary, the evidence has satisfied them that the defendant bought the stock in question in good faith and at what he believed to be its full value and a fair price, and that he did not use the circumstances or necessities of the plaintiff as a means of extorting from him either the purchase of the stock, or its purchase at an improper or insufficient consideration, and that he was actuated by a desire to accommodate the plaintiff and relieve him of his embarrassments by making with him the agreement of which the purchase of the stock was a part." Burke asked for a rehearing, and the arbitrators listened to another long argument, but remained unshaken. Corrigan then appealed to the Ohio courts. The case was carried up to the State Supreme Court, which by unanimous verdict decided in Rockefeller's favor (December 22, 1902).[76]

Decades later the closest surviving friend and business associate of Frank Rockefeller, when questioned by the author as to this case and the accompanying breach between the two brothers, indicated by his melancholy taciturnity that he believed Frank had been in the wrong.[77] "I have an opinion," he said sadly. "But I loved Frank, and will say nothing to injure his memory. I cannot speak." One of Rockefeller's advisers has left a sharp verdict upon Frank.[78] "I

[74]I have used briefs of both Corrigan's and Rockefeller's attorneys.
[75]*Opinion of the Arbitrators, Corrigan vs. Rockefeller*, 1, 2.
[76]67 *Ohio State Reports*, 366.
[77]Confidential Cleveland source.   [78]Confidential New York source.

knew and liked him for his best traits. But I thought his method was always to try to milk his abler brother." Yet in spite of the clear equities of the case, it did great harm to Rockefeller. Many newspapers played it up with unpleasant innuendoes. Once more Rockefeller was presented as a man who cheated even his partners. Miss Tarbell in 1905 published an article in which she discussed the Corrigan case as an instance in which the magnate had despoiled a youthful associate.[79] Virgil P. Kline thereupon charged Miss Tarbell with a "partial and misleading" statement, and called attention to the plain verdict of the arbitrators and of two courts.

It is evident that neither the Merritts nor Corrigan came into court with perfectly honorable motives. It is common enough for men (and nations) to borrow money with gratitude to the lender, and when the time comes for payment to think their creditors mean and harsh. But in these instances the men used untenable allegations in a play for high stakes. Another case of the same period was not dissimilar. For years a Clevelander whom we shall leave unnamed[80] had been cashier of the Standard of Ohio, with a high salary and ample opportunities to buy stock. He speculated, embezzled, and was found short some $275,000. On his promise to make restitution, Rockefeller treated his lapse gently and retained him in his employ. At his death the company paid $1,000 for the expenses of his burial. But he had kept his embezzlement a secret from his wife, telling her when he sold his $100,000 home that William Rockefeller and others had led him into speculation with Standard securities, and betrayed him. His widow brought a perfectly absurd suit for damages against the Standard, which broke down when the true facts were exposed. But once more sensational journals, while it lasted, could treat Rockefeller as a despoiler of widows—because he had been too kind to an erring employee! Very similar, too, were the legal attacks made by a minister of the before-mentioned Baptist church in downtown New York, which Rockefeller long helped support, and upon which—its future hopeless—he finally foreclosed an overdue debt. This man, his worthless case defeated in the courts, filled the press with irresponsible statements, and even lodged in the Henry Demarest Lloyd papers a

---

[79]"John D. Rockefeller, A Character Study," *McClure's*, July, 1905.
[80]Flynn in *God's Gold* gives the name.

story whose obscenity was matched only by its utter mendacity.

Yet it would be an error to make too much of these cases. Rockefeller was right in believing that in the long run the true character of the suits would come out. The real gravamen of the popular indictment against him was the charge that he was using merciless methods to maintain an illegal and injurious monopoly. If that were sustained, public hostility would be justified; if it were not, public hostility would fade away. In comparison with this, all the other charges were trifles.

XLI

Rockefeller, Morgan, and the Steel Trust

ROCKEFELLER's huge new iron-ore holdings furnished him one of the most interesting problems of his career—and also one of his most remarkable business opportunities. It was an extraordinary fact that fate should suddenly toss into the hands of the petroleum magnate the richest mineral property of the Northwest. His wealth gave him great advantages in dealing with these ore fields. A process of business consolidation took place in this area with a rapidity which one historian calls "as inevitable as unexampled."[1] At the outset, in 1891–93, the ore fields—rapidly being enlarged by new discoveries—were held by numerous individuals and companies. While for a short time the Merritts had exuberantly believed that they could control all the really valuable mines, they soon found that many other owners had obtained important sites. For months on end the Duluth hotels were crammed with fortune-hunters, outfitters reaped a golden harvest, and the woods to the north and west rang with the shouts of exploring parties. Many strips were leased or bought. It seemed that the range would be held by hundreds of different owners. But the grim depression of 1893–97 worked a rapid transformation. By the time the economic storm fully ended, the ore fields were dominated by three great corporations, the Oliver Iron-Mining Company, the Minnesota Iron Company, and above all, Rockefeller's Lake Superior Consolidated Iron Mines. A fourth large-scale purchaser, James J. Hill of the Great Northern, was just entering the field.[2]

Rockefeller had always regarded industrial concentration as an

[1]H. R. Mussey, *Combination in the Mining Industry: A Study of Concentration in Lake Superior Ore Production*, 117.

[2]Folwell, *History of Minnesota*, IV, 30 ff.; Mussey, *Mining Industry*, 115 ff.

irresistible tendency of the times, and certainly the forces making for a consolidated ownership of these rich iron-ore deposits were unescapable. It might seem that, since enormous bodies of ore could be literally shovelled out from enormous beds, mining would be cheap enough to favor the small investor. But this was not true. Huge steam shovels had to be purchased, grades built and tracks laid, locomotives brought from the East, barracks erected for workmen, water, heat, and electric light provided, and a hundred unforeseen items of expense met. The long and severe winters retarded the work of development. At the beginning a keen competition for leases forced bidders to pay large royalties and guarantee heavy shipments. The market was uncertain, for ironmasters distrusted the ore. "It took us fifteen years before we had really finished adapting our steel mills to it," said Charles M. Schwab of the Carnegie Company.[3] After a costly outlay, mining companies often found the market glutted, orders few, and prices at bankruptcy levels. Indeed, in the four years 1893–97 this was the usual tale. Companies which bought supposed ore lands in haste paid a heavy penalty. The Duluth & Winnipeg Railroad, for example, paid $750,000 for what proved to be barren earth, and went into bankruptcy.

An expert upon the development of the Missabe cites as all too typical the experiences of the Biwabik Ore Company, which attempted to exploit the Biwabik Mine, owned by wealthy lumbermen and containing more than 20,000,000 tons of ore. The company unwisely agreed to pay 50 cents a ton royalty, take out not less than 300,000 tons a year, and exhaust the mine within twenty years. It incurred a heavy expenditure for equipment. Then a bitterly icy winter smote the Missabe, while the panic upset all the roseate anticipations of a keen Eastern demand. Although the company's lease was of great potential value, lack of funds compelled it to throw up its contract; while its successor, the Biwabik Bessemer Company, was soon forced into bankruptcy by heavy stripping costs and lack of capital.[4] The same fate overtook the Duluth Ore Company, which leased the Berringer Mine at a royalty of 50 cents a ton, agreeing to take out not less than 100,000 tons a year. When its market failed, it had to abandon the mine to Rockefeller's Con-

---

[3]Schwab to the author, June 15, 1939.
[4]Proceedings, *Lake Superior Mining Institute*, III, 23–25.

solidated. The story of nearly all the small companies along the Missabe, indeed, was one of disaster.[5]

II

The fact was that the industrial revolution in America had now proceeded so far that the day of the little man in the iron industry had forever vanished. To obtain ore leases before the panic, companies had agreed to make large annual shipments at a high royalty; and then after the panic broke they had to pay out perhaps $100,000 a year without selling a ton. Steam shovels broke down, storms paralyzed the mining work for weeks, railroad tracks were washed out, buyers refused to pay cash; and as a result all shoestring operators went to the wall. "The early years of Missabe history," writes H. R. Mussey, "are filled with the wreck of companies which attempted the impossible task of mining without adequate financial support." Who should buy the mines? Those who had ready capital naturally took them over—Oliver, Carnegie, Rockefeller, James J. Hill, Charlemagne Tower, and their associates.

The Oliver holdings constituted one of the first large blocks. Henry W. Oliver, a buoyant, enthusiastic industrialist, Scottish-born, who began life as a messenger boy with Carnegie in a Pittsburgh telegraph office, and had made a fortune in manufacturing plows and other farm implements, was a delegate to the Republican National Convention in Minneapolis in June, 1892. He mingled in the hotel lobbies with men whose talk ran to lumber, railroads, and iron ore. For the first time in his life he heard the musical syllables Missabe, and listened eagerly while Minnesotans told him of the rich stores of loose ore lying under the pine needles of the great forests not far to the north. Hurrying to Duluth, he found the hotels so jammed by prospectors and buyers that he had to sleep on a billiard table. He talked with the Merritts. Then, hiring a vehicle, he travelled by the rough corduroy roads, through gloomy woods and across glistening black swamps, to the red gashes in the earth which marked the site of the Missabe Mountain Mine. Here Lon Merritt expatiated on the vast wealth that men of capital could take out of the district, and Oliver was rapidly converted. He was a born speculator, who had already won and lost several fortunes. The

[5]Mussey, *Mining Industry*, 115 ff.

Merritts wanted an associate with money, while Oliver needed a new field for his energies. Before he caught his train home he had paid a modest sum for certain leaseholds on the Missabe. It was one of the best bargains of Oliver's long career.[6]

No sooner was he back in Pittsburgh than Oliver, enthusiastic over the rich new ore field, organized the Oliver Iron-Mining Company to open up his holdings. An old friendship existed between him and Henry Frick, chairman of the Carnegie Company. This was the summer in which Frick ruthlessly crushed the union organization at Homestead, and was shot by the anarchist Berkman. But when he recovered sufficiently to return to his office—early in August, 1892—he opened negotiations with Oliver for a share in the Missabe enterprise.[7] Both Oliver and the Carnegie interests wished to be assured of generous supplies of good Bessemer ore, and a partnership was logical. They agreed that the Carnegie Company should receive one half of the $1,000,000 capital stock in the new Oliver concern in return for a mortgage loan of $500,000, to be used for developing the fields. Frick, delighted over what he correctly regarded as the best stroke he had ever executed for the steel company, hastened to inform Carnegie, who was spending the summer at his Skibo retreat. He was astounded when the cautious laird, still sore over the results of the bloody Homestead encounter, sent back a frigid protest. He wrote on August 29: "Oliver's ore bargain is just like him—nothing in it. If there is any department of business which offers no inducement, it is ore. It never has been very profitable, and the Missabe is not the last great deposit that Lake Superior is to reveal." There were times when Carnegie's vision failed him.[8]

But the bargain was nevertheless struck. In fact, Frick as chairman of the company had full authority to make it. All that Carnegie could do was to impede the flow of capital into the enterprise, and to grumble over its prospects. He could not really cripple it. Thanks to the introduction of huge Oliver steam shovels, the Missabe's output of 29,245 tons of iron ore in 1892 was increased by 1894 to 1,913,234 tons. Carnegie's biographer is at some pains to excuse his lack of foresight, saying that he felt a profound distrust for the

[6]See sketch of Oliver, *Dictionary of American Biography.*
[7]George Harvey, *Life of Henry Clay Frick,* 188.
[8]James H. Bridge, *Inside History of the Carnegie Steel Company,* 259.

dashing Oliver, while he also believed that pioneering did not pay
—that it was best to let other men take the risk of developing ore
fields. Might they not sink huge sums in the mines, only to find
that some one had discovered even larger and cheaper ranges?[9]
Frick's biographer, on the other hand, expatiates upon Carnegie's
timidity in order to emphasize Frick's courage and imagination.
Certainly Carnegie seldom made a worse prophecy than when he
wrote the board of managers of his company in the spring of 1894:
"You will find that this ore venture, like all other ventures in ore,
will result in much trouble and less profit than almost any other
branch of our business."[10]

Rockefeller shrewdly took Frick's view. He and Gates held long
discussions upon the Missabe deposits, which Gates had carefully
inspected. Rockefeller also read reports from experts, and debated
the matter with various business advisers. His natural instinct was
to increase his holdings in the field. Ever since the first Lima-Ohio
venture, he had insisted upon large purchases of oil-bearing lands.
He was destined to maintain this policy as long as he remained
head of the Standard. He soon arranged to support the Barnsdall
interests, for example, to the extent of $6,000,000 in opening the
oil lands of the Osage Indians, asking in return only that Barnsdall
give the Standard an option on his whole product; with profits
which in the end became enormous. Quite by accident, he had been
led into the iron-ore business. But now that his company, the Consolidated, held some of the finest sites on the Missabe range, while
the railroad to Lake Superior was under his control, should he
back out or go boldly forward? His answer was never in doubt.
He wished to find diversified investments for his enormous income,
already perhaps above $10,000,000 a year and irresistibly expand-
ing. He had an instinctive faith in underground wealth. He had
acquired an important share in the cheapest sources of petroleum in
the world; why should he not turn to iron ore for a similar triumph?

"When the fright of the panic period subsided," he writes, "and
matters became a little more settled, we began to realize our situation. We had invested many millions, and no one seemed to want
to go in with us to buy stock. On the contrary, everybody seemed to

[9]Burton J. Hendrick, *Andrew Carnegie*, II, 13 ff.
[10]Harvey, *Frick*, 191.

want to sell. The stock was offered to us in alarming quantities
—substantially all of the capital stock of the companies came without any solicitation on our part—quite the contrary—and we paid
for it in cash."[11] By these stock purchases he rapidly added to his
holdings in the Consolidated, making his control absolute. But he
did not buy out all the minority owners. As we have seen, he steadily
renewed an option which permitted two of the Merritts to retrieve
their Consolidated stock at the very figure at which he had purchased it; that is, he carried it for them while it steadily rose in
value. Under Gates's astute management, the Consolidated increased
its ore holdings both by purchase and lease. At the time this was
done, it must be remembered, the market for ore was wretched, and
the future of the new range seemed to many experienced men a
gamble. No less a person than Charles M. Schwab has told the
author:

> Our experts in the Carnegie Company did not believe in the Missabe
> ore fields. They thought the ore was poor; that it was not only too fine
> to work, but was too lean, its iron content being smaller than that of the
> old fields. They ridiculed Rockefeller's investments in the Missabe. They
> couldn't understand why he, who had no knowledge of the iron business,
> should plunge so heavily; putting large sums of money into ores that
> were useless, at least for a long period to come. They clung to this atti-
> tude for several years. Our Carnegie Company acquired considerable hold-
> ings in the old fields. But Mr. Carnegie and I wanted to avoid the Mis-
> sabe range.

Unquestionably Rockefeller, as later events showed, was acquiring some remarkable bargains. But the whole history of the region
was one of bargain-hunting. From the time that upper Minnesota
was first opened its rugged pioneers had acquired valuable lands,
known to contain timber and found later to hold ore, for almost
nothing—using "half-breed scrip," soldiers' scrip, and false pre-
emptions. Other great areas were bought at public auctions where
the lumbermen agreed beforehand not to bid against one another.
W. W. Folwell describes how at Duluth in 1882 a timber-cruiser
made a ridiculously low bid for twenty-six pieces of land, other lumbermen refusing to compete with him. He actually represented a
group of wealthy Minnesota speculators who had paid him $20

[11]*Random Reminiscences,* 120, 121.

for posing as the purchaser, and who thus acquired a small fortune in timber alone; while it was later found that the tracts also contained 70,000,000 tons of ore! The Merritts leased wide tracts of enormously valuable ore land for fifty years from the State at 25 cents for every ton of ore. These instances were typical of dozens of others. When Minnesota permitted such transactions, it had little right to complain because Rockefeller, Carnegie, Oliver, Tower, and others bought or leased lands at the low prices prevailing in a depressed market.[12]

James J. Hill, beginning in 1897 to buy huge areas of ore land for his Great Northern Railroad, and evading all legal restrictions, was the perfect type of the bargain-hunter. His principal land corporation, the Lake Superior Company, acquired in about seven years, by purchase or lease, more than 65,000 acres in and along the Missabe range. A State law which forbade such corporations to hold more than 5000 acres was circumvented by the organization of subsidiary companies. Hill's outlay was of course very small in comparison with the real value of the ore-beds. For one set of holdings which aggregated about 25,000 acres, with a railroad thrown in, he paid only $4,050,000. Within a few years he was able to boast that he had acquired for his railway system ore deposits worth, at a general estimate, about six hundred millions! Tower's Minnesota Iron Company also acquired large properties on the eastern half of the Missabe range, to which its railroad extended, at very low cost. During the single year 1895 the company is believed to have gained control of 40,000,000 tons of ore for an expenditure of slightly more than $1,000,000—about 2½ cents a ton![13]

III

It was in January, 1895, that the Merritts' option for 55,000 shares of Consolidated lapsed, and this stock passed irrevocably into the hands of Rockefeller. This was the month in which he achieved full control of the Consolidated properties; and he and Gates were ready for expansion. Whenever a mine or leasehold that Gates desired came upon the market, he prepared detailed plans for its incorporation into the Rockefeller properties. Rockefeller carefully studied them, and nearly always approved them. At no time did the

[12]Folwell, *Minnesota*, IV, 14–34.   [13]*Idem*, 34.

Consolidated, or any other Missabe company in which Rockefeller bought shares, pay a dividend, but the value of the property steadily increased. By the beginning of 1897, Consolidated stock was worth $20 a share.[14] As month after month Rockefeller added new acquisitions to the large Merritt holdings, he became more and more clearly the master of the richest iron deposits in the world—and with this potentially the leader of the steel industry. The Oliver-Carnegie interests had important mines, as did the Minnesota Iron Company, and Jim Hill. But Rockefeller's tracts overshadowed them all. Upon these properties the whole future of American steel, in his opinion and that of Gates, depended. Eastern mill-owners watched him with increasing uneasiness, and Carnegie's biographer correctly states:[15]

It certainly looked as though the genius who had made himself supreme in the business of refining oil, and whose fortune was already expanding in a dozen directions, had caught the steelmakers napping, and had placed himself in a position to seize within his tentacles the industry which was rapidly becoming the most profitable in the world.

Indeed, the rise of Rockefeller as one of the potential chieftains of the steel industry was a spectacle which seized powerfully upon the imagination of most Americans. He and Carnegie seemed to confront each other like two armed barons of feudal days, meeting on the tented field with a crowd of retainers at their backs. Sensational newspaper writers attributed a grim personal rivalry to them. They were supposed to be lusting for each other's blood after the manner in which bellicose railway magnates had so long behaved. But while the battles of the New York Central and the Erie, of the Pennsylvania and the Baltimore & Ohio had involved millions, this new contest threatened to involve billions. The ruler of oil against the ruler of steel, the two richest men in the world, the two strongest industrial organizations ever built, locked in implacable combat—this was a vision which excited a host of Americans. For a time in the sixties, when Carnegie was trading in oil, the two men had been potential rivals; were they now to be antagonists in good earnest? If so, their struggle might well shake the industrial world.

[14]Gates, MS Autobiography, 331–336; *The Truth About Mr. Rockefeller and the Merritts,* 26.
[15]Hendrick, *Carnegie,* II, 16, 17.

As a matter of fact, Rockefeller and Carnegie were personally always on the best of terms, and equally averse to any "battle." Both always read with amusement the press comments on their supposed rivalry in benefactions. Charles M. Schwab later recalled their exchange of Christmas gifts one year—Rockefeller sending Carnegie a paper vest that had cost a few cents, and Carnegie favoring the

From a cartoon by Tom Bee in the Baltimore Evening Sun

The Race to Poverty

Rockefeller and Carnegie shown as rivals in philanthropy

abstemious Rockefeller with a bottle of his best whisky![16] Nevertheless, Rockefeller was not averse to making the most of his position.

"I was astonished," he later stated, "that the steelmakers had not seen the necessity of controlling their ore supply." And Carnegie's biographer confesses that this hiatus gave him the opportunity of inserting an effective entering-wedge. "To slip between the steelmakers and their raw materials—here was another opening for the talent that had constructed the greatest trust in the world."[17] Some

[16]Schwab to the author, June 15, 1939.   [17]Hendrick, *Carnegie*, II, 16.

of Carnegie's associates began to feel a certain nervousness lest the cool-headed oil magnate should decide to enter upon iron manufacture in rivalry with the Scot. Rumors began to circulate to the effect that Rockefeller's agents were actually looking for the best sites on the Great Lakes—at Duluth, Chicago, Cleveland, and other cities—for the erection of huge new steel mills. The great realms of cheap ore which he controlled, fields from which iron deposits could be shovelled out for a few cents a ton, gave him an invaluable asset; the brains of the "Rockefeller crowd" were hardly to be matched elsewhere in American industry; and Carnegie himself had publicly admitted that the Pittsburgh area was now less suited to steel manufacture than certain Northwestern districts.[18] Add to these advantages Rockefeller's great wealth—the ten to fifteen millions a year that he had to invest; the powerful grip that he was fastening upon Great Lakes shipping; and above all, his genius for organization, and the Carnegie group had genuine reason for worry.

But Rockefeller never for a moment thought of going into the manufacture of iron and steel. His desire was always to consolidate one domain before moving on to the conquest of another, and he perceived that to make sure of supremacy in ore and ore-transportation would require all his energies. He says in his *Reminiscences:*

When we realized that events were shaping themselves so that to protect our investments we should be obliged to go into the business of selling in a large way, we felt that we must not stop short of doing the work as effectively as possible; and having already put in so much money, we bought all the ore land that we thought was good that was offered to us. The railroad and the ships were only the means to an end. The ore lands were the crux of the whole matter, and we believed that we could never have too many good mines.

It was a surprise to me that the great iron and steel manufacturers did not place what seemed to be an adequate value on these mines. The lands which contained a good many of our best ore mines could have been purchased very cheaply before we became interested. Having launched ourselves into the venture, we decided to supply ore to every one who needed it, by mining and transporting with the newest and most effective facilities, and our profits we invested in more ore lands.

Rockefeller noted disapprovingly the rumors which ran through the American press in June, 1895. "Within six months," declared

[18] *Idem*, II, 18.

a Pittsburgh dispatch,[19] "it is quite probable that plans looking forward to the construction of a gigantic steel plant on the banks of Lake Erie, at a point near Cleveland, Ohio, will be well under way." Rockefeller, it added, would be joined by other millionaires in the undertaking. "The name of John Potter, late general superintendent of the Carnegie Steel Company in Pittsburgh, now with the Cleveland Steel Company, is coupled with the project." Actually Rockefeller was anxious to decrease his business cares, and he knew that to enter so strange, difficult, and speculative a business as iron and steel—a business so uncertain that even Carnegie had been eager some years earlier to sell out, and had been restrained only by the cool-headed Frick—would be risky in the extreme. He would face the competition not only of Carnegie and Frick, so strongly entrenched, but of the fast-rising Illinois Steel Company under Elbert H. Gary, and other strong corporations. The result would be just such a mutually destructive warfare as he had abhorred in the early years of the oil-refining industry. No mind was quicker to grasp the basic elements of a business situation than Rockefeller's. He perceived that wisdom dictated an agreement with the Carnegie-Oliver interests by which, in return for his promise to abstain from competition in iron and steel manufacture, they should promise to refrain from unrestricted competition in ore production.

In 1896 a bargain was therefore struck—and not so much a bargain as an alliance. Announced with dramatic suddenness, it startled the iron trade of the world. The plan had been born in the fertile brain of Oliver. It was agreed that the Carnegie-Oliver group should lease the principal mines of the Rockefeller organization for fifty years at the low figure of 25 cents a ton. They were to take a minimum of 600,000 tons a year from these mines, and an equal amount from their own shafts, and to ship the total of 1,200,000 tons over Rockefeller's railroad and the great line of ore-carrying vessels that Gates had been building up. At this time Rockefeller held the only properties on the Missabe which were being successfully worked by steam shovels. The rates to be paid on the railroad and the lake boats were to be determined by the market prices of the day. At the outset they would amount to $1.45 a ton for the entire haul between the Missabe railheads and Lake Erie ports. Oliver

[19]N. Y. *Herald,* June 7, 1895.

and Frick on the one side, Rockefeller and Gates on the other, assented to the plan. But it had to be approved by the boards of the companies involved, and by Carnegie as controlling owner of the Carnegie Company. The astute Scot, landing in New York from Europe, withheld his consent until he had made an arrangement with Oliver by which he shortly took the ownership of five sixths, instead of one half, of the Oliver Iron Mining Company, on terms which allowed him to pay for this magnificent property out of profits.[20]

Under the new arrangement, the Carnegie Steel Company gained an assured supply of inexpensive ore (for the usual royalty rate had been 50 or 65 cents a ton) of high quality; while Rockefeller gained an assured supply of freight for his railroad and steamship line. For the time being Carnegie kept out of transportation, and Rockefeller out of steel manufacture. It might seem that Rockefeller assumed the greater risks. The Carnegie group invested no capital beyond mining machinery and similar outlays, and if any of the ore-beds became prematurely exhausted, Rockefeller would shoulder the loss. But the Carnegie Steel Company promised in writing that it would keep off the Missabe range, would 'buy from Rockefeller alone so long as he could furnish the grade of ore required, and would purchase or lease no iron-bearing lands there. These pledges Gates, who conducted the negotiations for Rockefeller, regarded as "fundamental." He wrote Oliver: "One of the prime motives for making this lease was to withdraw yourselves and the Carnegie Company from competition in the purchase and leasing of Missabe properties." On the whole, the bargain was fair. Each side gained valuable advantages without making any real sacrifices.[21]

The moment the compact became known, it startled the iron-ore trade like a clap of thunder. Obviously, iron ore was going to be cheaper than ever before in the history of the world.

Up to this time Rockefeller and Carnegie had seldom met. They were entirely different in temperament, tastes, and, save for a common interest in philanthropy, in their outlook upon life. Yet they respected each other, and in making this alliance Carnegie was

[20]Harvey, *Frick*, 191–193; Hendrick, *Carnegie*, II, 19, 20;. Folwell, *Minnesota*, IV, 31; "The Carnegie-Rockefeller Deal," *Iron Age*, Feb. 18, 1897.

[21]Hendrick, *Carnegie*, II, 19, 20.

actuated in part by regard for his "fellow millionaire," as he once addressed him. "Carnegie was always favorable to a close understanding with Rockefeller," writes his biographer, "and urged that nothing should be done to make the oil man hostile to the Carnegie Steel Company." He had joined the ore pool of 1895 for one reason only—because Rockefeller had asked his co-operation. Personally he did not care for this pool. But he had directed President Leishman of the Carnegie Company to enter it, for by refusing "we should lose the friendship of Mr. Rockefeller. . . . I think Rockefeller is the coming man in ore, and it will be to our advantage to stand in with him. As his ownership in ore lands will be very large, I believe it will be more to our advantage to mine ore in his territory, paying him a royalty, than to attempt to purchase ore property for ourselves." The final phase of the debate within the Carnegie-Oliver-Frick circles upon this agreement of 1896 found Frick hanging back, while Carnegie was in favor of signing. He was supported by Henry M. Curry, in charge of ore contracts, and by President Leishman. The minutes of the Carnegie Steel Company preserve one colloquy:[22]

Curry: "If we make this agreement, it will have the effect of keeping Mr. Rockefeller out of the steel manufacturing business."

Frick: "If Rockefeller does not go into the steel business, somebody else will."

Leishman: "But very few people are hunting places to invest an income of fifteen millions."

The new compact made it clear that Carnegie was still lord of steel, and could now control the industry more completely than ever. At once other holders of Minnesota ore lands perceived that they must cut their prices to meet the new royalty rates. The market broke overnight. Panic seized many owners, and Oliver exultantly pointed to the opportunity before his associates. "We simply knocked the price of ore down from $4 to say $2.50 a ton," he boasted. "Now let us take advantage of our action before a season of good times gives the ore-producers strength and opportunity to get together." And this the Carnegie-Oliver interests did. While the ore trade remained depressed, Frick and Oliver reached out to seize the shares that stockholders of mining companies were throwing upon the

[22]*Idem*, II, 20, 21.

market. In particular, they sought the stock of the three most important independent companies. Oliver obtained more than 400 options at "astoundingly low prices," and Carnegie confirmed the purchases. The Carnegie interests also leased at 50 cents a ton the output of that Tilden Mine which the Merritts had so hastily pronounced worthless, and a letter of Frick's shows that they expected to take from it 400,000 tons of excellent ore a year.[23]

IV

We have spoken of Rockefeller's fleet of lake boats, and by that thread hangs a remarkable tale. The development of this fleet, like that of the mines and railroad, was primarily the responsibility of Frederick T. Gates. Setting himself to learn about ore-transportation, he soon mastered all its complexities. "He did all the work," says Rockefeller.[24]

If difficult, the business was also fascinating. Since for five months Lake Superior is locked in ice, intensive use must be made of the warm weather. Rockefeller's engineers devised great ore docks of unique construction at the head of Lake Superior—at Duluth, Two Harbors, and Superior. The railroad tracks were run out on heavy trestles for hundreds of feet to deep water. Whole trains of ore-filled cars were brought down from the Missabe, backed out on these structures, their hopper bottoms opened, and the ore dumped into bins on both sides of the trestle. An ore-carrying vessel ran alongside, its hatches were opened directly under the bins, and the ore was dropped into the hold. Ten thousand tons of the dry powdery Missabe ores could be loaded in half a dozen hours or less, and started for the ports of Lake Michigan or Lake Erie. Here the docks were equipped with huge unloading machines which thrust an automatic bucket into the hold of a ship, grabbed several tons of ore, and lifted it out to be dropped into waiting cars, which were at once whisked off to the steel mills. The speed, simplicity, and cheapness with which ore was transferred from the Minnesota pits to the Pittsburgh furnaces were marvellous.[25]

[23]Harvey, *Frick*, 194; Bridge, *Inside History*, 265.
[24]*Random Reminiscences*, 122.
[25]C. E. Van Barneveld, *Iron Mining in Minnesota*, 208 ff. Mr. Herbert L. Satterlee, who later married a daughter of J. P. Morgan, had as agent for Wetmore supervised the construction of some of the first piers of the Duluth, Missabe & Northern. He has described his experiences to me.

As soon as the Missabe Railroad was placed on its feet, Rockefeller and Gates saw that they needed their own ships to carry the ore. Of course no one in the Rockefeller organization knew anything about the construction of vessels. It was necessary to find some one who did—and Rockefeller thought at once of his old Cleveland acquaintance Samuel Mather, descendant of Cotton Mather and head of one of the great Western Reserve families, who operated ore-carriers on his own account. He had long been interested in mines in the Gogebic and Menominee districts. He had married a daughter of Amasa Stone, and was now regarded as the first citizen of Cleveland. Of course he was a competitor, but that did not matter. Gates let him know approximately what was desired. The rest was accomplished when one evening Gates brought him up to Rockefeller's house in New York just before dinner. "He said he could stay only a few minutes," recalls Rockefeller,[26] "but I told him I thought we could finish up our affairs in ten minutes, and we did. That is the only time I remember seeing personally any one on the business of the ore company." But a great deal passed in that ten minutes:

We explained to this gentleman that we were proposing to transport our ore from these Lake Superior lands ourselves, and that we should like to have him assume charge of the construction of several ships, to be of the largest and most approved type, for our chance of success lay in having boats which could be operated with the greatest efficiency. At that time the largest ships carried about five thousand tons, but in 1900, when we sold out, we had ships that carried seven thousand or eight thousand tons. . . .

This expert naturally replied that as he was in the ore-carrying trade himself, he had no desire to encourage us to go into it. We explained to him that as we had made this large investment, it seemed to us to be necessary for the protection of our interests to control our own lake carriers, so we had decided to mine, ship, and market the ore; that we came to him because he could plan and superintend the construction of the best ships for us, and that we wanted to deal with him for that reason; that notwithstanding that he represented one of the largest firms among our competitors, we knew that he was honest and straightforward; and that we were most anxious to communicate with him.

Mather still demurred, but Rockefeller and Gates convinced him

[26]*Random Reminiscences,* 123.

that they were going into the ore-carrying business no matter what he did, and were willing to pay a satisfactory commission if he would superintend the construction of the ships. He might as well have the profit as somebody else! Finally he yielded. The agreement was closed then and there, and its details were later worked out to the satisfaction of everybody. "He spent only a few minutes in the house," concludes Rockefeller, "during which time we gave him the order for about $3,000,000 worth of ships, and this was the only time I saw him. But Mr. Mather is a man of high business honor, we trusted him implicitly although he was a competitor, and we never had occasion to regret it."

Nine or ten shipbuilding companies were then in operation at various points on the Great Lakes. They were all independent and sharply competitive. Times were still hard, the works were wholly or partly closed down, and the employees faced a difficult winter. Rockefeller and Gates determined to relieve a large number of workers by building as many ships as possible and scattering the work widely. They therefore instructed Mather to write each firm of shipbuilders, and find how many vessels could be finished and outfitted at each yard by the following spring. He learned that twelve ships could be constructed, some firms undertaking one, some two. Accordingly, Rockefeller and Gates directed him to have a full dozen all-steel boats, of the largest capacity then believed practicable on the Great Lakes, built. Some were to be steamships, and some great ore-carrying barges for towing.

If Mather had announced in advance that he planned to build twelve ships, asking for bids on them, he would have had to pay very high prices. Instead, he kept the number secret. Plans and specifications (the vessels being substantially identical) were sent to the various firms, and each was asked to bid on one or two ships. The general supposition up and down the lakes was that Rockefeller was going to build two vessels at most! Every firm was naturally anxious to get at least one of the contracts.

The day before the final orders were let, all the bidders assembled—by invitation—in Mather's outer office. Here collected men who embodied forty years of shipping history on the Great Lakes. One was a representative of the old Globe Shipbuilding Company in Cleveland, the first house to make a success of iron craft; it had hired a former master-mechanic of the Grand Trunk Railroad, John Smith, as superintendent, and he had become famous from Buffalo to Duluth for his fine vessels. Another was a representative of the Cleveland Shipbuilding Company, in which the Hannas were dominant. Still others came from Toledo, Buffalo, Chicago, Milwaukee, and Bay City.[27] One by one they were called into the private office for special conferences covering all the details. Each man somehow gained the impression that *he* was going to be the successful bidder, and emerged with satisfaction gleaming in his eye; this elation being suddenly chilled, however, when—meeting his competitors later in the hotel lobby—he discovered that they also beamed with hope.

"At last the critical hour came," writes Rockefeller, "and at about the same moment each gentleman received a little note from Mr. Mather, conveying to him the tidings that to him had been awarded a contract sufficient to supply his works to their utmost capacity. They all rushed with a common impulse to the hotel lobby where they had been accustomed to meet, each keen on displaying his note and commiserating his unsuccessful rivals, only to discover that each had a contract for all he could do, and that each had been actually bidding against nobody but himself. Great was the hilarity which covered their chagrin when they met and compared notes and looked into each other's faces. However, all were happy and satisfied." One man, McVitty of Detroit, a canny Scot, had held out for higher prices than the others. He got the contracts for the last two vessels. Rockefeller noted with satisfaction in 1909 that most of these desperately competing firms had shortly united in one great corporation, the American Shipbuilding Company, which

[27]I have talked with various old shipping men in Cleveland. The files of *The Marine Review,* edited in Cleveland in this period, are a mine of information. John Smith had begun his notable career by making two iron car-ferries for the Grand Trunk. He opened a yard on Sarnia Bay, had fabricated iron shapes shipped from England, and built two ferries, the *International* and *Huron.* When iron shipbuilding in Cleveland began, the Globe Company, whose principal figure was Henry Darling Coffinberry, called him to take charge of its works. A son, Alfred G. Smith, became president of the American Shipbuilding Company. It may be mentioned that the shipping firm headed by Samuel Mather was Pickands, Mather & Company.

later furnished vessels for the Rockefeller line at a more uniform price.[28]

But who should operate the twelve new ships, the finest ore-carriers on the Great Lakes? The treaty of 1896 with the Oliver-Carnegie interests assured a heavy traffic, and made great efficiency imperative. Rockefeller and Gates asked Mather to take the fleet in charge. His obligations to others forbade. Then Rockefeller asked Gates, "Do you know of any experienced firm?"

"No," said Gates, "I do not know of any firm, but why not run them ourselves?"

"You don't know anything about ships, do you?"

"No," Gates admitted. "But I know a man who I believe could do it, although I fear you will think his qualifications are not the best. However, he has the essentials. He lives up-State, and never was on a ship in his life. He probably wouldn't know the bow from the stern, or a sea-anchor from an umbrella, but he has sense. He is honest, enterprising, keen, and thrifty. He has the art of master-ing a subject quickly even though it is new to him. We still have some months before the ships will be completed, and if we put him to work now, he will be ready to run the ships as soon as they are ready."

"All right," said Rockefeller. "Let's give him the job"—and they did.[29]

This man was L. M. Bowers, whom we shall meet again in treat-ing the Colorado Fuel & Iron Company; a shrewd, alert, hard-fisted businessman, who had been born in Broome County, N. Y., in 1847. He had gone through a varied business career, including a partnership in a wholesale grocery house in Binghamton, and five years in the real-estate and machinery-warehousing business in Omaha; and already he possessed independent means. He was an uncle of Gates. Many thought him narrow and stern—"one of those churchly fellows," recalled a Cleveland observer. Rockefeller now employed him as "confidential representative." His first duty was to see that the contracts for constructing the boats were carried

---

[28]*Idem*, 127, 128. Shipping men in Cleveland assured me that fair profits were made on the contracts; and that if Rockefeller had announced a program for working the plants to capacity, the builders would have advanced their rates outrageously.

[29]Conversation with Mr. L. M. Bowers, Binghamton, Jan. 27, 1937.

out. Visiting all the yards, he studied the craft minutely, and made shrewd suggestions about their design and equipment, which were adopted. As soon as the vessels were afloat he took charge, and, states Rockefeller, "managed these and the dozens which followed with a skill and ability that commanded the admiration of all the sailors on the lakes." In fact, he took to water with inborn aptitude. He had an ingenious mind, and invented a new anchor, with other devices which were widely adopted on lake and even ocean vessels. He at once planned the construction of much larger ships than any yet built—ships 500 feet long.[30]

By far the largest ore-carrying fleet in the world was soon owned by Rockefeller. His Bessemer Steamship Company, with offices in Cleveland, grew until before the end of the century it numbered twenty-eight vessels, which could carry 3,500,000 tons of ore down the lakes at one voyage. Then the demand of the mills for raw materials swiftly doubled its size. By 1901 Rockefeller owned nearly sixty ships. No other group of ore-carriers on the globe compared with it. At this date the Federal Steel Company, the Cleveland Cliffs Company, and the Lake Superior Iron Company also had important fleets. Some independent companies owned vessels. But in general the control of shipping tended to pass into the hands of the great mining companies, and both under the control of the great steel-manufacturing interests. An irresistible process of vertical integration was under way.

Bowers, obeying Rockefeller's instructions and his own inclination, did not use his huge fleet in ruthless rate-cutting. "I've always tried to make friends with my enemies," he said in old age. "I've always said that when your competitor makes money you do too; I've never wanted to drive a competitor out of business." He practised this philosophy. When it had become known that Rockefeller was building enormous new ships, independent carriers were in despair, picturing themselves as ruined. But Bowers quickly took pains to reassure them. "What's a good rate?" he asked. "What's

[30]Old-timers told him that craft of such size were impracticable; that they would break in two, would stick in the Soo Canal, would be too long for the docks. "Pooh, pooh!" replied Bowers. The first, the *General Orlando F. Poe*, was soon under way, and others followed. Each was named for some figure connected with Great Lakes history. Conversation with L. M. Bowers, Jan. 29, 1939; Rockefeller, *Random Reminiscences*, 129 ff.

a rate at which you can make money carrying ore?" "That doesn't matter," they gloomily responded. "You'll undercut us, whatever it is." Bowers explained that Rockefeller's company was not interested in putting them out of business, but merely in hauling the Rockefeller ores; they would be left the freight from other mines. So they agreed upon a rate.

"Now I'll keep to this," declared Bowers, "and you fellows keep to it. So long as it's kept we can all get along. But if you go under it, I'll ruin you as sure as you're born."[31]

The threat was effective, and the rate was fairly well maintained. When Rockefeller gave up the fleet, the shipping men presented Bowers with two fine porcelain vases.

Within a few general rules, Rockefeller and Gates gave Bowers almost absolute independence in fleet operation. The former saw few of the vessels, and made but rare suggestions. "I was never ordered to do anything, or supervised, or reported on," states Bowers. "Of course this was in line with my stipulation on taking the work." Bowers also looked after various of the magnate's affairs in Cleveland, and erected the new Rockefeller building on Superior Street. After Rockefeller's retirement he was instructed never to communicate with him. Soon thereafter Rockefeller came to see him personally about a shipping question, and his directions implied that they would follow the matter through together. "You are making me break the orders I have from your own office, Mr. Rockefeller," protested Bowers. "Oh, Mr. Bowers, I am getting along in years," jocularly replied Rockefeller. "I think I may really be allowed a little liberty by my office!"

v

As prosperity returned to the nation in 1897, the immense value of the Missabe mines began to grow evident—though even yet few men would have estimated them at more than a fraction of their real worth. The iron and steel business entered upon a tremendous boom period. Demand and prices rose rapidly during 1898–99. When the century closed no fewer than twenty-two new furnaces, with an aggregate capacity of more than 3,000,000 tons a year, were

[31]Conversation with L. M. Bowers.

being constructed by nine of the large steel companies. In the last weeks of 1899 pig iron and finished steel sold for more than twice what they had brought in January. A sharp price reaction in 1900 proved only temporary, for next year the march of the industry was resumed, and American iron and steel mills produced almost 18,-000,000 tons of metal. An era of optimism succeeded to the years of gloom.

By this time four powerful interests controlled by far the greater part of the Minnesota ore fields, although a number of smaller companies survived. The big four were Rockefeller's Consolidated Company; the Oliver Iron Mining Company (five sixths of it now Carnegie-owned); the Great Northern Railroad, represented by various corporations; and the new Federal Steel Company, a holding corporation set up in 1898. This last had been organized by Judge Elbert H. Gary of the Illinois Steel Company, and financed by J. P. Morgan. It had taken over, in a giant combination, all the ore lands of the Minnesota Iron Company, the Duluth & Iron Range Railroad, and a fleet of ore-carriers, Gary becoming its head. But practically all the soft-ore mining was still in Rockefeller's hands, for the Hill interests were slow in developing their holdings. The four organizations were so eager for expansion, and so ready to offer high inducements, that in general the small holders found it more profitable to lease or sell than to continue independent operations. Consolidation thus continued its advance.

Steel manufacture, now invading the world's markets with brilliant success, also clearly demanded reorganization into a few powerful units. Small mills were wasteful and vulnerable. Carnegie's interests had already practically swallowed up those of Henry Oliver. Peace had not yet been signed with Spain when Gary's Federal Steel Company was set up as a holding corporation which at once combined the Illinois Steel Company, the Lorain Steel Company, and the Elgin, Joliet & Eastern Railway with the just-mentioned iron deposits. This great aggregation, possessing rich ore fields, strong mills, an astute president, and J. P. Morgan's unlimited credit, was sufficiently powerful to run the Carnegie interests a close race. Its directors hoped to erect in the Chicago area a mightier structure than any in the Pittsburgh district. Yet they had a rival in their own field—the American Steel & Wire Company, capitalized at ninety millions. Its presiding genius was John W. ("Bet-A-Million") Gates, a former barbed-wire salesman who, becoming a speculative financier, had developed no little constructive talent. He had arranged a union of large Western plants, several of which specialized in barbed wire, woven-wire fencing, and nails, while others carried on general steel production.

In the East the Carnegie interests by no means lorded it alone. The Crucible Steel Company was incorporated in the summer of 1900 as a consolidation of about thirteen properties, and held a practical monopoly of the output of crucible steel on the continent. The Pennsylvania Steel Company appeared in the spring of 1901 as a merger of two large Eastern plants, and shortly acquired the stock of that Spanish-American Iron Company in which Rockefeller had been a leading owner. Prominent among the other steel consolidations of the day were the American Tin Plate Company, with a capital of fifty millions; the American Steel Hoop Company; the National Steel Company; and two creations of Morgan, the National Tube Company and American Bridge Company.

As Carnegie, Morgan, and Rockefeller all believed, consolidation in the steel industry should go much further, for the bevy of medium-sized companies might at any moment engage in a life-and-death war. It was natural for Carnegie and Rockefeller to watch the situation with similar feelings. Both were distressed by the apparent imminence of an era of destructive competition. Both were anxious to retire from business before a conflict really broke out. Both were keenly interested in distributing their fortunes, and already had wide philanthropic interests to supervise. Their situations were similar in yet another respect. Rockefeller had steadily lost touch with those partners—H. H. Rogers, William Rockefeller, Flagler—who were interested in copper, gas, railroads, and banking, and he neither needed nor desired their assistance in building a steel empire. In the same way, Carnegie was steadily approaching a total breach with H. C. Frick. The two men, jarring on each other temperamentally, had often quarrelled about policies —Frick always being the bolder, the more venturesome; and now Frick was engaging in enterprises outside the steel business which Carnegie distrusted. Indeed, he was associated with Rogers and William Rockefeller in various undertakings. Had Carnegie decided to remain an ironmaster and build his own domain to greater strength, he could not have felt certain of Frick's loyal aid. Since by 1900 Rockefeller was sixty-one, and Carnegie was a year older, the assistance of such younger men as Gates, Frick, and Schwab would be indispensable to any long-continued undertaking.

We thus have a situation which pointed to certain obvious conclusions. Further consolidation seemed essential to a healthy steel industry. It might be undertaken by Rockefeller, who owned the richest iron mines and the greatest fleet of ore-carriers, or by Carnegie, who controlled the strongest mills; but both were really too old, and too much interested in philanthropy. Others must do it. Meanwhile, the two aging leaders, credited by a great part of the public with ambitions which neither entertained, were maneuvering for position, each resisting encroachments, each anxious to exact a fair price for his holdings, but both ready to sell. For three years, 1898–1900, talk of buying and selling filled Wall Street offices, uptown clubrooms, and the financial columns of newspapers. In the end, a group of dynamic outside leaders did step in, and both men sold their properties to help form the United States Steel Corporation.[32]

Only students of industrial and financial strategy would find a detailed rehearsal of the forays and hesitancies, the offers and withdrawals, of these three years profitable. Nor is our information, despite the reams of gossip printed weekly, at all precise and dependable. It appears that in 1899 Rockefeller offered to sell all his mines, ore-field railroads, and steamships to the Carnegie Company for fifty millions,[33] a bargain price which Carnegie should have snapped at had he been really interested in expansion. But he declined. Two factors, besides his general reluctance to accept new burdens, entered into this decision. As Schwab said later, Carnegie was always dourly cautious.[34] "I thought the industry would expand so that we would need all the ore we could possibly get. But Car-

[32]On the birth of the Steel Corporation see Hendrick's *Carnegie;* Harvey's *Frick;* Herbert L. Satterlee's *J. Pierpont Morgan;* J. H. Bridge, *The Inside History of the Carnegie Steel Company;* Abraham Berglund, *The United States Steel Corporation;* and Arundel Cotter, *The United States Steel—A Corporation with a Soul.*

[33]Mussey, *Mining Industry,* 134. Mr. John D. Rockefeller, Jr., recalls no such offer.

[34]Schwab to the author, June 15, 1939.

negie was a pessimist. If you look at the record of his life you will see that he was always nervous about the future, always cautious. It was Bill Jones and I who kept the plant constantly expanding. We insisted on putting Carnegie in debt for additions, additions, additions. I always wanted the company to buy its own mines; Carnegie always held back." The other reason was equally elementary. "Our experts did not believe in the Missabe ore fields. They thought the ore was too fine to work well, and too lean, its iron-content too small. They ridiculed Rockefeller's investments in Missabe. They couldn't understand why he, without any knowledge of the iron business, should plunge so heavily in a new field, putting a fortune into ores that would be useless for years to come."

It is also evident that the compact made in 1896 between the Carnegie-Oliver group and the Rockefeller organization by no means operated perfectly. The essence of this bargain was that Carnegie and Oliver should keep out of ore-transportation on the lakes, while Rockefeller should keep out of iron manufacturing. But actually Harry Oliver soon broke this agreement. He began buying Missabe ores and shipping them East on independent vessels. This flat violation of the compact resulted for a time in an approach to open warfare. The Rockefeller organization intimated that it might set up its own steel mills in the Chicago area, to which it could bring ore cheaply, while it obtained a virtual monopoly of the ore-carriers.[35] In 1900 Gates and L. M. Bowers, acting for Rockefeller, plunged into the market, bought the entire whaleback fleet of about thirty vessels for $3,000,000, and chartered a dozen large steel ships besides. The Carnegie Company had attempted, all too late, to purchase the whalebacks, while its efforts to take over the Mitchell Line of Buffalo had been repulsed when Rockefeller obtained that important fleet. By this shrewd move, the Rockefeller organization placed itself in a position to fix whatever charges it pleased for ore haulage. It promptly raised the rates for hauling ore from Duluth to the Lake Erie ports to $1.25 a ton, and the Carnegie Company had to pay that high charge on all its shipments. Not to be caught twice, the Carnegie interests at once incorporated their own $5,000,-000 Pittsburgh Steamship Company; but they realized that it would

[35]Schwab told me details of this.

take time to build up a formidable fleet, and that they would still be vulnerable.[36]

Meanwhile, Carnegie, who from his thirty-third year had talked about an early retirement, had indicated quite clearly his desire to sell out. In 1897–1900 he weighed two possible plans. One was a scheme for amalgamating the Carnegie Steel Company and H. C. Frick Coke Company, and selling the property to the existing partners at a moderate figure—even $125,000,000 was mentioned. The other plan was for selling to outsiders, in which event he and Frick spoke of $320,000,000 for their joint holdings. It has sometimes been said that Rockefeller was one of the outsiders who made an offer! What really happened was that H. H. Rogers came to Schwab and others of the Carnegie group with a proposal to open negotiations, but made no definite financial offer. Some Carnegie men thought he represented Rockefeller, but that was not true; and he shortly told Schwab that he could not raise enough money for a purchase.[37] He was more prudent than the daring promoter William H. Moore. This gentleman talked to Carnegie of buying, was asked to furnish $2,000,000 for a ninety-day option, and actually laid down $1,170,000 —a sum which Carnegie pocketed when Moore proved unable to raise the $320,000,000 required!

But Carnegie, as all the world knows, did sell—sold in January, 1901, to J. P. Morgan and his associates in the great adventure that gave birth to United States Steel. The long-familiar story of the events preceding this transaction we need not rehearse. Morgan had been drawn into the steel business by his work in helping organize and finance the Federal Steel, American Bridge, and National Tube Companies. He had threatened an aggressive competition, and Carnegie, proving that he was not too old to fight, had struck back by announcing that he was about to erect a great tube factory at Conneaut on Lake Erie. The aroused Scot, boasting that he would go on to make barbed wire, tin plate, nails, and other wares in this huge plant, grimly quoted Richelieu to his associates: "First, all means to conciliate; failing that, all means to crush." To frighten John W. Gates and the American Steel & Wire

[36]Mussey, *Mining Industry,* 134; shipping periodicals.
[37]Schwab to the author, June 15, 1939.

Company, he announced that he would build a great rod mill in the Pittsburgh district. To intimidate the Rockefeller organization, he declared that his Pittsburgh Steamship Company would build boats so fast that it would soon smash Rockefeller's grip on the lake ore-carrying business. To show the Pennsylvania Railroad that he would no longer permit it to levy excessive rates on the iron products which he sent to the Atlantic ports, he put a corps of surveyors into the field to map a new route from Pittsburgh to the sea. The doughty laird was ready to wage war on every front at once.[38]

One of the closest observers of business in this period tells us that an actual panic broke loose among the millionaires of Wall Street. "We must stop Carnegie," they vociferated. "He will wreck us unless we call a halt. He is getting entirely too arrogant."[39] All the masters of capital then interested in steel besieged Morgan's office, begging the Jupiter of American finance to loose a few thunderbolts. Many of them also appealed to the Standard Oil interests, approaching the so-called "Standard Oil crowd"—that is, William Rockefeller, H. H. Rogers, and James Stillman. These men believed that, since Morgan had done so much to finance new steel companies, the problem should be left to him. And Morgan, urged forward by Schwab and John W. Gates, magnificently shouldered the responsibility. Frick and Carnegie had just severed their partnership. The Morgan interests bought the Carnegie Company and all its properties for a colossal consideration—$303,450,000 in bonds, with stock worth about $144,000,000 in the market and nearly $200,000,000 in face value. Never before had the world witnessed a sale of such magnitude. Would it assure the country of industrial peace, and would the future justify so high a capitalization?

The pressure of circumstances now rapidly forced Morgan to attempt a union of nearly all the great iron-ore and steel-manufacturing interests of the country. At first he seems to have believed that it would be necessary to include in his combination only those steel companies with which his name had already become identified. That is, Gary's Federal Steel interests in the Middle West and the

[38]A spirited sketch of this may be found in Hendrick, *The Age of Big Business,* 79 ff.; see also Harvey, *Frick,* 260 ff.
[39]Moody, *Masters of Capital,* 81, 82.

Carnegie interests in the East, with some smaller properties, could be united in an irresistible combination. But he and his partners soon perceived that it would be perilous in the extreme to leave any of the more powerful competitors outside. If John W. Gates and his American Steel & Wire Company remained in the independent camp, a constant threat of war would hang over the industry, for "Bet-A-Million" Gates, with his belligerent and speculative propensities, might soon be betting his whole fortune on a struggle with Morgan. That other daring promoter, William H. Moore, would be almost equally ready to use his steel properties in an assault upon the new combination. Indeed, he and Gates as kindred spirits might conclude a sort of Napoleon-Alexander I alliance in a war for booty.

In short, just as Rockefeller, after uniting all the units of the Cleveland sector of the oil-refining industry, had found it necessary to consolidate the other sectors, so now Morgan felt impelled to bring all the principal units of the steel industry into one combination; the greatest business aggregation which the globe had yet seen.[40]

VI

Above all, it seemed important for the Morgan group to obtain Rockefeller's Missabe ore fields and his powerful Bessemer Steamship Company. The holdings built up by Rockefeller and his astute lieutenants, Gates and Bowers, constituted the greatest single potential menace to the new steel combination. They comprised the richest iron mines on the face of the planet, and the most efficient carrying fleet the Great Lakes had yet seen; the Rockefeller organization had only to erect new mills at South Chicago or Cleveland to undersell any competitor. If Rockefeller sold to some third person the threat might become still more alarming. Morgan, prodded by Gary, made up his mind that it was all or nothing; every company of strong financial resources or connections must be included, and Rockefeller's holdings must be among them.[41]

The interesting story of Morgan's negotiations with other inde-

[40]See the *Report of the Commissioner of Corporations on the Steel Industry*, in three parts (1911).
[41]Moody, *Masters of Capital*, 86.

pendent interests does not here concern us. It is sufficient to say that Judge Gary, acting as principal intermediary, brought the John W. Gates group and the Moore brothers into the combination, these interests asking and receiving very high prices. But the problem of buying Rockefeller's properties presented some delicate features, for Rockefeller and Morgan had never had any personal relations, and were temperamentally antipathetic. In her life of Judge Gary, Ida M. Tarbell prints a conversation, undoubtedly reported to her by Gary himself, which took place in the Morgan offices just after Gary had explained in detail why Rockefeller's ore deposits were absolutely indispensable.[42]

"How are we going to get them?" demanded Morgan.

"You are to talk to Mr. Rockefeller."

"I would not think of it."

"Why?"

"I don't like him."

Undoubtedly Morgan spoke the truth. He never liked any rival, or any man who had acquired a degree of financial or industrial power which made him a great independent potentate. By nature he was arrogant and imperious, anxious always to play a dominating rôle, and unwilling to admit the equality of any contemporary figure. He had watched the rise of the Standard Oil with a dislike and irritation into which entered an element, probably unconscious but quite real, of jealousy. For his part Rockefeller, austere, self-contained, and coldly averse to the public gaze, disliked Morgan's ways: his regal pose, his huge expenditures on his yacht, art treasures, and private library, his versatile interests, his lordly glittering magnificence.[43] It was the Puritan against the Medicean prince, each incapable of understanding the other. In all the more desirable syndicates and promotions which he backed, Morgan never once admitted Rockefeller to the long list of initial participants—and Gates and the younger Rockefeller noted this fact in their tablets. Apparently the two magnates had thus far met but once. William Rockefeller knew Morgan well, and since William was ready to show a proper deference, Morgan took an attitude of condescending friendliness toward him. Once at William's home on the Hudson,

---

[42]Tarbell, *Elbridge H. Gary*, 118, 119.
[43]Various recorded conversations of Rockefeller corroborate this.

John D. Rockefeller and Morgan were introduced. "We had a few pleasant words," said Rockefeller later.[44] "But I could see that Mr. Morgan was very much—well, like Mr. Morgan; very haughty, very much inclined to look down on other men. I looked at him. For my part, I have never been able to see why any man should have such a high and mighty feeling about himself." There is a world of meaning in those four words: "I looked at him."

The story of what now happened has some comic-opera touches. Morgan swallowed enough of his imperious pride to make an approach to Rockefeller, asking for an interview at 26 Broadway. To this Rockefeller replied that he had retired from business and never went down to his office, but that he would be glad to see Morgan at 4 West 54th Street, at the latter's convenience—on the understanding that only matters of a personal nature were to be discussed! This was an ironic condition, for Morgan had no wish to make a purely social call. Taking the stipulation in a Pickwickian sense, he went uptown and laid his business before the unresponsive Rockefeller. Gary's biographer tells us how the financier reported this interview the next day. He came in excitedly, throwing his arms up in exultation, and shouting to Gary, "I have done it." The latter naturally replied, "Done what?"

"I have seen Rockefeller."

"How did he treat you?"

"All right."

"Did you get the ore lands?"

"No. I just told him that we ought to have them, and asked him if he would not make a proposition. How much do you think we ought to pay?"

What Rockefeller had apparently done, when Morgan—for once masking his imperious manner behind a show of gracious courtesy —had asked for a "proposition," was to tell him that John D. Rockefeller, Jr., and Frederick T. Gates were in immediate charge of his investments, and that he must see them. Some incorrect accounts of the sequel have found their way into print. The true story of what happened is simple if in its way dramatic.[45]

H. H. Rogers came to John D. Rockefeller, Jr., at 26 Broadway

---

[44]Rockefeller to W. O. Inglis, Sept. 20, 1917.
[45]John D. Rockefeller, Jr., to the author, April 3, 1939.

immediately after Morgan's call. He was closely in touch with Morgan, for as soon as plans for the great steel consolidation began to develop, the financier had called in important industrialists connected with the great independent steel companies to advise him —Rogers, Frick, Norman H. Ream, and others. "Would you like to go with me to meet Mr. Morgan?" asked Rogers. "I should be glad to," said John D. Rockefeller, Jr. He knew that Morgan wished to buy the Missabe mines and the ore-carriers, and that his father was willing to sell. A discussion, since Morgan had asked for "a proposition," seemed very much needed. The dapper, carefully dressed Rogers, handsome and magnetic, with the young man fresh from Brown—still only twenty-seven—proceeded to Morgan's office.

As they were ushered in they found Morgan talking with his partner, Charles Steele, about some legal papers. He did not raise his head or take any other notice of their entry. As soon as he had finished and dismissed Steele, Rogers stepped up and introduced the younger Rockefeller. Morgan, with the bull-like glare sometimes characteristic of him, fiercely ejaculated "Well"—and his "Well" could be and now was meant to be terrifying:

"Well, what's your price?"

If that assault was intended to take young Rockefeller off his guard, it failed. With great aplomb, the young man stood his ground.

"Mr. Morgan, I think there must be some mistake," he remarked. "I did not come here to sell. I understood you wished to buy."

The two confronted each other with unyielding gaze. For a moment it seemed that the interview was over. Then Morgan assumed a friendlier tone. He had requested Judge Gary to compute a fair price, and the judge had furnished him with "an outside figure" of $75,000,000 for the Missabe fields.[46] Morgan knew that the initiative was properly his, but was plainly uncertain how much he should or could offer. Finally young Rockefeller made a suggestion:

"If you are really interested in buying the properties, isn't it wise to find some man competent to advise you on their value?" And Rogers chimed in: "You need an expert steel man. Since you have confidence in Mr. Frick, why not turn to him?"

It was agreed that Frick should act as negotiator or adjustor in trying to arrange an agreement between Morgan and Rockefeller.

[46]Tarbell, *Gary,* 119.

Both men felt implicit confidence in his judgment and fairness. Rockefeller and his son would have found great difficulty in treating with the imperious Morgan, but the cool, impassive Frick, who never raised his voice above a quiet conversational tone, was a man of their own temperament. He was plain and unassuming, never forgetting that he had begun life in poverty. Particularly did the elder Rockefeller find in him congenial traits—his unemotional quality, his chill, precise intellect, his concentration upon business, his hatred of the imprecise and shortsighted. Frick was always friendly toward the Standard Oil. Half a dozen years later he wrote a long letter to President Roosevelt in an effort to arrange an amicable settlement of the government suit against the combination.[47] At Morgan's request, he called on the younger Rockefeller and Gates, and began negotiations. A number of interviews took place.

As it became evident that Morgan and Gary thought $75,000,000 the "outside price" while the Rockefeller organization demanded more, Frick went out to Pocantico Hills to talk with Rockefeller. Leaving his carriage at the entrance of the grounds, he walked inside, and found Rockefeller strolling about. They talked for some time, Frick urging an agreement. "As my son told Mr. Morgan," Rockefeller said, "I am not anxious to sell my ore properties. But, as you surmise, I never wish to stand in the way of a worthy enterprise. I do frankly object, however, to a prospective purchaser arbitrarily fixing an 'outside figure,' and I cannot deal on such a basis. That seems too much like an ultimatum. Now I want to ask you a question. . . . Do you or do you not agree with me that the price these gentlemen propose to pay is less by some millions than their true value?"[48]

Frick did agree, and candidly said as much. As a result of his talks with the two Rockefellers and Gates, he arrived at what all four thought a fair figure. Then he went back to the Jupiter of Wall Street.

"Mr. Rockefeller," he reported, "will sell the Missabe mines and the Great Lakes fleet if you will pay $5,000,000 more than the 'outside price' that Judge Gary set. I think that is fair."

Judge Gary was present. Astonishment and dissent were written on his countenance. "That is a prohibitive sum!" he exclaimed hotly.

[47]Harvey, *Frick*, 308, 309.   [48]*Idem*, 265.

But after spending nearly half a billion for the Carnegie properties, Morgan was not a man to boggle over minor sums. "Judge Gary," he expostulated, "in a business transaction as great as this would you let a matter of $5,000,000 stand in the way of success?"

"But I told you, Mr. Morgan, that mine was the *outside* figure."

"Well, put it this way: Would you let those properties go?"

"No," admitted Gary.

"Well, write out an acceptance."[49]

This was in March, 1901; and on April 2 the United States Steel Corporation sent out a circular to the stockholders, announcing that the Rockefeller properties had been included in the new amalgamation. Frick often expressed pride in having helped effect this arrangement. The price paid was actually moderate: $80,000,000 for the Missabe properties, half of it in preferred and half in common stock of the United States Steel, and $8,500,000 in cash for the ore-carrying fleet. Naturally, many observers at the time thought the sum colossal. These Missabe mines had never paid a dividend, and a few years earlier experts had been talking of them as Rockefeller's folly. The total of $88,500,000 was approximately one fifth of what Morgan had paid for all the far-flung properties of the Carnegie Steel Company, representing a lifetime of effort on the part of Carnegie and his partners; while Rockefeller's properties had been acquired within the last ten years, and represented an accidental and to him a very subordinate line of endeavor. But actually, as time soon proved, the payment was very reasonable.

VII

Years later, testifying before the Stanley Committee, Rockefeller remarked: "The price seemed wholly fair at that time, and was entirely satisfactory to me. It was not long either before the purchasers themselves realized that it was really very low." He went on, reminiscently: "I doubt, as I recall the circumstances, if anybody but Mr. Frick could have effected the transaction."

"And if it had not been effected?" he was asked.

"Then, in my opinion," he replied with deliberation, "the United States Steel Corporation could not have survived the stress of its formative period."

[49]Tarbell, *Gary,* 119, 120.

Four leaders in the age of big business.

Above: Henry Clay Frick and J. Pierpont Morgan. *Below:* H. H. Rogers
and Henry M. Flagler.

Charles M. Schwab

J. Pierpont Morgan

Andrew Carnegie

Wm. Rockefeller

Charles R. Flint

Composite Photograph of Industrial Organizers

Henry C. Frick

John W. Gates

August Belmont

The "Father of Trusts," Charles R. Flint, published his "Memories of an Active Life," in which he included a page of "industrial organizers," as seen singly and as a composite group.

It is said that Schwab remarked at the time that Rockefeller's mines were worth $500,000,000 on the basis of the ore merely in view; but that statement suggests hindsight rather than foresight, and was probably made years later. Rockefeller always felt that both sides had made a fair bargain, and that Frick had placed, for the year 1901, a fair appraisal upon the ore-beds. The Rockefellers and Frick had some later contacts; for Frick entertained the younger Rockefeller in Pittsburgh, and it is said once played a round of golf with Rockefeller, getting well defeated.[50]

For some years Rockefeller was one of the largest owners of stock in the United States Steel. Not long after its formation a piece of litigation made the New York press eager to obtain a list of stockholders, and reporters besieged the judge presiding over the case, who finally told an *Evening Post* man that the information was all a matter of public record in the capitol of New Jersey. *The Evening Post* scooped the other newspapers with a list of the chief stockholders. This was headed by the name of Bertram Cutler, otherwise lost to fame! For some days the press made Bertram Cutler a household phrase, printing jingles and caricatures about the great unknown. Then it came out that he was financial adviser to Rockefeller, who had put his stock in Cutler's name, and the sensation faded.[51] Rockefeller was for several years a director of the Steel Corporation, and while he never attended a meeting, so much weight was attached to his name that the London *Economist* treated his resignation in 1904 as "the sensation of the financial week"— though his son and H. H. Rogers remained on the roster. Schwab later thought that he withdrew because he resented the same tendency which led Schwab himself to resign. The board represented a variety of leaders drawn from various industrial spheres, who thought more of their special interests than of the welfare of the United States Steel. Thus when Schwab announced the intention of the Steel Corporation to put up some new mills in the Pittsburgh area, Marshall Field called at his office to protest that they ought to be built in Chicago. Schwab explained that the varieties of steel they would make were best adapted to the Eastern market. This made no difference; the imperious Field declared that he would

[50]John D. Rockefeller, Jr., to the author, April 3, 1939; Harvey, *Frick,* 361.
[51]Alexander Dana Noyes to the author.

resign if the mills were not erected in Chicago![52] But Rockefeller actually resigned merely in accordance with his policy of divesting himself of unnecessary responsibilities.

It is evident from any review of the formation of the greatest steel-manufacturing company the world had yet seen, the first billion-dollar corporation—indeed, the capital of the Steel Corporation as represented by stocks and bonds amounted to approximately $1,400,000,000—that both Carnegie and Rockefeller were anxious to withdraw from the field. Carnegie later declared that he knew well that he could have exacted a far larger price for his holdings had he retained them some time longer. "I could as well have had $500,000,000 in a few years," he wrote John Morley while the sale was pending.[53] Not long after the steel merger, Morgan, Stillman, and Carnegie crossed the Atlantic on the same vessel. The two former were friendly and congenial, but neither liked the Scot, whom they frostily kept at a distance. At last, however, Carnegie cornered them, and spoke to Morgan on the subject nearest his heart. "I ought to have had a higher price, Mr. Morgan," he said assertively. "I should have asked two millions more—you'd have given it!" "Oh, yes, I'd have given it," Morgan half humorously replied, "if only to be rid of you!"[54] Rockefeller similarly knew that he could have realized a larger sum than $88,500,000 for his ore fields and ore-carriers had he kept them some years longer. But both men were too old to care for the glory of conquering new industrial worlds. Both had large philanthropies in view, and valued the opportunity to obtain capital in forms givable to others. Both believed in industrial concentration, and had a strong faith in the economic and social utility of the work that Morgan was doing in integrating so much of the steel business.

Carnegie now made his final bow to the industrial world, and stepped off the stage forever. Rockefeller was nominally still an active figure, holding the presidency of the Standard Oil; but he also had given up all business save his inveterate pursuit of buying and selling stocks.

One last incident—and not the least dramatic—remains to be recorded. The man who had done more than any one else to seize

[52]Schwab told me this.
[53]Hendrick, *Carnegie*, II, 145.   [54]Burr, *Stillman*, 159.

the rich opportunities presented by the Missabe field was Frederick T. Gates. It was Gates who was responsible above all others for the efficient construction and management of the fleet of ore-carriers. He had spent millions, and tens of millions had flowed into Rockefeller's coffers in return. In the negotiations with Morgan, as carried on through Frick, he had constantly been one of Rockefeller's chief representatives. Doubtless it was he, thoroughly conversant with the wealth of the ore field, who had insisted on the additional $5,000,000. When the transaction was completed, and the final papers drawn for signing, he appeared before Rockefeller, and made a complete report. The president of the Standard heard him attentively, and as he paused showed genuine gratitude.

"Thank you, Mr. Gates—thank you!" he exclaimed, with cordial emphasis.

But Gates knew that his services had been worth a material return over and above his modest salary. He stood facing Rockefeller with a strange glint in his eyes.

" 'Thank you' is not enough, Mr. Rockefeller," he replied.

And Rockefeller saw to it that he received a reward commensurate with his sagacity and enterprise.[55]

VIII

Exactly what profit Rockefeller made out of his Missabe investments it is impossible to state, for no complete record exists of the sums which he and Gates put into buying and maintaining the mines, railroads, and docks. Not millions but tens of millions had been courageously spent in development work. For years they had gone without any return on their entire investment.[56] It would be conservative, however, to put the final profit at $50,000,000. In looking at this huge gain, emptied into a pocket already holding one of the world's greatest fortunes, admirers of the Merritt brothers have launched some of their most caustic sarcasms at Rockefeller. To him who hath shall be given! We may heartily wish that the Merritts had fared better, though it is probable that if they had reaped

[55]Mr. Jerome D. Greene and others to the author. Gates himself told this anecdote to a number of people.

[56]As Rockefeller says in *Random Reminiscences,* "Our profits we invested in more ore-lands"; for "we believed that we could never have too many good mines."

the $50,000,000 profit, little of it would have been devoted to public purposes—while nearly all of Rockefeller's fortune has been or is being dispensed for philanthropic objects. But the plain fact is that the Merritts could never have made much out of the Missabe holdings, for they lacked the huge capital required to fructify them. More money, brains, and industrial skill than they possessed were needed to give the Missabe the great values it attained.

Rockefeller's organization at 26 Broadway was now making—usually on December 31—an annual audit of the estate. At the close of 1901, thanks to this large payment for the steel properties, the fortune for the first time went above $200,000,000.[57]

[57]Records of John D. Rockefeller, Jr.

XLII

Rockefeller Drops the Helm

With all the properties of the Standard Oil being transferred to the New Jersey holding company, with the nation on the highroad of prosperity again, and with McKinley and Hanna in power in Washington, no reason existed why Rockefeller should not complete his retirement from business. In 1899 he was sixty years of age. His health was impaired. The constant struggles he had waged from 1865 to 1895, sufficient to break down any man who did not unite a strong constitution with a resilient spirit, had left a deep mark, and his letters after 1890 complain of digestive ailments and nervous fatigue. At the time of the Chicago World's Fair he was stricken with a nervous disease, generalized alopecia, which caused the loss of all his hair, even his eyebrows, and which was accompanied by a good deal of physical distress. At the same time he began to grow corpulent. Photographs taken in 1890 present a man still spare and erect, with abundant brown hair and mustache; those of half a dozen years later show him portly and stooped, his face deeply lined, his head crowned by a black skull-cap which he soon replaced by a wig. Once youthful-looking for his years, he now seemed old and worn.[1]

He had originally contemplated retiring early in the nineties. "Having begun work so young," he wrote later,[2] "I felt that at fifty it was due me to have freedom from absorption in active business affairs and to devote myself to a variety of interests other than money-making." However, the financial storm of 1893 and the

[1] Information from Rockefeller's associates; Doctors George Wilson and N. W. Winkelman, *Journal of the American Medical Association*, Vol. 86, pp. 142 ff.
[2] *Random Reminiscences*, 134.

ensuing depression kept him in harness. The Standard was under attack in the courts; the threat of the Pure Oil Company demanded counter-measures; the oil-producing industry was rapidly extending westward, whither Rockefeller was anxious that the Standard should follow it; and the competition of Dutch and Russian oil in Europe and Asia was growing keener. Rockefeller's investments, in these years of deflation and bankruptcy, needed solicitous care.

By 1896, however, he was able to cease going to 26 Broadway every weekday, and thereafter he gradually sloughed off his responsibilities for the Standard Oil. In his *Reminiscences* he gives 1894-95 as the general date when he gave up "association with the actual management of the company's affairs." But for several years he occasionally put his hand to the tiller. In 1907 he stated that he had rendered no substantial services for a decade, and had not entered the Standard offices for eight years,[3] so that we may accept 1897 as the date when he relinquished his guidance, and 1899 as the date of final severance. The Standard was now sailing on an even keel. Two of his main policies, that of continuous expansion and that of close attention to efficiency, would continue unchanged. He could drop out without anxiety as to his gigantic creation. To be sure, he was not wholly out of touch. Whenever industrial changes, legislative proposals, or court attacks seemed to menace the Standard's interests, he was likely to call upon his old associates for information. Important papers were sent him for any comment he cared to give. Little groups of Standard executives sometimes came to his house to ask advice. Counsel for the company—Dodd, Ledyard, or John G. Milburn—might call to talk over legal questions. John D. Archbold, living in summer near Pocantico, occasionally drove over, while Rockefeller saw his brother William frequently. But active direction of the company was left to Archbold, who was elected vice-president of the Standard of New Jersey, Rockefeller holding the presidency as a merely honorary post.

A younger, more physically vigorous head was really needed. In the years just after Rockefeller's retirement conditions in the oil industry underwent a momentous set of changes. In the half-decade ending with 1900 the production of crude oil in the Appalachian and Lima-Ohio fields still constituted about 95 per cent of the whole

[3]*Independent*, LXIII (July 11, 1907), p. 60.

national output. But the breasts of mother earth there were drying up; while after 1900 the development of new trans-Mississippi fields went forward at a pace which gave the industry an entirely new aspect. Drillers by thousands swarmed over Kansas, Indian Territory, Texas, and California. In 1904 the production of the Appalachian and Lima fields was less than half that of the entire nation, and in 1905 less than two-fifths. The total yield of crude oil shot up with tremendous rapidity, more than doubling in the first five years of the century. Then in 1905–6 came rich new strikes in Illinois, where a huge production suddenly developed.

And as the industry adapted itself to this enlargement of the sources of supply, it had also to make the most of the urgent new demands created by the automobile. The horseless carriage of 1895, stuttering along at fifteen miles an hour, was a curiosity; by the turn of the century it was a plaything of the rich; a few years more and it had become a general utility. In 1907 a magazine writer spoke of "the throngs of cars of every desccription upon Fifth Avenue" and of "the endless procession of automobiles faring out in the country of a week-end." The cars which grew from eight thousand in 1900 to two and a half million in 1915 in America alone ran largely upon Standard oil fuel and lubricants. Refineries had to be remodelled to give emphasis to gasolene as against kerosene. Instead of depots for tank-wagons, the company had to erect service-stations as ports of call for cars. And Rockefeller and Archbold did not read of what the Wright brothers accomplished at Kitty Hawk without realizing that there, too, lay a field for applying gasolene power.

As the oil industry thus entered upon a transformation, the place of monopoly within it took on a new character. Rockefeller had built up his great trust primarily to stop the chaotic price-slashing by a multitude of small refineries. For decades, while a few tens of thousands of dollars sufficed to build an effective kerosene-manufactory, he and his associates felt they had to be ruthless in dealing with newcomers; open the door to a few, and anarchy would overtake the industry again. But now that great new oil fields had been discovered, now that the automobile was fast making gasolene the principal product, now that oil-refining involved far more complicated processes and expensive machinery than before, and now that business was being organized in huger units in every field, no place existed for the small refinery. It was impossible to carry on effective competition without a large capital, like that of the Pure Oil Company. Such competition was less likely to be irresponsible and savagely destructive than in the old days. In a word, much of the old excuse for monopoly was gone; and Archbold's policies soon showed that competition was needed to keep prices down to a fair level.

II

It was highly unfortunate for Rockefeller's reputation that he failed to make public his retirement, which was announced neither to the press nor to business associates. Even in the oil industry men were slow to realize that Archbold was the real head of the Standard. Rockefeller should have compelled Archbold to assume the title of president, and have seen that his own abandonment of active responsibility was blazoned to the country. Newspapers would have pounced on the statement! It is easy to comprehend his reasons for retaining the empty title of president. The Standard was under heavy fire, and resignation might be construed as a retreat. His titular leadership seemed important to the unity and enthusiasm of the personnel. "No man," his associates told him, "can hold this able organization together as your name can." Since his prestige in the business world was equalled only by Morgan's and Carnegie's, the Standard was more formidable while he was its nominal chieftain. Archbold, who disliked prominence and about whom less was written than about any other industrial leader of the day, was especially insistent that he remain. It seemed as difficult for the Standard to do without his fame as for Rome of the early imperial era to do without Cæsar's.

And yet his course was a mistake, for it led to a gross popular misconception of his pre-eminence in all Standard affairs which continued down to 1911. This was fostered by editors, cartoonists, financial men, and politicians. They identified Rockefeller with all the Standard's acts long after he ceased to have any responsibility for them. His name provided the obvious label for the trust, and it was easier to stick to the old stereotype than to tell the discriminating truth. Writers who knew better clung so tenaciously to it that muckraking magazines in the decade 1900–1910 without exception pictured the old man who was playing golf, looking after his investments, and surpervising his benefactions as the controlling head of the Standard. Their readers assumed that he spent every day at the 26 Broadway office, though he had not crossed the threshold for years. The London *Economist* remarked in 1911:[4] "Every performance of the Trust is attributed to the sinister figure of Mr. John D. Rockefeller—a figure so subtle and a career so delusive that his critics are forced to find a parallel in romance." Romance indeed! At that time he had been completely out of the oil business for more than a dozen years!

A double injustice was done Rockefeller by this fiction. Archbold no sooner took charge than he gave the Standard a more belligerent direction in almost every department. As the Bureau of Corporations later showed, he raised prices sharply and widened the margin between the cost of crude oil and the charge for refined. He indulged in harsher competitive practices to wipe out marketing rivals at home. He sold oil at low cost abroad and made up for the loss by higher rates in non-competitive domestic areas. No one can read the Bureau reports without perceiving that the Standard's operations became much more aggressive in 1897, and continued so. At the same time, Archbold meddled with politics much more actively and indiscreetly than the Standard had ever done under Rockefeller. As nominal president, Rockefeller was inevitably though quite erroneously held responsible for these acts.

Meanwhile, H. H. Rogers, William Rockefeller, and others had erected beside the oil-producing, oil-refining, and oil-marketing organization properly called the Standard Oil a huge and ruthless financial mechanism in Wall Street which was naturally but improperly termed the "Standard Oil crowd." During the decade 1897–1907, the heyday of industrial promotions and consolidations, Rogers and William were ceaselessly busy with financial flotations and manipulations, often reckless in character. They used the dividends from their Standard Oil holdings, the profits of other enterprises, and the credit of Stillman's National City Bank. With their schemes and battles, often brutal and sometimes clearly contrary to the public welfare, Rockefeller had nothing to do. To his intimates he expressed outspoken disapproval. He deeply resented the deliberate

[4] July 1, 1911.

refusal of H. H. Rogers to make it clear that he had no share in these forays and adventures.[5] Yet because he was nominally head of the Standard, men naturally identified him with the justly hated "Standard Oil crowd."

One feature of these speculations particularly distressed Rockefeller. In the early years of the Standard, when it constantly needed money for expansion and he had been reluctant to pile up banking obligations, it had borrowed money from some large stockholders at 10 per cent a year. Later the Standard's surpluses allowed ample funds for growth, and the directors decided that all these accounts should be closed. But, as Rockefeller told W. O. Inglis, "one or two men"—apparently two—insisted that theirs should continue running:

And in after years, [these men] having these open accounts, they were used as a means of covering up their individual stock speculations by giving the check of the Standard Oil Company and passing the money through these individual loan accounts. It was charged by the public that the Standard Oil Company was engaged in stock speculations. One important reason for this charge was that the check of the Standard Oil Company appeared in settlements of these stock transactions, and it was not an unnatural suspicion therefore that the Standard Oil Company were dealing in stocks. But it was not true; and in a change of administration it was found out, and the account was closed.

I had protested against the continuance of the loan accounts, having closed my own and did all I could as an officer of the company, resulting in a severe arraignment of the parties years before these reports were circulated about the transactions being by and for the Standard Oil Company. Mr. Archbold was very much concerned after he became president in regard to these rumors, and through him or Mr. A. C. Bedford the real facts about the case became known, and he it was who furnished me with this information. . . . Regarding this, as well as certain copper schemes and Wall Street speculations in which I had not any interest, I was made to suffer before the public; and the real offenders kept quiet, and allowed me to take the shafts; but I do not regret that I patiently did so, without saying anything, and thus kept peace within our ranks; and in after years the facts became known, and I was fully justified.

The choice of Archbold as the new head had long been accepted as inevitable. He had proved himself one of the ablest leaders in American business, and Rockefeller had come to place complete re-

[5]Mr. John D. Rockefeller, Jr., to the author.

liance upon him. The youngest of the higher Standard officers, just fifty in 1898, he was also the most vigorous. His heart was entirely with the combination, for he had no outside enterprise like those of Flagler and Rogers, and no interest in society. He had long been the company's principal spokesman in public investigations, where it found his business expertness, quickness of mind, and skill in defense invaluable. Nevertheless, he avoided the limelight, and was content to labor indefatigably without public notice.

It was also logical to select him because he had plans of his own, some as statesmanlike as others were questionable, for developing the business and increasing the profits. So capably did he execute them that when in 1911 the courts dissolved the trust, one writer commented that while Rockefeller had been the architect of the Standard Oil, Archbold had been its constructor. He believed in a well-rounded, stabilized, and highly powerful organization, beyond the reach of effective competition, which should steadily improve its methods and product. He wished to increase the Standard's holdings in oil lands, to erect new refineries in Texas, California, and other areas convenient to regional markets, to extend the pipe lines, and to make better use of the by-products. He dreamed of a far greater and more efficient organization than that of 1899, and the dream was realized. In any list of the creative business builders of the first decade of the century, his name would stand high.

Of Archbold's executive capacity no question can exist, for he possessed imagination, energy, shrewdness, and decision. He also had a natural gift for inducing men to work in harmony. One of the most lovable of leaders, his ready humor, gaiety, and kindliness made him idolized by many associates. He was so buoyant, mercurial, and full of effervescent good spirits that it was a delight to sit at the 26 Broadway lunch-table or be invited to his house. Never so cautious as Rockefeller, he had learned from him that in a multitude of councillors there is wisdom; he believed in a large executive committee, and insisted that it hold daily meetings to present a variety of points of view. From Rockefeller he had also learned to hear all the evidence on a given issue, and to thresh a question over until certain that the right decision had been reached. He reserved his judgment until the end, and usually based it upon a consensus of opinion. He seldom made a business error, but he lacked Rockefeller's broad view and feeling of responsibility to society at large.

His associates thought him an ideal leader, unassuming, optimistic, and resourceful. They told many stories of his democratic bonhomie. Once as he walked whistling through the halls, an annoyed clerk thrust his head from a door and bellowed, "Cut out that noise!" Then, recognizing Archbold, he turned pale; but the chief merely laughed and apologized for making himself a nuisance. Many who frequented Archbold's home in the early nineties had no idea that this boyish, talkative, gay-hearted figure was second in command at the Standard offices, or after 1897 that he was first in command. One young fellow who had associated with Archbold's children decided to apply for a job. He went to 26 Broadway, asked for an interview, got it, and spoke to Archbold as an equal. "He talked to me as though he was entertaining the king of England," said this man later. "He asked me what part of the business I would like to be in." Beginning as a driver of a tank-wagon, the young man rose to be senior vice-president of the Standard of New Jersey —and his devotion to the head may be imagined. But though usually graceful and delightful, Archbold could lose his temper. He would explode in a sudden white flash, and woe to anybody in front of him! As an associate grimly remarked: "Not a man in the organization dared take issue with him when he got going."[6] In anger, his power of retort and invective was withering.

With Archbold, for a few years, Rockefeller kept in intermittent touch; the new captain was often at Rockefeller's house, and they had a half-social, half-business intimacy. "We were all very fond of him, he was so witty and jolly," says John D. Rockefeller, Jr. But their contacts gradually became rarer. The writer who states that for years Rockefeller "had a direct wire to Archbold's office and kept that functionary on the griddle" is in error. Rockefeller had no desire to interfere with the new head, nor would Archbold have permitted it.

III

By 1899 the older group of Standard captains was passing from the stage, and a new generation, responsive to the magnetic, aggres-

[6]Moore, *Archbold,* 210.

sive ways of Archbold, was coming forward. Charles Pratt had died in 1891. Bostwick was buried the following year. Oliver H. Payne had long since lost all contact with the Standard Oil, and so had William B. Warden. Flagler, H. H. Rogers, and William Rockefeller increasingly tended to occupy themselves with affairs outside the oil business, leaving that to Archbold and his associates.

Ever since their first Florida visit, Rockefeller had followed with interest Flagler's passion for the development of the peninsula. For the rôle of state-builder had seized Flagler's imagination, and rejuvenated his powers and enthusiasm. The wealth he obtained from the Standard Oil was used in a long series of constructive undertakings. In 1886 he purchased the Jacksonville, St. Augustine & Halifax River Railroad, to which he later added other short lines, improving them and combining them to make the Florida East Coast Railroad. In 1892 construction was begun southward from Daytona; in 1894 Palm Beach was reached; in 1896 through trains puffed into Miami, then only a clearing. Meanwhile, he built a string of splendid hotels along the line—the Ponce de Leon and Alcazar at St. Augustine, the Ormond at Ormond, the Royal Poinciana and the Breakers at Palm Beach, and the Royal Palm at Miami. He often urged Rockefeller to visit them, and later Rockefeller did. Flagler was also interested in people of small means who took up farming and fruit-growing, and spent large sums to assist them. To help finance all this he sold considerable blocks of Standard stock to Rockefeller during the nineties—stock that soon went much higher. His most costly achievement, the railroad to Key West, still lay before him.[7]

Rockefeller was impressed by the way in which these ventures transformed the character of his shrewd partner, who had once been interested in little except money-making. Flagler found a new zest in life, and evinced a new concern for humanity. Every section boss on his East Coast line became a personal friend; every man who set out an orange grove was cordially advised and aided. All along the railroad he provided schools, churches, and hospitals, insisting that strict secrecy surround his gifts. He had his troubles. His second wife (the first, Mary Harkness, had died long before) be-

[7]Edwin Lefèvre, "Flagler and Florida," *Everybody's Magazine*, February, 1901; H. S. Cutler, *Florida*, I, *passim; In Memoriam Henry M. Flagler.*

came hopelessly insane. The Florida legislature in 1901 passed an act making incurable insanity for four years a ground for divorce, and Flagler promptly remarried. For this he and the legislature were subjected to harsh criticism. He was sensitive over his increasing deafness. But he vastly enjoyed his labors in converting a realm of neglected jungle and swamp into a rich agricultural area, and in making the long coastal strip the most luxurious recreation-ground America had yet seen.

In the activities of H. H. Rogers, equally spectacular in their way, Rockefeller took a much more critical interest. Though nearly sixty when the century closed, Rogers was as full of fire, energy, and ambition as ever. He had become the transportation magnate of Staten Island, controlling its traction lines and ferries. He was still interested in gas companies. As the Standard poured out larger dividends, Rogers during the nineties had invested part of his share in the Anaconda and other copper properties; and in 1899 he formed the first $75,000,000 section of a gigantic trust, the Amalgamated Copper. Another part of his dividends flowed into the enterprises of E. H. Harriman, and he became a minor power in Harriman's Union Pacific. He was also a director in the Santa Fé, the St. Paul, the Lackawanna, and other roads, and in the United States Steel Corporation. With Harriman he was drawn into the life-insurance field, where he figured in the lurid scandal and investigation of 1905. His last great undertaking, the building of the Virginian Railroad from the rich coal fields of West Virginia to Norfolk, was a $40,000,000 enterprise which he pushed through by his own grit, ingenuity, and credit; and he gave it the same consuming energy that he had put into his early work for Pratt and Rockefeller. Meanwhile, in his restless leisure hours he gambled impartially at poker and on the stock exchange.[8]

Virile, arrogant, and ruthless in business, magnetic and witty in society, Rogers still had a lunar dualism—dark on one side, bright on the other. Rockefeller and other men downtown knew that he could be as cold and sharp as a Toledo blade. He was an astute organizer, a reckless plunger in finance, a cruel and implacable fighter. His fits of anger were notorious. But upper Fifth Avenue,

[8]*Harper's Weekly,* May 29, 1909; *Dictionary of American Biography.*

where both clubs and drawing-rooms welcomed his presence, found him a charming social ornament. He liked to appear at banquets and public meetings, and always appeared well. An old admiration for Mark Twain's *Innocents Abroad* helped bring him into intimate relations with the humorist, whom he met accidentally at the Murray Hill Hotel in 1893, when Mark Twain was financially embarrassed by his troubles with a patent typesetter and a publishing firm. Rogers took Mark's finances in hand to make him "stop walking the floor," and by his sagacity, prestige, and force restored order in the author's affairs. He made the creditors all wait until they could be paid alike, he protected Mark Twain's copyrights, and he invested the accumulating funds wisely. It was a fine service to a great man, and Mark Twain gratefully declared:[9]

"He is not only the best friend I have ever had, but is the best man I have ever known."

As his activities led him away from Standard Oil, Rogers did not grow more friendly toward Rockefeller and other old associates. He knew well that Rockefeller strongly censured his ruthless generalship in the copper war. To men both inside and outside the office Rockefeller never concealed his condemnation of the worst acts of the Amalgamated leaders, who vindictively battled with other copper interests, corrupted courts and legislatures in Montana, wrecked a great Eastern bank, and defrauded investors. One associate recalls hearing him speak out very bluntly even in a public elevator. Rogers resented this attitude. He was also irritated by Archbold's elevation to power, for temperamentally the two men were alien; and Rogers would have liked to head the Standard himself, though he knew that his gambling propensities, diversity of interests, and unhappy public reputation made any thought of his selection preposterous. Possessing a vein of jealousy, he did not hesitate, in his suave way, to belittle both Rockefeller and Archbold. As his copper raids aroused public hostility, he realized that his social position might be improved if he could divert part of the wrath to other men. All his life he possessed a talent for intrigue. His offices were a series of connecting rooms into which visitors could be brought without seeing one another. Not many years passed

[9]Albert Bigelow Paine, *Mark Twain*, 971 ff.; 1035 ff.; 1658 ff.

before, ushering Miss Ida Tarbell to a seat, he was ever so urbanely insinuating that while Rockefeller and Archbold were great men, they were much more sinister than his own charming self.[10]

William Rockefeller was closely associated with Rogers in the formation of the Amalgamated Copper Company—he being secretary and Rogers president—and other undertakings. But in these enterprises he remained, as in the Standard Oil, a secondary figure —a follower, not a leader. While Thomas W. Lawson in *Frenzied Finance* penned devastating portraits of Rockefeller and Rogers, he paid tribute to William as a kindly, honest, helpful man. He was "a solid, substantial, sturdy gentleman with the broad shoulders and strong frame of an Englishman"; "a man of few, very few words and most excellent judgment"; "rather brotherly than friendly, clean of mind and body"; "a good, wholesome man made in the image of his God." So William impressed even those who most harshly condemned the copper operations of Rogers and Daly in which he was implicated. The year 1899 found William approaching sixty, and giving less and less time to the Standard. He owned Rockwood Hall, not far from Pocantico Hills, and saw much of his brother, while his two sons and two daughters were always intimate with Rockefeller's four children.

A few words are necessary upon the "Standard Oil crowd." It was in the nineties that men really awoke to the imposing financial might of the Standard Oil. For two decades every one had known that it was a colossal industrial power. But its profits had gone in the main to expanding its own business, and not until after the panic of 1893 did the weight of its huge cash assets and its annual surpluses impress the public. The dividends distributed to stockholders in 1893–1901 inclusive amounted to more than $250,000,000. By far the greater part of these profits went to a little group of half a dozen men: the two Rockefellers, Rogers, Flagler, Archbold, and Harkness. Obviously, this group wielded an immense financial power, particularly as at their back the Standard was maintaining a flow of dividends which averaged about $40,000,000 a year. Thanks

[10]Ida M. Tarbell, *Harper's Magazine,* January, 1939. Miss Tarbell has told me of these interviews. She related to me that Rogers, speaking of Rockefeller's retention of the title of president, said: "We told him he had to keep it. These cases against us were pending in the courts; and we told him that if any of us had to go to jail, he would have to go with us!"

to Rockefeller's wisdom, the Standard had never allowed any finance capitalist to obtain a large share in its fabulous returns. Money borrowed in the early days for expansion had been promptly repaid, and no banker had been permitted to lay a controlling finger on any part of the property. By 1890 the Standard was itself a great money reservoir. John Moody correctly states that it "was really a bank of the most gigantic character—a bank within an industry, financing this industry against all competition, and continually lending vast sums of money to needy borrowers on high-class collateral, just as the other great banks were doing." If the principal stockholders acted in unison, no other bank or money reservoir in the country—save perhaps J. P. Morgan & Company—could exercise more authority.

Most observers, seeing this power within the stockholders' grasp, supposed then and later that they did act in unison. In particular, it was believed that most of them moved in concert with the National City Bank, which, as the City Bank, had from time immemorial been the financial arm of the raw materials' merchants of New York. The first important head of this institution on the north side of Wall Street had been Moses Taylor, who graduated from a mercantile business into finance, built the bank to affluence, and died in 1882 worth perhaps $50,000,000. Percy R. Pyne had succeeded him. Then, on Pyne's death in 1891, one of the true banking geniuses of the century, James Stillman, became president. Stillman, of New England blood though of Texan birth, had begun his career with a firm of South Street merchants, but had soon moved from trade into finance, for which he showed an inborn flair. Drab of personality, tight-lipped, cold, and passionless, he stood in striking contrast with such men as the imperious, many-sided Morgan and the brilliant, dynamic Harriman. Old-fashioned in his methods, never a promoter or manipulator, he brought to banking a consuming passion, and showed a positively uncanny wisdom and adroitness in making money multiply itself. He parted from his wife, made numerous enemies, and in the whole of his life seems to have made but one close friend, the shrewd attorney John Sterling. It was largely under Sterling's advice that in 1897 the National City Bank purchased the Third National, with the result that its deposits rose almost immediately above $100,000,000. As the financial resources of the bank increased, its head dreamed of making it the greatest power in the money world. He predicted early in the century that within twenty-five years it would hold a billion in deposits.[11]

The connection between James Stillman and William Rockefeller went back to 1884, when they had been thrown into association as directors of the Chicago, Milwaukee & St. Paul. Their friendship soon grew close. They were utterly unlike—William genial, warm-hearted, energetic, Stillman reticent, chill, and deliberate; but they were congenial. "I like William," Stillman once commented, "because we don't have to talk. Often we sit fifteen minutes in silence before one of us breaks it!" In truth, they understood each other instinctively, for both believed in centralization, in efficiency, and in looking far into the future; while each comprehended how useful the bank and the trust might be to one another. William Rockefeller had a large voice in managing the Standard's finances. Its surplus flowed naturally into the coffers of the City Bank. In time marriage cemented the tie between the two families, for Stillman's daughters Elsie and Isabel married William's sons, William G. and Percy A. Rockefeller. The fact that William G. shortly became treasurer of the Standard did not weaken the link between the trust and the bank, or the disposition of William Rockefeller and H. H. Rogers to work with Stillman in such ventures as the reorganization of the Union Pacific Railroad. Indeed, the funds of William Rockefeller and the National City Bank did much to make E. H. Harriman's spectacular railroad career possible.

During the dark years 1893–1895, when the Standard Oil often relieved the money tension in Wall Street by lending its idle millions, the channel usually employed was the National City Bank. Men began to call it "the Standard Oil Bank." One anecdote preserved by Stillman's biographer states that the Standard and the National City Bank furnished $20,000,000 of the sum which J. P. Morgan and August Belmont produced in 1894 to help the Treasury keep the government on a gold basis. The account may have substantial truth, for the Standard's huge export sales for gold gave it a vast credit abroad:[12]

[11]See Anna Robeson Burr, *The Portrait of a Banker: James Stillman, 1850–1918;* John W. Winkler, *The First Billion: The Stillmans and the National City Bank;* Frank A. Vanderlip, *From Farm Boy to Financier.*

[12]Burr, *Stillman,* 116, 117.

One night in Paris, James Stillman told the story in French to a French friend who found it interesting enough to take down in notes still extant.

"The Treasury begged Morgan for fifty millions, which he refused, thundering 'Impossible!' Then they came to me and I went 'round to see what I could do. He was greatly upset and overcharged, nearly wept, put his face in his hands and cried: 'They expect the impossible!' So I calmed him down and told him to give me an hour, and by that time I cabled for ten millions from Europe from the Standard Oil and ten more from other sources and came back. I told him:

" 'I have twenty millions.'

" 'Where did you get them?' And when he heard—'Il bondit de l'abîme de désespoir au pinnacle de bonheur—' " Here his French failed the narrator and he concluded, "and became perfectly bombastic and triumphant, as the Saviour of his Country."

Americans as the century closed were becoming aware of a momentous change in the conception and function of banking. Once, when finance capitalism was younger, it had been an adjunct of industry; now it was coming to own, control, and direct great industrial units. The amazing story of the reorganization and rehabilitation of the Union Pacific furnishes an apt illustration. To this road Morgan, who after the panic of 1893 had refinanced and taken control of a large part of the nation's railroad system, was strangely indifferent. E. H. Harriman, who had made a great success with the Illinois Central, joined hands in 1897 with Jacob Schiff of Kuhn, Loeb & Co. to rescue the bankrupt road. They agreed to bring in Stillman, and Stillman in turn convinced William Rockefeller of the possibilities in the line. Financed by the personal funds of William Rockefeller, H. H. Rogers, and perhaps one or two other Standard Oil figures, by Stillman and other City Bank men, and by Kuhn, Loeb, the railroad was quickly placed on its feet. Harriman saw just what was needed for its practical improvement. He rebuilt the roadbed, bought rolling stock, and made a decaying property into one of the world's most efficient carriers. With William Rockefeller and the City Bank at his back, after the death of Collis P. Huntington he seized control of the Southern Pacific. The battle between Harriman and James J. Hill in 1901 for control of the Northern Pacific was in great degree a bankers' battle, for behind Hill stood the Chase National Bank and the Morgan interests, and behind Harriman stood the City Bank and Kuhn, Loeb.

But no generalizations are more inaccurate than those which pass current in circles of financial gossip. Those who talked of the Standard Oil as a unified money power, or of "the Rockefeller crowd," were talking nonsense. The "Rockefeller crowd" actually consisted of two men, William Rockefeller and H. H. Rogers. At no time did John D. Rockefeller join William in an important investment outside the oil industry. On the contrary, he deliberately steered clear of William's operations, partly because he thought them too speculative—"William always judges everything by intuition and instinct; he doesn't act on analysis," he said once—and partly because he thought his brother should have a clear field.[13] He kept out of the Union Pacific. He did not put a penny into that Amalgamated Copper syndicate which sowed the wind and reaped the whirlwind. The merger in 1899 of the Consolidated Gas Company with the Edison Illuminating Company brought both, various writers have said, under the control of the Standard; actually it brought them under the control of William Rockefeller and Rogers. John D. Rockefeller had nothing to do with the merger, while the Standard, now directed by Archbold, was not interested in the manufacture and sale of gas in New York except in so far as it sold oil to the manufacturers.

Few legends have laid a more grandiose spell upon chroniclers than that of the Standard Oil alliance with the National City Bank. Various flaws may be found in the picture. But the chief is simply that Rockefeller, holding more than a quarter of the Standard's stock, had no part in the supposed coalition. He distrusted James Stillman even more than he did most bankers. During the panic of 1893 Stillman had asked how much ready money he could supply to help meet the stringency in Wall Street, and Rockefeller had offered a maximum of $5,000,000—"Up to that any sum you wish." He suspected afterward that Stillman, drawing large funds, had held them longer than necessary and used them for his own benefit. Throughout the nineties Rockefeller felt highly uneasy over William's efforts to keep a large part of the cash assets of the Standard Oil in the National City Bank. He opposed any alliance with finance capitalism. He feared that the funds, which drew little in-

[13]Mr. Henry Cooper to the author. Mr. Cooper once suggested that he invest some funds in the Chicago, Milwaukee & St. Paul. "No, that is William's," he replied.

terest, might be misused. At Standard meetings Rockefeller continually raised the question: "Why are these sums not used for expansion? If they cannot be used for expansion, why not invest them? And if we cannot invest them, why not put them out as call money? They would earn a better return." In this stand he was always supported by Archbold, Hunt Tilford, and others, and opposed by William and H. H. Rogers. He would win his point, but then the money would presently slip back into the City Bank, and a new showdown would be needed. The fact that the treasurer of the Standard was both Will's son and Stillman's son-in-law seemed to him highly unfortunate—particularly as the young man's judgment was unreliable and he drank to excess.[14] But he never quarrelled with Will; the two brothers were devoted to each other, spent much time together, and threshed out all their differences in the open.

A great combination uniting the wealth of all the Standard's principal stockholders with that of the National City Bank, Kuhn, Loeb & Co., the Union Pacific, and Harriman's other lines would have been a most dangerous combination indeed; but nothing of the sort ever existed. John D. Rockefeller's fortune stood on an absolutely independent basis.

As the old generation of Standard Oil leaders were drawn away from 26 Broadway, a group of somewhat different type took charge under Archbold. Fewer of them were self-made, or trained in the school of hard knocks; more were college-bred men of travel and reading, versatile in their tastes. Charles M. Pratt, for example, only forty-five in 1900, was a graduate of Amherst. His father having given him a careful business training, he became president of the Standard of Kentucky, and first secretary, then treasurer, and finally vice-president of the Standard of New Jersey. Like his father, he was essentially a merchant, interested above all in marketing. Clean-cut and handsome, cultivated and public-spirited, he was a

[14]Conversations of the author with Mr. Bertram Cutler, Mr. Henry Cooper, and others. Rockefeller was often credited with large holdings of National City Bank stock. Actually he owned very little of it; in 1906, as he told the mayor of Compiègne, France, about $300,000 worth. While William Rockefeller and Rogers supported Harriman (see George Kennan, *E. H. Harriman, A Biography,* II, 343 ff., for details), John D. Rockefeller invested liberally in the railroads of George J. Gould, Harriman's rival and enemy. Gould had an early fight with Harriman over the Colorado Fuel & Iron, a property which eventually passed into Rockefeller's control.

trustee of Amherst and Vassar, president for years of the Pratt Institute, and a leading citizen of Brooklyn. His younger brother Herbert, who managed the Kings County and Long Island refineries, was also a graduate of Amherst. Henry C. Folger held degrees from Amherst and the Columbia Law School. He became head of the manufacturing committee of the Standard, and then a director; but meanwhile he was building up the finest library of Shakespeareana in America, writing monographs on the drama, and pursuing mathematical studies. Alfred C. Bedford, a member of the manufacturing committee until 1907 and then a director, had gone from Adelphi College to study in England, Germany, and Switzerland —the family being English. He was prominent in the work of the Y. M. C. A., the Pratt Institute, and the Baptist Church. E. T. Bedford, who became a director in 1903, was interested in sports, and bred "Hamburg Belle," the mare which for a time held the world's record of 2.01¼. Walter C. Teagle, who joined the export department of the Standard in 1903, became its head, and was made a director in 1910, had graduated from Cornell University.

But important men of the older stamp remained with the company. One was Ambrose McGregor, his Scottish sagacity deepened by the years. One was the headlong, explosive James A. Moffett, Camden's protégé, who became president of the Standard of Indiana. The organization found his impetuous energy invaluable in many fields. James Smith, a Cleveland boy trained first by Sam Andrews and then by Ambrose McGregor, was sent from 26 Broadway to rebuild the Bayonne refinery when, in 1900, that great forty-acre plant was razed to the ground by fire; he managed it for eight years, and then became head of the manufacturing committee. John W. Van Dyke, Henry M. and Wesley H. Tilford, and Orville T. Waring were all veterans who remained active. So, too, did Frank Q. Barstow, who had been with Archbold in the old Titusville days, and who stayed in harness till his death in 1909.

IV

Early in the new century the simplicity which had characterized Rockefeller's life was decidedly modified by his creation of his wide Pocantico estate. It added to the three homes he had previously owned a beautiful new residence.

This new estate began modestly. He needed a place near New York for short summer sojourns and winter week-ends. In 1893 he therefore bought a little group of properties at North Tarrytown, N. Y., comprising part of the ridge which separates the Sawmill River from the Hudson. Seventeen or eighteen parcels in all, they cost a total of $168,705. On the slope of the principal eminence, Kijkuit Hill, was a comfortable wooden house of homely architecture, but with the broad piazzas and verandahs that he liked. While it had few charms besides spaciousness and coolness, the views it commanded were magnificent. Any one standing on the western veranda looked out over the Hudson just where the Tappan Zee makes it broadest. Gazing northward, his eye could follow the river to the portals of the Highlands; southward, far down toward New York Bay. The main structure of the house was two stories high, with an attic. Simply furnished, the place gave Rockefeller a pleasant place of retirement.

It also gave him a new employment. Piece by piece, he rapidly increased the property. He bought a large tract from Rufus A. Weeks for some $50,000, and a still larger one from the Parsons estate. Before the end of the century the holding consisted of more than 1600 acres. Meanwhile, he was busy transforming its aspect. As plots were purchased he demolished buildings, whisked away fences, and removed unsightly boulders. Ragged clumps of woodland were sheared down, bushes uprooted, and lawns planted. At intervals he broke the open, gently rolling slopes with patches of native forest, or by trees and shrubs which he himself set in. He built many miles of winding drives and bridle-paths, making the most of the points overlooking the Hudson, and opening wide vistas wherever needed. In his *Reminiscences* he wrote later that he had always delighted in this "old house where the fine views invite the soul and we can live simply and quietly."

Unfortunately, the house burned down in the summer of 1902. John D. Rockefeller, Jr., who was staying in it at the time, at once bought furniture for another cottage on the estate, somewhat nearer to Tarrytown; and the family occupied this place when at Pocantico for the next seven years. Meanwhile, the elder Rockefeller frequently spoke of placing a new house on the top of the Kijkuit hill, but did nothing about it. He never liked to burden himself with the detail of building operations. His son finally suggested Delano & Aldrich as architects to draw plans; and Rockefeller and his wife determined the general arrangement, and decided how many rooms would be required—making provision for visiting children and grandchildren as well as guests. But when the plans were completed, he did nothing to utilize them. "After a while," writes the son, "I became convinced that the reason he did nothing was because he hesitated to build so large a house, with the additional care which its operation would involve, but on the other hand was too generous to suggest a smaller house, which would not adequately accommodate children and grandchildren. I therefore suggested that the plans be redrawn to provide a house that would fully meet his needs and Mother's, and provide for such guests as they might want to have but go no further in size. This met with Father's immediate approval and seemed to be a great relief to him."

The house, moderate in size and Georgian in style, was immediately erected. Its guest rooms were in the third story, with dormer windows. John D. Rockefeller, Jr., and his wife supervised the construction, and also bought all the furniture, china, silver, glass, and works of art, employing the best advisers. The younger Rockefeller frequently told the architects and decorator that his ideal was a residence so outwardly simple that friends visiting his father, and coming from no matter how humble an environment, would be impressed by the homelikeness and simplicity of the house; while those who appreciated fine design and were familiar with beautiful furnishings would say, "How exquisite!" This combination of simplicity and beauty was attained. Rockefeller and his wife were delighted with the house. But after a time they felt that the dormer rooms were not adequate for guests, that the outlook on the entrance side was too restricted, and that the service entry was noisy. John D. Rockefeller, Jr., writes:[15]

To correct these defects, the house was taken down to the second story; the entrance front extended out to include the piazza, with stone arches and columns replacing the wooden ones; and a full third story with a mansard fourth story added, all of stone. The approach to the house was extended some five hundred feet by making an enormous fill that involved thousands and thousands of loads of dirt brought in by a caravan of teams; the building of a huge retaining wall to confine this extended

[15]Memorandum for the author.

fill. To overcome the noise at the service entrance, the entrance was dropped from the basement to the subbasement and approached by a long tunnel so that the deliveries were made underground and without noise. These changes involved the entire re-landscaping and planting of the area around the house, although that had been fully completed before,' and were of a most radical nature. They gave Father great satisfaction, however, particularly the large fill at the entrance and the excavation of the service tunnel, for difficult projects of that kind always interested him. In 1913 the practically rebuilt house was finished and again ready for occupancy.

Even after this mansion went up at Kijkuit, Rockefeller had no residence that compared with some of the great houses at Newport; with the stone palaces that Carnegie, Frick, and William A. Clark built on Fifth Avenue; with the houses of some of the steel magnates in Pittsburgh; or with the great establishments rising about Tuxedo. It could not be mentioned with George Vanderbilt's "Biltmore House" in North Carolina, William C. Whitney's Venetian palace on Long Island, Gould's "Georgian Court," or the chateau on Riverside Drive upon which Charles M. Schwab was reputed to have spent $7,000,000. Rockefeller kept no yacht like Morgan's *Corsair* or J. J. Astor's *Nourmahal*. It is evident that he derived his chief satisfaction at Pocantico not from the house, but from the grounds, which by 1908 approached 3000 acres in extent. To set out clumps of trees, to level hills, to build roads, to open wide views, delighted him more than anything else.

Here he could execute on sweeping lines what he had done at Forest Hill on a small scale. He grew young trees by thousands, especially evergreens, to be used in his planting schemes. When he bought a golf clubhouse at Lakewood, N. J., and converted it into another residence, he made a small fortune out of himself by selling it at $1.50 or $2 trees which had cost but five or ten cents at Pocantico. He frankly confessed the pride which he took in saving and moving large trees—trees of ten to twenty inches in diameter. "We build our movers ourselves, and work with our own men, and it is truly surprising what liberties you can take with trees, if you once learn how to handle these monsters. We have moved trees ninety feet high, and many seventy or eighty feet. . . . Perhaps the most daring experiments were with horse-chestnuts. We took up large trees, transported them considerable distances, some of them after they were actually in flower, all at a cost of twenty dollars per tree, and lost very few." Careful records showed that the tree-moving campaign of a whole season was sometimes accomplished with a loss of only 3 per cent. "We have grouped and arranged clumps of big spruces to fit the purposes we were aiming for, and sometimes have completely covered a hillside with them."

This passion for recontouring land and making fine vistas was one of the oldest and most constant of his life. Like Cyrus the Great, he always pointed with special pride to the trees planted by his own hand. Once he scored a genuine triumph:[16]

Others may be surprised at my claim to be an amateur landscape architect in a small way, and my family have been known to employ a great landscape man to make quite sure that I did not ruin the place. The problem was just where to put the new place at Pocantico Hills ... I thought I had the advantage of knowing every foot of the land, all the old big trees were personal friends of mine, and with the views at any given point I was perfectly familiar—I had studied them hundreds of times; and after this great landscape architect had laid out his plans and had driven his lines of stakes, I asked if I might see what I could do with the job.

In a few days I had worked out a plan so devised that the roads caught just the best views at just the angles where in driving up the hill you came upon impressive outlooks, and at the ending was the final burst of river, hill, cloud, and great sweep of country to crown the whole; and here I fixed my stakes to show where I suggested that the roads should run, and finally the exact place where the house should be.

"Look it all over," I said, "and decide which plan is best."

It was a proud moment when this real authority accepted my suggestions as bringing out the most favored spots for views, and agreed upon the site of the house.

Associates of Rockefeller testify that he became expert in all the craft of the landscape architect. "I am thinking of moving that hillock," he would remark, and gaze at it appraisingly. "Offhand, I would say there are just about 650,000 cubic feet of dirt there." He laid out a drive through a deep rock cut; he built a stone wall to hide a railroad. In these years he often kept at his planting, tree-moving, and road-building until he was exhausted. He would run the lines for new paths until darkness made it impossible to see the stakes and flags, and then tramp wearily home.

[16]*Random Reminiscences*, 24–28.

Obviously, in his recreations he was above all an outdoor man. His brother Frank had his large and finely fitted ranch in Kansas. His brother William not only owned Rockwood Hall and its 800 acres, but a summer camp of many thousand acres at Bay Pond in the Adirondacks, and a winter cottage at Jekyll Island, Georgia. All three brothers had the vigorous tastes of old William Avery Rockefeller.

v

Rockefeller's other recreations had insensibly changed. Even when past sixty he continued his bicycle riding and skating. But after retirement he ceased to drive fast trotters in Central Park or on the speedways. The stables at Pocantico contained good riding horses for the children, while he and his wife liked to drive a steady pair on sunny afternoons around the estate. Racing, however, was out of the question.

He still went occasionally to concerts, Mrs. Rockefeller and he subscribing to the Philharmonic. He may have attended the opera, for William had a box. But he almost never went to the theatre. His son recalls that when in 1901 Weber and Fields were convulsing audiences with "Hoity-Toity," Rockefeller was prevailed upon to go to the Music Hall to see them.[17] One feature of the show was their famous banking scene. Weber was to furnish the money for a bank in Monte Carlo, while Fields and Bernard were to give him a joint note for their interests. "A joint note," they explained, "is a note signed by three or more people who all become unreliable for the full amount." While spectators held their sides, Rockefeller sat grimly impassive. But when De Wolf Hopper came on with Lillian Russell in a more dignified bit of comedy, he was amused beyond words. Some years later Rockefeller was in Santa Barbara. His son took him to see William Gillette in "Sherlock Holmes," and that consummate bit of acting he greatly enjoyed. A taste for the theatre, however, was as little in his make-up as a taste for books. He still listened in the evening while Mrs. Rockefeller or Lucy Spelman read aloud, and the family recall his appreciation of Ian MacLaren's *Beside the Bonny Brier Bush*. Like Grover Cleveland, he was delighted by *David Harum*. He read the Bible, devotional

[17] Cf. Felix Isman, *Weber and Fields*, 276–277.

or inspirational books, newspapers, and sometimes the principal Baptist journals. But his best books were people.

His principal new recreation was golf, a game now rapidly coming into vogue. The first golf club in America had been the St. Andrews of Yonkers, which built a six-hole course in 1888. A Chicago club completed an eighteen-hole course in 1893, and by the end of 1895 the country had more than a hundred links. Though some prejudice long surrounded the game as a rich man's sport, by 1900 millions were taking a keen interest in the exploits of the Australian-born Walter J. Travis, who that year won the American amateur championship. The previous February, Rockefeller and his wife were staying at a hotel in Lakewood, N. J., with their friends the Johnsons of Spuyten Duyvil. Mr. E. M. Johnson, an enthusiastic golfer, often joined Rockefeller in playing quoits. Praising the magnate's dexterity, he urged him to apply it to golf. At last Rockefeller submitted to some instruction on a grassy field remote from public view. They took a caddy and a bag of clubs, and Johnson explained the principles of the game. His pupil's first three strokes were straight, true drives of a hundred yards—unlike most beginners, he did not try to shoot too far. For some days the two men practised in the lonely field, until on April 2, 1899, Rockefeller played his first game on the nine-hole course of the Ocean Country Club. He showed no embarrassment before the curious spectators, and covered the nine holes, some 2800 yards, in 64 strokes; not a bad mark when it is considered that he had to cross half a dozen bunkers, two brooks, and three roads, while the rather narrow course was tree-lined. Next day he did the course in 61 strokes. As his form improved he became more and more enthusiastic.[18]

He immediately put in four golf holes at Pocantico Hills, and in 1901 engaged one of the early golf architects, Willie Dunn, to lay out a course of twelve holes. These links were not easy, for the turf was heavy, while a Japanese lake in a setting of boulders offered a stiff hazard. A professional from Ardsley, Willie Tucker, came up regularly to give him lessons. At Forest Hill, meanwhile, he had a nine-hole course built, and was tutored by another professional, Joe Mitchell. Here the ground was much more level than at Pocan-

[18]Memorandum by Mr. E. M. Johnson.

tico. As it was the strokes, not the walking, in which Rockefeller was interested, he provided bicycles for all the players. "I like to play golf as much as possible," he explained, "so I save up energy."

A cartoon by Viafora in the New York Evening Mail

A popular conception of Rockefeller as a golfer

This practice he kept up at Forest Hill until the house burned down in 1918, and he forsook the place. In his last years there he even had men on the estate push his bicycle to save him exertion. His favorite companions at Forest Hill included Levi Scofield, Doctor Biggar, his brother-in-law W. C. Rudd, and the Euclid Avenue ministers, first Doctor Charles A. Eaton and then Doctor William W. Bustard.[19]

[19]For a good account of Rockefeller as golfer, see William Hemmingway, "John D. Rockefeller at Play," *Harper's Weekly*, Feb. 15, 1909.

Like Frederick W. Taylor, the father of scientific management, who braved a good deal of criticism by taking up golf in 1895, Rockefeller employed unusual methods to improve his game. He did not follow Taylor in inventing a special golf-club. But at the suggestion of a friend, he had a photographer come out from Cleveland and make a series of snapshots of his stroke. Studying these, he learned how to get rid of a slice. For a time he hired a colored boy to ejaculate, as he teed off: "Hold your head down! Hold your head down!" To improve his long shots, said the press, he had a caddy place a stone slab on his toes to hold them straight as he teed off. When this did not work, he took a wire croquet wicket and fastened his foot firmly before driving. By 1904 he was playing so well that he won a silver cup offered by Wallace De Wolf, at Pinehurst, N. C. Golf was by that time his principal amusement, and only very bad weather or an unusual pressure of business kept him off the course for at least an hour daily. E. M. Johnson writes:

Four inches of snow stopped us at Ardsley on December 4, 1904; so I was surprised three days later when Mr. Rockefeller telephoned me to join him at Pocantico Hills for a foursome with Mr. Rudd and Mr. McCormick. When I objected that we could not play in the snow Mr. Rockefeller said, "Just come up and see." I went up and found that on the day before he had sent out men with horses and snowplows and cleared the snow off five fairways, and that the five putting greens had been swept clean. We never had a finer game.

The writer adds some notes on Rockefeller's game:

In all our playing, which has been foursomes as a rule, so as to have a pleasant company, Mr. Rockefeller has arranged a handicap before the start. Then he is eager to see the best side win. It would be unthinkable for him to favor his own side in the handicapping. All through the game he is in jolly spirits . . .

In looking over the books—I have among my 37 scorebooks the records of 430 games played with Mr. Rockefeller—I find that the best score was made on October 30, 1912, a fine warm day, when he played with Messrs. Edgar L. Marston, Charles Brown, a young enthusiast who afterward won the championship of the Hudson Valley, and myself. The best scores were:

Mr. Rockefeller	4—4—3—4—6—4—6—4—4 —— 39
Mr. Brown	7—3—2—4—5—5—5—5—3 —— 39

Henry Clay Folger became a frequent partner of Rockefeller's at

Rockefeller as a golfer during the years between 1909 and 1925.

The top photograph shows him with Will Rogers.

From a photograph by Ira Hill.

Rockefeller at Pocantico.

With Mr. and Mrs. John D. Rockefeller, Jr., and four of their children.

Pocantico and Lakewood; he never talked about Shakespeare, but he played golf with enthusiasm. So did Father Patrick Lennon of Tarrytown, a handsome young Irish priest. But Rockefeller had to choose his companions cannily. Once Gates, commenting on his apparent loneliness at a Southern hotel, remarked that many men of cultivation in the vicinity would make agreeable associates. "You should not keep to yourself so much, Mr. Rockefeller," he expostulated. "You should call upon some of these men, who naturally wait for you to make the first gesture."

"Well, Mr. Gates," said Rockefeller, emphatically, "if you suppose I have not thought about the matter you are mistaken. I have made some experiments. And nearly always the result is the same —along about the ninth hole out comes some proposition, charitable or financial!"[20]

By 1905 Rockefeller had an automobile of American manufacture, for which the newspapers said he had paid $6000. He humorously remarked to a visitor: "I can do fifty miles an hour in that machine without turning a hair!" As he had no hair, this statement could be taken literally. The story is told in Cleveland that soon after 1900 a dealer brought a car out to Forest Hill, announcing that Rockefeller could have it for $10,000. "How fast does it go?" asked Rockefeller. The dealer told him. "Well, see how fast you can drive it back to town," the magnate remarked with a smile.

Landscape architecture, golf, and driving restored Rockefeller's health, which after the breakdown of the early nineties had never been as bad as newspaper articles asserted. In 1909, a writer for *Harper's Weekly* described him, then seventy, as "a hale and hearty athlete, bronzed by daily play in the sun, ruddy-cheeked and clear-eyed, as brisk and powerful and enduring as most men of fifty years." His muscular vigor sufficed for repeated drives of two hundred yards and more. Only five feet eleven, "his spare, sturdy figure is so well muscled and broad in the back that he seems six feet tall or even taller." Doctor Biggar liked to give the press brief statements upon Rockefeller's physical well-being. "He will live to be a hundred," he predicted. "He follows three simple rules. First, he avoids all worry. Second, he takes plenty of exercise in the open air. Third,

[20]One of Gates's Montclair neighbors repeated this story to me.

he always gets up from the table a little hungry." Every observer commented on his equanimity at golf; he "is never fussy over trifles, or shuffles about in frequent changes of stance, or wastes his own time and his antagonist's temper by much waggling of the club." He sometimes spoke of golf as a touchstone for both calmness and honesty:

"One of the best places to test a minister is on the golf links," he told his Cleveland Sunday school after announcing that he and the pastor were playing next day. "Even the best of them often lose their tempers there." And again he remarked sadly: "I am sorry to say that I have met ministers who did not hesitate to cheat a little on the links!"

VI

Rockefeller still belonged to two congregations. In summer he faithfully attended the Euclid Avenue Church, but since he spent most of his time in the East, the Fifth Avenue Church received most of his attention. The Cleveland church went through serious financial vicissitudes. Under the Reverend L. A. Crandall, who served 1889–92, its building was reconstructed, while other expenses overtaxed its resources. When the Reverend Henry C. Applegarth took charge in 1893, the church, as its historian writes, was "at its lowest ebb." Applegarth, an able preacher who remained seven years, and who placed it on a solid financial foundation, became a favorite visitor at Forest Hill. But he was never so intimate with Rockefeller as his successor, the Reverend Charles Eaton, a Canadian who became minister in 1900.

At the Fifth Avenue Church Rockefeller always held a position more formal and aloof than that which he occupied in the Cleveland congregation; but the church nevertheless played an important part in his life. He, William Rockefeller, and Bostwick were all trustees. Though he never taught in the Sunday school, Mrs. Rockefeller took a class of boys and kept it for many years; she would remain with a group until they became old enough to go to college, and then begin with a new one. Many of her pupils, looking upon her almost as a foster mother, spent much time at the Rockefeller house. Each spring her class went for an outing on the Palisades, crossing at the Fort Lee Ferry in a noisy body, while she followed in a landau, and a caterer brought a wagon of comestibles. Alta also remained active in the church. Besides managing her sewing school for girls, she taught a Sunday school class for boys which included Charles E. Hughes, Jr., and Albert Spalding.

The West Fifty-fourth Street house shortly became a busy center for all kinds of Baptist work. It was used for missionary meetings, charitable meetings, temperance meetings, and prayer meetings. Young people's organizations met there, as did the board of trustees. Ministers of the Fifth Avenue Church almost became members of the family circle. The pastor when Rockefeller settled in New York was Thomas Armitage, another Englishman, who served more than forty years. Living in a parsonage next the church, he was a close neighbor, and the children, because of the wrinkled homeliness of his long countenance, framed in side-whiskers, affectionately called him "Cousin Monkey." Visiting ministers were often invited to the Rockefeller house for Sunday dinner. Rockefeller would cordially remark after the sermon: "You have fed us; now let us feed you!" Prominent Baptists from all over the land—Jacob Gould Schurman, President Taylor of Vassar, Doctor Harper of Chicago, and others—were often entertained. Missionaries came and went, some of them becoming familiar figures: Edward Judson, for example, son of the great Adoniram Judson, and John E. Clough, a noted missionary to India. Mrs. Rockefeller's zeal for temperance made Frances E. Willard, J. Ellen Foster, and Frances E. Barnes, head of the Loyal Legion, frequent guests. The atmosphere of the house was full of religion and good works!

When Armitage retired from the pastorate, Rockefeller and his brother William served on the committee to choose a successor. Hearing of a brilliant young minister in Springfield, Mass., William Herbert Perry Faunce, they and their wives went up one Sunday to listen to him. They were anxious to arrive and depart unrecognized. At the church door the usher demanded: "You are strangers, are you not? Will you please give me your names?" As the service was just beginning, Mrs. Rockefeller, hastily leaning forward, put her finger on her lips and said: "Sh-h-h! You will interrupt the minister!"

A little later Rockefeller almost betrayed their identity. When the collection plate was passed he drew a ten-dollar bill from his pocket. Just as he deposited it he realized that the amount might attract attention, and hesitated. The result was that after the service an officer approached him, inquiring:

"Do you want change from that ten-dollar bill you put in the collection, sir?"

Doctor Faunce was called to New York, where he gave the Fifth Avenue Church fresh life. He was active in the world peace movement, and in various plans for social reform; he was fearless in assailing shams and corruption in the established order. But his administrative energies soon found a larger sphere. In 1899 the trustees of Brown University made him president—two years after John D. Rockefeller, Jr., had been graduated; and there he remained for thirty years, completing the development of Brown from a provincial college to a true university. He also was often at 4 West Fifty-fourth Street. In view of Rockefeller's friendship with Harper, Schurman, Taylor, and Faunce, four leading educators of the day, the magnate could not be said to lack intellectual contacts. After Everett Colby and Charles E. Hughes became trustees of Brown, a liberal group under Colby's leadership undertook to eliminate the charter provision excluding Catholics and Jews from the board of fellows and board of trustees; and Rockefeller, his son, and Doctor Gates all gave this successful movement earnest support.[21]

Faunce's most notable early successor was Doctor Charles F. Aked, a man of remarkable eloquence, who was called in 1907 from Pembroke Chapel in Liverpool. For some years New York had no preacher of greater declamatory power. He was extremely outspoken on all social questions, denouncing selfish plutocracy, and proclaiming his belief in Socialism "as the expression of human hope and zeal for human brotherhood, of the new spiritual life of the world." Various members thought that Doctor Aked had something about him of Dickens's Reverend Mr. Honeythunder, while others compared him with Newell Dwight Hillis, who also had a

[21]Mr. Everett Colby to the author. Doctor Schurman was often at Rockefeller's house. On his earliest trip to Europe Rockefeller met Andrew D. White on the steamer; he thus became interested in Cornell University, to which he made repeated gifts. George Schurman, a brother of Jacob Gould Schurman, was a member of the Fifth Avenue Baptist Church. President Taylor of Vassar had induced Rockefeller to act as a trustee of Vassar from 1888 to 1905; and Rockefeller frequently visited the college. He gave Vassar two buildings, Rockefeller Hall and Davison House, and helped erect a third, Strong House.

gift for the headlines.[22] At any rate, he was very different from the gifted man who succeeded him in 1911, Doctor Cornelius Woelfkin, a clergyman who was largely self-educated but who possessed rare cultivation and real intellectual depth. To him Rockefeller always felt a special devotion.

But no matter who was the pastor, the church always played a powerful part in Rockefeller's life. He found refreshment and sustenance in his simple elemental piety. "I can never be grateful enough for all that our church has meant to me," he told a friend in 1917. "Years ago in New York an associate of mine who was a member of a big and fashionable church was eager to have me go in with him. He said to me, 'John, you are too big for the Baptist Church.' I put my hands on his shoulders and replied: 'Henry, I *hope* I'm big enough for the Baptist Church.' "

VII

As the children grew up the Rockefeller circle was naturally expanded by marriage. Bessie's husband, Charles A. Strong, returned from his studies in Germany to become docent in psychology at Clark University in 1890. Later he was made associate professor at the University of Chicago, and then professor at Columbia. Strong was a man of learning and intellectual vigor, who wrote one notable book, *Why the Mind Has a Body;* and when he took up his residence in New York he added a good deal, despite his quiet ways, to the family life. His religious liberalism never disturbed Rockefeller, who believed that all men have a right to their own opinions, but the fanatical Doctor Strong all but drove his son from his door.

Late in 1895 Edith, the most individual, artistic, and unconventional of the children, married Harold Fowler McCormick (younger son of the inventor of the reaper), who had graduated from the Browning School and from Princeton. They had been brought together in musical and educational activities. Since the bridegroom was ill with a cold, the ceremony was performed at the Buckingham Hotel instead of the church, with a breakfast later at the West Fifty-fourth Street house. McCormick was soon occupied with his older brother

[22]In the San Francisco *Bulletin* of July 18, 1911, Doctor Aked asserted that Rockefeller had never offered the slightest interference with the character of his preaching.

in carrying on the harvester works. After the formation of the so-called Reaper Trust—the International Harvester Company—he became vice-president, treasurer, and ultimately president of that huge corporation. Edith of course went to live in Chicago, where five children were born to them before the marriage ended in divorce in 1921. The union brought the Rockefellers a number of interesting connections, including the James G. Blaine family—one of McCormick's sisters having married Emmons Blaine. That remarkable woman "Madame" McCormick, widow of the inventor, the supporter of numerous philanthropies and an extremely witty, strong-willed person, often visited at Pocantico or 4 West Fifty-fourth Street, bringing the breeziness of her vigorous personality.

Then in 1901 the two remaining children married. Alta had become engaged to E. Parmalee Prentice, an Iowan by birth, and a graduate of Amherst and the Harvard Law School. He was an attorney who had spent a dozen years practising in Chicago, where he was general counsel for the Illinois Steel Company. He came to New York in 1901, soon joining the firm of Howland, Murray & Prentice, later Murray, Prentice & Aldrich. A trial lawyer of clear mind and argumentative power, he participated in some noteworthy cases—for example, an important corporation suit against the Delaware & Hudson Company, and the difficult reorganization of the Colorado Fuel & Iron Company. He became particularly interested in questions of constitutional law, argued cases before the Supreme Court, and wrote two legal books, one on the commerce clause and one on Federal power over carriers and corporations. He also became interested in higher education, which he believed should train men for leadership, and should emphasize the classics rather than more practical studies. Retiring in 1924 from the bar, he turned to scientific agriculture, making the Mt. Hope Farm near Williamstown, Mass., famous for his experiments, and writing some remarkable volumes on cattle-breeding and the conquest of hunger.[23]

The marriage of John D. Rockefeller, Jr., to Abby Green Aldrich, daughter of Senator Nelson W. Aldrich, whose abilities were rapidly making him the undisputed leader of the Senate, was of course a notable occasion. An extremely talented and attractive young woman, she had become a great social favorite not only in Newport

[23]See his *Hunger and History* (1939).

but in New York and Washington. It would have been difficult for many years to say which was the more unpopular with the American masses, the father of the bride or that of the groom; and the press naturally published reams of matter on the union. Already, however, it spoke highly of the younger Rockefeller for his serious tastes and devotion to public duty. The Senator was not inclined to let the wedding be a small, quiet affair. A huge gray awning-pavilion was specially built at the summer home of the Aldriches at Warwick on Narragansett Bay. Here, in an immense chamber sixty feet wide and a hundred long, a thousand guests gathered. The bride was showered with costly presents. The same minister who precisely thirty-five years earlier had united Senator and Mrs. Aldrich, Doctor James G. Vose, performed the ceremony. Wine was served, and Doctor Faunce, a total abstainer, innocently remarked over a glass of champagne, "This is the most delicious ginger-ale I ever drank!" Thereafter, John D. Rockefeller, Jr., saw a good deal of the circle of elder statesmen close to Aldrich, notably Senators Platt of Connecticut, Spooner of Wisconsin, and Allison of Iowa; and Rockefeller, who himself met Aldrich a number of times, heard more about governmental affairs.

The Rockefellers, even after Doctor Strong resigned from Columbia and went abroad, kept two of their children near them. John and his wife in time settled down at 10 West Fifty-fourth Street, next door; while the Prentices took a house just at the rear, No. 5 West Fifty-third. Both houses were large. "Whatever are you going to do with this great big echoing mansion?" a Brown classmate of John D. Rockefeller, Jr., asked his wife, soon after they moved in. "Why, fill it up with children!" she replied.[24] Indeed, there were soon grandchildren in both domiciles. All of them thrived and grew except Edith's older son, John Rockefeller McCormick, who succumbed at Pocantico Hills to scarlet fever early in 1901, when not yet four. The death of this favorite grandson, the first named for him, was a serious blow to Rockefeller. But the family circle steadily expanded. As child after child arrived in John's household—Abby in 1903, John D. Rockefeller III in 1906, Nelson Aldrich in 1908, and later still Laurance, Winthrop, and David—the grandfather showed manifest delight in his patriarchal position.

[24]So the classmate told the author.

To Rockefeller these were in many respects years of fruition and happiness. His health had returned, bringing an elastic vigor. His family grew more varied and interesting as the years passed. He had thrown off his heaviest burdens, and hard as he still labored —for his secretaries have testified that he was a very busy man—he was no longer driven by urgent tasks or harried by anxiety. He had found fascinating new recreations in his landscape work and golf. Only one dark cloud marred his contentment. Public antagonism toward the Standard Oil monopoly, public repugnance toward the great experiment he had made in completely reorganizing an industry, was mounting higher and higher. With Theodore Roosevelt in the White House, huge corporate aggregations were the target of increasingly heavy attacks. The hatred of Rockefeller personally, far from showing any abatement, became grimmer and fiercer, and was often clamorous in intensity.

But he did not take this popular hostility with tragic seriousness. Mrs. Rockefeller kept a scrapbook in which she pasted newspaper clippings that particularly interested her. Some very abusive attacks upon her husband found a place there. Among the cuttings was a cartoon which John T. McCutcheon had drawn for the Chicago *Tribune* in 1905. The American Press Humorists' Association had just met in Cleveland. Rockefeller had thrown the Forest Hill grounds open to them; and when they brought him a badge as honorary member, he promptly conducted them, with a genial smile, to look at what he described as "a chestnut tree four hundred years old." They laughed. McCutcheon depicted Rockefeller as saying: "Well, now that I have been elected a humorist, I suppose I must make a joke." He doffs wig and coat, and squares to his desk. In a moment he electrifies the group by holding up the joke he has composed: "Mr. John D. Rockefeller entertained a large company at a champagne supper last night. The guests of honor were the Reverend Washington Gladden, Miss Ida Tarbell, and Thomas W. Lawson."[25] Evidently the Rockefeller family had enjoyed this good-natured fling.

[25]Chicago *Tribune,* Sept. 8, 1905.

BOOK FOUR

A MAN AND HIS MONEY

XLIII

Adventures in Spending

AFTER 1897 the wise use of his fortune, and not the Standard Oil business, was the dominant responsibility in Rockefeller's life. It, and all the problems of investment and philanthropy attendant upon it, grew without cessation. It had increased during the depression. It leaped forward again when prosperity returned with the Spanish War. In the seven years between the dissolution order in 1892 and the reorganization in 1899, the Standard paid nearly 130 per cent on the trust capital, or approximately $120,000,000, in dividends and "extra payments."[1] Rockefeller's share was between one third and one fourth, while his Standard Oil stock was now but a part of his productive estate. Early in 1899 the trust certificates, which had been worth $166 each at the time of the dissolution decree, sold at nearly $500. The increasing use of the internal combustion engine, the rapid spread of the automobile, and the discovery of new oil fields were about to give the fortune a tremendous new impetus. It truly threatened, as Gates constantly warned Rockefeller, to crush him and his children. And yet the magnate never agreed with Swift's statement that money is liberty, but great wealth is a jailer; his son testifies that he regarded the fortune as an opportunity, not a burden, and approached the problem of its use with the same cool determination that he had shown in approaching the reorganization of the oil industry.

Fortunes of the magnitude now controlled by Rockefeller and Carnegie were a novel apparition in American civilization. When John Jacob Astor closed his long life in 1848, the wealth he had amassed in fur trading and real estate was estimated at perhaps

[1]Taylor, MS History; N. Y. *Herald*, June 15, 1899.

$30,000,000; and his son, William B. Astor, "the landlord of New York," brought it to perhaps $50,000,000 before he died in 1875.[2] Old Commodore Vanderbilt was believed to have wrung from $90,000,000 to $100,000,000 out of steamboats and railroads before he passed to his tomb on Staten Island in 1877.[3] These fortunes had once dazzled Americans. But the two greatest industrialists of the new era, like Mr. Henry Ford years subsequently, counted their wealth not by scores but hundreds of millions. Carnegie's income from his steel company rose to about $25,000,000 a year just before he sold it, and the securities which Morgan gave him for his interest could be roundly valued at $500,000,000. At that date Carnegie's fortune was by far the largest in the country; but Rockefeller's holdings continued to grow until both his wealth and his benefactions much exceeded those of the steel king.

How could so enormous an accumulation of money be employed? To dissipate it would be easy enough; but it was intolerable to Rockefeller's systematic and careful mind to think of frittering it away. Nor could he spend it for personal whims of a philanthropic or pseudo-philanthropic kind; first because, unlike many rich men, he had no whims, and in the second place because he had an unconquerable instinct for giving in an orderly way upon the basis of fixed principles. While he had founded and heavily endowed a university, that made only a small reduction in the fortune. He constantly gave to a multiplicity of small causes—schools, hospitals, churches, and missions; but although Gates had systematized this giving, he was doubtful if it met the highest standard of usefulness. Year by year he and Gates were finding out, often by bitter experience, that some types of philanthropy simply did not yield adequate returns. Most millionaires, for example, liked to erect college buildings. Mr. Croesus-Jones would perpetuate his name by the Croesus-Jones Laboratory at the So-and-So Polytechnic Institute. Rockefeller gave money for buildings at Vassar, Brown, and numerous other institutions. But he found that they were sometimes rather a burden than an aid, for what colleges most needed were gifts for general

[2] A more conservative estimate of the elder Astor's fortune was $20,000,000. See Kenneth W. Porter, *John Jacob Astor, Business Man*, 939; James Parton, *John Jacob Astor*; Gustavus Myers, *History of the Great American Fortunes*.

[3] W. A. Croffut, *The Vanderbilts and the Story of Their Fortune*; Burton J. Hendrick, "The Vanderbilt Fortune," *McClure's*, November, 1908.

From the drawing by Orr in the Chicago "Tribune."

Rockefeller's reputation as a giver grows.

endowment. And among the hundreds of hungry colleges and universities, how find those which could make the best use of money, and how ascertain the precise sum which each deserved?[4]

As the fortune grew, it became necessary for him, his son, and Gates to plan philanthropies which should aggregate not millions but scores of millions, and should if possible fructify some important

[4]Gates indicates in his MS Autobiography that he repeatedly talked this problem over with Rockefeller. Later the General Education Board had in its offices a large map of the United States with pins for all the institutions of higher education. There were manifestly too many, and at some points they were too close together. John D. Rockefeller, Jr., to the author.

work along a nation-wide and even international front. He insisted that all the principles which he had laid down during the eighties must be maintained. His money should be given, whenever possible, to a work already well organized and of proved efficiency and utility. It should be given, in general, on conditional terms which would stimulate gifts by other men and organizations. It should foster in the beneficiary a spirit of self-help, not of dependence. And finally, the work done should be of a continuing character, which would remain vigorous after his aid had been withdrawn. But he had to think of formulating new principles as well. His philanthropies would have to be planned with more sweep and imagination. In their execution he would have to enlist eminent scientific experts. The main justification for his fortune would lie in using it with consistent wisdom for great public undertakings which clearly deserved support, but which were being neglected both by other philanthropists and by governmental agencies. What were the best of these undertakings?

II

In July, 1897, while Rockefeller was spending the summer at Forest Hill, Gates left the 26 Broadway office to join his family in the Catskills for a vacation. Several conversations with a young medical student whom he often entertained at Montclair had led him to plan some reading in medical textbooks in order to discover what was the existing state of knowledge among physicians. William Osler's masterly *Principles and Practise of Medicine,* then six years old, was being used in the College of Physicians and Surgeons in New York,[5] and he took a copy of the 1000-page volume with him. To his astonishment, he found it so delightful that he read every one of the close-printed chapters. As he remarked afterward, it is one of the few scientific treatises written by Americans which possess real literary charm. "There was a fascination about the style itself that led me on, and having once started I found a hook in my nose that pulled me from page to page, from chapter to chapter, to the end."[6]

[5] A part of Columbia University. The medical student was E. W. Huntington. Gates's father, it will be recalled, had studied medicine.
[6] Gates, MS Autobiography.

Gates had begun his examination of the book with certain marked preconceptions regarding medicine, formed while he was a pastor in Minneapolis. Attracted by the Northwestern real-estate boom, scores of physicians had settled in the city to practise. A number, including both allopaths and homeopaths, joined his congregation. At this time the homeopathic wing of the profession was conducting a vigorous crusade for support, and several Minneapolis members, after sending Gates all their propagandist pamphlets, called to inquire whether he had been convinced. When he pointed out the fallacies in their arguments, they asked him to read Doctor Samuel C. F. Hahnemann's *Organon,* the Bible of the homeopathic faith, and he did so. He thought it wildly absurd, and it depressed him to learn that thirty or more so-called medical colleges in the United States were teaching the doctrines. Then he looked into some of the claims of the allopathic group. Theoretically their practice was sounder, but he believed that their excessive use of powerful and dangerous drugs gave a certain excuse for homeopathy. Moreover, it seemed difficult to credit them with more cures, save in epidemics, than their rivals. Gates reached the radical conclusion that neither school was having much effect on the health of the community, and that if a science of medicine existed, it was probably not being taught in the United States. He writes:[7]

I used to meet occasionally the ablest and most prominent physician then in Minneapolis, a man of the regular school, who sometimes had patients in my congregation. He described to me one day with engaging frankness the actual character of his practise. He said that in ninety of every hundred of his calls, the patient would have recovered just as certainly and comfortably without him. One call and a harmless prescription was enough. Of the remaining ten he could make nine perhaps more comfortable, and would throw certain protections about the patient, but the disease must run a natural and predestined course, to recovery or fatality. There remained only the one case in a hundred, perhaps, in which medical science as commonly practised among us knew how to effect a cure. I may say that I have ever since been in the habit of telling this story to physicians trained earlier than 1900, and without exception found it confirmed by their experience.

Being thus convinced that medicine as taught and practised in the United States was at best largely futile and at worst very in-

[7]*Idem.*

jurious, Gates searched in Osler for proof or disproof. He thought he found a verification. Osler's pages indicated that of hundreds of diseases then recognized, the best medical practice did not as yet know any certain cure for more than four or five. For one reason, few disease germs had thus far been identified and isolated. Usually it was nature, and nature alone, that cured. Gates found a deep skepticism haunting Osler's pages. His chapter on any particular malady usually began with a definition of it, some account of its distribution throughout the world, and the history of discovery regarding it; he would then proceed to causes, symptoms, and probable course, using the results of innumerable post-mortems; "but when he came to the vital point, namely, the *treatment* of the aforesaid disease, our author . . . would almost invariably lapse into a feeble attitude of doubt, skepticism, and hesitation. He would suggest that such and such celebrated physicians at home or abroad had found this or that treatment to be helpful; such had not been his own experience, but perhaps this or that might be found to be useful in some cases." We need not accept Gates's summary of Osler or his gloomy view of the state of medical knowledge in 1897, both exaggerated.[8] But his conclusion that medical science needed a rapid stimulation and development in America was sound, and it was an important conclusion.

Particularly was it important in the brain of a man who possessed imagination, and who had direct access to Rockefeller. For Gates at once began to try to puzzle out some means of bettering the position of medicine, and to lay plans for applying part of Rockefeller's fortune to the object. It was perfectly true that the scientific study of medicine in America had been neglected. Nearly all medical schools as yet stood on a commercial or part-commercial basis; they were proprietary and money-making institutions. Since few of them had been endowed, and not one given adequate funds, medical research had been left to shift for itself. The faculties were teachers, not investigators. Gates became persuaded that if medicine were ever to be lifted to a proper level, advanced experimentation would have to be established on a permanent basis, and groups of

[8]Doctor Harvey Cushing's *Life of Sir William Osler* indicates that he was less pessimistic about the immediate effectiveness of American medical knowledge in 1897 than Gates indicates.

qualified men would have to be given opportunity, on ample salaries, for uninterrupted scientific inquiry.

For this purpose, he decided, an institute for medical research ought to be established in the United States. As he pondered the idea, he became possessed by the conviction that here lay an opportunity for Rockefeller to do the United States, and perhaps the world, an immense service. He knew nothing of the difficulties—the cost of research, the problem of finding experts, the certainty of attacks by many doctors and laymen. It was well that he did not, for an overmastering enthusiasm was needed. He writes:[9]

Filled with these thoughts and enthusiasm, I returned from my vacation on July 24, 1897. I brought my Osler book into the office at 26 Broadway, and there I dictated for Mr. Rockefeller, who was summering as usual at Cleveland, a memorandum. It enumerated the infectious diseases, and pointed out how few of the germs had yet been discovered, and how great the field of discovery, how few specifics had yet been found and how appalling was the unremedied suffering and fatality. It pointed out the usefulness of the Koch Institute in Berlin and the success of the Pasteur Institute in France. Pasteur's inquiries on anthrax had saved for the French nation a sum far in excess of the entire cost of the Franco-Prussian War.[10] Even if the proposed institute should fail to discover anything, the mere fact that he, Mr. Rockefeller, had established such an institute of research, if he were to consent to do so, would result in other institutes of a similar kind, or at least other funds for research being established, until research in this country would be conducted on a great scale, and out of the multitudes of workers we might be sure in the end of abundant rewards.

Both Rockefeller and his son were impressed by the suggestion. A little investigation showed that in this field the United States was lagging pitifully behind Europe. The Institut Pasteur, founded in Paris in 1888 with funds raised in several nations, had long been occupied not merely in treating persons bitten by rabid animals but in making fresh investigations into disease. Almost as famous as Pasteur's work was that of Robert Koch. Pasteur's early bacteriological studies on fermentation led to Lister's discovery of antiseptic surgery; while Koch's perfection of methods of cultivating and iden-

[9]MS Autobiography.
[10]In writing this Gates was probably thinking of Huxley's famous statement that it had saved more than the indemnity paid by France.

tifying bacteria led, in the eighties of the last century, to the discovery of the bacterial causes of tuberculosis, Asiatic cholera, typhoid fever, diphtheria and pneumonia, and ushered in the modern era of preventive medicine. In 1885 Koch was made director of the Institute of Hygiene in Berlin, and in 1891 the Institute for Infectious Diseases was founded there for him. Paul Ehrlich became director in 1899 of the well-equipped Institute for Experimental Therapeutics in Frankfurt a/'M., in which was discovered Salvarsan. In 1890 the Imperial Institute for Experimental Medicine was founded in St. Petersburg, and in 1891 the Jenner Institute, soon to become the Lister Institute, in London, modelled on the Pasteur Institute, was created.

But where were the centers of medical research in America, the skilled staffs, and the men whose discoveries could be placed beside those of the great Europeans? The few laboratories that existed—for example, the Carnegie Laboratory at the Bellevue Hospital Medical College in New York—were small, and their staffs and resources inadequate.[12]

III

For some time little came of Gates's memorandum. Very busy with other matters, he realized that the subject required the full time of an able man. He therefore introduced to Rockefeller a quiet, efficient Montclair attorney, Starr J. Murphy, as qualified to make inquiries among the principal medical men of the large Eastern cities regarding the feasibility of the suggested institute, and to study the foreign prototypes. Some months of labor by Murphy brought only a chilly response. Most medical men thought that an institute could do little, and that it would be more profitable to subsidize promising experimenters who were already at work here and there. Another impediment very unfortunately arose in certain events at the University of Chicago.

As the idea of the Institute first germinated in Rockefeller's mind,

[11]For good popular accounts, see Paul De Kruif, *Microbe Hunters;* W. W. Keen, *Medical Research and Human Welfare.*

[12]In 1900 an American Yellow-Fever Commission in Cuba solved by careful experiment the problem of one of the world's most terrible diseases. Gates was of course familiar with Doctor Walter Reed's work. At this time the outstanding institution of medical research was the Johns Hopkins Medical School.

he naturally thought of associating it with the University of Chicago. In 1894 an attempt had been made to affiliate the Rush Medical College with the new university. Rockefeller had discouraged the proposal, and his statements and letters had led him to suppose that it was completely dead. But to his surprise, he was informed in the early days of 1898 that official action had just been taken to connect the two institutions. The history and standards of Rush at that time rendered it a very unsuitable foundation upon which to rear an institute of research; and Rockefeller directed Gates to send an immediate and earnest letter of dissent to the university authorities. This letter, dated January 12, was hammered into shape at a long and careful conference between the two men. Rockefeller made it clear to Gates, and the latter intimated to Secretary Goodspeed, that if the university would wait until a medical branch of the highest type could be established there, the founder would probably endow a great institute of research in connection with it. The university authorities persisted in their stand. Rockefeller and Gates then sent another letter which set forth their own vision of a medical college "magnificently endowed, devoted primarily to investigation, making practice itself an incident of investigation." When they failed to receive the response they desired, Rockefeller gave up all idea of planting the proposed institute at the University of Chicago.

Mr. Murphy still continued busy with the problem. Rockefeller still thought of the institute as properly associated with some powerful university, and active negotiations were conducted for a time with Harvard. Little progress had been made, however, when John D. Rockefeller, Jr., broached the subject to Doctor L. Emmett Holt; and matters then took an entirely new turn.

Holt, an outstanding pediatrician of the time, was doctor to the younger Rockefeller's children, and a member of the Fifth Avenue Baptist Church; a man of dynamic personality and progressive outlook. He had been in Chicago treating one of the McCormick children, and during the return trip held what he later called a 200-mile conversation with young Rockefeller on the project. He promptly brought three friends, Doctor Christian A. Herter, Doctor T. Mitchell Prudden, and Doctor Hermann M. Biggs, into the discussion. Herter, who possessed inherited wealth, had a laboratory on the upper floor of his Madison Avenue house, where he devoted much time to scientific research; Prudden was professor of pathology at the College of Physicians and Surgeons; and Biggs was general medical officer of the city department of health.[13] All three felt a passionate faith in medical research, while Biggs knew much about its practical applications. Trained in Germany at the very time that bacteriological research was making its most spectacular advances, he had brought the new gospel home with a fervent belief in its possibilities. He had organized a department of pathology and bacteriology in the city health service, had introduced the use of diphtheria antitoxin into the United States, and was taking important steps to combat tuberculosis and other diseases.

The four men, Holt, Herter, Prudden, and Biggs, met early in 1901 at the house of John D. Rockefeller, Jr.[14] Their host began by recounting the result of Murphy's inquiries, which seemed to show that money could best be used to aid research men in existing laboratories.

"Suppose my father were to give $20,000 a year for ten years?" he asked. "What would you do with it to promote medical research?"

To answer this question was not easy. Other medical leaders had to be called in, and a series of meetings was held. One at the Arlington Hotel in Washington on May 1, 1901, was attended by Doctor William H. Welch, professor of pathology at Johns Hopkins. Next to Osler, he was probably the foremost figure in American medicine; great not for original ideas or discoveries, but as teacher, leader, and inspirer of others.[15] To this meeting Rockefeller sent an explicit offer embodied in a letter signed by his son. "My father," the letter ran, "is prepared to give for the purpose of medical research whatever amount may be required up to an average of twenty thousand dollars a year for ten years. This money he will

[13]I have been given much information by Doctor Herter's widow, Mrs. H. D. Dakin, and by Doctor Emmett Holt. Doctor Herter was professor of pathological chemistry at New York University and Bellevue Medical College.
[14]Mr. Rockefeller has described the meeting to me.
[15]The papers of Doctor Herter, which Mrs. Dakin kindly allowed me to examine, show that correspondence with Doctor Welch on scientific subjects went back to 1887. Welch had gone to the Johns Hopkins Medical School in 1884, and became dean in 1893; he assembled the great Johns Hopkins faculty, and perhaps even more than Osler he led the upward movement in scientific medicine in America. As Doctor Simon Flexner's forthcoming biography will make clear, he was keenly interested in bacteriology.

give to a committee which shall be appointed and which shall be empowered to formulate the policy, and direct the carrying on of the work."[16] Ten days later another meeting was held at the University Club in New York, attended by Doctor Theobald Smith, professor in the Harvard Medical School. It was he who, years earlier, while working for the Federal bureau of animal husbandry, had discovered that the Texas cattle fever was caused by a protozoan parasite carried by ticks. It was not difficult to free great areas of the tick, and thus save the cattle industry of the nation millions annually. And at a third meeting on May 25 in Doctor Holt's office, Doctor Simon Flexner, professor of pathology at the University of Pennsylvania, was present.

Of all this group, Doctor Flexner was destined to do the most important work for Gates's fundamental idea and for medical research. Born in Louisville in the midst of the Civil War, he had taken his medical degree in the University of Louisville and done postgraduate work at Johns Hopkins under Welch, whom he all but worshipped. He had studied at Strasbourg, Berlin, and Prague; he had worked in the Pasteur Institute. Then, after teaching for a time at Johns Hopkins, he had joined the faculty at Pennsylvania, where he also directed the Ayer Clinical Laboratory of the Pennsylvania Hospital. Keen-witted, industrious, passionately interested in science to the exclusion of almost everything else, he was a born research worker.[17]

Thus within a few months seven leading figures in American medical science had been drawn together as a group interested in using Rockefeller's gift to the best purpose in research. Most of the men were fairly young—Doctors Herter and Flexner in their thirties, Doctor Biggs forty-two, Doctor Holt forty-six; all were energetic. To Gates, who apparently believed that something like the institutes of Paris and Berlin could be created overnight, they at first seemed excessively timid.[18] He had little patience with the general idea that it would be best, at least for the time being, to employ the workers and laboratories already available; but this idea was accepted. Dur-

[16]Rockefeller Papers.
[17]Doctor Flexner, who was very modest, often said he owed everything to his teacher, Doctor Welch. John D. Rockefeller, Jr., to the author. Doctor Flexner has given me much information on the Institute.
[18]MS Autobiography.

ing May the conferees agreed that Doctor Welch should communicate with the leading medical institutions, find out what problems
they were investigating, and ascertain the needs of the investigators.
They also decided to call the new organization the Rockefeller
Institute for Medical Research. Within a short time they laid plans
for co-operating with the New York health department in a study
of the milk supply and its relation to child health, and made a money
grant to Doctor Flexner for study of the bacteriology of the dysen-
teric diseases, including certain summer diseases of children, and for
research in public health in five cities in this country.

IV

By the end of 1901 this tender scientific shoot had taken firm
root, and was beginning to put forth some leaves. Incorporation
papers had been received from the State. A board of directors, comprising the seven men who had performed the work of organization, had been set up. Doctor Welch was chosen president, Doctor
Prudden vice-president, Doctor Holt secretary, and Doctor Herter
treasurer.[19] Rockefeller had executed a legal pledge of $200,000, upon
which the directors might draw at any time during the next ten
years. Although he offered no intimation that another copper would
be forthcoming, every one knew that if the undertaking proved
hopeful his purse-strings would be unloosed. Apparently Doctor
Welch agreed with Gates in desiring a special Institute corps working under one roof. He wrote Doctor Herter on January 13, 1902:
"My talk with Mr. Rockefeller Saturday was most satisfactory, and
I think we can go ahead as fast as is desirable. If we can get together
a good working staff for a laboratory, this seems to me our next
move."[20] But at the outset twenty-three research workers were selected in nearly a score of American institutions and given modest
stipends, usually $500 or $600 a year. One man was sent to the Koch

---

[19]*The Rockefeller Institute for Medical Research: History, Organization,
etc.* (1934), p. 12. Hereafter cited as *Rockefeller Institute History.* According
to the N. Y. *Times,* June 3, 1901, several universities, particularly Columbia
and Harvard, made a spirited fight to gain possession of the proposed institute.
The Times declared: "It marks an epoch in the science of medicine in this
country." *The Tribune* predicted that the staff might see their work "grow to
be a great landmark in medicine, like that of the Pasteur Institute." June 2,
1901.
[20]Herter Papers.

The Scientific Directorate in 1908. *Left to right:* Doctor Flexner, Doctor Holt, Doctor Prudden, Doctor Welch, Doctor Herter, Doctor Smith, and Doctor Biggs.

The Scientific Directorate in 1932. *Left to right:* Cedric B. Smith, C. R. Stockard, Theobold Smith, Eugene L. Opie, William H. Welch, James B. Conant, Simon Flexner, and Francis G. Blake.

Boards of Scientific Directors of the Rockefeller Institute for Medical Research.

Board of Scientific Directors of the Rockefeller Institute in 1940.
Left to right: Ross G. Harrison, G. H. Whipple, Cedric B. Smith, W. B. Cannon,
A. R. Dochez, Herbert Gasser, J. B. Conant, and Wilfrid T. Longcope.

Trustees of the General Education Board in 1915.
Bottom row from left to right: Edwin A. Alderman, Frederick T. Gates, Charles W. Eliot,
Harry Pratt Judson, and Wallace Buttrick. *Middle row from left to right:* Wickliffe Rose,
Hollis B. Frissell, John D. Rockefeller, Jr., Eben C. Sage (Assistant Secretary), Albert
Shaw, Jerome D. Greene, and Abraham Flexner. *Top row from left to right:* George E.
Vincent, Anson Phelps Stokes, and Starr J. Murphy.

Institute in Berlin and two to the Ehrlich Institute in Frankfurt. Of course all discoveries were to be public property.

At frequent intervals the directors met with the younger Rockefeller, Gates, and Murphy to scrutinize the work and review the financial arrangements. These meetings were always completely harmonious, though Gates remained discontented with the program. The initial caution was natural, for an atmosphere of uncertainty surrounded the institute. No precise model existed anywhere in the world. The Pasteur, Koch, and Lister Institutes had all been planned on a more narrow scale than Doctors Welch, Flexner, and their associates thought proper for the American undertaking. While these European agencies had clung somewhat rigidly to pathology and bacteriology, the American organizers wished to be free to investigate any problem in biological science—pathology, bacteriology, immunology, biological chemistry, and so on—which might bear upon medicine. Still other elements of dubiety existed, the chief being the uncertainty whether an able research group could yet be assembled in one center.

But that phase of cautious exploration soon ended. As Gates writes, the directors quickly found that scattering small subventions over America and Europe did little good.[21] They determined to concentrate their work, building up their own staff under an expert head, for in that way alone could they carry through long-range projects, and co-ordinate a variety of different labors. Doctor Welch wrote Doctor Herter on January 30, 1902: "I am thoroughly alive to the importance of our presenting to Mr. Rockefeller the view of the Directors concerning the organization of an Institute. Our first work seems to me to secure or have in sight a Director and working staff. We cannot proceed until we get Theobald Smith's decision. I have written him to this effect. I think we should next learn whether Flexner would consider a proposal. I have had a letter from Mr. Rockefeller which indicates his readiness to consider favorably any proposal upon which we are agreed."

Obviously, placing the Institute on this new basis would require more money; and Rockefeller asked his son and Gates to find out how much the directors needed. On receiving full information, he promised in June, 1902, that he would give $1,000,000 to build,

[21]MS Autobiography.

equip, and temporarily operate a research laboratory.[22] He guaranteed nothing more—but it was evident that if they could show that they had laid a sound foundation, more would come. The directors looked about for a site possessing light, good air, and quiet. Above all, they searched carefully for a director; and, after canvassing various American names of prominence, decided that nobody was so well qualified as Doctor Flexner. No other single step did so much to assure the success of the Institute. He was reluctant to accept, for he was devoted to his work at the University of Pennsylvania, while he doubted whether American science had really gained an elevation which would support an ambitious institution for medical research.[23]

But the board, with Doctor Welch's enthusiasm as the most persuasive factor, insisted, and Doctor Flexner yielded. He went abroad in 1903 for some intensive study of chemistry in Berlin, especially under Professor Emil Fischer, while Doctor Herter spent some time in the Ehrlich Institute. Doctor Gates long afterward wrote:[24]

I hope that it may never be forgotten that it is to Doctor William H. Welch that we owe the priceless suggestion that Doctor Flexner be made the director of the Institute. Doctor Flexner was then forty years of age, at the maturity of his powers, already famous for important and successful research. He immediately developed administrative ability of the highest order, while at the same time pursuing his researches with as much zeal and success as if they had been his sole pursuit. The personnel of the Institute has of necessity been subject to constant change and replacement, as experts have passed out into private, consultative practise, or into teaching positions of high responsibility. But Doctor Flexner, always scanning this country and Europe for men of promise, has made the frequent replacements with unerring judgment. While sedulously maintaining the highest standards, he has multiplied the number of research savants and their assistants. All has been done with an attention to detail and a rigid economy, such as it has not been my lot to see in equal measure in any other large corporation, either in finance or in philanthropy. Doctor Flexner has every quality, without exception, of the masterful executive, while retaining the devotion and loyalty of his associates and subordinates. It is nothing but simple truth to say that the Rockefeller Institute of Medical Research has been no less fortunate in its great administrator, Doctor Flexner, than in its great founder, Mr. Rockefeller.

[22]Rockefeller Papers. [23]John D. Rockefeller, Jr., to the author.
[24]MS Autobiography.

The board's plan contemplated that each member of the expert staff should pursue a problem within his special field, care being taken to avoid overlapping or duplication; and that the group should possess complete freedom under Doctor Flexner's general guidance. At the outset, a building was rented at 127 East Fiftieth Street, where some $6000 was invested in equipment for investigations in pathology, physiology, pharmacology, and biological chemistry. Without ceremony, on October 15, 1904, the work began. The staff consisted, besides Doctor Flexner, of Doctors Hideyo Noguchi, Eugene L. Opie, and J. E. Sweet, all pathologists; Doctor S. J. Meltzer, physiologist and pharmacologist; and Doctor P. A. Levene, biological chemist.[25] This little force, as Doctor Flexner writes, "was largely untried, and it still had to win in actuality any considerable success as investigtors and leaders of men." They had been selected not to fit a prearranged plan of investigation, but with confidence that their initiative and talents would open up fruitful paths. "To be exact, they were not so much chosen as placed on probation in pursuance of a provisional plan . . . namely, the plan of centering activities about men, and not about subjects or departments."[26] It proved a wise plan, and to its essence the Institute has always adhered.

At the outset the staff worked under a natural but quite unnecessary tension, a certain feeling of hurry. "The first years," as Doctor Flexner put it, "were nervous ones for all concerned in the actual work, and I suspect the scientific directors did not escape this feeling of uncertainty which may be expressed by the slang phrase, the necessity of 'making good.' As I look back I am convinced that this necessity was overstressed; but then it must be recalled that the little handful of men were new at the job in every way. They had not worked together before; they had not before pursued research solely; they had not yet come into relation with the founder or his direct representatives, and they had not and could not have had any notion of those rare and wonderful relations that were going to be consummated between the scientific workers and directors."[27] As a matter of fact, some fruits were gathered at an early date. On

[25]*Rockefeller Institute History*, 12, 13.
[26]Memorandum by Doctor Flexner; Rockefeller Papers.
[27]*Idem.*

September 6, 1902, Doctor Welch was writing Doctor Herter: "Mr. Rockefeller, Jr., will surely be greatly interested in the important discovery of the specific cause of summer diarrhea of infants. Flexner will have told you all about it. It is in itself a sufficient return for all we have expended from the Institute funds."

Meanwhile, the board had chosen a site for the first laboratory on the brow of the rocky plateau overlooking the East River at Sixty-sixth Street. Rockefeller purchased the tract early in 1903. Here a carefully planned building, four stories of brick and stone, its back to the river, its two-pillared portico facing York Avenue, was erected. Opened May 11, 1906, it furnished excellent facilities for the work already undertaken in pathology, physiology, pharmacology, and biological chemistry, to which experimental surgery and experimental biology were later added.[28]

As the laboratories and staff were expanded, more money was needed—and Rockefeller gave it. "The first building," Doctor Flexner later recalled, "cost about $300,000, and hence left about $700,000 for maintenance. We estimated that by spending $70,000 a year we could operate for ten years—thought we would be on the safe side. We never asked Mr. Rockefeller's representatives for anything. They always came to us and asked: 'Suppose you had more money, what could you do with it?'" The founder made new grants to meet the costs of erecting and equipping the laboratory, and to enlarge its activities. But it soon became evident that additional facilities were needed—in particular, a hospital for the Institute itself, in which selected diseases could be constantly and minutely studied. Research workers had found the task of running from one part of New York to another to examine patients in different institutions highly troublesome. "It is very satisfactory," Doctor Welch wrote Doctor Herter early in 1907, "to learn of Mr. Rockefeller's interest in our plans for the Institute." The needs were laid before the founder, and beginning in 1908, he made a series of gifts which provided for a main hospital of sixty beds, and an isolation pavilion of nine beds under the direction of Doctor Rufus Cole. Increases in endowment were of course required for these activities, and Rockefeller supplied them. The number of diseases studied at any one time was limited and no

[28]*Rockefeller Institute History*, 13. Mr. John D. Rockefeller, Jr., found the site.

patient was admitted unless suffering from one of these maladies—all patients being taken free.[29]

The growth of the institution and its administrative funds required a more complex administrative organization. The original directors were therefore renamed "scientific directors"; they confined themselves to scientific duties. Business and general policies were transferred to a board of trustees, three of its members (Gates, John D. Rockefeller, Jr., and Starr J. Murphy) representing the Institute's fiscal interests, and two (Doctor Welch and Doctor Flexner) representing its scientific work.[30] No friction ever occurred between these two groups. Such difficulties as those which temporarily clouded the relations of Rockefeller and Doctor Harper were unknown. The scientists, who controlled their own expenditures absolutely, kept within their budget; while the founder never attempted the slightest interference with the Institute's work. As Doctor Flexner has testified:

> The Institute . . . has been expected to explore, to dream. Our founder and his advisers have said to us again and again, in effect: "Don't be in a hurry to produce anything. Don't worry about making good. We have faith that you will make good, and if you don't the next fellow will. It is faith—not mere hope—that this or that man will make the best use of his opportunities. Don't you worry. This thing may go on for generations; then suddenly somebody will give us a practical result."
> They have been too ready to praise, to encourage; too ready, including Mr. Rockefeller, to appreciate effort. Never has there been a syllable of question whether this or that could not be done; nothing but confidence has been expressed.

So scrupulous was Rockefeller in his hands-off attitude that he never but once inspected the Institute buildings. Years after the hospital was built he happened to be near that part of town with his son. "Father," suggested the son, "you have never been at the Institute. Let us take a taxi up there and look at it."

We shall return to the Institute's work later. It may here be noted

[29]Doctor Welch wrote Doctor Herter April 23, 1908: "A line from Flexner tells me the good news of Mr. Rockefeller's gift to the Hospital. I felt pretty confident, but it is delightful to have the assurance." Doctor Herter died late in 1910, the first loss among the scientific directors. "How he would have used and enjoyed the new and unique opportunities furnished by the Rockefeller Hospital!" Doctor Welch wrote Mrs. Herter Dec. 5, 1910. *Ibid.*

[30]*Rockefeller Institute History*, 14.

that the influence of Osler and Welch upon Rockefeller's benefactions was not confined to this agency. President Gilman of Johns Hopkins knew of the admiration which Rockefeller and Gates felt for Doctor Osler, and was aware that Gates had written to him in high terms. In February, 1904, the Baltimore fire destroyed many of the resources of the great Johns Hopkins Hospital. Gilman at once wrote Gates, reminding him of his letter to Osler, and asking if he could not interest Rockefeller in the unfortunate position in which the renowned school found itself. A few days later he received a telegram reading: "Our Mr. Murphy will be with you tomorrow." Starr J. Murphy duly spent some days making an accurate estimate of the Johns Hopkins losses. Several weeks passed. Then Gilman received a letter from the younger Rockefeller, which said in effect: "My father has carefully considered your losses, which total about $450,000. He wishes to know whether you would prefer to have a check for $500,000 or securities to that amount." The hospital selected the check; and this was the beginning of contributions to the institution which finally totalled $2,200,000.[31]

v

In the Institute, as in the University of Chicago, Rockefeller had found a use for tens of millions of dollars. Yet even these sums were but a beginning. As his fortune grew more gigantic, he sought still larger avenues of expenditure. Soon after the beginning of the century he established a great new benefaction, which at the outset operated largely for the benefit of the long-handicapped South. The history of this undertaking begins in one sense with 1899 or 1900, when Rockefeller, talking with his son and Gates, thought of setting up a generous trust fund to stimulate Negro education. In another sense it goes back much farther.

In the year that Rockefeller began to mold the Standard Oil combination into a trust, 1879, a middle-aged merchant named Robert C. Ogden became associated with John Wanamaker in Philadelphia. Three years older than Rockefeller, he came of God-fearing Quaker and Scotch Presbyterian ancestry. He had passed through

[31]Doctor Flexner's memorandum; John D. Rockefeller, Jr., to the author; Doctor E. L. Gilcreest, "Rockefeller, Osler, and Welch," San Francisco *Argonaut*, July 16, 1937.

stormy waters of business trouble, for his first choice as partner was unhappy. But Wanamaker gave him opportunity to make a brilliant success, and when in 1896 the company took over the old A. T. Stewart store in New York, he assumed charge. As a merchant Wanamaker had touches of sheer genius, achieving remarkable feats by a flamboyant inspiration. Ogden was quieter, more methodical, and industrious, less given to rhetorical slogans and colorful experiments. But behind his staid exterior was a broad vision and a shrewd, humorous mind. His judgment was so nearly unerring that Wanamaker used to say that his life would be insured cheaply at half a million. When he took control at Stewart's Tenth Street store, which many people thought too far downtown to attract trade, he gave it immediate prestige and success. Putting in a new stock and an expert staff, he made it pay so well that a second building soon had to be added to the first. The profits continued large until after Ogden's retirement in 1907.[32]

But this "retirement" was merely from one set of labors to another. For years he had been prominent in social and humanitarian work. Pennsylvania knew him well in this field. He had been the principal figure in relief work after the Johnstown flood; one of the leaders in succoring the Philadelphia poor after the panic of 1893; a collector of money for the Armenians and other oppressed peoples. He became a director of the Union Theological Seminary in New York, and in time chairman of the board. At an early date he had been intensely interested in the work of Samuel C. Armstrong at Hampton Institute for the colored race, and from that interest sprang a concern for the poor whites of the South as well. William H. Baldwin, the railroad executive and social reformer, had drawn him into the activities of the Tuskegee Institute. Of all the dozens of causes in which Ogden was interested by 1900, Southern education was the chief.

Rockefeller must have heard much of Ogden by this time; while earlier he perhaps saw something of a still more distinguished man engrossed in the same field—J. L. M. Curry. This robust Alabamian, who had fought in Mexico, served in Congress before the Civil War, sat in the Confederate House, and commanded a cavalry regiment during the conflict, was a Baptist. After Appomattox he

[32]P. W. Wilson, *Robert C. Ogden, An Unofficial Statesman.*

became president of Howard College in Alabama, and then professor in Richmond College, meanwhile being prominent in church affairs. In 1871 he was made a Doctor of Divinity by the Rochester Theological Seminary; in 1872 he was elected president of the General Baptist Association, a little later he was temporary pastor of the First Baptist Church in Richmond, and by the end of the decade he was perhaps the most prominent Baptist in the South. He declined a Cabinet position offered him by President Hayes, for what interested him most was education. Soon after the war the banker George Peabody had given more than $3,000,000 to stimulate teaching in the South; and in 1881 Curry was chosen agent—that is, field manager—of the fund. His work was interrupted by service as Minister to Spain under Cleveland, but he resumed it in 1888; and two years later he also became agent for the Slater Fund, a $1,000,000 endowment recently set up by John F. Slater of Connecticut for aid to Negro schools.[33]

Curry, who often came North on business, frequently attended Baptist gatherings in New York. As he was a friend of Doctor Armitage of the Fifth Avenue Church, Rockefeller very likely met and talked with him. If so, his vigor and idealism must have made a marked impression upon the capitalist. Alabama has fittingly placed his statue in the Capitol in Washington. No man did more for Southern education—to encourage the establishment of normal schools for both races, to stimulate cities and towns to set up public graded schools, and to arouse legislators to the crying need for good rural schools.

In the early summer of 1898 a number of men interested in Southern education met at Capon Springs, Va., a Blue Ridge resort.[34] At a second and larger gathering there the next year Curry was elected president of the group, and Ogden vice-president. Few newspapers North or South took any notice of these meetings, or of a third held in 1900. Ogden therefore resolved to see that the next one was larger and more enthusiastic, and that it was given adequate publicity. He hired a handsome special train from the Pennsylvania Railroad, sent out invitations to notable people, including

[33]Edwin A. Alderman and Armistead C. Gordon, *Life of J. L. M. Curry*.
[34]The first gathering was largely of churchmen. Burton J. Hendrick, *The Making of An American; Early Life and Letters of Walter Hines Page*.

John D. Rockefeller, Jr., and at a cost of $2500 a day, carried an array of influential men to the South. His undertaking met both suspicion and ridicule. Various Southern journals took a proudly scornful attitude toward the use of Yankee cash for their schools, while *The Manufacturers' Record,* organ of Southern industry, spoke of the train as having "the antique aroma of a minstrel troupe." The New York *World* ran headlines:[35]

MEN OF MILLIONS TO REDEEM THE SOUTH
Splendid Far-Reaching Plan in Which Young Rockefeller Is a Leader
MUCH HOPED FROM IT
Oil Trust Wealth May Be Poured Out to Educate Blacks
and the Poor Whites
SCHOOLS TO DOT SOUTHLAND

The younger Rockefeller had gone because his father and he were now keenly interested in the possibility of giving to Negro education, and this excursion train visited, with other points of interest, both Hampton and Tuskegee. Among the guests were Walter Hines Page, George Foster Peabody, Albert Shaw, John Graham Brooks, Bishop Doane, and William H. Baldwin. It was the last-named with whom John D. Rockefeller, Jr., talked oftenest and longest.[36] In 1902 and again in 1903 Ogden took similar excursion trains to the South. He was fired with the idea that the time had come for a broad-fronted educational renaissance, paralleling the industrial awakening in that section; that a sudden energetic impulse might create an irresistible tide. The new movement must enlist prominent Southerners as well as Northerners, and show a tactful regard for Southern susceptibilities. It must have no air of Yankee condescension, no flavor of Lady Bountiful on a slumming trip. The younger Rockefeller, who went on the first tour only, instantly caught the vision which Ogden and Curry had seen, and brought back a glowing story to his father.

One result of the Southern excursions and conferences was the organization in New York of the Southern Education Board, which

[35]April 28, 1901.
[36]So Mr. Rockefeller told me. Page was editor of *World's Work;* Shaw was editor of *The Review of Reviews;* Brooks was a writer and lecturer on economics; Peabody was an eminent banker; Doane was Episcopal bishop of Albany since 1869; Baldwin was president of the Long Island Railroad. They made up an impressive and influential group.

George Foster Peabody launched with a gift of $80,000 for two years' work, and for which Ogden selected the first board members.[37] Though its funds were meager, it carried on valuable activities during the next ten years. But a far larger enterprise grew out of the union of the "Ogden movement" with the nascent interest of the Rockefellers in Southern schools. After his talks with Baldwin, Peabody, and others, John D. Rockefeller, Jr., realized that it was important to give assistance to the whites no less than the blacks. This was a truth which Walter Hines Page—who later, in his address on "The Forgotten Man," vividly portrayed the needs of large Southern areas—helped to impress upon him. He thought earnestly upon the subject. He talked it over not only with his father and Gates, but with another arresting figure—Wallace Buttrick, chairman of the Baptist Home Mission Society, who knew Southern problems at first hand. Buttrick had begun life as a railway mail clerk, and educated himself by stern effort, graduating from the Rochester Theological Seminary. After holding pastorates in New Haven, St. Paul, and Albany, he had finally taken charge of the home missions, which included the grant of much assistance to Negro schools. He was an executive of sturdy common sense, keen comprehension of human nature, and winning geniality; not a scholar, but a practical man of the world. His enthusiasm and energy in any good cause were marvelously infectious. "He was the most unselfish worker I have ever known," testifies Abraham Flexner. Anxious to help both races in the South, he knew how to do it gracefully and effectively.[38]

VI

The first step in what was to prove one of the most far-reaching philanthropic enterprises of the century was taken on the evening of January 15, 1902. Six men met at the house of the venerable banker-philanthropist Morris K. Jesup—Ogden, Curry, Peabody, Baldwin, Buttrick, and John D. Rockefeller, Jr.; and they determined to form an organization for the promotion of education.[39] On February 27,

[37]Wilson, *Ogden*, 230.

[38]See N. Y. *Times, Tribune*, May 28, 1926, for obituaries of Doctor Buttrick; *Dictionary of American Biography*.

[39]Wilson, *Ogden*, 233. Baldwin had been head of the Committee of Fourteen dealing with vice-repression in New York, in the work of which Rockefeller was deeply interested.

1902, a larger group gathered at the younger Rockefeller's house on West Fifty-fourth Street for dinner. They included, besides the original six—four important new figures—Daniel Coit Gilman, Albert Shaw, Walter Hines Page, and Edward M. Shepard, the last-named acting as counsel.[40] Baldwin, whom Rockefeller had selected as leader of the undertaking, was elected president; a careful statement of purposes was read and signed by all; and plans were made for obtaining Federal incorporation under the name of the General Education Board. But the most memorable event of the evening was a financial announcement. Rockefeller, who had studied the matter with care, promised through his son that he would give $1,000,000 to be used during the next ten years for education without distinction of sex, race, or creed.[41]

It was an extraordinary charter that Shepard drew up. Far from confining the powers of the new body to the limited work at first contemplated, he drafted a perpetual charter which gave it authority to hold limitless capital, and to engage in any activities whatever in any part of the nation which could be construed as educational. Congress alone could grant such authority, and to Congress the Board applied. It was fortunate for it that Nelson W. Aldrich was then the most influential figure in the Senate. He took the bill into his highly efficient hands, and carried it through Congress without delay; the act of incorporation becoming effective January 12, 1903.[42] Thus was established an organization which shortly became the most powerful educational foundation in the world; one to which, within the next decade, Rockefeller was to give more than $50,000,000, and before his death, almost $150,000,000.

The four men whose ideas dominated the early work of the General Education Board were Baldwin, Buttrick, Gates, and John D. Rockefeller, Jr., for Curry died in 1903, while Ogden was largely engrossed with his own activities. At the outset it groped for an effective plan. After a rapid examination of the subject, it pledged itself to give the whole $1,000,000, without any particular public

[40]Alderman and Gordon, *Curry*, 372, 373. Shepard was a close friend of Peabody.
[41]*General Education Board Archives*. Rockefeller's pledge was embodied in a formal letter of March 1, 1902. I have had information from Mr. John D. Rockefeller, Jr., and others.
[42]Gates, MS Autobiography, 407, 408.

assistance, to build and improve schools in selected Southern counties. Its leaders quickly found that private philanthropy alone would be inadequate. The South had a thousand counties. The Board might shovel out thousands of dollars a year to each, and yet afford little real assistance. Its grants, moreover, would deaden the spirit of self-help, not stimulate it. A more carefully pondered program was indispensable.

After an intensive and thorough survey by a committee headed by Doctor Gates, the Board determined that the best way to improve the education of the South was not to pour money loosely into the counties, but to better the quality of the teaching. It could do this by furnishing information, initiative, and leadership rather than funds. Most country schools were taught by girls of seventeen to twenty-three, waiting to get married, who themselves had only a country school training. High schools must be widely established, their standards kept sound, and their graduates used for teaching. At the same time the assistance of the people ought to be enlisted— and in many districts they were as yet too poor to assist anybody with a dollar. They must be helped out of their poverty before they could form any real connection with a high-school system. This meant that somehow, and without loss of time, instruction must be given them in agriculture and domestic science.

Having completed its initial study, the General Education Board invited every State university to appoint a professor of secondary education, who should be a member of its faculty, working under its supervision, and yet have both his salary and expenses paid by the Board. These men were to travel over every county until they had covered the State; they were to discover in each the best place for a good high school, and look into ways and means—estimating the value of all the property in the county, the amount of the taxes, and the possibility of raising the assessments. Then, with the prestige of the State university behind him, the professor was to call a general meeting, explain the facts, present pictures of good high schools and statistics of costs, appeal to the community spirit of the citizens and their pride in their children, and show just how they could raise the money to build and maintain the high school.[43]

[43]*General Education Board: An Account of Its Activities, 1902–1914,* pp. 81 ff. The enlistment of State Universities began in Virginia in 1905; by 1910 eleven states had joined in the plan.

Doctor Buttrick, as secretary of the Board, supervised a long-continued and searching inquiry into educational conditions in the South. With the aid of field workers, he made a thorough examination of the school systems of all the States along the Atlantic seaboard, and several lying inland. Detailed reports were drawn up on school organization, supervision, and finance, on Negro education, on the number and pay of teachers, on normal-school education, and on allied topics. These documents were at first confidential; distributed among members of the General Education Board and filed in its archives, they were not made public. But within a few years, as the educational situation in the South materially improved, the information on some communities was published to assist other localities in meeting their problems. The same tact was shown in other ways. All the Board members agreed that it must never try to impose an educational program from the outside, but must cooperate with Southern spokesmen in working out a joint program. The success of the scheme was remarkable. Gates was able to write before his death:

The plan proved efficient beyond our most sanguine anticipations. All the Southern States without exception called for these professors of secondary education. Under their leadership the South had established in 1922 more than sixteen hundred new high schools, at a cost of over forty-six million dollars, all raised by local taxation. So fully has the need of high schools been supplied that for some years now our professors of education have been able to give their entire attention to enlarging the scope of the high schools, and improving the instruction given in them. This addition of over sixteen hundred high schools has stimulated the entire educational system of the South beyond the power of imagination to compass. It has multiplied many times the enrolment of the colleges and universities, and given their students a better preparation. . . . There is no school in the South of any kind, from the kindergarten to the university, that has not felt the new impulse.

Meanwhile, the Board had early reached the conclusion that no efforts could raise Southern education to the desired level until the economic position of the rural South was improved. The poverty of the section was appalling. The first years of the century found farmers of the Middle West in a far more prosperous condition than a decade earlier, and their wealth increased steadily until the end of the World War. But the Southerners, especially in areas bound hand and food by the one-crop system and filled with tenant farmers of meager resources, failed to obtain their due share of the new agricultural gains. While the average annual earnings of individuals engaged in farming in the State of Iowa were upward of $1000, the average earnings of those similarly engaged in the Southern States were as low as $150.[44] How could these poverty-stricken farmers be helped?

The Board sought advice in many quarters. By some experts it was urged to address itself to the rising generation, and to teach agriculture in the high schools. But for good and sufficient reasons this proposal was rejected. No trained teachers were available, no funds could be raised in the South to help pay such teachers, and the instruction would contribute nothing to its own support. Moreover, it was impossible to force the teaching of better farming into the curricula of neighborhoods which did not yet realize that their agriculture was highly deficient. Public schools simply could not be reconstructed until the public behind them in each district was convinced that they needed a drastic overhauling. The Board therefore determined to undertake the agricultural education not of the children, but of the existing generation of farmers. Once they were persuaded that a more scientific agriculture paid in hard cash, they would be willing to devote part of their enhanced income to better schools.

The Board having reached this decision, Doctor Buttrick spent almost a year in familiarizing himself with the best methods of teaching improved farming methods to adult farmers. He visited agricultural schools as far north as Quebec and Ontario, as far south as Texas, as far west as Iowa. By a stroke of good fortune, he found lecturing at the Texas State Agricultural College just the leader whom the Board needed to assist it—the able agent of the Federal Department of Agriculture, Doctor Seaman A. Knapp.

With his white sideburns, Knapp bore at first glance a startling resemblance to Chauncey M. Depew; and his firm jaw, domelike forehead, and keen eyes peering from under bushy brows stamped him with a look of vigorous leadership. His rugged frame and broad shoulders showed exceptional physical vigor. Alert, enthusiastic, and full of ideas, he was the foremost expert of the country

[44]*General Education Board Activities,* 21.

on farm demonstration work. In his long lifetime he had been farmer, editor, professor of agriculture, president of Iowa State College, head of a large colonization project in Louisiana, president of the Rice Association of America, and apostle of new farming methods throughout the West and South. He had helped to draft the law for Federal experiment stations in agriculture; he had done more than any one else to develop the rice industry of the Southwest. In his colonization work he had induced progressive Iowa farmers to come down to Louisiana, one to a township, and demonstrate the possibilities of good farming—a most fruitful innovation. The close of the Spanish War had found him, nearly sixty-five but still indefatigable, aiding the Agricultural Department in various capacities. He investigated rice culture in the Orient, and surveyed the rural resources of Puerto Rico. Then, when the armies of the boll weevil crossed the Mexican line and debouched upon Texas, he emerged as captain of the Federal forces resisting the invasion.[45]

The boll weevil had already devastated great tracts of northern Mexico. Its advance into Texas was seemingly irresistible, and panic gripped half of the State. For decades cotton had been the principal pillar of Texan prosperity, but now this source of wealth was threatened with destruction. Broad tracts were very rapidly abandoned, until some counties were almost depopulated. Then the intrepid Knapp in 1903 established a demonstration farm at Terrell, Texas, to show farmers how cotton could be grown despite the boll-weevil. It proved astonishingly successful. By using new scientific methods, growers could actually increase the yield of cotton over all previous figures. Observers shortly grasped the significance of his work; for if the production of cotton on weevil-infested land could be thus enhanced, what might not be done on pest-free farms? In the fall of 1903, Federal officers agreed to use $40,000 in employing experts under Knapp's supervision for farm-demonstration work. Knapp's

[45]Doctor Knapp's work has been given fairly full treatment in O. B. Martin, *Demonstration Work: Dr. Seaman A. Knapp's Contribution to Civilization;* A. C. True, *History of Agricultural Extension in the United States,* and *History of Agricultural Education in the United States;* and *Dr. Seaman A. Knapp: Proceedings of the Fourth Annual Convention of the Southern Commercial Congress.* A biography of Knapp is being prepared by Mr. Joseph Bailey, who tells me he believes that the entrance of the Rockefeller interests was invaluable in calling public and congressional attention to the extraordinary utility of Knapp's work, and in preserving it from bureaucratic indifference if not strangulation.

activities, as Buttrick saw, seemed a heaven-sent answer to the problem which the General Education Board was trying to solve.

Officers of the Board hastened to confer with Knapp. The costs of a large-scale experiment in demonstration work, the methods to be pursued, and the probabilities of ultimate self-support, were all thoroughly and cautiously canvassed. Knapp's point of view was precisely that which Rockefeller himself had always taken in his benefactions; he believed that the best form of help was that which stimulated self-help, and that a vitally rooted and self-continuing work was the proper goal of any well-planned philanthropy. He was sure that the demonstration work which he had in view would conform to just these specifications. Once it was vigorously begun in any State, county, or rural community, it would promptly enlist local support. It would spread from community to community, county to county, State to State, until agriculture and domestic arts would become accepted elements in the rural-school program everywhere.

Since the work was so important, and since its results promised to be so beneficent, why should not the Federal Government support it? Why should the General Educational Board enter a field which might rather be considered a national responsibility? The answer was simple: at that time the Federal Government held that it could spend funds only for interstate, and not intrastate, purposes. To be sure, after Doctor Knapp scored a spectacular success with his cotton-culture farm at Terrell, Congress made several special appropriations for extending the work, and similar farms were set up throughout the weevil-infested region. But these appropriations were based on the theory that the boll-weevil was an interstate menace, and for that reason only was a legitimate object of Federal concern. Federal money was simply not available for strictly educational uses within the States. The entrance of the General Educational Board into the farm-demonstration field was therefore a necessity if the work was to cover the entire South. Doctor Knapp, while still serving the Department of Agriculture, gladly agreed to direct the Board's activities in otherwise neglected areas. As the Board's historian later wrote, he entered into the undertaking "with all the vigor and enthusiasm of youth."[46]

[46]*General Education Board Activities,* 25.

Rockefeller had watched the Board's early undertakings with keen interest. At every stage his son had made oral reports to him while Gates had submitted written memoranda. He had talked with Buttrick and Starr J. Murphy. Doctor Gates speaks of his "very critical eye" for all documents laid before him. He approved of generous appropriations for the new work, rising from $37,500 in 1905-6 to $252,000 in 1913. The Department of Agriculture unhesitatingly made an alliance with the Board in promoting farm demonstrations. An agreement signed April 20, 1906, by Secretary Wilson and Doctor Buttrick, provided that although the farmers' co-operative work in which the Board engaged should be "entirely distinct in territory and finance from that carried on solely by the Department," nevertheless the latter "shall have supervision over the work and shall appoint all special agents for this extended territory in the same way that they are now appointed, and the said agents shall be under control of said department in every respect as fully as any of the agents of the department." Thereafter, farm-demonstration work in weevil-infected States was carried on by Government funds, while such work in noninfected States was carried on by the Board's funds; but control of both was placed in the hands of the Federal Department of Agriculture.

VII

Doctor Knapp's methods of winning the confidence of rural districts were as simple as they were effective. He would go to an intelligent and influential farmer.

"I have a cotton seed which has been carefully selected during a long period of years," he would explain. "It is a strong and quick-maturing seed. If you plant it and cultivate it properly you will more than double your yield. We have come to you as a leading farmer and would like to have you demonstrate its value. The demonstration, we believe, will not only convince you of the value of good seed and scientific tillage, but convince your neighbors."

Having gained the farmer's confidence, he would then broach the conditions to be met. The land must be plowed in the fall. Why? Because fall plowing gave mellowness to the soil. The rows of cotton must be planted wide apart. Again why? Because more than four fifths of the growth of any plant is derived from sunlight and air; if the rows were placed close together the cotton would be starved and smothered. The cotton must be cultivated six or eight times. Why? Because there was plenty of moisture down by the roots, and it must be kept there by breaking the top soil into a fine dust-mulch which retarded evaporation. Doctor Knapp's work was controlled by a few simple aphorisms. "Don't confuse people by elaborate programs," he would say; "the average man, like the crow, cannot count more than three." Again, he often remarked: "Do the next thing." He drew up a set of "Ten Agricultural Commandments" and circulated it widely in the South and West.[47]

The General Education Board fully appreciated Doctor Knapp's invaluable talents. He showed the farmers how to burn the boll-weevils with the stalks in the fall; to plow the land deeply; to plant good seed; to fertilize the soil. He showed them the advantages of a rotation of crops, alternating cotton, corn, cowpeas, and clover. He never ceased to inveigh against the system of mortgaging the cotton crop in advance to some factor or storekeeper who supplied groceries and clothing at outrageous profits. He stimulated the farmers to grow stock and make their farms self-sufficient in meat, eggs, milk, and vegetables. In Mississippi several of his representatives taught a group of farmers not only how to till the soil more efficiently, but to keep accounts. Then Doctor Knapp arrived.

"How many of you made your living last year?" he asked. They all had.

"How many two years ago?" he continued. Not one had done so.[48]

The area covered by this farm demonstration work rapidly expanded. In 1907 the Federal Government supported it in Texas, Louisiana, and Arkansas, these being the boll-weevil States; the General Education Board supported it in Mississippi, Alabama, and Virginia.[49] In 1908 the government added Oklahoma to its list; the Board added Georgia and the two Carolinas. As the boll-weevil spread eastward, the government enlarged its operations, taking over Mississippi in 1909, then Tennessee, then other States. By 1913 the Federal Government had eight Southern States and half of another on its roster; the Board had Maryland, Virginia, West Virginia, the two Carolinas, and northern Georgia under its care—and

[47]*Idem*, 46 ff.   [48]O. B. Martin, *Demonstration Work*.
[49]*General Education Board Activities*.

also Maine and New Hampshire, for it had now turned to the
North. By 1912, more than 106,000 farms and farmers were directly
reached by the new instruction—and from thirty to one hundred
neighbors visited each demonstration farm. A revolution in the sys-

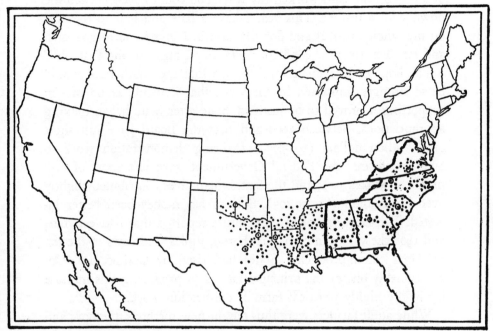

From Abraham Flexner's "The General Education Board, 1902–14."

Farm demonstration work as conducted by Rockefeller's General Education Board and the Southern States. Each dot represents a Demonstration
Center. Those west of Alabama were operated under Congressional appropriations. Later the work extended into Tennessee, Kentucky, West
Virginia, and Maryland.

tem of Southern agriculture had gotten well under way. One Alabama farmer, who made a little speech at a field meeting, spoke
for an army of his fellows when he said:[50]

"I was born in a cotton field and have worked cotton on my
farm for more than forty years. I thought no one could tell me
anything about raising cotton. I have usually raised one half a bale
an acre on my thin soil, and I thought that was all the cotton there
was in it for one season. The Demonstration Agent came along and

[50]W. O. Inglis, MS. Biography, 534.

wanted me to try his plan on two acres. Not to be contrary, I agreed; but I did not believe what he told me. However, I tried my best to do as he said, and at the end of the year I had a bale and a half to the acre on two acres worked his way, and a little over a third of a bale on the land worked my way. You could have knocked me down with a feather. This year I have a bale and half to the acre on my whole farm. If you don't believe it, I invite you to go down and see. Yes, sir, as a good cotton farmer I am just one year old."

The hope of Rockefeller and his son that the South itself would be so strongly impressed by the work that it would co-operate in supporting it proved to be justified. State after State began making appropriations. Between 1906 and 1915 the Board gave just short of a million dollars ($925,750) to bring demonstration work to Southern farms; the Federal Government gave just short of two millions ($1,922,300); and the States themselves contributed slightly over one million ($1,069,405). Seldom has money been better invested. The Department of Agriculture reported that between 1904 and 1908 the values in corn, hay, horses, mules, and cows in the ten principal cotton-producing States had risen by $421,000,000. Unquestionably one of the principal factors in producing this increase lay in the highly practical farm-demonstration work.

While adult farmers were thus taught new methods, the boys and girls in rural areas were not neglected. Doctor Knapp took up the idea of corn clubs for lads—a number had already been organized by county superintendents of education—and did his utmost to popularize it. Every club member planted one acre of corn on his father's farm by the use of demonstration methods, prizes were given, and the most successful boys were taken to Washington to shake hands with the President and Secretary of Agriculture. The neighborhoods soon noted that the boys raised much better corn, and in larger yields, than their fathers. Doctor Knapp similarly took up the idea of canning clubs for girls, and spread them broadcast throughout the South. The girls were taught to grow their own tomatoes, can them, and sell them, keeping careful account of costs and returns. By 1913 more than 90,000 boys and 30,000 girls had been enrolled in these clubs.

No race lines were drawn in the work done by the General Education Board. At an early date Oswald Garrison Villard raised the question whether a colored representative ought not to be included on both the Southern Education and General Education Boards. Robert Ogden, who succeeded Baldwin as president of the latter in 1905, took the conservative view that this was quite unnecessary. "The only direct responsibility that either Board has," he wrote, "is to the donors of the money that gives support to the one and capital for distribution to the other. Under these circumstances, there is no logical demand for representation in either Board from any person except the donors." To add a colored member would, he feared, heighten an all-too-prevalent misconception in the South. Many people believed that the Board was asserting a general control over education in the South, and that it was also assuming to establish the channels of philanthropy for Negro education; both beliefs being utterly erroneous.[51]

Nevertheless, the Board labored as energetically for Negroes as for whites. In his first report, Doctor Knapp wrote that since the greater part of the cotton crop is grown by colored laborers and tenants, "all our agents are not only instructed but of their own choice select colored tenant farmers as demonstrators, visiting them regularly and giving them every attention." At Mound Bayou in the Mississippi delta country, six demonstrations in 1907 were followed by forty-one the next year. The white agents and demonstrators who began the work of instructing the blacks were soon aided by graduates of Hampton, Tuskegee, and other industrial and agricultural schools. By 1911 thirty-two Negro demonstrators were at work. All over the South the colored race felt the general impulse toward more intelligent agriculture. As one Virginia Negro expressed it: "You done turned down de kivers and waked us up."

Doctor Knapp, working until the last, died in the spring of 1911; Robert C. Ogden in the summer of 1913. The passing of these two leaders ended the first phase in the history of the General Education Board. Knapp, in the opinion of Walter Hines Page, was one of the greatest men of his time, "the Benjamin Franklin of the countryside."[52] His practicality, modesty, and vision had won the hearts of the Southern people. After his death the Southern Commercial Congress held a special meeting to honor his memory, at which leaders in education, government, and business paid tribute

[51]Wilson, *Ogden*, 234.   [52]*Idem*, 248.

to him. As the Arkansas editor, J. C. Small, said, "Rather than stand upon the rostrum and direct or sit in the saddle and command, he preferred to walk between the plow handles and demonstrate his teachings, as neighbor to neighbor." Knapp had entered Arkansas, Small added, when the memory of Reconstruction days still fed a deep resentment. Overcoming all this sectional prejudice, he "extended a kindly hand to the eager student, and in the light of a new knowledge the Arkansas farmer has in ten years increased the agricultural wealth of his State $318,673,000." His last visit to New York, enfeebled by illness, had been to consult the Board upon means of expanding the work of the girls' clubs.[53] The death of Ogden removed an equally large-minded and great-hearted leader. "There is no man," said ex-President Taft, "whose sacrificing efforts in behalf of the humble and hopeless of his fellowmen deserve such unstinted praise as Robert C. Ogden."

But before these deaths, great additions had been made to the Board's funds, Gates had become chairman, and it had entered upon new paths. Rockefeller in June, 1905, gave $10,000,000 to it. He asked Gates to draw up the letter designating the purposes to which the funds were to be devoted, and Gates had no hesitation in dedicating the entire amount to higher education. Early in 1907 Rockefeller gave $32,000,000 more, and on July 7, 1909, increased his benefactions by an additional $10,000,000. The principal new activities of the Board were in advanced education. When elected head in 1907, Gates believed that he might carry out a great work of development and reformation. He had become pretty well acquainted with the 400 so-called colleges and universities, and thought he understood the governing factors in their growth. "I had a reasonably clear bird's-eye view of the whole field," he wrote later, "and while there was much to encourage, there was also much to regret. The picture was one of chaos. Most of these institutions had been located in a soil which could not sustain them as colleges; in spots they were injuriously crowded together. They were scattered haphazard over the landscape like wind-carried seeds." But we must reserve the story of the Board's work in higher education for another chapter.

[53]Mr. John D. Rockefeller, Jr., remembers this visit.

From a photograph by Brown Bros.   *From a photograph by Science Service.*

From the report of the Rockefeller Sanitary Commission.

Assistance to the South.

Above (left): Seaman H. Knapp, leader in farm demonstration work. (*Right*): Doctor
Charles Wardell Stiles, leader in the battle against the hookworm. *Below:* A dispensary
in Jacksonville, North Carolina.

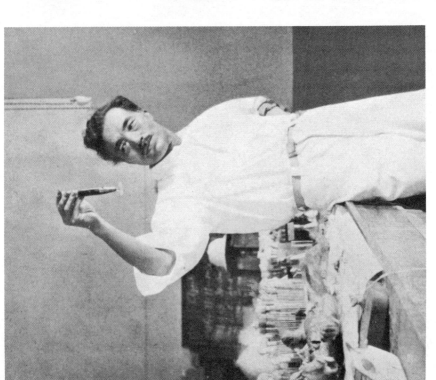

The struggle against disease.

Left: Doctor Hideyo Noguchi of the Rockefeller Institute for Medical Research.
Right: Pupils trained by Rockefeller funds in a native school, Ife, Nigeria.

VIII

Rockefeller and his aides had shown their ability to be pioneers in philanthropy. In two new directions, by 1905, they had broken away from the conventional paths followed in distributing a fortune. America has produced many men who knew better how to accumulate a fortune than how to give it away; men like Frank A. Munsey, who after long hesitation and confusion finally, in a gesture almost of despair, dumped his millions upon the Metropolitan Museum of Art. The usual course of perplexed multimillionaires was to give their money to colleges, universities, churches, hospitals, museums, and libraries. That course was easy; it threw the responsibility for a wise use of the funds upon other shoulders; and it usually resulted in ample advertisement of the gift and giver. To strike out on a new path required imagination, a quality with which Rockefeller and Gates were well endowed; but it also required a great deal of careful thought, investigation, and preparatory labor. Rockefeller remarked in his *Reminiscences* that he wished to apply in giving, as in industry, "the spirit of combination and co-operation"; and that he liked to work on "new, and, I hope, expanding lines, which make large demands on one's intelligence and study."

It was important, in dealing with so large a fortune, to employ it for purposes which would not otherwise be served by the government or by philanthropists of lesser means. It was important to use it with an eye not merely upon present needs, but upon underlying trends of the period and the growth of society; it should be geared to great dynamic forces just becoming evident. Both the medical research and the improvement of Southern farming and schooling met these requirements. No government and no other multimillionaire was going to provide $40,000,000 for advanced investigation of disease. The South could not aid its own farmers and teachers with sufficient rapidity, for the South was too poor; it would be trying to lift itself by its bootstraps. In opening these fields, Rockefeller, his son, and Gates aligned themselves with some great forces of the day. American science and American interest in public health had now reached a level at which work in medical research would fructify a broad area. New discoveries, new ideas in sanitation, would be eagerly utilized by an army of physicians, public health officers, and laboratory specialists. The South was just entering upon a social and economic renascence, while the time had come to give the new scientific knowledge in agriculture a broad popular application.

Two new roads had been broken; two gates had been thrown open. It was a beginning. Rockefeller, talking with Gates and his son, hearing of each new decision made by the independent agencies he had set up, and reading digested reports of their work, might feel satisfied that he was making fruitful use of his fortune. But much remained to be done, and still bolder enterprises had to be planned.

XLIV

Rockefeller vs. Public Opinion

THE year 1898 witnessed not only America's victory over decaying Spain, and the growth of a new prosperity, but an event in which Rockefeller took especial interest, the creation by Congress of an Industrial Commission. This was primarily the work of his old enemies in the Regions. Several years earlier Thomas W. Phillips of the Pure Oil Company had been elected to Congress and had induced it to pass a resolution creating a body to investigate the trusts and allied questions; but President Cleveland had vetoed it. It was brought up again, repassed, and approved by McKinley. Obviously the measure was born of a widespread dissatisfaction with the existing economic order, and portended an earnest effort at reform. The rapid proliferation of trusts had alarmed many Americans, while the immigration problem and labor unrest had frightened others.

Congress vested the commission with power to investigate almost every subject on the economic horizon—agriculture, labor, immigration, manufacturing, and industrial combinations. Nineteen men were authorized to collect facts and report; five Senators, five Representatives, and nine salaried laymen to be named by President McKinley. Under the chairmanship of Senator Kyle of South Dakota—onetime preacher, and former free-silverite and Populist—the body set to work. It was divided into subcommittees to deal with various subjects, but the trust question was reserved for the whole panel. Most of the Commission's time went into taking oral testimony. But as the months dragged on, it made increasing use of such trained investigators as Jeremiah W. Jenks, Emory R. Johnson, Samuel McCune Lindsay, John R. Commons, and William Z.

Ripley, who employed reports and statistics already in the government's possession.[1]

As Rockefeller, Archbold, and other industrial leaders were aware, the Commission might do much to mold public sentiment, and perhaps to initiate far-reaching legislation. For this reason corporation executives were eager to testify. The sugar trust, tobacco trust, Standard Oil, steel industry, and numerous other businesses presented their best spokesmen. Through such witnesses as Rockefeller, Archbold, Havemeyer, Duke, Gary, and William H. Moore, the apostles of business consolidation gave their side of the trust question—a side that had never been properly understood.[2] Because of the intense interest in the trust issue, the Commission presented a brief preliminary report on that subject in March, 1900; but not until 1902 did it bring out its final statement of findings and recommendations in the last two of its nineteen volumes. Upon the whole, the work of the body was disappointing. Like some of the British royal commissions, it made a great display of governmental interest in painful subjects, while in large part avoiding any real grapple with them.

Rockefeller doubtless heard from Archbold of the intense interest that 26 Broadway was taking in the inquiry. It is unlikely, however, that he learned of all the precautions that Archbold was taking. The new head of the Standard was on intimate terms with Senator Boies Penrose of Pennsylvania, a member of the Commission, and Senator W. J. Sewell of New Jersey, not a member. Both men were "safe." When the preliminary report was being drafted, Archbold urged Sewell to protect corporation interests. "It seems very important that this report should be wisely and conservatively shaped," he wrote. Representative John J. Gardner of Atlantic City was on the Commission, "and we think it very desirable indeed that you should have a word with him on the subject." Archbold believed he would act "judicially and sensibly," but "it seems very desirable to be as sure as possible."[3] Doubtless Sewell bestirred him-

---

[1]E. Dana Durand, "Methods of Government Investigation," *Quarterly Journal of Economics,* XVI, 564–586 (August, 1902). See also S. N. D. North, "The Industrial Commission," *North American Review,* CLXVIII, 708–719.

[2]Most of the Standard Oil evidence is in volume I of the Report.

[3]Archbold to Sewell, Dec. 29, 1899; quoted in *Hearst's Magazine,* XXIII, 697–707.

self; but if so, it was without effect. Gardner exhibited positive hostility toward the Standard Oil, and we shortly find Archbold writing Sewell that he wished an opportunity to talk with the stubborn Congressman.[4]

Meanwhile, on January 5, 1900, Archbold begged Penrose to see that his fellow-commissioners kept one dangerous proposal out of the preliminary report—the proposal that corporations should be required to publish the names and holdings of all stockholders, with full information upon receipts, expenditures, profits, and losses. What business had the public to know who held stock, and in what amounts? The demand for names, wrote Archbold, was "an unjust and unnecessary inquisition." And why should Tom, Dick, and Harry be told all about the receipts, expenses, and profits of a corporation? "A statement of assets and liabilities is all that can benefit the public." In the same way, numerous railroad heads and large manufacturers were trying to influence the Commission's action.[5]

Penrose obligingly sent Archbold an advance copy of the preliminary report as soon as one came into his hands. Later he explained that he would have done as much for anybody else directly concerned; for John Mitchell of the coal-miners' union, for example.[6] When Archbold and the Standard attorneys hurriedly perused the document, they were pleased by its mildness, for it contained no abusive language, and urged no prosecutions. It did suggest an increase in the powers of the Interstate Commerce Commission to cope with rebating. But after some general recommendations for protecting investors, the Commission offered only one important proposal bearing directly upon monopolies; and Penrose had apparently done what was expected of him, for this did not go farther than Archbold had thought proper. "The larger corporations—the so-called trusts—should be required to publish annually a properly audited report, showing in reasonable detail their assets and liabilities, with profit or loss; such report and audit under oath to be subject to Government inspection. The purpose of such publication

---

[4]U. S. Senate Committee on Privileges and Elections, *Campaign Contribution Testimony*, 62d Cong., 3d Session (1913), II, 1350. Hereafter cited as *Clapp Investigation*.

[5]*Clapp Investigation*, I, 151 ff., for Archbold's letters. Samuel McCune Lindsay has told me how much he and other experts resented the pressure of railroads, steel mills, and other organizations.

[6]Penrose in *Clapp Investigation*, I, 170.

is to encourage competition when profits become excessive, thus protecting consumers against too high prices, and to guard the interests of employees by a knowledge of the financial condition of the business in which they are employed."[7]

We may be sure that Rockefeller shared Archbold's relief over the moderation of this document. Rejoicing spread up and down Wall Street, and to the capitol in Trenton, where great holding-companies were being chartered more numerously than ever. "We think the report is so fair that we will not undertake to suggest any changes," Archbold wrote Penrose.[8] He was so sure of the Senator's friendliness that when Kyle died in the summer of 1901 he urged Penrose to take the chairmanship. Although Kyle had shown unexpected wisdom and caution, wrote Archbold, Penrose could do even better if he took the place. "This seems eminently fitting from every point of view. Your name as chairman would undoubtedly give to the report exceptional assurance of integrity and intelligence; you are the ranking Senatorial member of the Commission; the interests of your State are pre-eminent in the matter; and lastly, and we may hope not unfairly, we make it as a strong personal request."[9] He also asked Quay to do his utmost to persuade Penrose. When Penrose refused on the ground that he attended too irregularly, Archbold threw his support to Albert Clarke, who was elected.

The Industrial Commission had given the principal enemies of the Standard, as of other trusts, full opportunity to testify, and George Rice, Lewis Emery, Jr., James W. Lee, F. S. Monnett, and Henry Demarest Lloyd had eagerly seized it.[10] Many of the facts brought out were highly damaging to the Standard. These witnesses made it plain that the oil combination still profited from rebating. Emery and Lee testified that although both the president and general freight agent of the Pennsylvania Railroad had stated in 1890 that their line had permitted no discriminations, the auditors of the Pennsylvania immediately thereafter declared, under oath, that the discriminations against a single oil company in one year had ranged from three to twenty-eight cents a barrel, and aggregated more than

[7]*Industrial Commission Report*, XIX, 649, 650, gives this preliminary report.
[8]Archbold to Penrose, Feb. 21, 1900; *Clapp Investigation*, II, 1350.
[9]Archbold to Penrose, July 3, 1901; *Clapp Investigation*, I, 152; *Hearst's Magazine*, XXII (August, 1912), 10 ff.
[10]*Industrial Commission Report*, I, *passim*.

$24,000.[11] Indeed, the Commission collected evidence as to a vast amount of rebating in every great industry—coal-mining, flour-milling, meat-packing, and so on. Fierce local price-cutting to destroy competition was proved against the Standard, as also against the Tobacco Trust, the Salt Trust, and other combinations.

One high official of the Standard, in fact, admitted this price-cutting. "We are in the habit of fighting vigorously to hold our trade and to advance it," he said. "To the extent of holding prices down to cost until the rivals give way?" asked a Commissioner. "Yes."[12] The fact that the Standard practically fixed the price of crude oil (of course with some reference to the world market) was brought out.[13] A number of witnesses contended that the trust had cheapened the cost of oil products to the consumer, but another group argued—and with better evidence—that it had not been the chief factor in reducing prices, and had not lowered them as far as it should have done. The statement of dividends for 1882–1901, given by S. C. T. Dodd,[14] showed that profits had been excessively, and indeed egregiously, high, and indicated that the people had never been given a proper share of the economies effected by the Standard. Thomas W. Phillips put his inferences from the testimony in a crisp paragraph:[15]

The Standard Oil Company refined in the five years, 1894 to 1898, 82.3 per cent of the refined produced (Archbold, Volume I, 560), which, if this be the average proportion of the crude which they handled for nineteen years, would give them 641,731,379 barrels of crude oil. For this they paid the producers an average of 80 cents per barrel (Volume XIII, p. 670), or $513,385,379. From this source have come their enormous profits and undivided surplus, the high value of their capital, ranging from $600,-000,000 to $800,000,000, and the power which they are gaining over the railroads, the banks, and the industries of the country. These profits and financial power have been secured in addition to the large sums spent in order to maintain their monopoly, through crushing competition, purchasing and dismantling plants and pipe-lines, and subsidizing experts to refrain from the business. There are but two sources from which such profits have come—the consumer of the refined product, and the producer of the crude product.

[11]*Idem*, I, 287; 634; 635.   [12]*Idem*, I, 569.
[13]It had begun to do this in January, 1895; *Idem*, I, 436, 446, 571.
[14]*Idem*, I, 799.
[15]*Idem*, xix, 668. Phillips was a leader of independent oil interests.

The final review of industrial combinations was written largely by Jeremiah W. Jenks, and that of transportation chiefly by William Z. Ripley.[16] Both were judicious documents. In treating railroads the Commission assailed rebates, but offered a strong argument for legalizing pools, subject to Interstate Commerce Commission supervision. In dealing with industrial combinations all the members except Phillips agreed upon a mild program. The exposition which they signed showed clearly that the existing antitrust legislation had been ineffective; criticized it for not employing the remedy of publicity rather than attempting a direct destruction of the trusts; and pointed out the impracticability of effective legislation by forty-five States upon a subject which was almost invariably of interstate concern. The Commission, though asking that violations of the Sherman Act be prosecuted, and urging Congress and the States to pass laws "making both penal and criminal the vicious practice of discriminating between customers, and cutting rates or prices in one locality below those which prevail generally, for the purpose of destroying local competition," laid its principal emphasis upon publicity as a remedy.[17] In this it followed the general lead that Roosevelt was now giving. All corporations engaged in interstate or foreign commerce, it recommended, should be compelled to register with a bureau in the Treasury Department; their business and accounts should be reported to this bureau; and it should collate and publish all useful information. If this did not keep big business within due bounds, Federal incorporation might be required.

The Standard and other combinations had no reason to feel uneasy over the Commission's work. Its proposals were far from radical. No encouragement was given to the Bryan-LaFollette idea of exterminating the trusts; instead, regulation was held up as the guiding beacon. "Competition, when carried to an extreme," declared the Commission, "has very frequently led to the production of goods of inferior quality, to efforts to crowd down the wages of workingmen, to undue extension of credits, and to other wastes injurious to the community. So far as combination sets aside these

---

[16]Cf. W. E. Weyl, "Transportation," *Annals of the American Academy,* XIX, 474–481; May, 1902. Doctor Ripley's work was extremely valuable, and almost all his recommendations later became law. Doctor Jenks believed in the inevitability and value of great combinations, though he condemned monopolies.

[17]*Report,* XIX, 643–652.

harmful elements of competition, it is doubtless beneficial to industrial society, unless, by the exercise of monopolistic power, it exploits
the public and brings other evils even more serious than those of
excessive competition." E. Dana Durand wrote that most economists
would pronounce the recommendations remarkably sane and liberal.[18] And Rockefeller and Archbold might well have said "Amen."

One striking product of the Commission's work was little noticed
until years afterward. The most original economist of the nation,
Thorstein Veblen, levied heavily upon the report for the data of
his *Theory of Business Enterprise,* published in 1905. His thesis that
the great fortunes of modern times are in the main built up not
from productive efficiency, but from disturbances in the adjustment
between the industrial process and the business process, and from
manipulations of vendible capital and securities, had practically no
application to Rockefeller. But his treatment of the competition
between modern States as really a competition between powerful
corporations and financial captains owed much to a study of Standard Oil and its export policies. Veblen's essay in the *Journal of
Political Economy* on "An Early Experiment in Trusts," a treatment of Viking piratical enterprise in terms of modern capitalism,
possessed a satire too subtle for most readers.

II

The trustful letters of Archbold to Sewell and Penrose prove
that the political activities of the Standard had entered upon a new
phase. So long as Rockefeller was the active head, its rôle in politics,
though sometimes improper, had been primarily defensive. It had
sought protection against blackmailing legislation, court attacks,
and governmental regulation—which of course was seeking a good
deal. Rockefeller himself had avoided contact or communication
with politicians. But Archbold followed a far more aggressive course,
and had a reprehensibly large and frank correspondence with certain political leaders. No evidence exists that Rockefeller knew anything about Archbold's political activities; but he could have learned
all about them if he had asked, and such inquiry would have been
wise.

[18]Vol. XVI, 564–586; August, 1902.

The Republican organization had long been a mere appanage of big business in Pennsylvania, where Archbold easily found allies who were as stanch as Penrose. Chief among them was Joseph C. Sibley, who became the Standard's most trusted secret agent in Washington. "Archbold's jackal," the press later called him. He had been connected since 1879 with what became the Galena-Signal Oil Company, a Standard subsidiary, and by 1900 was chairman of its board. Essentially a cheap demagogue, he went into Congress in 1892 as a free-silverite from the Oil Regions. There he made blatant speeches, shocking the country by his description of President Cleveland as a combination of "brains, belly, and brass"; and in 1896 the Bryan Convention gave him a considerable vote for Vice-President. He and Archbold had been intimate for twenty years.[19] After Bryan's defeat he quickly dropped his radical ideas, exhibiting instead a marked friendliness toward big corporations. In 1900 he and Lewis Emery, Jr., ran a close race for Congress. The principal issue was naturally Sibley's connection with the Standard, and Archbold was deeply aroused by the campaign. He exerted all the power of the company, which owned about $100,000,000 worth of property and employed some 2500 men in the district; and he wrote President Cassatt of the Pennsylvania Railroad, urging him to assist in defeating "the old-time agitator." "Emery's election would certainly be a great misfortune, and I venture to ask that you do everything possible in the matter in Mr. Sibley's favor on the sure ground that all corporate and vested interests will have at least a fair consideration and treatment at his hands."[20] Sibley won, and by 1904 was head of the Committee on Manufactures.

For years "Joe" Sibley was a faithful lieutenant of the company. The yellow journals were perhaps unjust in treating him as a mere corrupt hireling, for like Camden long before, he had natural business and personal reasons for befriending the Standard. But he did make a contemptibly servile tool. Letters by the dozen fluttered from his Washington desk to 26 Broadway. Whenever Archbold wanted an attack headed off, a bit of lobbying done, or a Senator or Representative cajoled, he ordered Sibley to do the work. Just before this election of 1900, for example, Archbold learned that some

---

[19]Moore, *Archbold,* 244.
[20]Archbold to Cassatt, Sept. 6, 1900; *Hearst's Magazine,* XXII (1912) 35.

unnamed Representative was about to attack the company. See him at once, he requested Sibley, "and if it is at all possible guard against his explosion."[21] And Sibley volunteered his services in various ways with alacrity. "Had a long talk with Mr. B. a friend in the Senate, a Democrat," he writes on one occasion. "Had you not ought to have a consultation with him . . . ? If you want to see him I think I could arrange a call in New York." This was Joseph W. Bailey of Texas. He writes again in 1903: "A Republican United States Senator came to me today to make a loan of $1000. I told him I did not have it but would try and get it for him in a day or two. Do you want to make the investment?" And Sibley kept his patron fully informed of every new threat in Washington. "If at any time my long scribbles annoy you, chuck them into the waste basket," he begs. And still more effusively: "If you think of anything for me to do, let me know."[22]

Senator Quay was as effective a friend in Pennsylvania as Penrose, and Archbold did not hesitate to make requests of him. In 1899 Thomas A. Morrison of Southport, Pa., was a candidate for the supreme bench of the State. "If it proves possible and consistent for you to support him for the position," Archbold urged Quay, "I shall be greatly pleased. His abilities are so well known that I need hardly dwell on them."[23] Archbold supported still other candidates for Pennsylvania judgeships, such as John P. Henderson and John P. Elkin; and he contributed $15,000 to the campaign fund of the last-named in 1900. But he later defended his advocacy of these men, saying that he had never asked a favor of any judge anywhere outside of the plain practice of the law. "Any letters I may have written urging this lawyer or that for a judgeship have been governed wholly by a sense of fitness. . . ."[24] He did not define "fitness."

Quay was of course always eager to raise money for the Republican Party, and Archbold was always willing to give. Repeated contributions from 26 Broadway left the Pennsylvania boss still voracious. "Not because I think we should," Archbold once wrote him, "but because of your enticing ways, I enclose your certificate of deposit for $10,000." Again, an Oliver Twist demand for more

[21]Archbold to Sibley, May 22, 1900; *Clapp Investigation*, II, 1582.
[22]*Hearst's Magazine*, XXI, 2362 ff., June, 1912.
[23]*Idem*, XXII, 4 ff., September, 1912.
[24]Letter of Archbold to N. Y. *Evening Post*, Oct. 28, 1908.

wrung a complaint from the Standard's vice-president. "I will do as you say," he writes Quay, "provided you finally say you need so much. Please ask for payments as needed from time to time, not all at once." Between 1898 and 1902, Archbold transmitted not less than $42,500, and possibly more, to Quay for party uses.[25]

In Ohio, Rockefeller's old friend Mark Hanna could always be counted upon to support the Standard, and he expected the usual favors in return. The year 1903 found him contesting the Senatorial election with Tom L. Johnson. It was a heated campaign. Hanna received a generous contribution from Archbold, and thanked him prettily in a letter of September 15. "I want your people to help our State Committee liberally," he pleaded. "The demands on me are simply awful." September 22 found him writing once more. "I am 'holding the bag,' and this is going to be an expensive campaign. I can see where I will land before the thing is over, so I have no doubt I will have to call again. I feel a delicacy about this as it is my funeral. . . . There are many important questions in this fight. Should Johnson carry the Legislature, corporations will catch it, as I am their representative so called."[26] However, Hanna easily won. Other campaign contributions from the Standard went to Representative C. H. Grosvenor of Ohio, who got $1000 in 1900 "to aid in the good work," Senators Stephen B. Elkins and N. B. Scott of West Virginia, and Senator John L. McLaurin of South Carolina. Nearly all the large corporations were making similar gifts to the party chests, for public sentiment on the question had not yet crystallized, and no restrictive legislation was passed by Congress until 1907.[27]

But the Ohio leader with whom the Standard enjoyed the closest relations was Joseph Benson Foraker, who had been governor 1885-89, and who was elected to the Senate in 1897. An able lawyer and crafty politician, he represented all that was reactionary in politics. After Monnett brought his contempt suit against the Standard in 1898, Archbold made haste to employ the newly elected Senator as

[25] *Clapp Committee*, II, 1537–1539.
[26] Hanna to Archbold, Sept. 22, 1903; *Hearst's Magazine*, XXI, 2362 ff., June, 1912.
[27] *Cf.* E. M. Sait, *American Parties and Elections*. For the curious correspondence of Archbold and McLaurin, see *Hearst's Magazine*, XXIII, 2 ff., January, 1913.

Four political leaders connected with Standard Oil.

Above, left to right: Joseph W. Bailey and Joseph B. Foraker.
Below: Matthew S. Quay and Mark Hanna.

The Rockefeller estate at Pocantico, with the Hudson in the distance.

attorney.[28] Foraker prepared some briefs, one running to more than a hundred pages, advised various Standard officials, and conferred with Virgil P. Kline, the Standard's counsel in Cleveland.[29] No doubt, as Kline asserted later, his services had some value in bringing to a successful conclusion litigation which might easily have cost the company millions.[30] Foraker had a perfect right to accept such employment, just as numerous other Senators took (and still take) fat retainers from corporations, and just as he received employment from the General Electric Company, Ohio Traction Company, and other clients. But did he offer Archbold something more than his legal services? The evidence that he did seems overwhelming.

It is alleged that when first hired, Foraker talked with Monnett and warned him that, if he continued attacking the Standard, he would be driven out of politics.[31] However this may be, early in 1900 we find Archbold appealing to the Senator for help in dealing with measures before the Ohio legislature. On January 19 Archbold wrote both Foraker and Hanna for assistance in killing "a most malicious resolution for an investigating committee to be headed by Griffin, of Lucas, giving them power to investigate pretty much everything within the State, from the Supreme Court down." A month later he writes Foraker: "Here is still another very objectionable bill. It is so outrageous as to be ridiculous. But it needs to be looked after, and I hope there will be no difficulty in killing it." Early in March he begs Foraker for help against yet "another very objectionable bill," citing an opinion by the Standard attorney M. F. Elliott. "Perhaps it would be better to make a demonstration against the whole bill, but certainly the ninth clause, to which Mr. Elliott refers, should be stricken out, and the same is true of House Bill No. 500, also introduced by Mr. Price, in relation to foreign corporations, in which the same objectionable clause occurs." Im-

---

[28]Virgil P. Kline to Foraker, Oct. 6, 1908; *Clapp Investigation*, II, 1296, 1297.
[29]Foraker's Testimony, *Clapp Investigation*, II, 1300.
[30]*Idem*, II, 1298.
[31]Flynn, *God's Gold*, 355. Monnett did go over to the Bryan wing of the Democratic Party. When in March, 1903, it was reported that his brother-in-law, Smith W. Bennett, was a candidate for the Ohio attorney-generalship, Archbold wrote both Hanna and Foraker asking them to defeat him. *Hearst's Magazine*, XXI, 2376; June, 1912.

mediately after this, on March 26, he sent the Senator a certificate of deposit for $15,000![32] On April 17, remitting $14,500 more, Archbold wrote: "I need scarcely again express our great gratification over the favorable outcome of affairs."

And Foraker was clearly expected to keep similar watch in Washington and join the brigade of corporation-defenders there whenever needed. His services as counsel to the Standard ended in January, 1901. But he still remained ready to solicit favors from the company. In the first days of 1902 he wished to assist his friend, J. Linn Rodgers, of Columbus, Ohio, to buy *The Ohio State Journal*. Unable to furnish the money himself, he induced Archbold to lend him $50,000, taking stock in the newspaper as security. A certificate of deposit for this sum was forwarded on January 25. Unfortunately for Foraker, the Hanna group adroitly stepped in and bought the paper.[33] But the Senator was doubtless still grateful for the proffered loan when he received the following letter from Archbold, dated February 25, 1902:[34]

I venture to write you a word regarding the bill introduced by Senator Jones, of Arkansas, known as No. S. 649, intended to amend the act, "to protect trade and commerce against unlawful restraints and monopolies," etc., introduced by him December 4.

It really seems as though this bill is very unnecessarily severe and even vicious. Is it not much better to test the application of the Sherman Act before resorting to a measure of this kind? I hope you will feel so about it, and I will be greatly pleased to have a word from you on the subject. This bill is, I believe, still in committee.

It would be impossible to *prove* that Foraker, paid $44,500 in all during 1900 by the Standard Oil, received any of it for work as a lobbyist or legislative agent. It was merely for legal labors, he said;[35] and perhaps the sum was no more than other lawyers of equal eminence would have expected for an equal amount of advice

[32]Archbold to Foraker, Feb. 16, March 8, March 9, March 26, 1900; *Clapp Investigation*, II, 1539; *Hearst's Magazine*, XXI, 2209 ff., May, 1912.
[33]Foraker tells the whole story in *Notes of a Busy Life*, II, 333 ff.
[34]*Clapp Investigation*, II, 1277.
[35]Foraker said (*Clapp Investigation*, II, 1305): "Neither the Standard Oil nor any other company nor individual has ever paid me a cent on account of any public service, nor has that company or anybody else even suggested to me any compensation or reward of any kind in consideration of support for any bill or opposition to any bill, or for any action of any nature whatever."

and briefing. He and his wife published autobiographies in which, with great bitterness, they deny that he acted with any impropriety; and Mrs. Foraker wrote with transparent sincerity as well as wit and charm.[36] Archbold similarly denied that Foraker was ever employed in any capacity except that of attorney, or ever performed any censurable act. And yet these protestations leave us quite unconvinced. It is clear from the letters quoted that the Standard did attempt to obstruct proposed legislation both in Ohio and Washington, that it asked Foraker to assist it, and that it thanked him for the "favorable outcome." Archbold insisted that these obstructive tactics had been directed "against hasty, ill-digested, and predatory legislation inspired by interested antagonists or shaped by thoughtless demagogues," and not against fair measures.[37] But the fairness of the bills was a matter of opinion. And certainly the coincidence between the dates on which Foraker received his principal payments and his loan, and the dates on which he was asked to deal with undesirable legislation, arouses a suspicion that he sold his political influence.

Archbold should never have employed a Republican Senator from Ohio, the leader of an important party organization, to combat a suit conducted by the Republican Attorney-General of Ohio. He should never have written letters asking this Senator to use his influence to stop bills in the legislature and the Senate. He should never have advanced him $50,000 to help buy a political journal; the Standard was in the oil business, not the newspaper business. Archbold had able attorneys at his disposal without going to one of the leaders of the Republican Party, a man who even aspired for a time to the Presidency. The connection between the two proved highly unfortunate for both, for when its details were exposed it caused a national scandal which must always becloud the reputation of both men.

Archbold's campaign contributions raise another question of importance. Rockefeller had always been a loyal Republican, and from early manhood had given generously to the campaign funds of his chosen party. He never failed to vote the regular ticket—not even when, in 1904, he was sorely distressed by some of Roosevelt's acts.

[36]*Cf.* her delightful book *I Would Live It Again.*
[37]Moore, *Archbold*, 255.

Like other large corporations, the Standard Oil was expected to make generous gifts in years of a Presidential election. Matt Quay in 1888 and 1892 called upon most big Eastern businesses, and particularly those desiring tariff protection, for substantial sums. In 1896, when Hanna and Dawes were raising a fund of unprecedented size, the Standard contributed $250,000.[38] Undoubtedly Rockefeller strongly approved of this gift, for he believed that the demand for free silver was a menace to all American business, and feared Bryan's hostility to trusts. In 1900, with Bryan once more confronting McKinley, the Standard gave the Republicans the same amount. Then, less than a year after McKinley's re-election, Roosevelt entered the White House, and the party began to undergo a sea-change. The new President shortly launched an attack upon one great holding corporation, the Northern Securities Company; he called for more drastic railroad legislation; and he began to demand a Federal bureau which should apply pitiless publicity to the actions of big business. It seemed dubious whether the Standard would again make a handsome present to the coffers of the Republican Party.

A good deal of subtle maneuvering preceded the campaign of 1904.[39] Mark Hanna, eager to wrest the nomination from the much-distrusted Roosevelt, knew that he could count upon Archbold's loyal if tacit help. Quay was sulking in his tent, for Hanna had refused to stand back of him when his seat had been contested; and at Hanna's request, Archbold made various futile approaches to Quay. Meanwhile, Roosevelt was playing a not uncharacteristic rôle. Publicly, he treated the Standard and all its officers as abhorrent and untouchable, and rumbled vague threats against them. Privately, he made it plain that he knew the Standard was a real power, and that he was not unwilling to have its friendship. Very early in 1904 Sibley wrote Archbold that T. R. would be pleased to have the magnate lunch at the White House. "He urged strongly that you come over to meet him." When Archbold failed to respond, Sibley sent him fresh assurances that a palm leaf was being waved from the Executive Mansion. Roosevelt had said that he was de-

---

[38]Herbert Croly, *Mark Hanna*, 325; E. M. Sait, *American Parties and Elections*, 507.
[39]A good brief account is in Flynn, *God's Gold*, 382, 383.

lighted to hear from both Representative Sibley and Senator Aldrich
that the Standard Oil was well disposed toward him. Was this
merely some of Sibley's flattery, or routine politeness by Roosevelt,
or a bid for the favor of a corporation which influenced many conservative politicians, and employed great multitudes of voters? We
do not know. But Hanna's death soon made it unnecessary for
Roosevelt to woo anybody, while the Supreme Court's affirmation
of the Northern Securities decision gave him a new confidence in
dealing with the trusts.

As the Parker-Roosevelt contest got under way, the Republicans
made their usual request of the Standard organization. Cornelius
N. Bliss, treasurer of the national committee, paid a most polite
visit to Archbold and Rogers, and was shortly followed by Chairman Boies Penrose of the Pennsylvania State committee. Both assured the oil magnates that when it came to trust-busting, Roosevelt's bark would be much worse than his bite.[40] The leaders thereupon brought these requests before the Standard's directors, who
voted to give $100,000 to the national fund, and $25,000 to the Pennsylvania fund. Before sending the money, Archbold saw Bliss and
remarked:[41] "Our sympathies are with the Republican side, and
we want to help; but we do not want to do it without its being
known and thoroughly approved of by the powers that be." This
meant Roosevelt. Bliss assured him that he need hardly worry, and
soon afterward, as both Archbold and Penrose have testified, asserted that the President had been told of the gift, and was content.
Whether this was true it is now impossible to ascertain. But it is
certain that Roosevelt later vehemently denied that he had ever
said a word of assent. Instead, he produced a letter to prove that
he had directed Chairman Cortelyou of the national committee to
return the money. This epistle, dated October 26, 1904, was peremptory in tone. "I have just been informed that the Standard Oil
people have contributed $100,000 to the campaign fund," he wrote.[42]
"This may be really untrue. But if true, I must ask you to direct
that the money be returned to them forthwith." He went on to
assert that the Administration would treat the Standard just as

[40]See testimony in *Clapp Investigation*, I, 129–149 *passim*.
[41]*Idem*, I, 123.
[42]Testimony of Theodore Roosevelt, *Clapp Inquiry*, I, 178.

fairly as if it had taken the gift. "But I am not willing that it should be accepted, and must ask Mr. Bliss to return it."

If Roosevelt had made determined inquiries, he would have found that E. H. Harriman had donated $50,000 to the Republican campaign fund, and had collected for it $200,000 more. He would have learned that J. P. Morgan had given $150,000; that George J. Gould had contributed $100,000; and that James Hazen Hyde, H. C. Frick, and James Stillman were all donors. The Philadelphia banker E. T. Stotesbury, associated with J. P. Morgan, had collected more than $165,000. By setting some bookkeepers to work, Roosevelt could have learned that of the $2,195,000 collected to re-elect him, approximately 72.5 per cent had come from corporations—and chiefly big corporations.[43] But it was the Standard Oil, rather than other "malefactors of great wealth," which Roosevelt singled out.

The incredible spectacle of a national committee returning $100,-000 to a donor was never actually inflicted upon American nerves. Word was sent to Roosevelt that the Standard had given nothing; that the $100,000 was a personal gift from H. H. Rogers—and every one decided that this was highly acceptable![44] The formula proved perfectly satisfactory. Treasurer Bliss was so pleased that, according to Archbold, he even solicited $100,000 more, which the directors of the Standard declined to give.[45] As it turned out, the Republican Party got the spending of the $100,000, while Roosevelt had the satisfaction of waving it away with an air of Roman virtue. It is possible that Bliss and he had misunderstood each other. It is also remotely possible that, as the New York *World* said later, he had penned the letter so that if the fact of the gift ever came out he would have a perfect alibi![46]

Of the political activities of Archbold and the Standard, the public at the time knew little in detail. But it was aware that the corporation possessed willing allies in Senators like Hanna, Quay, and Elkins, and Representatives like Sibley and Grosvenor. It knew that the Standard kept on its payroll attorneys who were also in-

[43]Henry Pringle, *Theodore Roosevelt,* 356–358.
[44]*Clapp Inquiry,* 491, 519 ff.
[45]Testimony of Archbold and Rogers, *Idem,* I, 129 ff., 159.
[46]John L. Heaton, *The Story of a Page,* 319. Heaton quotes the N. Y. *Press,* an adherent of Roosevelt, to the same effect.

fluential politicians. It realized that, like other monopolies and quasi-monopolies, the corporation gave largely to party funds, pushed favored men for judgeships, worked in co-operation with machine leaders, and saw that dangerous bills were choked in committee. Americans were therefore not at all astonished when in 1908 William Randolph Hearst exploded the story of Foraker's varied services to Archbold; or when several years later the Clapp Committee showed just how obedient a tool Joe Sibley had been. From 1898 onward the sensational press was filled with highly colored tales of the Standard's political machinations, and everybody knew that they possessed some truth. Rockefeller was not informed of these activities. Archbold in 1902 wrote Sibley, who wished to talk with the philanthropist, that "Mr. Rockefeller never comes to business and I see him infrequently." But he could easily have found out what Archbold was doing; and as president of the company, he should have found out, and laid a restraining hand on the younger man's shoulder.

III

Throughout the first decade of the century the attacks of a great part of the press upon Rockefeller never ceased. Joseph Pulitzer, after making William H. Vanderbilt, Jay Gould, and J. P. Morgan the subjects of his just criticism, found the Standard endlessly useful as a whipping-boy, and was always coiling his lash around its shoulders. Hearst was equally pertinacious in assault. The old stereotype of Rockefeller as an inhuman vulture, a ceaselessly predatory despoiler of widows and orphans, had now been firmly imprinted upon the public consciousness. A hundred cartoonists drew pictures which made him as repulsive as a spider; a thousand copy-desk men wrote headlines in which greed, robbery, and oppression were associated with his name. To assail Rockefeller was to some extent a mere habit in which millions unthinkingly joined. In part it arose from a justifiable antagonism to monopoly and to the Standard's methods. But in part the ceaseless hue and cry was deliberately maintained by journalists who had learned that it boosted circulation and politicians who knew that there were votes in it.

An illuminating incident occurred in 1903. President Roosevelt was eager, as the year opened, to have his bill creating a Department of Commerce, with a Bureau of Corporations included, passed by Congress. An organized opposition had become evident. Roosevelt attacked it. He told Washington correspondents on February 7 that if Congress balked, he would call a special session. Cautioning them not to reveal the source of their information, he authorized them to state that six Senate members had received telegrams from John D. Rockefeller urging that no antitrust legislation be enacted. While he did not know the actual wording of the messages, they ran substantially as follows: "We are opposed to any antitrust legislation. Our counsel, Mr. ——, will see you. It must be stopped."[47] This news whipped up the storm that Roosevelt wanted, and on the wings of the gale the bill passed in just the form he desired. But word soon leaked out that Roosevelt was the author of the charge, and that he had given no evidence. No Senator could be found who had received any telegram from Rockefeller.[48] Many Congressmen decided that T. R. had made the story out of whole cloth, and Joe Cannon bluntly said so.[49]

As a matter of fact, Rockefeller had sent no telegram. But it can now be revealed that his son had done so. John D. Rockefeller, Jr., had recently seen a good deal of various Senators through Aldrich, and on February 6 had sent telegrams to Allison, Lodge, Hale, and Teller reading: "Our people are opposed to all the proposed trust legislation except the Elkins Anti-Discrimination Bill. Mr. Archbold, with our counsel, goes to Washington this afternoon. Am very anxious they should see you at once and shall much appreciate any assistance you can render them."[50] Archbold, however, saw only Aldrich, feeling it unnecessary to call on any one else. At the same time, the Standard people seem to have telegraphed various men in Washington to the effect that they were opposed to the Bureau of Corporations legislation. It will be made "an engine for vexatious attack against a few large corporations," they argued; it gave the right of Federal interference with State corporations "without giving any Federal protection whatever." Archbold had sent special protests to Joe Sibley and Senator Quay.[51]

[47]N. Y. *Times,* Feb. 8, 1903.   [48]Pringle, *Roosevelt,* 340, 341.
[49]L. W. Busbey, *Uncle Joe Cannon,* 216–232.
[50]Papers of John D. Rockefeller, Jr.
[51]*Hearst's Magazine,* XXII, October, 1912; N. Y. *American,* Feb. 12, 1903.

Roosevelt would therefore have been quite right if he had asserted that the Standard, and also John D. Rockefeller, Jr., were opposing his pet bill. But he was mistaken in accusing Rockefeller of sending telegrams, and the arrogant phrase he quoted, "It must be stopped," had been his own invention. Since his friend Lodge could easily have given him the true facts, it is evident that he had deliberately used the Rockefeller bogey to promote his special purposes.

Archbold had meanwhile taken pains to enlist certain journals. His correspondence indicates that after he took control, the Pittsburgh *Times, The Manufacturers' Record, The Southern Farm Magazine,* and *Gunton's Magazine* were all assisted.[52] Perhaps some of these aids had been begun under Rockefeller, as the financial assistance to the Oil City *Derrick,* the Titusville *Herald,* and the Bradford *Era* certainly had. Of all these journals, *Gunton's Magazine* was the most interesting. It was not to be treated lightly. Founded as *The Social Economist* in March, 1891, its early numbers included articles by President Seth Low of Columbia, Doctor Carroll D. Wright, and the Federal commissioner of navigation. Among the later contributors were John R. Commons, S. N. D. North, Edward Everett Hale, and the English labor leader, Tom Mann. After several years the name became *Gunton's,* and the last issues appeared in 1904 with such contributors as Stephen P. Duggan, James W. Garner, and Hubert Howe Bancroft. The files contain a good deal of valuable material.[53] Gunton was known when his magazine first appeared for two well-written books, *Wealth and Progress* and *Principles of Social Economics,* and as head of a school in New York called the Institute of Social Economics. Though hostile to the single tax and Socialism, he was by no means reactionary, for he believed that the advancement of the agricultural and wage-earning masses was the mainspring of all social and economic progress. He saw no danger to capital in strong labor combinations, and none to labor in powerful capitalistic combinations; and while he defended the movement toward concentration in industry as inevitable and healthy, he did not defend monopoly. *Gunton's* was no mere propagandist publication.

[52] Moore, *Archbold,* 234–259. But with the *Record* and perhaps others the assistance (as the treasurer of the *Record* assures me) lay merely in buying a large number of copies.

[53] All good economic libraries contain sets of the magazine.

The Manufacturers' Record was a highly conservative periodical devoted primarily to Southern industry, and probably a number of other corporations helped to support it. Evidently the relation between Archbold and its editor, Edmunds, was close. So was that between the Standard head and Thomas P. Grasty, editor of *The Southern Farm Magazine,* who received $5000 a year from the Standard treasury. "There is no doubt whatever," Archbold approvingly wrote Grasty on December 11, 1902, "of the excellent work being done by your publications, and by yourself and Mr. Edmunds on all the lines, and I feel that it would be almost an act of presumption to make any suggestion with reference to your course. If anything at any time occurs to us, we will not hesitate to speak of it, in response to your kind suggestion."[54]

Several important newspapers of conservative stamp, like the New York *Tribune* and Cleveland *Leader,* took a generally friendly attitude toward Rockefeller and the Standard. *Leslie's Weekly* printed favorable material,[55] while *The Nation* maintained a conservatively judicial attitude. But the flood of hostile news-stories and editorials, the general chorus of denunciations and jeers, overwhelmed these publications. Particularly was this true when the new literature of muckraking, with the comment, caricatures, and speeches which it inspired, reached its full roaring volume early in the century.

The history of the journalism of exposure in America can be traced back to the years just following the Civil War, when the excesses of capitalism had added vitriol to the ink of several public commentators. James Parton, Henry Adams, and Charles Francis Adams all wrote savagely of the Erie Ring and its political allies. Such a novel as *The Moneymakers* (1888), an anonymous and scathing attack on the methods of industrial leaders and the life of the plutocracy in New York and Cleveland, belonged to the general impulse. Some inspiration was doubtless drawn from Henry Labouchere's weekly, *Truth,* which made a business of telling the facts about financial as well as political corruption in England. Early in the nineties the new ten-cent magazines—*Munsey's, Mc-*

---

[54]See *Hearst's Magazine,* July–December, 1913, for Archbold's letters to editors.
[55]See, *e.g.,* H. C. McLean in *Leslie's* early in 1905.

Clure's, The Cosmopolitan—borrowed lessons from the sensational newspapers of Dana and the Bennetts, which had delved into personal and public scandals with vigorous realism, and from Pulitzer's *World,* which had conducted able crusades against various evils. It was no accident that *McClure's* was founded by a young man conducting a newspaper syndicate.[56] A highly personal note had already been put into magazine editing by young Edward Bok when he took charge of *The Ladies' Home Journal,* and this, applied to the depiction of prominent financial, industrial, and political figures, also played its part. The radicalism of the Populists, which gave the country Hamlin Garland's *Main-Travelled Roads* and B. O. Flower's trenchant magazine *The Arena;* the very different radicalism of the labor movement; the new sociology, which brought out the first scientific studies of poverty, and a new and more radical economics, preached by Richard T. Ely and others, all helped prepare the seed-bed for the full growth of exposure. By 1902 muckraking was in lusty flower.[57]

It is useless to debate who was the first muckraker—whether it was Lincoln Steffens, whose *Shame of the Cities* began in *McClure's* in October, 1902; or Mark Sullivan, who wrote in *The Atlantic* in 1901 on "The Ills of Pennsylvania"; or Ray Stannard Baker, who in the fall of 1901 published articles on the Northern Pacific and the Steel Corporation in *Collier's* and *McClure's.* The recipe was open to all, and supply and demand interacted perhaps more clearly than at any other time in our magazine history. Roosevelt, Bryan, LaFollette, Weaver, Tom Johnson, and Henry George had set in motion a great liberal impulse, which made men eager to learn more about the evils of the existing political and economic system, and to experiment with mild reforms. The rapid expansion of the high-school system had created a new reading public. The forces listed above had furnished a school of writers ready to attack any problem, no matter how difficult, and to try to throw new light into any corner, no matter how dark. The flood of muckraking ran strong for half a dozen years, until in the Taft administration, from a complex of causes, it weakened and ebbed. Many businesses

[56]See S. S. McClure, *My Autobiography,* 207 ff.

[57]Louis Filler, *Crusaders for American Liberalism,* 55 ff. The new fiction played its rôle in books like Frank Norris's *The Pit;* David Graham Phillips's *The Deluge;* and Brand Whitlock's *The Turn of the Balance.*

were savagely attacked. The Southern Pacific in Frank Norris's *The Octopus;* the meat-packing houses in Charles Edward Russell's *The Greatest Trust in the World,* and in Upton Sinclair's *The Jungle;* Amalgamated Copper in Thomas W. Lawson's *Frenzied Finance;* the glass factories, coal mines, and other businesses in John Spargo's *Bitter Cry of the Children;* the "patent medicine trust" in Samuel Hopkins Adams's articles in *Collier's.* But the greatest book produced by the muckraking movement was a history of the Standard Oil.

Rockefeller had overthrown the men of the Oil Regions; but in Ida M. Tarbell the Regions found a literary champion who gave them an enduring revenge. A daughter of Franklin S. Tarbell, who in 1860 had begun building wooden tanks for the petroleum producers, she had been reared first in Pithole and then Titusville, and had been graduated from Allegheny College in Meadville.[58] Her father had become a prominent if never highly prosperous oil producer; her able brother William Walter Tarbell, who read law after leaving Allegheny College, had helped organize an independent pipe line, had been active in the work of the Petroleum Producers' Protective Association, and had finally, in 1902, become treasurer of the Pure Oil Company.[59] Miss Tarbell, a brilliant woman of great force of character, had come to maturity amid the tumult and shouting of the wars between the Standard and the embattled independents. She had been deeply impressed, as a young girl, by the bitter antagonism between Association men and Standard men throughout the Regions. Her feelings had naturally been strongly enlisted in behalf of the former. In the panic of 1893 her father had been so hard hit that the family was compelled to mortgage its home. After Miss Tarbell, who had served on the editorial staff of *The Chautauquan,* went to Paris to study and to write articles, her mother wrote her of the turmoil which still pervaded the Regions, while her brother sent her vivid accounts of the battles fought by the Producers' Protective Association. In Paris, too, the English journalist H. Wickham Steed, at that time imbued with German Socialism, gave her a copy of *Wealth Against Commonwealth.* It crystallized her "clutter of recollections, impressions, in-

[58]Miss Tarbell has written a spirited autobiography, *All in the Day's Work.*
[59]D. R. Crum, ed., *Romance of American Petroleum and Gas,* 335, 336.

dignations, perplexities," into some approach to a pattern. She had always vaguely cherished the idea of writing a novel about the turbulent life of the Regions, and it was natural that, after becoming a staff contributor of *McClure's,* her mind should turn to the subject as suitable for a series of articles. She proposed the undertaking to S. S. McClure at Lausanne in 1900; and though he was at first dubious, he quickly caught her enthusiasm and authorized her to go ahead.[60]

The time, the magazine, and above all, the writer, conspired to make *The History of the Standard Oil Company* the most spectacular success of muckraking journalism, and its most enduring achievement. Miss Tarbell's first article appeared in November, 1902. Roosevelt had been in power for a year, and the fall elections that month showed how warmly the country had taken to his policies. He had just shocked Wall Street by ordering Attorney-General Knox to begin a suit against the Morgan-Hill-Harriman creation, the Northern Securities Company. His annual message this year called upon Congress to supply the executive with new weapons against monopolistic combinations. The work of the Industrial Commission had whetted an appetite for more facts about the trusts. Moreover, Rockefeller, his life, his personality, his activities, had become a figure of compelling interest to Americans. Who was this man, so retiring and secretive, who had piled up one of the greatest fortunes in history, defied the rooted conviction of Americans on the subject of competition, and was now giving in unprecedented sums? Miss Tarbell smote the iron when it was hot. And she had an excellent anvil: S. S. McClure and John S. Phillips had given their magazine a circulation and prestige such as no monthly of equal solidity and literary quality had ever enjoyed in any nation of the world. Directly or indirectly, it reached nearly the whole literate public of America.

Miss Tarbell, thanks to her books on Mme. Roland, Napoleon, and Lincoln, and her miscellaneous articles, already enjoyed a well-earned reputation as writer. Into her work on the Standard

[60]Tarbell, *All in the Day's Work,* 203–206. An interviewer of Miss Tarbell says (*Public Opinion,* May 27, 1905): "Originally the experiment of dealing with the Standard Oil by means of intermittent articles was expected to extend over eight numbers of *McClure's Magazine;* but it developed with many more articles and extended over three years."

she threw the utmost industry and earnestness. The task required
not a little courage. A legend had grown up that the Standard
crushed every company or individual in its path. More than one
adviser warned her: "Go ahead, and they will get you in the end."[61]
Even her father declared that they would ruin the magazine. "I
soon discovered," she writes, "that . . . I must work in a field where
numbers of men and women were afraid, believing in the all-seeing
eye and the all-powerful reach of the ruler of the oil-industry."
Save in one important respect, her labor was as searching and complete as four years of toil and an ample expense fund could make
it. She went through the mountainous testimony collected by State
and Federal inquiries; the records of courts; newspapers of the
Regions and outside cities. She travelled widely. She interviewed
various people, including one Standard leader, H. H. Rogers. This
engaging leader sent her word through Mark Twain that he would
be glad to talk with her, and they held a number of conferences in
his office at 26 Broadway. His ostensible motive in this was to help
her make the story fair and complete; his real motive, as Rockefeller always believed, was to divert as much censure as possible
from himself to Rockefeller and his associates. With his handsome
face, his gift for acting, his dashing, magnetic manner, his fluent,
persuasive speech, he half convinced her that Jorkins was the wicked
partner, not Spenlow. All her references to him are indulgent. But
Miss Tarbell did not extend her personal inquiries widely. The
principal deficiency of her preparatory labors was that she did not
search out many of the hundreds of veterans of the oil industry,
both supporters and opponents of the Standard, whom she might
have seen. Later historians must always regret that she did not make
a wider inquiry for the one kind of evidence—oral evidence—which
was rapidly disappearing.

Readers today are likely to find *The History of the Standard Oil*,
with its sober, factual method, difficult to read; and nine people
out of ten who talk of the book actually know it only at second
hand. But in 1902-4 the public had a background of knowledge
which lent the articles a stirring interest. Men like Lee, Phillips,
Rice, Monnett, and Emery, now forgotten, were vivid public figures; events like the Hepburn investigation and the battles of the

[61] *All in the Day's Work*, 206.

Pure Oil pipe line were fresh in everybody's mind. Long before the history was published in two volumes in 1904 it had made a deep impression upon the public mind; all the deeper because Miss Tarbell was not, like Lloyd, an emotional partisan, but a painstaking, industrious investigator, who strove to document every part of her narrative. When it made its final appearance the 550 pages of text, though containing few footnotes, were buttressed by 240 pages of source material arranged in appendices. The gravamen of her indictment was simple. Rockefeller and his associates, she argued, had built up a combination which was admirable in its organized efficiency and power; but nearly every step in the construction of this vast industrial machine had been attended by fraud, coercion, special privilege, or sharp dealing, which had tended to debase the whole standard of business morals in America.

Her book was received with an explosion of applause. Press, pulpit, and political leaders alike praised it. The only important dissenting voice came from the reviewer in *The Nation,* who attacked the work as sensational, ignorant, and deliberately unfair.[62] Indeed, taken as a whole, and with due allowance for two facts —first, that Miss Tarbell never pretended to be impartial, but wrote as a representative of the Oil Regions, and second, that she had a faulty sense of what constituted evidence—it merited the praise it received. It was easily the best piece of business history that America had yet produced. It collected an immense mass of data, arranged it clearly, and cast the history of the Standard into a pattern which nearly every subsequent writer has followed. Critical readers of today will detect the bias running through it, while at important points its conclusions are demonstrably erroneous. Miss Tarbell accepted the Henry Demarest Lloyd fable of a prosperous oil industry in 1872 thrown into confusion and depression by the South Improvement scheme, although in fact the industry was then depressed and chaotic. She placed the responsibility for the South Improvement plan upon Rockefeller and his associates, though it actually originated with the railroads. She blamed the collapse of early efforts of the Regions men to organize upon Rockefeller's machinations, when the cause lay chiefly in their own bickerings and greed. She treated rebating as the special sin of the Standard,

[62]N. Y. *Nation,* LXXX (1905), 15, 16. The writer was D. Macly Means.

though practically all refiners, including some of her heroes, accepted rebates. She assailed the immediate-shipment order given by the Standard when Bradford production ran wild, though the best evidence is that the combination was striving heroically to meet an impossible situation. She gave new currency to the preposterous charges of the Widow Backus; she offered nearly as one-sided an account of the Vacuum Oil affair as Lloyd, hinting that the leaders in the trust did really commit "lawless and relentless acts."[63] Nevertheless, much of her indictment of Standard methods was absolutely irrefutable. At one point, moreover, her book was actually too mild, for she made less than she might have done of the excessive prices and profits of the trust.

Though Standard men winced under the applause which greeted Miss Tarbell's history, Rockefeller stood firmly by his belief that no answer ought to be vouchsafed. The book could be left to the verdict of a later, better-informed, more impartial generation. "Not a word! Not a word about that misguided woman!" he remarked when somebody spoke of her.[64] A little later he showed a justifiable resentment when Miss Tarbell published in *McClure's* (July, August, 1905) a two-part article quite unworthy of her. She mercilessly assailed Rockefeller's father; she accused the oil magnate of perjury; she told the Corrigan story in *ex parte* fashion as proof that he had "squeezed" an old friend; she referred to his religion and his benefactions as "hypocrisy"; she asserted that he gave little in proportion to his wealth; and since she could not attack his extravagance, she spoke of his parsimony. She analyzed his features: "Concentration, craftiness, cruelty, and something indefinably repulsive are in them." She took a sinister view of his recreations: "There is little doubt that Mr. Rockefeller's chief reason for playing golf is that he may live longer in order to make more money." And she, or the editors of the magazine, placed immediately after the article a selection from Ruskin on Judas Iscariot. It was following

---

[63]*The Standard Oil*, II, 87 ff. Miss Tarbell writes of it as "the case on which is based the often-repeated charge that Mr. Rockefeller, to win his point, has been known to burn refineries." In her interview in *Public Opinion*, May 27, 1905, Miss Tarbell said of the whole Standard Oil story: "There was something to be said on the other side; there always is. If I were writing a hundred years later, it is possible that I should see the whole matter differently."

[64]Flynn, *God's Gold*, 389, 390.

From "Life," New York City, July 6, 1911.

Miss Tarbell and the other critics leave "St. John of the Rocks"
unperturbed.

the publication of this character study that Rockefeller spoke bitterly to a friend of "Miss Tarbarrel," and then passed hastily to another subject.[65] Her attacks upon his aged father deeply pained him. He thought his father's life no business of the public, and intensely resented the fact that one New York editor announced a reward of $8000 for information on the old man, and that trained writers searched wolfishly for gossip about him.[66]

Close in the wake of Miss Tarbell's *History* came another attack which heavily injured Rockefeller in public esteem. *Everybody's Magazine,* then edited by John O'Hara Cosgrave, began in July, 1904, a series of articles on Amalgamated Copper by Thomas W. Lawson, the Boston stock-market operator who had been associated with H. H. Rogers and William Rockefeller in forming the flagrantly lawless copper trust. "Personally," wrote Lawson in an advertisement scattered broadcast,[67] "I knew that $100,000,000 were lost, thirty men committed suicide, and twenty previously reputable citizens went to the penitentiary, directly because of Amalgamated." The melodrama that he promised was more than provided. A Barnumesque self-advertiser, brainy, handsome, and unscrupulous, he really knew the inmost secrets of business corruption.[68] His articles, written with verve, pungency, and narrative power, even affected the American stock market, while columns of matter from them were cabled to the London press. Full of thrilling incidents, of verbatim conversations with masters of finance, and of bits of local color, they told expertly of one of the most outrageous episodes in financial manipulation since the old Erie days. He related how he, H. H. Rogers, and William Rockefeller had become partners in the copper amalgamation, "the Judas of corporations," which prostituted the government of Montana, waged bandit wars around its mines, and left havoc all along its Apache trail in Wall Street. Here and there his tale was exaggerated, while he frankly admitted a motive of revenge in some of his lurid portrayals of former associates. But his indictment of the "System" of organized speculation and thimble-rigging which made Amalgamated Copper possible was

[65]Confidential source. Conservative journals frequently alluded to "Miss Tarbarrel"; for example, *The Northwestern Miller,* April 12, 1905.
[66]Flynn, *God's Gold,* 378.
[67]N. Y. *Evening Post,* June 21, 1904.
[68]Louis Filler, *Crusaders for American Liberalism,* 171 ff.

perfectly sound; and his statement that three great insurance companies, the New York Life, the Equitable, and the Mutual Life, were an integral part of the "System," helped precipitate the much-needed insurance investigation.[69]

Of course John D. Rockefeller never had the slightest connection

"*Frenzied* Lawson: "*Darn your 'big stick'! Get a meat AX!!*""

Cartoon by Steele in the Denver "Post," 1904.

Lawson's defamation of Rockefeller: He had nothing to do with the "System" which Lawson described, yet cartoonists portrayed him as its head.

with Amalgamated Copper. He disapproved of it, and to intimates spoke in stern condemnation of it. The sprincipal figures in that organization, besides Rogers, William Rockefeller, and Lawson, were Stillman, James R. Keene, and F. Augustus Heinze. Rockefeller had handed active control of practically all investments over to his son and Gates, who felt a strong repugnance for ventures like the Amalgamated. In his narrative Lawson should have made it perfectly clear that he never spoke a word to Rockefeller, never handled a

[69]See the section on insurance, *Frenzied Finance*, 413–485.

dollar from him, and knew nothing about his activities. Instead, he repeatedly spoke of "the Standard," and only less frequently of "the Rockefellers," in a way which led readers to conclude that the elder Rockefeller had entered the Amalgamated. Lawson really knew so little about the Standard that he was ignorant that Archbold was now its active head.[70] He knew so little about Rockefeller that he was unaware that the magnate had long since ceased to visit 26 Broadway. But he was determined above all to make a sensation. In one chapter he told how he had insisted on making William Rockefeller's son, William G., the treasurer of Amalgamated, because "not one in ten thousand but will think William G. is the senior Rockefeller." In the same way, he wished readers to think that the greatest of all the Rockefellers was implicated. He continually wrote of "the Standard" as if the company had shared in the copper operations, and quite gratuitously libelled its former head. "John D. Rockefeller can be fully described as a man made in the image of an ideal money-maker. . . . An ideal money-maker is a machine the details of which are diagrammed in the asbestos blueprints which paper the walls of hell."[71]

At one point in *Frenzied Finance* Lawson did admit that Rockefeller "was considerably worked up," and was "so opposed to the whole Amalgamated affair" that they feared his anger.[72] Yet in the next pages he was again writing of "the Rockefellers" and "the Standard." Millions gained from the book a hazy impression that John D. Rockefeller played a part in this deplorable affair. Careless writers even today repeat the fiction that the Standard Oil Company was implicated in it. Neither had anything whatever to do with the Amalgamated. That was the enterprise of H. H. Rogers and William Rockefeller. This aggressive pair, acting as individuals and not Standard Oil partners, shared the responsibility with Lawson, Stillman, and the rest; and the elder Rockefeller and Archbold

[70]See the absurd statement, p. 7, that H. H. Rogers, William Rockefeller, and John D. Rockefeller, "and included with them their sons," were the active heads. Archbold was *the* head; there was no other.

[71]P. 21. Nothing in Lawson is stranger than his inconsistencies. Though accusing William Rockefeller, whom he knew intimately, of heartless villainies, he heaps praise upon him as "a good, wholesome man made in the image of his God." With no knowledge whatever of John D. Rockefeller, he abuses him foully.

[72]Pp. 347, 348.

keenly resented their failure to make it clear that no other Standard man was concerned.

Once, in October, 1904, the Standard Oil gave the press a strong denial of some of the current accusations. "It is not true," it declared, "that the Standard Oil Company, Mr. John D. Rockefeller, or any officer of the Standard Oil Company has taken part in securing the nomination of any of the candidates for office. It is entirely untrue that there is any Standard Oil party banded together for speculation in stocks." This evoked replies from Lawson and Miss Tarbell. The former made an absurd statement. "Judge Parker's nomination was entirely because of Senator Pat H. McCarren," he declared, "and McCarren has been for years in the employ of Standard Oil and H. H. Rogers." Miss Tarbell said that as to the stock-speculation charge, a glance at the directorate of important companies was sufficient. "It is well known that the Standard Oil crowd is in nearly everything." What was "everything"? Rogers and William Rockefeller were directors in half a dozen corporations, but neither Archbold nor John D. Rockefeller was actively concerned with any save the Standard Oil itself.[73]

IV

As an accompaniment to the chorus of magazine attacks, the year 1905 brought news of fresh legal assaults upon the Standard. Kansas in particular was in arms against the combination. A little oil had long been taken out of that State. In 1903 the production leaped to a million barrels, and the next year it exceeded four and a quarter million. Prospectors, wildcatters, brokers, and speculators swarmed over the southeastern counties. As more and more gushers came in, and the tax upon storage facilities grew heavier, trouble ensued. The wells were about 500 miles from the Gulf. By 1904

[73]N. Y. *Herald*, Oct. 27, 28, 1904. John Morley, it is related, once sat beside Edith Rockefeller McCormick at a dinner. He had heard much from Andrew Carnegie about Rockefeller, and asked her many questions. She finally suggested that he write a biography of her father. "Oh," replied Morley, "an Englishman could never do it. It will have to be done by an American. And you have excellent biographers on your side of the ocean." "Whom would you suggest?" demanded Mrs. McCormick. "Well," said Morley, "I have lately read an excellent life of Lincoln by one of your writers. She is Ida M. Tarbell—why not ask Miss Tarbell to do it?"

the Standard had thrown pipe lines into all the fields, and had two large refineries at work, one at Neodesha, the other in Kansas City. In fact, the Standard had good reason to welcome the Kansas supply, for the flow in Pennsylvania and West Virginia was decreasing at a calamitous rate. Before the year ended an eight-inch pipe line was started northeast, to run 600 miles to Whiting and give the Kansas field a world market. To meet the situation until this was finished, the Standard erected scores of tanks holding from 30,000 to 50,000 barrels of oil apiece. This meant a tremendous outlay—$15,000,000 was the usual estimate; and Miss Tarbell writes, "the expenditure was made with the splendid, quiet efficiency which characterizes the Standard Oil Company's great operations." But even so, the corporation could not keep pace with the torrent of petroleum, and begged the well-owners to restrict the flow.[74] Instead, they speeded it up until at times it reached 35,000 barrels a day, and prices fell heavily.

An oil-producers' association shortly sprang into existence, which charged the Standard with coercion and land-grabbing. To furnish relief, the indignant governor, Edward Hoch, proposed a State refinery; and when constitutional difficulties arose, the Kansas authorities circumvented them by declaring that since they had a right to operate penitentiaries and keep the convicts employed, they would build an oil refinery as a workshop in connection with a new penitentiary! The Standard was meanwhile accused of attacking independent refiners in Kansas, and of using its strength to exact special favors from the Santa Fé and "Katy" railroads. The legislature retaliated by placing pipe lines under State jurisdiction, while the attorney-general began a prosecution under the State antitrust law. All this filled the newspapers and magazines with articles antagonistic to the Standard Oil practices in the West.

Still more spectacular was the attack which developed in Missouri under the leadership of a handsome young attorney-general, Herbert S. Hadley, who was swept into office at the same time that the reformer Joseph W. Folk was elected governor. His blows were directed at the Waters-Pierce branch of the combination. Sev-

[74]Production fell in 1908 to 1,800,000 barrels; *Annual Report, Kansas Bureau of Labor and Industry.* See Miss Tarbell's two vivid papers in *McClure's,* "Kansas and the Standard Oil Company," XXV, 469 ff., 608 ff., September, October, 1905.

eral years earlier, at the beginning of the century, Texas had taken effective action against Henry Clay Pierce and the branch of the Standard which he supervised so resourcefully and ably, but also so arrogantly and harshly.[75] The Waters-Pierce Corporation owned pipe lines running clear across the State and into Mexico, and did a heavy distributing business all the way from St. Louis to the Gulf. The Texas authorities, learning of its relations with the Standard, filed suit against it. They had no difficulty in proving a violation of the antitrust law, and in convicting Pierce's organization of illegal rebating as well. In May, 1900, the company was ousted from Texas. This was a staggering blow to Pierce, for his Mexican as well as Texan trade was at stake; but, gifted at subterfuge, he and Representative Joe Bailey worked out a new plan. The old company was dissolved, a new one was chartered under the Missouri laws, and Pierce gave his check to the Standard Oil for all the shares it had owned in Waters-Pierce. Holding the receipt as proof that the company was now independent, he swore to the Texas authorities that Waters-Pierce was not allied with any other company in violation of the State antitrust laws; and he was allowed to recommence business.[76]

But competitors remained suspicious of him. The new company looked and behaved just like the old one, and it was as difficult as ever for independents to stand up against it. All the way from St. Louis to San Antonio its salesmen had an uncanny knowledge of the operations of rivals. Perhaps the Standard was no longer interested in the company; but somehow Pierce still bought practically all his refined oil from the Standard plants. Moreover, men selling in the Southwest found the Standard of Indiana their largest rival in some areas, and the Waters-Pierce outfit the largest in others; but they never met both companies in the same district. After the Republic Oil Company of New York replaced the independent firm of Scofield, Shurmer & Teagle in 1901, the situation became more complicated. The Republic was as harsh in its business practices as the Waters-Pierce Company, but the two nevertheless seemed to get on admirably. They never undercut each other's prices, never fought each other for customers. Were Waters-Pierce and the Republic Oil

[75]Frederick Upham Adams, *The Waters-Pierce Case in Texas: Battling with a Giant Corporation*, passim.
[76]W. H. Gray, *The Rule of Reason in Texas*, 15.

truly the independents they pretended to be, or were they "bogus" competitors, and actually arms of the Standard Oil?

It was not long before the alert and intrepid Hadley stumbled upon some suggestive facts relating to the oil industry. He found that the Standard Oil sold no kerosene or gasolene in St. Louis—that was Waters-Pierce territory; while Waters-Pierce sold no products in Kansas City—that was Standard territory.[77] Yet they were supposed to be rivals! He found other evidence that the State had been partitioned for selling purposes. It cost 17 cents a barrel to ship kerosene from Kansas City to St. Louis, but 22 cents a barrel to ship it from St. Louis to Kansas City; the Kansas City refinery which sent oil to Waters-Pierce being a Standard plant, while the only St. Louis refinery was an independent company. Hadley learned that the Republic Oil Company had its offices at 75 New Street in New York, the "back door" of 26 Broadway. Whenever Hadley talked to an oil man, he heard gossip which enhanced his suspicions.[78] And as a result, on March 29, 1906, he filed a *quo warranto* suit in the Supreme Court of Missouri charging the Waters-Pierce Company, the Standard of Indiana, and the Republic Oil Company of New York with being members of a combination to fix prices, restrain competition, and deceive the public by posing as independents.[79] Forthwith, a deluge of letters from all over the State descended upon him, volunteering information to support his suit.[80]

Men read of the Kansas and Missouri attacks upon the Standard Oil in the very months in 1905 in which, by hundreds of thousands, they were reading Ida M. Tarbell's *History of the Standard Oil* and Lawson's *Frenzied Finance*. The newspapers were full of attacks on the Standard as a heartless monopoly. Roosevelt's new Bureau of Corporations, headed by James R. Garfield, had made a much-publicized report upon the so-called Beef Trust in March, just as the President was being inaugurated;[81] and it was common knowl-

---

[77]N. Y. *Herald,* Jan. 8, 1905. Hadley, a Kansas City man, talked with the Standard Oil manager in his city.

[78]"Governor Hadley of Missouri," *Independent,* April 8, 1909.

[79]218 *Missouri Reports,* 1 ff.

[80]N. Y. *Herald,* Jan. 8, 1905; Margaret A. Clapp, "Waters-Pierce Ouster Suits in Missouri and Texas," 9.

[81]This report found that the "Big Six" packing companies held no monopoly, and that profits had been less than the public supposed. See *The Nation,* March 9, 1905; N. Y. *World,* March 4–15, 1905, for comment.

edge that it intended to report next on the petroleum industry. Indeed, the House passed a resolution calling for an investigation of the situation in the Kansas oil field. Complaints of the high prices of kerosene and gasoline were incessant. Every one suspected the Standard Oil of unwholesome if not highly sinister political activities. Rockefeller was still president of the Standard, and still identified by nearly all Americans with its daily activities and its continuing policies. His public reputation touched its nadir of discredit in these months; and the fact was advertised to the whole world by the extraordinary controversy over "tainted money" which suddenly broke upon the American public.[82]

[82]It should be said that Rockefeller always took pride in the fact that Standard Oil stock was never listed on the New York Stock Exchange while he was active head of the company, and was never an easy means of speculation. He bought a seat on the Stock Exchange in 1883, which he held for more than fifty-four years; but he entered its building only once, and then only to comply with its rule that a prospective member appear before its committee on admissions.—N. Y. *Herald Tribune*, May 25, 1937.

XLV

Tainted Wealth

THE newspaper sensation over "tainted money" which enlivened the spring and summer of 1905 must be reckoned among the most curious episodes of the muckraking era. It flared up when a number of Congregational ministers, notably Washington Gladden, protested against the acceptance by the Congregational Board of Foreign Missions of $100,000 from Rockefeller. A three months' wonder, it died away when the most excited participants found, to their chagrin, that the Board had actually solicited the money. While it lasted it caused the millionaire much pain, though he appreciated the humorous aspects of the affair. The public quickly forgot the controversy. Yet it had certain noteworthy results. It confronted the recipients of philanthropy with a serious question of ethics, which had never before been dragged into the open; it gave journalism an immortal phrase; it caused Rockefeller's associates to abandon his policy of silence; and unhappily for the churches, it led him to defer for a decade any large-scale grants to foreign missions.

Until this time Rockefeller had confined his philanthropies rather closely to the United States, and in so far as they touched religion, chiefly to the Baptist Church. Doctor Gates believed that the fortune was far too great to be held within these limits; that it should benefit all the world, and flow into many denominational channels. To this position Rockefeller was himself coming. It was singularly unfortunate that his first effort to cross the old boundaries should arouse a venomous attack.

The origin of the gift was simple. Rockefeller had for decades given generously to Baptist missions, his church using the money to send abroad missionaries, educators, doctors, and nurses, and to equip churches, schools, colleges, and hospitals. He had insisted upon an intelligent expenditure of funds. The Congregationalists looked with natural envy upon the opulence of their sister denomination. It happened that in Boston the Congregational secretaries occupied offices near those of the Baptists, and the two groups often lunched together. But how could the poorer sect—for its missionary activities were in dire straits—reach Rockefeller? Some one recalled that Mrs. Rockefeller as a girl had been a Congregationalist, and that Lucy Spelman still belonged to the church. Miss Spelman's pastor approached her, she spoke to her sister, and the subject was brought up at the family breakfast table, where the Rockefellers discussed their philanthropies. But Rockefeller did not respond, declining the application without referring it to his staff.

Several months later the younger Rockefeller and Gates learned of the failure of these approaches, which they regretted; and they resolved to revive the question at the earliest opportunity. In April, 1902, Mr. Rockefeller, Jr., wrote to James L. Barton, the able and hardworking secretary of the Congregational Board—doubtless the man responsible for the request to Miss Spelman. Doctor Barton without delay called at 26 Broadway for a discussion, and set forth the urgent needs of the Congregational missions in strong terms, emphasizing the fact that at no point did these activities compete with Baptist missions. More than two years of intermittent negotiation then ensued. The younger Rockefeller and Gates were honorably anxious to extend the scope of the family's benefactions in the mission field, particularly for higher education; the Congregational Board was honorably anxious to receive some of the money. The Congregational minister in Gates's town of Montclair presently took a hand in the matter; and in the fall of 1903 Barton delivered an eloquent address there on mission activities, which was followed by a conference at Gates's home, with Starr J. Murphy, a Congregationalist, in attendance. Some months later Barton addressed a long letter of appeal to Rockefeller, and sent it to Gates. Apparently it asked for too much, for Gates requested a fresh conference at 26 Broadway, of which he writes:[1]

[1] MS Autobiography, 377, 378. The full title of the Congregational organization is American Board of Commissioners for Foreign Missions. Its present secretary, D. Brewer Eddy, D.D., has furnished me valuable information.

We welcomed the secretary most cordially, and he immediately opened up his budget of needs . . . The original sum, he explained, for material equipment had been in round numbers two hundred thousand dollars. By unsparing use of the knife they had cut this down to one hundred and sixty thousand. Would not Mr. Rockefeller give this sum in this emergency, for grounds, buildings, and equipment, absolutely essential? The budget which he had brought with him involved many items in both hemispheres. We discussed every item exhaustively, and at the end of several hours, Mr. Murphy and I were able to cut out of the budget about sixty thousand dollars which was to be spent in merely sectarian rivalry, as we thought. This left one hundred thousand and for this sum we promised to support a letter of appeal from the secretary to Mr. Rockefeller, who was then sojourning at Lakewood. It became my duty to write a private letter favoring the secretary's appeal. This letter afforded me a long-coveted opportunity to try to open up Mr. Rockefeller's philanthropy . . . to all countries of the world, and to all worthy religious and humanitarian agencies everywhere.

A few days after Gates mailed his letter,[2] Rockefeller instructed him to send the Boston secretaries $100,000. This was probably the largest gift from a living donor which the Congregational Board had received for current use in its whole history. Made by a Baptist, it ran completely athwart denominational lines, then an extraordinary occurrence. As any one with imagination could see, it opened up fascinating possibilities. From this precedent Rockefeller might rapidly go on to aid all other denominations, and thus begin a new and lustrous era in the history of American missions. It was the rule of Rockefeller's office, laid down by himself, never to announce his gifts publicly. That was left to the recipients. His office force always obeyed the injunction not to let the left hand know what the right did, and never even made an estimate of the sum total of the gifts.[3] But in this instance Rockefeller and Gates awaited the Boston announcement with eagerness, for they wished to see how quickly other denominations would apprehend its significance.

But seldom has a well-laid scheme gone more tragically agley. The news reached the Congregational denomination in such fashion as to create a false impression that the gift had come unasked, and that the mission authorities were not particularly grate-

[2]Gates's letter, which mingled spiritual and temporal considerations in singular fashion, is published in the N. Y. Times, April 17, 1905.
[3]Gates, MS Autobiography, 380.

ful. Gates's formal notification that the $100,000 was available was dated February 11, 1913. Two days later Barton sent a letter thanking him and Murphy, but not Rockefeller. On the fourteenth the Prudential Committee unanimously voted its approval of the acceptance of the gift. Gates indicated that Rockefeller wished his donation to be acknowledged just as the Board acknowledged all others; and a public statement was prepared for the next or April issue of the monthly *Missionary Herald*. Unfortunately, this was too brief to mention the negotiations leading up to the gift. Still more unfortunately, it offered an expression of thanks to God, but none to Rockefeller! And most unhappily of all, it declared that the Board announced the gift "with joyous surprise"—as if it had come quite unexpectedly! Moreover, before this notice appeared the weekly *Congregationalist* heralded the news to all its readers; and its notice likewise failed to mention that the Board had anxiously sought the gift, or to say a word of gratitude.

Then came the explosion. No sooner had the gift been announced in *The Congregationalist* of March 18, 1905, than a group of about thirty men, most of them Congregational ministers, met in Boston and signed a formal protest, requesting the Board to return the money to Rockefeller. This was presented to the Prudential Committee of the Board, which referred it to a subcommittee for report; but meanwhile its publication in the press unloosed a flood of public discussion. The ground stated by the protest was that the Standard Oil Company, of which Mr. Rockefeller was head, "stands before the public under repeated and recent formidable indictment in specific terms for methods which are morally iniquitous and socially destructive," and that the acceptance of such a gift "involves the constituents of the Board in a relation implying honor to the donor, and subjects the Board to the charge of ignoring the moral issues involved."[4]

One of the most powerful fulminations against the gift came from Doctor Gladden, moderator of the National Council of Congrega-

[4]The full text of the protest is in *The Congregationalist*, April 1, 1905, with "A Dissenting View" by Doctor Gladden, and "An Approving View" by Doctor Amory H. Bradford. The latter made it plain that the incident arose out of "a noble enterprise in its extreme need making its appeal" to Rockefeller, and added: "To that appeal he yielded, not in any way making the Board his partner, and not asking it to give him any approval." The gift was for eight collegiate institutions and certain publication work.

tional Churches, and deservedly the most influential minister of the sect. Broad in vision, fearless in temper, highly cultivated, and gifted with an eloquent voice and pen, he had long argued that Christianity must be made a vigorous social force.[5] Nobody in the American pulpit had attacked public and private corruption more forcefully. For years an assailant of monopoly, he had often expressed his hostility for the Standard. On March 26 he preached a sermon in Columbus, Ohio, which was one long invective. Rockefeller's wealth, he said, was tainted. "The money proffered to our board of missions comes out of a colossal estate whose foundations were laid in the most relentless rapacity known to modern commercial history. The success of the business from the beginning to now has been largely due to the unlawful manipulation of railway rates." The government was about to join battle with "the corporate greed which has entrenched itself in this stronghold and has learned to use the railways for the oppression and spoliation of the people." How could good citizens accept largess "from the man who more completely than any other represents the system they are summoned to fight"? Right-thinking Congregationalists did not want it. "To accept it will be to work the contempt of millions of honest men; to reject it will strengthen our churches in the affection and respect of millions. . . ."

The phrase "tainted money" was a flash of genius, and the whole press took it up. No subject had so swiftly captured the American imagination since Spanish War days. The press teemed with articles, letters, and editorials for and against Rockefeller. Every American of prominence was asked to express his views. H. H. Rogers, Starr J. Murphy, and S. C. T. Dodd spoke out on one side; William Jennings Bryan on the other.[6] Simeon E. Baldwin of the Connecticut Supreme Court uttered a long judicial opinion in *The Congregationalist*. Edward Everett Hale declared that he would gladly take the money,[7] and Doctor Russell H. Conwell, the founder of Temple University, expressed his belief that Rockefeller "is a generous Chris-

[5]See Gladden's *Applied Christianity* (1887), and *Social Salvation* (1901).

[6]See N. Y. *Herald, Tribune*, April 1, 1905, for Rogers's statement: N. Y. *Evening Post*, April 7, 1905, for Dodd's. Gladden had said that "the Standard now controls about two thirds of the railroads of this country," and Dodd showed that this was preposterous. Bryan's comment is in N. Y. *Tribune*, Sept. 22, 1905.

[7]Brooklyn *Eagle*, April 12, 1905.

tian man."[8] While the debate raged, it was announced on June 28 that Rockefeller had given a million dollars to Yale, and two days later that he had donated ten millions to the General Education Board. No responsible person proposed that these sums be rejected! "Gifts of ten millions," wittily remarked the New York *Sun*, "deodorize themselves."

The discussion, while diverting, was of course perfectly futile. But on the whole, the weight of considered opinion was adverse to Doctor Gladden. Judge Baldwin, after asking whether it would be Christian to say to even the gambler or rumseller that his sacrifice was unacceptable to God, asserted that the managers of a church or charitable corporation could not safely pronounce a verdict on an accused person—"they have none of the powers of a court of justice." Doctor Lyman Abbott's *Outlook,* in a much-quoted editorial entitled "Judge Not," remarked that it absolutely declined to sit on any man and decide whether the balance of his moral ledger was on the debit or credit side. Moreover, it positively refused to condemn his good deeds because of his evil deeds; it would co-operate with him in what was good, and rebuke him in what was bad. Hundreds of newspapers and magazines (among them the Baptist *Examiner*) pointed out that a man was supposed to be innocent until legally pronounced guilty, and no court had ever found Rockefeller guilty of the crimes which Doctor Gladden charged. President Alderman of the University of Virginia, speaking at a banquet just after that institution had received $100,000 from Rockefeller, remarked: "They are as good dollars as were ever seen!" President L. Clark Seelye of Smith declared that he knew of no reason why either missionary societies or colleges should not accept Rockefeller's gifts with gratitude; and Graham Taylor, the eminent social worker, echoed him.

The shriller voices on each side were indications of the intensity with which public opinion was now divided upon Rockefeller. Robert M. LaFollette demonstrated his Christian charity in a Chautauqua address at Galesburg, Ill.[9] "I read yesterday that Rockefeller had been to prayer-meeting again," he said. "Tomorrow he will

[8]Baptist *Commonwealth*, June 29, 1905.
[9]See N. Y. *Herald*, July 27, and N. Y. *World*, Aug. 20, 1905, for LaFollette's two utterances on Rockefeller.

be giving to some college or university. He gives with two hands, but he robs with many. If he should live a thousand years he could not expiate the crimes he has committed. There is only one way —eternity the time; and as to the place, you can guess that. He is the greatest criminal of the age." The once-noted Baptist evangelist, George F. Pentecost, preached on thirty pieces of silver, and published an article in *The Arena* full of moral thunderings and Biblical examples; while the Reverend Charles A. Crane of Boston called Rockefeller "chief of modern plunderers." On the other hand, the Pittsburgh coal operator J. B. Corey circulated broadcast a letter to Bryan's *Commoner* in which, after explaining that thirty years of close business contact with Rockefeller and the Standard had convinced him of their complete uprightness, he declared that Bryan was unworthy to loose Rockefeller's shoe-latchets.[10] A number of conservative organs seized the opportunity to denounce muckraking in angry terms. As a matter of fact, Miss Tarbell's two articles on Rockefeller's character, with their spiteful tone, bits of scandal about his father, and unpleasant comment on his personal appearance since his loss of hair, had aroused a widespread revulsion. They were "sinister" and "indecent," said *The Presbyterian Banner*.[11] "Is it envy, uncharitableness, or what not," demanded *Harper's Weekly*, "that induces spasms of attack upon men who get rich and give away money?"[12]

The real utility of Doctor Gladden's crusade lay in directing the attention of thoughtful men to a question which was—and always will be—worthy of earnest thought: Were the churches too dependent upon and obsequious to wealthy men? Both Protestant and Catholic sects had long shown a manifest deference to rich members. An Episcopal rector, Doctor Bliss, who had investigated the relations of wealth and religion, declared:[13] "The fifty-two Baptist churches in Manhattan and the Bronx, with the 19,738 members and property valued at $6,000,000, present almost the one sensational instance in New York City of a denomination ruled by one wealthy man." Baptist leaders categorically denied that any such domination

[10]Pittsburgh *Leader,* April 20, 1905, and other newspapers.
[11]July 27, 1905. Much press comment was equally acid. The N. Y. *Times* published indignant letters on the subject.
[12]*Harper's Weekly,* Aug. 5, 1905.
[13]*The Independent,* LX (1906), 135–142.

existed.[14] Yet the Episcopal Church was notoriously under the influence of J. Pierpont Morgan. The Catholic Church showed manifest pride in Charles M. Schwab and Thomas Fortune Ryan. Few congregations of any sect in large Eastern cities but displayed espe-

Wealth and the Churches: John T. McCutcheon portrays a passing sensitivity in the Chicago *Tribune*.

cial pleasure and interest when a millionaire entered the fold; few in Middle Western towns and villages failed to place the local rich man in the best pew. The New York *Evening Post* and Springfield *Republican* very properly commended Doctor Gladden for raising this issue,[15] and declared that it must be met in accordance with the

[14]See the article by Doctor John B. Calvert, president of the State Baptist Missionary Convention, refuting Bliss's statements; *Independent*, LX, 141, 142 (1906).

[15]*The Congregationalist and Christian World*, April 1, 1905, gives quotations to this effect from a number of journals.

highest ethical standards. "It is practically impossible," said *The Evening Post,* "for a religious denomination to look to a man as leader and chief contributor to its various enterprises, to seek his counsel and his aid, to accord him the standing of membership both in name and deed, and at the same time denounce his wrongdoing."[16] This was true. It was too much to expect the Baptists to accept large sums from Rockefeller, the Episcopalians from Morgan, or the Catholics from Schwab, and still feel free to criticize improper acts by the donor. Nor was it healthful for churches to pursue avidly the means of paying for splendid edifices, highly salaried ministers, and costly organs and choirs.

These larger aspects of the subject deserved more attention than they received. It was to Doctor Gladden's credit that after some untenable charges at the outset,[17] he tried to lift the debate to an impersonal plane. When the Congregational Association of Ohio, holding its annual meeting at Oberlin in May, drew up resolutions censuring Rockefeller by name, Gladden moved to strike out the reference, and this was done. But most of the discussion assumed that the churches were above criticism—that it was Rockefeller alone who was being questioned and assailed. Not a little solemn hypocrisy entered into the uproar. A celebrated New York pastor delivered in resounding phrases his verdict that the tainted money of Rockefeller ought to be returned. Yet only a short time before he had visited Rockefeller's private office to solicit funds for a benevolence through Gates, and had received many thousands of dollars. A leading Congregationalist minister of New England, formerly a Baptist in Cleveland, joined in the condemnation. Yet Rockefeller's files contained a recent letter from him pleading eloquently for a favorite cause! Gates writes:[18]

An aggravated case was that of an eminent Presbyterian divine, the head of an important interdenominational alliance. He had annually written Mr. Rockefeller for its support over his own signature, and with his own hand had endorsed the checks that had always been sent to him

[16]April 7, 1905; May 18, 1905, discussing Doctor Robert Stuart McArthur's warm defense of Rockefeller.

[17]For example, Gladden accused Rockefeller of perjury in his famous disclaimer of connection with the "Southern" Improvement Company. Murphy in the N. Y. *Sun,* May 7, 1905, refuted Gladden's charge.

[18]MS Autobiography, 384.

personally. He was a friend of Colonel S. C. T. Dodd, himself a Presby‑ terian, one of the best of men, who had given its legal organization to the Standard Oil Trust. . . . Only just before the controversy this emi‑ nent divine, with his treasurer, had visited Colonel Dodd at 26 Broadway to get through him an introduction to Mr. Rockefeller, whom they wished to solicit in person. After this man had appeared among Mr. Rockefeller's public maligners, he had nothing better to reply to Mr. Dodd's immedi‑ ate and sharp arraignment than that he had never asked or received any money from Mr. Rockefeller, and that he had only intended to introduce his treasurer and let him do the talking. Colonel Dodd was shown his annual letters of appeal. They bore his signature, and the answering checks all bore his autograph endorsement.

Suspicion that this hypocrisy was abroad led a good many min‑ isters to point out the relevancy of certain well-known Bible texts: those, for example, about casting the first stone; about plucking the beam out of one's own eye before dealing with the mote in your brother's; about judging not lest ye be judged; and about asking no needless questions for conscience's sake. The Chicago *Chronicle* recalled that Christ had rejoiced when the robber Zaccheus gave half his money to charity, and had not hesitated to accept the gift of a woman of the town. "When Christian ministers get to be holier than Jesus Christ they ought to watch sedulously against transla‑ tion."

While the controversy gathered intensity, the Congregational secretaries in Boston remained silent. Rockefeller and Gates waited impatiently for them to explain that Rockefeller had not pressed the money upon them—that they had solicited it. Instead, the press on March 27 published an interview with Secretary James L. Barton, in which it reported him as saying that the gift had been voluntary and unsought.[19] Finally Gates took the matter up with the Congregational minister in Montclair. To this gentleman he gave the details of the various early approaches to Rockefeller's home, of the itemized appeal, of the letter to Rockefeller, and of the check in response. All this Gates threatened to expose to the Associated Press.[20] The minister begged for time to write to Boston,

[19]N. Y. *Times,* March 28, 1905. "Unsolicited and spontaneous" were the words attributed to Barton.

[20]MS Autobiography, 385. Files of the Board, kindly searched for me by Doctor Enoch F. Bell, show that Barton wrote Gates on March 23 of the storm: "It will soon blow over. Every member of the Prudential Committee and

and on April 18 the Board of Foreign Missions announced that the gift of $100,000 had been solicited by representatives of the sect. At once the whirlwind of Congregational wrath began to subside, most of the excited preachers and editors displaying a new calmness. And the Prudential Committee, overriding Doctor Gladden, had meanwhile decided that the money ought to be accepted![21] Gates has well described the final course of the affair:[22]

Some months later, at the meeting of the triennial National Conference of Congregational Churches, a languid public attention was briefly turned back to the tainted money controversy. Doctor Gladden, President of the Council, publicly reviewed with great power, eloquence, and passion the whole question, mainly attacking the conduct of the secretaries. But the Council refused to be excited. Resolutions both for and against accepting questionable money were alike laid on the table, and to use the descriptive word of Doctor Gladden, the whole issue was "dodged." Even the attempt to rebuke the secretaries for soliciting Mr. Rockefeller was sidestepped. As for Mr. Rockefeller personally, there was not a member of the Council but felt in his heart a secret sympathy for the innocent victim of his own large-minded generosity. Doctor Gladden himself withdrew his aspersion of Mr. Rockefeller's motives. "Mr. Rockefeller had not thrust his offering on the Board. . . . If this fact had been clearly stated at the outset the attitude of many minds would have been different."

The controversy in the end did Mr. Rockefeller more good than harm. But it hurt missions. All the great missionary boards, except the Baptists, were frightened off. All continued for many years to do their work with meagre resources and in a crippled way. Of the major denominations, two or three dared to come to us, always armed with a resolution of their boards of control unanimously approving and directing the appeal. To all such Mr. Rockefeller gave freely.

every member of the Board feels profoundly thankful to Mr. Rockefeller for his gift, and there is no expectation that any other attitude will be taken." And on April 1, after his unfortunate interview, Barton telegraphed Gates: "I am preparing a statement and will mail you a copy tonight to Montclair. . . . Eager to correct every false impression." He did correct it, but very tardily.

[21] N. Y. *Times, Evening Post,* April 11, 12, 1905. Doctor Gladden commented: "No discrimination is henceforth to be made. The pirate or the train robber may bring his booty to the Treasury of the American Board . . . and, if sufficiently large, it will be described as a 'magnificent gift.'"

[22] MS Autobiography, 386, 387. In *The Independent,* LXVII, 781–874 (1905), Doctor Barton published an article, "The Correspondence on the Rockefeller Gift," which gave the whole story of the negotiation with Mr. Rockefeller beginning April 17, 1902, and ending with the acceptance of the gift on Feb. 14, 1905. Gladden's version of the episode, differing markedly in emphasis from Gates's, is in his *Recollections,* 398–409.

Rockefeller's son also suffered from attack. He happened a little later to make a talk on "Christianity in Business" to the Y. M. C. A. at Brown. In this he defended consolidation and the elimination

From "The Literary Digest," May 6, 1905.

This cartoon, widely reprinted in 1905, was based on a sentence in a speech by John D. Rockefeller, Jr.: "The American Beauty rose can be produced in all its splendor only by sacrificing the early buds that grow up around it."

of uneconomic competitors on the ground of the greatest good to the greatest number; remarking that the American Beauty rose in all its perfection is produced only by cutting away the early buds which surround it. The Episcopal Bishop of Michigan, Doctor Charles D. Williams, delivered a sermon in St. Bartholomew's fiercely attacking him ("a young scion of greed and wealth, possessed of more wealth than ideas"), and his doctrine. This brought a spirited rejoinder from the Reverend George T. Dowling, rector emeritus of St. James's Episcopal Church in Brooklyn. He assured

Bishop Williams that the younger Rockefeller, in conducting the men's class in the Fifth Avenue Baptist Church, evinced more ability than any pastor in his acquaintance, while the purity of his life had inspired universal respect. As for the American Beauty rose, he asked Doctor Williams to compare the great trunk lines from New York to Chicago which carried passengers in eighteen hours, at a fare of $35, with the ten budding railroads, long since absorbed, which several decades earlier had charged $150 for the trip and consumed three or four days. Bishop Williams, to his credit, made a manly apology.

The whole uproar had pained Rockefeller, but never really upset his equanimity. He made no public statement. To friends he even jested about the matter. The delightful "Madame" McCormick paid him a visit that summer. One evening Samuel Harper, also a visitor, saw him approach her with a twinkle in his eye. "I have a good joke on you, Mrs. McCormick," he remarked. "What is that, Mr. Rockefeller?" she inquired. "Well, you know that gift of $100,000 I made to the Congregational Board?" "Yes." "And you know how they denounced it as tainted money?" "Yes." "Well," said Rockefeller, "I gave it to them in bonds of the International Harvester Company!"[23]

Various newspapers had published highly imaginative accounts of Rockefeller's depression and melancholy as the attack raged. He "thirsts for sympathy, hungers for a kind word," declared a writer in the Philadelphia *Public Ledger,* adding that he had lost interest in golf, and become deeply morose. This correspondent related how "the richest man in the world sits by the hour at Forest Hill, his chin sunk on his breast, or walks for hours, always alone except for his guards, always in gloom."[24] But a reporter for the New York *Sun* saw him as he really was at the Euclid Avenue Church. He appeared in excellent health, chatted gaily with friends, and cracked some jokes before the Sunday School service. When it opened he made a little speech, for he had just arrived from the East. He referred to his love for the church. Then he stopped, ran his piercing eyes over the assemblage, and gaily remarked:

"I've talked too long, I am afraid. There are others here who

[23]Doctor Samuel Harper to the author.
[24]Philadelphia *Public Ledger,* July 21, 1905.

wish to talk. I don't want you to think I'm a selfish monopolist!"[25]

Early that autumn Cleveland business men indulged in a spontaneous demonstration of respect. *The Plain Dealer* had printed an editorial headed "A Square Deal Needed." Church friends had given out interviews in his behalf. Many people of the city keenly resented the slurs upon a man whom they knew well. On September 26 more than four hundred citizens, including city officials, merchants, bankers, attorneys, and manufacturers, visited Forest Hill as an emphatic gesture of esteem. Nearly all the leading men of Cleveland were there. They alighted at the entrance, where old Patrick Lynch kept the lodge, and walked across the half-mile lawn to the house. Rockefeller came down the porch steps to greet them, and as Andrew Squire and L. E. Holden made speeches in his praise, showed great emotion. They thanked him for giving, among other philanthropies, the land for Rockefeller Park, and recalled that it was only after prolonged pressure that he had consented to let his name be attached to it. "It is always the tree which bears the fruit that gets the clubs," said Holden. Rockefeller made a brief reply, recalling how he had arrived in the city fifty-two years before as a country boy, and urging his business hearers to think of other objects than money. "What shall the fruitage of your work be? Hospitals, churches, schools, asylums, anything and everything for the betterment of your fellows."

And in a private letter Rockefeller wrote: "I am happy to say I am in the best of health, and never enjoyed life more, with all its opportunities for doing good in the world."[26]

II

While the clamor was at its height, Gates sent Rockefeller a letter pointing out the plain lesson upon the ill-effects of the policy of secrecy. Doctor Gladden and most of his followers, he declared,

---

[25]N. Y. *Sun,* July 25, 1905.

[26]*Journal and Messenger,* Aug. 10, 1905. Rockefeller said in 1917 that Mrs. S. J. Life went all the way to Columbus, Ohio, to "excoriate" Gladden after his attack, while her brother, a Princeton graduate, wrote him a long argument. "Sometime after that Doctor Gladden admitted to Mr. F. T. Gates that he was wrong and that he regretted his attacks." Inglis, Conversations with Rockefeller. Various commentators pointed out that Gladden never protested against large gifts by the manufacturers of Peruna in Columbus, Ohio, to the Congregational Church.

were sincere and benevolent men. If they were misled, whose fault was it? Silence under attack had always been treated as a confession of guilt. No man or company, no matter how strong, could afford to defy the public opinion of the nation; and if Rockefeller continued to advise an ostrich policy, tempests would recur with increasing violence. "I wrote with considerable warmth," recites Gates,[27] "and Mr. Rockefeller replied with corresponding coolness." As a matter of fact, Gates might well have spoken even more sharply. Half of the current criticism of Rockefeller arose because he had never announced his retirement, so that men blamed him for what Archbold, H. H. Rogers, Pierce, and others were doing. The tainted-money controversy had been in part a product of the reticence surrounding the mission gift. The wide acceptance of Miss Tarbell's "character study" was largely a result of Rockefeller's refusal to countenance any reply to her history of Standard Oil. Along a lengthening front, the policy of silence was responsible for misunderstanding, suspicion, and hatred. So general was the revolt among Rockefeller's associates that Virgil P. Kline and the Standard's diplomatic agent abroad, William H. Libby, had joined Dodd, Rogers, Starr J. Murphy, and others in public replies to Doctor Gladden. Rockefeller knew that his son did not believe in the old policy.

And while replying frigidly to Gates, Rockefeller gave way. He asked Gates to see Archbold; and it turned out that he had sent Gates's letter to the head of the Standard, and had frankly yielded the whole question. The fact that a hostile report by the Bureau of Corporations was pending made protective action seem imperative. Joseph I. C. Clarke, long a staff writer on *The Herald,* a playwright, and a man of wide contacts, was shortly employed by Archbold as publicity agent for the Standard. In his naïve autobiography Clarke tells us that before accepting the modestly paid post ($5000 a year at first, later $6000) he investigated the history of the Standard, and decided that the outcry against it was absurd; that most of the clamor came from men worsted in the battle of business by stronger, more brilliant intellects! With a staff consisting of one stenographer, one office boy, and one man who pasted clippings, Clarke set to work answering every attack on the company. Reporters who had

[27]Gates, MS Autobiography, 385, 386.

once found the door shut in their faces were received with a smile, a cigar, and a funny story. He ate lunch at the directors' table in the large dining room at 26 Broadway; he conferred frequently with Archbold, a "blackheaded bunch of human dynamite," and the erect, haughty Rogers. Before long he became blindly devoted, for he even convinced himself that Archbold's political letters as published by Hearst contained nothing improper.[28]

From the time of this tainted-money battle the Standard ceased to accept passively all the attacks rained upon its head; it struck back. *The Nation's* review of Miss Tarbell's *Standard Oil,* indicting the book as sensational, misleading, and ill-informed, was reprinted and scattered broadcast. Articles friendly to the combination and to Rockefeller blossomed out more frequently in important periodicals. For example, when F. S. Barde published in *The Outlook* in 1905 an attack on the Standard's tactics in Kansas, John J. McLaurin countered with a long essay which he presented as what the Standard thought a "fair and unprejudiced" statement of facts. This emphasized the herculean efforts of the Standard to provide facilities for the torrential flow in Kansas, denied any unfairness toward independent producers or refiners, and asserted that the company had no responsibility for the rise in freight rates.[29] *The Cosmopolitan* published a friendly interview, "John D. Rockefeller on Opportunity in America," and an article by Alfred Henry Lewis which included a full quotation from Ledger A.[30] A staff writer of *The Woman's Home Companion* explained "How the World's Richest Man Spends Christmas," while Archbold presented a long defensive article in *The Saturday Evening Post.*[31] Harold J. Howland contributed to *The Outlook* in the fall of 1907 an impressive exposition of the Standard's might, intelligence, and efficiency. That same year Gates made a public statement, perfectly accurate, though it met with much jesting and incredulity, that Rockefeller's fortune was less than $300,000,000—"only three hundred, poor man!" said people. And in 1909 wide publicity was given to a list of his larger public benefactions, amounting to more than $112,000,000.

[28]Joseph I. C. Clarke, *My Life and Memories,* Chapter XXXVII.
[29]For Barde's article see *Outlook,* LXXX, 19-32 (1905); for McLaurin's, LXXX, 427-431. The periodical literature on the Kansas situation is enormous.
[30]*Cosmopolitan,* XLIII, 368-372 (1907); XLV, 610-621 (1908).
[31]*Woman's Home Companion,* December, 1905.

Meanwhile, a well-promoted circulation was attained by Gilbert Holland Montague's 150-page volume, *The Rise and Progress of the Standard Oil Company,* first issued in book form in 1903. The Standard had nothing to do with its preparation, though it unquestionably aided in its distribution. Montague, as Ricardo Scholar in Economics at Harvard, had used the Hepburn and other investigations to prepare two long articles for *The Quarterly Journal of Economics* on Standard Oil History, which were reprinted unchanged.[32] But antedating Miss Tarbell's book, his exposition of the rise of the Standard differed widely from hers. Montague found the principal secret of the trust's supremacy not in lawless and immoral acts, but in superior efficiency. Conditions in the industry, he declared, had made a march toward monopoly inevitable. "If the Standard Oil Company were not the largest refiner, its most powerful rival would certainly have seized the same control over transportation that the Standard Oil Company in fact secured." He attributed the huge profits of the Standard to its enormous economies in transportation and manufacture, while he reached the comforting conclusion that after all the combination was no monopoly, no omnipotent monster. "The power of the Standard Oil Company is tremendous, but it is only such power as naturally accrues to so large an aggregation of capital; and in the persistence with which competition against it has continued, in the quickness with which that competition increases when opportunity for profit under existing prices appears, and in the ever-present possibility of competition which meets the Standard Oil Company in the direction of every part of its policy, lie the safeguards against the abuse of this great power."

Pre-eminent among the magazines which printed material favorable to Rockefeller was *The World's Work,* whose editor, Walter Hines Page, was one of the truest liberals in the country. The issue for September, 1908, contained a long article by F. N. Doubleday, a shrewd observer, entitled "Some Impressions of John D. Rockefeller." For years, wrote Doubleday, he had heard of Rockefeller as an ogre. Then he met the man; and "I confess I found him exactly the reverse of what my reading had led me to expect, and

[32]Preface to Montague's book. The Rockefeller Papers contain an interview with him by Mr. W. O. Inglis.

my experience created the desire to try to convey the impression I had received to others." At some length the publisher described Rockefeller's benefactions, his personal kindliness, his methods of work, and his sense of humor. The way in which the magnate had been lynched by mob opinion in America struck him as remarkably like the way in which Dreyfus had been lynched by French hysteria. This same year *The World's Work* published two articles by C. M. Keys on the Standard Oil, both favorable, in a series on great corporations. And in October, 1908, it began issuing Rockefeller's recollections, brought out the following year in book form.

These reminiscences attracted international attention. "La defense d'un milliardaire" was the heading the Paris *Temps* put over its summary of the first installment by "le roi des petroles"; "Wenn Milliardaire Bücher Schreiben" was the caption in the Leipziger *Neueste Nachrichten.* Simultaneous publication of the *Random Reminiscences of Men and Events* was arranged in England, Germany, France, Italy, and other nations. In composing this rambling, informal volume Rockefeller had the literary assistance of Starr J. Murphy. It contained the fullest account the world had yet seen of his early business career, written with sparkle and human interest; a few episodes from his later business career—for example, some account of L. M. Bowers and the lake shipping venture; an outline of the principles upon which he had acted in business; two chapters on the difficult art of giving wisely; and a pleasing description of his recreations in landscape-gardening and forestry. The book encountered a mixed reception. But, published with well-selected illustrations, it was widely read, and did more to make Rockefeller a human figure than tons of Sunday supplement articles. William James had occasion in 1909 to write Rockefeller about a proposed gift for mental hygiene. He added: "I have had much pleasure in reading your charming and interesting autobiographical papers, and I trust that you and a certain portion of the public are now feeling much more affectionate toward each other than was ever before the case. This is what I proposed to you many years ago! Expansiveness wins a way where reserve fails."[33]

A not unimportant contribution to Rockefeller's defense was made by William Hoster, who as correspondent of Hearst's New

[33]June 1, 1909; courtesy of Mr. Clifford W. Beers.

York *American* accompanied the millionaire in 1906 to Compiègne. His letters presented Rockefeller in an attractive light, emphasizing his simplicity and quiet strength. Another contribution was made by Thomas A. Edison, who declared in *Pearson's Magazine* that, far from being overpaid for his services, Rockefeller had never been paid half enough. Charles W. Eliot made numerous kindly utterances. Help was lent even by Elbert Hubbard, the famous peddler of success hokum, whose brochure on the Standard Oil in 1910 was a weak reply to the muckrakers. Part of it was in the worst of taste, notably a passage assailing Miss Tarbell. But a little of it had merit, as when he explained the scope which the Standard's organization gave to talent, dilated upon the loyalty of its employees, and pointed out that a great part of the money it earned was brought from abroad and invested in American industry. Equally to the point were his remarks about the change in business ethics since 1885, and the impropriety of trying offenses of that period by the standards of twenty years later. "In that year I well recall how the firm for which I worked had a shipment of heavy chemicals arrive on the docks from Liverpool. The goods had not been removed from the lighters before we had bids from three different railroads and two canal-lines to transport the shipments to Buffalo. The reduced bids came in the form of rebates for 'cartage,' 'lighterage,' 'dockage,' or 'commissions.'"

Few elements in the history of American democracy are more distressing than the abusiveness which has always characterized much of our press and our political leadership. The torrent of billingsgate has smitten men great and small. Washington while President was assailed in the foulest terms, while no reader of Sandburg's *Lincoln* can fail to be appalled by the indecent denunciation to which the emancipator was subjected. In this very period Theodore Roosevelt was being attacked as harshly by the conservative press as Rockefeller was denounced by muckraking periodicals. It would be a mistake to take seriously the scum of libel which always floats on the stream of public discussion; but attacks by men like Gladden were more important. They arose, beyond doubt, from two misconceptions. In the first place, such men had swallowed whole the tales of Henry Demarest Lloyd about the Widow Backus, the Buffalo "explosion," and other sensationalized episodes. Gladden would not have attacked Rockefeller harshly as an architect of monopoly, for he knew that the country was full of monopoly; he was attacking Rockefeller because he seemed an oppressor of helpless and struggling individuals. In the second place, they assumed that Rockefeller's philanthropies were taken out of a Standard Oil slushfund, and were distributed in Rockefeller's name to absolve the sins of both. They did not know that his gifts stretched back to his earliest earnings, and had consistently grown with his income. Had Gladden given nearly one tenth of the first $50 he earned to church and charity? It would be interesting to know.

Instances in which a stereotype, completely falsifying the real man, has imposed itself upon public opinion for long periods of time, to be removed only by patient scholarship and slowly increasing knowledge, are too numerous to need illustration. In British history the reputation of Cromwell as a brutal regicide, who himself lusted after tyrannic power, remained substantially unshaken until Carlyle once and forever destroyed it; in American history the reputation of Andrew Johnson as an ignorant, quarrelsome pothouse type of politician persisted until scholars like James Schouler substituted the portrait of one of our few statesmen Presidents. Even great literary men, who possess special advantages for presenting themselves fairly, have been victims of the stereotyped image—as witness Cervantes, Fielding, Boswell, and Poe. Lowell in one of his essays gave public thanks to Austin Dobson for rehabilitating the author of *Tom Jones:* "He has rescued the body of Fielding from beneath the swinish hoofs which were trampling on it as they once trampled the Knight of La Mancha, whom Fielding so heartily admired." Malice, jealousy, hearsay, do their worst with most prominent men, and in a muckraking era they may do great injustice. Partial accounts must be met by impartiality; tradition must be sharply cross-examined until it reluctantly stammers out a confession that it has no evidence for its tales.

With his son and Gates urging him forward, Rockefeller after 1905 began to appear more frequently in the public view. He gave out occasional interviews; he allowed his infrequent speeches, beginning with a talk to the young men's Bible Class of the Fifth Avenue Church, which appeared in the New York *Evening Mail* in the fall of 1906, to be widely republished. It was noted that he never spoke querulously, never once let an indignant or chiding word escape him. He never publicly alluded to any assailant. When badly misquoted in some remarks upon the French people after his return from France in 1906, he gently remarked that he supposed that the reporters had misunderstood what he had said. Actually a copyreader had inserted a misleading caption which was telegraphed broadcast as part of the story. But the New York *Times* commented editorially on his charity and moderation. When he testified in the Federal court in Chicago in 1907, newspapermen were annoyingly pertinacious, but he indulgently commented that he understood their position. "I respect every man who has to work and is trying to get along." Norman Hapgood in *Harper's Weekly* noted to his credit that he had never, during all the muckraking period, made an impatient or denunciatory comment, and never in all his public appearances betrayed any irritation.

But the great body of American public opinion continued bitterly hostile. He was president of the Standard Oil, and the public regarded the Standard Oil as a hateful, corrupting, and predatory organization. Its marketing organization touched everybody, whereas the activities of Morgan and Carnegie affected people only indirectly. Until the monster was slain by the trust-busters, or voluntarily changed its form and its policies, no press agents and no friends could do much to brighten Rockefeller's reputation.

XLVI

Big Stick vs. Standard Oil

B Y THE spring of 1904, when Roosevelt's new Bureau of Corporations produced a report on the Beef Trust which was widely assailed as a whitewashing document, the discussion of monopoly had grown more vigorous than ever. Conferences upon trusts, attended by economists, politicians, and publicists, were frequent.[1] State and national party conventions passed resolutions on the subject. Newspapers and magazines were full of articles. Book after book appeared; some, like George Gunton's *Trusts and the Public* in 1899, and J. H. Bridge's *The Trust, Its Book,* in 1902, favorable to combinations, and some, like John Moody's *The Truth About the Trusts* in 1904, and Richard T. Ely's *Monopolies and Trusts* in 1900, antagonistic. By this time the extreme *laissez-faire* school, as long represented by Mark Hanna and Nelson W. Aldrich, had been driven into the background.[2] The central debate raged between the aggressive group which, under Bryan and LaFollette, demanded extermination,[3] and the school which, with Theodore Roosevelt its principal apostle, called for a combination of destruction and regulation; for breaking up the "bad" trusts, but tolerating the "good" ones.

[1] For example, see printed proceedings of the *Chicago Conference on Trusts* (1900). Most "trusts" were now holding companies.

[2] In 1890 Senator Aldrich offered an amendment to the pending Sherman Antitrust Bill for exempting "combinations or associations made for the purpose of lowering the cost of production" in other ways than by reducing wages. See *U. S. Congress, Bills and Debates Relating to Trusts* (Washington, 1902).

[3] Successive volumes of Bryan's *Commoner Condensed* offer the best means of studying his views on trusts. See also his "A Remedy for Trusts," *Public Opinion,* XXXVIII (1905), 645–648.

555

Seldom in an economic debate have the opposing views been more interestingly related to the background and personalities of the debaters. Rockefeller undoubtedly followed the discussion with deep interest. Bryan's doctrine was distinguished by his emphasis upon simon-pure human emotion instead of dry economic theory, and his over-simplification of the problem. Away with those who saw any good in great industrial combinations! Politically, they were corrupting agencies, subsidizing parties in order to obtain special privilege. Financially, they opened the door to stock-watering and loathsome manipulation. Socially, they crushed deserving small businessmen, and closed the gates of advancement to the rising generation. The eloquent Nebraskan believed they should be attacked on all fronts at once. To smash the rebates on which they thrived, the government should take over the railroads. To lower their prices, tariffs should be abolished on trust-produced articles. Interlocking directorates should be rigidly prohibited. And as his principal measure, a Federal licensing system should be set up for all corporations engaged in interstate commerce which controlled 25 per cent or more of the output of their particular industries—each license dependent upon good behavior.

Thus Bryan would keep business units small, maintain fair competition, and equalize opportunity. LaFollette, who took much the same position, shortly proposed that control of 40 per cent of any business should be treated as proof of unreasonable restraint of trade. And William E. Borah decried any idea of merely regulating monopolies: "Whenever you establish that condition in this republic you establish two classes, those who have property and those who have none, and you tear down the only ladder by which the child born upon the outside can ever raise himself to power on the inside."

But Roosevelt, like Taft after him, did not wish to wrench the hands of the industrial clock back to the centennial year. Although he had gained a smashing victory over the monopolistic holding-company device in the Northern Securities decision, he felt that great possibilities for good inhered in the new "age of combination." It would be realistic, he believed, to accept the fact of powerful business units, to make the most of their enterprise and economies, and to regulate them. Only the pernicious combinations, the tyrannical monopolies, should be dissolved. Wisdom called for new laws to be written in accordance with the facts of the new century. "It is generally useless," he told Congress in his annual message of 1905, "to try to prohibit all restraint on competition, whether this restraint be reasonable or unreasonable, and where it is not useless it is generally hurtful." To pass harshly coercive enactments against all types and forms of combination would merely bring the government into contempt. It was positively immoral, he declared two years later, to keep on the statute books so archaic an antitrust measure "that the law itself provides that its own infraction must be the condition precedent to business success." Roosevelt also refused to accept the Bryan-LaFollette theory that the trusts must be punished with the speed of a lynching party. He warned the nation against haste, and informing Congress in 1906 that he regarded the agitation against trusts as four-fifths wrong, asked for moderation. Failing "to see any immediate and complete solution of all the problems" involved, he was unwilling to rush forward with a cocksure remedy.[4]

Holding these tenets, Roosevelt developed his program for dealing with big business more carefully than his impetuosity of manner indicated. At first his principal specific for its evils was publicity —and the establishment of the Bureau of Corporations in 1903 made possible a truly pitiless publicity. Then he struck at important abuses related to the trust problem; in particular, the Elkins and Hepburn Acts of 1903 and 1906 practically abolished rebating, so fertile of evil. Meanwhile, he was moving toward the principle of controlling and advising big business by Federal commission. His annual message in 1905 spoke of the need for some regulatory agency to be created by Congress, and thereafter he harped upon "direct affirmative action rather than negative prohibitions." He constantly kept in mind the distinction between good and bad combinations, and the importance of protecting the one while destroying the other. In the end he advocated a system of Federal charters for interstate corporations, and suggested that the government be empowered to appoint receivers for all industrial units caught violating the law.

[4]See Roosevelt's annual messages to Congress 1901, 1905, 1906 and 1907, and the inaugural address in 1905. The Roosevelt Memorial Library in New York contains a scrapbook compiled by William Wirt Mills upon Roosevelt and the trust question.

With the help of his attorney generals, Roosevelt applied his distinction between good and bad trusts by prosecuting some twenty-five alleged monopolies.[5] Foremost among these was the great oil monopoly. His letters and speeches show a deep animosity for both the Standard and Rockefeller, whom he mistakenly believed to be in full control. "I never changed my attitude toward the Standard Oil in any shape or way," he told the Clapp Committee. "It antagonized me before my election, when I was getting through my Bureau of Corporations bill, and I then promptly threw down my gauntlet to it. . . ." His confidential epistles show that he lumped Rockefeller with Harriman and Heinze as malefactors of great wealth. And then Roosevelt liked big game. He agreed with the Autocrat of the Breakfast Table: "It is not great to have money, but fine to govern those who have it"—and Rockefeller had more of it than anybody else.

Of Rockefeller's opinion of Roosevelt we know little. He voted for T. R. in 1904, as for Taft in 1908; he tried to avoid any public comment upon the President. During the panic of 1907 he spoke in confidence to a reporter: "The runaway policy of the present Administration can have but one result. It means disaster to the country, financial depression, and chaos." When the reporter published this, he was deeply hurt. "I could have cried for that young man," he said. Roosevelt resented the statement fiercely, and wrote the head of Bryn Mawr that Rockefeller was "giving out interviews denouncing me." But whatever Rockefeller thought of the President personally, his attitude toward the big stick and the antitrust suits was never in doubt. He believed that the monopoly he had created, stabilizing a once chaotic industry, had benefited the country, and that Roosevelt's attacks on it were prejudiced and unfair.[6]

II

In the years 1906–9 the Standard underwent a veritable drumfire of government prosecutions. Law officers all over the land assailed it. Rockefeller and other officers were pursued by subpœna-servers, haled to the witness stand, and threatened with dire pun-

[5]Pringle, *Roosevelt,* 427.
[6]Flynn, *God's Gold,* 428; Joseph Bucklin Bishop, *Theodore Roosevelt and His Times,* II, 44; John D. Rockefeller, Jr., to the author.

ishment. A Federal judge stepped into the limelight with a $29,-240,000 fine. By midsummer of 1907 the national government had seven suits pending against the Standard and its various subsidiaries, while others were being pushed by Texas, Minnesota, Missouri, Tennessee, Ohio, and Mississippi. The "trust" had a myriad of enemies, and hardly a single friend. It is true that all these prosecutions were but a part of the general trust-busting campaign of the period, and that Roosevelt also inspired suits against the tobacco combination, fertilizer combination, powder combination, and others, while the Interstate Commerce Commission investigated Harriman's great railroad combination with manifest hostility. It is true that the disclosures of the New York insurance investigation in 1905, and the discovery that the sugar trust had robbed the government of millions in customs duties by false weights, did as much to shock public opinion as any charges of monopoly. But Rockefeller felt that the Standard was made a particular scapegoat, and agreed with James J. Hill's hot condemnation of the forays of "political adventurers."

The government's pitiless publicity for the Standard began in 1906. On May 2 the Bureau of Corporations filed a report on the transportation of petroleum which had been apprehensively awaited by Standard executives.[7] Rockefeller knew of their eager interest and doubtless saw an early copy, though later that month he sailed for France. The government published a crisp, readable summary in the Monday morning newspapers, where it caught the attention of the whole country.

This report was focussed upon the long-standing alliance of the Standard with various railroads, and the special advantages it gained from them. But it also gave attention to a number of interesting related subjects—crude-oil production, pipe lines, refining, the distribution of products, competitive methods, and foreign trade. The total effect was an impressive indictment of the Standard as a monopoly resting primarily upon transportation privileges. The fact was established that the combination refined a good deal more than four fifths of all the oil manufactured in the country, this

[7]*Report on the Transportation of Petroleum*, May 2, 1906, xxvii and 512 ff. The author has profited from a careful "History of the Bureau of Corporations" in manuscript, by Philmore Groissier.

giving it unquestioned price control. Emphasis was laid on its ownership of practically all pipe-line transportation in the Appalachian, Lima-Indiana, and Mid-Continent fields, the three areas which up to that date had furnished nearly all the American crude. It was shown that the largest Standard plants were situated at or near the great centers of distribution, and received their crude oil by pipe. Independent plants, on the other hand, were for the most part situated in or near the crude-oil fields, and therefore sold their wares at a disadvantage. The Bureau admitted that the combination owed much to the consummate ability of its officers. But it also owed a great deal to "discriminations in freight rates, both published and secret, interstate and State, which give the Standard monopolistic control in the greater portion of the country, and which so limit competition as to practically prevent the extension of the business of any independent to a point which even remotely endangers the supremacy of the Standard."[8]

Specifically, the Bureau made two basic charges with respect to the Standard's position in the transportation field. The first was that it had habitually obtained, and was then receiving, *secret* rebates and other illegal discriminations from the railroads. The second was that it also obtained unjust *open* discriminations in rates.

Both charges were supported by detailed evidence. In 1904, declared the Bureau, the Standard had saved not less than $750,000 by secret rebating, and these discriminations were by no means few and accidental. Instead, they had been "so long-continued, so secret, so ingeniously applied to new conditions of trade, and so large in amount as to make it certain" that the Standard and the railroads had concerted them.[9] As for the open rates, some of them were glaringly unjust. Independent refiners had been shut out of the New England area for a decade because the New York, New Haven & Hartford and the Boston & Maine had refused to join in prorating oil (that is, giving through rates on it) which came from west of the Hudson. The Standard meanwhile reached New England points easily by its superior water facilities. In New York State, the Standard received special rates on various railroads from its Olean refinery. It controlled the whole vast section south of the Ohio River through a combination of secret rates and open discrimina-

---

[8] *Report*, xx.   [9] *Ibid.*, xxi.

tions from its great Whiting refinery. Similarly, discriminating open rates on crude oil in the Mid-Continent area gave it a decisive advantage over the independent Kansas refineries. On the oil it shipped from California it had received rebates amounting to $100,000 in 1904.

This report, a telling blow at the Standard, and a most effective stroke in favor of new railroad legislation, was given prominence in newspapers from the Atlantic to the Pacific. President Roosevelt underlined its meaning by a scathing message of transmittal to Congress, in which he roundly denounced the Standard's activities. The heads of the company immediately issued a flat denial of all the charges. While M. F. Elliott, counsel for the Standard, criticized the government for a one-sided exploitation of hostile data, ignoring a mass of friendly evidence, Archbold and Rogers joined in declaring that the Standard had co-operated fully with the Bureau, which was true, and that the report was hasty and partial. "We say flatly that any assertion that the Standard has been or is now engaged in practices which are unlawful is both untruthful and unjust."[10] They were supported in these denials by various railroad heads, including President W. H. Newman of the New York Central, President Tuttle of the Boston & Maine, and Vice-President Thayer of the Pennsylvania.[11] When the two latter accused the Bureau of "absolute misstatement of facts," and "outrageous perversion of the facts," its head, Garfield, replied in a long letter of May 16 to President Roosevelt.[12]

This wordy war over the question whether the Standard had been accepting rebates involved such intricate technicalities in rate-making that a full discussion is impossible. But it is clear that the main charges were valid. Archbold and Rogers declared that when the New England railroads refused to pro-rate, they were simply doing what long-recognized natural conditions forced them to do. To this Tuttle added that the Boston & Maine actually *was* pro-rating. Thayer of the Pennsylvania declared that the "secret rates" on Olean shipments were not secret at all, but open. The Standard, pointing

[10]N. Y. *World*, May 5, 1906.
[11]See statements in N. Y. *World*, May 5, 6, 1906; *Wall Street Journal*, May 7, 1906.
[12]*The Railway World*, January, 1908, spoke of the report as reaching "the nether depths of baseless and unfair misrepresentation."

out that its real transportation strength lay in its immense pipe-line system, on which it claimed to have spent $50,000,000, asked: "Are we to have no advantages because we construct these pipe lines?" Possibly at some points the Bureau's indictment was over-drawn. Having been fiercely assailed for treating the "beef trust" too gently, Garfield may have determined to make his second re-port sternly uncompromising. But public opinion pronounced an unequivocal judgment in his favor. Even *The Wall Street Journal* declared that "Commissioner Garfield, whose report on the beef trust was regarded as playing into the hands of that monopoly, has squared himself by his courageous criticism of the Standard Oil."[13] Most of the evidence spoke for itself. Roosevelt shortly delivered a speech on the trust question full of fiery denunciation; and the report, as he had planned, helped to batter a path for the Hepburn Rate Bill that summer.

It is significant that even while the Standard and the railroads denied Garfield's main assertions, they took action to cancel most of the rates which he had condemned. In submitting his report, Garfield was able to assert that most of the secret rates and some of the open discriminations "were abolished by the railroads shortly after discovery," and furnished a long list of these rate-changes. The New Haven, for example, began to pro-rate on oil, thus saving about eight cents a hundredweight to independent refiners of Penn-sylvania and Ohio who were shipping into New England. The published rates on oil shipments from Whiting to points in Michi-gan and northern Indiana were advanced by two or three cents a hundredweight. In California secret rates were abolished, and dis-criminations adjusted. But despite these changes, Garfield reported that enough rate-favoritism remained to keep the independents at a disadvantage, and the President emphasized this in his public utterances. In response, the Senate swiftly passed the Knox Bill giving the Interstate Commerce Commission jurisdiction over the pipe lines as common carriers, and these provisions shortly became part of the Hepburn Act. With the threat of indictments hanging over their heads, the Standard and the railroads continued to make fairer rate adjustments.

Great was the rejoicing among independent producers and re-

[13]May 7, 1906.

finers all over the land. By scores they wrote in to congratulate Garfield, and jubilantly assured him that for the first time in many years they were getting equality of treatment from the nation's transportation lines.

III

Meanwhile, the suit of Attorney-General Hadley in Missouri to prove that the Standard of Indiana, the Waters-Pierce Company, and the Republic Oil Company were parts of one monopolistic combination was filling a vast amount of newspaper space. Overwhelming testimony was brought out during 1905 that these companies had a close working arrangement. Then Hadley decided to begin hearings in New York;[14] but of thirty-four subpœnas which he issued in January, 1906, only eight were immediately served. One was for Rockefeller, who could not be found. Newspapermen joined in an excited hunt. Reports were published that he was hiding in New York, at Lakewood, N. J., in Europe—even that he was cruising in South American waters with H. H. Rogers's son. Finally the hue and cry was given up in March, when other officers furnished all the needed information, and explained that he had no active touch with the business. It then became known that he had been in New York or at Lakewood all the time.[15] Archbold, William Rockefeller, the two Tilfords, and Rogers were finally brought to the stand, but they made most unwilling and obstructive witnesses. The exhibition given by H. H. Rogers was particularly outrageous. He admitted that he was a director of the Standard of Indiana, but that was all.

"Are you familiar with the business of the company you are a director of?" Hadley demanded.

"I know it's in the oil business, but I'm not familiar with the details," Rogers replied.

"You feel reasonably confident it's in the oil business?"

"I judge so from what I've heard," flippantly returned Rogers.

[14]218 *Missouri Reports*, 8. N. Y. *Herald*, Jan. 6, 1906; N. Y. *Tribune*, Jan. 13, Feb. 13, March 8, 1906.

[15]N. Y. *Herald, Tribune, Evening Post*, Jan.–March, 1906. Hadley magnanimously announced, when told that Rockefeller wished to see a grandson born in New York: "If Mr. Rockefeller wishes to hold his grandson in his arms I will declare a truce and allow him to come over from New Jersey without interference."

And as Hadley pressed him to say more about his knowledge of the business, he exclaimed:

"I may modestly say that I am familiar with dividends when they are declared!"

Rogers's manner added insult to his stubborn refusal to furnish information; for as he declined to answer each question, he rose with dignity, made a bow to the Commissioner, and suavely murmured that he regretted to remain silent "by advice of counsel." Hadley methodically had each question certified to the Supreme Court of New York for a ruling. And gradually the persistent attorney general made progress. Armed with new rulings by the New York and Missouri courts, he soon brought Rogers back in a more submissive mood.[16] Representatives of the Standard were compelled to admit ownership of the three companies "in trust," and H. M. Tilford, with incredible professions of ignorance, reluctantly furnished some facts as to the working arrangements of the group. When Hadley closed the New York hearings on March 26, 1906, he had proved that the Standard not only owned a great part of the Waters-Pierce stock, but enjoyed ample opportunities to influence the Waters-Pierce management. And in September Pierce himself was put on the stand in St. Louis. The way was plainly being paved for a court decree which would break up this Standard Oil combination in Missouri, and impose heavy penalties on the participants.

New storms were bursting about the Standard throughout the summer and fall of 1906. The ink was hardly dry on Roosevelt's signature to the Hepburn Act and Attorney-General Hadley had hardly returned to his Missouri office when Rockefeller left on the *Deutschland,* accompanied by Doctor Biggar, to visit Mrs. Strong's bedside. Within a few weeks he had settled in Compiègne, riding his bicycle up and down the main street, strolling with his granddaughter, and chatting through an interpreter with the inhabitants. But news was cabled in July that an indictment had been handed down in Ohio against him and other officers of the Standard of Ohio for violation of the State antitrust law; that the Interstate Commerce Commission was on the warpath against the combination; and that trouble of the gravest character was brewing in Texas.

Despite his daughter's illness, Rockefeller enjoyed his stay in

[16]New York newspapers, March 25, 1906.

Compiègne. He chatted frankly with William Hoster, who was struck by his interest in hygiene, and the enthusiasm with which he talked of diet, exercise, sleep, and drugs. "Beyond question in prime physical condition now for a man of his years," wrote Hoster, "the King of Petroleum neglects not the smallest detail to preserve his condition unchanged." Hoster asked him if he had ever studied medicine. "No," Rockefeller replied, with a humorous side-glance at Doctor Biggar. "Not much. But I have studied doctors." Rockefeller liked to question the townsfolk—peasants, fishermen, dock laborers, market women, and shopkeepers—upon homely matters like the cost of living, their income and savings, their clothing and food. To beggars he was adamant. Writes Hoster:[17]

A ragged, barefooted urchin approached and held out his hand. The appeal was unmistakable. Rockefeller looked at the lad steadily, but made no response. The boy continued to hold out his hand. At length a bystander interfered.

"Don't you see," he said, speaking in French, "that there will be no penny? Have you no self-respect? Go away."

The boy slunk off.

"What did you say to him?" asked Rockefeller.

"I asked him if he had no self-respect," said the bystander.

"That was fine!" exclaimed the richest man in the world. "Self-respect—that's it! That's the way we make citizens out of the immigrants who come to our country."

Hoster expostulated with Rockefeller because of his inaccessibility to newspapermen who could do something to soften the harsh public judgment upon him and his work. "It is your own fault, Mr. Rockefeller," he complained. "You refuse to see reporters or to make known your side of the case." And Rockefeller was half-acquiescent. "So it's all my fault," he said, looking quizzically at Hoster. "Well, perhaps it is." Nevertheless, he refused to let Hoster print an interview. "I cannot break a rule of fifty years' standing," he declared.[18] "A man is judged by his acts more than by his views and opinions, and so do I wish to be viewed."

Yet he was glad to have Hoster publish some *obiter dicta* that when pieced together were as good as a formal interview. A friend came to Compiègne to ask money for a certain charity. "I am not

[17]N. Y. *American*, June 23, 1906. Rockefeller took a deep interest in learning all about Joan of Arc while at Compiègne.

[18]N. Y. *American*, July 30, 1906.

a beggar," he said apologetically in opening the conversation. "Stop right there," exclaimed Rockefeller. "I am a beggar, and proud of it. In my time I have collected millions of dollars, I suppose, for

Rockefeller's new attitude toward the public.

His bland self-defense portrayed by the cartoonist of the Indianapolis *News,* November 23, 1908.

charitable purposes, and I am as proud of my success in that line as I am of anything in my career. I would have made a good preacher had I been a better man!" Again, he told Doctor Biggar: "Capital and labor are both wild forces which require intelligent legislation to hold them in restriction." To the mayor of Compiègne, on whom he called with a gift for the poor fund, he said: "You must know that I am not nearly so rich as the newspapers have represented me to be. It is foolish for any one to believe that any man in the United States is worth a billion dollars. I am not worth one third of that amount." And he added, with feeling: "I have been credited with owning all the banks, trust companies, insurance companies, and railroads in the United States. The fact is that I do not control a single concern of that kind—and never did, except a small railroad in the West." He spoke with pride of the cordial relations between the Standard and labor.[19]

And when he returned to the United States in midsummer, leaving his daughter desperately ill, he showed that he had learned something from Hoster. To reporters in New York he made a statement which indicated that he was anxious to be better understood. Europe was very pleasant, he added, but despite the abuse which he continually met he liked the United States better. In Cleveland he gave another interview which was interpreted as an abandonment of his policy of seclusion. "I hope the time will come when some of the people will know others of the people better," he said. "You newspaper men can do much toward making some of us better acquainted with the others." His conciliatory attitude amazed many observers. "Oil King Acts Like Political Candidate," ran one headline.[20]

The clouds had thickened ominously while he was abroad. On June 22 Attorney-General Moody had announced that the government would prosecute the Standard Oil with all its might, and that every possible case against it would be brought to trial. The subject had been discussed at a mysterious night meeting in the White House, when all the lawyers among the President's advisers conferred with him. It was the principal subject again at a regular Cabinet meeting, where according to press reports it was considered for three hours in all its phases.[21]

One of Rockefeller's first acts after his return was to enter a plea of "Not Guilty" in the Ohio conspiracy suit. When reporters asked if he did not consider the warrant a joke he hastened to show that he had more respect than Rogers for judicial process. "Oh, no, by no means a joke, but I certainly think it will not amount to anything when the case comes to trial." Then in September came news that a suit had been filed in Texas to oust the Waters-Pierce Com-

[19]*Ibid.*   [20]New York and Cleveland papers, Aug. 5, 1906.
[21]N. Y. *Times,* June 23, 1906.

pany, and to fine it more than $5,000,000 as part of the Standard
Oil monopoly, this prosecution being a natural outgrowth of the
Missouri case. Special interest attached to rumors that an "unholy
alliance" between Senator Joe Bailey and the Standard interests
would be exposed. And in November a shower of blows fell upon
Rockefeller and the corporation. Within three days that month he
learned that his daughter had died in France; that a grand jury
in Ohio had found another indictment against him; and that Attorney-General Bonaparte, acting through Special Counsel Frank
B. Kellogg, had begun a prosecution of the Standard of New Jersey
under the Sherman Anti-Trust Act. At about the same time it was
announced that the Standard of Indiana had been indicted for
accepting rebates in violation of the Elkins Act.[22]

Of all these attacks, the suit to dissolve the Standard under the
Sherman Act, filed November 18 in the Circuit Court of Missouri,
was the most important. The defendants named were the Standard
of New Jersey, the sixty-five or more corporations which it was
alleged to control, and seven individuals—the two Rockefellers,
Flagler, Payne, Archbold, Rogers, and Pratt. The charges had the
broadest character. Rockefeller and his partners, they declared, had
conspired at an early date to control the oil industry through
restraints upon interstate commerce. The trust agreements of 1879
and 1892, the evasion for seven years of the Ohio dissolution decree
of 1892, and the erection of the New Jersey holding company in
1899, had been successive milestones in the history of a brazen
monopoly. The government charged that the Standard had gained
its dominant position not by superior efficiency, but by unfair and
immoral acts—rebate-taking, local price-cutting, operation of bogus
"independents," improper control of pipe lines, and so on.

Thus opened the greatest antitrust case in American history. It
was plain that the time was now at hand when it would be decided
whether the great Standard Oil combination or the Department
of Justice was the stronger. Early in 1907, the Interstate Commerce
Commission published a fierce indictment of Standard methods.[23]

[22]See Philadelphia *Press,* Nov. 16, 1906, for this series of blows.
[23]This was a report, sent to Congress Jan. 28, of investigations under the
Tillman-Gillespie resolution of March, 1906. The I. C. C. accused the Standard of accepting secret railroad rates; maintaining a system of espionage over
competitors; setting up fake independents; and unjust local price-slashing. See
summaries in N. Y. newspapers, Jan. 29, 1907.

The Roosevelt administration, the officials of a dozen States, and the great majority of the American people had decided that the combination was a pernicious monopoly and must be broken up. By evasion and obstruction, it might postpone the decision—but not for long. Beyond the act of dissolution the government did not look; it did not inquire whether it would be effective or ineffective, its results good or bad. But as once in their history the American people had said they were tired of kings, as later they said they were tired of slavery, so now they were tired of flagrant monopolies. They would suffer them no more.[24]

"Darkest Abyssinia," declared Archbold later,[25] "never saw anything like the course of treatment which we experienced at the hands of the Administration." But the American electorate stood behind the Administration, and the handwriting was plain on the wall.

IV

The first of several heavy shocks which the Standard sustained in 1907 was the report of May 20 by the Bureau of Corporations upon the position of the company in the oil industry—a document which arraigned the Standard as an unabashed violator of Federal and State laws.[26]

In 400 pages, the Bureau undertook to prove that the Standard held absolute dominance in the oil industry of the land. It showed that during 1904 the combination had refined more than 84 per cent of the crude oil treated in America; that it had produced more than 86 per cent of the country's illuminating oil; that it held 86 per cent of the export trade in illuminants; that its pipe lines transported nearly 90 per cent of the crude oil of the older fields, and 98 per cent of the Kansas crude; and that it controlled more than 88 per cent of the sales of illuminating oil to American retailers. The only competitors in 1904 had been about seventy-five small refineries, whose total consumption of crude did not equal

[24]Even the London *Times*, Nov. 17, 1906, expressed warm approval of "the courageous manner in which the President is tackling what Americans believe to be the greatest, the most pernicious, and most strongly entrenched of all the oppressive trusts."

[25]Clapp Investigation, I, 133.

[26]*Report on the Petroleum Industry,. Part I: Position of the Standard Oil Company in the Petroleum Industry*, May 20, 1907, xxi and 396 ff.

that of its Bayonne plant! About one fifth of these independents drew their oil through Standard pipe lines, and were capable of little effective competition. The Standard's vast system of pipes had but one noteworthy competitor, the Pure Oil Company, and its business was not one twentieth that of the Standard.

How was this almost absolute sway over a vast industry maintained? Not by ownership of the sources of supply, for in 1905 hardly one sixtieth of the total production of crude oil came from wells owned by the Standard. The key factor was domination of transportation in one form or another. A widely ramified system of railroad discriminations had enabled the combination to control the gap between the refinery and the consumer. Ownership of the great 40,000-mile pipe-line system gave it control over the gap between oil well and refiner. Every attempt to lay a competing pipe line had been bitterly opposed. By vexatious litigation, by pre-emption of the right of way, by the aid of railroads, by buying up crude oil in the limited areas reached by new pipes, the Standard had been able to prevent the rise of any formidable competitor.[27] Its comprehensive pipe-line system had also given it a strategic position for its refineries near the largest distributing and exporting centers. Apart from transportation, the Standard was assisted in holding a monopolistic position by its huge and efficient marketing machinery and its unfair prices:[28]

It uses very generally the bulk system of delivery to retail dealers by tank wagons—a cheaper, safer, and far more convenient method of delivery than by barrels. This not only reduces the cost of marketing greatly, but also has eliminated largely the jobber from the business. Dealing thus directly with the retailer, the Standard is enabled to arrange such local price differences as it may desire for the purpose of destroying local competition, without disturbing its prices over any large section of its trade. The tank wagon system of the Standard is as complete as its system in other branches. The Bureau received returns on this subject from over 5300 retail dealers throughout the country. Of the towns in which tank-wagon deliveries were reported, such deliveries were made by the Standard in over 97 per cent.

The Bureau called attention to the failure of the Standard pipe lines to comply with the Hepburn Act. Though they were required to file rate-schedules, some of the most important lines had not

[27]*Report,* xviii, xix.   [28]*Report,* xix, xx.

done so at all, while others had offered only a partial and evasive compliance. Having prevented the rise of independent pipe lines, wrote Commissioner Smith, the Standard now plainly intended to nullify the common-carrier requirements of the new rate law. In his letter of transmittal, Smith assailed the monopolistic character of the Standard in sweeping terms.[29] His conclusions were a direct call for prosecution under the Sherman Act:

In brief, the history and present operation of these Standard interests show throughout the past thirty-five years a substantial monopolization of the petroleum industry of the country, a deliberate destruction of competition, and a consequent control of that industry, by less than a dozen men, who have reaped enormous profits therefrom. The commercial efficiency of the Standard, while very great, has been consistently directed, not at reducing prices to the public, and thus maintaining its predominant position through superior service, but rather at crippling existing rivals and preventing the rise of new ones by vexatious and oppressive attacks upon them, and by securing for itself most unfair and wide-reaching discriminations in transportation facilities and rates, both by railroad and by pipe-line, while refusing such facilities as far as possible to all competitors.

On the heels of this report came the decisions in the Missouri and Texas cases against affiliates of the Standard Oil. On May 24, the findings of the commissioner appointed to collect testimony in the Missouri suit were presented to the court. He had compressed into a moderate-sized volume the principal facts gained from more than 3000 printed pages of testimony. The commissioner found the three accused companies guilty of an illegal agreement to lessen competition, control prices, and deceive the public by posing as independents. He recommended that the charter of the Waters-Pierce Company be rescinded, that the other two companies be forbidden to do business in Missouri, and that each be fined $50,000.

Throughout the West a burst of applause greeted this report. Naturally the three companies hastened to publish vehement protests and to file a long list of exceptions. But though the Standard of Indiana and the Republic carried the case up to the Federal Supreme Court, their ouster from Missouri was affirmed.[30] In view

---

[29]The Wall Street column of the N. Y. *Tribune*, May 21, 1907, remarked that in view of the prodigious strength of the Standard, "Wall Street considers with something akin to dismay the 'nerve' of the President in investigating it."

[30]See 218, *Missouri Supreme Court*, October term, 1908, for verdict; 224 *U. S. Reports*, 270, for affirmation.

of the fact that the Waters-Pierce Company had its entire corporate life in Missouri, and that extinction of its charter would gravely injure minority stockholders who had protested against the illegal acts, it was given a special dispensation. The court allowed it till early in 1909 to prove that all connection with the Standard Oil had been terminated.

The Texas case provided more fireworks. At the outset it, too, had been a simple ouster suit, for Hadley's evidence showed that the Waters-Pierce Company had been violating the Texas antitrust law. But it quickly took on political complications of the most tempestuous order. Texas officials enlisted the aid of a disgruntled former secretary of Waters-Pierce. It soon appeared that he had taken from the company files certain important documents, which tended to show that Joseph W. Bailey had been a tool of the Standard. Late in 1906 the Texas attorney general served notice on the Waters-Pierce offices to produce the correspondence between counsel for the Waters-Pierce Oil Company and Bailey, and various specified vouchers for payments to the latter. At once a burst of rage came from Bailey's supporters, and a burst of cheering from his enemies; the trust fell into the background, and the burning question of the day from the Sabine to the Rio Grande was whether Joe Bailey was an honest man.

Bailey was a spectacular figure, tall, deep-chested, with handsome features, and an organ voice.[31] Immaculately dressed in the style of the old Southern régime, he prided himself on his knowledge of constitutional law, and his alertness as a debater. He had usually taken the progressive side in public affairs, and when Roosevelt compromised on the railroad bill, his scorn had been scorching. Texas was proud of him, as Maine had been proud of James G. Blaine; but like Blaine, he had a weakness for spending money on a grand scale. He had been elected to the House in 1890, was minority leader just before the Spanish War, and in 1901 went to the Senate. Now he was a candidate for re-election. In the House he had learned to know Joe Sibley. He had also become friendly with ex-Governor David R. Francis of Missouri, who was a friend of Henry Clay Pierce. When in 1900 Pierce was looking for assistance in reinstating his company in Texas, Francis had seen that

[31]See Sam Hanna Acheson, *Joe Bailey, The Last Democrat*, 139 ff.

the two men met in St. Louis. Pierce explained that he needed help in what he thought was a perfectly legitimate enterprise. To this Bailey replied that the people of Texas would not and ought not to tolerate the methods of the Standard Oil: "I would rather go back to the tallow candle than do it." This elicited from Pierce so emphatic a denial that his company was any longer part of the Standard Oil combination that Bailey promised his assistance.

"And what will be your fee?" asked Pierce. "This is a political matter," returned Bailey in his grandest manner. "I sell my legal knowledge, but not my influence. There will be no fee." But he and Pierce became so friendly that in order to avoid a forced sale of some Kentucky property, on April 25, 1900, he borrowed $3300 on what purported to be a demand note.

All these facts now came out. By strenuous labor, Bailey partially cleared his reputation—but only partially, and that at the expense of Henry Clay Pierce, who no longer had any. The Senator contended that Pierce had given his word in 1900 that the Waters-Pierce Company was no longer connected with the Standard. He proved that, when he had first learned from the Missouri hearings that Pierce had lied to him, he had demanded an explanation, and had then offered to assist the attorney general in a prosecution. As for the $3300, he argued that the demand note was signed in good faith. He had not the slightest notion that Pierce had put it on the books as a company payment. As a matter of fact, just after his election to the Senate Bailey had borrowed $1700 more. He was left a damaged figure, while public opinion in Texas was more inflamed than ever against Pierce, who was promptly indicted for perjury, and who for more than a year gave Texas a wide berth.[32]

The decision in the ouster suit was what everybody expected. The Waters-Pierce Company was found guilty of violating the antitrust law every day since its re-establishment in 1900; and on June 1, 1907, it was ejected from Texas, and fined $1,623,900. In vain did it appeal to the Federal Supreme Court. The decision was confirmed, and in the spring of 1909 it paid its fine and interest, amounting to more than $1,800,000—officers carrying bills for that amount

[32]S. H. Acheson in his life of Bailey takes the view that he was guiltless of wrongdoing; 230 ff. See also F. U. Adams, *The Waters-Pierce Case in Texas: Battling with a Giant Corporation;* and W. L. Crawford, *Crawford on Baileyism* (1907).

in a suitcase to the State Capitol![33] Before the year ended the property of the company was sold to a friend of Pierce named Fordyce, and soon a new company, the Pierce-Fordyce Oil Association, was running the old Waters-Pierce business in the State. The Southwest was grimly satisfied with this victory over the Standard—and, indeed, to defeat the hardfisted Pierce was a genuine achievement. At once Mississippi sued the Standard for $1,480,000 in penalties under the State antitrust laws.[34]

v

But if the Texas case was spectacular, far more so was one which immediately followed it, bringing Rockefeller himself to the witness stand; the Alton case under the Elkins Act, which Judge Landis's fine made a *cause célèbre*. By this time it had been abundantly proved that the Federal laws against rebating really had teeth. Despite the efforts of Joseph H. Choate, the New York Central had recently been found guilty of giving rebates to the Sugar Trust.[35] It was therefore not a light charge which government prosecutors made in alleging that in 1903–5 the Standard of Indiana had taken rebates on hundreds of carloads of oil shipped from Whiting to East St. Louis over the Chicago & Alton.

The case involved some intricate questions of fact. According to the government, the Standard had paid the Alton but six cents a hundredweight, though the rate-sheet filed with the Interstate Commerce Commission designated eighteen cents as the correct charge. But the Standard replied that nobody ever paid the eighteen-cent rate, which had long been superseded, and that six cents was both customary and reasonable. The company pointed out that from 1891 to 1905 the rate for carrying oil from Chicago to East St. Louis was six cents; that the railroads applied the Chicago rates to all points in the so-called Chicago Switching District; and that Whiting was in this district. The Standard also argued that the Chicago & Eastern Illinois had duly filed with the Interstate Commerce Commission

[33]Philadelphia *Public Ledger*, April 25, 1909; 212 U. S. Reports, 86–112.
[34]Philadelphia *Press*, July 24, 1907; this suit was also to oust the company.
[35]Philadelphia *Press*, N. Y. *Times*, Nov. 16, 1907. The Sugar Trust was fined $300,000, while between October, 1905, and March, 1907, various concerns were assessed $586,000 in penalties.

a six-cent rate from Whiting to East St. Louis; that it could ship over this line as readily as over the Alton; and that it was therefore absurd to deny that the two rates should be the same. Finally, it alleged that the Alton had filed an "application sheet" with the I. C. C. giving notification of the six-cent rate to Whiting. Federal attorneys denied this, and charged that the Standard alone knew of the six-cent rate. To the Standard's assertion that since no other oil company shipped between the two points, discrimination could not exist, the government replied that the special rate had prevented the rise of any competition. The Standard argued that as glycerine was carried between the two points for six cents, and bricks for five, oil ought not to pay more. But, declared the government, the issue was not the reasonableness of the rate, but its discriminatory character.[36]

Kenesaw Mountain Landis, presiding over the trial, had but recently been appointed to the Federal bench. He was a headstrong liberal of forty-one, who had been secretary to Walter Q. Gresham. The Administration did not wish him to insist on Rockefeller's presence in the courtroom, for if the magnate testified he might gain an "immunity bath," which would shield him in the far more important case pending under the Sherman Act. Excessive zeal on the part of Federal inquisitors had thus caused a breakdown of the suit against the beef trust. The attorney general hastily took steps to explain his wishes to Landis. But at the moment Landis was irritated by the difficulties a subpœna-server had met in trying to reach Rockefeller. "I'd do anything in reason to oblige the President," he said in effect, "but Rockefeller is making a monkey out of my process-server, and I'm going to bring him before this court to vindicate its dignity!"[37] And so he did. On a sweltering day in early July Rockefeller and his brother William pushed their way, with the aid of two dozen brawny policemen, through a fiercely curious crowd swirling about the Federal Building in Chicago. They took the elevator to the sixth floor, and there met another throng

[36]I have used the briefs of the Standard Oil attorneys. See also the pamphlet reply, "The Directors of the Standard Oil Company to its Employees and Stockholders," signed by C. M. Pratt, secretary.

[37]Confidential Chicago source. In the beef trust case, the main issue became one of procedure in obtaining evidence; and out of the involved mass of technicalities grew the "immunity bath" decision. See William Z. Ripley, *Railroads: Rates and Regulations,* 550.

so tightly packed that they actually tore the buttons off Rocke-feller's coat. William exploded, as the mob surged about him, "An outrage! I never heard of such treatment." But Rockefeller main-tained his unvarying placidity, and grinned genially at newspaper-men.[38]

For fifteen minutes, with politeness and suavity, Rockefeller told Judge Landis what he did not know about the secrets of the Stand-ard of Indiana. As he had now retired for nearly a decade, and his touch with the Ohio and New Jersey companies had always been far closer than with the Indiana concern, his ignorance was not astounding. While electric fans droned and cameras clicked, the suffocating crowd listened intently. The press reported him "the coolest looking man in the room." Despite the heat, he stayed long enough to take in some sharp impressions. Most of his Chicago attorneys were overawed by the court, and acted cautiously. But a brilliant junior, Moritz Rosenthal, made a terrific assault upon Landis's procedure; and the magnate was so impressed that he in-sisted on retaining the young man for other work of importance, and advanced him on a successful career. When the hearing ended, Washington reported that the Department of Justice was much irritated. Landis, to indulge in a grand-stand play, had given Rocke-feller immunity, under the recently passed Knox Act, from all crim-inal prosecution, while his testimony had been worthless.[39]

On August 3, 1907, the country was startled to read that Judge Landis, following a verdict of guilty by the jury, had fined the Standard of Indiana $29,240,000—assessing the maximum penalty of $20,000 each for the 1462 counts based on as many carloads of oil. Landis's bizarre name, lank form, and Lincolnesque features instantly became famous. The text of his decision, delivered before

[38]N. Y. *Sun,* July 7, 1907. The *Sun* reporter wrote of Rockefeller: "Every motion he made was slow and dignified. His step was slow. His replies to the questions of the court were even slower, some delay being caused when he took time to look at Attorney Miller before answering." Landis put most of the queries, reading from a list in his hand. Pratt, as treasurer of the Standard of New Jersey, was compelled to furnish much financial information. Later, in an attorney's office, Rockefeller said: "It seemed to me a shame that we had to give out all that information." Flagler replied: "Well, John, you know the time has come when we had to give up this policy of 'silence is golden.'" Said Rockefeller: "Well, Henry, it always worked very well when I was in the chair." Charles T. White to the author.

[39]See Philadelphia *Press,* Aug. 4, 1907, for this irritation.

another huge crowd, contained stinging reproaches and accusations, which the audience greeted with uproarious laughter.[40]

This famous fine had a very mixed reception. Half of the newspapers warmly applauded it, though they regretted with the New York *Press* that the Standard would go on robbing the public just the same. But an equally large number of journals criticized the penalty savagely. They called it claptrap, a play to the galleries, a piece of opera bouffe, mere sensationalism, "yellowism in the judiciary." The New York *Times* declared that Landis's decision was not merely very bad law, "but also a manifestation of that spirit of vindictive savagery toward corporations that, until recently, possessed the minds of a large number of the people and of persons in high authority." *The Nation* was acidulous in its comment, *The Outlook* noncommittal, and *The Independent* highly favorable. Attorneys generally were almost stunned, though few of them believed that the fine would ever be collected. Perhaps the most scathing attack on the decision came from *The Railway World:*[41]

> The conclusion of the whole matter is that the Standard Oil Company of Indiana was fined an amount equal to seven or eight times the value of its entire property, because its traffic department did not verify the statement of the Alton rate clerk that the six-cent commodity rate on oil had been properly filed with the Interstate Commerce Commission. There is no evidence, and none was introduced at the trial, that any shipper of oil from the Chicago territory had been interfered with by the eighteen-cent rate, nor that the failure of the Alton to file its six-cent rate had resulted in any discrimination against any independent shipper—we must take this on the word of the Commissioner of Corporations and of Judge Landis. . . .
>
> Under the old criminal law, the theft of property worth more than a shilling was punishable by death. Under the interpretation of the interstate commerce law by Theodore Roosevelt and Judge Kenesaw Landis, a technical error of a traffic official is made the excuse for the confiscation of a vast amount of property.

Rockefeller was not disturbed by the decision. Though every one had known that Landis would begin reading his decision at ten o'clock that morning, he went out to play golf on his Forest Hill estate as usual. It was a cloudy day; "but never mind," he said, "the barometer is going up." A Cleveland newspaperman and one from

[40]N. Y. *Tribune, Sun,* Aug. 4, 1907, describe the scene.
[41]*Railway World,* January, 1908.

Philadelphia were among his guests. His first drive went into a bunker. "It seems to me that golf is a game you have to learn over again every time you play," he said plaintively. The party was half-way down the long nine-hole course when his friends saw a messenger running across the wood-encircled glade. They were more excited than Rockefeller, and eyed the magnate as cats watch a mouse while he unfolded and read the message. Would the game stop? Would Rockefeller indulge in some outburst of indignation? Characteristically, all he said was: "Well, shall we go on, gentlemen?" And he proceeded, with deliberation, to drive 160 yards. At the next hole somebody mustered up courage to ask, "How much is it?" Rockefeller gave the figure, and added: "The maximum penalty, I believe. It is your honor. Will you gentlemen drive?" And, according to *The Plain Dealer,* he finished the nine holes in fifty-three, a good mark for him.[42]

His indifference was wise, for within two years the decision was reversed. The Standard immediately appealed. In August, 1908, Judge Grosscup of the Federal Circuit Court found that Landis had grossly erred, and ordered a retrial. Because Grosscup assailed Landis's procedure in fixing the fine as an "abuse of judicial discretion," the latter refused to sit in the case. Roosevelt, dismayed by this turn of affairs, expressed public apprehension of a miscarriage of justice, and asked the attorney general to call Frank B. Kellogg to the government's aid. But all this was in vain. When the retrial took place, Judge Anderson instructed the jury that "the Government has failed to prove its charge," for the documents it had introduced did not show "that there was a definite fixed rate of eighteen cents." After a verdict of "not guilty," the government paid the costs. Roosevelt was deeply angered, and his feeling that the courts were an obstacle to progress inspired a remarkable message to Congress, full of vehement phrases.[43]

VI

Two days after Landis's fine, the Bureau of Corporations brought out its last excoriation of the Standard in a report on prices and

[42]Cleveland *Plain Dealer,* Aug. 4, 1907. Mark Sullivan in *Our Times,* III, 496, 497, quotes Rockefeller: "Judge Landis will be dead a long while before this fine is paid."

[43]Pringle, *Roosevelt,* 478; Sullivan, *Our Times,* III, 497.

profits in the oil industry.[44] Once more it was released on Monday morning, with a digest giving newspapers its high points. The fact that it had been timed to appear just after the Landis bombshell seemed to Archbold and Rockefeller new proof that Roosevelt was conducting a sinister campaign of persecution. They believed that he was trying to work up a largely artificial fever of public indignation.

It was evident that this report had a special interest to tens of millions of American consumers who used Standard Oil products. Were they paying more than they should? To this question the Bureau uttered an emphatic "Yes." Commissioner Smith assured the nation that when the Standard boasted of its great services in reducing costs, it was deceiving the public. Of course the price of oil had fallen; but the report ascribed the fall in the period 1866–74 to competitive conditions, and in more recent years to automatic factors like the building of pipe lines. It pointed out that the few independents which survived did a profitable business at rates much lower than the average Standard Oil prices.

Commissioner Smith conceded that the Standard possessed much greater efficiency than its rivals, but he added that the difference had been exaggerated. By controlling a huge pipe-line system and handling an enormous volume of oil, it did business more cheaply than any smaller concern. In the local collection of crude oil by pipe line the Standard's operating costs were estimated at not more than 5 cents a barrel, while those of the Pure Oil Company were nearly 8 cents. The Standard saved even more on its operation of the great trunk pipe lines; so that its total advantage in pipe-line transportation came to 31 cents a barrel, or about three fourths of a cent a gallon. It made additional savings by the superior efficiency of its refineries, but none in marketing. The total economies through superior efficiency perhaps reached about 1½ cents on each gallon of oil processed. But Commissioner Smith objected that the Standard did not hand on this saving to the public. According to his detailed figures, it charged the American people a normal competitive profit, plus the cent and a half, plus an additional sum! Five of its largest plants, he declared, had been making an average profit

[44]*Report of the Commissioner of Corporations on the Petroleum Industry, Part II: Prices and Profits;* Aug. 5, 1907.

of 2.3 cents a gallon on refining and marketing alone.[45] The Bureau naturally expatiated upon the high earnings piled up by the Standard, which it computed at $790,000,000 for the years 1882–1906 inclusive.[46] It pointed to the high profits of the Waters-Pierce marketing subsidiary, which reached 47.2 per cent in 1904, and of the Lima and Whiting refineries, which in that year paid 37 and 45 per cent respectively on investment.[47]

Rockefeller had handed over the active management to Archbold in 1897; and the fact stands clear in the report that 1897 marked a sharp change for the worse in the Standard's price policies. According to the Bureau, the profit on the capital of the whole system in 1882–96 (when Rockefeller was in control) had averaged 19 per cent. When it is remembered that the capitalization contained not a cent of water and was indeed understated; when it is recalled that until Frasch succeeded in 1886 in making the Lima production usable the industry was regarded as highly speculative, and even after that embodied elements of unusual risk; when it is considered that a host of American businesses, from country stores up to the Ford plants, have made equal profits over extended periods, and that the exceptional brains and energy of the Standard leaders deserved exceptional rewards, careful observers will hesitate to call this 19 per cent exorbitant. But in 1897 the rate of profit began rising sharply, and in the years 1903–5 reached 68 per cent—which was very exorbitant indeed.

No doubt the sharp turn in 1897–98 from depression to prosperity and the general rise in prices had something to do with the upward trend; but the policy had unquestionably altered for the worse. The Industrial Commission Report shows that the margin between crude-oil prices and prices of illuminants for domestic sale, though subject to many fluctuations, grew generally narrower in the eighties and nineties. The tables of the Bureau of Corporations point to the same fact. But after Rockefeller dropped the helm the margin broadened. From September, 1897, to the end of 1899, it was 5.3 cents a gallon; in 1900–1902 it was 6 cents; from the beginning of

---

[45]*Report,* xxxiv; the five plants were at Lima, Whiting, Sugar Creek, Neodesha, and Florence.

[46]"And possibly much more"; *Report,* xxxii

[47]*Report,* xxxii.

1903 to June, 1905, it was 6.6 cents.[48] Of course this was not all profit, for many charges had to be figured into the margin. But the steady rise in prices was significant. Since this rise coincided with an immense expansion of business resulting from widening of the oil fields and increased use of internal-combustion engines, the result was a colossal, even an egregious, rise in profits.

As to foreign trade, Commissioner Smith reported that the Standard's price policy "has apparently been to sacrifice the interests of the American consumer for the purpose of securing the Standard's foreign business." Particularly had the disparity between foreign and domestic prices become marked in 1902–5. More than half of the illuminating oil produced in the United States was exported, and nearly nine tenths of this was sent out by the Standard. While American prices were sharply advancing in the years 1897–1905, foreign prices were declining. This decline, said the Bureau, was not caused by an oversupply of oil abroad, for the amount of oil produced in foreign countries 1904–5 had actually decreased. The fault lay with the Standard, which had charged monopoly prices at home, while in Europe it had given the Briton, German, and Frenchman the benefit of competitive prices.[49] Here again the aggressive policies of Archbold were plainly responsible.

The price-slashing tactics used by the Standard to stamp out independents in the United States also came in for a well-justified attack. Since the Standard sold most of its kerosene and gasolene directly to retailers by tank-wagons, it could raise or lower prices in one district without disturbing those in another. Where its monopoly was unchallenged, it kept prices firm; elsewhere it cut them according to the rivalry it met. Facts collected from more than 5000 retail dealers near the end of 1904 showed some startling discriminations. For example, the Waters-Pierce Company retailed oil in St. Louis, where it had to face strong independents, for little or no profit, while in Texas it demanded a wholly exorbitant return. In California the Standard transported oil from its great refinery near San Francisco and sold it throughout the southern part of the State for several cents a gallon less than in the Bay area. Even within the same districts, price disparities were often enormous. In south

[48]Prices had reached their peak in 1903, when the Standard had taken advantage of the heavy use of fuel oil following the anthracite strike. *Report,* 11 ff.
[49]This is discussed in great detail in the *Report,* 321–440.

Texas, for example, nine towns in one month showed oil selling at a profit margin below 3 cents, and twenty-one towns at a margin exceeding 6 cents.

Landis's fine and this report on oil prices stung the Standard into issuing a forty-page pamphlet in its own defense. On August 20 postmen deposited copies on editorial desks all over the East, while bundles were scattered broadcast to stockholders and prominent citizens. The brochure reprinted a variety of press comments attacking Landis, and presented reasons for terming the Bureau report "a wholly false deduction from incomplete facts."[50] At the same time, spokesmen at 26 Broadway explained in detail why they believed Commissioner Smith to be prejudiced and inaccurate. Their profits, they argued, had not been excessive, for if all the properties, good will, and managerial capacity of the Standard were capitalized at a proper figure, they would yield only a moderate return. The Bureau was accused also of neglecting many factors of peril and loss. It had said nothing of the risks of carrying stocks of oil paid for, but for which no ready market could be found—and in Kansas alone the Standard had lost millions in falling prices on the huge quantities it had too generously bought. Even when prices were steady, the carrying charges on 30,000,000 or 40,000,000 barrels of stored oil were heavy, while losses by fire, evaporation, and leakage added to the bill. The Standard was building tanks, costing $65,000 to $75,000 each, at the rate of one a day. Its transportation and labor costs, too, were greater than the Bureau had estimated, and were rising fast.[51]

Turning to prices abroad, the Standard admitted that they were lower than in the United States. But this was mainly due to a disparity in quality much greater than Commissioner Smith had indi-cated, amounting to more than 2 cents a gallon instead of one. Moreover, the fierce competition of the Russians and Dutch, with their advantages of geographical position, cheap labor, and govern-

[50]N. Y. *Times, Tribune, World,* Aug. 21, 1907. The pamphlet called the re-port of May, 1906, "a tissue of old representations," intended to influence action on the Hepburn Bill. It asserted that the Landis verdict was obtained "upon the most hair-splitting technicality, aided by the rigorous exclusion of evidence that would have removed all presumption of guilt."

[51]Philadelphia *Press,* N. Y. *Tribune,* and *World,* Aug. 6–30, 1907.

ment aid, made price concession absolutely necessary. Since the United States Steel Corporation and International Harvester Company notoriously sold products at lower prices abroad than at home, why should the Standard not protect its export trade? As for the uneven charges in the United States, "we are not responsible for prices charged by retailers of oil. It will have to be admitted that many retailers do not adjust their prices to correspond with fluctuations in wholesale prices."[52]

No unbiased reader of the Bureau report today can doubt that in essentials its charges were justified; that under Archbold Standard profits were exorbitant, that it made improper concessions to the foreign buyer at the expense of American customers, and that its price-slashing policies were unfair. At certain points Doctor Smith doubtless tried to prove too much. Subsequent inquiries into prices and profits have shown that the subject is full of pitfalls. An investigation by the Twentieth Century Fund showed that in 1937 the standard package of cigarettes cost 3.86 cents to manufacture, while consumers paid an average of 14 cents, not including State and local taxes. Yet this margin was much less preposterous than it seemed. The same organization found that in 1936 New York City motorists paid 17.5 a gallon for gasolene that cost 5.5 cents on the Gulf, plus 1 cent for freight to New York and terminal and processing charges there. Yet it showed that the 11-cent spread could be explained without charges of greed.[53] Commissioner Smith was too quick to ascribe the far slighter spread between kerosene costs and prices in 1897–1907 to Standard Oil extortion. Conservative organs like the New York *Times* and *Wall Street Journal* criticized him sharply. Yet the gravamen of the report was unquestionably justified. Archbold's aggressive policies had rendered the Standard's position much less defensible than under the wiser, more moderate

[52]The Standard, no doubt correctly, accused the government investigators of going to work in a prejudiced spirit. Its spokesmen published (N. Y. *Tribune*, Aug. 13, 1907) a colloquy which had taken place between a Bureau of Corporations agent and an English oil-dealer, in which the agent asked for help in "downing the Standard."

[53]See N. Y. *Times*, Sept. 8, 1939, for editorial on the work of the Twentieth Century Fund upon distribution costs. It found that one type of men's hats that cost $3.74 to make sold for $10 at retail; yet this extreme margin did not necessarily point either to waste or undue profits.

Rockefeller; though it should be added that no evidence appears that Rockefeller, who was still nominally president, ever protested against these aggressive policies.

The two Federal reports of 1907 produced an immediate effect. Independent refiners were soon testifying that the revelations had brought about a substantial improvement in their business. In 1909 Congress practically repealed the retaliatory duty which had shut out imports of petroleum from abroad.

VII

The sharp but brief panic of 1907 was now at hand. Within a fortnight after Landis's fine, prices of stocks began declining in Wall Street, and before September many securities had dropped to alarming levels. Standard Oil, after showing temporary strength, fell rapidly from around 500 to around 420.[54] The primary cause of the relapse lay in a world-wide fever of overexpansion and speculation, based on inflated credits. Numerous Eastern banks and trust companies were in an unsound condition. Promoters like Morgan and Harriman, speculators like Rogers and William Rockefeller, had recklessly overcapitalized various enterprises. Water had been pumped into the United States Steel, the International Mercantile Marine, Western mining properties, and railroads. But the titanic battle between Rockefeller's organization and Roosevelt, accompanied by detailed evidence of lawbreaking and fiery Presidential speeches, had also helped to shake confidence. So careful an observer as the London *Economist* declared on August 31 that Roosevelt's trust-busting policy was contributing to the incipient depression, and that the Standard in especial was being harried too cruelly. "It is difficult to avoid the conclusion that the company is not now receiving what may be called fair treatment in its fight with the government."[55] In October a genuine panic was precipitated by the crash of a combination of banks, copper interests, and other enterprises under two daring gamblers, F. Augustus Heinze and Charles W. Morse, followed by the stunning collapse of the Knicker-

[54]Landis's decision brought a sharp two-day fall in most stocks, but Standard Oil dropped only one point. But on August 9 it fell to 466, the lowest price in eight years. N. Y. *Evening Post,* Aug. 10, 1907.

[55]*The Economist* also denounced the Landis fine as excessive and unreasonable.

bocker Trust Company. By the beginning of November banking facilities throughout the nation were half paralyzed.

Nobody who had observed conditions closely was surprised by the panic. Rockefeller had been warned of it months in advance by his financial adviser, Henry E. Cooper. Before joining the staff, Cooper had devised a statistical compilation which showed the general financial and economic condition of the country, basing it on twelve items which to his mind pointed to a storm; and he felt certain that a sharp reaction was ahead. Rockefeller, following his rule of purchasing on a descending and selling on an ascending market, was then buying Union Pacific stock at every downward quarter point. Cooper told him: "I think your present policy is a mistake. The red flags are waving all along Wall Street. We are headed for a panic as sure as fate. Why not wait for your Union Pacific stock? It is now selling at around 140; mark my words, in a little while you can get it at 100." "No," said Rockefeller, "I have always done my buying according to my fixed rule, and I shall keep on doing it."[56] Union Pacific actually went below 100 when the panic struck; nevertheless, Rockefeller was right in clinging to his principle.

In the steadying measures undertaken immediately after the smash of the Knickerbocker Trust, Rockefeller played an important part. His first step was to make a public statement. "Mr. Gates telephoned me from Montclair," he later recalled, "asking if he could not come up to my home and get some expression of opinion from me which could be published throughout the country and thus relieve the situation. I said there was no need of his coming up; I could manage through the Associated Press. I was still in my bathrobe—Mr. Gates's call had roused me from bed. I called up Melville E. Stone, general manager of the Associated Press, and told him that the credit of the country was all right, and that if necessary, I would give half of all I possessed to restore the balance. That message was published throughout the country next morning." It was followed by a flood of telephone calls to Pocantico, and the reporters at once came out.

"Would you really give half the bonds and securities you own to restore credit?" they asked.

[56]Mr. Henry Elliott Cooper to the author, Nov. 30, 1939.

"Yes," Rockefeller said, "and I have cords of them, gentlemen, cords of them!"[57]

He also made a special trip to 26 Broadway, a gesture—since he had not been seen there for years—which attracted much favorable notice. Meanwhile, the government greatly increased its bank deposits, and offered $150,000,000 in bonds to help provide a basis for additional banknotes. J. P. Morgan, as the leader of large financial interests intent upon stopping the deflation, boldly grappled with the situation; and Rockefeller gladly gave him all the assistance within his power. Calling on October 24 at the Union Trust Company, Rockefeller deposited $10,000,000 to help save the trust companies and other threatened institutions. He then proceeded to Morgan's office to assure him of his readiness to give further assistance.[58]

He also lent money to numerous hard-pressed friends and acquaintances. "They always come to Uncle John when there is trouble," he humorously remarked. Large sums were furnished his brother to help the latter protect his interests, and, doubtless at some sacrifice of pride, William sent Henry E. Cooper a list of securities as coverage. Cooper was not quite satisfied with it, and asked for additional collateral. On hearing of this, Rockefeller gently chided him. "Now, Mr. Cooper," he said, "don't be too rigorous. Remember, William is a very rich man."

While the panic was at its height, Rockefeller was approached for an advance of several millions by a leader in downtown New York who represented to him that an important public situation would suffer if the money were not provided. His name cannot be given, but nearly every one would recognize it. Rockefeller furnished the loan for what he thought the public benefit. Sometime later Cooper received information which convinced him that this man had used the money, not to protect the threatened public situation, but to buy securities in the Street—the Stock Exchange being temporarily closed—at distress prices. He had subsequently resold them for large profits, which he pocketed. Filled with indignation, Cooper took his evidence to Rockefeller, and explaining it to the old gentleman, declared with heat: "You ought to get after him

[57]Rockefeller to W. O. Inglis, Oct. 9, 1917; Rockefeller Papers.
[58]Herbert L. Satterlee, *J. Pierpont Morgan, An Intimate Portrait*, 473 ff.

hard!" But Rockefeller preserved his accustomed equanimity. "No, Mr. Cooper," he said, his voice serene, but his eye more steel-like than usual, "we will do nothing. But we shall not forget it!"[59]

Before the year closed, the panic, essentially a financial rather than industrial disturbance, was history. Its disturbance to business had done something to cripple Roosevelt's power—but the government suit against the Standard was still being pushed with determination. The day of its final disposition was not far distant.

[59]Mr. Cooper to the author, Nov. 30, 1939.

XLVII

The Supreme Court Writes Finis

ARLY in 1908 Rockefeller went to Augusta, Ga., to escape the coldest weather and play golf. On the way down he learned that "Pitchfork" Ben Tillman, who had so often jabbed him metaphorically in the Senate, was on the train, and he introduced himself for a long talk. According to Tillman, he admitted that grave abuses existed in business and should be remedied, but believed that reform might have come "without all this agitation and feeling of distrust." He gave Morgan and himself credit for helping to rescue dozens of banks in the recent panic. "Now that was a pretty nice thing to do, wasn't it?" he inquired. The Senator said that he wished he could arrange an interview between Roosevelt and Rockefeller. He also made a plea for the poor whites of the South, remarking that Northern millionaires who were aiding the Negro so generously might well do as much for the yeomen farmers and mountaineers, "poverty-stricken and illiterate."

Rockefeller seemed responsive to this, and Tillman astonished everybody by giving the reporters some praise of the millionaire: "He is the greatest optimist I have ever met. He gets more sunshine out of life than any man I have seen in a long time."

One newspaper dryly remarked that Rockefeller had a good deal to be optimistic about. But his serenity indeed struck every observer. With only one important anxiety, the growing invalidism of Mrs. Rockefeller, he had arranged his life in a pattern which entirely suited him. An important element in his contentment was his ɪm-plicit confidence in his son, now his principal lieutenant in managing the fortune and planning benefactions. The rarest of bonds united the two men. Their devotion to one another was profound. While Gates was valuable to Rockefeller, the son could be termed invaluable. Gates's remarkable qualities, his creative imagination, shrewd business capacity, and enthusiastic energy, were marred by obvious faults; for he was opinionated, egocentric, and prone to intoxicating himself by his own rhetoric. But the son's gifts of conscientiousness, unselfish public spirit, unresting industry, and practical sagacity were offset by no defects which impaired his father's confidence. When he recommended a course, the elder Rockefeller almost invariably approved.

And the son spared no pains to keep close to Rockefeller. Constantly meeting interesting and important people, he reported his conversations in detail. Receiving a huge mail, he made it a point to show letters of unusual interest to his father. Nothing ever touched their mutual understanding. Even when Rockefeller doubted the wisdom of a course urged by his son, he first demurred and then yielded—he seldom disagreed. "Mr. John is a wonderful man," he used to say to intimates.

The personal office at 26 Broadway was operated efficiently and thoroughly. The son and Gates, aided by Henry E. Cooper from 1907 to 1912, Jerome D. Greene in 1912–14, and Bertram Cutler for a far longer period, managed the huge holdings in railroad, industrial, and banking securities. Meanwhile, they explored avenues of philanthropic activity. Men with good causes came from all parts of the world. Pleas poured in by every mail. The younger Rockefeller had a much greater facility in meeting people than Gates, and went to many more dinners and gatherings. He knew most leading citizens of New York, most prominent educators and social workers in the country, and hundreds of leaders in labor, agriculture, public health, and the church. He rapidly became an expert in many forms of "welfare" work. Although the elder Rockefeller was seventy in 1909, he continued to give protracted labor to his benefactions. His daughter-in-law recalls how frequently he was closeted for hours with his son and how conversant he was with details. Doctors Flexner, Buttrick, Vincent, and others came to dine socially, and he would chat with them about their work. And Gates's friends recall how earnestly he prepared for his meetings with Rockefeller. He worked for days assembling his data on business and philanthropic matters, and emerged from long and rigorous examination in a state of exhaustion.

But Rockefeller had no cares which he could not devolve upon his office—above all, upon his son; and his life was systematic rather than strenuous. It was marked by no expansion of interests. Intellectually he had always been narrow, and he remained so. He evinced no desire to use his wealth, as Carnegie did, to consort with men of mark and power. Knowing that he was not highly cultured, he would have felt something artificial in intimate association with people of purely intellectual tastes. His golf companions were jovial people like Doctor Biggar, Doctor Eaton, and Father Lennon, who told stories amusingly and discussed little beyond current affairs. He did not read much; he did not travel. A more active, disciplined life, mentally and socially, would have benefited him. But those who saw him never doubted that he had a very superior mind, keen, lucid, and masculine, and that it was always busy.

Rockefeller had always been in great degree self-withdrawn. He always kept inner resources of thought and interest. When he spoke, in his slow, measured fashion, he was likely to say something arresting. He always formed his opinions for himself, they showed original insight, and they sometimes pierced to the heart of a subject in a way that startled lesser people. He had the power of looking at persons and situations in a fresh, unhackneyed light, and his independence of books and men kept that power unimpaired. Those who talked with him felt that he constantly approached affairs on new planes, by new angles; that he saw deeper into them than others could; and that the result was an astonishing faculty of *origination*. He carried with him, too, a breath of moral austerity. He had a seriousness which made the character of some ministers who came to the house seem shallow. As the artist, Sargent, said, those who regarded him closely felt: "Here is a man at peace with God." Even at seventy, his personality carried a striking force, a sense of vital power.

II

The press was still filled with a strange mélange of stories favorable and unfavorable. The announcement in May, 1908, that he was giving another $500,000 to the Institute for Medical Research to build its hospital elicited approving comment from doctors; especially as the letter of gift stated that he made the grant "in grateful recognition of the services of Doctor Simon Flexner" as director and as discoverer of a cure for epidemic meningitis.[1] Doctor Flexner's serum, announced a few months earlier, was making it possible to save three patients out of four. The annual reports of the General Education Board showed how much it was doing for Southern farming and education. When Cardinal Logue in June visited the estate of James Butler near Pocantico, Rockefeller took pains to call, was photographed with the prelate, and told reporters that the visit was a memorable occasion. "A very kindly, gracious gentleman," said the Cardinal. Rockefeller's first installment of his autobiography appeared almost simultaneously with the news that the Court of Appeals had set aside Landis's spectacular fine.

More and more frequently, he managed to make a favorable appearance in public. While he was in Augusta, the Cleveland Grays, a military company which he knew well, passed through on their way home from Havana. Rockefeller went down to the station to greet them, filled his car with their suitcases, and was prominent at a barbecue in their honor. The Augusta *Chronicle* printed an editorial praising his part in the reception. When he left the Bon Air Hotel he told a reporter: "I like Augusta because the people here treat me as a human being." Both in Augusta and at Hot Springs, Va., he visited congregations of Negro Baptists—for he always liked Negroes. He received reporters cordially. The result appeared in friendly sketches like that published by the New York *Globe* on May 16, 1908. Rockefeller was not the harsh, irritable man of the cartoons, said the writer, but serene, genial, and companionable. He was also obviously one of the ablest men in the country. "He is taller than the average man and very sturdily built. Every movement is slow, firm, and certain. There is never any frittering, any nervousness. And it is this very substantiality that makes him so impressive."

Clarke was the publicity agent of the Standard—Rockefeller had none. Still, some of Clarke's work benefited the nominal president of the corporation. His hand perhaps appears in the New York *World's* display article of May 10, 1908, on twenty-five years of the Standard Oil, full of praise for the organization and its founder. "One by one," declared the story, "the falsity and exaggeration of

[1]N. Y. *Times,* May 31, 1908.

the charges made by interested rivals and demagogues of every class are being made plain"—a remarkable statement to appear in *The World*. We are tempted to see Clarke's touch again in a statement by Carnegie on his golf matches with Rockefeller. "Our last game was hotly contested," said the Scot. "In fact, we were so excited over some especially good work that we lost count of the score." Carnegie intimated that Rockefeller had taken advantage of this to give himself an extra point! When the General Education Board in 1908 elected Carnegie and President Eliot trustees, and announced a new list of gifts to colleges and universities, the press totted up the accounts of the rival philanthropists. It computed that Carnegie's benefactions exceeded $140,000,000, while Rockefeller still lagged behind with about $110,000,000.

Yet the attacks on Rockefeller were as fierce as ever. Senator La Follette, in a speech against the Aldrich Bill for banking reform, named ninety-three men who he said completely controlled banking, industry, and commerce. Morgan and Rockefeller headed the list, which did not include Carnegie—for Carnegie's retirement, unlike Rockefeller's, was everywhere known. The statement foreshadowed the Pujo or "money trust" investigation of 1912.

One attack actually aroused sympathy for Rockefeller. The New York *World* on February 2, 1908, published a sensational story entitled, "Secret Double Life of Rockefeller's Father Revealed." This purported to show that William Avery Rockefeller had adopted the alias of Doctor William Levingston; that before the Civil War he had married a young woman, Margaret L. Allen, in Ontario; that he had removed with her in 1867 to Illinois, living in several places there; that for many years he had divided his time between a brick cottage in Freeport, Ill., and a 480-acre ranch on the banks of the Park River in Walsh County, N. Dak., not far west of the Minnesota line; that he had died in Freeport on May 11, 1906; and that he was buried there in an unmarked grave. His widow was said to be still living in Freeport. The evidence included alleged photographs of Doctor Levingston, and title-deeds showing that some Dakota land granted to him by the government was later conveyed by William Avery Rockefeller to his son-in-law, Pierson D. Briggs.[2] William Avery Rockefeller certainly owned a ranch in Dakota. But

[2]The Freeport *Standard* assembled some corroborative evidence.

there is no clear proof that he and Doctor Levingston were identical, for the photographs and legal papers are not conclusive. Frank Rockefeller and William Rockefeller's son Percy both issued denials that William Avery Rockefeller was dead, and Frank said that he lived in close retirement to protect himself from cranks. The author has received information from Frank's daughters indicating that the old man died on his Dakota ranch, in the summer of 1909, when he was a hundred. But even this is uncertain, and the mystery surrounding his last days is not likely to be pierced.

Much more important to Rockefeller and the Standard Oil was William Randolph Hearst's great exploit in 1908. That year found the publisher supporting an Independence League Party which had nominated T. L. Hisgen for President. Speaking at Columbus, Ohio, on September 17, Hearst announced that he was going to read certain sensational letters "written by Mr. John D. Archbold, an intimate personal friend of Mr. Rockefeller and Mr. Rogers." He proceeded to regale the crowd with some of those discreditable letters from Archbold to Foraker, Sibley, and Hanna which we have already reviewed. They created a national furor. The press flamed with headlines. In Memphis a fortnight later Hearst read some more correspondence apparently implicating Joe Bailey. At last Archbold was paying the penalty for his unprincipled conduct. Asking Foraker to kill "objectionable" bills and Hanna to defeat a dangerous man, he had simultaneously paid money lavishly in campaign contributions and "legal fees." As the months passed Hearst, publicly thanked by Roosevelt, issued other damaging Standard Oil letters.

It appeared that Archbold had employed at 26 Broadway a Negro, Willie Winkfield, whose fondness for craps kept his pockets always empty. Willie hit on the idea of rifling Archbold's letter-files and selling important epistles to the press. Through a fellow employee, he established relations with the New York *American*. Before long Willie was staying after hours to steal letters and carry them uptown; they were immediately photographed; and early next morning they were restored to the files. Hearst began chuckling over them in 1904. He kept them secret for several years because, in injuring Foraker, Quay, Penrose, and Bailey, they would help Roosevelt—and he detested T. R. When finally brought out they were too belated to be fully effective, and had no influence on the campaign of 1908. Moreover, Hearst did much to spoil their ultimate effect by forging at least five epistles. In 1912 he collected the whole correspondence in *Hearst's Magazine,* with an elaborate commentary from his own pen; and late that year a writer in *Collier's* showed that these five letters, dated between 1898 and 1904, had been written upon a kind of typewriter first placed upon the market in 1905, and had all been given spurious signatures. Four of these forged letters purported to have been sent by Archbold to Quay, Hanna, and Penrose, while one was from Congressman Grosvenor to Archbold. No reason existed for the forgeries, for the publisher had an ample supply of genuine documents; but he could not resist the temptation to gild his lily.

Yet after these facts had been exposed, and after the excuses of Foraker and Bailey had been heard, the letters still profoundly shocked most Americans. With the Clapp Committee material, they strengthened the demand for strict control of campaign funds. They also shocked the Standard organization. Every one recognized their impropriety. One day when the excitement was at its height an officer of the Standard of Indiana entered the quarters of its head, J. A. Moffett. He was busy opening his mail, which he read carefully, tore up, and tossed into the waste-basket. It was well known that he had a memory that instantaneously photographed any document. "Bill," he said to the caller, "wouldn't it have saved a lot of trouble if Archbold had had a letter-file like mine?"[3]

A word should be said about the campaign of 1908. On October 30 Rockefeller innocently announced that he would vote for Taft. At once a roar of delight came from the Democrats, a cry of anguish from the Republicans. Bryan made an exultant speech. Taft declared in Buffalo that he did not want Standard Oil support. Roosevelt issued an angry statement that Rockefeller's announcement "is a perfectly palpable and obvious trick." "This is terrible," ironically exclaimed the New York *Evening Post.*[4] "We never felt the fiendish malignity of the Standard Oil before." It suggested that stringent orders be given election officials not to receive Rockefeller's ballot for Taft. Either Taft's name should be scratched out and that of Bryan substituted, or it should be burned publicly in front of the polling-place!

[3]Doctor William Burton to the author, Nov. 14, 1939.   [4]Oct. 30, 1908.

III

The summer of 1907 had found seven Federal and six State actions pending against the Standard or its subsidiaries.[5] But one suit loomed high above all others in importance: the suit begun in the

From the cartoon by Berryman in the Washington "Evening Star."

Rockefeller announces his support of Taft, 1908.

Federal Circuit Court of Eastern Missouri in the fall of 1906 to dissolve the entire combination as a conspiracy in restraint of trade. Seventy-nine corporations and individuals were named as defendants. The center of attack, however, was the New Jersey holding company, with its stock in nine Standard Oil companies and sixty-

[5]See list in Philadelphia *Press,* Aug. 11, 1907.

two other corporations. Roosevelt was determined to break up this combination once and forever. Frank B. Kellogg, as special prosecutor, spent most of 1907 in accumulating evidence before a Federal examiner; and the second chapter of the suit began in May, 1908, when the Standard opened before the same officer the presentation of its case. The Standard's attorneys included John G. Milburn and M. F. Elliott of New York, John G. Johnson of Philadelphia, and Moritz Rosenthal of Chicago.

As one witness after another testified before Examiner Franklin Ferris, an imposing amount of evidence was piled up. Counsel for the government succeeded in obtaining admissions, for the first time, of (1) the ownership by the Standard of New Jersey of recognized subcompanies; (2) the use of these subcompanies in managing the oil business by areas; (3) the Standard's monopoly of the export trade; (4) the fact that ten men, or their estates, owned far more than a majority of the holding company's stock; and (5) that the Standard's net earnings within eight years had been nearly one-half billion, and within a quarter century almost a billion dollars. The records of the trustees in liquidation after the Ohio decree of 1892 were procured, and the means by which the trust had been maintained virtually intact for seven years elucidated. Facts to prove actual restraint of trade were elicited. Several old enemies of the Standard appeared—for example, Josiah Lombard, now with the Tidewater, and Robert D. Benson. A younger man, Walter W. Tarbell, testified upon the Standard's relations with pipe lines. The picturesque Anthony Brady gave information upon the transfer of the Manhattan Oil Company to the Standard in 1907. Various oil men furnished evidence upon espionage, and W. H. Tilford himself presented data proving that competitors were shouldered out of the European market.

On the other hand, the great combination made some telling points in its defense. It tried to rebut the government charges of price-slashing to put competitors out of business. Evidence had been offered upon price-cutting in thirty-seven towns and cities, ten of them in South Carolina and six along the Hudson. The Standard attorneys showed that in some instances the price-cutting had been begun by independents; that in other instances the evidence was weak; and that in still others it could be disproved. The old charges that the Standard improperly varied its prices from locality to locality, and that these prices had been excessive, were vigorously denied. It was shown that in densely populated areas kerosene and gasolene could naturally be sold at lower figures than in sparsely populated districts; while evidence was presented that the rise in the price of petroleum products 1895–1906 was less than the rise in other commodities.

In one department, that of lubricants, the Standard conclusively proved a sharp price-reduction. Through the Galena-Signal Company, it had enormously improved quality while lowering costs. The government itself used Standard lubricants in the navy and for the machinery digging the Panama Canal. They had become absolutely indispensable to industry the world over. More than nine tenths of the American and Canadian railways used them; many of the English and Continental railways; and factories in all parts of the globe. One prominent railroad had long suffered an average of 128 hotboxes daily, but thanks to the Standard's researches, it had cut this number to about 40 a year. A trunk-line witness testified that before the Galena oils were introduced it was necessary to lubricate through trains every hundred miles—often every fifty; but that now a train ran a thousand miles with one lubrication. Railroad officers paid tribute to the Standard for its expert advice upon lubrication problems. And evidence was presented that in the ten-year period 1897–1906, railroads using its lubricants had reduced the costs per ton mile as much as 80.43 per cent—the figure reported by the Union Pacific.

Rockefeller appeared on the witness stand in the new Custom House in New York on November 18, 1908, to begin his three days' testimony. He had been carefully coached. Day after day early that month brokers, lawyers, and traders on lower Broadway paused and stared as they saw him, wearing mittens and a paper waistcoat, enter No. 26. Reporters inferred that he was "attending to business again," but actually he was being drilled by Standard attorneys. Public interest had been whetted to a keen pitch, though nobody expected much illumination. "Rockefeller Will Tell All—Yes He Will!" ran one sarcastic headline. At the appointed time a crowd jammed all the corridors. The setting was not impressive. The room was small. Examiner Ferris made a dull presiding officer.

Down in front five of Rockefeller's lawyers, keenly alert, bent their heads together. Near them sat Kellogg, short, gray, nervous-mannered, and efficient-looking. Reporters fidgeted at tables. Back of them stood the spectators—and then: "Mr. Rockefeller enters. An old man—not an aged man. He is under no embarrassment. He is grave, but in his rather small light-blue eyes there is humor. He sits down and throws one leg easily over the other. There is no tremor in the long hand that he lays upon the table. He has an air of polite deference. A man with a strange, phenomenal, most unusual face!"[6]

Questioned by his own lawyers on the first two days, Rockefeller gave an historical account of the Standard Oil combination. He spoke with a blandly reminiscent air, like a country gentleman regaling friends with some tale of the good old times. Archbold, Tilford, Moffet, and others had been crisply businesslike; he was benignly discursive. In a gently soothing discourse, he undertook to show that the Standard Oil empire had been built up by benevolent assimilation. *The World* remarked that he had achieved a new triumph in raising the witness chair into a seat of wisdom.[7] It listed the new definitions he had given business. *"Railroad Rebate:* A voluntary compensation paid by the railroads for ample services rendered at a great disadvantage to the beneficiary of the rebate." *"Trust:* A philanthropic institution created by the benevolent absorption of competitors to save them from ruin, combined with the humane conservation and ingenious utilization of natural resources for the benefit of the people." *"Riches:* Results of incessant borrowing from friends and uniform kindness. to competitors."

This recital finished, Rockefeller was questioned closely for five hours by Kellogg. His swift change to taciturnity amused the press:[8]

John D. Rockefeller's memory was bright as a coin from the mint while his own lawyer was interrogating him. During the two days on the witness stand there was scarcely the minutest detail that he could not recall for forty years back. But on the third day, when the government counsel began a cross-examination, he hadn't a memory as long as a shoestring. His mind was as opaque as an oyster-shell. Just think of it; in a single night that bright, clean mind vanished! Oh, the pity of it!

[6]N. Y. *Evening Mail,* Nov. 21, 1908.
[7]Nov. 21, 1908.   [8]Wheeling *Register,* Nov. 21, 1908.

From cartoon by Morris in the Spokane "Spokesman-Review."

Rockefeller on the witness stand, 1908. *Above:* As his enemies hoped he would look. *Below:* As he actually appeared.

But on the whole his three-day appearance made a favorable impression. The Milwaukee *Free Press* discussed his "new-found humility." The Louisville *Times* remarked that on the witness stand he was "a more attractive character than he has always been regarded as being in the Standard Oil presidency." The Cincinnati *Times-Star* ruminated: "It is barely possible that the curious old man has been misrepresented . . . and that the world owes him an apology." The New York *Telegraph* praised his affability. "And what a story it is that he tells! We shall search the fairy-tales of all the ages for another such romance. It is the epic of this age."[9]

Taft had not been in the White House nine months when, on November 20, 1909, the Circuit Court gave a decision which entirely upheld the government. The Standard of New Jersey was ordered to divest itself of all subsidiaries within thirty days. Taft publicly congratulated Kellogg on his "complete victory."[10] The Standard immediately appealed the case to the Supreme Court, where it was first argued in March, 1910, and reargued in January, 1911.

Shortly before Johnson and Milburn filed the Standard Oil briefs in the Supreme Court in 1910, a bill to establish the Rockefeller Foundation as a national corporation was introduced into Congress. With the reasons which led Rockefeller and his advisers to ask for Federal incorporation we deal elsewhere. What concerns us here is the fact that the bill met immediate and unremitting hostility from the Taft administration. Attorney-General Wickersham thought that its philanthropic pretensions cloaked the most sinister designs. The measure was "an indefinite scheme for perpetuating vast wealth," which he pronounced "inconsistent with the public interest." He urged Taft to recall how unfortunate had been the English experience with the indefinite charters of the monasteries and other medieval institutions, and how stringent had been the laws which resulted. He solemnly warned the President: "The power which, under such a bill, would be vested in and exercised by a small body of men, in absolute control of an income of $100,000,000 or more, to be expended for the general indefinite objects described in the bill, might be in the highest degree corrupt in its influence."

[9]Many similar comments may be found in the press, Nov. 21–23, 1908.
[10]Henry Pringle, *William Howard Taft*, II, 661.

Of course Rockefeller had nothing but the public welfare in view in this conception of a great agency, controlled by the best trustees obtainable, to which he would assign the bulk of his fortune for philanthropic objects. Its purpose was not to perpetuate wealth, but to distribute it. This wealth was not to be kept in a few hands, but given to the whole world. In John T. Flynn's words: "As Rockefeller had been the most thoroughly constructive and most honest of all the great captains of industry, he now proposed to make the most impressive use of his great fortune in the cause of humanity." Wickersham's suspicions did him no credit. Yet they were naturally shared by others. Here was one arm of the government, the Supreme Court, considering whether Rockefeller's great industrial creation should not be broken up as flagrantly violative of the laws of the land; there was another arm, the Congress, considering acceptance from Rockefeller of the greatest gift in history for human betterment. The paradox struck the imagination. Wickersham asked Taft if it was appropriate that, when the government was "seeking in a measure to destroy the great combination of wealth which has been built up by Mr. Rockefeller," it should "create and perpetuate in his name an institution to hold and administer a large portion of this vast wealth?"

"I agree," Taft replied, "with your . . . characterization of the proposed act to incorporate John D. Rockefeller"—which was not at all what the act proposed. The result was the withdrawal of the Foundation Bill, and its reintroduction later with amendments limiting the powers granted. It failed, and a charter was then obtained from New York.[11]

The final brief of Johnson, Milburn, and their associates was an extremely able argument. It roundly denied the existence of any monopoly. "Here," it declared, "we have acquisitions through separate transactions from time to time of various plants and properties more or less competitive, or not at all competitive in some instances, more than thirty years ago as accretions to an existing business; then growth by enlargements and creations; no exclusion at any time of others in connection with either of these processes; and the question is, is there present monopolizing or an attempt to monopolize?" The answer was no. The widening distribution of oil

[11]Pringle, *Taft, II*, 662, 663.

fields, now found in Louisiana, Texas, California, Kansas, Illinois, Oklahoma, and other parts of the Union, gave new firms ample opportunity to enter the business. Numerous independent refineries existed and were growing. The brief quoted the testimony of Walter W. Tarbell of the Pure Oil Company:[12]

Q. Mr. Tarbell, for a number of years you have lived alongside of the Standard Oil Co., have you not, in many different localities in the transaction of your business? A. We are in a number of points where they are doing business; yes, sir. Q. At many points? A. Yes, sir. Q. In Europe and in this country? A. Yes, sir. Q. And your business is growing? A. Yes, sir. Q. And you have made money? A. Yes, sir. Q. And you are a prosperous concern? A. Well, I think we are. Q. And you are expanding and developing the whole time? A. It is necessary to do so if we stay in the business.

The final decision was handed down, after Taft had become irritable over the delay, on May 15, 1911. Chief Justice White, heavy of body and mind, mounted the bench. As he began reading his 20,000-word opinion, all his colleagues seemed in good humor save the irascible Justice Harlan, who alone dissented. White, in characteristically turgid language, stated the case and pointed out the irreconcilable conflicts of law and fact in the briefs.[13] He went on to say that all parties agreed that the controversy was controlled by a correct conception of the first two sections of the Sherman Act. His own interpretation was that the "standard of reason" of the English common law in monopoly cases should be the legal standard; that the Sherman Act meant "to prevent undue restraints of every kind and nature." Harlan vehemently objected to reading "standard of reason" and "undue" into the law. Its prohibitions, he declared, were absolute.[14] All the judges agreed that the Standard had violated the Sherman Act. No one could survey the history of the combination, asserted White, without concluding that "the very genius for commercial development and organization" which created the trust had soon begotten an intent to set up a monopoly. The object of the Standard had been "to drive others from the field and exclude them from their right to trade."

Within six months, declared the court, the Standard must divest

---

[12]*Brief for Defendants on the Facts.*
[13]*221 U. S. 1; Supreme Court Reporter, 502.*   [14]*221 U. S. 90.*

itself of all its subsidiaries. It should do this by transferring back to the stockholders of the original companies all the stock they had exchanged for shares in the New Jersey corporation. The companies and their officers were enjoined from doing anything to re-establish the combination.

Forty years earlier, in the fall of 1871, Rockefeller had begun to build his edifice. It had risen with amazing speed, expanded with prodigious vigor, awed the whole industrial world, and taught business a hundred memorable lessons. Now the courts had decreed not its destruction, but its separation into thirty-odd component parts—many of them giant in size.

IV

And what were the results of the dissolution?

Even enemies of the Standard could not but feel admiration for the magnificent strength to which it had attained. In 1906 its plants, scattered from sea to sea, had consumed more than 68,200,000 barrels of crude oil. Its 88,000 miles of pipe lines netted the country, and it pumped oil direct from Oklahoma to Bayonne. Its tank farms contained 75,000,000 or 80,000,000 barrels of stored oil. On an average day it poured nearly 35,000 barrels of illuminants and gasolene into the markets of the world. It sold nearly 4,000,000 barrels of lubricants annually. It turned out enormous quantities of by-products, such as 300,000,000 candles of 700 different kinds every year. Its fleet of tankers numbered 78 steamers and 19 sailing vessels.

As the automobile business grew in America, the importance of domestic trade as compared with the foreign business had increased. Nevertheless, even in 1906 the foreign trade was still 63 per cent of the whole Standard production. All over the world the officers whom Rockefeller had taught to combat Russian and Dutch oil were ceaselessly busy maintaining and widening the American market. The Standard sold lamps for almost nothing to the poor of crowded lands. In one year it distributed in China alone 850,000 complete lamps, with wicks and glass chimneys, for 7½ cents apiece. In a single year it sold a half million of the more expensive Rayo lamps. The Standard's case oil was carried on the backs of coolies in Burma, burros in Spain, camels in Arabia, llamas in Peru. Races brown, black, copper-colored, and white peered into the flame of Standard burners fed by Standard kerosene. This vast foreign trade had played a greater rôle in American economy than most men dreamed. In the period since Rockefeller founded the Standard, it was estimated to have brought into the United States more than one and a half billion dollars in gold; a stream which had helped nourish all American trade and industry, and made hundreds of thousands of homes prosperous.

Now the empire had to be divided. Before 1911 ended the combination was separated into thirty-eight companies, which had no common officers or directors; the stocks of thirty-three subsidiaries being distributed to shareholders in the New Jersey company on December 1. This act involved the use of some complicated fractions. The denominator in each instance was 983,383, the number of outstanding shares in the Standard of New Jersey; the numerator was the number of shares it held in each subsidiary. Thus every share in the Standard of New Jersey entitled its owner to 994/983383 of a share in Swan & Finch, and 599994/983383 of a share in the Ohio Oil Company, these being the two extremes! At once several firms specializing in Standard Oil securities sprang up in Wall Street.

The segregation of the stocks was accompanied by spectacular changes in the official personnel of various companies. Rockefeller resigned his nominal presidency of the Standard of New Jersey, and was succeeded by Archbold. William Rockefeller resigned as vice-president and director, and his son William G. Rockefeller as assistant treasurer. H. H. Rogers had died in May, 1909; Flagler, long inactive, gave up his directorship. In short, all the original partners were now out. Henry C. Folger, who had been secretary of the New Jersey company, became head of the Standard Oil of New York, with H. L. Pratt under him as vice-president; his old place being taken by Charles T. White. To assist him in managing the Standard of New Jersey, Archbold had three able vice-presidents: J. A. Moffett, A. C. Bedford, and Walter Teagle. The Standard of Indiana passed under the guidance of McGregor's old protégé, Cowan. Still other changes might be listed. But nearly all the new executives had been trained in the Rockefeller school, and bore the strong imprint of the founder's aims and ideas.

The best opinion of the day was that the results of the dissolution could not be clearly predicted, and that years would be required to prove whether it was beneficial. Yet in one respect it immediately bore happy fruits. For a host of younger executives it meant a new freedom, and threw open the gates to fresh achievements. The leadership at 26 Broadway had begun to show evidence of age and conservatism. It moved slowly and cautiously; many thought it had devised too much red tape, and that the combination was suffering from an excessive centralization of authority. The rule that every expenditure involving $5000 had to go before the national officers meant delay and trouble. Insufficient encouragement was given to initiative. But now in company after company the older leaders retired, and new ones stepped forward to show their mettle. "We felt the change all along the line at once," says William Burton, soon to be head of the Standard of Indiana. "The young fellows were given the chance for which they had been chafing."

This happened as the market for automobile gasolene was rapidly expanding and new fields were being found in the West. A striking illustration of the release of new energies was furnished by Burton's development of his famous method of "cracking" oil. He had begun his experiments in this field about 1910. The cracking of oil under pressure was not new, for Sir Boverton Redwood in England had taken out a patent on pressure distillation long before. But Burton applied the idea on a new scale at the Whiting works, with improved apparatus and fresh methods. After successfully operating a 100-gallon still for several months, he built a 3000-gallon still that was equally efficient. Then he asked the Standard of Indiana for authority to erect one hundred pressure stills of 6000 gallons each, at a total cost of $800,000. At a board meeting he explained just what he wanted. L. J. Drake, the vice-president under Cowan, demanded: "Billy, do you know what you are doing?" Burton looked Drake squarely in the eye and replied: "Yes, I do." "Then," said Drake, "I move that the appropriation pass."

"We would never have made the rapid progress we did in cracking oil if we'd had to go to New York for every dollar we spent," said Burton later. "They would never have let us. As it was, when some of the New York officers learned what was happening they said: 'You'd better be careful—you'll blow the State of Indiana into Lake Michigan.'"

Great care was taken in building the hundred large stills. So sound was the basic idea and so strict were the precautions that the battery ran for three years without a serious mishap. The new method quickly won general acceptance. When Burton obtained his patent in 1913, he assigned it to the Standard of Indiana. This corporation licensed the other Standard companies in using it, but withheld it from independent refiners until, after the lapse of about a decade, litigation by the Texas Company threw the patent-right open to everybody. In other words, just as for long years the Standard Oil Trust had enjoyed the exclusive use of the invaluable Frasch process, so for about a decade the Standard companies held exclusive rights to the equally important Burton process.[15]

As this indicates, while the dissolution meant an enhanced initiative, for some time it carried little or no increase in competition. The various companies had divided their fields either territorially or functionally. They continued for years to respect the eleven old territorial divisions, though functional lines were less easily maintained. The Standard of Indiana long took pains not to cut into areas held by the Standard of Ohio, and vice versa. The Standard of New York, which had been the great exporting agency of the combination, now increased its distributing business in New York State; but it and the Standard of New Jersey tried not to trespass on each other's limits. The shares of the thirty-odd companies were so largely owned by the same small group that, in theory at least, the old chieftains could control the directorates and hence the policies. Rockefeller himself, despite his large benefactions, was credited at the time of the dissolution with 244,500 of the 983,383 shares of stock in the Standard of New Jersey. But actually the main factor in company policy was a common-sense realization that unrestrained competition would be idiotic. Old comradeships also counted for much. Ostensibly, the exchange of information among the Standard companies ceased. The officers were warned on no account to write letters to each other containing technical or commercial information. But a great deal of friendly visiting and consultation among Standard men inevitably went on, and information was guardedly exchanged. Long after the holding company was dead the "Rockefeller spirit" gave the old elements a sense of fraternalism.

[15]Doctor William Burton to the author, Nov. 14, 20, 1939.

A year after the dissolution, the principal Wall Street specialist in Standard securities, C. H. Pforzheimer, told his customers that the essence of the combination persisted. "It is clear that the disintegration has not altered appreciably the mutual commercial or trade relations of the various former subsidiaries of the Standard Oil of New Jersey. Indeed, they will continue to transact business with each other in the same manner that they did before the dissolution. Already it is obvious that each and every company is operated as efficiently and profitably today as before the disturbed intercorporate relations—through stock control." He pointed out that the great merits of the Standard combination had been "the rare skill and proficiency constantly displayed in handling its vastly expanding and diversified production," and "the natural co-ordination existing between the companies." The first had been accentuated, while the latter was hardly weakened.[16]

Some observers had expected prices of refined oil to drop, and profits and stock values to decline. Actually, oil went up, dividends increased, and shares soared. The highest dividends ever paid by the Standard of New Jersey had

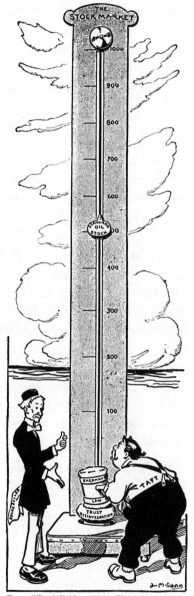

From "Puck," New York City, Aug., 1912.

Taft's trust busting sends up the value of Standard Oil shares.

[16]Carl H. Pforzheimer (25 Broad Street), *Standard Oil Issues* (November, 1912).

been 48 per cent in 1900 and 1901. In other years preceding dissolution the rate had ranged between 36 and 45 per cent. But in the first eleven months of 1912, twenty-six of the thirty-four companies in the old combination paid dividends amounting to 53 per cent of the outstanding capital stock of the old Standard of New Jersey. Still other dividends were paid in December. In other words, the units made more money after competition was nominally restored than before! The value of Standard securities also increased sharply. According to Pforzheimer, in the first month of 1912 stock in the New Jersey company sold at 360–375 a share; in October at 590–595. Simultaneously, stock in the Standard of New York rose from 260–275 to 560–580; Atlantic Refining stock from 260–300 to 610–620; Galena-Signal stock from 215–225 to 240–245; and South Penn Oil from 350–375 to 800–825. Similar rises might be traced in other stocks. Particularly spectacular was the exhibition made by Standard of Indiana. Anybody who had a share in January, 1912, found $3500 bid for it; by March the bid was $5400. Then each share received a stock dividend of twenty-eight shares; and in October the bid on twenty-nine shares was $9500! Why this tremendous rise in values? Partly because of trade expansion; partly because the dissolution furnished information which enabled the public to see how much the major companies were really worth. While Wilson's election brought a fall, the gains for the year remained impressive. Another stock specialist soon reported:[17]

All things considered, the year 1912 was probably the most prosperous in the oil trade since August 27, 1859, when petroleum was first discovered near Titusville. . . .

The Standard Oil Companies, beyond all others, are reaping the benefit of this increased activity, for they are better fitted to take care of this increased demand, and the most rigid economies are practised in all their plants. They have reduced the loss in refining to an absolute minimum, and no new machinery is too expensive if its resultant saving can be demonstrated. For example, with few if any exceptions no so-called independent plant has installed the continuous-process stills. In this process refined oil is running out at the same time crude is being admitted to the still. As the Standard group has hardly a plant which is not so equipped, the saving from this item alone must run into the millions.

[17]F. S. Smithers & Co. (44 Exchange Place), *Standard Oil Companies* (September, 1913). See *Bradstreet's,* May 20, 1911, for the business optimism engendered by the Supreme Court decision.

The Standard organization was still largely intact when the World War began. In that war, as Lloyd George put it, "The Allies floated to victory on a sea of oil"—and the Standard companies did their full share in providing the sea.

As the years passed, the units of the great Standard flotilla inevitably drifted apart. Stock ownership became widely diffused; old leaders gave way to new. As fields were opened in fresh areas, more capital came in. Automobiles were sold in tens of millions, the world market expanded, and the industry became more competitive. The principal companies engaged in refining and marketing began to "integrate backward" and obtain direct control over crude oil; the production and transportation companies combated this by integrating forward to control their own markets. In short, economic developments brought about a breakdown of the old Standard Oil monopoly which laws and courts had been unable to attain. But it should be noted that the competition which resulted has been primarily a service-competition, not a price-competition. Reduction of charges, all factors considered, has been illusory. Any motorist who finds at his crossroads four service stations of four different companies, selling substantially the same gasolene at precisely the same prices, and battling for trade by variations in washroom facilities, has reason to ponder upon the proper limits of competition.[18]

Beyond question, the vindication of the Sherman Act by the 1911 decision was indispensable. The American people are committed to the theory that, in industries not natural monopolies, and not subject to strict government regulation, a reasonable competition must at all costs be preserved. The breakup of the oil and tobacco combinations under Taft established an invaluable principle. But it is certain that the mere passage of laws will not solve difficult problems of industrial organization, and that, as the history of the Clayton Act, the Federal Trade Commission, the trade association move-

[18]*Cf.* H. T. Warshow, ed., *Representative Industries in the United States,* 551 ff. For the total failure of the dissolution decree to reduce costs of refined oil, see U. S. Senate Committee on Manufactures, "High Cost of Gasolene and Other Petroleum Products," Senate Report No. 1263, March 3, 1923; Federal Trade Commission report on "Advance in the Price of Petroleum Products," 1920. See also Joseph E. Pogue, *Economics of Petroleum* (1921); John Ise, *The United States Oil Policy* (1926); George Ward Stocking, *The Oil Industry and the Competitive System* (1925).

ment under Hoover, and the N. R. A. all shows, the working out of a proper adjustment between competition and combination must be a long, slow, and painful process. Any visitor to the great Western oil fields finds that the question of the desirability of making competition the regulatory force in the petroleum industry is today most perplexing. Fierce and reckless competition in one oil pool after another has led to excessive drilling, costly duplication, appalling waste of gas, incomplete recovery of oil, and other losses terrific in magnitude, accompanied by recurrent periods of glut, financial prostration and bankruptcy. It is not strange that in the oil industry as a whole the demand for a saner control has led to a resurgence of the same tendencies toward combination which Rockefeller represented; that in 1938 a petroleum expert, W. J. Kemnitzer, published a volume which he called *The Rebirth of Monopoly: A Critical Analysis of Economic Conduct in the Petroleum Business,* and in which he accused twenty major companies, many of them never Standard units, of acting in unison. The dissolution was in one sense a condemnation of what Rockefeller had accomplished. But some values of the great experiment in industrial organization which he had conducted, some uses of that huge object-lesson in efficient consolidation, were permanent.

v

Even yet, Rockefeller was not quite through with inquiries and litigations. In 1911 the Stanley Committee, appointed by the House of Representatives to investigate the Steel Corporation, held hearings in Washington. Leonidas Merritt was suddenly placed on the stand to give some confused, inaccurate, and undocumented testimony on the Missabe affair. When questioned he showed himself, as Paul De Kruif admits, "amazingly ignorant," and had no clear memory of his "lamentable business entanglements." As the events of which he testified took place years before the Steel Corporation was formed, several committee members were irritated. Augustus P. Gardner of Massachusetts, though known as a sharp critic of big business, interposed. He asked why they should waste time over these irrelevancies, adding that the use made of Merritt's testimony seemed to him most unjust to Rockefeller. Chairman Stanley then explained that he was "a poor country fellow"; that he had "picked up this little incident from my journey in Minnesota"; that he did not know what it meant, but that he thought Rockefeller's acts had been "circuitous and strange and incomprehensible." Gardner responded with manifest indignation: "I do not think that justice is being done to the people who are ostensibly defendants in this quasi-judicial proceeding."

The press, which had already taken up the Merritts' story—*The World*, for example, having printed in 1910 a lurid article by Alf Merritt's daughter Hepzibah entitled "What Rockefeller Did to Us" —made the most of this testimony. But Rockefeller's attorneys, warned at the last minute, presented his side of the story. As Paul De Kruif says, Lon Merritt's recollections of the vital transactions were so jumbled that spectators sometimes thought he was "one of those shrewd witnesses who forget—intentionally."[19] In order to answer distorted versions of the Missabe operations completely, Gates in 1913 brought out his pamphlet on the truth about the Merritts, an exposition which in essentials has never been controverted.

Then, too, in 1912 litigation arose over the control of the old Waters-Pierce properties, and a settlement was finally effected by which the Standard Oil interests relinquished their holdings. It was announced on February 1, 1913, that Pierce and his associates had bought more than two thousand shares in the Waters-Pierce Oil Company from Rockefeller and his former associates at $1500 a share. In the course of this litigation Rockefeller had to testify before a commissioner. Samuel Untermyer, attorney for the Waters-Pierce interests, cross-examined him. Keen-witted, shrewd, sharp of tongue, Untermyer had no rival at the American bar as an interrogator. But in this instance he was completely baffled. Rockefeller's attorney, George Welwood Murray, rubbed his hands delightedly as the magnate repeatedly outmaneuvered the questioner. After a two hours' struggle, Untermyer exclaimed in despair: "I submit, Mr.

[19]*Seven Iron Men,* 201 ff. Two attorneys, Rush Taggard and Judge Dillon, advised Lon Merritt. Mr. De Kruif quotes Gates as saying (p. 205): "To me, Messrs. Dillon and Taggard had nothing but praise for the good faith in which Mr. Rockefeller acted."

Commissioner, that the witness has not answered a single question." Almost the only positive statement wrung from him was his remark, when asked about the signing of some Waters-Pierce proxies, "I sign proxies every day."

"His was the ablest mind I ever encountered on the witness stand," said Untermyer later. He added that Rockefeller had shown an uncanny power to divine the ultimate object of the simplest queries. "He could always read my mind and guess what the next six or seven questions were going to be. I would start with interrogations intended to lay a foundation for questions far in the future. But I always saw a peculiar light in his eyes which showed that he realized my intention. I have never known a witness who equalled him in this clairvoyant power."[20]

Rockefeller had enjoyed the fencing. At the end he approached Untermyer, shook hands, and remarked with a faintly quizzical note:

"I must apologize to you, Mr. Untermyer. You must have found me very dull!"

But this was his last appearance in a great legal case; he was now free to devote himself to his investments and philanthropies.

The World War came on; the tumult and shouting over the trust problem died away as far more exigent tasks demanded attention. When the guns were silent again and the country entered on its post-war boom, the Sherman Act was for a time almost forgotten. Few suits were pressed to a conclusion. Adverse reports by the Federal Trade Commission on the Aluminum Trust and Sugar Institute were ignored, while the courts took a changed view. Said William E. Humphrey of the Trade Commission: "It is not that the courts flout statutory law, but that they interpret it in harmony with economic law. They are changing with the people and the times." The concentration of business control increased until in 1933 more than half the corporate wealth of the nation was owned by 594 companies. So powerful were the forces which Rockefeller had exemplified! This was an unhealthy situation, and the New Deal days brought a much-needed reaction; but the fresh antimonopoly

[20]For Untermyer's statement, see his obituary, N. Y. *Herald Tribune,* March 17, 1940. Mr. Murray gave me a full account of the episode.

campaign was never marked by the heat, impatience, and denunciation of the time of Theodore Roosevelt. The American people had learned much. They looked more tolerantly upon Rockefeller's objective of a completely controlled and efficiently integrated industry. What they chiefly condemned, in retrospect, was not the aim, but the unfair and unsocial practices which had accompanied the achievement and maintenance of that aim.

XLVIII

Stewardship

THE art of stewardship was in one sense—the deepest sense of the word—the art in which Rockefeller most excelled. It is not enough, says La Rochefoucauld, for a man to have great qualities; he must also have the management of them. Or as Sainte-Beuve puts it: "Empire in this world belongs not so much to wits, to talents, and to industry, as to a certain skilful management and the art of applying a continuous administration to all a man's other gifts." Rockefeller possessed not only great talents, but the capacity to keep them in effective focus. Students of his career as an industrialist must be impressed by the almost unerring accuracy of his course in conquest and organization. After the South Improvement fiasco he conquered the kingdom of oil with hardly a misstep, and before forty stood sovereign in that domain. In later life, called upon to direct the greatest fortune ever placed in one man's hands, he managed it with equal effectiveness. It would have been easy to make a random, fumbling, stupid use of these hundreds of millions. But, so adroitly and surely that we are likely to underrate the thought and effort required, he chose the proper ministers to manage his benefactions; gave the right guiding touches; and employed his wealth with much the same sagacity shown in his business career. Conceivably, the money *might* have been spent to better advantage; but certainly no similar sums ever *have* been better spent.

There is much which touches the imagination in this spectacle of the aged industrialist, armed not with expert knowledge but with his ingrained Baptist Puritanism, high intentions, and native penetration, acting as the largest almoner in history. Obviously, he owed much to his associates. As in early life part of his success had been due to Flagler, Payne, McGregor, Archbold, and Pratt, so in his philanthropies he owed an even greater debt to his son, Gates, Starr J. Murphy, and others. But then he had trained his son and chosen Gates! If the public thought of him after 1900 as brooding over the attacks on the Standard and its ultimate dissolution, the public was much mistaken. He knew that his industrial creation had served its main purposes: it had stabilized the oil industry, accelerated its development, kept it continuously profitable, and standardized its products. He knew that whatever lessons it furnished in the large-scale organization of industry would not be obliterated. For him the principal concern of his life after 1900 was the wise distribution of the money which, as he said, "God gave to me." He did not bring to this task the adventurous interest he had felt in refashioning an industry, but he did bring many of the same qualities of foresight, patience, wariness, and enterprise.

Obviously, the story of his philanthropies, if pursued in all its details, would become overwhelming. Rockefeller created or helped create a half dozen principal agencies—a university, an institute for medical research, a board for educational work, an international health board, a board for social studies, and a "foundation" of the broadest scope. To each many chapters might be devoted. Historical volumes will yet be written on most of them. The biographer must perforce be eclectic and interpretive in facing this mass of detail. He must content himself with some account of Rockefeller's personal relation to the agencies; of the principal men who aided him; of the objects they held in view; and of their successes and failures, taken in the large view.

II

Rockefeller was never quite a billionaire. Shortly after the dissolution, one of the year-end inventories of his fortune showed that it amounted to $815,647,796.89.[1] Probably when the stock market was highest before the recession of 1913 it would have totalled about $900,000,000. (He had of course given such large sums that if the estate had been kept intact it would have far exceeded a billion.) As he had believed in constant expansion in business, so now he

[1] Records of John D. Rockefeller, Jr.

believed in an ever-expanding philanthropy; there must be no halt, no suspension of effort and enterprise, until most of his wealth was gone.

The investment of the fortune was given circumspect care. Rockefeller had organized a small group which managed it under his direction somewhat as the best investment-trusts are managed today. The executive expenses were never as high as are those of investment-trusts of similar magnitude, and the results compared favorably with the efforts of these bodies. Most of the fortune remained in Standard Oil securities. Rockefeller's belief in them was so firm that his office never recommended any change, regarding them as a sacrosanct part of his property. When the dissolution suit neared its climax, Henry E. Cooper thought the stock of the Standard of New Jersey had reached its highest levels, and if consulted would have recommended lightening the holdings. But later he admitted Rockefeller's superior wisdom, for soon after the dissolution the Standard of New Jersey paid a "special dividend" of $40 a share and its values soared. After the decree, the stocks of some of the pipe lines were sold—and wisely; but Rockefeller was glad to keep the shares of other oil companies. A part of the fortune, particularly after the issuance of the Liberty Loans, was always in United States bonds. Another small part Rockefeller kept in cash and liquid Wall Street loans, using it to seize investment opportunities when the stock market was low, and to assist financial institutions in time of national distress. The remainder of his estate was placed in widely diversified investments. No attempt was ever made to dominate any one investment field; Rockefeller remained to the last essentially an industrialist, and refused to become a manipulator.[2]

To the eve of the World War, railroads were the principal vehicles of investment in America, and Rockefeller relied heavily upon them. To be sure, he had some industrial holdings apart from his oil companies. He kept controlling interests for a time before the war in American Linseed Oil and Colorado Fuel & Iron, while his block of International Harvester stock was at one time worth $25,000,000 or $30,000,000. He had an early holding in United States Leather, and a little later a large interest in General Motors, which he bought before the first reorganization, and on which he made

[2]Henry E. Cooper to the author, Nov. 30, 1939.

remarkable profits. He also owned a good deal of stock in United States Steel and Consolidation Coal, a large mining company of Kentucky and West Virginia. After 1906 he became the largest holder in the Equitable Trust, a company which the Equitable Life had to surrender following the insurance investigation, and which Alvin Krech, with the backing of Rockefeller and George Gould, took over. When the Bankers' Trust Company was founded he took a substantial interest in it, $30,000,000 or more, and again made extraordinary profits on the venture. The American Shipbuilding Company of Cleveland was for years largely under his ownership. He of course possessed a good deal of real estate. But until after the war, railroad securities held a place in his fortune next to his stock in the oil companies—though at a long remove.[3]

The heavy purchases which he had made in George Gould's railroads gave his staff a good deal of trouble. They included the Missouri Pacific, the Western Pacific, and the Western Maryland, the history of all of which was chequered. Before the war he also bought complete control of the important Wheeling & Lake Erie. Henry E. Cooper, who gave special attention to railroads, had no faith in the junior securities of this property, and was anxious to extricate his chief from it. Again and again it trembled near the verge of bankruptcy. But its head was William McKinley Duncan, a stubborn Scot (related to William McKinley) who was determined to keep it afloat. "By God!" he used to declaim, "I'll never let this road go again into a receivership." Finally he lifted it to a fair level of prosperity, which enabled Rockefeller to dispose of his shares at a favorable price.[4] At about the same time the precarious Western Maryland securities were sold to the Baltimore & Ohio at a satisfactory figure. The bonds and stock which Rockefeller held in the Western Pacific—the unnecessary line that Gould threw from Salt Lake City to San Francisco—were kept at a loss. But the Missouri Pacific securities were easier to get rid of, and a small profit was probably realized on them.[5]

[3]The treasurer's reports of the Rockefeller Foundation, published annually, show in detail what securities were received from the fortune.

[4]Rockefeller paid Duncan a special reward; Cooper thinks $150,000.

[5]Information from Henry E. Cooper, Jerome Greene, Bertram Cutler. After 1915 Rockefeller owned large quantities of securities of the New York Central, the Santa Fé, the Southern Pacific, the Northern Pacific, and the Great Northern.

A good deal more might be said of Rockefeller's investments, but it would lead us into a morass of details. Early in the century he traded heavily and profitably in Consolidated Gas of New York. Later he invested largely in Virginia Chemical, another valuable property. He held a fair-sized interest in some Cleveland banks. In the great years of syndicate flotations before the World War he participated in a good many of the Blair & Co. enterprises, and in some of J. P. Morgan's—including the ill-fated International Mercantile Marine.[6] But enough has been said to illustrate the point that his investments were diversified. Using his membership on the Stock Exchange, he regularly bought and sold stocks, carefully studying values and trends. He never purchased on margin, always paying cash and registering his stock. He never, despite a statement by C. W. Barron, "jammed" the market. He never departed from his fixed rule of buying stocks on a decline, a certain amount at every eighth-point down, and selling on a rise, a certain amount at every eighth-point up. But he liked to "back his judgment," as Barney Baruch has put it; and he sometimes borrowed large sums, even $15,000,000 or $20,000,000, posting bonds as security, and then used these sums in the market with great courage.

When Rockefeller's office was fully organized it became the general rule that bond investments up to $2,000,000 might be made without consulting him, but that any larger transaction required his consent. A little group—his son, Gates, Cooper, later Jerome Greene, later still Bertram Cutler—studied offerings and decided on policies. In most instances, when he was consulted he would approve their investment proposals without any prolonged investigation. He would telegraph: "If you think it wise, go ahead." In this he simply followed his lifelong rule. Having selected counsellors in whom he felt confidence, he gave them almost unlimited responsibility. If an investment turned out badly, he never complained; while if it turned out exceptionally well, he was chary of praise.[7] The office was carefully organized, and always had ample

[6]Another Morgan promotion in which Rockefeller invested was the Chicago City & Connecting Railways Collateral Trust. His total investment in the I. M. M. reached eight or ten millions. According to his staff, Morgan never gave him any large percentage of the best promotions.

[7]High profits were made in General Motors, Bankers' Trust, the Equitable Trust, and other ventures, while shares in Continental Oil and Standard of Indiana made spectacular records.

From a photograph by Ira Hill.

Rockefeller with his son, grandson, and great-grandson.

Rockefeller and John D., Jr.

statistical information available. Cooper not only devised a special mode of analyzing industrial conditions, but made a habit of travelling frequently from coast to coast to inspect railroad properties. He moved only by day, and sitting at a window desk, with the division superintendent at his side, and often the president or general superintendent as well, he noted down facts and figures. These he embodied in long written reports to Rockefeller. When he left his place was taken by Bertram Cutler, who had entered the office as a stenographer and bookkeeper about 1900. In his long career, which still continues, Mr. Cutler proved of the greatest value to the fortune and the philanthropies. He possessed a marvellous grasp of financial detail, and a wizardlike intuition in dealing with investment opportunities. In constant touch by telephone and telegraph with Rockefeller until the latter's death, he offered him the best possible advice in complex situations.

Cooper and Bertram Cutler both saw a good deal of Rockefeller personally. The first-named occasionally went to 4 West Fifty-fourth Street while Rockefeller was breakfasting, to talk about investments. "He spoke confidentially in these chats," states Cooper. "But never once did I hear him utter anything which would lead me to think: 'Well, after all, the old gentleman is pretty sharp.' Not once did I see the slightest indication of a desire to take unfair advantage of anybody." While Gates sometimes seemed hard and contriving, Rockefeller was often too indulgent: "He was excessively easy on people in business." The same judgment is expressed by Mr. Cutler: "He was too gentle with people with whom he dealt." He was rigorously analytical, and to Jerome Greene seemed frigidly unemotional, but he was never hard.

He evinced a remarkable memory and great persistence. Once in a difficult business situation he said to Cooper: "Don't you think we could get these different interests to unite in some common action? Why not see what you can do?" Cooper was rebuffed. "Very well, we'll drop the matter," said Rockefeller. Several years passed, and Cooper forgot the subject. Then one day Rockefeller unexpectedly spoke up at breakfast. "Mr. Cooper, do you recall those interests which we tried to unite? Why not approach them again?" This time Cooper met with success. Rockefeller liked the frequency with which Cooper and Greene turned in able reports. Gates had given a frosty welcome to all promoters, a tribe whom he always distrusted. Cooper and Greene, on the other hand, were ready to talk with any accredited banker, broker, or industrialist who wished to enlist capital. They seized some attractive opportunities, and Rockefeller approved of their course.

III

But what of the benefactions? Did adequate imagination and enterprise as well as care go into them? The first great undertakings, as we have seen, were the University of Chicago, the Rockefeller Institute for Medical Research, and the General Education Board. How fast and far did they grow?

For the University, Rockefeller had come by 1900 to expect a magnificent future. His faith in its destiny was in no way better expressed than by his insistence upon acquiring large tracts of land for expansion. In 1898 he and Marshall Field bought two blocks for athletic purposes; in 1901 he bought another block and a half. Then he instructed the University business manager, working with his office, to purchase for him, as quietly as possible, all the land fronting south on the Midway Plaisance from Washington Park to Dorchester Avenue, about three quarters of a mile. Late in 1903 he was able to give the institution tracts which had cost him $1,500,-000. While his agents were completing the purchase of practically ten entire blocks north of the Midway, Rockefeller commissioned them to make similar purchases on the south. The result was the acquisition there of another ten-block area. In all, Rockefeller spent between $3,000,000 and $4,000,000 for these long strips of land. This step, taken on his own initiative, without consulting the trustees, furnished a spacious setting for the beautiful buildings, many of them replicas or adaptations of the finest structures at Oxford and Cambridge,[8] and ample room for future growth.

For numerous purposes—buildings, new departments, a legal library, publications—Rockefeller continued giving to the University. He even sent out his own engineer to erect a heat, light, and power plant.[9] But he remained troubled by the inability of the institution to keep within its budget. Despite the agreement made

[8]Goodspeed, *History*, 336, 337.   [9]*Idem*, 342.

with him in 1897, the deficits continued large. In a period of seven years he had to pay over almost $1,600,000 to meet them. This was in spite of his large gifts to endowment ($3,000,000 in 1900–1902, for example). Year by year the situation became graver. Finally, some decisive action had to be taken. The trustees' committee on the budget was summoned to New York in the closing days of 1903 to confer on the subject with John D. Rockefeller, Jr., and Gates. (These two men were also trustees, the former serving thirteen years, the latter fourteen.) A careful memorandum on the results of the conference was drawn up. It embodied the views of every one present. After stating that the tendency had been "steadily and alarmingly toward an increased deficit," this document laid down the principle that until it was wiped out by retrenchment or fresh endowment, the University must rigidly decline to enlarge its work or increase its expenses.

To President Harper, who had also come on to New York, this was a heavy blow. He frankly held the view that, while a bank or factory had to balance its books precisely, no such mechanical rule should bind a growing university; that for it a deficit was a sign of health.[10] But the memorandum declared that the principle which the budget committee had laid down was not a step backward. The University officers must demonstrate their ability to give the institution assured financial stability before it could command the confidence which would invite large gifts. This was not a criticism of Harper's policy alone. The trustees, including the younger Rockefeller and Gates, candidly acknowledged that they were in part to blame for the deficits, for they had approved plans for expansion which involved unexpected costs. Nevertheless, the ardor and impetuosity of the gifted president, who so nobly dreamed dreams and saw visions of greatness for his University, were the main root of the difficulty. Gates writes:[11]

Nothing but a clear vision of the public interest could have sustained Mr. Rockefeller in these trying years. He was grateful for the generous response of Chicago in the earlier years of Doctor Harper's presidency. He saw students entering the university in numbers increasing annually by hundreds. He saw the State universities of the West imitating the University of Chicago in their ideals and resources, and the gradual rise in the Middle West of a great and powerful university system. He knew

[10]Doctor Samuel Harper to the author.   [11]MS Autobiography, 369–373.

that Doctor Harper's temptations and weaknesses were the faults of his strength. While he was painfully aware that the budgets annually presented to us in advance were not the least restraint upon expenditures, yet he knew that after all there was little waste. All these facts I felt it my duty to keep before Mr. Rockefeller while at the same time I was warning the university authorities, one and all, at the instance of Mr. Rockefeller, of the inevitable results of debt and default. And so Mr. Rockefeller was patient.

But not too patient. When in 1904 . . . he thought the time had come and the interests of the university and the public required that the trustees assume authoritative and complete control of the finances, and live up to the budgets and not transgress them, the threatened blow fell and there was no faltering. The trustees themselves were convinced that the hour had struck, and were from that time zealous for complete financial reform.

President Harper was staggered by the turn of events:

It was a tragic moment, about the first of January, 1904, at a meeting of the trustees in Mr. Rockefeller's private office, when one trustee after another, in Doctor Harper's presence, declined, each personally and in turn, to endorse Doctor Harper's appeal for more money, in face of the usual overexpenditures of the previous year, contrary to a specific written agreement. Doctor Harper fully realized that the conflict with Mr. Rockefeller, always a friendly conflict, was over, and that it was he who had lost. His saddest plaint was, "The trustees all went back on me," for that, with no lack of personal fidelity, was true. After an overnight private conference with his father, Mr. John D. Rockefeller, Jr., formally announced the next morning, to the assembled board, the discontinuance of further endowment gifts from his father until the university budget could show a clean balance sheet.

In the next two years, indeed, Rockefeller added nothing to endowment, though he did contribute $545,000 toward current expenses. Gates writes: "There was no break at any time in the friendly social relations between the Rockefellers and Harpers." This was true. But a marked coolness had grown up between Gates and Harper, which only great self-restraint on both sides prevented from breaking into open antagonism. It is evident that Harper thought Gates meddlesome and officious, while Gates believed that Harper was often careless and sometimes inclined to force Rockefeller's hand.[12]

[12]"We note with pleasure," Gates wrote Harper, Jan. 7, 1903, "that the proposed new journal is to cost no more than $400 or $500 a year, and that there is to be no increase in this over the expenditures for the same department under the budget of past years." Harper Papers.

"I was thinking over your statements to me at luncheon yesterday on my way home," Harper writes Gates on June 25, 1904. "If my memory serves me correctly, you must have some wrong figures in your mind. You said something like the following: 'The deficit amounts to 15 per cent on the total sum. Anybody ought to be able to make a budget that would be closer than that. I could make one myself.'" He protested that the deficit was not so great. But, he continued, "the importance of holding things inside of the budget, and especially the emphasis you laid on getting rid of the permanent deficit, are greatly appreciated, and . . . our strength and attention will be devoted to these two points from this time forward."[13] Gates's resistance to some of Harper's plans for adding a strong medical school to the University was also a sore point between them.

Yet the genius of Harper was no less indispensable to the University than the generosity of Rockefeller or the loyalty of the trustees; and it was a tragic fact that he was removed so early from the scene of his brilliant activities. He had been suffering from a hidden malady, cancer. He complained repeatedly to Gates and others during 1903 of lassitude; and in March, 1904, an operation was performed for appendicitis. The physicians, hoping that they might be wrong, at first refrained from telling him that microscopic examination of the appendix had indicated a cancer. But before long the news had to be broken to him.

Early in 1905 an examination convinced the doctors that the growth had increased, and that an early operation was imperative. He immediately wrote Rockefeller and Gates. The physicians, he told the latter, "have asked me to decide before the operation whether in case they find the malignant growth it is to be removed even at the risk of life, the chances being three to ten for life, or whether they should cover the matter over and allow the end to come gradually as in similar cases in which operation is not performed. I am therefore proceeding to arrange all my affairs on the supposition that there is but a slight chance for recovery from the operation." He added: "It is as clearly a case of execution announced beforehand as it could possibly be." A few days later he was heroically writing Gates: "I have recovered very considerably from the effect of the first announcement and am myself in most par-

[13]*Idem.*

ticulars. I have met my classes today as usual, and have lectured to the freshmen."[14]

When Rockefeller heard the news, he was profoundly affected. Gates wrote the president that he "is distressed beyond words. He cannot bring himself even yet to attempt to express his feelings. He had a talk with me over the 'phone this morning, the purport of which was that you yourself would know far better than any words of his could express what is in his heart."[15] After this sad intelligence he sent Harper more frequent notes than before, all warmly sympathetic. Knowing that the president's salary had been modest, he insisted upon the privilege of helping meet the medical expenses.[16] He sent word to Mrs. Harper that if the president did not obey his doctors, she must telegraph him, "and I will come on at once." He urged Harper, in a letter of more length than usual, to see if osteopathic treatment might not yield some benefit, saying that he had been markedly aided by it: "I can do twice as much work as I could last winter before I took the treatment, and with greater ease."[17] Mrs. Rockefeller had been on intimate terms with the Harpers, writing characteristically vivacious notes to Mrs. Harper and exchanging limericks with the family. She was overwhelmed. "Love and sympathy prompt me to tell you both," she wrote, "how much you are in our thoughts, and that our prayers are heavily laden with petitions." She begged to be commanded: "Nothing that you can ask will be too much."[18]

Harper and his wife paid their last six-day visit to Forest Hill in August, 1905, though the hand of death was visibly on him. His sole thought was of the University which he must so soon leave in other hands, as he showed when afterward he wrote Gates a long letter:[19]

Mr. Rockefeller is in good health. The reaction has come in the matter

[14]Harper to Gates, Feb. 3, 8, 1905; Harper Papers.
[15]Gates to Harper, Feb. 11, 1905; Harper Papers.
[16]Harper sternly insisted on financial independence, living frugally. Once when he proposed to become director of the Congress of Arts and Sciences of the St. Louis Exposition, at a remuneration of $50,000, in order to provide for his family, Rockefeller interposed. It was plain that Harper would be over-tasked. Rockefeller offered, and Harper properly accepted, a temporary trust fund for the family.
[17]Rockefeller to Harper, June 30, 1905; Harper Papers.
[18]Mrs. Rockefeller to Mrs. Harper, Feb. 9, 1905; Harper Papers.
[19]Harper to Gates, Aug. 19, 1905; Harper Papers.

of attacks for tainted money, and they are receiving letters of sympathy by the hundred as well as clippings from all over the country. He believes that this is all providential, and that he is to be thoroughly vindicated. It is a subject, however, which still occupies a large part of his mind.

He discussed with me informally many matters at the university; also his recent gifts. I have never known him to be more genial or communicative. At the same time, it was clear that anything like business propositions was not what he was expecting. He has tremendous confidence in you, and the success of the Ten Million gift has strengthened his confidence. I am fully convinced that you can persuade him to take another step forward in university matters this autumn if you will contrive a plan and put it before him. . . .

You will be glad to know that we brought out the budget of the university, including the School of Education, with a surplus of $26.

Heroically laboring to the last, administering, teaching, publishing new books, Harper set an example of Christian fortitude which is an imperishable part of the history of one of the world's greatest universities. On January 10, 1906, in the fiftieth year of his life and the fifteenth of his presidency, he died. American education had suffered an irreparable loss, for intellectually he was at the height of his powers. For years he had insisted that one of the University's most urgent needs was an adequate library building to house the splendid and fast-increasing collection of books, many of them kept in part of the decaying structure used as a gymnasium. Immediately after his death, Rockefeller and his son discussed the means of carrying out his wishes. On January 16, 1906, the younger Rockefeller telegraphed the president of the board of trustees: "If the trustees favor the erection of a University library in honor of Doctor Harper, my father will join with the doctor's many friends in Chicago and the East in a contribution toward it." Appropriate action was taken by the University authorities and alumni. The building was completed and occupied in 1912, Rockefeller having given $655,000, and a host of other donors $385,000, toward its erection.

In his reminiscences, Rockefeller pays a warm tribute to Harper. He speaks deprecatingly of the cartoons which portrayed the educator as pursuing the millionaire for gifts, cartoons as erroneous as they were annoying. "He never once either wrote me a letter or asked me personally for a dollar of money for the University of

Chicago. In the most intimate daily intercourse with him in my home, the finances of the University of Chicago were never canvassed or discussed." He mentions Harper's exquisite personal charm, his genius for organization, and his lofty idealism. "The world will probably never realize how largely the present splendid university system of the Central Western States is due indirectly to the genius of this man."[20] Harper's instinct for fruitful innovations has indeed exercised a profound influence. But the rapid growth of the Universities of Illinois and Wisconsin was in part attributable to the resolve of Altgeld and LaFollette, men who hated Rockefeller, that the democracies should build seats of learning as powerful and influential as any raised by the barons of wealth.

The new head of the University, Harry Pratt Judson, was a very different man from Harper; not a gifted creator, not endowed with imagination and thrust, he possessed a talent for conservation and consolidation. He gave the institution a prudent and economical management. Convinced of the wisdom of balancing the budget, he built upward by careful steps. But the indispensable decision had been taken before he assumed the presidency. In December, 1905, as Harper lay dying, the budget committee, visiting New York, found themselves, as the University historian writes, "in a new atmosphere."[21] Rockefeller promised to add more than a million to the endowment. During 1906 he actually gave more than $3,000,000 to the University, of which $2,700,000 went into endowment. The following year, 1907, he added $1,400,000 to endowment. The deficits were then ending. The last was met in 1908, when the younger Rockefeller expressed his father's deep satisfaction in a letter to the president of the trustees. At last the financial stability of the University was assured.

And within two years Rockefeller demonstrated the warmth of his gratification by giving, upon his own initiative, $10,000,000. In a letter just before Christmas, 1910, he notified the trustees that he had set aside, as a final grant, securities of that value, to be delivered in ten equal annual instalments. Expressing his complete satisfaction with the strength, scope, and elevation attained by the institution, he declared: "This gift completes the task which I have

[20]*Random Reminiscences*, 178–180.   [21]Goodspeed, *History*, 290.

set before myself." The University should thenceforth be supported and expanded by the many, not the few:[22]

In making an end of my gifts . . . and in withdrawing from the board of trustees my personal representatives, whose resignations I enclose, I am acting on an early and permanent conviction that this great institution, being the property of the people, should be controlled, conducted, and supported by the people, in whose generous efforts for its upbuilding I have been permitted simply to co-operate; and I could wish to consecrate anew to the great cause of education the funds which I have given, if that were possible; to present the institution a second time, in so far as I have aided in founding it, to the people of Chicago and the West; and to express my hope that under their management and with their generous support, the University may be an increasing blessing to them, to their children, and to future generations.

The only stipulation which Rockefeller made was that at least $1,500,000 of his last gift should be used in erecting and furnishing a University chapel. "As the spirit of religion should control and penetrate the University, so that building which represents religion ought to be the central and dominant feature of the University group." The fruit of this paragraph was the beautiful edifice which since his death has been named the Rockefeller Chapel, one of the finest structures of its kind in the world.[23]

The trustees, in drawing up a suitable minute of thanks, pointed out that within twenty-one years Rockefeller had given the institution approximately $35,000,000, as against $7,000,000 contributed by others. Such grants from one hand were unprecedented. But unique as they were in amount, they were still more remarkable for the spirit in which they had been bestowed. He had never permitted the University to bear his name, and had consented to be called founder only at the urgent request of the trustees. He had never suggested an appointment or removal, and never interfered indirectly or directly with the freedom of the institution; even when religious doctrines had been voiced which traversed his known views, he had made no sign of irritation or apprehension. The

[22]For this letter see *Science*, XXXII, Dec. 30, 1910. While Rockefeller personally gave no more to the University, his son and his benevolent boards in the years 1910–1932 gave approximately $41,500,000. John D. Rockefeller, Jr., to his father, April 25, 1932; Rockefeller Papers.

[23]Goodspeed, *History*, 292, 293.

minute added, in words which the University historian calls re-strained and moderate:[24]

In contemplating the severance of this long-continued relationship, so gracious on his part, and rendered so delightful by so many acts of personal courtesy, the trustees are unable to express their appreciation of munificence so vast exercised in a spirit so fine. It is the conjunction of the act and the spirit of the act which has made it possible to create and maintain the university, and the trustees hope that through the ages to come the University of Chicago, by training youth in character and in exact learning, and by extending the field of human knowledge, may justify all that has been done by the founder.

IV

Gates tells us in his autobiography that one day he was walking down Broadway with Charles W. Eliot. He remarked to the president of Harvard that the Rockefeller Institute for Medical Research was the most interesting agency in the world—that nothing was so exciting and fascinating as its work. President Eliot stopped short in the street, turned to him, and said with emphasis: "I myself feel precisely so. The Rockefeller Institute is the most interesting thing in the world!"

They might well have said so. Before the World War began, the Institute had firmly established itself, and its work had commanded the attention of scientists all over the globe. It had become the best-equipped institution for studying the cause and cure of disease to be found in any land. We have noted that in 1910 it opened its new hospital, a substantial seven-story building just south of the original laboratory on the East River. Half of the sixth floor and all the seventh were devoted to laboratory facilities, with operating room and electro-cardiograph room on the roof. Only those patients whose diseases were being studied by the staff were admitted to this hospital, or to the isolation pavilion close at hand. As the work grew, in 1916 a new laboratory, a large six-story structure, was erected just north of the existing group. The Institute also bought a 780-acre farm near Princeton for the development of animal pathology under Doctor Theobald Smith and plant pathology under Doctor Louis O. Kunkel.

The first great discovery at the Institute was, as we have seen, in

[24]*Idem*, pp. 345, 346.

the treatment of epidemic meningitis. This disease, becoming active in New York in 1905, spread rapidly throughout the country. It was truly a deadly malady, for about four cases in five terminated fatally. Doctor Simon Flexner discovered that it could be transmitted to monkeys and that the curative serum he had produced in horses would cure the disease in these animals. With this experimental knowledge to go on, the antimeningitis serum was applied to the treatment of the disease in man—in children chiefly, who are the common victims. Of the first 400 cases treated with the serum, nearly four-fifths recovered. The Institute sent the serum all over this country and before long to every foreign land where meningitis prevailed.

Then came other discoveries of equal value. Infantile paralysis, a scourge of childhood throughout the earth, had always been among the most mysterious of ailments, its cause, its means of dissemination, and its cure alike unknown. One child in every three whom it attacked died. Half of the survivors were crippled for life. In 1907 the disease broke out in America, having been brought there from Norway and Sweden. Landsteiner, then of Vienna, later at the Rockefeller Institute, first successfully inoculated monkeys with the disease; Flexner and his associates first succeeded in securing monkey-to-monkey passage, and later determined its virus nature, and the fact that the virus both enters and leaves the central nervous system by way of the mucous membrane of the nose.

Besides Simon Flexner, two members of the Institute staff soon achieved a world-wide fame: the bacteriologist Hideyo Noguchi, and the surgeon Alexis Carrel. Noguchi, born in Japan in 1876, had graduated in medicine at Tokyo University, and occupied research and teaching positions in his native land before he came to America in 1900.[25] He served for three years under Doctor Simon Flexner at the University of Pennsylvania, and after a year in Copenhagen became one of the original staff of the Institute. He became deeply interested in the bacteriology of yellow fever, paresis, rabies, Oroya fever, trachoma, and other diseases. In the technique of bacteriology he was extraordinarily skillful and resourceful, and his many contributions were recognized by degrees from numerous universities and decorations from governments. Meanwhile Doctor Noguchi

[25]Rockefeller Foundation, *Annual Report,* 1928, pp. 32-34.

had begun his investigation of the diseases caused by spiral micro-organisms, including syphilis. He discovered the spirochete in the brain of human beings who had succumbed to paresis in hospitals for the insane; he also found that certain cases diagnosed as yellow fever are caused by a special spiral organism—leptospira—and not by the virus that is the cause of true yellow fever. He cultivated the rod-shaped organism causing the fatal Peruvian Oroya fever, and identified the insect whose bite transmits it to man. He likewise identified the micro-organism which produces trachoma.

In the end Noguchi gave his life for science. He had studied yellow fever in Mexico, Peru, Ecuador, and Brazil. Under the aus-pices of the Rockefeller Foundation, he wished to continue his work in Africa; and though not in good health he insisted, despite the protests of friends, on an expedition to Accra on the Gold Coast. From the fall of 1927 until early in May he labored in enervating heat. He was ready to take his materials back to New York when, on the eve of sailing, he was stricken with yellow fever and died. No microbe hunter of his time had been more indefatigable or successful; and he held an honored position in the great line founded by Pasteur, Koch, and Lister.

Very different but equally fruitful were the achievements of Doc-tor Carrel, who, born in France and educated at the University of Lyon, joined the Institute in 1906. Working on animals, he perfected a method of suturing (sewing up) arteries and veins without letting them become obstructed by blood-clots; this enabled him to trans-plant kidneys, spleen, and other organs; he resected arteries, veins, and nerves; and he applied to operations on the thoracic cavity a new method of intra-tracheal insufflation developed at the Institute by Doctors Auer and Meltzer, which made it possible to maintain respiration without any muscular inflation or contraction of the lungs. He led the way in operations on the heart. As a surgeon he united consummate anatomical knowledge with in-credible dexterity. One of the early results of his labors was the con-trivance of a method of coping with "hemorrhage of the new-born," which had killed one infant in every thousand. In the dead of night, he was awakened by the father of a baby which was at the point of death. He laid the two side by side; joined an artery in the father's arm to a vein, frail as wet tissue-paper, in the child's leg; and let the man's blood flow into the tiny body. The hemorrhage instantly stopped.

Before the World War, Carrel had successfully cultivated in glass vessels the cells of warm-blooded animals, thus affording an invaluable method for the study of the form and activities of cells outside the body. These tissue cultures also made it possible to cultivate in test tubes those minute, elusive viruses, common causes of severe diseases in men, animals, and plants, which even the strongest microscopes fail to make visible. In 1912 Carrel was given the Nobel Prize for his success in suturing blood vessels and in transplanting organs. Then came the World War and the Carrel-Dakin solution for the treatment of wounds; and after it another long series of surgical experiments and discoveries, ending with the mechanical heart which he perfected with the aid of Colonel Lindbergh.

A widespread fame also attended the brilliant work of Jacques Loeb, who became head of the department of experimental biology in 1910. Long before the Rockefeller Institute reached its twentieth birthday, it had established itself beside the best European institutes. The founder's gifts to it presently reached a total of more than $50,000,000. Its staff expanded until it numbered scores of experts. The trustees, including Gates, Jerome D. Greene, and the younger Rockefeller, who ultimately became president of the board, worked in close harmony with the scientific directors, headed by Simon Flexner. Medical men honored the names of devoted servants who gave up their lives in its work—of Howard B. Cross, killed by yellow fever in Vera Cruz in 1921, and Doctor W. A. Young, a gallant Englishman at Accra who followed Noguchi to the grave in 1928. Scientists everywhere followed with care the publications issued by the Institute—*The Journal of Experimental Medicine,* which it took over in 1906, just a decade after Doctor Welch founded it at Johns Hopkins; the *Monographs;* and the large volumes of *Studies.*[26]

Perhaps one of the most exciting discoveries was that of Peyton

[26]See the official pamphlet, *Rockefeller Institute for Medical Research, History, Organization,* etc. (1934). This lists 22 members of the Institute; 12 associate members; 28 associates; 58 assistants; 8 fellows; and 20 other employees. John D. Rockefeller, Jr., was president of the corporation and the board of trustees; Simon Flexner was vice-president of both; and Raymond B. Fosdick secretary of both. Doctor William H. Welch died in 1934.

Rous in 1910 that certain tumors of a destructive (cancerous) nature are caused by viruses. First found in the tumors of fowl, they were soon identified in tumors of such small mammals as rabbits. The joint investigation of two chemists, Jacobs and Heidelberger, and two pathologists, Wade Hampton Brown and R. M. Pearce, yielded the drug tryparsamide, which has a curative action on syphilis of the nervous system, and especially on the highly prevalent and fatal sleeping sickness of the Congo. In the hospital especial attention was directed to the study of pneumonia. The germ (pneumococcus) was found by Cole and his associates to be divided into distinct immunological types which they called types I, II, and III. A curative serum was perfected for the highly fatal type I pneumonia, and the fatality, in 431 cases (up to 1930) was reduced to 10 per cent, a lower figure than has been secured with any other type of treatment.

The success of the Institute brought other agencies of the kind into existence; and it may be noted that the first of them was founded by Rockefeller's son-in-law and daughter, Mr. and Mrs. Harold F. McCormick, who set up in Chicago an institute for research in infectious diseases. The very journals which had denounced Rockefeller's business operations most unrelentingly were warmest in praising his work for medical science. Thus the New York *World* enthusiastically commended a new gift to the Institute in 1914. "Hardly any service is even imaginably greater," it said. And when Carrel received the Nobel prize, the Hearst press suggested that Rockefeller deserved half a dozen such awards. The New York *Evening Journal* had already remarked editorially:[27]

All that has been said of Rockefeller's actions *accumulating* may be true, and,—what is more probable—nine-tenths of it may be false. But this surely is true. Rockefeller uses his money *for all the people*. He is doing as an individual what the nation as a whole has not intelligence to do. He considers himself a responsible custodian of the millions that he had dipped up from the golden stream of opportunity. And humanity will be better off because of his work when he shall have been dead ten

[27]N. Y. *World*, June 29, 1914; *Evening Journal*, June 3, 1912, Jan. 9, 1913. Nathan Straus, himself a well-known philanthropist, stated in the *Evening Journal* (Jan. 11, 1913) that he agreed that Rockefeller deserved a Nobel Prize. The year before he had seen in Palestine a hospital, once taxed to the utmost to care for meningitis patients, but now closed. He was told that the Rockefeller Institute's new serum had made the hospital tenantless. "All honor then to John D. Rockefeller, whose benefactions are stamping out disease all over the world."

thousand years. His dollars fight diseases, man's enemies, and ignorance, man's greatest enemy.

V

Until long after the World War, the General Education Board continued to give money to State departments of education in the South for the support of agents used in rural education, Negro education, and secondary education. But its expenditures in this field gradually diminished. By 1924 it was evident that the purposes for which the grants had originally been made had been substantially achieved. The Federal Government had taken over the farm-demonstration work. The States had awakened to their responsibility for good secondary instruction. As the principal officers of the Board —Doctor Buttrick, the chairman, Doctor Wickliffe Rose, the president, and Abraham Flexner, the secretary—stated that year: "Interest in schools has been widely awakened, laws have been improved, even though they are still by no means generally satisfactory, steadily increasing taxes have been and are voted by the people, the State departments have strengthened and improved their personnel." When the Board began its work, no State department of Education had possessed a professional staff, adequate funds, or proper quarters; by 1924 most of them had all three. The Board was then assisting scores of people in important Southern educational posts to take leaves for advanced study in the best universities. They returned to their labors with enlarged ideas and quickened energies.[28]

Having done this much, what else could the Board undertake? A whole world of labors. Apart from the remnants of its Southern activities, it was soon expending its energies in three principal directions: in improving the work of colleges and universities, in raising the standards of American medical schools, and in making surveys to ascertain the possible existence of other needs in education. When it touched colleges and universities on the one side, and medical schools on the other, it touched two very sensitive spheres. Its activities were soon receiving vigorous criticism as well as warm praise.

Rockefeller in his second gift to the Board had directed it to do what it could "to promote a comprehensive system of higher education in the United States." Its first task was to study the field. As

[28]General Education Board, *Annual Report,* 1923–24, pp. 28, 29.

Doctor Abraham Flexner says in his history of the first dozen years of the Board, 1902–14, it scrutinized all the higher institutions in the country—their number, origins, purposes, location, resources, potential strength, "and, with the utmost particularity, their relations to their respective communities, educationally and otherwise."[29] Obviously, the nation had far too many weak, ill-nourished institutions. About 700 schools, exclusive of technological institutions, called themselves colleges or universities. Ohio, with fewer than 5,000,000 people, boasted of forty, or about twice as many as the whole German Empire of 65,000,000. Many were hardly more than secondary schools, while others offered only one or two years of true college work. In 1913, only twenty-five enjoyed an annual income of a half million or more, and one fourth of the 700 received less than $100,-000 a year from all sources. Only a small number of them were definitely articulated with the secondary schools of their respective States; only a few were wise enough to confine themselves to really needed work which they were well equipped to perform, the remainder being dangerously overextended. In their location, their programs, and their personnel they often evinced a total absence of planning. Even when a number of them had been established by the same denomination they seldom had co-operative relations, while a larger unity among all the institutions of a single State had not even been proposed. Observers, as Doctor Flexner wrote, found their emotions oscillating between disgust and admiration:[30]

Local, institutional, or denominational pride, vanity, or self-interest, propped up tottering, feeble, or superfluous institutions, some of them established in this or that State or county for no better reason than that a small town wanted one, or a rival denomination already had one. Of course worthier motives in abundance also played their part. Many of these schools, seriously defective according to modern ideas, had done good work under the pioneer conditions that have only lately passed away; splendid devotion and self-sacrifice had gone into their making, and their graduates had become important factors in the development of their respective communities.

The Board, on a highly selective basis, undertook to extend assistance to what it thought the most deserving institutions. By 1924 it had contributed more than $20,300,000 to 134 colleges and uni-

[29]*The General Education Board, 1902–14,* pp. 108, 109.
[30]*Idem,* 111.

versities on condition that they raise nearly $76,500,000 more—which they were rapidly doing. The Board (Gates was chairman until May, 1917, and was succeeded by Buttrick) acted upon certain broad general principles. First, it gave only to schools of proved stability and on the stipulation that others also give liberally. Second, it showed a preference for centers of wealth and population as the natural capitals of higher education in America. In the third place, it asked that efforts be concentrated, in general, upon the strengthening of endowments. Finally, it undertook a systematic and sympathetic co-operation with all religious denominations; this being entirely natural, for the Board was in part the heir and outgrowth of the Baptist Education Society.[31] These basic principles might be called an amalgamation of the ideas of Rockefeller and Gates, though in their application the counsel of such Board members as Charles W. Eliot, Walter Hines Page, Edwin A. Alderman, Albert Shaw, Anson Phelps Stokes, George E. Vincent, and the younger Rockefeller was invaluable.

The plan of conditional giving worked wonders. Not that the Board ever "required" any institution to raise a certain sum. On the contrary, the college always took the initiative, notifying the Board that it meant to collect certain amounts for such-and-such purposes, and inviting a contribution. Sometimes the Board gave half the total, sometimes one third, sometimes one fourth. We find it granting a weak institution, Maryville College, $40,000 on the understanding that the college would raise $20,000 more. We also find it granting Harvard $500,000 for general endowment toward a total of $10,000,000. Much more typical were the grants made in 1919 to Vassar, Smith, Wellesley, Bryn Mawr, and Holyoke; $500,-000 each, the colleges to raise $1,500,000 more respectively. The Board never drew any denominational lines. It gave alike to Knox, which was Presbyterian; to Hobart, which was Episcopal; to Allegheny, which was Methodist; to St. Olaf, which was Lutheran; to Carleton, which was Congregational; to Swarthmore, which was Quaker; and to Fordham, which was Catholic. It did not refuse its aid to State-supported institutions. For example, in 1924 it gave liberally to William and Mary, maintained by Virginia. Its conditional donations aroused more effort than had been thought pos-

[31]*Idem*, 7, 143 ff.

sible. Not only did the campaigns to match its grants enlist immediate support, but they stimulated a continuing interest shown in
subsequent gifts and bequests. "Under the stimulus of your pledge,"
wrote one president, "a local movement was begun, local resources
were developed, alumni and friends were aroused, and we secured
not only a million dollars, but twenty-five hundred investors in our
educational enterprise."[32]

With the gifts, as an aim which gave peculiar satisfaction to Rockefeller, went an insistence on better financial administration. It was
impossible to give wisely to a college or university without obtaining
a fianncial statement from it. Many of these statements showed a
sad confusion; some a still sadder mismanagement. Walter Hines
Page was impressed by the incompetence of various academic authorities. "They accept all sorts of gifts—unproductive land, embarrassing annuities, and the like; and they manage their affairs rather
with a sort of blind trust in Providence than with clear entries on their
ledgers. Often their assets are really liabilities in disguised forms."[33]
Numerous institutions had no proper system of bookkeeping, no
annual audit, no distinction between current funds and invested
capital. Even careful institutions had "borrowed" from their endowments in time of stress and so dissipated their resources. With no
desire to act as financial policeman, but simply to make sure that
the money it gave would be safeguarded, the Board had to call for
drastic reforms. In particular, they asked for full assurances that
trust funds would not be used to meet current expenses. As time
passed the Board's officers, when requested, made detailed examinations of academic finances, and a volume by one of the secretaries,
Trevor Arnett, on *College and University Finance,* was widely distributed. Rockefeller made repeated gifts to the Board; $10,000,000
in 1905, $32,000,000 in 1907, and $10,000,000 again in 1909. One
later grant was especially noteworthy. The close of the World War
brought such a sharp increase in living costs that the purchasing
power of academic salaries, always meager, was cut in half almost
without warning. Costs of administration had similarly increased.
Institutions of higher education faced a grave financial crisis. Largely
at the instance of George E. Vincent, Rockefeller just before Christmas in 1919 gave the Board securities worth approximately $50,-

[32]*Idem,* 154.   [33]Burton J. Hendrick, *Training of an American,* 378.

000,000, the principal and interest to be used primarily in co-operation with institutions which were trying to increase their salaries. The result was a distinct rise in the scale of academic remuneration. Within five years, nearly four fifths of the grant had been distributed among about 170 colleges and universities as additions to endowment, while they were raising some $83,000,000 more. What this meant to a host of struggling teachers and their families could not easily be overestimated.

And what else did the Board undertake? The answer is that it took up many labors, reaching into far corners of the land; but the most striking were in the field of medical education. For a number of years three men dominated the active work of the Board: Gates, Buttrick, and Abraham Flexner. They worked in the utmost harmony. They brought to their labors a lighthearted adventurousness. The docket which went to the trustees was drafted by Flexner, and then amended by Gates and Buttrick; and in general no action was taken except by agreement of all three. Flexner was full of ideas, Buttrick of enthusiasm, energy, and questions. "I'd sometimes come out of Buttrick's office feeling like a squeezed sponge," relates Flexner. Gates liked to operate on the grand scale, and was impatient of petty proposals. "That is retail business—other people will look after it," he would remark contemptuously when a small scheme was laid before him. The three made a remarkable triumvirate, proposing bold plans, talking them over endlessly, exuberantly amending and enlarging them, and finally either tossing them aside or making a courageous decision.

One of their plans amounted to little less than a thorough reorganization of American medical education. Gates had long been passionately interested in medical progress. Flexner, while an expert for the Carnegie Foundation, had written profoundly influential books on *Medical Education in the United States and Canada* (1910) and *Medical Education in Europe* (1912). Both men were distressed by the fact that most American medical schools were still proprietary profit-making institutions, that equipment and teaching staffs were usually wretched, and that even where good teachers existed, they obtained an adequate income only by combining general practice with their lectures. They discussed the matter again and again. They drew the hard-working, single-minded, unselfish Buttrick

February 26, 1920.

Dear Mr. Rockefeller:

Your latest gift to this Board of $150,000,000 for the purpose of raising the salaries of teachers in higher institutions of learning is a momentous event in American educational history. The new price levels and the consequent decline in the value of endowments have caused a crisis in our educational affairs, and your gift brings aid to this situation on an unexampled scale.

All who are concerned for the future of American education must be profoundly moved by an act which promises such beneficent consequences. It will afford direct relief to many higher institutions of learning which are indispensable to American educational welfare and to the development of intellectual leaders; in our judgment it will also stimulate others to make similar contributions in the same cause.

The results which should be achieved by a gift of this magnitude are so important that no expression of thanks can be adequate; at the same time we wish to offer you our earnest and warm appreciation of your generous wisdom, and to express our deep sense of responsibility in connection with the disbursement of this great fund. It shall be our task so to distribute it among educational institutions as most effectively to carry out the wise purposes of the donor.

The General Education Board thanks Rockefeller for

we shall rely in turn upon those institutions to make use of it in accordance with their aims in such manner as to satisfy the expectations and ideals of American public opinion.

Frederick T Gates *Trevor Arnett*

Wallace Buttrick *Abraham Flexner*

Albert Shaw *John D. Rockefeller Jr.*

Starr J. Murphy *Harry Pratt Judson*

Edwin A. Alderman *Wickliffe Rose*

Jerome D. Greene *Charles P. Howland*

Frank E. Spaulding

James H. Dillard

George E. Vincent.

Members of the General Education Board.

his gift of fifty millions to improve academic salaries.

into their parleys. Finally, one day in Gates's office something like the following colloquy took place:[34]

Flexner.—"Mr. Gates, it will take hundreds of millions to reorganize medical education in the United States the way it should be reorganized."

Gates (feet characteristically on desk, gesticulating with cigar).—"Mr. Rockefeller cannot do it all. But he can start the ball rolling. The rest will follow."

Flexner (with determination).—"If Mr. Rockefeller will start it rolling, I think by hard work I can get a good deal of the remainder."

Gates (enthusiastic but guarded).—"How much? What sum is in your mind?"

Flexner (with an air of caution).—"Fifty millions will do as a start."

This was far from "retail business." And enlisting Rockefeller and the trustees, they rapidly realized a great part of their dream. The plan was to create strong medical schools, operated in conjunction with well-equipped hospitals and clinics, and abreast of the finest European models, at key points where they might serve as examples. Existing institutions were to be utilized and other givers enlisted. The Board began by making large grants to the medical departments of various universities, notably Johns Hopkins, Yale, and Washington; more than $5,000,000 up to the summer of 1919. Meanwhile the war had emphasized the medical weaknesses of the nation. Only with the greatest difficulty were competent directors found for the 150 American base hospitals, while the medical corps was never strong. Rockefeller on September 20, 1919, gave securities worth more than $20,000,000 "for the advancement of medical education in the United States," and followed it with other large donations.

One by one sterling schools were erected in strategic centers. Already, in 1916, the Board had pledged its aid to the University of Chicago in creating a complete medical department. As a result of gifts from numerous sources, including $1,000,000 each from the Board and the Rockefeller Foundation, a great medical center was set up in Chicago, possessing resources of almost $15,000,000 at the outset. It was equally important to assist the South. The Board did this by appropriating to the struggling medical school of Vanderbilt University $5,500,000 in two years; a sum sufficient

[34]Doctor Abraham Flexner to the author.

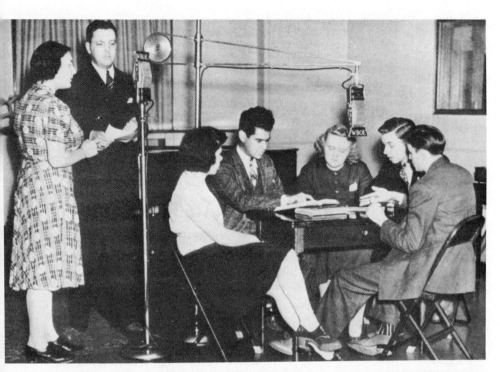

From a photograph by James Meli.

Rockefeller Foundation activities in the North.

Above: Broadcasting a discussion over a school station, Cleveland. *Below:* Master blacksmith at Clinton, N. J., instructing pupils in making I-bolts.

Rockefeller Foundation activities for the Negro.

Above: A class in the Summer Demonstration School, Fisk University, Nashville.
Below: Instruction of an industrial arts group at Beaver Dams, N. Y.

to place the institution firmly on its feet, and to create a new standard of medical education in that area. Another gift of $5,000,000 enabled the University of Rochester to launch in 1919 a medical school which, thanks to the generosity of George Eastman and other donors, had total initial resources of about $11,000,000. It immediately became one of the best medical centers of the East. In assisting it, Flexner and Gates were actuated partly by a desire to stimulate Columbia and Cornell Universities to take as advanced a position in the field as Chicago. And these institutions did not tarry long. The Board soon joined the Rockefeller Foundation in contributing $2,000,000 to the fund which enabled Columbia University and the Presbyterian Hospital to rear their magnificent medical center in upper New York; while still larger gifts were later made to the Cornell center, an equally impressive institution on the East River.

The Board even co-operated with the State University of Iowa in erecting a fine medical school. Gates was reluctant, fearing that they would be embroiled in politics. As Mr. Flexner says, he had an electric intellect, but also one that was very cautious; when he made up his mind, it was either with complete enthusiasm or a total lack of it. The university officials had asked for a pathological laboratory. "No," said Flexner in effect, "that is too small—it will get you nowhere. What you need is to reorganize your whole medical school, at a cost of $5,000,000 or more." The dean was fearful, though himself enthusiastically favorable. "We can't persuade the Iowa farmers to furnish so much money," he said. "But won't the farmers of Iowa buy a dollar for fifty cents?" demanded Flexner. "We'll give our half at once." In 1922 they did give $2,500,-000 to help Iowa build and equip a splendid medical school in the heart of the Mississippi Valley, and the farmers gave as much more. Nor was this all—but the full story of the Board's achievements cannot here be told.[35]

The work of giving the best medical schools full-time teachers is a chapter in itself. It began in 1913, when the Board, upon a request from Johns Hopkins, appropriated $1,500,000 to enable that university to establish a full-time staff in the departments of medicine, surgery, and pediatrics. The innovation was quickly pro-

[35]See General Education Board, *Annual Reports,* 1914–1940, for full data.

nounced a great step forward. Yale and Washington Universities followed in organizing similar staffs. The reform rapidly affected other institutions, though the Board emphasized the fact that only well-endowed and highly developed institutions could afford to adopt it. As it spread, Mr. Flexner was commissioned soon after the war to prepare a comparative study of medical education in America and the principal nations of western Europe. His penetrating volume (*Medical Education,* 1925) furnished a much-needed spur to further effort, for it showed that the clinical side of medicine was still feebly developed in the New World, that a sound relationship between medical schools and hospitals was far too uncommon, and that much of our medical research and teaching did not meet the highest ideals of science.

In some labors the General Education Board encountered heavy criticism. Southern politicians long remained suspicious of it. Though most colleges and universities welcomed its aid in financial reorganization, a few resented its stipulations. Many weak institutions were disappointed when it declined to help them. Numerous educators, including able and sincere men, believed that colleges exposed themselves to grave perils in accepting its bounty, some dreading Rockefeller's interference, some the influence of the Standard Oil, some the bureaucracy of a moneyed institution. They pictured this richly endowed Board as a paralyzing influence, destroying initiative and compelling timid presidents and deans to conform to fixed rules. Not a few officers and teachers of medical schools were bitterly opposed to the principle of the full-time staff, and reason exists for believing that some individuals who secretly disliked the plan accepted it merely that their schools might get the Board's money.

But the work as a whole was beneficial. Much of it paid magnificent returns upon the sums invested. And the basis for most criticisms of the Board was demolished when the founder and its officers acted in one direction to destroy the "dead hand" requirements which had limited grants to specific purposes, and in another direction to do away with conditional grants. In 1920 Rockefeller wrote to the Board: "If in any gifts heretofore made to you by me there are any restrictions or limitations as to the specific purpose for which they are to be used, I hereby revoke such restrictions."

This showed a wise development in his point of view.[36] The Board in turn, by letters retroactive in effect, gave various institutions greater freedom in the use of funds once granted for specific purposes; a library, a laboratory, an endowment. In the same way, the making of gifts conditional upon certain acts (say the installing of a full-time medical staff) was gradually abandoned. Donations were frequently offered to colleges and universities in contemplation of certain aims, but never upon a rigid requirement of them. The resultant freedom benefited education and the Board alike.

[36]See Raymond B. Fosdick's comment, *The Rockefeller Foundation: A Review for 1937*, p. 8.

XLIX

The Opened Purse

A FUNDAMENTAL fact regarding Rockefeller's wealth, quite elementary to any economist, must be clearly grasped. Vast as it seemed, it was tiny in relation to the world's needs. As direct charity it could accomplish little. But used as a germinating agency, a leaven or stimulant, it might cause wonders to be performed. Nine hundred millions seems a huge amount of money. But when Rockefeller died the Federal Government had spent seven hundred millions upon one defensive item, the Pearl Harbor Naval Base. President Vincent of the Rockefeller Foundation pointed out in his report for 1917 that although the Foundation's endowment had a book value of $120,000,000, its annual income would pay the current expenses of the national government for only seven hours; its principal for only five days. The public functions of New York City could be supported for only twelve days out of the Foundation's income, while the current Red Cross program would consume that income in seventeen days. If the Foundation tried to meet the whole bill for private charity in the United States, he estimated that its annual revenue would carry the budget for but twelve and a half days.[1]

In short, the resources of all Rockefeller's benevolences, when measured against the needs of the government, or charity, or public health, or education, were very limited. If the money were simply parcelled out to deserving agencies as they asked for it, the results would be slight. The gifts might even do harm by drying up existing sources of income for good works. The way in which Rockefeller demonstrated his wisdom as a philanthropist was by striking

---

[1] *The Rockefeller Foundation, A Review for 1917*, pp. 5, 6.

at the root of various needs; by promoting great object-lessons in charity; by initiating valuable programs which others could carry on; by stimulating men to act and to give.

Rockefeller, who never gave without a plan, clearly perceived this, as he perceived other basic principles in philanthropy. He came to realize, for example, that his wisdom and that of his advisers was less valuable to the future than the wisdom of future generations. It would be a mistake to make a rigid allocation of money for specific purposes which might soon be outmoded. Some men who had done that in the past had become time's laughing-stocks. He knew the history of British as well as American trust funds, and as Raymond B. Fosdick later wrote, would have agreed with Sir Arthur Hobhouse's comment on medieval foundations—that nations cannot long tolerate "the spectacle of large masses of property settled to unalterable uses." He came also to accept the equally important principle that no foundation, no matter how broad its terms, should be set up in perpetuity. "Perpetuity is a pretty long time," he remarked.[2] When he died the General Education Board was approaching liquidation, and it was understood that the other boards he had created would in no long period expend their principal and dissolve.

II

Controversy attended nearly all of Rockefeller's acts. It raged even about the creation of his greatest and freest philanthropy, the Rockefeller Foundation. After roughly a decade of experience with the Institute and General Education Board, he and his advisers felt that they had demonstrated the soundness of the principle of entrusting large sums to able and public-spirited trustees. He wished to begin giving unprecedented sums to a new agency of larger scope. The General Education Board was restricted by charter to the United States; this new organization should have the world as its field, and all aspects of human need as its prospect. For two main reasons a Federal charter appeared desirable. It seemed stronger, safer, and more dignified than State incorporation; moreover, the Board had one. A suitable bill was therefore prepared and introduced.

But hardly had this bill been reported favorably (March 10, 1910)

[2]*The Rockefeller Foundation, A Review for 1937*, pp. 7, 8.

from the Senate Committee on the District of Columbia than a wild storm burst about it. In this tempest two elements were discernible. One was the opposition of politicians and editors to whom anything connected with Rockefeller was anathema; who, as the Chicago *Inter-Ocean* remarked, would have denounced a bill permitting

From the Philadelphia "Star."   *Cartoon by Robert Carter in the "New York American."*

Two views of the Rockefeller Foundation, 1910.
Some cartoonists regarded it with fantastic suspicion; others
treated it more generously.

him to donate his whole fortune to the government, or to retire to a monastery. The other was more respectable. It lay in the opposition of thoughtful critics who were genuinely disturbed by the vagueness of the proposed charter, the possible magnitude of the foundation's tax-free resources, and the perpetuity implied in the grant. Rumor stated that a quarter billion, a half billion, even a billion would be given the foundation. In its power to do anything "to advance civilization" some men saw all kinds of dragons and chimeras dire.

The fact was that the bill might well have passed without a syllable changed. As *The Nation* said,[3] its terms spoke of sagacity and large-mindedness. "All of that talent for making large combinations and for creating an instrument of centralized control which went to the accumulating of Mr. Rockefeller's vast fortune seems now to have been applied to devising this magnificent scheme." As Congress would create the Foundation, so Congress might abolish or alter it at any time. But some really constructive suggestions were made by Edward T. Devine, editor of *The Survey,* and President Schurman of Cornell. Devine proposed that the government should be given a voice in selecting the trustees, that the expansion of the endowment through compound interest should be forbidden, and that the agency should be required to spend all its funds within a century or two.[4] Schurman objected to "a self-perpetuating and irresponsible board, wielding enormous powers."[5] The widespread opposition caused the bill to be laid aside. But the next year Jerome D. Greene volunteered to go to Washington and renew the effort to obtain a Federal charter. The result was the introduction of a new bill of more restricted character.[6] It provided that the fund should be limited to $100,000,000, that income should not be accumulated, that after a century Congress might direct the distribution of the remaining principal, and that certain Federal and university officers should have a veto power over the selection of new Board members. In short, the measure was now hedged about by even too many prohibitions.

It was no misfortune that in this new form it failed to pass. It got through the House early in 1913 by a vote of 155 to 65, but was caught in the Senate log-jam at the end of the session; unanimous consent was required to bring it to vote, and a few Senators always objected. A Western newspaper remarked that Rockefeller had been represented by "the most powerful lobby ever seen in Washington." The lobby was Mr. Jerome D. Greene! When Congress adjourned,

[3]March 10, 1910. [4]*Survey,* March 12, 1910.
[5]See his pamphlet, "Speech Before the Cornell Congress, April 22, 1910." The N. Y. *Times,* March 26, 1910, called the objections "a mare's nest." *Hampton's Magazine,* May, 1910, pp. 732, 733, argued that the Standard Oil, dissolved by the courts, would reconstitute itself as the Rockefeller Foundation! Starr J. Murphy's full explanation before the Senate Committee is in *61st Cong., 2d Sess., Senate Report 405.*
[6]For approving editorials, see *Survey,* Jan. 14, 1911; *Outlook,* Jan. 7, 1911; *Independent,* Feb. 8, 1912.

Rockefeller's staff turned to the New York legislature. That body passed a bill, practically identical with that first proposed to Congress, which became law May 14, 1913.

"To promote the well-being of mankind throughout the world"— so ran the basic terms of the charter. The original trustees comprised the elder Rockefeller, Gates, Simon Flexner, Jerome D. Greene, C. O. Heydt, Harry Pratt Judson, Starr J. Murphy, Wickliffe Rose, and John D. Rockefeller, Jr., who was destined to serve for twenty-seven years. The younger Rockefeller was the first president, becoming chairman of the board when in 1917 George E. Vincent left the University of Minnesota to accept the presidency; Greene was secretary and executive officer. "There was a brief time in my little room at 26 Broadway," Greene later remarked, "when one secretary with a four-drawer file constituted the staff and equipment of the Rockefeller Foundation."[7]

It was characteristic of Rockefeller that, though specially invited, he refused to attend the first meeting of the trustees or any other; and that although asked to become honorary president, he declined to hold any official relation with the Foundation. His rule was never to meddle. In an early gift he reserved the right to designate the uses to which about $2,000,000 of income annually should be devoted, but within three years this limitation was withdrawn. His gifts to the Foundation were made substantially in five large blocks. In 1913 he gave $34,430,000; the following year, $65,570,000 more; in 1919, slightly more than $50,000,000; and in 1929, the merger of the Laura Spelman Rockefeller Memorial with the Foundation added $53,006,000. Some small interspersed gifts brought the total in this period to $235,000,000. But while Rockefeller made the Foundation the principal engineer and agent of his benefactions, he kept his hands entirely off the management. He took the keenest interest in its work and that of the Board; Abraham Flexner states that his strong sympathy illustrated the converse of Lowell's line, "The gift without the giver is bare."[8] But save in informal conferences with his son, he refused in any way to advise or comment.

The first meetings of the trustees were devoted to a discussion of the policies and labors which were most likely to offer permanent

[7]MS address of John D. Rockefeller, Jr., as retiring chairman of the board, April 3, 1940.
[8]Mr. Flexner to the author.

and far-reaching usefulness. It was generally agreed that the advancement of public health through medical research and education, including the demonstration of known methods of curing disease, afforded the best prospect for an initial step. On June 27, 1913, the trustees therefore created the International Health Commission. Its aims were set forth in a resolution beginning: "Whereas, the Rockefeller Sanitary Commission, organized in 1909 for the eradication of hookworm disease in the United States, has found more than two million people in the Southern States to be infected with the disease . . ." By this preamble hangs a tale—the story of a great emancipation.

III

If controversy dogged Rockefeller's work, so also did drama. In a striking chapter of *Our Times* Mark Sullivan relates how in 1902 a reporter for the New York *Sun,* listening to a lecture in Washington by Doctor Charles W. Stiles of the Federal Health Service upon the "uncinariasis americana" or hookworm, exploded that parasite into fame by a news-story headline: "Germ of Laziness Found?"[9] Almost nobody had heard of the hookworm, but Doctor Stiles declared that he had recently found it widely prevalent in the South, where its devitalizing effects led to chronic indolence. The press at once took up the "bacillus" supposedly responsible for human laziness. Cartoonists drew fanciful sketches of the animal; jokesters linked it to our Weary Willies and Rip Van Winkles; merry jingles studded the press. The idea that a disease-germ gave rise to that delightful springtime desire to loaf and go fishing, that lazy office boys and sleeping policemen had simply been bitten by a microbe, delighted Americans intensely.

The hookworm, as a matter of fact, was very far from a joke. Doctor Stiles had first encountered the parasite while a student in Europe, finding that the hookworm disease afflicted many people in Italy, France, and southern Germany. In the United States the ailment had never been recognized in its true character. Yet when Stiles returned home, a little study convinced him that it was actually very common. Hearing of the widespread practice of "clay-eating" associated with "chronic anemia" or "continuous malaria"

[9]*Our Times: Pre-War Years* (III), Ch. 9.

in the South, he became certain that the real cause was the hook-worm. This intestinal parasite, a worm about a third of an inch long when grown, produces an incredible number of eggs. They hatch when deposited on the soil, and while still invisible to the eye, enter the human body, usually through the bare feet. Thence they make a long journey through the body until they reach the small intestines, to which they cling with a little hook—whence their name —and give forth a poison which produces the disease, meanwhile laying more eggs. As many as 4500 worms have been expelled from a single person. They have been known to live in human beings for ten years, and are so common that large parts of the warmer zones of the earth are polluted by them. The lassitude common in China, India, and large parts of Latin America is in great degree attributable to them.[10]

Stiles began to expound his belief—to preach a crusade. In 1896 Doctor Osler rebuked him for declaring that the disease existed in America, but Stiles replied: "Wait and see." Support came from an unexpected quarter. In 1899 a talented young army surgeon, Bailey K. Ashford, treating hurricane victims in Puerto Rico, found that great numbers of the emaciated scarecrows were really hookworm victims. By simple doses of thymol to kill the parasites and Epsom salts to expel them he cured thousands of the sufferers.[11] Stiles's conviction as to the prevalence of the disease in the South was fortified by Ashford's work, by the discovery of hookworm cases among students at the University of Texas, and by his own careful observations. He continued his campaign of publicity and agitation. He pointed to the tremendous economic losses. But for years, even after the *Sun* reporter had created a fleeting national sensation, he accomplished little. The complacent American people simply would not awaken to the grave malady. Then he met Walter Hines Page. Travelling with him in 1908 through the South on a train used by Roosevelt's Commission on Country Life, he pointed out to the editor a typical dirt-eater lounging on a platform: scrawny, yellow-skinned, pot-bellied, misshapen, apathetic—a human wreck.

"His condition is due to hookworm," Stiles told Page. "He can

[10]*American Journal of Tropical Diseases and Preventive Medicine,* April, 1914, I, 669 ff.; Rockefeller Sanitary Commission, Publication No. 61.

[11]"A Ten Years' Campaign Against Hookworm Disease in Porto Rico," *Journal of the American Medical Association,* May 28, 1910, LIV, 1757-1761.

be cured by fifty cents worth of drugs, and in a few weeks' time be turned into a useful man."

Page was astonished and excited, for the regeneration of the South and the elevation of its people had long been his greatest passion. The principal reason why Stiles had as yet accomplished so little lay in his lack of funds. But Page, long associated with Rockefeller's work, knew where to turn for aid. What ensued is admirably related by Mark Sullivan:

Stiles and the rest of the Commission on Country Life, returning from their tour, stopped at Cornell University. At a reception in their honor Stiles heard a voice booming behind him, "Where is Stiles?" He turned and was introduced to a plump, jolly-looking man, Wallace Buttrick, at that time secretary of the General Education Board, an organization through which Rockefeller carried on some of his philanthropic activities. Buttrick told Stiles: "Walter Page says you know something which I must know immediately; let us go to my room." Stiles and Buttrick talked hookworm almost all night.

Back in Washington Stiles was settling into the routine of his office when a telegram came to him from Doctor Simon Flexner; Flexner was director of the laboratories of the Rockefeller Institute for Medical Research, and his telegram invited Stiles to New York for a conference. Stiles went, armed with specimen case, microscope, drawings, photographs, and statistics. At Rockefeller's office Flexner introduced Stiles to Frederick T. Gates, Rockefeller's chief adviser in his philanthropies. Stiles told his story, Flexner and Gates listening quietly. After about forty minutes Gates interrupted, rang for a messenger, and sent for Starr J. Murphy, whose place in the Rockefeller hierarchy of benevolence was described as "personal counsel and benevolent representative." When Murphy appeared, Gates said: "This is the biggest proposition ever put up to the Rockefeller office. Listen to what Doctor Stiles has to say. Now, Doctor, start from the beginning and tell Mr. Murphy what you have told me."

After several more conferences, Gates called Stiles to his home one night and told him: "The Rockefeller office will support this work."

The next step was the organization of the Rockefeller Sanitary Commission, with Stiles, William H. Welch, and Simon Flexner as the medical members, and nine lay members. Wickliffe Rose, a Tennesseean of broad culture and fine personality who, after a distinguished academic career, had become general agent of the Peabody Fund, was appointed administrative secretary, and Stiles as scientific secretary. In October, 1909, it was announced that Rockefeller had given $1,000,000 for a ten years' war on the hookworm. "It is a peculiar pleasure to me," he wrote, "to feel that the principal activities of your board will be among the people of our Southern States. It has been my pleasure of late to spend a portion of each year in the South and I have come to know and to respect greatly that part of our country and to enjoy the society and friendship of many of its warm-hearted people. It will, therefore, be an added gratification to me if in this way I may in some measure express my appreciation of their many kindnesses and hospitalities."[12]

Already, for many months in 1908–9, Rockefeller's representatives had studied the prevalence of the disease and made plans for dealing with it. Headquarters were set up in Washington. With practical wisdom, a plan of co-operation with the health authorities of the Southern States was adopted. The procedure was for the commission to appropriate a certain sum to the State officials and to choose an executive officer to direct the work. This officer divided the State into districts, each under a physician as inspector; infected persons were treated by their local doctors; and special provision was made for care of the indigent.[13]

The tact shown in this approach was much needed. The hypersensitive South was inclined to resent the jeering and patronizing tone with which some Northern journals wrote of the hookworm, and a large body of Southern spokesmen heaped abuse with proud facility upon Rockefeller, Stiles, and the Commission. But this prejudice rapidly abated. By 1913 approximately 900,000 people had been examined, and 500,000 who were infected had been treated. Whole communities were being restored to health. It was still estimated that the South had 2,000,000 cases of the disease; but by 1927, when about 7,000,000 people in all had been treated, its incidence had been greatly reduced in the United States. As Doctor Eliot said, the work was "the most effective campaign against a wide-spreading disease which medical science and philanthropy have ever combined to conduct." Page regarded it as effecting a veritable social revolution. The cause of the long backwardness of the Southern people had

[12]For Rockefeller's letter see *Science*, Nov. 5, 1909, N. S. XXX, 635, 636.
[13]*Virginia Health Bulletin*, June, 1910; *Bulletin of the North Carolina Board of Health*, Dec., 1910; W. H. Glasson, "The Rockefeller Commission's Campaign Against Hookworm," *South Atlantic Quarterly*, April, 1911, X, 140–150.

at last been explained—and found removable. It was not malaria, it was not climate, it was not the "poor white" element; it was the

COMING!

To Roxobel, Kelford and Powellsville.

BERTIE CO. HOOKWORM DISPENSARIES.

HOOKWORM GREATLY MAGNIFIED

The County Commissioners have so arranged with the North Carolina Board of Health that the towns of Roxobel, Kelford and Powellsville will secure the services of The State and County Free Hookworm Dispensaries.

Dr. Covington, a state specialist on these diseases, and Mr. Conner, an expert microscopist, will be in attendance at these dispensaries on the days and dates printed below.

Everybody should visit these dispensaries on the dates given below, be examined and see if they have any of these diseases. If you have, medicine will be given that will change you from a tired, indolent, despondent kind of a man to one who goes about his work with a vim and a rush, always finding pleasure in everything. Ask any of the thousands who have already been treated in this county. They know. All this without any cost to you whatever. All is paid for by the state and county. Come, bring your wife and children with you, let them see the different varieties of worms that often infect people. See the hookworm eggs under the microscope and hear talks on this disease.

Remember the dates as this will be your last opportunity to be examined and treated free of all cost.

In visiting the dispensaries do not neglect to bring with you a very small box on which you have written your name and age containing a small specimen of your bowel movement as only in this way can an examination be made. In making this examination, if present, any of the worms are found, whether it be the tape worm, round worm, or any of the other various varieties.

The name of the Rockefeller Sanitary Commission did not appear on the announcements like these. People were allowed to think that the campaign was purely a state enterprise.

same disease that had for centuries retarded the people of India, China, and Central America. "The hookworm," he wrote,[14] "has

[14]Walter H. Page, "The Hookworm and Civilization," *World's Work*, XXIV (1912), 504–518.

probably played a larger part in our Southern history than slavery or wars or any political dogma or economic creed"—and now the hookworm was being abolished. Not only that, but in destroying it Doctor Stiles and the Commission were promoting general sanitation in the South, lessening the ravages of typhoid and other diseases, and stimulating a spirit of neighborliness and courage.

As Mark Sullivan writes, the hookworm is now one with Nineveh and Tyre. The nation has forgotten it. Yet the success of this battle inspired the Rockefeller Foundation in 1913 to carry the same fight to other lands. The parasite flourished in areas belting the earth and containing a thousand million people, while in some nations the infection touched 90 per cent of the population. It was a weighty factor in retarding the economic, social, and moral progress of mankind. Hence the Foundation set up the International Health Commission to extend to other countries the eradication of the hookworm, and to follow this up by the establishment of agencies to promote public sanitation and scientific medicine. Wickliffe Rose was appointed director-general. Of the work which this extremely able man did until 1923, when he became president of the General Education Board; of the labors of other devoted men, like Colonel F. F. Russell, who succeeded Doctor Rose as director of the International Health Commission, and John A. Ferrell, director for the United States, we can make but the barest mention here. One widely known servant of the Board, Victor G. Heiser, director for the East, has described part of its work in an autobiography which has reached millions.[15]

IV

The history of the Rockefeller Foundation falls into three main phases. The first was an initial period, 1913–16, of exploration and experiment, during which the International Health Commission and a cognate enterprise, the China Medical Board, were launched. Under this latter board a modern medical college and hospital were built in Peking. Some experiments with techniques were also conducted, and Jerome D. Greene presented to the trustees in 1916 a careful memorandum on research. The second period was opened

[15]The International Health Commission, like all the other Rockefeller agencies, published careful annual reports.

by the appointment of George E. Vincent as president in 1917. It witnessed the adoption and prosecution of a more concentrated program, effort being focussed in the main upon the advancement of public health and medical education. Most of the Foundation's income in this second period was spent upon the International Health Commission and China Medical Board, with a third agency created in 1919: the Division of Medical Education, renamed a decade later the Division of Medical Sciences. This period of concentrated activity lasted down to 1928. "The aim always kept in mind," President Vincent wrote, "is not to assume governmental or social functions, but to show that certain things can be done successfully, and then as soon as may be to turn these over to the community."

The third period, 1928 to the present, has been one of labor on a wider front, comprehending the medical sciences (with special attention to psychiatry), the natural sciences (especially experimental biology), the social sciences, and the humanities. This represented a natural evolution. In 1918 Rockefeller had founded a new charitable corporation, the Laura Spelman Rockefeller Memorial. Under the direction of Beardsley Ruml, a brilliant and fertile-minded leader, it had been developing research in the social sciences on an extensive scale. Within half a dozen years Doctor Ruml and his associates had appropriated twenty million dollars for various purposes, chiefly the development of university centers of research in America and abroad, and assistance to research councils and conferences through fellowships and other aids. Then in 1928 occurred a great merger. The Foundation took over the Laura Spelman Rockefeller Memorial with its social-science program, the natural-science program of the General Education Board, and the humanities program of the General Education Board. A new era in the worldwide activities of the Rockefeller philanthropies was opened. This first step toward unification under the Foundation permitted a better co-ordination of activities, a firmer handling of policy, and quicker shifts in strategy.[16]

But a statement in these general terms does little to indicate the wide range of the Foundation's activities, the variety of the ways in

[16]See the MS "History of Foundation Program, 1913–1936," a 28-page résumé, in Rockefeller Foundation archives; annual reports of the Foundation.

which it tried to leaven the whole lump. Some single undertakings had the qualities of an epopee: for example, the work of the Inter-

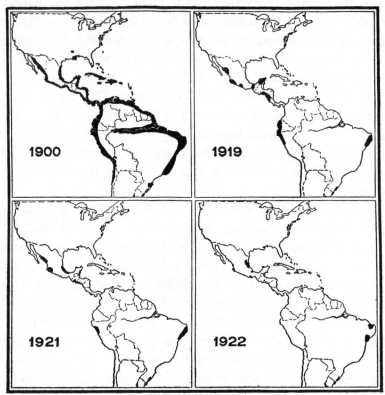

The battle against yellow fever.

The Rockefeller Foundation, through the International Health Commission, long furnished world leadership in the battle against yellow fever. It began a vigorous campaign in Ecuador in 1918. By 1925 the disease was making practically its last stand in the New World in Brazil. Many governments are carrying on the struggle on the basis of years of co-operative work with Rockefeller Foundation scientists.

national Health Commission in helping stamp out yellow fever all over the globe—a battle in the midst of which William Crawford Gorgas, organizing the campaign on the west coast of Africa, laid down his life. President Vincent's summary of the work in 1921 sufficiently indicates the scope of activity in the second phase:

During the year 1921 the Rockfeller Foundation (1) continued a quarter-million annual appropriation to the School of Hygiene and Public

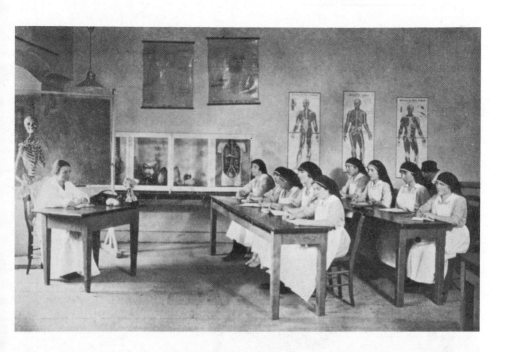

Rockefeller activities in public health.

Above: Classroom in Strasbourg School for Public Health. *Below (left):* Inspecting a water tank in Mexico. *Below (right):* Administering a dose of chenopodium to a boy in New Guinea.

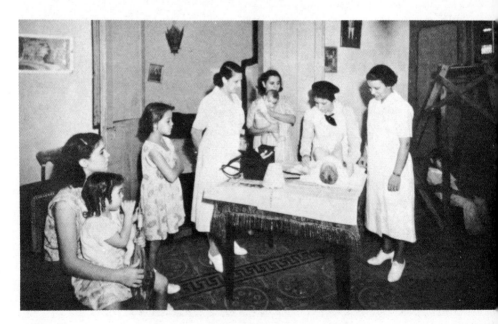

Activities of the Rockefeller Foundation.

Above: Public health nurse at work in Greece. *Below:* Instructing student nurses in the technique of home visiting, Cuba.

Health of Johns Hopkins University, (2) pledged two millions to Harvard for a school of health, (3) contributed to public health training in Czechoslovakia, Brazil, and the United States, (4) aided the Pasteur Institute of Paris to recruit and train personnel, (5) promoted the cause of nurse training in America and Europe, (6) underwrote an experimental pay clinic in the Cornell Medical School, (7) formally opened a complete modern medical school and hospital in Peking, (8) assisted 25 other medical centers in China, (9) promised a million dollars for the medical school of Columbia University, (10) contracted to appropriate three and one half millions for the building and reorganization of the medical school and hospital of the free University of Brussels, (11) made surveys of medical schools in Japan, China, the Philippines, Indo-China, Straits Settlements, Siam, Syria, India, and Turkey, (12) supplied American and British medical journals to 112 medical libraries on the continent, (13) supplemented the laboratory equipment and supplies of five medical schools in Central Europe, (14) defrayed the expenses of commissions from Great Britain, Belgium, Serbia, and Brazil, (16) continued a campaign against yellow fever in Mexico, Central and South America, (17) prosecuted demonstrations in the control of malaria in ten States, (18) co-operated in hookworm work in 19 governmental areas, (19) participated in rural health demonstrations in 77 American counties and in Brazil, (20) neared the goal of transferring to French agencies an antituberculosis organization in France, (21) provided experts in medical education and public health for counsel and surveys in many parts of the world, and rendered sundry minor services to governments and voluntary societies.

President Raymond B. Fosdick's report for 1938 shows the immense range of labors, touching forty-two countries in all parts of the world. They included:[17]

Vaccination of more than a million people in Brazil with an effective virus against yellow fever developed by the International Health Division; work to combat a severe outbreak of malaria in North Brazil; investigations of influenza, the common cold, tropical anemia, and other ailments; maintenance of a school in the Fiji Islands to train doctors for Oceania; large grants to the State Institute of Public Health in Stockholm and the Nursing School of the University of Toronto; support of psychiatrical and neurological work in London, Montreal, St. Louis, New York, Stanford, Baltimore, and other centers; the grant of $750,000 to Yale for its Institute of Human Relations; appropriations to a number of universities, from Leeds to California, for work in developing the new field of molecular biology; a grant of $1,500,000 to the University of Chicago toward an endowment fund for research in the biological

[17]This is my own résumé from the report.

sciences; a grant to the University of Illinois for studies in nutrition; battles against malaria in Cuba, Egypt, Greece, India, and other lands; support of the medical school of the American University of Beirut, of the Peiping Medical College, and of the China Medical Board, Inc.; a long list of grants to agencies trying to promote better international relations—the International Information Committee in Stockholm, the Institute of Economics and History in Copenhagen, the Council on Foreign Relations, the Institute of Pacific Relations, the Foreign Policy Association, the Graduate Institute of International Studies in Geneva; support of mass education in China; aid to agricultural schools and rural reconstruction in the same harried land; grants to the Social Science Research Council and American Council of Learned Societies; assistance to a long series of agencies for research and training in public administration—the National Institute of Public Affairs, Harvard's Graduate School of Public Administration, work in public administration at the Universities of Chicago and Southern California, and the Pacific Northwest Council of Education, Planning, and Public Administration; contributions for the development of Chinese studies in various American universities; an appropriation for an annual Handbook of Latin American Studies; grants for archæological work; assistance to the Library of Congress in microfilming; promotion of the drama by assistance to the regional dramatic work at the University of North Carolina and Western Reserve University, and to the National Theatre Conference; grants to the Museum of Modern Art in forming a library of motion picture films, and to the World Wide Broadcasting Foundation in experimenting with radio programmes of educational and cultural value.

All this seems a bit bewildering. But study of President Fosdick's 514-page report shows that it had been carefully planned, and fell into orderly coherence under half a dozen headings: the medical sciences, the social sciences, the natural sciences, public health, the humanities, and rural reconstruction in China. The aim was to guide and stimulate rather than to complete definite projects; and a cardinal rule of the Foundation was to withdraw from undertakings as soon as they were in a position to develop independently. By 1938 Rockefeller's philanthropic work had been fairly well integrated. Under the guidance of his son and others, the unification begun in 1928 had been carried forward step by step. Since the Rockefeller Foundation and the General Education Board were State and Federal incorporations respectively, it was not practicable to give them formal union; but they now had the same executives and trustees, and were managed almost as one.

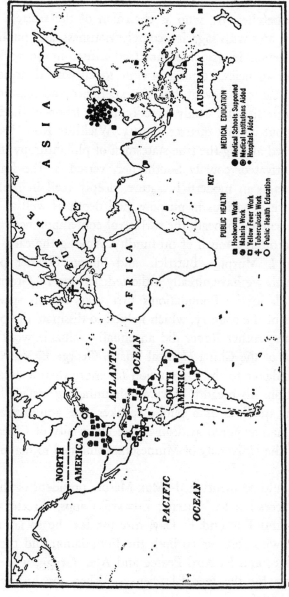

From the Review of Rockefeller Foundation Activities for 1919.

Worldwide activities of the Rockefeller Foundation in public health and medical education, 1919.

Like the General Education Board, the Foundation was fortunate in its principal officers. It enlisted a number of men of high organizing and administrative ability. In the roster must always be placed John D. Rockefeller, Jr., who as chairman of the trustees labored indefatigably, and with sagacity, conscientiousness, and public spirit, until his retirement in 1940. He immersed himself in the work of this and the other agencies, keeping in close touch with their activities; other officers came and went, but his experience and self-sacrificing zeal gave continuity and steady direction to the labors of the Foundation throughout its first quarter-century. Wickliffe Rose deserves to be remembered among the true statesmen of philanthropy in America. This cultivated, courtly Southerner, versed in the Latin and Greek classics as in modern literature, deeply read in philosophy, gentle of spirit, tenacious in purpose, had depth as well as breadth of mind. He saw far beneath the surface of contemporaneous trends; his ideas had often a touch of profundity. Among the early trustees Gates, Starr J. Murphy, Buttrick, and Simon Flexner possessed qualities which we have already indicated. Jerome D. Greene did a valuable work in the Foundation's first years by his speeches in various parts of the country, which helped to dissipate the prejudice against it; his brother Roger did an equally valuable work as resident director of the China Medical Board. George E. Vincent gave sagacious guidance to the Foundation for more than a decade. His ripe cultivation, his breadth of view, his unfailing tact and charm, his magnetic qualities as a public speaker, the administrative experience he had acquired as dean at the University of Chicago and president of the University of Minnesota, combined to make him an ideal head.

Others should be mentioned—Max Mason, president of the Foundation in succession to Vincent; Edward Capps, director for the humanities, and Edmund E. Day, director for the social sciences; Rufus Cole, who ably served both the Foundation and the Rockefeller Institute; and Richard Pearce and Alan Gregg, who were in turn directors for the medical sciences. When the history of the Rockefeller benefactions is fully written, a place of special distinction will be reserved for Raymond B. Fosdick. An attorney who first achieved notice as commissioner of accounts (an investigative post) in New York City, he spent 1913 in Europe studying police organization as a representative of the Rockefeller Bureau of Social Hygiene. Varied service in important public posts followed. For a time he was under secretary-general of the League of Nations. He became a trustee, one of the most active and resourceful, of all the important Rockefeller philanthropies—the Medical Institute, the General Education Board, the Spelman Fund, and the Rockefeller Foundation. When Max Mason resigned in 1936, he was the logical choice for president of the Foundation. Under his energetic guidance the General Education Board is terminating its activities, and the Foundation is carrying forward a many-sided work.

V

The Rockefeller philanthropies have made certain mistakes in both policies and personnel. Both the Foundation and General Education Board have gone hopefully up some roads that turned out to be blind alleys. The comprehensively planned studies in industrial relations which W. L. Mackenzie King began for the Foundation in 1914, for example, had to be thrown aside. Public suspicion and hostility developed; his program was made the subject of inquiry by the United States Commission on Industrial Relations under Frank P. Walsh; and so much public criticism arose that in 1917 the project was dropped. The Walsh investigation put a damper on foundation activities in the social sciences for some years. Looking back over the history of both the Foundation and the Board, students can see some sharp changes of direction which constitute a virtual admission of error in judgment. Money has now and then been wasted. A few unwise appointments to office have been made; friction has occasionally developed in internal management. All foundations have been criticized, and often with justice, for a tendency toward the development of inertia, insulation, and conservatism; it is contended that they become stiffly bureaucratic and timidly cautious. The organizations created by Rockefeller have shared in this criticism, though little in their history thus far justifies it.[18]

[18]Frederick P. Keppel, *The Foundation: Its Place in American Life;* Harold C. Coffman, *American Foundations;* W. A. Orton, "Endowments and Foundations" in *Encyclopædia of the Social Sciences,* V, 531–537. Foundations are criticized by Cornelia J. Cannon and Hans Zinsser in articles in the *Atlantic Monthly,* Sept., 1921, and Feb., 1927, respectively (CXXVIII, 289–300; CXXXIX, 246–250); defended by H. S. Pritchett in the *Atlantic,* Oct., 1929, CXLIV, 517–524, and Edwin R. Embree, a very able officer of the Rockefeller philanthropies, in *Harper's,* Aug., 1930, CLXI, 320–329.

One reproach long levelled against the Rockefeller Foundation was that "potentially if not actually" it was dominated by the founder and his son. For years this criticism was valid; when the Walsh investigation took place only two of the trustees were not either on the Rockefeller payroll or in the "official family." By 1936 the board of trustees was clearly independent, but some doubt still existed whether the powerful executive committee was not, like the finance committee, dominated by the official family. Yet even if valid, the criticism had little weight. For if the younger Rockefeller had the power to dominate, he never exercised it. "Time and again," writes one observer,[19] "Mr. Rockefeller, Jr., has been outvoted on the boards of his father's donations." His colleagues give striking instances of this; for he always insisted that they treat him precisely as they treated each other, and some of them took President Harper's pride in dissent. Moreover, as a sharp critic of foundations remarks, the younger Rockefeller "is a man of such catholic and impersonal interests and of such statesmanlike qualities" that his influence has been strongly beneficial.[20]

Upon this subject Mr. Rockefeller, Jr., has made a frank statement to the author. "The philanthropic boards which my father established," he writes, "usually began in a small way and developed gradually. Since they were the immediate outgrowth of his own personal philanthropies it was only natural that, generally speaking, they should have been manned at the outset by members of our 'official family' and those with whom we had been working along similar lines. However, as rapidly as capable and interested men were found outside this group they were added to the boards, in which members of the 'official family' gradually and properly became a minority." He adds that this principle has also pertained to the committees of the boards, except that he has been chairman of several of the Finance Committees. This was largely because he had means of knowing more than other trustees about the companies in the securities of which the original gifts had been made. "As my father's son, and his representative most closely related to the development of these boards; as a trustee for the longest period of time, I have naturally and properly felt a peculiar responsibility

[19]"John D. Rockefeller, Jr.," *Fortune,* July, 1936, XIV, No. 1.
[20]E. V. Hollis, *Philanthropic Foundations and Higher Education,* 80.

to the founder for the wise use of the large sums of money he gave to the boards. It is significant that with at least some of the officers and directors my interest in a project has been more apt to prejudice its favorable consideration than to forward it, so wholly independent of the founder and his so-called 'official family' have they been."

Another early criticism of some Rockefeller gifts, as of other foundations, was that the conditions imposed were unduly rigid. This, too, had some validity. But the trust instrument of the Rockefeller Foundation itself was so liberal that many attacked it for excessive breadth, and Rockefeller's letters of 1920 quoted above did much to nullify restrictions that experience had proved to be unwise. The assertion that Rockefeller's agencies, like those set up by Carnegie, Rosenwald, Harkness, and others, have tended to become bureaucratic and cautious, has been particularly emphasized. The tendency perhaps exists; but there are strong counter-tendencies. The Rockefeller funds have a really impressive record for work on what John Dewey calls "the growing edge of things." The Medical Institute has kept a pioneering spirit. The General Education Board, by giving $6,000,000 to the Lincoln School in New York, has exercised a highly progressive influence on primary and secondary education.[21] The Board has similarly made grants for experimental college programs: to Sarah Lawrence, Bennington, Swarthmore, the General College of the University of Minnesota, and so on. It has helped to broaden legal education as well as to raise the standard of medical education. All around the world the Rockefeller Foundation has been a great pioneering agency in health and medicine.

No doubt foundations are in many respects "status quo" agencies. Beyond question their heads prefer to avoid controversy; though the Laura Spelman Rockefeller Memorial in 1924 laid down twelve principles to guide foundations in controversial fields, and they have been used by all the Rockefeller trusts and many other foundations. Holes may be picked in foundation programs, and fault found, as Harold J. Laski and E. C. Lindeman have shown,[22] with trustees and officers. But the Rockefeller agencies have justified themselves. They have undertaken much-needed labors in fields which no existing agency, governmental or private, would have entered. They

[21]*Idem*, 62.
[22]Harold J. Laski, *Dangers of Obedience*, 150–177; E. C. Lindeman, *Wealth and Culture*, passim.

have blazed trails in many directions; they have set on their feet projects which others have then carried forward; they have added

A Rockefeller Foundation activity.
Poster used by Commission for Prevention of Tuberculosis in France.

immeasurably to the resources of health, economic well-being, and culture in this all too insane world.

And few critics, no matter how much they dislike the principle of the private funding of wealth for the general welfare, have ever denied that the Rockefeller benefactions have been created in a singularly enlightened spirit. Setting aside the debate on the principle, it must be admitted that the distribution of the fortune has been admirably accomplished. Rockefeller always dealt with his wealth in humility, not in arrogance. He never used it to minister to his vanity or power. Regarding it objectively, he never let personal prejudices or predilections impair the wisdom of its employment. He applied careful planning to the principles that should guide his giving; but once the money was given, he took the view that it was no longer his own. Unlike Carnegie, he did not appoint personal favorites to trusteeships. Unlike Leland Stanford, Jonas Clark, and many another, he never meddled with the men in control. Unlike James B. Duke, he never for a moment mingled private commercial interests with philanthropic acts. His attitude was ideal, and it permitted the placing of his philanthropies on the very highest plane. The American people, as we have said, felt no great gratitude to Rockefeller for the distribution of a fortune which many regarded as largely a historical accident. But reflecting citizens have properly felt a very warm gratitude to him and his son for the painstaking care, the wisdom, the unselfishness, and the fine public spirit with which the distribution has been made.

For the purse has been opened wide. During his lifetime Rockefeller devoted to public uses approximately five hundred and fifty million dollars, while most of the remainder was made over to the son for a continuance of the work. The fortune has long since ceased to be one of the greatest American accumulations. It is still shrinking. According to Gates, Rockefeller took a warm and constant pleasure in his philanthropic activities. It delighted him to give, and delighted him still more to hear about the results of his giving.[23] He was entitled to take a deep satisfaction in the thought that he was an agent in doing so much good: in helping to heal the sick, to raise the standard of life, to enlarge the frontiers of science, and to enrich the human mind.

[23]Gates writes (MS Autobiography, 394): "I think Mr. Rockefeller gets more, far more, than the usual amount of satisfaction in his philanthropy. There come to him many appreciative letters that are heartfelt and sincere. Many a fond mother is ready to pour out her heart's blood in gratitude for the salvation of children through discoveries of the Institute. Some of these letters no one can read without te. "

L

Exeunt Omnes

"'T IS OUR fast intent to shake all cares and business from our age; conferring them on younger strengths, while we unburthened crawl toward death." So Lear; so John D. Rockefeller. But life is always more eventful than men anticipate; the web of human relations constantly offers new tangles; and, living on through a terrible war, a wild boom, and a savage depression, Rockefeller encountered both unforeseen troubles and unexpected satisfactions before he quit the stage.

One dark and controversial page remained to be written into his life. On April 21, 1914, the country was shocked to learn that the previous day a conflict had broken out between militia and striking coal-miners at Ludlow, Colo.; that the workers had been routed with six men killed; and that when the guardsmen had fired the tents sheltering the strikers' families, two women and eleven children lying in pits underneath had been suffocated. It was a heart-rending incident. For days afterward little battles raged through the coal-mining areas of the State. As correspondents sent out long news stories, it became clear that a virtual civil war was under way. The governor hastily summoned the legislature in special session, and called upon President Wilson to restore order with Federal troops. A labor struggle that had been intermittently waged for years had suddenly reached a tragic climax.[1]

On one side stood the Colorado Fuel & Iron Co., the Rocky Moun-

[1] See U. S. Commission on Industrial Relations, *Report on the Colorado Strike,* by George P. West; Samuel Yellen, *American Labor Struggles* ("Bloody Ludlow"). The strikers were accused of shooting at the militia from their tent colony, with fatal consequences to the women and children when the shots were returned.

tain Fuel Co., and scores of lesser mining corporations; on the other stood a heterogeneous population, chiefly Greeks, Slavs, Italians, and Mexicans, living in isolated communities dominated politically and economically, in many instances, by the companies. The chief immediate issue in the strike was recognition of the United Mine Workers of America. The employees had also demanded a 10 per cent increase in wages, an eight-hour day, the right to trade outside company stores, and the enforcement of long-neglected State labor laws. Behind all this lay a larger issue: the demand of the workers for emancipation from an economic, political, and social autocracy which in many localities seemed unendurable. When the nation learned that Rockefeller and his son owned about 40 per cent of the stock of the Colorado Fuel & Iron, which admittedly gave leadership to some lesser corporations, the animosity with which many people regarded the magnate leaped up anew. He was still oppressing the common man, still grinding the faces of the poor!

Grave abuses had long existed in southern Colorado, where large corporations had undertaken to develop rich coal deposits in isolated and unsettled territory. The companies had built up mining camps in what was originally a waste of mountains and canyons. At the outset it had been necessary for the owners to provide housing, stores, amusement places, and churches; they had unavoidably performed the chief functions of civil government and supervised the principal activities of community life. This had been quite proper for the early pioneering years. But most companies had attempted to continue their all-inclusive control long after the excuse for it had ended. "This domination has been carried to such an extreme," wrote George P. West in his report on the strike for the United States Commission on Industrial Relations, "that two entire counties of southern Colorado for years have been deprived of popular government, while large groups of their citizens have been stripped of their liberties, robbed of portions of their earnings, subjected to ruthless persecution and abuse, and reduced to a state of economic and political serfdom." Some rhetorical exaggeration appears in this statement, while the companies varied widely in their practices. The Rocky Mountain Fuel Co., among others, was far more illiberal than the Colorado Fuel & Iron. But the abuses were serious. And when the miners attempted to resist, they were met by a grim, dogged opposition to unionization. Strong unions were needed to break down the autocracy and establish collective bargaining. The United Mine Workers claimed 400,000 members. The operators of most of the important coal-mining States west of the Mississippi had long been working under contract with this body. But when it tried to organize the southern Colorado field it encountered a fierce, unyielding hostility.

No leaders were more prominent in this opposition to unionization than L. M. Bowers, chairman of the board of the Colorado Fuel & Iron, and J. F. Welborn, president of the company. Both were men of integrity, courage, and ability, but both showed an inveterate hostility to any interference with the open shop, and Bowers took rigid views of labor management. He belonged to a dying age in the relationship of capital and labor. The Colorado Fuel & Iron owned twenty-five mines and two groups of coke ovens, in which it normally employed from 5500 to 6000 men. From the point of view of those who believed in a paternalistic labor system, these men were not ill treated. Wages had been advanced by 5 per cent in 1907, and again in 1912. An eight-hour day had been instituted in the mines early in 1913. The company stores, according to Welborn, made no profit, furnishing the workers with goods of as good quality as could be obtained elsewhere, and at as low a price. A $300,000 hospital had been erected at Pueblo, Colo. (where the Rockefellers controlled important steel mills), which treated workers without charge; and each mining camp had its doctor, who furnished the families with medical treatment at one dollar a month. Pay was said by the company to average slightly less than $1000 a year, as against $600 a year for coal-miners in Illinois. But nevertheless grievances existed—complaints of poor housing, arrogant mine bosses, unjust rules; and no way existed of getting a fair hearing or treating with the owners on equal terms. Bowers and Welborn had sternly forbidden any union activity on the company premises.[2]

Bowers, a man of rugged force, prided himself upon the influence he exerted over other corporation heads, and his ability to bring stern business and banking pressure upon the "little cowboy gov-

[2]See Testimony of J. F. Welborn Before the U. S. Commission on Industrial Relations, Dec. 4–7, 1914 (342 pp.); Testimony of L. M. Bowers, May 27, 1915 (114 pp.). Files of *The Survey* are enlightening.

ernor," E. M. Ammons. The United Mine Workers had launched an energetic new campaign in southern Colorado in 1913. Under Frank Hayes, a magnetic leader, they made such rapid progress that a convention of Colorado and New Mexico locals had decided to strike unless the employers consented to a closed union shop, with a written trade agreement. Bowers, Welborn, and the other company heads refused even to confer with the union leaders. The result was that some 9000 miners dropped their tools in September, 1913, and carried their families and possessions to tent colonies on land leased by the union. Armed Baldwin-Felts guards were then hired to protect mine property. Violence had soon flared up. Governor Ammons had ordered the militia into Las Animas and Huerfano Counties, and, under officers like the bull-faced K. E. Linderfelt, many soldiers ceased to be neutral, and passed from the protection of strikebreakers to the intimidation of strikers. Some of them felt a blind hatred for the excitable workers and the paid "agitators" arousing them. The Ludlow explosion had been a logical sequel.

Public opinion at once declared itself strongly on the side of the workers. It could hardly do otherwise. To be sure, the question of the closed shop or open shop had two sides, for many miners did not want to join a union. The question of responsibility for the Ludlow affray also provoked a heated debate. Governor Ammons declared that the militia had been attacked by lawless strikers, who used the tents as cover;[3] the labor leaders asserted that the troops were mere company hirelings. But weighing the larger issues, the American people never felt a moment's doubt that the strikers were in the right, and that the corporation autocracy in southern Colorado must be broken down. The companies had repeatedly attempted to gain political domination in order that they might defy State laws, block unfavorable new legislation, estop injured workers from collecting adequate damages, and deal roughly with union organizers; and these activities constituted an ugly story.

Very naturally, the American public also laid the principal blame for the outbreak on the two Rockefellers. They were by far the most important industrialists concerned; they were eminent philanthropists, and yet they had done little to terminate this distress-

[3]E. M. Ammons, "The Colorado Strike," *North American Review*, CC, 35-44 (July, 1914).

ing situation. Something has been said by John **T. Flynn** and others in extenuation of the elder Rockefeller. Now almost seventy-five, he had long before surrendered practically all his business cares to others. He had never been really interested in the mines anyhow. An unprofitable investment into which he had been led by George Gould, he regarded them merely as red-ink items in a ledger; for never in the fourteen years of his control had the common stock paid a dividend. Nevertheless, he had approved the choice of Bowers as the principal officer; and Bowers later testified that, when hired, he had a perfect understanding with the elder Rockefeller as to labor policy. We cannot wholly exculpate Rockefeller. A more direct responsibility lay with his office force—with John D. Rockefeller, Jr., Gates, and Starr J. Murphy. All three had served at times as directors, the younger Rockefeller doing so for fourteen years. Of course they were extremely busy men, for the management of the fortune was a huge task, while the benefactions offered still heavier cares. But they had not bent upon Bowers and Welborn the critical scrutiny which these executives needed. Moreover, for weeks after the strike began they had adopted a definite policy of supporting the officers on the spot against all critics, while they had failed to inform themselves on many important details of the management.

The younger Rockefeller and his aides were soon ready to acknowledge that they had committed mistakes, though they protested that they had always done what they thought at the time was right. The fierce storm which beat about them made their course difficult. On the open-shop question they could not surrender what they thought was a just principle. They did not wish to throw loyal, able, and hard-working subordinates to the wolves. But a few weeks after Ludlow the younger Rockefeller was generously anxious to turn a new page in company history.

Federal troops soon restored order in Colorado. Meanwhile, President Wilson, the House Committee under Mines and Mining, and the new Federal Commission on Industrial Relations were all displaying a stern interest in the affair. Labor groups were deeply aroused, and they had the support of radical elements in insisting that far-reaching reforms were needed. For weeks in 1914 files of labor sympathizers paraded in front of 26 Broadway and 10 West

Fifty-fourth, carrying banners and placards, while the anarchists Emma Goldman and Alexander Berkman staged a demonstration in Tarrytown. The press was full of articles on Colorado. Thoughtful journals like the *Survey* and conservative organs like the New York *Evening Post* were highly critical of the mine-owners. A report by a subcommittee of the House Mines Committee sharply assailed Bowers and Welborn, and suggested that, if the corporations did not take a more reasonable attitude, stringent Federal intervention would be necessary. On the issue of the closed shop, Mr. Rockefeller, Jr., refused to yield. He declined to submit the dispute to arbitration, asserting that the troubles had been fomented by outside agitators, that most of the miners really opposed the strike (about 40 per cent of the Colorado Fuel & Iron men had joined it), and that the closed shop would be unjust to non-union men. In December, 1914, the conflict was won by the companies and the strike called off by the union.

But the younger Rockefeller realized that some constructive action had to be taken. He knew that the *New International Yearbook* for 1915 accurately summed up public opinion of affairs when it stated: "This momentous dispute showed clearly the evils of absentee capitalism, its abuse of power, its disregard of responsibilities and of human rights, and its exploitation of labor."

The Commission on Industrial Relations shortly summoned Welborn, Bowers, and others to testify on the strike. It also called the two Rockefellers, Charles W. Eliot, and Jerome D. Greene to give evidence on the activities of the Rockefeller Foundation in the industrial field. The younger Rockefeller and Greene made an especially creditable appearance, their testimony dispelling many misconceptions, and indicating the strong desire of the Rockefeller office to act liberally.[4] But the elder Rockefeller disappointed lib-

[4]The younger Rockefeller's testimony was given Jan. 26, 27, 1915, and fills 118 pages. Mr. Greene's was given Feb. 2, 3, 1915. He made an interesting remark upon Rockefeller: "I have never known, with the exception of President Eliot, a man with whom I have been associated who is more completely dominated by the idea of coming to his decisions by conference and consultation on the part of men who he thinks will be independent and fearless in the expression of their opinions. He does not care where a suggestion comes from. He is perfectly willing to reverse his own opinion the next minute, even if the office boy or any one else suggests the idea, which on its intrinsic merits is better than the idea he previously followed."

eral observers. Possessing no acquaintance with the new social philosophy in America and feeling skeptical of its value, his utterances on the stand seemed the echo of a distant past. To be sure, he was more kindly and well disposed than most representatives of the paternalistic school. He declared that he believed capital and labor to be partners, that he favored good wages, that he would welcome his employees as stockholders, and that he thought they might well be represented among the directors. But as Bowers testified, and as he showed in his confidential conversations with Inglis, he was suspicious of labor unions and had no understanding of collective bargaining. He believed that any correct scheme of profit-sharing should also include loss-sharing in hard times. He no more than George Pullman or Commodore Vanderbilt understood that private property is often affected with a public interest, and that in any industry the workers have rights no less than the owners. It was fortunate that his son was more progressive and liberal.

For the younger Rockefeller pushed forward a program of reforms which had far-reaching results. L. M. Bowers was gently ousted from the Colorado Fuel & Iron. As Mr. Rockefeller puts it, "he was not ready to go forward into the new day," and it was "a painful duty" to obtain his resignation. He had gone to Colorado reluctantly. He had shown unblenching nerve and great ability there. Though reactionary in labor matters, he was a Christian gentleman who always tried to be just. "I shall never forget the three or four hours I spent with him at my house," recalls Mr. Rockefeller, "trying to get him to retire amicably; for he could be an unpleasant enemy." He did retire. But resentment rankled in his breast, and to the distress of his relative Gates, for years he showed keen hostility toward Rockefeller. This was fortunately dispelled when one summer the father and son, being near Owego, begged permission to call, and paid so gracious a visit that he forgot his ill-feeling. Meanwhile, Welborn had quickly adapted himself to the new point of view, and was soon responsible for some striking improvements in labor conditions.

But changes in staff were not enough. The younger Rockefeller had quickly decided that it was important to get an expert man to explore the situation at first hand and submit recommendations. At the suggestion of President Eliot, he summoned W. L. Mackenzie

King, former Minister of Labor in Canada and author of the famous Industrial Disputes Act of 1907, to New York. They talked for several hours, after which King spent the night at the younger Rockefeller's house, and the elder Rockefeller came in to dine with them. "It was my intention to ask King to suggest an expert adviser," says Mr. Rockefeller. "But his ability, fairness, and energy so impressed me that I requested him to undertake the task." They agreed in their initial talk that some organization must be developed in the mining camps which would assure the employees of a clear, fair means for stating their case—of "easy and constant conferences with reference to any matters of difference or grievance." King had travelled all over the Dominion settling strikes. He saw in the Colorado dispute a remarkable opportunity to apply his favorite principles of conciliation and arbitration in industry, and accepted the younger Rockefeller's offer. It was arranged that beginning October 1, 1914, he should head a new department of the Rockefeller Foundation for the study of industrial relations on a worldwide scale, with no time limitations; Colorado being his first assignment. The Foundation also appropriated $100,000 for relief among the miners of the whole State.

By December 17, 1914, such progress had been made that President Welborn was able to announce to the public and the miners that a plan would be instituted for enabling workmen and company officers to discuss all complaints. The younger Rockefeller and King believed that lack of personal relationship had been the main source of the bitter conflict in Colorado. In the era of small-craft industries such relationships had been easily established. But the Colorado Fuel & Iron employed so many thousands of men in its collieries, iron mines, lime quarries, and steel works, and on its railroad, that contact was difficult. The principle of representation was adopted to solve the problem, plans being made for effecting a personal relationship through agents elected by the employees and the management. The details of this "industrial representation plan," which was established in the coal mines in 1915 and the steel works in 1916, have been described by Mr. Rockefeller in his volume *The Colorado Industrial Plan*. Into the weaknesses and merits of the plan—its virtues clearly preponderating—we cannot go here.[5] It is

[5] See T. R. Fisher, *Industrial Disputes and Federal Legislation*, Ch. V.

sufficient to say that, despite serious defects, it was an experiment which offered many interesting lessons to industry, and which marked a praiseworthy advance beyond the archaic system existing before the strike. While it did not furnish a permanent solution of the problem, it could be called a success.

Along with the new scheme went important minor reforms. Miners were allowed to hold meetings on company property, and before many years passed nine tenths of them belonged to unions. More competitive stores came in, while workers were allowed to hire their own ministers and doctors. The younger Rockefeller put a sharp stop to the political activities of company officers. Doctor Ben Selekman in his report of 1924 for the Russell Sage Foundation described clean, attractive communities with good housing facilities, and a general state of content. Two visits to the area by the younger Rockefeller had meanwhile produced a happy effect. He had gone out in 1915, while the district was still full of resentment, had toured all the camps and towns, had taken pains to eat, talk, and fraternize with the workers, and had made many speeches. In the spring of 1918 he and his wife returned, again visiting the steel mills and all the camps, and finding a greatly changed atmosphere. Mrs. John D. Rockefeller, Jr., talked with hundreds of women, played with the children, and did all that she could to prove that the owners were keenly interested in the workers' welfare.

Still another step taken by the younger Rockefeller showed his increasing independence. The storm aroused by the Colorado affair seemed to him to make it imperative to find some means of putting his family's side of the dispute before the public. He was urged by various advisers to hire advertising space, to subsidize docile writers, and even to buy a newspaper. Arthur Brisbane, long an admirer of the elder Rockefeller, gave him better advice—to employ Ivy L. Lee as his representative. At this time Lee was publicity expert for the Pennsylvania Railroad. Mr. Rockefeller, Jr., asked President Rea to release him, arguing that his work in the Colorado imbroglio was certain to benefit industry as a whole. Never had the elder Rockefeller been willing to take such a step. But Lee, commencing work June 1, 1914, at $1000 a month, proved so valuable that the connection was made permanent, and his successor, Mr. T. J. Ross, still ably serves the Rockefeller interests.

To many observers the appointment seemed unfortunate. Lee, shrewd, polished, and plausible, had been so notoriously the servant of some dubious corporate interests that newspapermen eyed him with suspicion. Dubbing him "Poison Ivy" Lee, they believed him skilled in making the worse appear the better reason. Yet he was a man of ability, who had worked out some sound principles in publicity. He never denied unpleasant stories, never indulged in recrimination or debate, and never asked editors to retract. Ignoring attacks on his client, he offered positive material calculated to put him in a better light. He knew that newspapermen wanted a story as much as they despised a puff, and constantly tried to give them real news without too many frills or overtones. He could be devious at times in dealing with the press, but Mr. Rockefeller has testified that he always gave the family honest and candid advice. Within a decade men were remarking how much Ivy Lee had done for the elder Rockefeller's reputation. He had done something; but the son, hardworking, conscientious, the very soul of generosity and public spirit, had done infinitely more.

And what was the elder Rockefeller's position in the Colorado troubles? He left the active direction of affairs entirely to his son. No doubt he at first thought Bowers perfectly right. "I have watched and have studied the trade unions for many years," he told W. O. Inglis in 1917. "My ideas about them are not those held by some others. But my son will see; others will see; times change, but men change very little. It is hard to understand why men will organize to destroy the very firms or companies that are giving them the chance to live and thrive; but they do it. . . . Soon the real object of their organizing shows itself—to do as little as possible for the greatest possible pay." This was the spirit of 1870. While the storm of criticism was still at its height, the younger Rockefeller caught a severe cold and went to Pocantico to recover. He kept in touch with Starr J. Murphy by telephone, and discussed the changing situation with his father. The elder Rockefeller never tried to stop or impede his son. But he remained unconvinced of the propriety of any concessions to unionization; he questioned the employment of any publicity agent. He was for standing firm on the old ground.

Yet in some ways he showed a generous spirit. When the younger

Rockefeller first went to Colorado, the father was much concerned. He told a friend that he would have given a million dollars to keep John away from danger. But he breathed not the slightest hint of his uneasiness to his son. In due time he admitted that the visit had been wise; that it had both helped to educate the younger man, and conduced to a better understanding of the family. He likewise reconciled himself to Ivy Lee's appointment. He even came to admit that the industrial representation scheme was good, and to encourage its introduction into the oil companies. The man who had done most to put the scheme into effect in the Colorado Fuel & Iron was Clarence J. Hicks, a gifted associate of John R. Mott in Y. M. C. A. activities, who had performed valuable work as a supervisor of industrial relations for the International Harvester Company. The younger Rockefeller selected him and sent him out to Colorado. Later A. C. Bedford, of the Standard Oil of New Jersey, asked him to make a study of industrial relations for that company; and he was finally employed to manage its industrial representation plan. In the Standard Oil of Indiana some complaints by a minister meanwhile led the younger Rockefeller to inquire of Colonel Robert W. Stewart whether the employees were really contented. As a result, W. L. Mackenzie King was sent out to make an extensive study, and an industrial representation plan was developed. Stewart was at first reluctant, but he soon accepted it with enthusisam, and put all his tremendous energy behind it. And there, and in many other companies which adopted it, the elder Rockefeller followed its progress with approval. "He was very happy over it," remarks his son.[6] However conservative and limited in some ways the magnate might be, he showed readiness to learn; and his son was a teacher in whom he felt implicit confidence.

II

Trouble had come to Rockefeller, and so did bereavement. The illness of Mrs. Rockefeller, a semi-invalid from the beginning of the century, had long done much to restrict his social contacts. Beginning in 1910, she was for the most part confined to her bed. A

[6]John D. Rockefeller, Jr., to the author. W. L. Mackenzie King never sought to impose his own plan upon a company. He tried rather to help it systematize, improve, and extend whatever work in employee relations it was already doing.

heavy cloud thereafter rested upon the household. Charming in her mixture of gentleness and fun-loving alertness, she had always been half the life of the family. She suffered from a variety of ailments and from some organic derangements, but the most serious difficulty was an excess of white corpuscles in the blood which produced the effects of pernicious anemia. Long days of pain made her at times somewhat exacting. Those who visited the home at this period testify to Rockefeller's unwearying assiduity in waiting upon her and meeting all her wishes. He paid constant visits to her bedside. When guests came to dinner he frequently excused himself to take her a flower, or to tell her something interesting which they had said. "He was the most affectionate and thoughtful man in illness and sorrow I have ever known," records his son. "No woman could have been more tender."

They went in June, 1913, to Forest Hill, intending to return in October. But Miss Spelman became sick, and when she recovered, Mrs. Rockefeller was too weak to be moved. The three deferred their return from time to time until after the first Monday in February, 1914, fixed by the Ohio statutes as tax-listing day. The result was a disagreeable incident. Rockefeller had remained unwillingly, preparing more than once to leave, but being detained by the doctors. Early in February notice was served that he must declare all his property, including money invested in stocks, bonds, and annuities. When he failed to file a return, the deputy tax commissioners made out one which included intangible property valued at $311,040,337; and the tax assessed on this return was certified to the treasurer of Cuyahoga County for collection. Rockefeller's attorneys thereupon brought a suit in equity to enjoin the treasurer against collection, their principal ground being that Rockefeller was a legal resident of New York, not Ohio.

All this seemed to Rockefeller ungenerous treatment on the part of Cuyahoga County. "With one hand they try to wring money out of me by an unjust lawsuit," he told Inglis, "while they hold out the other for a gift." He had little doubt of the outcome—and indeed first the district and then the circuit court decided unreservedly in his favor. But when the summer of 1914 came on, he did not feel like returning to Forest Hill, to be badgered by process servers and reporters. He and Mrs. Rockefeller remained at Pocantico, where the activities of I. W. W. demonstrators made it necessary to close the gates and instal watchmen at the estate. In June he and some members of the family made a brief trip to Maine. Then came the World War. Rockefeller and the Rockefeller Foundation were both soon making large gifts to Belgian relief and the Red Cross, and considering other activities. It seemed well to stay near New York. Mrs. Rockefeller was a little stronger when on September 8, 1914, as she neared her seventy-fifth birthday, they celebrated their golden wedding. The children and grandchildren gathered at Pocantico; a gala dinner was served. On her birthday Rockefeller brought a band out from New York to play her favorite music. Thereafter she seemed to improve. Throughout the fall and winter she remained at Pocantico, her husband close to her side. "I have had but one sweetheart," he used to say, "and I am thankful to say that I still have her."[7] But the end was near at hand.

Early April in 1915 found Rockefeller, his son, and his daughter-in-law at a hotel in Ormond, Fla., on a brief Southern trip. Mrs. Rockefeller had been as well as usual. But on the morning of the 12th a telegram announced that she was dying, and immediately afterward came word that she was dead. A heart attack was responsible. By hurried packing the three caught a train which left Ormond at noon. All along the way they found sympathetic knots of people gathered at the stations, while railroad officials and train-men made it clear that they felt for the sorrowing old man. The funeral was held at the Pocantico house on April 15, a brief service with only the family, the servants, and a few intimate friends present. At its conclusion the body was not removed. "Mother looks so beautiful lying there in bed," said the son, "that we simply cannot take her out of our house today. She looks as if she were merely sleeping." The following day she was placed temporarily at rest in the Archbold mausoleum at Sleepy Hollow cemetery. Not until August—after Governor Willis had removed the two deputy tax-commissioners who had caused Rockefeller so much annoyance—was the body taken to Lakeview Cemetery in Cleveland.

Thereafter Rockefeller's household was in charge of Mrs. R. A. Evans, a second cousin and an old and valued friend. Since she had lived most of her life at Strongsville, Ohio, the whole family had

[7]Flynn, *God's Gold*, 463; Inglis, Conversations with Rockefeller.

seen much of her. When Mrs. Rockefeller's illness reached a serious stage she was asked to take charge of domestic affairs. A hearty, spontaneous, sagacious woman, with a rich fund of common sense and a cheerful, sunny nature, she became a great favorite with all the children and grandchildren. After she arrived Rockefeller felt freer to take short excursions and to have friends come for dinner or stay a few days. She soon became indispensable, and was an ideal hostess and companion throughout the later period of his life.

One by one, in these years, Rockefeller's old associates were dropping away. Flagler's death on May 20, 1913, cost him a heavy pang, for of all the partners he had been the nearest and dearest. Rockefeller could look back on more than fifty years of friendship with him—to the day when, armed with his own and Harkness's money, Flagler had raised an Achilles' shield over the youthful Standard Oil; to the years when he had been the Marshal Ney in Rockefeller's Napoleonic schemes; to the talks in which, pacing Euclid Avenue together, they had planned the details of the great trust. After spending more than $40,000,000 on the railroads, hotels, steamships, and orange groves of Florida, Flagler had lived to see his greatest enterprise, the East Coast Railroad, triumphantly carried across the islands to Key West in 1912. He died full of years and a great public figure. It was unfortunately not so with John D. Archbold, whose tempestuous career came to an untimely end on December 5, 1916, before he had attained three score and ten. Rockefeller, always deeply attached to the gay-hearted, resourceful, loyal little man, mourned him deeply. And a still harder blow came in 1922, when William Rockefeller suddenly died. An entry in a journal which Rockefeller kept intermittently in the years 1918–24 records the sad event:[8]

On the morning of June 16, following our return from the delightful tour to the old homes, brother William went to his city office as usual, and on the following day, with no sign of fatigue. On the afternoon of the 17th, however, he determined to walk uptown and was overtaken by the rain. The next morning, the 18th, at one o'clock he suffered a severe chill. On the following afternoon we visited him in his home and he appeared to be better. We had a few moments of pleasant conversation, which proved to be our last meeting with him. He grew steadily worse, and although we did our utmost, exhausting all the resources humanly

[8]This journal, filling only a few pages, is in the Rockefeller Papers.

possible—calling upon the best skill of the Rockefeller Institute—it was unavailing, and he passed peacefully away on Saturday morning, June 24, at five o'clock. Brief, appropriate services were held on Monday afternoon, without singing or eulogy—the simple reading of the scriptures, followed by prayer—the immediate family only being present, with the exception of some of the men who had long been in our offices, and people from brother William's estate. It . . . left a deep impression upon all who were present.

One aide in the benefactions, Starr J. Murphy, died suddenly while visiting Rockefeller at Ormond, Fla., in the late winter of 1921. This genial, widely read attorney had been useful to Rockefeller in many ways, especially in the work of the philanthropic agencies. His reports on the organization and work of Yale and Harvard were memorable documents, which are still often cited in both universities. He had assisted in setting up the Laura Spelman Rockefeller Foundation, and, as a capital raconteur, had often been a prized guest. John D. Rockefeller, Jr., fearing the shock to his father, was about to hurry down to Florida when he received a reassuring message by telegraph: "Dear Mr. Murphy has gone. We shall miss him sadly. We must close up the ranks and press forward." At that time Frederick T. Gates was still invaluably active, though he had resigned as president of the General Education Board in 1917, becoming merely a trustee. He gradually fell into the background, devoting much of his leisure to writing the vigorous autobiography from which we have quoted. Nevertheless, he may be said to have rounded out a full forty years, 1888–1928, in assisting Rockefeller and his son in distributing the immense fortune at their disposal. Early in 1929 he too died. Rockefeller sent Mrs. Gates a letter of which we may be sure every word was written with heartfelt sincerity, for he realized the great debt he owed the man:

I am deeply shocked and saddened to learn of the passing of your dear husband, my companion, friend, and invaluable helper for long, long years in our business and philanthropic undertakings. Too much cannot be said of his most helpful service in these relations. He will be greatly missed by the multitudes whose lives have been blessed as a result of the beneficent influences in which his labors in connection with those of others of our associates have done so much toward uplifting our fellow men and relieving worldwide suffering. Those of us who remain unite in paying the highest tribute to his beloved memory.

One domestic trouble, the quarrel with his brother Frank, gave Rockefeller great sorrow for many years. The two men were never made to agree. Many of the intellectual and temperamental differences which had created such a gulf between William Avery Rockefeller and his wife Eliza Davison were discoverable in the brothers. Frank—genial, adventurous, quick to love and to hate—had always disliked John's stoic, repressed ways, and shown jealousy of his superior intellect and greater success. He used to quarrel gustily with his brother, denounce him fiercely, and then come to him in contrition. "Can you ever forgive me, John?" he would say.[9] The families had always been intimate, for Frank's country place at Wickliffe, Ohio, was only seven miles from Forest Hill, and the children visited back and forth, while Frank's daughters later went East to school. But after the Corrigan lawsuit the two men came to a complete breach. Frank, always hotheaded and quick-tongued, his natural irascibility sometimes inflamed by drink, made cutting remarks. He asserted that John had taken a cruel advantage of him and Corrigan. The two men ceased to speak, while Frank gave denunciatory and threatening interviews to the press, and even took the bodies of his children from the Forest Hill burial plot because he would not have them rest near his brother. During his final illness in 1917 he remained implacable. "You can understand the depth of his animosity," said a close friend, "when I tell you that his greatest fear during those last days was that John might try to come and see him!"[10]

John never did. The quarrel was ended only by death. But Rockefeller journeyed to Cleveland for the funeral, and stood beside his brother's open grave. The breach had never diminished· the cordiality between the families of the two men, and the children continued to visit each other frequently, showing unabated affection. No doubt Rockefeller would have liked many times to hold out his hand to Frank, for he never cherished a resentment; but he felt sadly sure that Frank, all the more stubborn because in the wrong, would reject it.

[9]Inglis, Conversations with Rockefeller.
[10]Confidential Cleveland source.

III

Yet on the whole Rockefeller's years of retirement were placid and happy. Keeping healthfully busy, he never allowed himself to become overburdened. He cultivated the equanimity and serenity which he had inherited from his mother; and he tried to plan his life as he had once planned an industry and later his benefactions. He was a living contradiction of Cato's remark: "All want to attain old age, and all grumble when they get it."

Early in the century stories were widely circulated that he lived in constant apprehension. His brother Frank gave the Washington *Star* an interview in which he said that "the fear of kidnapping has become a mania" with John; that "armed men accompany him everywhere ready to repel any effort to capture him." Ida M. Tarbell in the fall of 1903 went to the Euclid Avenue Church, where for the first time she saw Rockefeller. He impressed her as a most striking figure; apparently very old, "but what power!" She adds: "The impression of power deepened when Mr. Rockefeller took off his coat and hat, put on a skullcap, and took a seat commanding the entire room, his back to the wall. It was the head which riveted attention. It was big, great breadth from back to front, high broad forehead, big bumps behind the ears. . . . Wonder over the head was almost at once diverted to wonder over the man's uneasiness. His eyes were never quiet but darted from face to face, even peering around the jog at the audience close to the wall. . . . Mr. Rockefeller, for all the conscious power written in face and voice and figure, was afraid, I told myself, afraid of his own kind."[11] In a magazine article she emphasized this apparent fear. At the same time, other writers were circulating tales that Rockefeller's digestion had been completely shattered. He lived on bread and milk, they declared; he had said that he would give a million dollars to have a good stomach again!

The fact was that Rockefeller never showed any apprehension of attack and often made his best friends uneasy by his constant exposure of himself. He never had a bodyguard. While in earlier days he kept a revolver at his Euclid Avenue house, he probably never fired it once. His children were often worried by his demeanor. "I

[11] *All in the Day's Work*, 235, 236.

never knew a person so devoid of any slightest semblance of fear with reference to himself," remarks his son. In Georgia, said the Augusta *Chronicle* in 1913, he walked the streets, used the trolley cars, and drove about the country roads unattended. "He enters unostentatiously into our charities; goes about his way as his will suggests; enjoys himself at the barbecues and in the country; attends a public meeting now and then; joins in on public affairs like banquets; adversely criticizes nothing." At church in New York and Cleveland the ushers took care to place anybody who acted like a crank where they could watch him, but no other precautions were taken. The idea that Rockefeller lived in fear was absurd.

And equally absurd were the stories about his digestion. Except for a time in the early eighteen-nineties, it remained excellent. If he ate bread and milk, it was because he had always been fond of that dish. He never lost his teeth. To the end of his life they, like his eyes and his hearing, were excellent, and in his last year, at ninety-eight, he was allowed a varied menu, including poultry of all kinds, fish, lamb, and a variety of vegetables.

Throughout the final decades his pride and confidence in his son were one of the principal elements in his contentment. Relations between some of the personal agents employed by the two men were not devoid of jealousy and friction; one of Rockefeller's secretaries, Mitchell, became a sharp critic of several of the son's aides. But never the slightest shadow marred the mutual trust and affection of the two men. Whenever Rockefeller spoke of "Mr. John," a note of happiness came into his voice. At the time of the Industrial Relations hearings, the coolness, sense, and sincerity of the younger Rockefeller on the witness stand made a strong impression on the father. A full report was read to him. "Well," he said at the end, "I've been on the stand myself. Mr. John conducted himself admirably. He gave his testimony with more shrewdness and ability than I used to do."[12] (He might have added, with more candor!) Any criticism of "Mr. John" pained him inexpressibly. A visitor to Pocantico heard him remark, at a time when both men were being heavily assailed: "They have no right to attack Mr. John. All my life I have been the object of assault. But they have no ground for striking at him!" On another occasion the same visitor saw him

[12]Mr. Harry D. Sims to the author.

pick up a copy of the *Masses* from his library table. "A very interesting publication," he said. "I don't mind what they say about me and other rich men. But I resent their attacks on my son!"[13]

In 1915 Duveen & Co. bought J. Pierpont Morgan's magnificent collection of Chinese porcelains, long exhibited at the Metropolitan Museum. John D. Rockefeller, Jr., was offered his choice, and being a connoisseur of Chinese ware was eager to purchase a considerable number of pieces. As a very large sum was required, he was in no position to buy them without borrowing. He therefore wrote his father describing the extraordinary opportunity, which could never recur, and asking for a loan of the necessary amount. Rockefeller refused. His æsthetic tastes in such fields were totally undeveloped, he had not the slightest understanding of the instincts of a collector, and the expenditure seemed to him an extravagance. "I then wrote him," relates Mr. Rockefeller, Jr., "that I had always lived modestly, had never spent money on gambling, horse racing, drinking, or fast companions; that the acquisition of Chinese porcelains was my only hobby and a great pleasure; that I made no purchases without the advice of competent experts; and that, while the sum involved was large, I felt the price was the best obtainable, and I hoped he would reconsider his decision." Rockefeller thereupon immediately reversed his decision; and instead of lending the money to his son he did more—he gave it to him.

But the younger Rockefeller relates a still more striking instance of his father's implicit confidence, and of his readiness to perform a large act in a large way:[14]

During the War, I happened to be the chairman for Greater New York of the United War Work Campaign, which represented a consolidated effort to raise funds for the eight welfare organizations that were ministering to the American soldiers both at home and abroad. Thirty-five million dollars was the goal set for Greater New York. We got up toward thirty millions; then the Armistice was declared and it was exceedingly difficult to go further. I called upon three or four of the rich men of the city in the hope of interesting them to join me in underwriting the remaining five millions, feeling confident that the money would come in as a result of the momentum of the campaign even after the campaign itself had closed. In this effort I was unsuccessful. Not being in a financial

[13]Mr. Harold V. Milligan to the author.
[14]Memorandum for the author.

The Rockefeller Memorial Chapel at the University of Chicago.

Rockefeller Center in New York.

position to underwrite the amount myself, I called Father on the telephone at Lakewood and laid the matter before him. He had already contributed to the fund with great generosity. I told him that if the five million dollars were underwritten I felt morally sure the underwriter would not be called upon to pay much if any of the amount, but that he might be called upon to pay it all.

Father did not reply as many men would have under similar circumstances, that he had already done more than his share. . . . After listening to my statement, he simply said, "Do you think it is all right, John?"

I replied, "Yes, Father, I do."

Whereupon he said: "I will back you to any amount."

I had to ring off, because I could not speak, even to thank him. Even now I cannot recount this incident without getting all choked up, so overwhelming, so unprecedented, so inspiring was the confidence Father showed in me. One can imagine with what satisfaction I was able ultimately to tell Father that the entire amount had been raised and that no part of his underwriting would be called for. It is just such confidence as this that has bound men to Father during his entire life. . . .

It pleased Rockefeller to see his grandchildren carefully reared. He often emphasized the importance of this in his letters. For example, in 1909 he wrote his son: "I know that you and Abby will be careful to educate the children in financial matters as we sought to educate you, that they may understand the value of money and make the very best use of it." The younger Rockefeller and his wife brought up their five boys and one girl in exemplary fashion. "I say to them with perfect frankness," Mr. Rockefeller, Jr., once remarked,[15] "that wealth will go only to those of them who show fitness and ability to handle it wisely; that neither their father nor grandfather will leave them money unless they give evidence that they know how to lead decent, useful lives and that they will make good use of any property." Alta's children were trained with equal circumspection. Edith was the temperamental and erratic member of the family. Though Rockefeller disapproved strongly of some of her acts and wrote her several sorrowfully reproachful letters,[16] he was very fond of both her husband and her children. Harold Mc-

[15]Albert W. Atwood, "The Rockefeller Fortune," *Saturday Evening Post,* June 11, 1921.

[16]One written on April 9, 1921, pleaded with her to spend more time with her children; to consider "the importance of the constant, jealous, watch-care of the mother." He concluded: "I am not lecturing. I am not scolding. I love you, Edith dear; and I am still hoping." Rockefeller Papers.

Cormick, gay, hearty, and spontaneous, swept all barriers away whenever he came to pay a visit, and was a great favorite with every one. It is recorded that he was the only man who could march into Mrs. Rockefeller's room and unconcernedly light and puff a cigarette there—for she disliked smoking. The son Fowler McCormick became an equal favorite, and when he passed through stormy waters Rockefeller made his loyal affection for the young man extremely plain.[17]

But it was "Mr. John" upon whom Rockefeller always leaned most strongly, and who was the special stay and comfort of his declining years. "What a providence," he wrote the son in 1918, "that your life should have been spared to take up the responsibilities as I lay them down! I could not have anticipated in the earlier years that they would have been so great, nor could I have dreamed that you would have come so promptly and satisfactorily to meet them, and to go beyond, in the contemplation of our right attitude to the world in the discharge of these obligations." And he continued, with a display of feeling rare in either his letters or speech: "I appreciate, I am grateful, beyond all I can tell you. There is much for you to accomplish in the future. Do not allow yourself to be overburdened with details. Others must look to these. We will plan and work together. I want to stay a long time to help do my part. I hope you will take good care of your health. This is a religious duty, and you can accomplish so much more for the world if you keep well and strong."

It was a very real and close partnership in which the two men were united from the beginning of the century until 1937. At first "Mr. John" was the junior partner, but gradually he assumed senior responsibilities, and after 1920 the burden was almost entirely his. A long series of letters might be quoted showing how constantly and carefully he advised his father. Space will unfortunately suffice for only a few typical epistles. One, written by the son on August 22, 1914, indicates how capably he offered business guidance:

On Sunday last, at Warwick, I was present in the morning at a conference on Mr. Morgan's yacht attended by Mr. Morgan, Mr. Davison, Senator Aldrich, Senator Lippett, who took Mr. Aldrich's place in Washington, and Mr. Walters, who is so largely interested in Southern rail-

[17]Mr. Harry D. Sims and others to the author.

roads. The prevailing opinion was one of discouragement. The New York men felt that with the recent decision in the freight rate case the railroads of the country were generally facing bankruptcy, particularly those which had short-term obligations soon to be taken care of. They felt it would be most difficult to secure new capital for the very urgently needed railroad extensions in this country. Furthermore, the opinion prevailed that if the present plan of President Wilson to force through his anti-trust legislation (which there seems no hope of blocking) is carried out other lines of business will be bound and gagged much as the railroads are. Such action would destroy all initiative on the part of capitalists, which never more greatly needed encouragement than at this time when the commerce and finances of the country are suffering such a check as a result of the European War.

The impression made upon me by the conference is that it is the part of wisdom to accumulate cash at present rather than to be tempted to be buying bargains, and that furthermore, for the present at least, railroad securities are going to be much less attractive and promising for an invest-ment than formerly. I am wondering whether municipal and government bonds and bank and trust companies stocks may not prove a safer form of investment for the present, at least.

Another letter, representative of many, relates to the conduct of the Pocantico estate. It was sent during the wartime fuel shortage, and one reason for quoting it lies in its refutation of a widely cir-culated story that Rockefeller tried to profiteer on his surplus supply of coal. He left the matter to his son, who wrote him on Feb-ruary 5, 1918:

I have already sent you a copy of the letter which I wrote Mr. Law. . . . I too very much wish we might have been allowed to distribute our surplus coal in our own community, but since Mr. Law has the power to com-mandeer our supply, and since he at first asked for 100 tons and then 150, it seems to me that our attitude might be misunderstood were we to insist on making the distribution ourselves to the exclusion of sending any coal to Ossining for its general needs. Mr. Ellis agreed with this view, as I hope you will under the circumstances. You will note what I said to Mr. Law about the question of price. I have yet to hear from him upon that point.

Of the multitude of letters upon the work of the various benevo-lent corporations, one dated May 23, 1928, is of special interest as describing the first steps taken toward unification:

We have been overwhelmed with grief at the death of Dr. Noguchi, the great Japanese scientist of the Rockefeller Institute staff, who, as you have read in the papers, died in South Africa, where he went to study yellow fever. Equally sad has been the death of Mr. James C. Colgate's youngest daughter. . . .

Last night all the trustees of the four philanthropic boards, with the exception of three—two of whom were abroad, the third being Mr. Gates, who did not feel able to undergo the fatigue incident thereto—dined with me at our house. There were thirty of us at the dinner. The purpose of the gathering was to receive the report of the Interboard Committee, which has been at work over a year on plans for reorganization and consolidation. The report of the committee, which I have discussed with you from time to time and with which you have been in fullest accord, was, after full and valuable discussion, unanimously adopted. Mr. Fosdick, the chairman of the committee, has been very able and indefatigable in his study of this vexed question, and presented his case in a masterly way last night. I feel that this is a very important step of progress in our philanthropic boards, and that the results that will ultimately be worked out in unification of the organizations will be a great improvement over the methods now in use.

And one of the crowning steps in this work of unification is chronicled in a letter which the younger Rockefeller sent his father on December 6, 1935:

Things are shaping very rapidly looking toward the election of Mr. Fosdick as the President of both the Rockefeller Foundation and the General Education Board when our meetings occur the latter part of next week. The trustees of both boards have been informally approached regarding the matter and are practically unanimous in their desire to offer him these posts if he will accept. It will mean a financial sacrifice to him that will result in practically cutting his present income in two. It will also mean that he will have to resign from all his outside activities and relationships and from now on regard himself as the spokesman of the two Boards only. These sacrifices he is, however, ready to make in view of his profound interest in the work of the Boards and his belief in the great possibilities for usefulness which lie ahead of them. President Mason of the Foundation has shown a fine spirit throughout and will do everything he can to help his successor. It has taken weeks and months of constant planning, also countless interviews, to bring this end about, but if it can be ultimately attained, it will be well worth all it has cost. Please regard the matter as very confidential until after the meetings next week. I wanted, however, to have you have this advance information of how things were going.

A letter of the son on April 25, 1932, informed Rockefeller that the chairman of the trustees of the University of Chicago had recently sought him in New York, and put to him two questions: first, whether the elder Rockefeller felt satisfied that the people of Chicago and the Middle West had demonstrated, in the twenty-one years since he withdrew his trustees, that they regarded the University as their own institution, its support their peculiar duty; and second, whether the two Rockefellers would be willing to have the University elect John D. Rockefeller 3d as a trustee. It will be recalled that when in 1910 Rockefeller had made the University his final direct gift, the total of his donations to it had reached about $35,000,000. Mr. Rockefeller, Jr., described what had happened thereafter:

Since that time, because the trustees of our several philanthropic boards have felt that the University of Chicago offered one of the most important and strategic centers for certain types of work, these boards have pledged to the University over $35,500,000, and I about $6,000,000. During this second period the people of Chicago and the West have added to the resources of the institution in round figures $38,500,000. The total amount pledged from all sources during this second period is $80,000,000, of which all has been paid except $14,000,000, a portion thereof being conditional, hence not due. In this period, therefore, your boards and your son have given 52 per cent of the funds received by the University, while 48 per cent has been received from other sources. By comparing these percentages with those quoted above, it appears that while before your withdrawal you had contributed about five sixths of the funds, and other people only about one sixth, since your withdrawal your boards and family have contributed a trifle over one half, while the general public has given only slightly under one half.

To this Rockefeller replied that he was greatly pleased with the showing made by the University. "Clearly, the institution is no longer regarded as our institution, but rather as belonging to the people of Chicago and the Middle West. I am satisfied that the purpose which led me to write my letter of December 13, 1910, has been accomplished, and that my action in withdrawing my support and my representatives at that time has fully justified itself." He closed by saying he perceived no reason why his grandson should not become a trustee.

IV

Down to the accidental burning of Forest Hill in December, 1917, Rockefeller usually followed a settled routine. He went South for the coldest weather. Then late in March he would return to Lakewood, N. J., where he owned "Golf House," a former country club of modest size with very plain rooms. In April he would proceed to Pocantico, remaining there until late May or early June, when he went by train to Forest Hill. This breezy knoll overlooking Lake Erie was still his favorite home, and he would linger there until the sharp frosts of autumn sent him back to Pocantico. Of his house in the city he now made little consecutive use, and during much of the World War its lower floors were occupied by a Red Cross unit organized by his daughter-in-law.

The direction of the estates gave him a great deal of pleasant activity. Even at Forest Hill he sometimes employed fifty or sixty men, while at Pocantico the payroll often numbered 200 or 300. Until well past eighty he loved to plant and transplant trees, to plan vistas, and to lay out drives. At Forest Hill he had opened a limestone quarry, which supplied rock for buildings and crushed stone for roads and paths. That estate had nearly twenty miles of private road, while Pocantico offered much more, the drives leading to every corner of the great domain, and being carefully built to make the most of the landscape. Rockefeller prided himself upon his expertness in all the operations at his estates. When Elbert Hubbard visited him in 1914 at Forest Hill to write a rather fulsome essay, the magnate inquired what East Aurora was doing to provide good roads. "Use a nine-pound brick on a concrete base," he advised, "and make sure that your roadway is well drained. Water is the great enemy of a road." Hubbard's last glimpse of him was working, shovel in hand, to show three Italians how to scatter gravel.[18] He kept fifteen or sixteen cows at Forest Hill, had several thousand chickens hatched each spring, and though he drove less and less, was fond of the dozen horses still maintained there. Doctor Samuel Harper once disturbed him greatly by pointing out that the drainage of his barns was poor.

After the burning of Forest Hill, Pocantico received most of his attention, while his son also spent much time and money on it. Some very exaggerated stories of the size, cost, and magnificence of this estate got into the press, and have thence been copied into books. Writers have even spoken of 8000 acres; actually the estate

[18]*The Fra*, XII, No. 5; February, 1914.

never contained more than 3000. Some have estimated the total expenditures at $50,000,000 or $60,000,000; the younger Rockefeller places the whole investment at not above $6,000,000.[19] The principal additions after 1910 were made by the son. He bought large areas on both sides of the Putnam Division of the New York Central, and agreed in 1917 to have the railroad run around instead of through this property. Wishing the 300 acres on which St. Joseph's Normal College stood, he bought that tract, and gave the college ample funds to rebuild in another place. A commodious house had been erected for the son, while eventually provision was made for the married grandchildren who wished to live there. Many of the original farm buildings on the estate were repaired or remodelled; other buildings were put up. One of the handsomest was a recreation house and gymnasium which, with children's play apparatus, bowling alleys, and swimming pool, cost perhaps $750,000. The garage housed fifteen or twenty cars and trucks used on the estate. Various stories of elaborate importations of trees and shrubs are inventions. But the fine taste of John D. Rockefeller and his wife did give Pocantico some remarkable features: for example, an exquisite Japanese garden, with Ginkgo trees and Japanese shrubs and flowers, surrounding a picturesque Japanese lake. A large group of dwarf-orange trees, several hundred years old, each planted in a tub, was brought from a nobleman's estate in France. Fine native trees and shrubs were of course abundant.

Yet if Rockefeller had many homes and one rarely beautiful estate, his way of life remained simple. He had systematized his employments. He rose early; before the World War he was up at Forest Hill by six A.M. He liked to walk barefoot on the dewy grass.[20] Then he read the morning paper with great thoroughness, breakfasted, went through the mail with his secretary, and about ten emerged for some golf. If the weather was cool he wore a paper vest; if hot, a pith helmet. Guests were welcomed before he went on the green, and often came up after he began to play. He once spoke proudly of "the little reception I have on the golf course from ten to noon." A reporter in 1913 watched him greet two strangers. "Mr. Rockefeller," explained the man, "we are from Texas." Rockefeller knew

[19]Mr. Rockefeller to the author; this naturally does not include maintenance.
[20]So old servants at Forest Hill told me.

how Texans regarded him since the Waters-Pierce exposures. "I'm awfully sorry," he said genially as he took off his hat, "but I didn't put on my horns this morning." He and his companions always played nine holes, and often twelve. His game was remarkably steady, but if a mashie shot went badly he sometimes refused to count it and took another! While he could drive the ball 175 yards on occasion, he was best at putting. To save his strength he pedalled a bicycle between holes, and as he grew older, had it pushed by his caddy; while half-way through the course malted milk was served.

Returning to the house about noon, he bathed, lunched, and lay down for a short rest. The afternoon he gave in part to business—answering letters, studying reports, buying and selling stocks; in part to directing work on the estate; and in part to an automobile drive. One car, a Peerless, he used for fifteen years; later his chauffeur, Phillips, drove either a Simplex or a Lincoln. At Pocantico there was an organ, on which he liked to have somebody—perhaps his Swiss attendant, John Yordi, perhaps his grandson, Fowler McCormick—play simple old tunes. After another ten-minute rest and a brief period with his secretary, Rockefeller was ready to dress for dinner, which was served promptly at 7:30. He always wore formal clothes, and always sat a full hour though he ate but little. Guests were usually present—sometimes a dozen of them: ministers, social workers, college presidents, men connected with the benefactions, and Standard Oil executives. Doctor Bustard of the Euclid Avenue Church and Doctor Woelfkin of the Fifth Avenue Church were favorite companions. He also saw a good deal of such old Standard officers as Van Dyke, who outlived him. Besides the inner circle of executives in the philanthropies, like Doctors Buttrick and Vincent, who came often to the house, an outer circle of men visited him less frequently. We find Doctor W. H. Welch writing the younger Rockefeller in 1916: "It was a real delight to talk with him, to find him so vigorous in mind and body, and also to find him so thoroughly informed and keenly interested in the philanthropic activities which he is supporting, and deriving, I think, pleasure and satisfaction from them. I carried away a lively impression of his great kindness of heart, of his wisdom, and of his strength of character."

His secretaries testify that he never suffered from a moment's boredom. Estate management interested him intensely; so did golf;

so did the stock-market, in which he traded with acumen. He went over stock quotations carefully with his secretary, had his aides prepare memoranda on various corporations, and kept in touch with Messrs. Cooper and Cutler by telephone or telegraph. Messengers frequently trotted out on the golf course with notes upon sudden market shifts. He liked to receive advance intimations from friends, advisers, and old Standard Oil heads of anything big that was going on in the business world. He read little, but could talk for long periods. Doctor Samuel Harper once spent an entire evening describing the Soviet system as he listened with intense interest, and he confessed next morning that it had given him a wakeful night. But, he said, he thought that the capitalist system, with all its faults, would survive.[21] Most evenings saw him absorbed, after dinner, in Numerica—a game in which little square counters were used in an attempt to build four stacks of consecutive numbers from 1 to 13. It was only rarely in the final years that Rockefeller's mind was seen to have suffered from the semi-isolation of his life; chiefly when he fell into a state of almost beatific optimism and sweetness astonishingly unlike the stern practicality of his prime.

For some years he liked the Hotel Bonair at Augusta, Ga., as a winter resort. The golf links were good; the Georgians were friendly. President Taft and his suite came more than once, and he and Rockefeller greeted each other with pleasant, genial politeness. But as the magnate grew older he found Augusta sometimes too chilly for golfing comfort. A friend recommended Seabreeze, just below Ormond, and Rockefeller (after characteristically cautious inquiries of the weather bureau) made hotel reservations. Alighting one February morning at Daytona, he drove over. "Ah, Mr. Sims," he said to his secretary, "it's just like June!" Here he was perfectly content. Mr. Sims retains a vivid picture of him and Doctor Biggar in a private dining-room overlooking the Atlantic, sipping milk, eating boiled ham slowly, and chaffing each other in the most entertaining fashion.

Before long (in September, 1918) he purchased "The Casements" on the River Road at Ormond; a relatively small, unpretentious building with gray-shingled walls and many large windows. Here again he gave careful attention to the grounds. Beautifully land-

[21]Doctor Harper to the author, Feb. 21, 1937.

scaped, they descended in terraces to the Halifax River, with fine flower gardens. He played golf with old cronies and such new friends as General Adelbert Ames, using the public links. On Sunday mornings he attended the non-denominational Ormond Union Church, to which he was a generous contributor. After the services he stood on the lawn distributing bright new dimes among the children, with much good advice. He gave dimes also to golf companions, to guests at "The Casements," and to casual visitors; in fact, they became famous. A good many people thought the dime-giving a rather childish publicity feature and suspected Ivy Lee; actually it was his own idea, a rite that put people in good humor, bridged awkward moments, and enabled him to point a lesson in thrift. For years he presided over the annual charity bazaar at the Hotel Ormond, where crowds bid joyously for the odds and ends auctioned off for the benefit of the local poor. He liked to have the Florida people call him "Neighbor John," a name of his own invention; and he was as neighborly as his years, dignity, and natural reserve permitted.

Innumerable people have set down their impressions of the world's richest man in his last twenty-five years. They are without exception pleasant impressions. No longer, as in the earlier years of his life, did he lack the quality of being easily likable. He did not grow old with the rosy patriarchal grace of nonagenarians like John Bigelow; but he retained vigor of mind and tenacity of purpose almost to the end, while he gained in affability. The press had now ceased to publish articles with such harsh titles as "Rockefeller: Man or Monster?" and a kindlier picture of him slowly gained currency. He found his pleasures in simple interests. He liked flowers, scenery, and children, the little daughter of his chauffeur becoming a favorite. He enjoyed simple newspaper jokes, which his daughter Alta clipped out and sent him. He made constant use of two simple (and once well-known) inspirational volumes called *The Optimist's Good Morning* and *The Optimist's Good Night;* while on a higher plane he read the books of Doctor Jowett of the Fifth Avenue Presbyterian Church and of Harry Emerson Fosdick, and knew the sermons of the great English Baptist, Spurgeon.

Like Dickens's Silas Wegg, he took a powerful sight of notice of passers-by; and in much Wegg's simple-hearted way. Before retirement he had been too busy and perhaps too shy (for his daughter-in-law states that he really was shy) to exhibit a social instinct that lay deeply innate in his character; but now it burst to the surface. Old inhibitions were loosed, and he became almost indiscriminately friendly. On train journeys, at hotels, and on his daily rides he struck up acquaintance with all sorts of people, for to him, as to Wordsworth and Lincoln, a porter or plowman was as well worth knowing as a governor. He frequently took the young people who were working at the Hotel Ormond for drives, using two cars. "We were just the help at the hotel," writes one, "but never once did he miss an opportunity to be nice to us." Ever since he became prominent his house had been full of guests; now it was more crowded than ever. "It is a great pleasure to me to meet real people, men and women who are at work in the world," he told W. O. Inglis in 1917. "That is why I have so many persons of this sort as guests for a few days. It is a complete change for the clergymen, teachers, and others; and these new faces, new minds, are helpful and agreeable to me." He drew much pleasure from planning his daily drives. "Who was that nice young man we met at church last Sunday?" he would ask his secretary. "Let's ask him to drive with us—call him up." On roads leading out from Forest Hill he liked to halt and talk with farmers. "Stop," he would tell his chauffeur. "Look at that fine field of wheat. Let's find out what the farmer's methods are." And later he would discuss whatever he had learned about the use of potash or nitrates with his estate superintendent.[22]

Every visitor remarked upon his unquenchable liking for jests. Once a humorous catch-phrase which was running across the United States seized his fancy; and his secretary saw him go up to the housekeeper with a button in his hand, ejaculating: "Here's a button; won't you sew a shirt on it?" While not witty, he had a grave jocularity which raised many a laugh. A Cleveland attorney, John A. Cline, tells of playing golf with Rockefeller and two other companions. These three men led off with drives of about two hundred yards each. Cline felt on his mettle. He dug in his heels and swung with all his power. The ball moved six inches, while he went flat on his back. Without a smile, but with a droll note in his voice,

[22]Mr. N. A. Quilling has described to the author how regularly, in his drives about Cleveland, he would unobtrusively distribute to a group of needy pensioners bills folded in neat little packets.

Rockefeller remarked: "What you need when you play, Cline, is a feather-bed attachment." Once William Rainey Harper's son Samuel, who occupied the chair of Slavic studies at the University of Chicago, was driving near Pocantico. He telephoned, and Rockefeller invited him to lunch. As he was about to drive away, the magnate asked him how his car ran. "Oh," said Harper, "I can get eighteen miles to the gallon out of this Franklin." Rockefeller threw up his hands in a mock gesture of despair: "Why, Mr. Harper," he exclaimed, "you will ruin me!"

Another friend stayed overnight at Pocantico. After breakfast, Rockefeller excused himself. In his grave, deliberate way he remarked: "If you will pardon me, I will go upstairs and get to work, and"—here a twinkle came into his eye—"see if I can do something to keep the wolf away from the door."[23]

His displays of shrewdness were as frequent as those of humor. He had a way of dropping unexpected remarks that revealed a good deal about his own character. Everett Colby recalls that, riding with him one day in the Adirondacks, they passed a boy driving a sled with barrels. The boy was whistling and kicking up his heels. Rockefeller remarked in his slow, drawling way: "Everett, that young man will never be a success in life." "Why?" demanded Everett. "Because he is not thinking of driving his horse, and that is his business," returned Rockefeller. Mr. Colby also recalls a talk with Rockefeller about lending money. The magnate described how ungratefully he had sometimes been treated: "I have lent and given people money, and then seen them cross the street so that they would not have to speak to me!" And he admonished his son, who sat near him: "John, never lend money to your friends; it will spoil your friendships." Various stories are related to illustrate his quick grasp of financial detail. Doctor George E. Vincent recalls that on their drives near Ormond Rockefeller and he used to visit an old Scandinavian who, after an adventurous life, had settled down on the Florida coast. The grizzled sailor chatted amiably with Rockefeller on many subjects. After several visits, Rockefeller on the homeward drive remarked to Vincent, apropos of nothing: "He has just about $75,000." He had pieced together bits of information from the old sailor.

[23]Mr. Harold V. Milligan to the author.

Rockefeller when past ninety.

Rockefeller in Florida.

The upper photograph shows him on a terrace overlooking the Halifax River.

Yet on many observers the dominant impression he made in his last years was of unworldliness, or other-worldliness. That was the impression which John Singer Sargent formed when he painted his two portraits of Rockefeller; and one canvas presented him looking almost like a medieval saint—for he averred that so Rockefeller struck him. This might be set down as an artist's eccentricity. Yet Jo Davidson, the exceptionally hard-headed sculptor, formed a very similar impression. "Maybe you have strolled along the left bank of the Seine," he wrote after making a bust of Rockefeller, "and picked up an ancient volume bound in dusty leather. You handle it. It belongs to another world. You open it. The print at first is difficult to read. The s's look like f's; the spelling is strange. But you read on and you come to a phrase familiar, human, appealing, and it acts like as an open sesame. That to me is John D. Rockefeller."

As he passed from the seventies into the eighties, he remained remarkably active in his routinized life. To his previous enjoyments he added long automobile trips, the first of which was taken just before his eightieth birthday in 1919. Leaving Tarrytown on June 16 with his brother William, he was driven 185 miles to Binghamton. "The next day," he recorded in his journal, "we proceeded to Owego, where we had a most pleasant visit with Mrs. Life, motoring thence to the old home and cemetery, and on to Ithaca, where we had lunch. From here we journeyed to Moravia, visiting the scenes of our boyhood, which was spent in this little town from the age of three to ten; from Moravia to Watkins Glen, where we spent the night and the following day. On the 19th we returned to Pocantico, (after) lunching at the Owego House with Mrs. Life and Miss LaMonte, and paying a visit to the old homestead, which concluded a most delightful trip and the first excursion of its size undertaken by the writer in a motor-car." During each of the next four years he repeated this journey to the Richford-Moravia-Owego region. In 1924, after covering 500 miles in three days, he wrote that "the trip this year to the boyhood homes seemed more precious and pleasurable than ever"—a rare touch of sentiment. At this time the Moravia house was used for sheltering convicts from Auburn who were working on the highways. A few days after the visit, under date of July 22, 1924, Rockefeller made the last entry in his journal:

We learned by the newsprints this morning that the old house in which we spent part of our boyhood, three miles north of Moravia Village, was destroyed by fire during the night, supposedly from a defective chimney. This was the scene of our first business venture, when we engaged in the raising of a flock of turkeys.

v

Of public affairs, as the World War gave way to the Great Boom, and that in turn to the Great Depression, he was an interested spectator. A stanch Republican to the last, he steadily voted the regular party ticket, and deplored the accession of Woodrow Wilson to the presidency. He thought the Administration too deferential to labor and too hostile to business. "I wish some day that we might have a real businessman as President," he sighed. As he had opposed the war with Spain in 1898, so he was reluctant to see America enter the World War. Having built up a great worldwide business, he regarded the waste and destruction of the conflict as appalling, and wished to see it limited and shortened as much as possible. But he made no public statement on the subject. When war came he supported the government wholeheartedly, and believed that the utmost possible material aid should·be sent·to the Allies. But he thought that a war of blockade and economic attrition would be better than a plunge into bloody fighting. "We can hold the Germans relatively harmless," he told Inglis on September 8, 1917; "erosion will weaken them more and more every month."

But he gave to public objects during the war upon a scale which did much to break down the old hard, invincible hatred of his name. He also subscribed heavily to the liberty loans. Late in 1917 it was said that his contributions to the Red Cross, Y. M. C. A., and other war-work organizations, together with his bond subscriptions, reached $70,000,000. "It was brought to my mind today," he told Inglis on December 3, "that I am paying two thirds of my income in taxes, and that I have already given away for war purposes more than the amount of my gross income for the year. That is, the war has cost me for the year one and two thirds the amount of my income; to say nothing of the millions which the Rockefeller Foundation has given." But he hastily added that he did not speak in complaint. "How silly it would be to compare that with the personal sacrifices so many men have made." The Foundation, co-operating with the Belgian Relief Fund, played a large part in sustaining the

Belgian people. It gave the Y. M. C. A., K. of C., and other camp and community welfare agencies very nearly $11,000,000, and the American and International Red Cross $10,665,000. In doing this the Foundation invaded its principal, and Rockefeller insisted upon reimbursing it to the extent of $5,500,000. The press naturally saw to it that his larger donations were well publicized, and the effect of this was soon noticeable. Mr. John T. Flynn writes: "As drive succeeded drive and patriotic donations were called for at public meetings, in theatres, churches, immense subscriptions by John D. Rockefeller produced thunderous applause. Men were applauding and cheering the name of Rockefeller."[24]

After the war two distinguished visitors from Belgium came to Pocantico to thank Rockefeller for the aid he had tendered. An account of these visits is found in Rockefeller's journal:

Oct. 9, 1919.—On this day we record a notable event. Cardinal Mercier, Primate of Belgium, accompanied by Archbishop Hayes of the New York diocese, of the Catholic Church, paid us the honor of a visit and took tea. They were escorted to Pocantico and introduced by Mr. George Gillespie. The purpose of the visit was to express personal thanks for the work which we tried to accomplish through our food ships which were sent to the relief of Belgium by the Foundation during the earlier period of the World War. We were assisted in receiving by Mrs. Abby Rockefeller, Mrs. Evans, Mrs. Wehrle, Miss Litta Grimm, and Mr. Inglis. The Cardinal readily engaged in most friendly and brotherly conversation, and spoke with the deepest emotion of our efforts in connection with the work of relief, when his country was starving and our Government had not yet been able to organize for its assistance. We in turn tried to express our high appreciation of the Cardinal's beautiful and most courageous conduct during the trying days of the War.

Oct. 26, 1919.—On Sunday evening—at Kijkuit—we were honored by a visit from King Albert of Belgium, accompanied by his aide, Count Guy d'Oultremont. These distinguished visitors were brought from the city by Mr. John and Mrs. Abby Rockefeller, who, with Mrs. Evans and Mrs. Wehrle, aided in entertaining at dinner. The King shared with us about four hours of his time, having several other engagements for the evening. We were deeply impressed by his delightful personality and most cordial and democratic manner. The dear children, all of whom spoke with him and shook his hand, will long remember his pleasant and kindly remarks. After walking with Mr. John in the garden he came into the house quite

[24]*God's Gold,* 466. He made a gift to the town of Pasteur's birth, Dole, which named the Avenue John D. Rockefeller after him.

informally through one of the door windows from the west verandah. The dinner was informal and the King seemed content to delay—indeed, he did delay for nearly half an hour after Mr. John informed him that his car was at the door—deliberately chatting and smoking his cigar. He was good enough to say upon leaving that his visit to America would not have been complete without this call at our house. (We may remark here that some three years previously he had presented us with a bust of himself which we highly treasure.) We felt it a great honor to have him take the trouble to come to our home, especially as there were so many desiring him, and he was about to leave for Europe within a few days.

Neither Rockefeller nor his son favored American entry into the League of Nations. But after that agency was set up, the Rockefeller Foundation cordially co-operated with various of its international undertakings; for example, it supported for five years the disease-reporting service of the Health Section, and for three years the program in the international exchange of health personnel. Moreover, John D. Rockefeller, Jr., gave $2,000,000 for erecting a fine library building for the League, and $500,000 for a library fund.

In all the varied activities of his son after the war Rockefeller took the keenest interest; but it was an entirely passive interest except when his help was especially requested. He did lend active assistance when his son espoused the cause of the liberal element in the Baptist Church, as against the Fundamentalists. Doctor Woelfkin and both Raymond B. and Harry Emerson Fosdick were of course highly liberal in outlook. They grew alarmed in 1920–21 lest the Fundamentalists, who, as Raymond B. Fosdick wrote, "are thinking in terms of the Middle Ages," should gain control. When the Northern Baptist Convention in 1921 voted in favor of accepting a gift of about one and a half millions which had been offered with a proviso that it should be used only for ministers and missionaries holding the Fundamentalist creed, the younger Rockefeller protested vigorously. He thought it deplorable that the church should eagerly grasp a donation which thus limited freedom of faith and of thought within its ranks. The elder Rockefeller, who had long espoused the principle of giving with no unnecessary conditions attached, agreed with him; and he at once took steps to make sure that if the Fundamentalists did gain an ascendancy, they could not lay hands on any of the Rockefeller donations. This attitude contributed to the maintenance of the fine liberal tradition of the Baptist Church. In these same years Rockefeller approved and abetted the leading part which his son took in the Interchurch World Movement, and followed with interest his speeches during the campaign of 1920 to raise $330,000,000 for all the Protestant denominations.

The aged magnate also supported his son in the heated contest of 1928–29 to eject Colonel Robert W. Stewart from the chairmanship of the board of the Standard of Indiana. This was a sequel to the shocking oil scandals which had involved Albert B. Fall, E. L. Doheny, and Harry Sinclair. It appeared that a sum of $300,000 which Sinclair had paid to Secretary Fall had been derived from the receipts of a mysterious Canadian company called the Continental Trading Corporation. Sinclair and Stewart, who had been connected with it, declined to explain its funds. Sinclair was sent to jail for contempt. Senator Nye sent the record of Stewart's testimony before the Senate investigative committee to the younger Rockefeller, and, with strong press support, appealed to him to take some action. On May 9, 1928, after an investigation of his own, Mr. Rockefeller, Jr., made public a letter requesting the resignation of Colonel Stewart. But Stewart prepared to fight for his place; and the following January he formally announced his candidacy, while President Seubert and various directors of the company gave him their support. A fierce fight for proxies was already raging. To strengthen his son's committee, Rockefeller on January 30, 1929, publicly commended his fight against Stewart and called on the colonel to resign. Despite the fact that the family had only a small interest in the company, the younger Rockefeller, with the aid of his counsel Thomas M. Debevoise, the banker Winthrop W. Aldrich, and others, obtained a two-thirds majority of the proxies. In this process the prestige of the elder Rockefeller was all-important. Charles M. Higgins, for example, one of the largest stockholders, had long been a warm friend of Stewart; but because of his loyalty to Rockefeller he unhesitatingly placed his large block of stock at the son's disposal.[25] On March 7, 1929, Stewart was ignominiously ousted—a notable victory for sound ethics in business.

The autumn of this year brought the great crash in Wall Street. Rockefeller made one of the last of his public appearances when on October 30 he issued a statement that the current business situation

[25]Mr. Higgins to the author.

did not warrant the severe stock-market panic, and that he and his son were buying common stocks in large amounts. It was a well-meant gesture, but no such straw could stay the avalanche. Late in 1930 the two Rockefellers joined in giving $1,000,000 to the Emergency Employment Committee of New York City; another million followed in 1931, and additional gifts for unemployment after that. When in 1932 the younger Rockefeller electrified the public by a letter to President Nicholas Murray Butler reversing his stand on prohibition, and urging repeal of the Eighteenth Amendment, his father made no public statement. But, with much sadness over the failure of prohibition, he assented to the change of front. The support which the Rockefellers gave to the Anti-Saloon League and other temperance or prohibition organizations had always been much exaggerated. Dinner-table gossip in New York after the World War estimated the total sum in the tens of millions. It was to place such rumors at rest that the younger Rockefeller had furnished the New York *Tribune* an interview, published March 7, 1919, in which he said that the family gifts to the Anti-Saloon League over twenty years aggregated just $350,323.67. The ratification of the Eighteenth Amendment had gratified Rockefeller, but he was willing to accept the evidence that it had proved a failure.

From 1920 onwards Rockefeller was an appreciative watcher of the long list of benevolent activities which made his son one of the most useful citizens of the country. The principal items in this roster are widely familiar. The gift of two millions to the Cité Universitaire in France; the restoration of Rheims Cathedral, and the repair of the palaces at Versailles and Fontainebleau; the grant of $500,000 for the Shakespeare Memorial Theatre at Stratford-on-Avon; the gift of $4,000,000, including land, to the United States for Acadia National Park; the donation of $500,000 for Jewish farm development in Russia; special aids to Lincoln School, the Ethical Culture School, and a long list of colleges; the expenditure of $2,360,000 for building and maintaining International House at Columbia; the building of similar houses at California and Chicago; the grant of $600,000 for the improvement of Rockefeller Hall at Brown University with the stipulation that it be renamed W. H. P. Faunce Hall; the conveyance of fifty-four acres of land to New York City in 1930 for one of its most beautiful parks, with additional gifts later; the offer to the nation of 30,000 acres in the Jackson's Hole area in Wyoming; the assistance given to the creation of Palisades Interstate Park, with its beautiful cliff scenery; the transfer to public ownership of The Cloisters and George Gray Barnard's collections therein; gifts of $3,500,000 to the New York Public Library and $2,500,000 to the Hampton and Tuskegee Institutes; a donation of $1,540,000 toward restoring the Imperial University of Tokyo, ruined by fire; the establishment with an endowment of $21,000,000, of the International Education Board, devoted especially to all forms of science; and that splendid historical enterprise, the restoration of Williamsburg to its appearance in old colonial days—these are but the principal benefactions. Nor should we omit mention of an enterprise partly commercial in character, though it had its inception in a desire to aid the Metropolitan Opera—the building of Rockefeller Center in midtown Manhattan on the neglected site of the Elgin Gardens, given generations earlier by Doctor David Hosack to Columbia University. Twelve acres in area, this "city within a city" represents an investment of more than $100,000,000; and it has benefited alike the university, the municipal treasury, and the city's appearance.[26]

The benefactions have been invariably credited to the elder Rockefeller by his son. The son laid the plans and made the decisions; the father's accumulations supplied the money. These labors represented a remarkable association, the spirit of which was finely expressed by the son in the letter which he wrote his father on July 7, 1933, just before the latter's ninety-fourth birthday:

I have tried to do what I thought you would have me do. I have striven to follow in your footsteps. I have endeavored to use wisely and unselfishly the means that you have so unselfishly placed at my disposal. . . . In all these years of effort and striving, your own life and example have ever been to me the most powerful and stimulating influence. What you have done for humanity and business on a vast scale has impressed me profoundly. To have been a silent partner with you in carrying out these great constructive purposes and benefactions has been the supreme delight of my life.

VI

On Sunday morning, May 23, 1937, at 4:05 o'clock, Rockefeller died at "The Casements." His health had been good to the last,

[26]See the little volume, *The Last Rivet* (Columbia University Press, 1940).

though he tired easily and had to be given constant attendance. In his last few years he had limited his physical exertions to sitting in the sun a few hours a day, to half-hour rides in his automobile, to brief walks, and to chats with his frequent visitors, who had included such notables as Mme. Galli-Curci, Mary Garden, Sir Malcolm Campbell, Harvey Firestone, and Will Rogers. Male nurses had constantly attended him, and he had used a wheel chair a great deal. "The Casements," like his other residences, had contained much of the equipment of a small hospital. But his hearing and sight remained excellent, he ate with appetite, and his voice remained strong. Just before he died he was displaying a keen interest in plans for some remodelling at "The Casements," and for an air-conditioning system at Lakewood. Death was due to sclerotic myocarditis, or hardening of the heart muscle.

He left a net estate of $26,410,837, of which $16,630,000 was taken by Federal and State taxes. About two-thirds of the estate was in United States Treasury notes. At death he owned only one share in a Standard Oil Company—a share of Standard of California common, which he had retained for sentimental reasons because it was Certificate No. 1. Most of the property which he had not given to the various philanthropies had passed to his son and to other heirs long before his death. The chief individual beneficiary of the residuary estate was a granddaughter, Mrs. De Cuevas, who was singled out because her mother, Bessie, had not been living when he determined to make large gifts to his children. It may be noted that his probated estate exceeded very slightly that of $23,247,161 left by his rival in wealth and philanthropy, Andrew Carnegie.

On May 24 the body left Ormond and was brought northward, reaching Pocantico on the twenty-fifth. The next day funeral services were conducted at the home by Doctor Harry Emerson Fosdick, who delivered a brief but moving eulogy, and the Reverend Mr. Lester P. Bent of the Pocantico Hills Union Church, who read the service. While this was taking place the carillon of the Riverside Church played "Lead, Kindly Light," and other favorite hymns; and elsewhere a singularly impressive tribute was being paid. For five minutes, at the hour the services began, work ceased in all the wide-flung offices and shops of the companies which had made up the Standard empire. In Philadelphia and Cleveland, in Whiting and St. Louis, in Oklahoma and California, machinery stopped and employees paused. Overseas, in the offices of the Anglo-American Oil Company and the old German and Italian subsidiaries, the moment was noted. For those five minutes the Standard Oil Trust, legally dissolved nearly thirty years before, took life again to pay honor to its founder.

The body was taken to Cleveland, where on May 27 a short service was conducted in Lakeview Cemetery. The son and grandchildren stood beside the grave until it was filled. No more fitting spot for his burial could have been found. In this beautiful cemetery, its wooded slopes overlooking the blue waters of Lake Erie, lie many of the men who made the Western Reserve great, and whom Rockefeller had known well in life. Here are political figures like James A. Garfield, Mark Hanna, and John Hay. Here are business leaders like Leonard Case, Amasa Stone, and Samuel Mather. Here lie such old friends and loyal associates of Rockefeller's as Ambrose McGregor, Will Cowan, Stephen Harkness, and Oliver H. Payne. Here are such oldtime rivals and enemies as Jim Corrigan and William C. Scofield. No one can tread the shaded walks of the great burial ground without feeling moved by the tumultuous and constructive history of a crowded pioneering period which its gravestones represent.

Rockefeller was at peace, his hand stilled. But that day thousands of students poured into the classrooms and libraries of the University of Chicago. Scores of scientists toiled in the finely equipped laboratories of the Medical Institute above the East River, peering through microscopes or busy with test-tubes. Throughout China graduates of the Peking Union Medical College were struggling to give health and life to areas where disease had walked unchecked. Over vast districts of Africa, Asia, and South America experts were trying to stamp out the last vestiges of yellow fever, and to imprison the dread forces of malaria. In our Southern States men were busy building on the firm basis laid by the General Education Board when it had helped to revitalize agriculture, and by the Rockefeller Foundation when it had led in destroying hookworm disease. Hundreds of thousands of students that day were using facilities pro-

vided by the Board or the Foundation. The long arm of the benefactions was training physicians, stimulating research in psychiatry,
ameliorating the hardships of persecuted men in totalitarian lands,
aiding field work in archæology, astronomy, and biology, and helping to support economic institutes. Through a thousand channels
the beneficent activities which Rockefeller's money had helped to
create were pushing forward and widening the boundaries of civilization. The work that he had done lived after him.

LI

Epilogue

THE story of Rockefeller's life is one of the great romances of American history; but it is not a story which invites swift and easy judgments. For one reason, it is extremely complex; for another, it raises highly debatable economic issues. "Each great industrial trust," writes the English economist Alfred Marshall, in *Industry and Trade,* "has owed its origin to the exceptional business genius of its founders. In some cases the genius was mainly constructive; in others it was largely strategic and incidentally destructive; sometimes even dishonest." He correctly ascribes the Standard Oil Trust to a combination of exceptional constructive ability and astute destructive strategy. The pages of its history—some of them very dark, some brilliantly creditable—show the two elements inextricably mingled. They also show that, as Marshall elsewhere states, "general propositions in regard to either competition or monopoly are full of snares." While some journalists and some politicians will utter sweeping and dogmatic statements upon an industrial aggregation like the Standard Oil, and upon the work of a great business leader like Rockefeller, economists will regard these glib verdicts with distrust. Too many unsolved problems are opened up by such an industrial organization, and too many difficult issues are raised by such an individual career.

Yet on the basis of the facts recorded in these volumes, one judgment may be ventured. It is that the extremes of praise and blame heaped upon Rockefeller were both unwarranted. His enemies during his years of power treated him as one of the arch-criminals of the age. His admirers during his later years of philanthropy lauded him as one of the world's greatest benefactors. Neither estimate possessed historical truth, and neither touched Rockefeller's greatest significance to civilization.

This is not to say that much of the criticism heaped upon Rockefeller and the Standard Oil was not entirely valid. The great combination made a cruel use in its early years, and particularly in 1875–79, of railroad rate discriminations. It practised espionage. It employed bogus independent companies. It used "fighting brands" and local price-slashing to eliminate competitors. Its part in politics was sometimes reprehensible. It paid less attention than it should have done to systematic price-reduction. All this can be set off against its constructive achievements: its elimination of waste and introduction of manifold economies; its application of the Frasch process, the Burton cracking process, and the Van Dyke patents; its standardization of products on a high level of quality; its development of valuable by-products; its ready assistance to other industries, particularly in improving lubricants; its efficiency in home distribution, and its bold vigor in conquering world markets. A fairly heavy indictment can be drawn up to offset the credit items.

But it is clear that for various reasons the indictment was overdrawn. In the first place, because Rockefeller established the earliest of the great trusts a fuller and fiercer light of publicity beat upon it than upon other combinations. The constant investigations and suits placed him and the Standard under a gigantic, pitiless lens. Subsequent combinations were less severely treated. In the second place, the fact that the early investigations took place before the American public realized that combination was an irresistible tendency of the age led to a natural misconception. People thought of the trust as a conspiracy, a dark plot born in greed. Not until later did they see that the formation of trusts, pools, and cartels was a world-wide movement born of industrial conditions and in large part as natural as the upheaval of the tides. In the third place, Rockefeller was singularly unfortunate in some of his enemies, and particularly in the attacks of Henry Demarest Lloyd. Such fabrications as the Widow Backus story, and such distortions as the tale of the Buffalo "explosion," did him a gross injustice, and led to the invention of a totally false stereotype of the man. Finally, Rockefeller was open to harsher attack than most captains of industry because he touched directly the lives of the masses. Carnegie sold his steel to railroads

and industries which passed on his charges to an uncomprehend-
ing public; Rockefeller sold gasolene and kerosene to every family
—and most families were ready to believe the worst whenever oil
went up. Altogether, it is not strange that the accusations against
Rockefeller and the Standard Oil were very decidedly exaggerated.

It is plain that the place Rockefeller holds in American industrial
history is that of a great innovator. He early caught a vision of
combination and order in an industry bloated, lawless, and chaotic.
Pursuing this vision, he devised a scheme of industrial organization which, magnificent in its symmetry and strength, world-wide
in its scope, possessed a striking novelty. The opposition which he
met was massive and implacable. Producers, rival manufacturers,
courts, legislatures, Presidents, public opinion, fought him at every
step. He and his partners marched from investigation to investigation, from suit to suit, under a growing load of opprobrium. But
they moved imperturbably forward. They believed that the opposition was mistaken and irrational. In their opinion it represented a
wasteful anarchy; the full victory of this competitive *laissez-faire*
individualism would mean retrogression, confusion, and general
loss. They kept grimly on. The day came when, with Taft in the
White House, the government finally won its battle against Rockefeller and the Standard Oil. But by that time intelligent men were
comprehending that the struggle against Rockefeller's movement
for industrial consolidation was not a struggle against criminality;
it was largely a struggle against destiny.

The dominant ideal of pioneering America was one of utter
independence and self-sufficiency. Long after the new industrial era
was far advanced, men clung to the old faith in a self-balancing
system of private ownership, small-unit enterprise, and free competition, and to their belief that this system would give every man a
reward roughly proportionate to his industry, integrity, and ability.
They were slow to perceive that the industrial system was not self-
balancing; that it grew less so decade by decade. They were slow
to perceive that men were less and less independent, more and more
interdependent. They were reluctant to admit that free competition
was steadily becoming more restricted, and that its character was
inexorably changing. It was ceasing to be a competition of small
businesses and individual firms, and becoming a competition or-

ganized by great aggregations. They finally had to confess the truth which Donald Richberg wrote in 1940, and which might have been stated a generation earlier: "Ours is the competition of great collective organizations of capital and labor, the competition of huge corporations and large labor organizations. It is the competition of industries with other industries, the competition of overpowering advertising and propaganda." Nor was it altered merely in the scope of the units involved. It was for various reasons no longer a *free* competition in the sense in which it had been free in 1860, or 1880.

Rockefeller was a realist; one of those realists who, as Pareto teaches, have a better grasp of realities than the intellectuals who operate with theories and ideals. Partly by intuition, partly by hard thought, he divined the real nature of economic forces, and the real motives operative in American industry. He and the other leaders of the "heroic age" in American business development thus constituted the guiding elite, in a modern sense, of our industrial society. Many of the forces and elements in that society were irrational and wasteful; Rockefeller wished to impose a more rational and efficient pattern, answering to his own intuitions and deductions. Behind this desire he placed an intellectual keenness, a skill in organization, and a dynamic personal force which were not surpassed, and possibly not equalled, by those of any other industrial captain in history. He was not a product of economic determinism, for he rose superior to it; but he wished to give the economic world a form in which determinism would meet fewer obstacles. He expressed the full potentialities of a movement which shattered the old industrial order, and he naturally incurred the hostility of the masses.

Rockefeller's economic vision, and the courage shown in his fidelity to it, deserve commendation. He knew that he was carrying through a great experiment, and he believed the experiment sound and fruitful. As our national history lengthens and we gain a truer perspective, the importance of this experiment becomes clearer. It is true that some of his methods were open to criticism; but then it must be remembered that he had to use the weapons and implements of his time. Few books are more needed, in the study of our past, than a thorough examination of the development of business ethics in America. Such standards are progressive, and the steps by which they have improved from generation to generation constitute a fascinating topic. Henry Lee Higginson once told a Harvard class that when he entered the banking and brokerage business, men accepted as perfectly correct practices which the best firms a generation later sharply condemned. In 1870, when a rich customer placed a heavy order for stocks, the broker felt it proper to order a few hundred shares on his own account and thus profit from the rise. By 1900 good brokers condemned such an act. By 1940 it would have been punished by very severe penalties. In talking with Samuel Harper, Rockefeller once remarked that his trust had committed acts in the seventies and eighties which advancing business standards had later made clearly improper. When the history of our business ethics is written, it will doubtless be found that some correlation exists between boom periods and business laxity, between depression periods and an advance in morals. It will also be found that business honesty is correlated with social maturity. An old, long-settled, and fairly static community has better standards than an adolescent, fast-changing district; an old industry has higher ethics than a new industry. All this must be remembered in appraising Rockefeller's weapons and the use he made of them.

The question of motive enters into any consideration either of economic vision or of business ethics; and it is important because some writers of the muckraking school have grievously misconstrued the motives not only of Rockefeller but of a whole generation of business leaders. They sum up these motives in the word "greed," as if it were greed which led Carnegie to build steel mills, Rockefeller to organize the oil industry, Westinghouse to develop the electrical industry, and Ford to manufacture motor cars. If we wish to misuse the word greed we can apply it in many contexts. We can say that Shakespeare was greedy for fame, Lincoln greedy for political power, and Duse greedy for applause. But such a word means nothing in the analysis of motive. What these figures were really interested in was competitive achievement, self-expression, and the imposition of their wills on a given environment. And these were precisely the motives which actuated Carnegie, Westinghouse, and Rockefeller. We have quoted early in this biography a statement by Rockefeller that "achievement" was his great aim, and the statement was true. The word greed may seem apposite to industrial leaders because they accumulated large fortunes. But any careful analysis of the work of the best leaders shows that money was not the central object, but a by-product. Greedy men exist, but they seldom accumulate colossal fortunes, for greed tends to defeat itself in complex business operations. The corner grocer may be greedy, the political boss, the literary hack. But greed usually stops with the few hundred thousand dollars that purchase satiety. The men who built the really towering economic structures were not thinking primarily of dollars, or they would have halted at the first story.

And one great fact to be borne in mind when studying Rockefeller and his fellow-captains of industry is pointed out by Van Wyck Brooks in *America's Coming of Age.* It is the fact that American business has typically been a more optimistic, light-hearted venture than in other lands, and the best businessmen have been great adventurers. The giants of the "heroic age" of industry can aptly be compared with the famous Elizabethan captains—with Drake, Hawkins, Cavendish, Frobisher, Cabot (some of whom were canny businessmen too). In business, as I have pointed out, Americans of the nineteenth century found the Great Game. They played it with zest and gusto, they enjoyed it even when it was perilous, and they took its ups and downs with equanimity. As Herbert Spencer said in 1882, for Americans it was the modern equivalent of war. If it was hard-hitting and ruthless, so is war; and even when the blows were hardest, it remained a game. "Business in America," wrote Brooks, "is not merely more engaging than elsewhere, it is even perhaps the most engaging activity in American life." Of all its leaders, none showed more boldness or swiftness than Rockefeller, and none more equanimity in accepting defeats and victories. Love of the game was one of his motives, particularly as his keen eye saw a pattern in the game that less discerning men missed.

We have said that his place in the history of business was that of a great innovator; and that is also his place in the history of philanthropy. This man who remolded one industry and offered a design for remaking others crowned his activities by the colossal grant of some $550,000,000 to various objects. But the unexampled scale of his gifts is not their most striking feature. What made his donations arresting and memorable was in larger part the skill with which he planned and organized them. From the beginning his gifts were made thoughtfully and conscientiously. The huge foundations which he, his son, and their aides set up, governed by able men working in greater and greater independence, have become models for large-scale philanthropy in this and other lands. Their aims, administrative mechanism, methods, and not least of all, their spirit, offer lessons which have been widely copied. Foundations had existed long before—but never any quite like these. His emphasis upon ameliorative work at the fountain-heads of evil, upon the use of money to stimulate men to self-help, and upon the establishment of *continuing* activities, has been of the highest value.

A correct appraisal of his rôle as philanthropist will avoid the excessive praise which many have given him because of the sheer amount of his benefactions. The size of his fortune, as we have said, was a historical accident. There was obviously no true sense in which he had earned his billion dollars,[1] any more than Carnegie had earned his half-billion. Only the special economic, legal, and fiscal situation in the United States between 1865 and 1914 made such huge accumulations possible. Rockefeller always recognized this fact, and always regarded himself as a trustee rather than an owner. His statement at the University of Chicago that "God gave me the money" is sometimes quoted as an arrogant utterance; like Napoleon's statement in putting on the iron crown of Lombardy, "God has given it to me—let man touch it at his peril"; like George F. Baer's statement that God had given the anthracite business to a picked group of men. Actually Rockefeller made that statement in a spirit of utter humility. He devoutly believed that God had made him a trustee for these hundreds of millions, not to be kept but to be given wisely and carefully. And it is for the wisdom, the conscientious effort, and the vision which he and his son lent to the task of distribution—a laborious and difficult task—that gratitude is really due them. The animating generosity, too, is to be counted to his credit. For we must not forget that Rockefeller began to give as soon as he began to earn.

---

[1]The word "billion" is here used in a general sense; Rockefeller never possessed that much at one time, though much more than that sum passed through his hands.

It is earnestly to be hoped that no such fortune will ever again pass into a single grasp. The American people have determined that such aggregations of wealth are incompatible with the best interests of the land. And yet it would be a bold critic who would say that this fortune was an unhappy accident. It passed into the hands of a man who had proved the possession of certain strong liberal impulses. As an ill-clad youth earning a few dollars a week, his own necessities poorly met, he had given a substantial part of his meager wage to charity. Few indeed are those who make such sacrifices for altruistic objects as are recorded in Ledger A. He had given from the outset without regard to religion or race, to Catholic and to Negro. He kept on giving more and more as his income grew. The fortune went to a man who had also proved a remarkable capacity for planning and organizing; who knew how to call expert and farsighted assistants to his side; and who was so devoid of egotism that, having once given funds to agents whom he trusted, he cut himself off from all further control over the money. The United States has in one form or another wasted a great many billions of its wealth. Indeed, waste is a conspicuous part of our national life. It was perhaps a happy accident that a single billion passed into the temporary control of a man who, with his son and his expert counsellors, tried to show how much of public welfare and advancement could be purchased by its careful use.

The life of Rockefeller, we can say again, is not one which invites swift and dogmatic judgments. The lessons which men draw from it will vary according to the preconceptions with which they approach the subject. Some will give a heavier weight to the debit items in the ledger than others. But it can safely be said that the prime significance of Rockefeller's career lies in the fact that he was a bold innovator in both industry and philanthropy; that he brought to the first a great unifying idea, which he insisted should be thoroughly tested, and to the second a stronger, more expert, and more enduring type of organization. It can be said also that by virtue of his organizing genius, his tenacity of purpose, his keenness of mind, and his firmness of character, he looms up as one of the most impressive figures of the century which his lifetime spanned. His fame went around the world, and it will be long before the world forgets it.

APPENDICES

APPENDIX I

PRODUCTION OF APPALACHIAN OIL IN BARRELS
(From *Derrick's Handbook*)

	Pennsylvania and New York	Southeastern Ohio	West Virginia
1859	8,500		
1860	650,000		
1861	2,118,000		
1862	3,056,000		
1863	2,631,000		
1864	2,116,200		
1865	2,497,700		
1866	3,597,500		
1867	3,347,300		
1868	3,715,800		
1869	4,215,000		
1870	5,659,000		
1871	5,795,000		
1872	6,539,100		
1873	9,893,786		
1874	10,926,945		
1875	8,787,514	200,000	3,000,000
1876	8,968,906	31,763	120,000
1877	13,135,475	29,888	172,000
1878	15,163,462	38,179	180,000
1879	19,685,176	29,112	180,000
1880	26,027,631	38,940	179,000
1881	27,376,509	33,867	151,000
1882	20,776,041	661,580	91,000
1883	23,128,389	47,632	126,000
1884	23,772,209	90,081	90,000
1885	20,776,041	661,580	91,000
1886	25,798,000	703,945	102,000
1887	22,356,193	372,257	145,000
1888	16,488,668	297,774	119,448
1889	21,487,435	318,277	544,113
1890	28,458,208	1,116,521	492,578
1891	33,009,236	424,323	2,406,218
1892	28,422,377	1,193,414	3,810,086
1893	20,314,513	2,602,965	8,445,412
1894	19,019,990	3,184,310	8,577,624
1895	19,144,390	3,694,624	8,120,125
1896	20,584,421	3,366,031	10,019,770
1897	19,210,786	2,877,193	13,078,011

APPENDIX II

TABLES OF YEARLY AVERAGE PRICES OF CRUDE AND REFINED

(From Tarbell, *History of the Standard Oil,* II, 383; by courtesy of the Macmillan Company)

(All quotations up to 1899 are from the Oil City *Derrick;* all quotations for 1900–1903 are from the New York *Commercial.*)

TABLE OF YEARLY AVERAGE PRICE OF CRUDE

In the following table is presented the highest and lowest price of oil, the months in which these quotations occurred, and the general average for each year. The "average" as estimated is usually the mean price between the highest and lowest quotations of a given time. It is sufficiently accurate for general purposes of comparison. It would be an almost impossible task to determine a "true average" from the reports of the daily sales that are now on record. Previous to 1875 the quotations are given for points along Oil Creek, and they hardly represent what the producer actually realized for oil at the wells. From 1875 onward the trading in oil was placed on a more satisfactory basis by the general adoption of pipe-line certificates, and the exchange quotations show very closely the value of the oil at the wells. When the certificate was finally purchased by the refiner, it was subject to a uniform charge for pipage of the oil from the wells to the nearest shipping point.

Year	*Highest Month*	*Price*	*Lowest Month*	*Price*	*Average*
1859	Sept.	$20.00	Dec.	$20.00	$20.00
1860	Jan.	20.00	Dec.	2.00	9.60
1861	Jan.	1.75	Dec.	.10	.52
1862	Dec.	2.50	Jan.	.10	1.05
1863	Dec.	4.00	Jan.	2.00	3.15
1864	July	14.00	Feb.	3.75	8.15
1865	Jan.	10.00	Aug.	4.00	6.59
1866	Jan.	5.50	Dec.	1.35	3.75
1867	Oct.	4.00	June	1.50	2.40
1868	July	5.75	Jan.	1.70	3.62½
1869	Jan.	7.00	Dec.	4.25	5.60
1870	Jan.	4.90	Aug.	2.75	3.90
1871	June	5.25	Jan.	3.25	4.40
1872	Oct.	4.55	Dec.	2.67½	3.75
1873	Jan.	2.75	Nov.	.82½	1.80
1874	Feb.	2.25	Nov.	.62½	1.15
1875	Feb.	1.82½	Jan.	.75	1.24¾
1876	Dec.	4.23¾	Jan.	1.47½	2.57⅝
1877	Jan.	3.69⅜	June	1.53¾	2.39⅜
1878	Feb.	1.87½	Sept.	.78¾	1.17⅛
1879	Dec.	1.28¾	June	.63⅛	.85⅝
1880	June	1.24¾	April	.71¼	.94⅛
1881	Sept.	1.01¼	July	.72½	.85¼
1882	Nov.	$1.37	July	$0.49¼	$0.78½
1883	June	1.24¾	Jan.	.83¼	1.05⅞
1884	Jan.	1.15⅝	June	.51¼	.83⅝
1885	Oct.	1.12⅝	Jan.	.68	.88⅜
1886	Jan.	.92¼	Aug.	.59¾	.71⅜
1887	Dec.	.90	July	.54	.66⅝
1888	Mar.	1.00	June	.71⅜	.87
1889	Nov.	1.12½	April	.79½	.94⅛
1890	Jan.	1.07⅝	Dec.	.60¾	.86⅝
1891	Feb.	.81⅜	Aug.	.50	.66⅞
1892	Jan.	.64⅛	Oct.	.50	.55½
1893	Dec.	.80	Jan.	.52⅞	.64
1894	Dec.	.95¾	Jan.	.78½	.83¾
1895	April	2.60	Jan.	.95¼	1.35¼
1896	Jan.	1.50	Dec.	.90	1.19
1897	Mar.	.96	Oct.	.65	.78⅜
1898	Dec.	1.19	Jan.	.65	.91⅛
1899	Dec.	1.66	Feb.	1.13	1.29⅜
1900	Mar.	1.68	Nov.	1.07	1.35¼
1901	Nov.	1.30	June	1.05	1.21⅛
1902	Dec.	1.44½	Mar.	1.15	1.23
1903	Dec.	1.88	Mar.	1.50	1.58¾

APPENDIX III

Assets, Earnings, and Dividends of the Standard Oil Combination

(From Brief on the Facts for the Defendant in U. S. *vs.* Standard Oil **Co.**, pp. 145 *et seq.*)

Year Ending Dec. 31	Total Net Assets	Total Net Earnings	Percentage of Earnings to Net Assets	Total Dividends	Percentage of Dividends to Net Assets
1883	$72,869,596.46	$11,231,790.56	15.413	$4,268,086.50	5.857
1884	75,858,960.19	7,778,205.73	10.253	4,288,842.00	5.654
1885	76,762,672.19	8,382,935.50	10.921	7,479,223.50	9.743
1886	87,012,107.37	15,350,787.68	17.642	7,226,452.50	8.305
1887	94,377,970.83	14,026,590.96	14.862	8,463,327.50	8.967
1888	97,005,621.27	16,226,955.94	16.728	13,705,505.50	14.129
1889	101,281,192.66	14,845,201.39	14.657	10,620,630.00	10.486
1890	115,810,074.50	19,131,470.84	16.519	11,200,089.00	9.671
1891	120,771,074.79	16,331,826.29	13.523	11,648,826.00	9.645
1892	128,102,428.18	19,174,878.30	14.968	11,874,225.00	9.263
1893	131,886,700.68	15,457,354.05	11.720	11,670,000.00	8.849
1894	135,755,449.44	15,544,325.54	11.450	11,670,000.00	8.596
1895	143,295,602.88	24,078,076.60	16.803	16,532,500.00	11.537
1896	147,220,399.90	34,077,519.10	23.147	30,147,500.00	20.478
1897				33,000,000.00	(newspaper report)
1898				30,000,000.00	(newspaper report)
1899				33,000,000.00	(newspaper report)
1900	205,480,449.09	55,501,774.52	27.011	46,691,474.50	22.723
1901	210,997,066.13	52,291,767.61	24.783	46,775,390.00	22.169
1902	231,758,405.58	64,613,365.45	27.880	43,851,966.00	18.921
1903	270,217,921.85	81,336,994.27	30.101	42,877,478.00	15.868
1904	297,489,225.47	61,570,110.75	20.697	35,188,266.00	11.828
1905	315,613,261.55	57,459,356.08	18.206	39,335,320.00	12.463
1906	359,400,193.31	83,122,251.76	23.128	39,335,320.00	10.945

APPENDIX IV

Rockefeller's Gifts, 1855–93; From Data (Not Quite Complete) in the Rockefeller Offices

(The record of Rockefeller's donations, especially before 1880, is often incomplete, and these totals must not be taken as representing all his gifts. But they have been compiled as carefully as possible from his accounts.)

1855 (first entry November 25)	$2.77	1875		$460.08
1856	19.31	1876	clearly incomplete	608.00
1857	28.37	1877		200.00
1858	43.85	1878		23,485.65
1859	72.22	1879		29,280.16
1860	107.35	1880		32,865.64
1861	259.97	1881		61,070.96
1862	283.06	1882		61,261.75
1863	292.03	1883		66,722.97
1864	671.86	1884		119,109.48
1865	1,012.35	1885		140,543.18
1866	1,320.43	1886		155,413.42
1867	669.14	1887		284,116.52
1868	3,675.39	1888		169,822.63
1869	5,489.62	1889		123,592.47
1870	2,635.79	1890		303,542.78
1871	6,860.86	1891		509,779.84
1872	6,930.68	1892		1,353,520.70
1873	4,770.58	1893		1,472,122.52
1874	4,841.06			

APPENDIX V

THE STANDARD'S LABOR POLICY

Material upon the Standard's labor relations is scanty. All observers agreed that Rockefeller insisted upon good wages and kindly treatment, and that labor troubles were rare; also that unions were discouraged. Cleveland papers in 1877 reported several demonstrations by discontented employees. But *The Leader* of September 4 explained this by saying that the Standard had found itself with more employees than it needed, and "rather than discharge some in the hard times, they thought it would be wiser and kinder to keep all, and allot the work so that all could earn at least a support." The result had been misunderstanding and dissatisfaction. U. G. Swartz in his history of the Whiting plant in the *Stanolind Record* emphasizes the fact that wages were always higher than in neighboring steel mills and packing plants. New York newspapers show that in June, 1891, coopers in the Standard's barrel factory at Bayonne struck for $2.50 a day instead of the $2.25 they were getting. But strikes were clearly very rare.

In 1905 Rockefeller gave an interview in Cleveland which the New York *Herald* published (September 17). He said that the Standard's freedom from labor disturbances was easily explained. "Every head of a department in the Standard Oil has explicit instructions to treat all employees with absolute fairness. When that policy is carried out there will never be any danger of strikes." But *The Herald* reporter declared that the Standard, while generous in wage-policy, maintained "a secret service department." Its agents mingled with the workers, and kept careful watch for labor agitators. When one was found, he was transferred to some other plant, where he would be hampered by lack of acquaintances; in extreme instances only was he discharged. The New York *World* of May 10, 1908, warmly commended the Standard's labor policies. "It is and has been almost wholly free from strikes and lockouts, and this because it has always paid good wages and had a kindly care for its men. . . . Promotion is strictly on merit. . . . A pension system has been many years in operation." Nevertheless, the liberal activities of John D. Rockefeller, Jr., in promoting the industrial representation system in various of the former Standard companies, indicate that numerous employees became discontented with the paternalistic system.

APPENDIX VI

THE WIDOW BACKUS STORY

A remarkable series of affidavits bearing on this story was published in the Oil City *Derrick* of February 18, 1905. They included a sworn statement of H. M. Backus, brother of Fred M. Backus, ridiculing the widow's tale; and similar statements by Peter S. Jennings, who represented Rockefeller in the negotiation, Charles H. Marr, who represented Mrs. Backus, and Edward Malony, superintendent of the Backus Oil Works. H. M. Backus estimated the total proceeds of the sale at from $155,000 to $160,000; Malony says the company realized about $133,000 with a good deal still to be sold. From Backus's sworn statement we quote:

Q. In actual money value—speaking now of the construction of the plant—what could the works be replaced for at that time?

A. . . . I think the plant could have been built for about one-third of what they gave us for it. It could have been erected for about $20,000. You see they only bought the construction, and they paid well for that. . . .

Q. Did you ever hear that Mr. Rockefeller made an addition of some thousands of dollars to the price asked by Mrs. Backus, because she was a widow?

A. Yes, sir. I understood that when the proposed purchasers met, Mr. Rockefeller said, "Gentlemen, I want you to give this woman a good round price for that property." That is what I was told by one of the men who was there, and he was not very friendly to Mr. Rockefeller, either.

We quote also from Charles H. Marr's statement:

I conveyed to Mrs. Backus and the other stockholders the proposal of Jennings, and it was at once accepted by them, and the price thus agreed on was shortly thereafter paid. The negotiations extended over a period of from two to three weeks, and were conducted on behalf of the Backus Oil Company by myself. During their pendency Mrs. Backus frequently urged me to bring them to a conclusion, as she was anxious to dispose of the business and relieve herself of further care and responsibility therewith.

We quote further from Edward Malony's affidavit:

Mrs. Backus was anxious to sell and was entirely satisfied with the sale after it was concluded. I know the fact that about a year and a half previous she had offered to sell out the stock of the Backus Oil Company at from 30 to 33 per cent less than she received in the sale referred to, and the value of the works and property had not increased in the meantime. I was well acquainted with the works of the Backus Oil Company and their value. I could, at the time of the sale, have built the works new for $25,000. . . . The negotiations were pleasant and fair, and the price paid was in excess of the value and satisfactory to Mrs. Backus and all concerned for her.

APPENDIX VII

ORIGINAL MEMBERS OF THE STANDARD OIL TRUST

(From Walter F. Taylor, MS History of the Standard Oil, 177, 178)

I. Companies held in their entirety by the trust: Acme Oil Co., New York; Acme Oil Co., Pennsylvania; Atlantic Refining Co. of Philadelphia; Bush & Co. (Limited); Camden Consolidated Oil Co.; Elizabethport Acid Works; Imperial Refining Co. (Limited); Charles Pratt & Co.; Paine, Ablett & Co.; Standard Oil Co., Ohio; Standard Oil Co., Pittsburgh; Smith's Ferry Oil Transportation Co.; Solar Oil Co. (Limited); Sone & Fleming Manufacturing Co. (Limited).

II. Companies a controlling interest in whose stock was held by the trust: American Lubricating Oil Co.; Baltimore United Oil Co.; Beacon Oil Co.; Bush & Denslow Manufacturing Co.; Central Refining Co. of Pittsburgh; Chesebrough Manufacturing Co.; Chess, Carley Co.; Consolidated Tank Line Co.; Inland Oil Co.; Keystone Refining Co.; Maverick Oil Co.; National Transit Co.; Portland Kerosene Oil Co.; Producers' Consolidated Land and Petroleum Co.; Signal Oil Works (Limited); Thompson & Bedford Co. (Limited); Devoe Manufacturing Co.; Eclipse Lubricating Oil Co. (Limited); Empire Refining Co. (Limited); Franklin Pipe Co. (Limited); Galena Oil Works (Limited); Galena Farm Oil Co. (Limited); Germania Mining Co.; Vacuum Oil Co.; H. C. Tine & Co. (Limited); Waters-Pierce Oil Co.

Acknowledgments

THE author has had the benefit of a large body of materials assembled upon John D. Rockefeller and his work by Mr. John D. Rockefeller, Jr., and generously placed at his disposal. Mr. William O. Inglis, a trained writer and journalist, spent several years in collecting notes for a biography, including verbatim records of a large number of conversations with Rockefeller. These have been invaluable. Mr. Inglis has also given me much advice, and read large parts of my book in manuscript. The brief manuscript history of the Standard Oil prepared by Walter F. Taylor, essentially a legal history, was likewise placed at my disposal. Mr. Rockefeller, Jr., provided for further research, which was most ably executed by Mr. Frank E. Hill, Miss Helene Maxwell, and Mr. David K. Rothstein, three expert and impartial workers. The surviving papers of John D. Rockefeller (his business correspondence was never extensive, and has largely been destroyed) were open to me, as were some dozens of volumes of bound newspaper clippings.

The author is indebted to Miss Ida M. Tarbell for advice and information, and for the loan of important materials. He is indebted to Mr. John T. Flynn for similar favors. Professor Paul H. Giddens, historian of the early years of the oil industry, helped him search for materials, and read a large part of the proofs. Writers on John D. Rockefeller and the Standard Oil will always owe much to the books of these three authors.

In the former Oil Regions the author received the assistance of a large number of men and women. He must especially mention Miss Grace Emery of Bradford, Pa., daughter of Lewis Emery, Jr.; Theo L. Wilson of Clarion, Pa.; M. M. Lutton of Franklin, Pa.; W. H. Andrews of Meadville, Pa.; S. Y. Ramage of Oil City, Pa.; John H. Scheide of Titusville, Pa.; and the helpful curator of the Drake Museum at Titusville.

In western New York the author was assisted by numerous people, including Mayor Frank Smith of Ithaca; Professor Morris Bishop of Cornell; and Doctor Cornelius McCarthy of Auburn. He was aided in Pittsburgh by President P. H. Curry of the South Penn Oil Company; Leland D. Baldwin of the University of Pittsburgh; and by officers of the Carnegie Library and the Historical Society of Western Pennsylvania. He was assisted in Philadelphia by Julian P. Boyd of the Pennsylvania Historical Society, Henry W. Bikle of the Pennsylvania Railroad, William G. Warden, Jr., S. R. Kamm, and William M. Potts. In West Virginia he received help from Festus P. Summers, C. H. Ambler, and Mrs. Annie Camden Spilman, whose permission to quote from the Camden Papers he gratefully acknowledges. Samuel Hopkins Adams of Auburn, N. Y., kindly gave the author information. So, also, did N. A. Quilling of Georgetown, Ky., who had assisted Rockefeller in business and charity in Cleveland.

In Cleveland he profited from the assistance of Joseph A. Schlitz, who gave unsparingly of time and advice; of William H. Kendall, who was equally kind; of Doctor William M. Burton, former president of the Standard of Indiana; of Charles Arter; and of numerous present and former officers of the Standard Oil of Ohio. He received valuable aid from Miss Alice M. Rockefeller, Mrs. William F. Nash, and Mrs. Walter S. Bowler, daughters of the late Frank Rockefeller. And he must particularly acknowledge the unselfish counsel of Charles C. White, who read the proofs of the whole work and helped correct many errors.

A full list of those in and near New York who have aided in the preparation of this biography would fill pages. The author can mention only a few names. He owes much to various men associated with John D. Rockefeller. In addition to Mr. Rockefeller, Jr., who has been unsparing in assistance, and who has been as anxious as any one that the subject should be treated critically and with unsparing honesty, they include the late Charles M. Higgins, Walter Teagle, Henry Cooper, George Welwood Murray, Bertram Cutler, Thomas M. Debevoise, and Robert W. Gumbel. He received valuable light upon the subject of the biography from Charles T. White, Everett Colby, and J. W. Saybolt. Various men connected with the great benefactions, notably Abraham Flexner, Simon Flexner, Jerome D. Greene, Henry James, and Raymond

B. Fosdick, gave indispensable information and criticism. Among others who aided the author were Francis H. Brownell, chairman of the American Smelting & Refining Company; Burton J. Hendrick, Richard T. Ely, Herbert L. Satterlee, Rolland H. Maybee, Sam C. Halper, Harry Barnard, W. Dixon Ellis, James N. Fleming, Harry Harkness Flagler, and Mark D. Hirsch. Mr. Charles M. Schwab kindly talked at length with the author. Particularly valuable help was given in the final preparation of the manuscript by Louis M. Hacker, to whose expert knowledge of American economic history the book owes much; by Miss Sylvia Black; by Louis Filler; and by Frank E. Hill, who contributed much to the literary form.

The author gratefully acknowledges the assistance of the Public Library of Cleveland; of the librarian of Columbia University, C. C. Williamson; of the Congressional Library; of the library of the University of Wisconsin, which opened the Henry Demarest Lloyd Papers to him; and of the staff of the University of Chicago, who gave great assistance in collecting material on the early history of the University, and who permitted him to use the William Rainey Harper Papers. He acknowledges also the help of President Harper's son, Doctor Samuel Harper, and of Edgar J. Goodspeed and C. T. C. Goodspeed, sons of the late Thomas Wakefield Goodspeed. For the use of the manuscript autobiography of the late Frederick T. Gates, and for incidental information, he is indebted to Franklin H. Gates of Montclair, N. J. To all these, and to many more, the author feels a gratitude which he can ill express.

INDEX

Index

Acme Oil Company, I, 486, 487; controls Oil Regions refineries, 488; II, 42–44, 57–58, 77; and the Buffalo case, 78; 182

Adams, Jr., Charles F., I, 299; chairman, first railroad commission, 300, 302; on Standard Oil, 683; II, 333

Addicks, J. Edward, I, 678–679

Aldrich, Nelson A., II, 358, 458–459, 485, 513, 516–517, 555, 592

Alexander, Hewitt & Company, merged with Standard Oil, I, 366

Alexander, McDonald & Company, I, 499, 501, 658, 674

Alexander, Scofield & Company, I, 193; rebates, 257; 295, 308; and Rockefeller, 328; merged with Standard Oil, 366, 373–374; II, 45. *See* Scofield, Shurmer & Teagle

Allen, N. M., editor, Titusville *Courier*, I, 341, 408, 423, 464, 465, 466, 472, 565

Amalgamated Copper Company, formed, II, 358; and H. H. Rogers, 436–437; and "Standard Oil crowd," 438, 442; *Frenzied Finance*, 526 ff.

American Baptist Education Society, established, II, 209; and F. T. Gates, 210–211, 214, 218, 223; Rockefeller's interest in, 225; and University of Chicago, 226–227, 228, 230–231; and General Education Board, 635

American Lubricating Oil Company, I, 653, 656

American Petroleum Company, II, 31

American Steel Barge Company, II, 365, 374–375

American Steel and Wire Company, II, 411–412, 415, 417

American Transfer Company, I, 442–443, 462; merged with United Pipe-Lines, 495; 545; expanded, 598; 652; and Pennsylvania Railroad, II, 130

Andrews, E. Benjamin, II, 216, 226, 286

Andrews, Samuel, refiner, I, 130, 178–179, 186–187; and Rockefeller, 184, 188–190, 268, 274; Standard Oil superintendent, 292, 393–394, 476; quits firm, 480–481; II, 444

Andrews, W. H., and Billingsley Bill, II, 110–111

Andrews, Clark & Company, formed 1863, I, 179; 182; and Rockefeller, 183, 184; expansion, 185–186; dissolved, 189

Anglo-American Oil Company, II, 31, 33

Archbold, John D., rejects South Improvement plan, I, 328; 331; early career, 340–341; 352, 397, 407, 408, 431, 460; joins Rockefeller, 479–480, 486; and independents, 488, 492, 502; described, 510–511; 542, 592; Standard Oil trustee, 614; 651, 671, 672, 676, 677; and J. E. Addicks, 678–679; II, 5, 21, 35; at Hepburn Investigation, 42–43, 44; and E. G. Patterson, 62–63; 68; on George Rice, 71–72; 76–77; and the Buffalo case, 78–79, 83, 85–86; and Billingsley Bill, 111; 117; New York investigation, 121; and Congressional investigation, 128 ff.; 145, 153, 163, 175, 182, 183, 186, 189, 287, 328, 329, 332; Ohio investigation, 350–351; Standard Oil vice-president, 356; directs policies, 428 ff.; and "Standard Oil crowd," 442–443; and Industrial Commission, 499 ff.; in politics, 505 ff.; 548–549, 561, 563, 568–569; price policy, 578 ff.; and Hearst exposures, 593–594; Standard Oil president, 604; death, 679

Armitage, Dr. Thomas, II, 455, 482

Armour, J. Ogden, I, 133, 140

Armour, Philip D., II, 194, 260, 341

Arnold, Frank B., chairman, New York Senate Investigation, II, 118, 121–122

Arter, Frank A., I, 269, 369, 370, 379

Atkinson, Edward, and "Aladdin Oven," II, 20

Atlantic & Great Western Railroad, as oil-carrier, I, 180–181; and Oil Regions, 177; absorbed by Jay Gould, 255

Atlantic Refining Company, I, 322, 339, 486, 503, 510, 526; II, 608

Atlas Company, absorbed by Standard Oil, II, 77

Atwood, Luther, chemist, I, 151–152

Aurora Iron Mining Company, II, 368; value, 377

Babcock, Paul, I, 666–667, 676

Backus, Fred M., I, 350, 393, 653

Backus, Mrs. Fred M., transaction with